FOCUS ON CAPITAL
New Approaches to Developing
Latin American Capital Markets

Kenroy Dowers

Pietro Masci

Editors

Published by the Inter-American Development Bank
Distributed by The Johns Hopkins University Press

Washington, D.C.
2003

© 2003   **Inter-American Development Bank**
1300 New York Avenue, N.W.
Washington, D.C. 20577

Produced by the IDB Publications Section.

To order this book, contact:
IDB Bookstore
Tel: 1-877-PUBS IDB/(202) 623-1753
Fax: (202) 623-1709
E-mail: idb-books@iadb.org
www.iadb.org/pub

**Cataloging-in-Publication data provided by the
Inter-American Development Bank
Felipe Herrera Library**

Focus on capital : new approaches to developing Latin American capital markets / Kenroy Dowers and Pietro Masci, editors.

p. cm.   Includes bibliographical references and index.
ISBN 1931003491

1. Capital market—Latin America.   I. Dowers, Kenroy.   II. Masci, Pietro.   III. Inter-American Development Bank.

332.673 F597—dc21   LCCN 2003102343

Contents

Foreword v
Acknowledgments vii
About the Authors ix
Overview xv

Part I. Introduction

Chapter 1
Developing a Strategy for Reforming Capital Markets
in Latin America and the Caribbean 3
    Kenroy Dowers, Felipe Gomez-Acebo, and Pietro Masci

Part II. Factors Affecting the Development of Capital Markets

Chapter 2
Globalization, Technology, and Regulation in Capital Markets:
Strategies for Latin America and the Caribbean 37
    Reena Aggarwal

Chapter 3
Internet Technology and the Development of Securities Markets 65
    Georg Wittich, Ethiopis Tafara, and Robert J. Peterson

Chapter 4
The Impact of the Macroeconomic Environment on Capital Markets
in Emerging Latin American Economies 91
    Valeriano F. Garcia and Luis Alberto Giorgio

Chapter 5
Institutional Investors and Capital Market Development 119
    Karen Goldstein Rossotto

Part III. Issues in the Implementation of Capital Market Strategies

Chapter 6
Promoting Regional Capital Market Integration 159
    Ruben Lee

Chapter 7
Accounting and Auditing Standards 213
    Pietro Masci and Ivan Sotomayor

Chapter 8
Enhancing Market Infrastructure in Emerging Economies 239
    Andrew Hook

Chapter 9
Demutualization of Exchanges as a Strategy
for Capital Market Regulatory Reform 269
    Roberta S. Karmel

Chapter 10
Developing Bond Markets: A Comprehensive View 295
    Clemente del Valle

Chapter 11
Designing a Derivatives Complement to Cash Markets
in Developing Countries 335
    Andrea M. Corcoran, Ronald B. Hobson, Gregory J. Kuserk,
    Karen K. Wuertz, and Derek West

Chapter 12
Access to Financing for Small and Medium Enterprises 389
    Hannes Takacs and Kinga Korcsmaros

Chapter 13
Developing Capital Markets in Latin America and the Caribbean:
Ethical Issues 415
    Osvaldo R. Agatiello

Chapter 14
Corporate Governance and Capital Market Development:
Recent Experiences in Latin America... 437
    Mike Lubrano

Chapter 15
Human Capacity Development for Capital Market
Professionals in Latin America and the Caribbean... 463
    Catherine Chandler-Crichlow

Part IV. Conclusion

Chapter 16
Pragmatic Issues in Capital Market Development in Emerging Economies...... 487
    Kenroy Dowers, Ruben Lee, and Antonio Vives

Index 517

Foreword

During the past two decades, despite suffering damaging financial crises, the countries of Latin America and the Caribbean have introduced important reforms in their financial markets, encompassing changes in the legal and regulatory framework, ownership patterns, and market infrastructure. The regulatory frameworks have evolved from monopoly and public ownership settings lacking specific regulations, toward scenarios where private participation prevails, with supervision, regulation, and competition playing complementary roles. However, although legal reforms, regulation, and supervision are pivotal features in reform processes, financial and capital markets in the region have fallen behind, and have not provided necessary financing to enhance competitiveness and spur economic growth.

Without effective legislation and enforcement to promote reform and political vision accompanied by strong leadership, the situation could become worse, restraining market discipline and further reducing the capability of the economies of the region to operate effectively in an increasingly global economy. Moreover, several factors—the region's poor performance compared with other parts of the world; the diversity of experience across countries; the complexity of public policy dynamics; and the scarcity of human, financial, and institutional resources—complicate the ability of countries to implement adequate policies.

The Inter-American Development Bank Group, which includes the Bank as well as the Multilateral Investment Fund (MIF) and the Inter-American Investment Corporation (IIC), has actively promoted financial sector reform and recently has concentrated efforts on domestic capital market reform. A large number of specific and diverse operations have been approved during the past decade for capital market development in the region, amounting to more than US$9 billion. This includes projects that impact capital markets, such as pension reform, support for national securities commissions, development of primary and secondary mortgage markets, and insurance.

In February 2001, a roundtable on capital markets offered an additional push to the activities of the Bank in the area of capital market development. Almost at the same time, the Private Sector Department of the Bank was authorized to enter into specific financing operations aimed at developing local capital markets in the region. In addition, the MIF has been providing financial support for specific technical cooperation in various countries, including a continental training program for securities supervisors. Recently, the MIF launched a program, as part of its Cluster Action Plan, aimed at supporting the competitiveness of countries in Latin America and the Caribbean through the adoption of internationally accepted standards, particularly in the area of accounting and auditing.

Focus on Capital: New Approaches to Developing Latin American Capital Markets is part of the Bank's strategy in the area of local capital market development. The book analyzes the status of the markets in the region and identifies the technical and political challenges to making capital markets functioning and efficient.

The fundamental message of the book is that capital market development constitutes a value, an asset that belongs to the overall Latin American and Caribbean community, and that policymakers have to provide vision, leadership, and commitment to move ahead. In its dialogue with the countries, the Inter-American Development Bank will continue to support reforms to build vibrant capital markets, to increase the efficiency benefits of regional economic and financial integration, and to allow full participation in the global economy.

Carlos M. Jarque, Manager
Sustainable Development Department
Inter-American Development Bank

Acknowledgments

The idea of producing a book on capital markets in Latin America and the Caribbean came following the *Capital Market Roundtable: A New Focus for Capital Market Development in Latin America and the Caribbean,* which the Inter-American Development Bank hosted in February 2001. The event inspired more in-depth work on the expansion of capital and financial markets in the region with the objective of articulating, mostly to regional policymakers, the overall picture as well as the relevant specific issues for capital market development.

Kenroy Dowers and Pietro Masci of the Inter-American Development Bank coordinated and edited the book. The authors represent a wide range of disciplines, institutional and professional backgrounds, and global experience. This *peleau* was deliberate to provide variety in the perspectives and experiences that would contribute insight and guidance in formulating dynamic capital market strategies under different situations.

The authors benefited from valuable contributions and comments from numerous individuals. They extend special thanks to those who provided feedback: Lynnette Asselin, Edgardo Demaestri, Kim Staking, and Aimee Verdisco of the Inter-American Development Bank; Raul R. Herrera of the Inter-American Investment Corporation; Noritaka Akamatsu, Mario Guadamillas, Leora Kappler, Cally Jordan, and Melinda Roth of the World Bank; Randall Dodd of the Derivatives Study Center; Eija Holttinen of the Bank of Finland; Tanis McLaren of the Ontario Securities Commission; David Mazza of Citibank; Gary Stephenson, individual consultant in clearance and settlement systems; Augusto F. Cauti, legal expert; and Benjamin M. Rowland, PhD, a former IDB and World Bank staff member and an independent consultant and policy advisor to governments and institutions in the Latin American and Caribbean region.

The editors and the authors are grateful for the research assistance of Juan Jose Durante, Rose Maria Garcia, Diego Sourrouille, and Rodrigo Iñaki Trelles Zabala, who conducted research on selected issues, compiled and analyzed relevant data, and developed tables and figures. The publication benefited from the able administrative assistance of Martha Chavez, Veronica Ferraro, and Liliana Lopez.

The editors are indebted to the overall guidance provided by Barbara H. Rietveld, Graciela Testa, and Grace Guinand. Finally, a great thank you to our editor, Sandra Gain, who has helped to improve the final product.

About the Authors

Osvaldo R. Agatiello is a legal and economic consultant to international organizations and development cooperation agencies, specializing in Latin America. He was undersecretary for projects and technical cooperation and advisor to the Vice-Minister of Economy of Argentina in the 1990s and a member of Argentina's foreign debt team in the 1980s. He holds a PhD in international economics from the Fletcher School of Law and Diplomacy and an SJD from the University of Córdoba in Argentina.

Reena Aggarwal is a professor of finance with the McDonough School of Business at Georgetown University, specializing in stock and emerging markets, microstructure of stock exchanges, and initial public offerings. She has published in several important journals and was an academic fellow at the Securities and Exchange Commission. She has spent time in Brazil and Chile examining stock markets and privatization programs. She holds a PhD in finance from the University of Maryland.

Catherine Chandler-Crichlow is president of International Leadership Associates, Inc., and has more than 25 years experience in human capacity development, technology-based distance education, and leadership development. A graduate of Harvard University and the University of Toronto, she has held executive positions in various public and private sector firms. She is currently a senior advisor to the Toronto International Leadership Centre for Financial Sector Supervision.

Andrea M. Corcoran is director of the Office of International Affairs of the U.S. Commodity Futures Trading Commission. She is a frequent contributor to legal, economic, and regulatory journals on derivatives issues in the United States and abroad and an adjunct professor at Georgetown University Law Center. She holds a degree in law from Harvard Law School and a BA from Stanford.

Clemente del Valle was recently appointed superintendent of the Comisión Nacional de Valores in Colombia. He joined the World Bank in 1997. He coordinated the recent publication of the World Bank and International Monetary Fund's *Developing Government Bond Markets Handbook* as well as the annual Organisation for Economic Co-operation and Development and World Bank forum for government securities.

Kenroy Dowers is an investment officer at the Inter-American Development Bank (IDB). Previously he was a financial sector specialist at the IDB and senior risk analyst with Freddie Mac. He holds an MBA in finance and a PhD in financial economics from the State University of New York and a BSc from the University of the West Indies.

Valeriano F. Garcia holds a PhD from the University of Chicago. He has been a principal economist and executive director at the World Bank. He has done extensive empirical work on open macroeconomics and financial sector issues, and currently heads Washington International Advisers, a consulting firm based in Washington, D.C., and Buenos Aires.

Luis Alberto Giorgio is a financial analyst at the Inter-American Development Bank. A graduate of the University of Minnesota and the University of Buenos Aires, he was deputy director general of the Center of Latin American Monetary Studies and managing director of the Center for Monetary and Banking Studies of the Central Bank of Argentina. He has taught monetary and banking courses at the Anahuac University (Mexico) and the University of Buenos Aires.

Karen Goldstein Rossotto is a senior counsel in the Division of Investment Management of the U.S. Securities and Exchange Commission. She served as a professional staff member with the U.S. Senate Banking Committee's Subcommittee on International Finance and Monetary Policy. She holds a BA in economics and political science from the University of Wisconsin, a JD from Cornell University Law School, and an MSc in financial and commercial regulation from the London School of Economics.

Felipe Gomez-Acebo is a financial specialist with the Inter-American Development Bank, working as a task manager for projects in Argentina, Bolivia, Brazil, Chile, Paraguay, and Uruguay. He was a capital market development specialist with the Bank and held executive positions in the Spanish stock exchange system. He holds an MBA from ESADE of Barcelona and a master's degree in law from the Universidad Autónoma de Madrid.

Roberta S. Karmel is a professor of law and co-director of the Centre for the Study of International Business Law, Brooklyn Law School. She is a director of the Mallinckrodt Group, Inc. and Kemper National Insurance Company, and was formerly a commissioner of the U.S. Securities and Exchange Commission and public director of the New York Stock Exchange. She has written more than 30 articles for legal journals and writes a regular column for the *New York Law Journal*.

Kinga Korcsmaros is a senior consultant at the Vienna Exchange/Consulting and International Projects Division, and leads the Small and Medium Enterprise Finance Competency Center. She holds a master's degree from the University of Salzburg (Austria) and has worked on several international projects as a consultant in financial and capital market development, small and medium enterprise finance, and telecommunications.

Gregory J. Kuserk is a senior economist with the Office of the Chief Economist at the U.S. Commodity Futures Trading Commission. He has authored a number of papers on the market microstructure of exchanges and serves as the commission's expert on over-the-counter derivatives markets. Mr. Kuserk holds a master of science degree in agricultural economics from the University of Delaware and a bachelor of business administration degree from the University of Notre Dame.

Ronald B. Hobson is a senior economist with the Office of the Chief Economist at the U.S. Commodity Futures Trading Commission (CFTC). He has worked in various capacities for the CFTC for more than 25 years. He has a master's degree in economics from the University of California at Los Angeles.

Andrew Hook is an international consultant in the financial sector. He has been regional director of the Americas at Thomas Murray, U.K. He has worked at the International Monetary Fund and the World Bank. After earning an MBA at Columbia University in 1977, he joined the Federal Reserve Bank of New York as an international economist. He has worked in South America, the Middle East, and South East Asia.

Ruben Lee is the founder and managing director of the Oxford Finance Group, a research firm. He was a fellow at Nuffield College, Oxford University, and worked in capital markets in New York and London for Salomon Brothers International. He has published widely on many topics concerning financial markets, including most recently a book entitled *What Is an Exchange? The Automation, Management, and Regulation of Financial Markets.*

Mike Lubrano leads the Corporate Governance Unit in the Global Financial Markets Department of the International Finance Corporation. He received an MPA from the Woodrow Wilson School at Princeton University, a JD from New York University School of Law, and a BA from Harvard College.

Pietro Masci is chief of the Infrastructure and Financial Markets Division at the Inter-American Development Bank. He has held other positions at the Bank and worked with the Inter-American Investment Corporation and World Bank. He worked at the Italian Treasury on external borrowing and management of public debt. Mr. Masci holds a degree in economics and political science from the University of Rome and an MBA in finance from the George Washington University.

Robert J. Peterson is an attorney in the Office of International Affairs at the U.S. Securities and Exchange Commission (SEC). Before joining the SEC, he was an attorney in private practice at the law firm Fulbright and Jaworski in Washington, D.C. and a management consultant with A.T. Kearney in Chicago. He received a law degree and a master's degree in international relations from the University of Chicago.

Ivan Sotomayor has been a practicing accountant since 1984, serving a diversified client base in the United States and Latin America. He has been an advisor to the Colegio de Contadores Publicos Autorizados in Panama and the Federación de Colegios de Contadores Publicos in Peru. He received a BS in economics from California State University and an MBA from Golden Gate University.

Hannes Takacs heads the Consulting and International Projects Division of the Vienna Exchange and has more than 10 years of experience in consulting and international development. He specializes in capital markets and small and medium enterprise development, and has developed the meta exchange concept to create a regional capital market without losing the identity of the local exchanges.

Ethiopis Tafara is an assistant director with the Office of International Affairs at the U.S. Securities and Exchange Commission (SEC). Prior to joining the SEC, he was an attorney with the U.S. Commodity Futures Trading Commission (CFTC) and counsel to CFTC Chairperson Brooksley Born. Mr. Tafara was an attorney in private practice with the law firm Cleary, Gottlieb, Steen, and Hamilton in Brussels, Belgium, and is a graduate of the Georgetown University Law Center and Princeton University.

Antonio Vives is deputy manager of Private Enterprise and Financial Markets of the Sustainable Development Department at the Inter-American Development Bank. He holds a degree in chemical engineering from Universidad Central de Venezuela, and a master's degree in industrial administration and a doctorate in finance (corporate finance and capital markets), both from Carnegie Mellon University (Pittsburgh, United States).

Derek West is director of Strategic Planning and Business Development at the National Futures Association. He develops business opportunities related to regulatory programs and services intended to ensure marketplace integrity, protect market participants, and help members of self-regulatory organizations and other market participants meet their regulatory responsibilities. He holds a degree from the University of Ottawa, Canada.

Georg Wittich has been president of the Bundesaufsichtsamt für den Wertpapierhandel (BAWe) since October 1994. He represents the BAWe at several committees of the International Organization of Securities Commissions (IOSCO), and was elected vice-chairman of the Technical Committee of IOSCO for 1996 and 1997. He studied law at the University of Kiel, University of Freiburg, and University of Munich, Germany, as well as at the École Nationale d'Administration in Paris, France.

Karen K. Wuertz is a senior vice president with the Strategic Planning and Development of National Futures Association. She is licensed as a certified public accountant in the state of Illinois and holds a master's degree in management from Kellogg Graduate School of Management at Northwestern University and a bachelor of science degree in accounting from the University of Illinois.

Overview

Financial markets have a significant impact on economic growth and competitiveness. Experts, practitioners, and policymakers generally agree that the development of financial markets both precedes and facilitates economic performance. Thus, the relationship between financial development and economic growth is neither one-dimensional nor mechanical because developing financial markets without considering the real economy is not sufficient to ensure economic growth. For instance, U.S. financial and capital markets have grown because of the strong economy and companies' need for financing to grow and compete. The German economy grew despite the lack of a capital market because there was a solid banking system.

Although there is much to learn about the relationship between the financial and productive sectors, there is clear evidence that a well-functioning financial system positively influences growth and macroeconomic stability as well as encourages poverty reduction. However, a strong, export-oriented productive sector defines the scope of a financial system and requires that the financial sector become more sophisticated and complete. Furthermore, financial and capital markets, particularly in emerging market economies, constitute a "public good" that deserves the attention of policymakers and the expenditure of public resources. Policymakers need to find the right balance between allowing the real productive sector (which is typically outward oriented) to advance and devising a strategy for financial market development that facilitates the expansion of the real sector. Local capital market development is part of such a strategy.

Why is local capital market development important, especially now? It improves the efficient allocation of resources and reduces information asymmetries. The justifications for local capital market development refer to the need to reduce the risk of financial crises that result from an excessive reliance on external borrowing—for example, to avoid foreign exchange risk, reduce contagion, and decrease short-term external borrowing. In fact, as financial crises dwarf the role of financial intermediation, the problems of asymmetric information become even more severe, leading to greater public mistrust of financial institutions.

In addition, local capital market development allows emerging markets and particularly Latin American countries to use domestic resources for national fiscal evolution, avoiding the risk that globalization and information technology will deplete these countries' scarce savings by allowing them to be attracted to industrial countries. Thus, fostering local capital market development in Latin America and the Caribbean can be an important mechanism for completing financial sector development, facilitating economic growth, and reducing financial instability and crises.

Local capital markets embody market infrastructure, the legal and regulatory framework, and organizations and institutions. These markets function effectively through competition and enhanced information by using existing instruments, such as equity and bonds, and by creating new ones. The markets therefore ultimately permit economic growth and constitute a relevant development target.

Many Latin American and Caribbean countries can easily be included in the category of those that have not developed a fully functioning capital market and have suffered grave and recurrent crises. There is an extensive literature on capital market development in emerging markets in general and in Latin America and the Caribbean in particular. The literature provides analysis, insights, and recipes for building vibrant capital markets in the region.

Building on this literature and experience, the overarching goal of this book is to provide a forward-looking perspective on the issues that affect capital markets in emerging market economies. To this end, the book presents a set of critical issues that constitute the ingredients for a policy initiative to ensure local capital market development. The issues raised are addressed in a synergistic rather than isolated fashion, recognizing that the challenge for policymakers and regulators is to minimize interference with the functioning of markets but allow continuous oversight to detect problems and make appropriate interventions.

The Message of the Book

This book answers several questions: What is the status of market development in Latin America and the Caribbean? Which strategic initiatives foster market development? Who are the key players in the development of local capital markets? How are capital market institutions and organizations built? And how can trust and confidence be assembled and sustained to support the development of a capital market?

The book's authors assume that capital market development is a relevant initiative for policymakers to embrace. That is, ensuring the stability of the financial system and developing a capital market are worthy objectives of public policy. In pursuing these objectives, the political decision to reform the financial sector rests with the highest level of government, while the finance ministry has the day-by-day responsibility to build the necessary consensus among parties, design a long-term strategy, and monitor implementation.

In shaping the public policy interventions to develop capital markets, the governing authorities need to recognize that they must abstain from interfering with market functioning. Instead, their sphere of action must be limited to removing market imperfections and shortcomings—by providing vision and direction, ensuring good economic management, promoting the disclosure of information, avoiding monopolistic practices, and building institutions.

Thus, governments are not supposed to intervene to adjust asset price volatility but rather to eradicate the causes of excessive price swings that threaten the functioning of the financial and capital markets. Governments also can help market players realize that the rules are in place and that they are on their own to "play the game." The same right balance needs to be found between market functioning, regulation, and self-regulation—keeping in mind that the appropriate mix is constantly changing and thus needs to be monitored by interest groups that have the ultimate stake in the functioning of the market.

In accord with this balance, this book is both theoretically grounded and focused on operational issues in Latin America and the Caribbean. A combination of endogenous and exogenous factors has created a situation whereby the region's economies are hampering the export-oriented productive sector and directing insufficient resources to it. This makes the task of policymakers daunting and may create the wrong expectation that initiatives to reform the financial sector and local capital markets could entirely solve problems related to growth and resources directed to the productive sector. Policymakers need to find a balance between the two sectors. Moreover, the characteristics of Latin America and the Caribbean—such as the region's diversity—make the task of creating efficient capital markets more challenging than in other regions.

Latin America and the Caribbean faces a dire economic and financial situation in comparison with other regions, as is shown in table 1. The picture becomes even more distressing when the economic losses from the crisis in Argentina, which are not reflected in the table, are taken into account. Yet even though the average financial market development indicators for Latin America are well below worldwide averages, some countries in the region are at a level similar to that of industrial countries.

The regional integration of financial and other markets, which would be the long-term answer to many problems, constitutes the ultimate objective for the region's capital markets. However, for the time being, domestic interests still prevail and national and regional institutions continue to be feeble. The regional aspect of creating the critical mass to build a viable capital market requires leadership, a long-term view, and thinking beyond national borders.

The start-up role assigned to the public sector must be taken into consideration in the midst of these special circumstances and difficulties. The key challenge for

Table I | **Financial Market Development Indicators: Latin America and the Rest of the World**
(Percent)

Indicator	Latin America	Caribbean	Developed countries	Middle East and North Africa	South and East Asia	Sub-Saharan Africa	Transition economies
Bank credit to the private sector over GDP	24.20	43.20	75.90	41.00	44.30	14.40	26.40
Overhead costs	5.90	4.70	2.60	2.30	2.60	5.50	5.60
Net interest margin	5.80	4.50	2.50	2.70	3.10	5.70	5.40
Stock market capitalization over GDP	17.20	29.00	65.90	36.00	81.60	16.30	14.30
Stock market value traded over GDP	3.81	2.67	42.18	12.70	46.00	1.66	25.90

Source: The Latin American Competitiveness Report 2001–2002, World Economic Forum and Harvard Center for International Development.

public institutions is that the dynamics of capital markets are incredibly complex and the resources—human, financial, and institutional—are scarce. The challenges at hand include multiple and changing goals, and various and emerging topics, stakeholders, and decisionmakers. Government leadership is essential as markets evolve in response to new challenges and as institutions respond to new issues.

Investment in human capital and regional integration are the two key components of the public policy strategy for capital market development. The need for a skilled pool of professionals, experts, and practitioners to deal with capital market issues requires a forward-looking attitude, given the intricacy of the issues and their continuous evolution. Moreover, decisions about these issues (for example, the determination of financial standards) are made outside the substantive reach of emerging market countries. Governments in Latin America and the Caribbean thus face the intimidating challenge of building solid national institutions while markets become globalized and decisions are made beyond national boundaries. In this respect, the task requires hefty resources and the benefits will be realized far in the future.

The Structure of the Book

The book has four parts. Part I introduces the themes and topics. Part II describes the factors that affect the development of capital markets. Part III covers the issues in implementing capital market strategies. Part IV offers conclusions.

The introductory chapter that constitutes part I discusses the evolution of capital markets in Latin America and the Caribbean. It formulates the main components of a strategy for further development on the basis of three pillars: an enhanced regulatory framework, modernization of market institutions and actors, and support for regional efforts and activities. Assuming that an appropriate foundation for market activity is in place, the strategy focuses on increasing market activity and liquidity, broadening investor participation, and expanding the types of instruments traded.

The four chapters in part II review key factors underlying the development of capital markets. Chapter 2 examines the current status of emerging markets in relation to the progress that has been made during the past decade. It analyzes the key factors in the development of securities markets in both industrial and developing markets: globalization and regionalization of financial markets and increased competition; the role of technology in creating new types of trading platforms and the widespread use of the Internet in providing financial services; and the changing regulatory structure dealing with globalization, technological innovation, and the changing structure of securities markets. The chapter raises key policy questions and strategies for capital market development.

Chapter 3 looks at the impact of Internet technology on the development of securities markets. The chapter discusses the relevance for policymakers, regulators, and market participants of the early lessons many capital market regulators have learned regarding securities activities on the Internet. It centers on those areas that have seen the greatest growth and innovation and to which regulators have paid the most attention—that is, the use of the Internet by investors, exchanges, issuers, and market intermediaries; system capacity, resilience, and security; liability for hyperlinks and information contained on websites; the growth of day trading; and the unique enforcement concerns posed by Internet chat rooms and information stored by Internet service providers. Securities regulators have various options for using the Internet to better protect investors and promote market efficiency and transparency. The chapter states that the most significant lesson is that the fundamental principles of securities regulation do not change, regardless of the medium used to buy, sell, and market securities. The recommended focus is on the type of information made available to investors to protect them; enhance market fairness, efficiency, and transparency; and reduce systemic risk—rather than the manner in which that information is delivered.

Chapter 4 provides policymakers and financial experts with an overview of the most relevant issues related to the effect of macroeconomic policy, institutional arrangements, and other exogenous structural factors (such as market size) on the development of capital markets in emerging economies, with particular emphasis on Latin America. The chapter analyzes the constraints that the macroeconomic environment imposes, which are characterized by the impact of exogenous factors on the effectiveness of capital market performance. The chapter highlights the negative impact of financial regulations that give preferred status to banking over capital market investment and financing instruments.

Chapter 5 examines the relevance and role of institutional investors in fostering capital market development. On the basis of the experience of the United States and other countries that belong to the Organisation for Economic Co-operation and Development, the chapter provides policy guidance on how governments and policymakers can further encourage the growth of domestic institutional investors in Latin America and the Caribbean while capitalizing on the sector's potential benefits for the region's capital markets.

The chapters in part III review several important issues for developing strategies to implement capital market reform and offer guidance for building a capital market strategy. The issues addressed include regional integration, the bond and derivatives markets, international trends in clearance and settlement systems, and the role of corporate governance in fostering capital market development. Moreover, this part of the book goes considerably beyond many texts on financial sector reform by tackling the elusive topics of human capacity development and ethics.

Developing an approach to regional capital market integration is one of the most crucial topics in Latin America and the Caribbean. Chapter 6 examines the costs and benefits of and typical barriers to integration. It identifies the principles and methods that might be employed to promote integration, including regulatory standardization and harmonization, multiple listing, links and mergers between stock exchanges and other types of market institutions, technical interfaces, and information sharing. The chapter describes the success or failure of attempts to promote integration in different regions, identifies the elements of a strategy to promote integration, and discusses the optimal role and functions of policymakers, private sector entities, government agencies, regional bodies, and international financial institutions.

Chapter 7 emphasizes the role of information disclosure and accounting standards and practices in capital market development. It discusses accounting standards as an essential component of the global and regional public good. It identifies the peculiarities of accounting in emerging market countries, particularly in Latin America and the Caribbean; describes the debate between the two prevalent sets of accounting standards (the U.S. Generally Accepted Accounting Principles, or U.S. GAAP, and the International Accounting Standards, or IAS); and discusses the national standards of each country and reviews the progress of the process of convergence. The chapter describes the situation in Latin America and the Caribbean and makes public policy recommendations that point toward a long-term goal of accounting convergence between U.S. GAAP and IAS and the role of multilateral financial institutions.

Chapter 8 discusses the key risks in clearance and settlement systems and addresses the application of international standards in developing such systems. The chapter focuses on the challenges policymakers face in building market infrastructure in emerging economies. The underlying motive is that developing or upgrading capital market infrastructure is a responsibility of the public sector and part of the public policy agenda directed at developing capital markets. Designing and operating infrastructure that functions with a minimum of errors and delays and that can interact with other financial and information systems is a major challenge for policymakers in emerging economies, particularly in Latin America and the Caribbean. At the same time, policymakers need to regard this particular activity as part of the larger strategy of capital market development, providing the right incentives for the private sector to be part of this initiative, but at the same time not falling into the trap of thinking that infrastructure alone is sufficient for capital market development.

Demutualization is discussed in chapter 9, and this is somewhat of a departure because the focus is on the rationale for demutualization and the key issues developing countries must consider when thinking about the decision to demutualize. The chapter establishes that demutualization is fundamentally a strategic decision that Latin American and Caribbean countries are probably a few years behind in addressing. The chapter highlights some of the key trade-offs regulators must confront in developing a newly demutualized exchange, using lessons learned by established exchanges.

Chapter 10 highlights the importance of bond market development for the entire economy and financial system, and especially for building a sound domestic capital market. The authors explain the various steps and components for establishing a self-sustaining bond market. The chapter advocates that policymakers should be fully aware that development has to be addressed in a comprehensive way, taking into account that it is a long-term process and requires a strategic plan and a firm commitment to market practices.

Although derivatives markets are a long way off for many emerging econo-mies, some countries have introduced exchanges and others have introduced syn-thetic instruments that are traded either over the counter or as direct relationships between counterparts. Chapter 11 reviews the characteristics of derivatives markets and discusses the balance among regulation, market oversight, and self-regulation. Derivatives markets constitute a complement for cash markets. However, policy-makers should include derivatives markets as part of their strategy for capital mar-ket development and recognize the trade-off between markets and the role of the government.

Chapter 12 looks at the broader relationship between small and medium-size enterprises (SMEs) and financing, and focuses on the scope of capital market so-lutions for providing financing to SMEs. The chapter demonstrates that financing SMEs depends on the stage of development of the SME in its life cycle. Furthermore, the potential role for SMEs would be more in the context of an advanced stage of de-velopment. Many stock exchanges, mostly in industrial countries, are establishing in-novative structures to help SMEs gain access to capital markets. But it seems that in emerging market countries and in Latin America and the Caribbean, there is no clear indication of the potential for SME exchanges to meet the financing needs of SMEs.

Chapter 13 shows that ethical behavior—mostly as a form of self-regulation with disciplinary enforcement as well as a moral stigma—glues together the various elements that make a capital market work. Many reforms of legal and regulatory sys-tems, as well as the introduction of international standards, take for granted an insti-tutional ethical foundation that may not exist in Latin America and the Caribbean. Trust is the cornerstone for ethics. Legal enforcement, which is always regarded as a fundamental requisite, provides only an imperfect and partial substitute for trust. In this respect, trust is a public good that deserves equal if not greater attention than market infrastructure, legal systems, and benchmarks.

Chapter 14 explains why the relationship between capital market develop-ment and corporate governance is neither trivial nor linear. It is part of a loop, with a continuous interaction of factors that make up the machinery of corporate gover-nance but are also outside the typical definition of corporate governance. The chap-ter looks at the initiatives in corporate governance in emerging market countries and Latin America. An important element of the analysis is devoted to the trade-off between public law (law issued by a traditional legislature) and private law (contracts and self-regulation). As do other parts of the book, the chapter advises policymakers to find the right balance between public and private and between regulation and self-regulation, which is more of an art than a science and requires continuous attention and revision.

Human capital is essential for making reforms work. Without dedicated and skilled professionals, no system can function and prosper. The challenge for emerging market countries is not only to invest in human capital but also to mitigate the risk of losing trained people, because they may be attracted elsewhere. Chapter 15 offers an innovative model for human capacity building that is specific to capital markets in Latin American and Caribbean economies. On the basis of an analysis of the region's needs, the chapter spells out the factors that need to be considered in generating an agenda to improve human capacity building.

Part IV has two main objectives: to synthesize the book's main findings and to identify the practical issues that must be considered in building capital market strategies. The conclusion provides guidance for the countries of the region, including the roles of government, the private sector, and multilateral development banks. In this sense, the conclusion articulates practical measures to facilitate capital market development and to strengthen the roles of the relevant players in Latin America and the Caribbean.

What Is Next?

The various chapters of the book constitute individual areas that need to be tackled to attain the goal of developing a capital market in an emerging economy. One of the shortcomings of many strategies for capital market development—more than getting the sequencing wrong—is failing to fully understand the links between the various components and how the development of efficient capital markets requires an overall strategy as well as plans for each component. Macroeconomic and structural policies, accounting practices and standards, bond market development, market infrastructure, derivatives markets, corporate governance, ethics, human capital, regional integration, and technology are not isolated mechanisms. Instead, they are all parts of an integrated approach that must be understood, designed, orchestrated, implemented, and monitored. Policymakers need to follow this whole approach synergistically to ultimately strengthen the institutions that support the functioning of capital markets. Ideally, the parts of this whole together compose a unified matrix of policies that governments can pursue. This matrix can guide the actions of governments and stakeholders as well as frame the support that international financial institutions can offer to meet the goal of building a better financial system.

PART I

INTRODUCTION

■CHAPTER 1

Developing a Strategy for Reforming Capital Markets in Latin America and the Caribbean

Kenroy Dowers
Felipe Gomez-Acebo
Pietro Masci

History appears to indicate that a good financial system has five key components: sound public finance and public debt management, stable monetary arrangements, a variety of banks, a central bank to stabilize domestic finances and manage international financial relations, and well-functioning securities markets.

In the past decade, the countries in Latin America have undertaken important reform programs that in general have brought macroeconomic stability and improved the performance of the first four key elements. Inflation and government deficits have been reduced, monetary growth is under better control, and external debt as a percentage of both GDP and exports has fallen. However, although the region's financial markets have been liberalized, their activity presents a picture of steady decline that has impaired their functioning and efficiency. Increasing attention has been directed to this key element and to the role that capital markets play in stimulating or supporting economic development. This chapter addresses the functioning of securities markets and the need for a comprehensive strategy to direct reforms and key variables.

Capital markets help to mobilize national savings, channeling them into potential productive projects and attracting international funds and investors. This process provides access to capital at lower cost and facilitates the growth of companies and of the economy as a whole. In particular, stock markets ease resource mobilization and can improve economic efficiency and accelerate long-run growth.

Capital markets could be more advantageous to other sources of financing (such as bank financing) by providing companies with alternative funding mechanisms to support rapid growth relative to those that depend solely on internal sources of funds. Loans are inappropriate for risky venture capital projects. Throughout the world, there is a trend away from bank-dominated systems and toward mixed systems. Countries in the region require a shift away from bank dependence through the growth of a complementary capital market–based financial industry to increase access to long-term financing and lower its cost.

Capital markets help the financial sector achieve efficient allocation of resources and economic growth. These functions include clearing and settling payments, pooling funds to facilitate investment and achieve diversification, transferring economic resources over time, pooling and sharing risk, making price information available, and providing ways to deal with incentive problems when there is asymmetric information. Investors are usually reluctant to relinquish control of their savings for long periods; however, many high-return projects require a long-run commitment of capital. Capital markets solve this problem through risk pooling and instruments that permit diversification and maturity transformation, allowing savers to have liquid assets while firms have permanent use of the capital raised by issuing equities.

Capital markets have additional functions, including providing more democratic access to capital, presenting financial support to innovators and entrepreneurs, and reducing the risk of contagion based on problems within one firm or industry that could spread to the overall economy. Equity and debt markets, in particular, serve to enhance corporate governance through increased monitoring of management performance, reduced agency cost, information dissemination, and increased efficiency of investments and management decisions. The possibility of takeover increases the pressure, promoting management efficiency.

Diversified financial systems result in more dynamic and efficient capital allocation processes. The efficient management of economic risk and uncertainty allows for long-term commitments to capital investments, leading to greater capital formation and accumulation. Thus, capital market development constitutes a form of public good, and government is required to step in to promote its development and act as a regulator to reduce information asymmetries and increase efficiency.

In the past decade, many countries in Latin America and the Caribbean have adopted policies aimed at creating or improving domestic capital markets to realize some of these specific benefits. A precondition to the success of these policies is to build on a foundation of political, legal, and macroeconomic stability. Moreover, realizing the benefits depends on the level of development, liquidity, depth, and completeness of the markets.

The focus on development of the domestic capital market in emerging countries can be divided into two stages or generations.[1] In the first generation, the focus

---

[1] The concept of first- and second-generation capital market reforms is used in this chapter to underscore differences in the emphasis and focus of the types of policies, programs, and activities applied to create viable capital markets.

was on creating a good foundation for market activity. Thus, the main preoccupation was the introduction of an appropriate legal and regulatory framework for the operation of stock and debt markets. During the first stage, attention was directed at the delicate balance between creating a legal/regulatory environment that stimulates capital market activity and establishing safety, discipline, and soundness. Another component of the first generation of reforms was the development of market institutions to expand trading. Visible elements of the first phase include enactment of capital market regulation, introduction of trading mechanisms, creation of a securities regulatory body, clearance and settlement systems, and investor education.

During the first phase, another important development was the creation and growth of institutional investors, such as pension funds, mutual funds, and insurance companies, and the increasing need of financing for the companies. This growth has responded to changing circumstances, including a more predictable macroeconomic and political environment, more resources available to individuals planning for their future, more sophisticated risks (such as aging disabilities), and the opening of markets with increasing commercial and financial opportunities.

The second generation of reforms in capital market development adopts a different focus. It presumes that the foundation has been laid or is well under way, and attention moves to increasing market activity and liquidity, broadening investor participation, and expanding the types of instruments traded. The elements of the second-generation reforms are also driven by vast development in technology and increasing investor sophistication.

This chapter explores the impact of these second-generation reforms on the full development of capital markets in Latin America and the Caribbean. The analysis presents some of the critical ingredients required for developing a strategy to increase capital market activity in emerging countries. It examines the factors affecting local capital markets in Latin America and the Caribbean and provides the elements of a strategy to promote their development.

Literature Review

The development of financial markets is widely acknowledged to be one of the crucial issues facing emerging markets with an impact on economic growth. For Levine and Zervos (1996), stock market development is positively associated with economic growth. Levine (1997) and Beck and Levine (2001) find a positive causal impact of financial development on productivity and economic growth. Demirgüç-Kunt and Levine (1996) show that the level of stock market development is good at predicting economic growth. Caprio and Demirgüç-Kunt (1997) confirm that long-term credit is scarce in emerging countries and more so for smaller firms that could obtain term finance in developed countries. Long-term credit is associated with higher productivity.

Boyd and Smith (1996) show that the endogenous evolution of debt and equity markets in the development process provides an economy with more efficient capital markets. Levine and Zervos (1998) exemplify that equity market liquidity is correlated with rates of economic growth. In that vein, Al-Yousif (2002) studies time series and panel data for 30 developing countries in 1970–99. The results support the view that financial development and economic growth are mutually causal, but the relationship cannot be generalized across countries because economic policies are country specific and depend on the efficiency of the implementing institutions. Wurgler (2000) finds that financially developed countries boost investments more in their growing industries and reduce it more in their declining industries. Therefore, the efficiency of financial markets allows a better allocation of capital and determines economic growth.

Taking the perspective of global markets, Rodrick (1999) examines the relation between openness to trade and economic growth, and introduces the role of the financial sector in a standard cross-country analysis. Rodrick finds that the relationship between openness to trade and economic growth is weak. In contrast, Bekaert, Harvey, and Lundblad (2001) find that financial liberalization is associated with higher real growth. Rajan and Zingales (2001) illustrate the role of openness and interest group politics in financial market development. Bekaert, Harvey, and Lumsdaine (2002) show that integration is accompanied by a significantly larger equity market, more liquidity, and more volatile stock returns, and is more correlated with world market returns. Integration is associated with a lower cost of capital, improved credit rating, real exchange rate appreciation, and increased economic growth.

Regarding the specific policy choices that spur capital market development, the research examines the relevance of legal regulatory reform, property rights, the role of institutional investors, and effective corporate governance. La Porta and others (1997, 1998) confirm that the legal environment and enforcement matter for the size and extent of capital markets. They study the quality of laws governing investors' protection and enforcement and confirm that a weak legal system has a negative impact on financial development and economic growth. Demirgüç-Kunt and Maksimovic (1998) illustrate that in countries with an efficient legal system, a greater proportion of firms uses long-term external financing. On the relevance of institutional investors for capital market development, Gompers and Metrick (1998) analyze the holdings of individual investors in the United States and confirm the role of institutional investors in capital market growth, determination of asset prices, and liquidity. Impavido, Musalem, and Tressel (2001) demonstrate that the development of contractual savings institutions has a significant impact on the financing patterns of firms across and within countries and a comparative advantage in supplying long-term finance to corporations.

On the role of corporate governance reform for fostering capital market development, La Porta and others (2000) look into investor protection as a factor in capital market development. Lopez-de-Silanes (2001) indicates that the legal system, that is, rules and enforcement, matters for the size and extent of a country's capital market. He develops indicators of investor protection and the legal system based on a cross-sectional review of countries in 1999. Various authors have explored how institutional inheritance affects financial development, for example, Coffee (2000), Rajan and Zingales (1999), and Stulz and Williamson (2001).

Capital Markets in Latin America and the Caribbean

In reviewing the development of domestic capital markets in Latin America during the past decade, it is necessary to review the macroeconomic situation during the period. With some exceptions, during the 1990s, sound macroeconomic policies, market liberalization, and the privatization of state enterprises restored economic growth in Latin American and Caribbean countries. Real gross domestic product (GDP) growth averaged 3.3 percent a year during the decade (World Bank 2001).

Net equity investments in the largest Latin American countries increased from $7.3 billion in 1989 to more than $61 billion in 2000 (IMF 2001a). During the same period, external borrowing increased from $417 billion to $809 billion, but it declined as a percentage of both GDP and exports of goods and services, compared with 1989. Public sector borrowing also declined from 40 percent to 4 percent, reflecting the impact of privatization on fiscal policy. However, the countries in the region still rely on external financing to sustain growth. The structural current account deficit (almost $48 billion in 2000) is nearly exclusively financed through direct investment, with only a small portion of financing stemming from portfolio investment. Savings in 1999 represented 18 percent of GDP, compared with 34 percent in Asia. Fiscal policy has led to mixed performance with respect to budget deficits as a percentage of GDP, with some countries (for example, Mexico) showing stabilization below 2 percent, while others present a declining but high budget deficit (for example, Argentina and Brazil).

Decline in Local Capital Markets

The improving macroeconomic situation has not grown in tandem with activity in the region's financial and capital markets, which have been marked by numerous market crises, weaknesses, and volatility. We use size and liquidity indicators to measure the development of stock markets. Market capitalization equals the total value of all listed shares in the market at market prices. It is assumed that the size of the stock market is positively correlated with its ability to mobilize capital and diversify risk.

Secondary market liquidity shows roughly the capacity of the market to fulfill the roles of attracting capital inflows and providing allocation efficiency, risk diversification, information, and price discovery. Without liquidity, the markets lose the transformation function, lessening the interest of potential investors who might not be able to access their funds quickly. In addition, without liquidity, primary markets do not develop efficiently. The diversity of the instruments used also represents an indicator of market development.

Emerging financial markets are small relative to mature markets and generally small relative to GDP. In the year 2000, around half of the $2.7 trillion in emerging market capitalization was in Asian markets; the Latin American share was about 20 percent. As figures 1-1 to 1-5 show, relative to other countries, domestic capital markets in Latin America and the Caribbean are underdeveloped with respect to market depth, quality, and ability to attract domestic and external resources.[2] Box 1-1 compares traded activity for selected countries in Latin America and the Caribbean with countries with more advanced capital markets. After the emerging market crises of the late 1990s, Latin American exchange problems have tended to worsen rather than improve.

A number of factors have caused the decline of local markets in Latin America. The cost of operating in the stock market (for example, measured by fee levels or time for liquidation) is proportionately higher in Latin America and the Caribbean than in other regions. The region's stock exchanges do not substantially affect large companies that are able to raise funds abroad. However, small and medium-size start-up companies, which generate new employment, are not able to obtain financing. Even when money is available locally, taking a company public in Latin America is often not considered worth the effort because local exchanges lack capital, liquidity, and risk-tolerant investors. This is especially true for new economy or Internet companies, which do not become profitable for several years. These factors have led a growing number of Latin American blue chip firms to delist their shares on local stock exchanges.

---

[2] On the size and scope of financial markets in developing countries, see Levich (2001).

Figure 1-1	**Equity Capitalization in the World, 1991–2001** *(Trillions of U.S. dollars)*

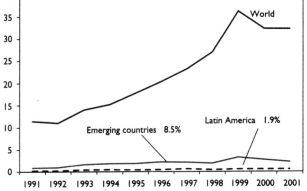

Source: IFC (various years).

Figure 1-2	**GDP per Capita and Market Capitalization in Selected Countries, 2000** *(Percentage of GDP)*

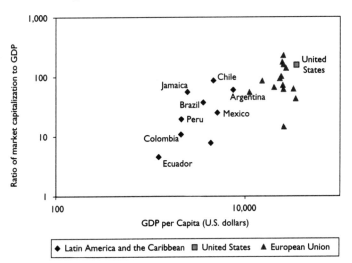

Source: IFC (various years).

Figure 1-3	Market Capitalization in Selected Countries, 1991–2000
	(Percentage of GDP)

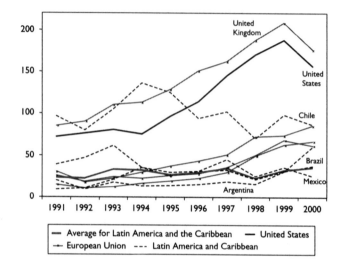

Figure 1-4	Value Traded in Selected Countries, 1991–2000
	(Percentage of GDP)

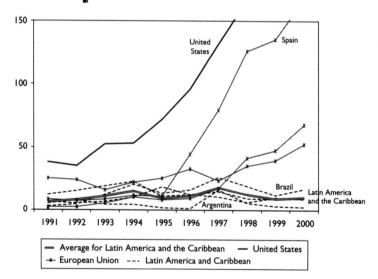

Source: IFC (various years).

Figure 1-5	**Turnover Ratio for Selected Countries, 1991–2000**

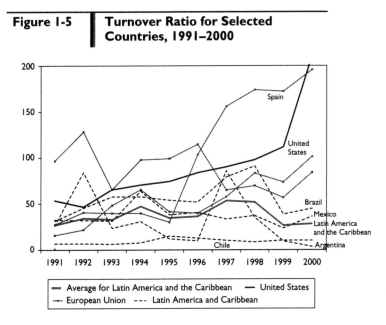

Source: IFC (various years).

During the first half of the 1990s, these shortcomings were largely offset by international portfolio investment. Fund managers and investors in industrial countries invested heavily in emerging countries through equities, bonds, and project finance based on the expectation that economic growth and market returns in those economies would exceed growth in the United States and Europe. Furthermore, it was hoped that international portfolio investments would provide opportunities for risk diversification due to the low cross-correlation between rates of return in emerging markets and industrial countries.[3] Unfortunately, those expectations have not been realized. The U.S. stock market outperformed other markets in 1987–99—data returns for the Europe, Australia, and Far East index (EAFE); Standard and Poor's; and Morgan Stanley Capital International (MSCI) versus the National Association of Securities Dealers and Automated Quotations (NASDAQ)—as did the U.S. bond market.[4]

Since the emerging market crises, access to international capital markets has been more difficult for Latin American countries. In 2000, for the first time in a

---

[3] In general, by holding an asset whose returns are not correlated with the returns of another asset, investors can raise the overall return on their portfolios without equivalent increase in risk.

[4] Investors have not completely abandoned the companies of emerging countries, but only 8.5 percent of all global funds' assets are stocks classified as those of emerging countries, after a peak of 12.5 percent in 1994.

Box 1-1	Trade Activity

The data on Latin American stock exchanges present a picture of decline. Over the period 1991–2000, the number of listed companies on Brazil's São Paulo Stock Exchange declined by about 19 percent, from 570 to 459. Argentina's stock exchange has experienced an even greater decline, falling by 27 percent, from 174 to 127 listings.

In the same period, the value traded on the Argentina Bolsa went from $15,679 million in 1992 to $50,956 million in 1997 and declined to $4,189 million in 2002. In 2000, on average, stock market capitalization in Latin America was about 34 percent of GDP. In the United States, it was almost 200 percent, while it was well above 80 percent in Europe.

Liquidity, measured as turnover of the capital of the companies listed over GDP, is about 10 percent in the major Latin American exchanges, more than 200 percent in the United States, around 70 percent in Europe, and more than 130 percent in Spain.

decade, the region had a decrease in foreign direct investment, reflecting the completion of many large-scale privatization projects (see table 1-1). Foreign direct investment continued to rise and offset the disappointing performance of bank lending and portfolio investment. Emerging Latin American and Caribbean countries are at this point investment-starved due to high levels of public sector debt, which reduces the resources for local capital market development, while making international investors nervous and therefore leading to capital outflows.

Moreover, the political events of September 11, 2001, the Argentina crisis, and various setbacks in the U.S. stock market have accelerated the slowdown in growth and increased asset price volatility, playing an important role in determining the terms and conditions under which Latin American market entities can access international capital markets. The increasing role of mature market developments in the

Table 1-1	Net Flows of Private Capital to Western Hemisphere Emerging Markets, 1993–2001 *(Billions of U.S. dollars)*

Private capital	1993	1994	1995	1996	1997	1998	1999	2000	2001
Private capital flow, net	37.4	47.1	44.0	66.4	70.6	71.3	43.2	42.5	27.1
Direct investment, net	12.2	22.8	24.2	40.3	56.2	60.6	64.1	61.6	67.2
Portfolio investment, net	45.5	65.0	0.8	38.8	25.9	18.7	11.1	4.6	0.9
Other private capital flows, net	−20.3	−40.7	19.0	−12.7	−11.5	−8.0	−32.0	−23.8	−41.0

Source: IMF (2001a, 2002).

conditions of market access reflects the lack of a significant, dedicated investor base and the dominant role of crossover investors in Latin American financial markets.

The role of crossover institutional investors is particularly important in transmitting the effects of asset price volatility from mature to emerging markets. Crossover investors typically hold most of their investments in mature markets and invest a relatively small fraction of their holdings as claims on emerging markets.[5] During a period of uncertainty about emerging market developments and/or increased risk aversion, investors reduce or eliminate investments in emerging economies. A recession in the United States would reduce capital flows to Latin America and the Caribbean due to deterioration in the region's prospects for exports, smaller inflow of funds from crossover investors, and weaker business prospects. A lower international interest rate would be unlikely to be sufficient to change the scenario.[6]

In this difficult environment, Latin American countries with severe domestic imbalances, somehow hidden by the now ending exceptionally favorable external environment of the 1990s, might have to confront more supply constraints and see little increase in net flows. This scenario emphasizes the importance of reform of domestic capital markets in the region.

Factors Affecting Market Development

The past decade witnessed severe financial crises in emerging economies—most notably, the devaluation of the Mexican peso in 1995 and the Thai baht in 1997, the Brazilian crisis of 1998, and the Argentina crisis of 2001—that highlight the risks of investing in emerging markets. In addition, the expectations of low correlation in investing internationally do not fully apply for many securities in emerging countries. These two factors have made investors wary of investing in international and, in particular, emerging capital markets.

The demand for securities from emerging markets depends on expected returns and the stage of development of the market infrastructure, especially the legal and regulatory framework and the level of transparency under which listing firms operate. In Latin America and the Caribbean, the securities that have successfully attracted international investors have been characterized by international activity, application of international standards in accounting and auditing, and simultaneous listings

---

[5] According to 1995 data, 1 percent of domestic equity holdings by institutional investors in the G-7 countries is equivalent to slightly more than 1 percent of global stock market capitalization but to 66 percent of the market capitalization of the Latin American economies.

[6] Furthermore, the events of September 2001 will certainly have an adverse impact on the global economy.

Box 1-2 | **Depository Receipts**

There is an increasing shift toward depository receipts. A growing number of Latin American equities are being traded away from their home markets to the depository receipt market, predominantly American Depository Receipts (ADRs) and Global Depository Receipts (GDRs).

A depository receipt is a negotiable security that generally represents ownership of shares in a company domiciled in one country (for example, an emerging market) that are held by a depository custodian bank, which issues a certificate that can be traded in another country (mostly in the United States), and that represents a claim on the underlying shares. ADRs, which trade in the United States, were introduced in 1927 and are the oldest form of depository receipt. Before 1990, there were few depository receipt programs from emerging countries. However, during the 1990s, emerging market companies accounted for a majority of new programs and capital raised in most years.

ADRs were developed to address some of the concerns of U.S. investors interested in investing abroad but reluctant to purchase foreign stocks. ADRs eliminate many of the disadvantages of holding non-U.S. shares because they do the following:

- Trade in accordance with U.S. clearing and settlement conventions
- Are quoted in U.S. dollars and pay dividends in U.S. dollars, thus avoiding exchange risk
- Eliminate global custodian safekeeping charges and can trade freely on the major U.S. exchanges.

The advantages of a depository receipt program for companies include the following:

- Access to capital markets outside the home market
- Expansion of the shareholder base
- Increased potential liquidity by enlarging the market for the company's shares that may increase or stabilize the local share price
- Enhanced shareholder communications.

While these developments are driven by the maximization of the valuation of the company and are good for shareholders, the negative implications for the stock exchanges in the Latin American region include reducing volume and liquidity.

---

in the United States and/or Europe. However, few Latin American companies, typically in the telecommunication and media sectors, are able to reach that level and are truly integrated and capable of raising resources through American Depository Receipts (ADRs) and Global Depository Receipts (GDRs) (see box 1-2).

Substantial amounts of trading activity have shifted from Latin America to the United States. In 1995, ADRs trading in Argentine stocks totaled $15.7 billion, more than three times the total amount transacted on the Buenos Aires market. Mexican ADRs totaled $54.4 billion, that is, one and a half times all stock trading in Mexico. Chilean ADRs were $11.6 billion, slightly more than total trading in Santiago. For specific stocks, ADR trading exceeds the volume of domestic transactions in the same security in their respective home markets, shifting price discovery to the New York Stock Exchange (NYSE). In 2000, for Mexican companies, the value of trading on the NYSE (the majority listed as ADRs) totaled $54.0 billion, compared with $45.3 billion in the domestic market. The value for Brazil was $69.4 billion; Argentina, $7.9 billion; and Chile, $5.3 billion,[7] compared with $101.2 billion, $6 billion, and $6.1 billion in their respective markets. Under these circumstances, the recently created *comisiones de valores* (securities and exchange commissions) are financially strapped because their revenues depend on stock market activity that has been steadily declining. This phenomenon erodes the independence of the commissions and threatens their long-term survival.

Privatization and mergers and acquisitions also contributed to the state of capital markets in the 1990s. The trend has been the acquisition of Latin companies by foreign firms, such as AES, Telefónica, Repsol, Endesa, and Banco Santander Central Hispano (BSCH). These acquisitions have led to the removal of local companies from national exchanges, as listings were consolidated with those of the parent companies in exchanges outside Latin America. The problem is dramatic in Argentina, where delisting by foreign companies of their Argentine subsidiaries has resulted in a 50 percent reduction in market capitalization over the last few years.

A similar process of consolidation has swept through the banking sector in Latin America, but with a more limited impact on the development of local capital markets. Many of the acquiring firms are based outside Latin America and the Caribbean, and bank consolidation across Latin American countries is limited. Under these circumstances, some newly listed companies, especially Internet companies, have had their initial public offerings in mature markets, ignoring the local markets (see box 1-3).

Although economies in Latin America and the Caribbean have grown during the past decade, investors have not been directed toward the region's capital markets. They require good liquidity and shareholder protection, which are crucial elements in evaluating a company. This implies that fund managers favor those emerging companies that apply international financial standards in their statements and represent global growth companies in well-identified sectors. Furthermore, fund managers consider the emerging market stocks of companies that are fully integrated into the global economy, which receive attention and investments regardless of the fact that

---

[7] Non-U.S. value of trading by geographic region (NYSE web page).

| Box 1-3 | Impact of the Internet on Capital Market Activities in Latin America |

Recently, the Internet and initial public offerings (IPOs) have become part of the Latin American landscape. The following are some noteworthy examples.

- Starmedia, one of the most successful Latin American Internet companies, raised $330 million in two public offerings on Wall Street. Its shares, listed in the NASDAQ, initially sold at $5 and traded for as much as $60, although they have recently lost much of their value as a result of a generalized cooling of the Internet sector. Starmedia did choose not to list on any exchange in Latin America.
- El Sitio, an Internet portal and service provider based in Buenos Aires, also raised millions of dollars through an IPO on NASDAQ.
- Yupi Internet Inc., another portal company, raised start-up money in the United States with the goal of serving Latin American countries. It intended to sell shares to the public in the United States, not in Latin America.
- Ibolsa, an Internet company, sells and buys shares over the Internet. Its customers are the Latin American community living in the United States. Ibolsa represents a vehicle for Latin American investors. Ibolsa is under the jurisdiction of the U.S. Securities and Exchange Commission and is also listed on NASDAQ.

they are emerging market companies. Investors are attracted to securities with the best returns, easiest access, and highest quality in terms of standards and services (corporate governance, disclosure, and market regulation). Similarly, local companies do not regard their capital markets as the answer to their funding needs because of the high cost of capital, short tenure, adversity to risk, and lack of liquidity. Issuers go where they get the lowest cost of capital, which is tied to demand by investors.

It seems safe to state that, in the past two decades, most Latin American and Caribbean countries have undertaken several courageous reforms. However, the various actions have not been connected at the national level and certainly even less at the regional level. For instance, privatization was motivated by cash needs and not seen as a component of capital market development. Government bond markets emerged more to provide resources for the needs of the public sector than as a building block for the capital market.

Structural changes are taking place, and some Latin American governments are taking encouraging steps toward building a solid financial system and stronger capital markets. Despite the shortcomings, capital market flows have assumed an increasingly important role compared with international bank flows (see table 1-1). This shift reflects the diversification of banks into financial services and the increased role of institutional and multinational investors. For the change to be sustainable, however, local capital markets will need to become more attractive to investments. Ideally, domestic capital markets must also be seen as one of the most effective ways of protecting against market turbulence and contagion.

Given the relevance of capital markets, current circumstances raise several critical questions. What should be the role of the public sector in market development? What is an appropriate sequence leading to capital market development? What areas should be targeted as crucial second-generation reforms? While the private sector plays a pivotal role in the development of capital markets, Latin American governments must take bold and unequivocal steps to ensure that local markets can prosper.

A Strategy to Promote the Development of Capital Markets in Latin America and the Caribbean

Second-generation reforms for capital markets assume that the foundation and fundamentals for capital market activity are in place. The goal of these reforms is to create mechanisms to increase market activity and liquidity, broaden market participation, and increase the variety of instruments traded to make the markets more attractive to investors. We propose that a suitable capital market strategy should focus on the proper functioning of three basic aspects: building an enhanced regulatory framework; broadening the role of market institutions and actors; and supporting regional efforts and activities for capital market integration.

Enhanced Regulatory Framework

For many countries in the region, it is necessary to restructure the regulatory framework to ensure market viability. The regulatory framework should guarantee that the incentives and structure of the market are consistent with efficiency, fairness, and safety. Market participants, rather than governments, should be mainly responsible for establishing and enforcing market regulations. Nevertheless, adequate official oversight should be provided to verify that the rules are indeed fair and evenly enforced and information asymmetries minimized. For some countries, particularly small, emerging economies, the battle between self-regulation and optimal supervision depends on regulatory capacity.

The legal regulatory structures currently in place seek to increase security and investor protection and, to a lesser extent, to encourage internal competition between market institutions. However, this approach has been insufficient because of the lack of market depth. A new focus is necessary to strengthen the market, support external competition, and ensure that the regulatory framework meets international standards. The regulatory authorities have to foster market confidence and growth. Their function is critical for making the market attractive to individual and institutional investors.

The regulatory framework should address three important and related issues: a reliable legal and judicial system, good corporate governance, and transparency and disclosure. However, harmonization is necessary to make the restructuring successful and obtain balanced and efficient markets. Further, the focus should be on advancing the legal basis for all three regulatory objectives.

A reliable legal and judicial system is essential for the development of a sustainable capital market because a reliable system encourages appropriate market incentives, allows equitable and reasonably affordable access to legal remedies for dispute settlement, and guarantees oversight of market functioning. Any judicial incapacity regarding the enforcement of contracts would increase uncertainty and reduce the attractiveness of the market. Therefore, effort should be dedicated to enhancing the regulatory institution responsible for oversight of the securities market. Countries should establish or strengthen their Comisión Nacional de Valores (CNV, Securities and Exchange Commission), which may require choosing between a securities regulator and an integral approach to financial market regulation.

Good corporate governance ensures protection of the rights of shareholders (particularly minority shareholders); equitable treatment of the participation of shareholders and stakeholders in decisions relating to management compensation, mergers and acquisitions, dividend policy, and other significant corporate actions; and dissemination of appropriate information to the investor community. Fair treatment implies that voting power and dividends should be proportional to the number of shares held and that disclosure announcements should not discriminate among shareholders. Good governance also increases the role of boards of directors, ensuring fair and autonomous selection, training commensurate with responsibilities, and sufficient motivation to create value for shareholders. Regulations promoting these criteria make a capital market more attractive for investors. The recent cases of Enron, Global Crossing, and WorldCom demonstrate that, even in a sophisticated capital market like that of the United States, corporate governance and oversight play a crucial role in the functioning of the market and in the trust and confidence of investors. In Latin America, traditionally the protection of minority shareholders and corporate governance in general have been ineffective, but there is consensus on the need for modernization. Some countries have already changed, and others are in the process of changing, the regulations.[8]

Implementation of principles and practices that promote transparency and disclosure and allow comparability in relation to international best practices is directly related to corporate governance and sets the foundation for regional integration and harmonization.[8] Public disclosure is the key to increasing transparency in the market. Disclosure should start when a firm issues securities to the public and should continue thereafter. Listing, initial offering, and disclosure requirements should occur on a timely basis. Listing requirements deal with the minimum disclosure requirements for a firm to list in the market, while initial offering requirements refer to the disclosure mandated for a firm to issue new securities. The initial offering disclosure should involve information that allows investors to evaluate the overall condition of the firm and more specific information about the new issue, such as the amount of capital to be raised, its purpose, and how the offering price was determined. Disclosure requirements should also include periodic reporting on important corporate developments that may affect the company's business and stock price. Rating agencies and credit bureaus also have an important role in promoting a transparent information environment.[10] However, disclosure will be effective only if the financial information is based on accounting principles and practices well understood by investors. Harmonization of accounting standards will be especially helpful in attracting foreign investors.

Reform could include utilization of the principles for securities regulation established by the International Organization of Securities Commissions (IOSCO). These principles, developed through global consensus, are essential to ensure that international standards for market activity are maintained. The principles have specific applications and guidelines for all market actors, from regulators and enforcement agencies to market participants. Regulatory reform should also seek to create an environment that encourages the participation of new potential issuers of securities. The Association of the Securities and Exchange Commissions of the Americas (COSRA) encourages its members to adopt IOSCO's core principles for securities supervision, international accounting standards issued by the newly revamped International Ac-

---

[8] See OECD (1999).

[9] Policymakers are considering utilizing opacity as an advanced version of transparency. Opacity is defined as the lack of clear, accurate, formal, and easily discernible and widely accepted practices in the world's capital markets and national economies. Opacity poses an obstacle to economic progress as it results in lost opportunities for investment and higher costs of capital. This concept is being advanced and promoted by PricewaterhouseCoopers and other policymakers. For more information, refer to www.opacityindex.com.

[10] For a regulatory model based on public disclosure and self-imposed market discipline, see Strahota (1996).

counting Standards Board (IASB), and the corporate governance principles of the Organisation for Economic Co-operation and Development (OECD 1999). However, each country or region should adapt the principles to suit its own markets. The one-size-fits-all approach to regulation would be inappropriate.

A key problem many domestic capital markets face is the need to increase market liquidity. In this regard, regulations that focus on improving liquidity should be designed to do the following: increase the efficiency of securities trading; improve the role of organized markets and the concentration of operations in those markets; develop internal markets in relation to external ones and allow remote members free entry to markets; establish a strong market maker; and institute a comprehensive market perspective that includes the submarkets that currently exist in each country. It is also crucial to eliminate dispersed regulations (established with other goals) that could hamper market competitiveness. With respect to the activity of the regulator, improving market competitiveness depends on the quality of regulation and, above all, on enforcement capacity. International institutional investors consider enforcement one of the main elements when deciding where to invest.

There is encouraging evidence that countries in Latin America are moving toward regulatory regimes that meet the standards of foreign investors. Brazil is at the forefront in defining and implementing a strategy for local capital market development and is acting on several fronts. The Commissão de Valores Mobiliarios (CVM, Securities and Exchange Commission of Brazil) has instituted developments to make it difficult for controlling shareholders to coerce minority shareholders into selling their stakes in public tender offers. By increasing the minimum level of approval for such decisions (from 50 to 67 percent), CVM is signaling that Brazil intends to protect the rights of shareholders and evolve into a modern financial center. The government is taking action to shape the local government bond market, increase its liquidity, and lengthen the tenor of corporate issuers. The accounting profession is also taking decisive steps toward introducing accounting and auditing standards that are aligned with international best practices. Brazil is also working on the other end of capital market development: the access of small and medium-size companies. The São Paulo Stock Exchange (Bovespa) has launched the Novo Mercado, a trading environment that is intended to attract companies that have the highest standards and are hungry for capital (for example, technology companies like Microsiga Software constitute one of the Novo Mercado targets).[11]

---

[11] The increased volume of trade activity in the stock exchanges of Brazil and Mexico in the year 2000 seems to suggest that reform efforts pay off.

The Novo Mercado is a listing segment designed for trading shares issued by companies that voluntarily undertake to abide by corporate governance practices and disclosure requirements in addition to those already requested by Brazilian legislation. The inclusion of a company in the Novo Mercado implies the company's adherence to a series of corporate rules, known generically as "good practices of corporate governance," which are more rigid than those required by current legislation in Brazil. These rules, consolidated in the Listing Regulation, increase the rights of shareholders and enhance the quality of information commonly provided by companies. In addition, the creation of a Market Arbitration Chamber for conflict resolution between investors and companies offers investors a safer, faster, and specialized alternative. The main innovation of the Novo Mercado, compared with the current Brazilian legislation, is that nonvoting shares may not be issued. A similar initiative is under way in Chile, with the Ley de Oferta Públicas de Adquisición de Acciones (Initial Public Offering Law), which was approved in December 2000. The law establishes public share offers and corporate governance, giving stronger protection to minority shareholders.

The government of Mexico has proposed legislation to allow swift action on insider trading and greater protection for minority shareholders, based on the assumption that greater shareholder protection could double market capitalization and attract five times the number of companies currently listed. At the same time, the country is revitalizing the local bond market. The upgrade of Mexico's sovereign debt rating by a major ratings agency in August 1999 helped to increase investors' confidence, and in 2000, the Mexican government made its first privatization through the stock market. Chile is also expected to increase the corporate issuance of inflation-indexed units.

Another encouraging sign is the growing amount of funds (mostly pension funds) managed by institutional investors. Mexico introduced the private pension system in 1997 and already manages $28 billion, around 5 percent of GDP. Argentina created pension funds in 1994, and they have accumulated resources totaling $21 billion (7.4 percent of GDP). Brazil, which has not yet privatized its social security system, holds more than $175 billion in mutual fund assets. Chilean institutional investors and insurance companies hold more than $45 billion. These funds, presently mostly invested in government securities, seek diversified investment opportunities within local markets.

The situation for the smaller countries in the region is characterized by increasing cross-border intraregional activity. Countries in the subregions of Central America and the Caribbean have launched regional capital market development programs, which include collaboration on market infrastructure, coordination of the legal regulatory framework for trading and market activity, and cross-listing agreements. More work is needed in this area along the lines described in the section on regional integration.

Market Institutions and Actors

To increase market competitiveness, countries should also focus on enhancing primary and secondary market institutions. The primary market needs good transparency and disclosure as a main requirement. In addition, development of the primary market relies on standardized and uniform securities issuance methods and established initial offering requirements, specifically regarding information that allows investors to evaluate the condition of the firm issuing the securities. However, these rules should not impose any unnecessary restrictions on the mechanisms of public offering. It is also important to explore other types of instruments that could be introduced in the marketplace using venture funds, securitization, and products that help small and medium enterprises gain access to capital markets. Efforts should be made to implement standards that subscribe to international best practice and allow for wider dissemination among the public.

For secondary market activity, market institutions must play a central role in increasing liquidity. A market without liquidity cannot develop its functions. In an ideal regulatory framework, with the holding structure or the equivalent tailored to the country's needs, market institutions should act as "champions of the security industry." However, these institutions must also graduate from being merely "the meeting point of supply and demand" to being "the meeting point of potential demand and supply." This can be achieved through the following channels: transformation of market institutions into venture capital leaders, creation of virtual meeting points between possible suppliers and demanders, and massive education of investors.

An important element in the process is the market infrastructure, comprising the systems and institutions that facilitate the trade, transfer, and custody of securities. Market infrastructure that functions well reduces obstacles to trading flows and custody and builds controls for systemic risk. Efficiency and reliability are the main concerns. There are many recommendations for what constitutes best practice; some examples are the G-30 recommendations and the revisions suggested by the International Society of Securities Administrators, the Lamfalussy standards, and the conclusions of the task force between the Committee on Payment and Settlement Systems and IOSCO.

Although much has been done in recent years, the following improvements to reduce transaction costs and attract potential investors and issuers are still necessary:

- A computerized, automatic, matching trading system to enhance market transparency despite the fact that this system is not the best suited to increasing liquidity for large orders
- Systems to facilitate the comparison of trade details between the counterparts (again, computerization is cost-efficient for all but the smallest markets)
- Clearance and settlement systems to accomplish settlements by a delivery versus payment system with same-day funds
- Risk control systems to reduce the operational risk and problems with lost transactions, bad record keeping, or computer problems
- Independent central depository systems for the safekeeping of securities, with an independent registry of registries to encourage immobilization and dematerialization and facilitate the settlement process and other aspects of custody.

All these systems represent the steps in a market transaction. They should grow together in order to establish an active and dynamic market.

Market institutions include private sector members and perform important public sector goals. Institutions can play a central role in advancing the reforms to enhance liquidity, as has been the case in several European countries. Isolated interventions by the public sector lack sustainability; market innovation has to come from within the markets themselves. Only market institutions, as intermediary associations, can combine interests that have the necessary amount of leverage and sustain a competitive drive. They boost the integration processes that generate the critical mass needed for the survival of these markets. Hence, public sector support for organized markets should be seen not as a subsidy for a private project, but as a measure to provide the financial systems of the region with a relevant development instrument.

Simultaneously, market institutions have to ensure wide access for broker-dealers by providing incentives for their activities while ensuring that self-regulating structures are created to monitor these activities. However, the present situation is far from perfect, as in many cases there are important structural deficits (particularly in small, concentrated markets) that lead to development of fragmented markets and club structures. These structures reduce market integrity and hinder market competitiveness. The trend in many countries is toward the creation of holdings that bring markets together as well as clearance and settlement agencies to avoid insufficient internal competition. These holdings also allow markets to dispose of redundant structures by sharing systems and professional management. Moreover, they reduce the requirements for collateral, allowing for a better use of capital.

For example, Brazil and Colombia have integrated all the regional stock exchanges on a national level. In Brazil, trading of stocks will be carried out on the São Paulo Stock Exchange, while trading of bonds will be conducted on the Rio de Janeiro Stock Exchange. The other regional exchanges will concentrate activities on developing the market and providing services to local markets. This trend toward increasing consolidation among financial institutions as a way to remain competitive has been facilitated by technological advances such as the Internet and online trading. In Argentina, consolidation of the exchanges has been slow. However, an agreement was signed in March 2000 between the market institutions and the national authorities to redefine the market structure.

It is essential that market institutions offer instruments that meet the needs of investors and particularly those of institutional investors that dominate emerging markets. These investors demand that instruments present identifiable risk features, sufficient liquidity, appropriate tenure, and comparable returns. This is a daunting task for many domestic markets, as they cannot compete with the international products offered to institutional investors. However, with increasing innovation and commitment to develop products—such as pooled instruments, project financing vehicles, and bonds (government, municipal, asset-backed, and corporate)—it should eventually be possible to attract more institutional investors to Latin America's domestic markets. For example, Brazil and Mexico have been making efforts to build and lengthen government bond yield curves. The next challenge is to create liquid secondary markets and develop corporate debt.[12]

Institutional investors who can operate in domestic currencies are critical for capital formation and for increasing the growth of domestic savings. In Latin America, the reform and privatization of social security—shifting from pay-as-you-go pension systems to fully funded pension schemes—have opened big opportunities for long-term growth in the stock markets and fostered the development of financial instruments with long-term horizons. Private pension funds are growing at a fast pace (see box 1-4); however, excessive regulations have delayed the benefits and restricted the activity of funds. In Mexico, pension funds are not allowed to invest in stocks. In Argentina, the maximum amount authorized to invest in stocks is 35 percent, but regulations regarding the credit ratings of eligible companies have limited the investment in equities to 14 large listings, reducing the possibilities of diversification. Therefore, investments in stocks reach only 19 percent of total assets. These regulations and the high real interest rates on government bonds concentrate the investments in public sector liabilities.

---

[12] The lack and/or high level of the risk-free rate discourages the formation of other fixed-income assets.

| Box 1-4 | | Pension Funds |

The growth of private pension funds has been one of the most important developments in domestic capital in Latin America and the Caribbean. Their resources are rapidly becoming the major source of domestic long-term capital and can contribute to the development of financial markets.

Latin America's private pension funds are currently estimated to have more than $85 billion under management. Brazil does not have a private system, but corporate pension funds are valued at around $75 billion.

Pension Fund Assets under Management, 1994–2000
(Millions of U.S. dollars)

Country	1994	1995	1996	1997	1998	1999	2000	2001
Argentina	525	2,497	5,323	8,827	11,526	16,787	20,381	20,786
Brazil	55,081	62,693	73,454	83,444	82,029	71,230	74,755	67,958
Chile	22,296	25,143	27,198	30,525	30,805	34,501	35,886	35,460
Colombia	38	265	802	1,367	2,110	2,887	3,584	4,951
Mexico				615	5,801	11,509	17,012	27,146
Peru	260	583	949	1,510	11,734	2,406	2,752	3,622

Source: International Federation of Pension Fund Administrators (FIAP).

Financial innovation is another key for the maintenance of competitive capital markets. The relatively more developed markets in the region must be able to provide new techniques and a greater number and type of financial instruments. In these economies, there is an important unmet demand for risk management and investment services that needs to be addressed. Expanding the use of derivatives and developing new instruments, such as securitization and guarantees, should be encouraged.

Given the increasing importance of small and medium enterprises to economic activity, efforts must be directed to supporting their growth and development by creating suitable market structures to increase their access to financing and capital. These developments could include programs for specific types of initial public offerings for these entities, specialized trading facilities (similar to the Nuovo Mercato in Italy and the Neuer Markt in Germany), and government-supported finance programs.

Regional Capital Market Integration

Regional integration is a crosscutting issue that is critical for the development of many sectors in Latin America and the Caribbean. Given the lack of depth and critical mass in most of the region's markets, regional capital market integration is an important policy consideration. The main benefits of capital market integration are that competition lowers transaction costs, allows larger regional firms to exploit economies of scale, and creates more liquid, efficient, and broader securities markets, lowering prices for all financial services. In general, discussions on this issue focus on the importance of common trading systems. While this is an important dimension, it can sideline more critical issues that have greater implementation potential.

Today's technological and communication advances affect the integration process and its increased liquidity. The simplest strategy is to build cooperative initiatives between different markets with open trading systems. The strategy would include the following elements:

- Trading systems that could operate in the interested markets, so that market and remote members would have access only to their respective market, but with the possibility of seeing the activity of each and every one of the markets that are part of the single trading system
- Media systems in which agencies (such as Reuters and Bloomberg) spread information about various markets jointly, in the various currencies
- Routing orders that would allow crossing connections
- Clearance and settlement procedures that would also allow accounts to cross borders.

A strategy of capital market integration based on these elements could facilitate increased liquidity without the need to harmonize individual legal systems or consolidate relevant regulatory frameworks and agencies. In such a setting, the market actors are responsible for boosting performance in the various markets.

Over time, this structure could motivate market members to progressively increase the degree of cooperation and integration, including legislative and regulatory initiatives aimed at promoting integration; sharing information between the regulators of the jurisdictions in the region; harmonizing regulation between jurisdictions; establishing a system of mutual reliance between the regulators; and creating a legal environment in which mutual recognition between regulators and home-country control is accepted and enforced (see box 1-5 for recent developments). To be successful, the integration strategy should also have high-level political support, ambitious but realistic targets, and adequate financing.

Creation of a unified market will require developing a more holistic process, taking into consideration macroeconomic and fiscal concerns, exchange rates, financial sector policy, and cross-border issues. In developing this strategy, it will be neces-

---

Box 1-5	**Recent Developments in Capital Market Integration**

- The Ibero-American Securities Markets Institute was founded in May 1999 to facilitate cooperation and exchanges among the regulatory bodies that supervise securities markets in Spain, Portugal, and 15 Latin American countries. Other objectives include fostering their development and promoting legal harmonization in the area.
- The Argentine, Brazilian, and Uruguayan stock exchanges signed an agreement that will allow them to interconnect their operations in the future.
- The new euro-based Latin American stock market, LATIBEX, began trading in 2000. This new exchange, established with Spanish capital, is designed to help generate financing in European markets for firms in the region.
- The Brazilian and Mexican stock exchanges are participating in negotiations among 10 world stock markets led by the NYSE to establish a common stock market that would allow 24-hour trading around the world.

---

sary to address specific considerations relating to the benefits of integration, the region or regions to which the strategy should apply, barriers to integration, and methods for removing them.

Conclusion

Although Latin American and Caribbean economies have implemented programs and policies to foster the development of capital markets over the past decade, the evidence demonstrates that many of the markets are still fragile and lack depth and liquidity. This chapter has discussed several factors that explain the current status of capital markets in the region and presented a strategy for governments to fully develop capital markets. We support an approach that encourages increased market activity and liquidity and advocate advancing a second generation of legal and regulatory reforms. These reforms should emphasize the adoption of internationally accepted accounting standards, development of good corporate governance, and increased transparency and disclosure to encourage supply and demand of securities to take place in local capital markets.

The roots of the encouraging movement toward capital market development, undertaken by the largest countries of the region, are driven by government's recognition that local capital market development constitutes a public good that needs to be pursued. Political will and leadership are the crucial ingredients for success. However, different from the past, it is crucial that government understands that capital market development is not the summation of various actions, but requires a holistic approach to be pursued with a long-term view and perseverance.

Implicit in the strategy is the potential role for international financial institutions to support the development of capital markets. These institutions can foster and facilitate the articulation of a vision of the role of capital markets as an appropriate component of public policy. Once each country reaches political consensus and clarifies the role of capital markets, further support could be directed to developing the regulatory environment. At the same time, international financial institutions could provide support for the goal of moving toward regional capital market integration and for initiatives that seek to harmonize practices in subregions.

Integration of Latin American and Caribbean markets and/or integration with a large global block (for example, as in the case of Mexico with the United States) are becoming the trademark for the success of emerging markets. In addition, the trade benefits of integration allow economic convergence and a reduction of the cost of capital, which lead to increased competitiveness.

Bibliography

Allen, Franklin, and Gale Douglas. 2000. *Comparing Financial Systems*. Cambridge, Massachusetts: MIT Press.

Al-Yousif, Yousif Khalifa. 2002. Financial Development and Economic Growth: Another look at the Evidence from Developing Countries. *Review of Financial Economies*.

Annamali, N. 2001. *Small Financial Systems: Regulatory Unions as a Way Forward*. Washington, D.C.: World Bank.

Bank for International Settlements. 2001. Electronic Finance: A New Perspective and Challenges. *BIS Papers* No. 7, Basle.

Barro R. 1991. Economic growth in a cross-sector of countries. *The Journal of Economics*.

Barth, James R., Gerard Caprio Jr., and Ross Levine. 2000. *Banking Systems around the World: Do Regulation and Ownership Affect Performance and Stability?* Milken Institute, World Bank and University of Minnesota.

Beck, Thorsten, and Ross Levine. 2001. *Stock Markets, Banks, and Growth: Correlation or Causality*. Washington, D.C.: World Bank.

Bekaert, Geert, Campbell R. Harvey, and Robin L. Lumsdaine. 2002. Dating the Integration of World Equity Markets. *Journal of Financial Economics.*

Bekaert, Geert, Campbell R. Harvey, and Christian Lundblad. 2001. Emerging Equity Markets and Economic Development. *Journal of Development Economics.*

Blaschke, W., M.T. Jones, G. Majnoni, and S. Martinez Peria. 2001. Stress Testing of Financial Systems: An Overview of Issues, Methodologies and FSAP Experiences. IMF Working Paper, International Monetary Fund, Washington, D.C. June.

Bortolotti, Bernardo, Marcella Fantini, and Domenico Siniscalco. 2001. Privatization: Politics, Institutions and Financial Markets. *Emerging Markets Review.*

Boyd, John, and Bruce Smith. 1996. The Coevolution of the Real and Financial Sectors in the Growth Process. *The World Bank Economic Review* 10(2).

Caprio, G. 2001. Finance for Growth: Policy Choices in a Volatile World. World Bank, Washington, D.C.

Caprio, Gerard Jr., and Aslï Demirgüç-Kunt. 1997. The Role of Term Finance: Theory and Evidence. Policy Research Department, World Bank, Washington, D.C.

Caprio, G., P. Honohan, and J. Stiglitz, eds. 2001. *Financial Liberalization: How Far How Fast?* Cambridge, Mass.: Cambridge University Press.

Choi, J. Jay, and John A. Doukas. 1998. *Emerging Capital Markets.* London: Quorum Books.

Claessens, Stijn, Daniela Klingebiel, and Sergio L. Schmukler. 2001. The Future of Stock Markets in Emerging Economies: Evolution and Prospects. Unpublished.

Coffee, John. 2000. Convergence and its Critics: What are the Preconditions to the Separation of Ownership and Control. Mimeo. Colombia University.

Crotty, James, and Lee Kang-Kook. 2002. Is Financial Liberalization Good for Developing Nations? The Case of South Korea in the 1990s. *Radical Political Economics* 34, pp. 322–34.

Dattels, P., and P. Bestus-Cardiel. 1995. The Microstructure of Government Securities Markets. Monetary and Exchange Affairs Department, International Monetary Fund, Washington, D.C. June.

Del Valle, Clemente, M. Batlay, and E. Togo. 1998. Overview of Fixed Income Securities Markets in Developing Countries. Capital Markets Development Department, World Bank, Washington, D.C. December.

Demaestri, E., and P. Moreno. 2001. Financial Market Development in Latin America and the Caribbean—Support from the IDB Group (1990–2000). Inter-American Development Bank, *Infrastructure and Financial Markets Review*. March.

Demirgüç-Kunt, Aslï, and Ross Levine. 1996. Stock Markets, Corporate Finance, and Economic Growth: An Overview. *The World Bank Economic Review* 10(2).

Demirgüç-Kunt, Aslï, and Vojislav Maksimovic. 1998. Law, Finance and Firm Growth. *The Journal of Finance*.

Dowers, K., F. Gomez-Acebo, and Masci, P. 2000. Making Capital Markets Viable in Latin America and the Caribbean. Inter-American Development Bank, *Infrastructure and Financial Markets Review*. December.

Economic Commission for Latin America and the Caribbean (ECLAC). Various years. *Economic Survey of Latin America and the Caribbean*. Santiago, Chile: ECLAC.

Financial Stability Forum. 2000. Report of the Follow-up Group on Incentives to Foster Implementation of Standards, Meeting of the Financial Stability Forum. 7–8 September.

Fischer, Bernhard. 1998. *Institutional Investors, Saving and Capital Markets in Emerging Economies*. Nomos Verlagsgesellschaft Baden-Baden.

Gompers, Paul A., and Andrew Metrick. 1998. Institutional Investor and Equity Prices. Working Paper 6723. National Bureau of Economic Research.

Guadamillas, M., and R. Keppler. 2000. *Securities Clearance and Settlement Systems: A Guide to Best Practices*. Washington, D.C.: World Bank.

Haque, Nadeem U., Robert B.H. Hauswald, and Lemma W. Senbet. 1999. Financial Market Development in Emerging Economies: A Functional View. Unpublished.

Harwood, A., ed. 2000. *Building Local Bond Markets: An Asian Perspective*. Washington, D.C.: International Finance Corporation.

Ho-Hahm, Joon, and Frederic S. Milshkin. 2000. Causes of the Korean Financial Crisis: Lesson for Policy. Working Paper 7483. National Bureau of Economic Research. January.

Howard, Alison, Robert Litan, and Michael Pomerleano. 1999. *Financial Markets & Development. The Crisis in Emerging Markets*. Washington, D.C.: The Brookings Institution.

Impavido, Gregorio, Alberto R. Musalem, and Thierry Tressel. 2001. Contractual Savings, Capital Markets and Firms' Financing Choices. Financial Sector Development Department, World Bank, Washington, D.C.

Institute of International Finance. 2000. Comparative Statistics for Emerging Market Economies. Institute of International Finance, Washington D.C. April.

_____. 2001. Capital Flows to Emerging Market Economies. Institute of International Finance, Washington, D.C. January.

Inter-American Development Bank. 2001a. Proceedings of the Roundtable *A New Focus for Capital Market Development in Latin American and the Caribbean.* Washington, D.C., February 5–6.

_____. 2001b. *Summit of the Americas. Strategic Programs.* Washington, D.C.

International Finance Corporation (IFC). Various years. *Emerging Stock Market Fact Book.* New York, NY: Standard and Poor's.

International Monetary Fund (IMF). 2001a. *Global Economic Outlook.* Washington, D.C.: International Monetary Fund.

_____. 2001b. *International Capital Markets.* Washington, D.C.: International Monetary Fund.

_____. 2002. *Global Economic Outlook.* Washington, D.C.: International Monetary Fund.

International Monetary Fund and World Bank. 2001. *Guidelines for Public Debt Management.* Washington, D.C.: International Monetary Fund and World Bank.

Jacome H.L.I. 2001. Legal Central Bank Independence and Inflation in Latin America during the 1990s. IMF Working Paper. Monetary and Exchange Affairs. December.

La Porta, Rafael, Florencio Lopez-de-Silanes, Andrei Shleifer, and Robert W. Vishny. 1997. Legal Determinants of External Finance. *The Journal of Finance.*

_____. 1998. Law and Finance. *Journal of Political Economy.*

_____. 2000. Investor Protection and Corporate Governance. *Journal of Financial Economics.*

Lamfalussy, Alexandre. 2000. *Financial Crises In Emerging Markets.* New Haven, CT: Yale University Press.

Lee, J. Y. 2000. *The Role of Foreign Investors in Debt Market Development: Conceptual Framework and Policy Issues.* Washington, D.C.: World Bank.

Lee, Ruben. 1998. *What Is an Exchange?* New York, NY: Oxford University Press.

_____. 2001. Promoting Regional Capital Market Integration. Prepared for the Roundtable "A New Focus for Capital Market Development in Latin American and the Caribbean," February 5–6, Inter-American Development Bank, Washington, D.C.

Levich, Richard. 2001. The Importance of Emerging Capital Markets. *Papers on Financial Services.* Washington, D.C.: Brookings Institution.

Levine, Ross. 1997. Financial Development and Economic Growth: Views and Agenda. *Journal of Economic Literature.*

Levine, Ross, and Sara Zervos. 1996. Stock Market Development and Long-run Growth. *The World Bank Economic Review.* 10(2):323–39.

_____. 1998. Stock Markets, Banks and Economic Growth. *The American Economic Review.*

Lopez-de-Silanes, Florencio. 2001. *The Politics of Legal Reforms.* J.F.K. School of Government, Harvard University and NBER.

Love, Inessa. 2000. Financial Development and Financing Constraints: International Evidence from the Structural Investment Model. Unpublished.

Mathieson, D.J., and G.J. Schinasi. 2000. International Capital Markets: Developments, Prospects and Key Policy Issues. International Monetary Fund, Washington, D.C. September.

_____. 2001. International Capital Markets: Developments, Prospects and Key Policy Issues. International Monetary Fund, Washington, D.C. August.

MEFMI, South African Debt Office, the World Bank. 2000. *Sovereign Debt Management, Cash Management and Domestic Market Development: Case Study, Malawi.* Washington, D.C.: World Bank.

McInish, Thomas H. 2000. *Capital Markets. A Global Perspective.* Malden, MS: Blackwell Publishers.

Merrill Lynch. 2002. *Size and Structure of the World Bond Market: 2002* Merrill Lynch.

Mishkin, Frederic S. 2001. Financial Policies and the Prevention of Financial Crises in Emerging Market Countries. Working Paper 8087. National Bureau of Economic Research. January.

Morck, Randall, Bernard Yeung, and Wayne Yu. 2000. The Information Content of Stock Markets: Why Do Emerging Markets Have Synchronous Stock Price Movements? *Journal of Financial Economics.*

Obstfeld, Maurice, and Alan M. Taylor. 2002. Globalization and Capital Markets. Working Paper. National Bureau of Economic Research.

Organisation for Economic Co-operation and Development (OECD). 1999. *Principles of Corporate Governance*. Paris: OECD. May 26–27.

Rajan, Raghuram, and Luigi Zingales. 1999. The Politics of Financial Development. Mimeo. University of Chicago.

_____. 2001. The Great Reversals: The Politics of Financial Development in the 20th Century. Unpublished.

Rodrik, S. 1999. *Determinants of Economic Growth*. Washington, D.C.: Overseas Development Council.

Rousseau, Peter, and Sylla Richard. 2001. Financial Systems, Economic Growth and Globalization, Working Paper Series 8323. National Bureau of Economic Research.

Shleifer, Andrei, and Daniel Wolfenzon. 2002. Investor Protection and Equity Markets. *Journal of Financial Economics*.

Stiglitz, Joseph E. 1993. The Role of the State in Financial Markets. *Proceedings of the World Bank Conference on Economic Development*. Washington, D.C.: World Bank.

Strahota, Robert. 1996. Securities Regulation in Emerging Markets: Some Issues and Suggested Answers. Paper presented at the SEC's 1996 International Institute for Securities Market Development in Washington, D.C.

Studart, Rogerio. 2000. Financial Opening and Deregulation in Brazil in the 1990's Moving toward a New Pattern of Development Financing? *The Quarterly Review of Economics and Finance* 40.

Stulz, Renee, and Roham Williamson. 2001. Culture, Openness and Finance. Working Paper. Ohio University.

Sundaranjan, V., P. Dattels, I.S. McCarthy, M. Castello-Branco, and H.J. Blommestein. 1994. The Coordination of Domestic Public Debt and Monetary Management in Economies in Transition—Issues and Lessons from Experience. Monetary and Exchange Affairs Department, International Monetary Fund, Washington, D.C. December.

Van Horne, James. 2000. *Financial Markets Rates and Flows*. Upper Saddle River, NJ: Prentice Hall, Inc.

Vittas, Dimitri. 2000. Pension Reform and Capital Market Development: 'Feasibility' and 'Impact' Preconditions. Development Research Group, World Bank, Washington, D.C.

World Bank. 1997. *Private Capital Flows to Developing Countries. The Road to Financial Integration.* New York, NY: Oxford University Press.

_____. 2000. *World Bank Development Indicators 1993–2000.* Washington, D.C.: World Bank.

_____. 2001. *Global Development Finance.* Washington, D.C.: World Bank.

World Bank and International Monetary Fund. 2001. *Developing Government Bond Markets: A Handbook.* Washington, D.C.: World Bank and International Monetary Fund.

Wurgler, Jeffrey. 2000. Financial Markets and the Allocation of Capital. *Journal of Financial Economics.*

Yago, Glenn, Thomas Hall, and Michael Harrington. 2000. *Think Locally, Act Globally. Capital Power Restructuring and Global Economic Growth.* Milken Institute.

Zask, Ezra. 2000. *Global Investment Risk Management.* New York, NY: McGraw Hill.

PART II

FACTORS AFFECTING THE DEVELOPMENT OF CAPITAL MARKETS

CHAPTER 2

Globalization, Technology, and Regulation in Capital Markets: Strategies for Latin America and the Caribbean

Reena Aggarwal

This chapter examines the current status of emerging markets with respect to the progress made during the past decade. It analyzes key factors affecting the development of securities markets in both developed and developing markets. These include:

- Globalization and regionalization of financial markets and increased competition
- The role of technology in creating new types of trading platforms and widespread use of the Internet in providing financial services
- The changing regulatory structure for dealing with globalization, technological innovation, and the changing structure of securities markets.

The chapter raises key policy questions and offers strategies for capital market development in Latin America and the Caribbean.

Capital markets allow for efficient capital raising and allocation of limited resources. Well-functioning primary and secondary capital markets provide issuers the ability to raise capital and investors the ability to invest in diverse financial instruments at low transaction costs. This helps to lower the cost of capital for issuers so they can compete globally; it also helps to increase savings that will be channeled into productive investments. Thus, capital markets lead to overall efficiency and economic development and growth. They also play an essential role in improving corporate governance, disclosure standards, transparency in the marketplace, and accounting standards. The optimal amount of transparency and regulation leads to credibility and therefore growth of capital markets. A sound regulatory framework is the cornerstone of vibrant financial markets (box 2-1).

Box 2-1	The Role of Capital Markets

- Resource channel
- Capital formation
- Efficient allocation of capital
- Economic development
- Investment opportunities for citizens and institutions

Several Latin American securities markets have made major strides in the past decade. This is clear from the increased access of large Latin American blue chip companies and governments to global financial markets. This access reduces the cost of capital for these companies and makes them more competitive at the global level. Ultimately, this means economic growth in the country and the region. However, success has also led to some problems for local markets.

When capital raising and trading move out of the country, local exchanges suffer in the form of lower capitalization, lower volume, and lack of liquidity. In addition to dealing with the issue of large blue chip companies, there should be a strategy to help small and medium-size companies raise capital. These companies are the engines of future growth. The region has made important advances in the past decade; however, a lot more needs to be done in terms of formulating a strategy to integrate into the global financial marketplace, address technological issues, continue to develop the appropriate legal and regulatory infrastructure, and strengthen the development of financial intermediaries.

The global economy and the availability of the Internet are reducing the role of financial intermediation. Exchanges could lose their traditional sources of revenue and must develop strategies to add value or face the consequence of becoming obsolete. For example, listing fees will not be a major source of revenue in the future; instead, the competitive position of the exchange will depend on the trading volume that it attracts. The role of stock market intermediaries, such as market makers and specialists, will be reduced in certain cases. Markets will not revolve around intermediaries or exchanges; the most important determinant of success will be who attracts trading activity.

This chapter raises the politically sensitive question of whether every country, especially every smaller country, needs its own exchange. If so, then at the minimum, countries should consider the possibility of sharing services between exchanges in the region to reduce costs and make the exchanges efficient.[1]

---

[1] Part of this work draws on Aggarwal (2001).

Globalization and technological innovations provide both opportunities and challenges for market development and also for regulators. The window of opportunity is small because of intense global competition; however, Latin American markets are well positioned to exploit it. Latin America has several large companies that are actively traded and of interest to global investors. However, if markets truly become global, there will be little need for these companies to trade on the local domestic exchange. Therefore, local exchanges must develop a strategy to attract liquidity and global investors. Caribbean countries are developing a regional approach, and this is appropriate for their long-term strategy.

The Current Status of Emerging Capital Markets

Emerging markets have made significant progress in market infrastructure, institutions, and regulation. Computerized trading systems have been set up with expanded capacity and transparency. Market capitalization and trading volume increased significantly during the past 15 years. World market capitalization increased almost 10 times, from $3.39 trillion to $32.26 trillion between 1983 and 2000; for the U.S. markets, it increased from $1.9 trillion to $15.1 trillion. The most dramatic increase was for emerging markets, from $67 billion to $2.74 trillion (see table 2-1).

The rise in trading volume provides evidence of increased liquidity in the markets. Worldwide trading volume increased 40 times, from $1.2 trillion in 1983 to

Table 2-1 | **Market Capitalization and Trading Volume, 1983–2000**
(Billions of U.S. dollars)

	Market capitalization			Trading volume		
Year	World	United States	Emerging markets	World	United States	Emerging markets
1983	3,389	1,898	67	1,228	797	25
1986	6,514	2,637	238	3,574	1,796	83
1989	11,714	3,506	738	7,468	2,016	1,166
1992	10,933	4,485	991	4,783	2,082	628
1995	17,788	6,858	1,911	10,227	5,109	1,046
1998	26,948	13,451	1,855	22,575	13,148	2,415
1999	36,149	16,635	3,152	30,360	18,574	3,111
2000	32,260	15,104	2,740	47,870	31,862	4,052

Source: IFC (1992, 1995, 2001).

Box 2-2	Second-generation Regulatory Challenges

- Development of financial intermediaries
- Development of institutional investors
- Role of self-regulatory organizations
- Investor protection
- Risk management
- Financial engineering
- Cross-border regulation

$47.87 trillion in 2000; for the United States it increased 40 times, from $797 billion to $31.86 trillion. For the same period, emerging markets saw the most dramatic increase of 162 times, from only $25 billion to $4.05 trillion (table 2-1).

Several factors explain the growth of emerging markets, including privatization, participation of foreign institutional investors, increased domestic investor base, and more issuers going to the market. Clearance and settlement systems have also become more efficient. The regulatory framework has undergone some major changes, with countries issuing new securities laws and setting up independent regulatory agencies with a reduced role for the state.

However, many emerging markets now need to start addressing "second-generation" capital market development issues (box 2-2). These include development of financial intermediaries that have staff with financial sector skills, an enhanced domestic institutional investor base, self-regulatory organizations, and mechanisms for investor protection. Risk management at all levels of the financial structure is extremely important but severely lacking in emerging markets. Emerging markets must also think about introducing new financial products that are suitable for local markets and develop financial engineering. This will require investment in human capital.

Innovation is also important for competing in the global marketplace, and the regulatory structure should be supportive of such innovation. Both industrial and developing countries have to work together to address cross-border trading issues. Some countries are making good progress on all these issues, while others lag behind. For example, Chile has been able to develop institutional investors, and Brazil is paying attention to corporate governance issues, with the São Paulo Stock Exchange (Bovespa) starting a new tier for companies that meet high corporate governance requirements.

Questions about how to regulate financial markets in the face of major transformations are being studied and debated at many levels, even in developed markets.

In the United States, NASDAQ is in the process of demutualizing and the New York Stock Exchange (NYSE) is considering it, while the U.S. Securities and Exchange Commission (SEC) is reassessing the role of self-regulatory organizations (SROs). There is considerable consolidation taking place in the financial services industry, blurring the distinction between banking, insurance, and the securities industry. This requires enhanced cooperation between regulators, even within the same industry. The concept of domestic markets will not be significant when the industry becomes truly global in nature. Issuers will raise capital wherever it is cheapest, and investors will invest their money wherever it is most profitable and transaction costs are low. Globalization is at the root of some of the change, but technology is at the heart of many of the changes and is clearly the major force in today's marketplace. These developments are posing interesting challenges for regulators. However, there is no one-size-fits-all approach to regulation that will work for all jurisdictions.

Globalization

Globalization is changing the nature of capital raising and securities trading. It is creating opportunities but also posing challenges. There is no question that emerging markets are becoming integrated into the global financial system; the questions are whether those markets are ready and how they will be affected. Physical trading floors are being replaced by electronic trading systems, and the Internet is playing a crucial role in the globalization of markets. Internet use is expected to grow by 60 percent in one year on English-language sites and by 100 percent on non-English sites (Zarb 2000). Information is available quickly and cheaply, foreign markets are one mouse click away, and individual investors have as much access to the market as institutional investors. Issuers look beyond national boundaries to raise capital wherever it is cheapest. Investors also want to invest globally in order to earn higher returns and diversify their portfolios. The rapid pace of global mergers in the financial services industry makes the importance of global competition clear among financial intermediaries.

Figure 2-1 shows that U.S. equity markets accounted for 78 percent of world capitalization in 1970; however, by 2000, their market share had dropped to 46 percent (World Bank 2002). The share lost by the United States was due to the rise of trading in emerging markets. During this period, several new stock exchanges opened, particularly in the transition economies, and the stock markets of Latin America and Asia expanded and opened up. The globalization of markets is also evident from the growth of depository programs that have been increasing in terms of both number

---

Figure 2-1 | **Change in Market Capitalization, 1970, 1999, and 2000**

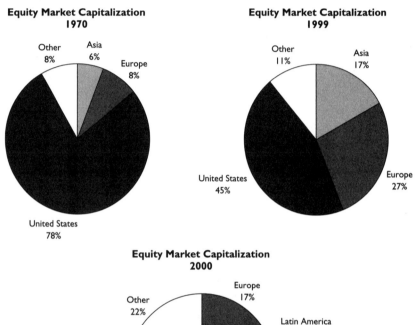

Equity Market Capitalization 1970

Other 8%
Asia 6%
Europe 8%
United States 78%

Equity Market Capitalization 1999

Other 11%
Asia 17%
Europe 27%
United States 45%

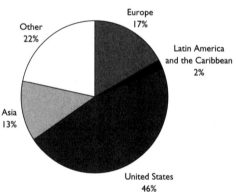

Equity Market Capitalization 2000

Europe 17%
Other 22%
Latin America and the Caribbean 2%
Asia 13%
United States 46%

Source: Bank of New York's website; for 2000, World Bank (2002).

of issues and size of the market (figure 2-2). There are large depository programs in several emerging markets, with more being added every year. Emerging market companies that trade in the United States have been some of the most actively traded stocks there.

The impact of globalization on Latin America specifically can be seen in a number of ways. Mexico is an excellent example. There are 24 Mexican companies

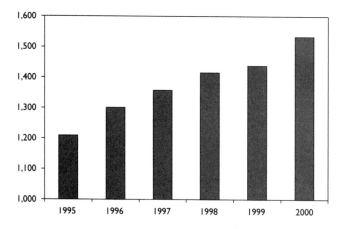

Figure 2-2 | **U.S. Depository Receipt Programs, 1995–2000**
(Number of programs)

Source: Bank of New York's website; for 2000, World Bank (2002).

listed on the NYSE, 33 trade in the over-the-counter (OTC) market, eight in London, one on NASDAQ, and two on Amex (Calderon 2000). Teléfonos de México (Telmex) and Grupo Televisa were in the top-20 list of depository programs by dollar volume. Telmex is one of the most active stocks traded on the NYSE. Almost 80 percent of trading activity in stocks such as Telmex, Cemex, and Televisa takes place outside Mexico. Most Mexican stocks tend to be dual listed and at least continue some trading in the home market. This is different from the experiences of some other countries, such as Israel, where there are 152 companies listed on foreign markets, 123 in the United States and 29 in Europe. Only 22 of these stocks are dual listed on the Tel Aviv Stock Exchange. Recently, the Securities Authority of Israel has started taking steps to encourage Israeli companies to dual list in Tel Aviv. These steps include recognition of a U.S. prospectus and filings. It is also important for Latin American regulators and stock exchanges to continue to encourage dual listing so these issuers do not completely bypass the home market.

The trading activity of foreigners has gone up significantly on the Mexican Bolsa. As figure 2-3 shows, in 1995 foreign investors owned 27 percent of Mexican capitalization; this increased to 43 percent by 1999 and 44 percent in the first seven months of 2000. Currently, eight foreign brokers and one foreign independent fund manager operate in Mexico (box 2-3). The significant participation of foreign investors and financial intermediaries in the Mexican market and the issuance of American De-

Figure 2-3	Acquisition of Mexican Securities by Foreign Investors, 1995–99
	(Foreign ownership as percentage of market capitalization)

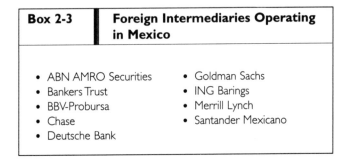

Source: Calderon (2000).

pository Receipts (ADRs) in Mexico and Global Depository Receipts (GDRs) in foreign markets are evidence of the globalization of capital markets.

Challenges Posed by Globalization

The challenges of globalization are evident in Latin America, as shown in box 2-1. The loss of trading activity in blue chip stocks, low liquidity, and decrease in the number of primary offerings are raising questions about the future of Latin bourses. This concern is clear from the data presented in table 2-2.

Box 2-3	Foreign Intermediaries Operating in Mexico

- ABN AMRO Securities
- Bankers Trust
- BBV-Probursa
- Chase
- Deutsche Bank

- Goldman Sachs
- ING Barings
- Merrill Lynch
- Santander Mexicano

Table 2-2 | **Change in Listings and Market Capitalization in Selected Countries, 1990–2000**

Country	Percentage change in listings, 1990–2000	Market capitalization (percentage of GDP)
Argentina	−30.17	19.7
Brazil	−19.34	20.7
Chile	+20.83	101.1
Mexico	−14.49	34.5
Peru	−3.40	21.2
United States	+28.36	180.8

Source: IFC (2001).

The number of listings has dropped by 30.17 percent in Argentina, 19.34 percent in Brazil, 14.49 percent in Mexico, and 3.40 percent in Peru (table 2-2). Chile is one of the few examples in Latin America with an increase in listings. The size and scope of the stock market continue to be small relative to the overall economy. Market capitalization as a percentage of gross domestic product (GDP) ranges from an average of 15.6 percent in Eastern Europe, to 25.5 percent in Latin America, and 38.5 percent in Asia. The stock market in Chile is quite large in size relative to the economy and is an exception in Latin America. In the United States, the market capitalization rate is 180.8 percent of GDP, and the picture is similar for annual trading volume as a percentage of GDP. It was 11.1 percent in Latin America, 11.4 percent in Eastern Europe, and 63.5 percent in Asia, but a high of 154.9 percent in the United States.

Cross-ownership of markets, mergers and acquisitions, alliances and partnerships between exchanges, cooperation between regulators, and demutualization of exchanges are all considered part of the globalization strategy. Harmonization of accounting standards, listing requirements, qualification of financial intermediaries, and regulation are at various stages of development. These changes are expected to increase efficiency and reduce costs for the global investor. Some of these strategies become even more important for emerging capital markets that must identify strategies to compete in the global marketplace and ultimately contribute to the economic development of the country and the region.

Some traditionally structured exchanges have begun to question the appropriateness of their membership ownership and governance structure. Business is moving at a fast pace, and stock exchanges do not have the luxury of obtaining the approval of their membership for every change. Stock exchanges need to be flexible and quick in making decisions and well financed to compete globally and invest in both technology and human capital. These factors are motivating exchanges to demutualize and restructure into for-profit organizations in which access to trading will be separated from ownership of the market.

In the world of the Internet, it is unclear what value-added services a stock exchange can provide that cannot be provided in alternative ways at a cheaper cost. Stock markets have to respond to change and innovate in order to survive. Traditional methods of trading securities will soon be outdated. The typical sources of revenue (fees for listing, transactions, and information) may not continue to exist. There is no reason to believe that listing will continue to be a major source of revenue.

Similarly, technology has already made information inexpensive, and exchanges do not have the luxury of keeping this as a major source of revenue. Winners will use design and cost to attract trading volume. Demutualization should make exchanges more flexible to respond to some of these challenges and continue to be competitive.

Policymakers and regulators will have to consider the impact of restructuring a membership organization on the regulatory functions of the market authorities, particularly in managing conflicts of interest. The counterargument to the "acting responsibly" argument is that there will be considerable conflict of interest if the major exchanges proceed with their announced intentions to demutualize. One possibility might be to maintain SROs within exchanges, but in a subsidiary with a "Chinese wall" separating trading and member surveillance from day-to-day operations. In a more dramatic option, SROs might become stand-alone firms for hire by their former parent companies.[2] The securities commissions and others in the industry worldwide are currently studying these various options. As exchanges have been challenged to meet the demands of multinational issuers and international investors, they have converged to form regional and global alliances. These alliances and partnerships become particularly important for emerging markets in order to reduce costs and offer more services to their clients. So far, there has been a lot of talk about alliances and partnerships and even mergers. In reality, due to political, social, and economic differences, it is hard to make these structures functional. Major differences in regulation between countries make harmonization across borders difficult. Even Europe has found it complicated to achieve integration, which has evolved over decades. For example, the merger talks between the London Stock Exchange and Deutsche Bourse did not come to fruition.

---

[2] "For-Profit Stock Markets Raise Regulatory Concerns," Dow Jones News Service, September 3, 1999.

Box 2-4 | **Alliances and Partnerships in Emerging Markets**

- African Stock Exchanges Association (ASEA): Botswana, Egypt, Johannesburg, Mauritius, Morocco, Swaziland, Tanzania, Uganda, Zambia, and Zimbabwe
- Federation of Euro-Asian Exchanges (FEAS): Amman, Bulgaria, Dhaka, Egypt, Istanbul, Karachi, Lahore, Tehran, Ukraine, and others
- Iberoamericana (FIABV): Argentina, Brazil, Chile, Costa Rica, Ecuador, El Salvador, Mexico, Peru, Portugal, Spain, Uruguay, and Venezuela
- European (FESE): European exchanges, including Bucharest, Cyprus, Latvia, Lithuania, and others

---

Alliances among markets have similar missions and objectives. Box 2-4 gives examples of alliances and partnerships in emerging markets. For example, the Federation of Euro-Asian Exchanges (FEAS) includes 21 stock exchanges, with the Istanbul Stock Exchange taking a leadership role. Its mission statement states:

> The mission of FEAS is to create [a] fair, efficient and transparent market environment, with little or no barriers to trade, between the FEAS members and their operating regions. Harmonization of rules and regulations and adoption of new technology for trading and settlement, by member securities markets, will facilitate the objectives of FEAS by promoting the development of the member markets and providing cross listing and trading opportunities for securities issued within FEAS member countries.

Through alliances and partnerships, exchanges are trying to create common trading platforms, clearance and settlement procedures, listing standards, capital reserve requirements, qualifications for financial intermediaries, and risk management systems. The International Federation of Stock Exchanges (FIBV) is an important trade organization for securities markets. FIBV acts as a central reference point in the process of international harmonization (cross-border trading and public offerings) among its members and lobbies public bodies about the markets. FIBV also supports emerging markets in their development according to global standards.[3] The securities commissions of many countries have adopted the standards set for harmonization and market integration by the International Accounting Standards Committee (IOSCO). The Council of Securities Regulators of the Americas (COSRA) continues to play an important role in

---

[3] See http://www.fibv.com.

Table 2-3 | **Market Linkage Discussions**

Market	Linkage discussions between exchanges/electronic communication networks
NYSE	Toronto, Tokyo, Paris, Amsterdam, SEHK, Australia, Brazil, Brussels, Mexico
NASDAQ	All electronic communication networks trade NASDAQ stocks, Osaka, Deutsche Bourse, London, MarketXT joint venture
London	Deutsche Bourse, NASDAQ, OM
Tokyo	South Korea, Thailand, Philippines, Singapore, NYSE, NASDAQ
SE of Hong Kong	NASDAQ
Paris	NYSE
Brazil BOVESPA	London, Lisbon, NYSE, Argentina
Australia	NASDAQ, NYSE, Far East
Toronto	NASDAQ, NYSE

the region to achieve the same objective. Cooperation is needed among regulators of different countries and market participants in order to make global trading a reality.

There has been discussion about creating a global equity market at the initiative of the NYSE that includes emerging markets such as Brazil and Mexico (table 2-3). The Tokyo Stock Exchange is in discussion to form its own alliance with the emerging markets of Asia, including South Korea, Thailand, and the Philippines. Globalization of securities markets has become possible because of technological innovations. The next section examines the impact of technology on securities markets.

Technology

Technology has made obsolete the traditional "brick and mortar" exchanges that formerly needed a physical location. Trading floors are no longer required, person-to-person contact in conducting transactions is not needed, and information can be transmitted rapidly without physical contact between the transacting parties. This has led to an increase in cross-border trading and therefore raised issues of jurisdiction. Technology has also resulted in the development of new types of trading systems that have become easy to set up because of lower barriers to entry. These include automation of existing stock exchanges, creation of new automated exchanges, and growth of new independent trading systems.

The 1990s saw the decline of floor-based exchanges and the emergence of electronic securities markets. Electronic exchanges in Latin America have emerged

Figure 2-4 | **Order Book Execution**

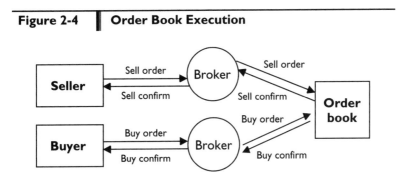

along with exchanges that have a physical location. A similar trend has been occurring in Europe. For example, two-thirds of all trading in Germany takes place on Deutsche Bourse's electronic trading platform, Xetra.[4] Buy and sell orders are entered into an electronic order book, and transactions are done when bid and ask prices match, as shown in figure 2-4.

Alternative Trading Systems

Another innovation in trading systems has been the increase in the importance of alternative trading systems (ATSs) and electronic communication networks (ECNs). These new trading systems have captured a significant share of the trading volume of traditional exchanges. ECNs account for 35–40 percent of trading in NASDAQ stocks, particularly the largest stocks. ECNs are similar to an electronic order book; they are automated proprietary trading platforms with no market makers or specialists. Investors can anonymously enter orders into the system, which then matches buy and sell orders. If a matching within the ECN does not occur, then the order is routed to other ECNs or exchanges, as shown in figure 2-5.

ATSs provide services somewhat similar to an exchange, but they are not an exchange and neither are they regulated as an exchange. They have raised the question of what is an exchange and how an exchange differs from other trading systems. A number of issues regarding the operation and regulation of ATSs have arisen that will need to be addressed by emerging markets in the near future.

Electronic order books and ECNs work particularly well for the execution of small orders in highly liquid stocks. However, for large block trades and for trading in less liquid stocks, the role of market makers/dealers/specialists becomes important and should be integrated within an electronic limit order book or an ECN. The

---

[4] *Vision and Money: E-Trading,* January 2000.

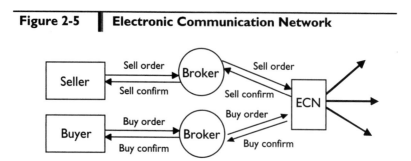

Figure 2-5 | **Electronic Communication Network**

U.S. stock exchanges have been extremely successful and have been the envy of the world; however, the structure of traditional stock exchanges in the United States leaves a lot to be desired in terms of their market microstructure. The advent of the Internet and the emergence of ECNs are changing the structure of the markets. The nonelectronic structure of the U.S. markets was ideal for the operation of ECNs, allowing investors to trade anonymously. ECNs lower the costs of transacting by reducing or eliminating the spread, providing faster execution, and cutting out some of the intermediation functions. For instance, ECNs moved first to offer after-hours trading. Based on their experience and economies of scale, traditional stock exchanges are well positioned to offer similar and even better services than ECNs, but they need to act soon because ECNs are becoming aggressive and starting to enter the fixed-income and the derivatives markets.

Major market participants—for example, investment banks, investors, traditional retail brokers, e-brokers, and data providers—are investing in ECNs (box 2-5). Even European firms are starting to invest in ECNs. Instinet, owned by Reuters, has operated as an ECN since 1969. New entrants include Island (Datek Online), Redi-Book (Fidelity, Spear Leeds, and Schwab), Brass (Merrill Lynch, Goldman Sachs, and Morgan Stanley Dean Witter), and Archipelago (Goldman Sachs, JP Morgan, and Merrill Lynch). ECNs have adopted different strategies. For example, Instinet's focus so far has been on institutional investors (now it is also entering the retail market), while Island started in 1996 with a focus on retail investors benefiting from the increase in stock market activity during the past three years. Tradepoint was the first European ECN to register as an exchange, but liquidity in Tradepoint has been a major problem. ECNs that are able to pool large amounts of liquidity will dominate the marketplace.

New trading systems are already operating in many parts of the world. In addition to ECNs, other ATSs have emerged. The term ATS describes different types of alternative trading platforms, with ECNs being one category. POSIT is an electronic crossing system, owned by ITG, which executes orders at the midpoint of the bid and

Box 2-5	Ownership of Electronic Communication Networks
Electronic communication network	**Owner**
Instinet	Reuters
Island	Datek Online Waterhouse Securities Vulcan Ventures
Redibook	Spear, Leeds & Kellogg
Tradebook	Bloomberg Bank of New York
Archipelago	Terra Nova E*Trade Goldman Sachs JP Morgan American Century
BRUT	Automated Securities Clearance Goldman Sachs Merrill Lynch Morgan Stanley Dean Witter Knight/Trimark
Strike	Bear Sterns DLJ Paine Webber Cantor Fitzgerald

ask price. Optimark is another system that allows investors to execute transactions based on optimizing preferences. Primex is yet another system designed as an electronic auction market. Large financial intermediaries that have adequate financial resources sponsor the new systems and have already started expanding globally. It is not clear who will eventually win the race among ATSs. For now, the same financial intermediary is taking positions in several systems in order to keep its options open. Regulators will need to contend with these new ATSs (exemplified by the numerous ECNs).

Regulation of Alternative Trading Systems

Trading systems perform tasks similar to an exchange, channeling orders from the originator to the execution site and transforming orders into trades. The process involves disseminating the pre- and post-trade data to the market. Regulators are concerned about the microstructure of new trading systems, their trade execution rules, the impact on the price discovery process, and issues of fairness and competition. ATSs may be owned and operated by a single intermediary (for example, Instinet) or by a group of intermediaries (for example, Archipalego). However, they do not fall under the umbrella of an exchange and therefore are not obligated to meet the same set of responsibilities as an exchange and are not required to perform several functions, including the SRO role.

Compared with trading systems, exchanges must comply with many more regulations. They must provide trade execution capabilities, centralize trading, and engage in price discovery. They are also required to file proposed rules with the securities commission and to have a process for obtaining public comments. These regulations make it difficult for them to respond quickly to the market environment, competitive pressures, and new business opportunities. Registered exchanges are required to have adequate capacity and must publicly disseminate pre- and post-transaction information. These concerns raise the question whether ECNs have unfair regulatory advantage over exchanges in the United States. These trading systems are also for-profit organizations, while exchanges have traditionally been nonprofit member organizations. However, the ownership structure is changing rapidly.

The proliferation of new trading systems has ignited the debate in the United States, Canada, Europe, Australia, and even some emerging markets as to how ATSs should be regulated. Are they exchanges, brokers, or dealers? Do they have competitive advantages over exchanges? As they become more and more important, how should they be integrated into the markets? Can they and the exchanges be regulated in a manner that would not stifle innovation? The SEC in the United States published a major concept release in May 1997 to explore ways to respond to the technological developments in financial markets. The U.S. SEC recognized that ATSs already trade more than 30 percent of NASDAQ orders and could potentially become the major market for certain securities. However, ATSs are regulated as broker-dealers and not as exchanges. The definition of an "exchange" was revised under Rule 3b-16 to mean any organization, association, or group that:

- Brings together orders of multiple buyers and sellers
- Establishes uses and nondiscretionary methods under which such orders interact with each other.

Specifically excluded are routing systems and single market-maker systems. Under this new framework, the U.S. SEC seeks to encourage innovation; it allows SROs to operate new pilot trading systems for up to two years without requiring SEC approval.

The emergence of several trading systems has led to fragmentation, and liquidity has become dispersed in small pools rather than consolidated in one place. This situation prompted the U.S. SEC to examine the issue in detail and provide guidelines. Under the new guidelines, ECNs are allowed to continue operating as broker-dealers or apply to become an exchange.

ECNs have several advantages in becoming an exchange, such as not being regulated by a competitor (NASDAQ or the NYSE); not needing to reroute orders for best execution purposes; and being able to earn tape revenue by posting quotes. In addition to normal supervision of the market operator, markets often require coordination of regulatory activities for each ATS, surveillance, and establishment of minimum regulatory requirements. One possible response to this development is to consolidate the SROs that exist now in U.S. markets and create a single, central SRO. This option should remove the conflict of interest concerns and satisfy those opposed to the NYSE's announced intention to keep its SRO in-house after it takes for-profit status. Although a central SRO might lose some of the nimbleness and expertise that the current SROs have, it still should be considered an alternative.

Trading systems are a natural platform for cross-border trading. The technology exists to make financial markets truly global and integrated. Technology can easily make round-the-clock trading a reality. However, in spite of all the progress, the regulatory barriers to cross-border trading remain high. Commissioner Laura Unger of the U.S. SEC has pointed out, "The only real impediments to global market are regulatory, not technological. Specifically, what is lacking is an appropriate framework for that market to work in." She also remarked that the U.S. SEC has ample authority and jurisdiction over the activities of foreign markets and broker-dealers in the United States, but the real issue is "to what extent the Commission should exercise that authority" in the global marketplace.[5]

Securities Regulation

A strong legal and regulatory framework is essential for a well-functioning capital market. It is not sufficient to have laws and regulations—their enforcement is critical. Many emerging markets have begun to set up an acceptable regulatory framework, but enforcement has been lacking. This section discusses some approaches to globalization, focusing on the role of self-regulatory organizations in the regulation of capital markets.

---

[5] "The Global Marketplace, Ready or Not Here it Comes," speech by Laura Unger at the Third National Securities Trading on the Internet Conference, New York, January 24, 2000; http://ww.sec.gov/news/speeches/spch344.html.

Cross-Border Trading

International organizations such as IOSCO have played an important role in setting regulatory standards for capital markets. IOSCO has long promoted the importance of interdependence among regulators in dealing with the increasing globalization and integration of securities markets (IOSCO 1998). Harmonization of rules with regard to qualifications of financial intermediaries, capital requirements, registration of new securities, listing requirements, trading systems, and clearance and settlement will make it less costly for market participants to transact business. However, it is important for each country or region to adopt principles that suit its own markets.

In 1998, IOSCO established 30 principles of securities regulation that are aimed at achieving three objectives:

- Protecting investors
- Ensuring that markets are fair, efficient, and transparent
- Reducing systemic risk.

These objectives form the general foundation for effective regulation. The challenges become particularly complicated for emerging markets that lack liquidity and face several human and financial constraints. There is no one supra-regulator that would have jurisdiction over global capital markets. This idea has been suggested, but would be extremely difficult to implement. In the European Union, these issues have been difficult to resolve in spite of the common social, political, and economic background of the European Union countries. Europe is the only region in the world that has issued the Investment Services Directive, which spans several countries and lays down provisions for cross-border trading. Hence, it is difficult to imagine agreement on a supra-regulator at an international level.

Exchanges and regulators are forming alliances/partnerships to reduce barriers to trading within member countries. These alliances include harmonization of regulation, adoption of similar trading platforms, and clearance and settlement systems. If each country has its own regulator, several issues arise (Domowitz and Lee 1998). Which country should have jurisdiction over what institutions? What if a trading system is physically located in one jurisdiction but is incorporated in another? Where are securities listed? Which country are investors from? Which country do the financial institutions involved in the transaction belong to? Several approaches have been suggested for dealing with the regulatory framework in the global marketplace, but no consensus has been attained.

The U.S. SEC's Concept Release had set out to address the issues of foreign-market access in addition to the ATSs.[6] However, the issues related to ATSs were important and complicated enough that the discussion of foreign markets was deferred for another time. The U.S. SEC proposed three nonexclusive approaches:

1. *Mutual recognition approach.* This approach would mean reliance on a foreign market's primary regulator. This would work only for those countries whose rules and regulations are similar. Most emerging markets would not be included in this approach. There would be a great deal of politics involved in determining countries whose regulations are comparable. The developed markets would select countries whose regulation is comparable to that of their markets. In the United States, the concern is that foreign markets could operate with fewer regulatory burdens than U.S. markets. This would be anticompetitive for U.S. exchanges that would, in turn, want their regulatory burden reduced. It would even be possible for U.S. exchanges to register in the foreign country under less regulation and still operate in the United States. Europe has adopted this approach.
2. *Exchange registration approach.* The domestic regulator applies the same rules and regulations to foreign and domestic exchanges operating in the country. As globalization proceeds, exchanges could face several sets of regulations, making this a costly approach.
3. *Access provider regulation.* The United States considered the possibility of regulating access providers, such as exchanges and broker-dealers that provide investors with access to foreign markets.

On the Internet, the U.S. SEC's view has been that foreign exchanges and broker-dealers should post a prominent disclaimer and refuse to transact with U.S. investors. The foreign market should also not allow access to U.S. investors indirectly through its own members. In March 1999, the U.S. SEC issued an exemption to London-based Tradepoint Stock Exchange to provide access to securities listed on the London Stock Exchange. This exemption was granted based on Tradepoint being a limited-volume exchange in the United Kingdom. The primary market of a country could not be considered a limited-volume exchange. Even in this case, only qualified institutional investors have access to all securities; other public investors only have access to securities registered under the U.S. Securities Act in the form of American De-

---

[6] For details, see U.S. SEC Release No. 34-38672; International Series Release No. IS-1085; File No. S7-16-97.

pository Receipts or ordinary shares. Even as an exempted exchange, Tradepoint is required to provide substantial information to the U.S. SEC.

Regulators have attempted to create a regulatory wall around cross-border trading, but this is not sustainable. Investors and issuers both suffer from such artificial barriers. However, regulators have to make sure that there is sufficient investor protection. They also realize that citizens of the country demand more and more opportunities to invest in foreign markets. Ben Steil, in a letter to the U.S. SEC, argues that exemptions based on low volume are flawed.[7] The exemption suggests that investors trading on less liquid systems are somehow better off than those trading on a more liquid one. He also argues that U.S. institutional investors already have access to foreign markets through electronic brokerage systems.

Rationale for Self-Regulation of Financial Markets

Policymakers realize that markets should be allowed to operate with minimum intervention by regulators. Investors and issuers feel confident in participating in stock exchange transactions only if they can be assured that transactions are executed according to a predetermined set of rules. SROs have played a key role in the regulation of markets; however, the tensions inherent in the system are also apparent. SROs can set rules that include regulation of market transactions, regulation of market participants, resolution of disputes, enforcement of actions, and precommitment of resources. SROs should have the responsibility for regulating and monitoring stock markets. They should develop qualification standards for market intermediaries, rules for these firms to participate in the market, and rules for dealings with customers and clients and should ensure that members fully comply with these rules and with securities laws and regulations.

Self-regulation can effectively combine monitoring by private entities with oversight by government regulatory agencies. The role of self-regulation varies from country to country. In some countries, only one SRO operates, but in others more than one SRO may exist. Even in the United States, there is discussion about the potential for a single SRO rather than each exchange being an SRO. According to the Report of the SRO Consultative Committee (IOSCO 2000):

> SROs should be able to have the authority to create, amend, implement and enforce rules of conduct with respect to the entities subject to the SRO's jurisdiction and to resolve dispute through arbitration or other means.

---

[7] Letter by Benn Steil dated July 16, 1998, to the U.S. SEC, http://www.sec.gov/rules/othern/f10-101/steil.html.

SRO rules and regulations will only complement the statutory requirements that already exist.

There are costs associated with operating an SRO, and the industry directly or indirectly bears these costs. Many stock exchanges in emerging markets with low liquidity are rightly concerned about the costs of the SRO function. These costs are associated with human capital, training of employees, and the need for updated technology, among others factors. In the early stages of development of the SROs, it is quite likely that that there will be considerable duplication of effort by the SRO and the government regulator. The securities commission may have to continue performing the same functions as the SRO until it becomes credible and market participants are satisfied by its fair policing activities. If the SRO is able to conduct its operations effectively and efficiently, then the government regulator should be able to reduce its budget and pass the savings to market participants. It takes time for SROs to establish credibility based on their track record.

Self-regulation ensures that transactions are executed by member firms according to preset rules and conditions. Regulation of member firms ensures that the admission criteria are set clearly and firms can become members only if they satisfy minimum capital requirements, creditworthiness, risk management capability, and other requisites. Rules are also laid down about conducting business and ethical standards. The procedures for sanctions in case of noncompliance are also laid out. Dispute resolution is an important part of the SRO's responsibilities (box 2-6).

SROs have a business interest in making sure that their markets function smoothly. Reputation capital is very important in this business. Therefore, SROs have incentives to implement rules that are consistent with the business model. The industry has a business interest in operating a fair, transparent, and competitive market in

---

Box 2-6 | **Regulation by Self-regulatory Organizations**

Regulation of market transactions

    Effective surveillance of markets
    Information disclosure and dissemination

Regulation of member firms

    Criteria for membership (capital requirements, risk management, and
        technical requirements)
    Rules for conducting business
    Compliance with rules
    Sanctions

today's global, efficient market. SROs are also typically closer to market participants and usually have more flexibility than government agencies do in responding to market needs and creating appropriate rules. The combination of commercial interest and proximity to the markets makes SROs suited to carry out some of the regulatory role. They are in a position to set rules, enforce the rules, and resolve disputes that arise from those rules. Flexibility is extremely important in today's fast-changing financial world. Government agencies typically do not have the financial resources and human resources necessary to carry out all aspects of the regulatory function. It is also easier for the market to self-police itself. Self-imposed rules are more easily accepted than those imposed by a third party, particularly if marketplace competition is fierce and technology allows market participants to quickly take their transactions to the government agency.

However, there are major challenges with the implementation of self-regulation. SROs are generally the stock exchange, clearing agencies, and sometimes other professional associations. This model of regulation assumes that the industry has the capability to police itself. Self-regulation also assumes that the industry has the incentive to operate fair and efficient markets and requires competition among market participants so that they will monitor each other. If conflicts of interest undermine the role of self-regulation, the benefits of controlling the activities of members and enhancing investor and issuer confidence may not be highly valued. In emerging markets, there is typically only one stock exchange, so there is no competition. Issuers and investors do not have the option of using an alternative if they are dissatisfied.

Global competition threatens countries with low liquidity because they do not have enough trading volume and liquidity to support the emergence of other trading systems or new exchanges in their markets. Even in a developed country with competition, such as the case of the NASDAQ stock market, collusion between dealers is possible, to the detriment of investors. SROs can be driven by the short-term interests of their own market. For example, if exchanges are interested in obtaining more foreign listings, they may establish more lenient listing requirements for foreign issuers.

In emerging markets, there is also concern that SROs may not have enough resources (financial and human capital) to carry out effectively their responsibilities. And it might be problematic if only a handful of financial intermediaries are members of the SRO or have too much influence. The governance structure of the SRO plays a major role in determining the effectiveness of its oversight activities. If more than one SRO has overlapping surveillance and enforcement activities, then market participants have to abide by several sets of rules, incurring substantial costs.

The SRO approach might not be prefect, but it is better than other options. A costly alternative would be to have the securities commission perform all the regulatory functions. SROs are closer to the industry; they are more flexible and therefore have several advantages. Oversight by congress and the securities commission could help resolve the conflict of interest problems.

Strategic Issues and Recommendations

Competition among exchanges is heating up on a global scale. Securities markets are undergoing tremendous changes. It is not clear who the winners will be five years from now. Will the traditional stock exchanges survive? How will the role of exchanges be modified? What additional value-added services will they provide? Will every country have a stock exchange, and does every country need a stock exchange? How will exchanges in Latin America and the Caribbean compete with the big players? Will there be regional markets? It will be interesting to see what kinds of alliances and partnerships become fruitful and how consolidation in the industry shapes up.

Emerging markets should have a strategy in order to compete in the global marketplace. Integration in the global system is a fact; the issue is how best to prepare for it. Regulators must encourage the development of strong, competitive markets. They must continue to encourage innovation and foster competition at the international level. International cooperation is a necessity. The risks of financial failure will not be borne by one country alone, as is evident from several examples (such as Barings, Long-Term Capital, and the Asian crisis). Risk management and monitoring at the global level are required. The consolidated risk of financial intermediaries and timely dissemination of information are needed. Regulators need to share information in order to carry out effective surveillance and enforcement and achieve harmonization. Harmonization does not mean that each country would lose its legal and regulatory identity. However, if the standards of emerging markets are perceived to be weak relative to those of developed countries, integration might be difficult.

This section identifies key questions and recommends a strategy related to the three broad issues discussed in this chapter: globalization, technology, and regulation.

Globalization

What are the benefits of globalization, and how can the region exploit them? Globalization has brought a number of benefits to local markets. For example, many companies in the region have successfully raised capital in other countries. The stocks of Latin American companies have generated considerable investor interest and have become some of the most actively traded stocks, even in New York. This in turn has helped to lower the cost of capital. It is important to embrace policies that will continue to allow these companies to raise capital globally. The entrance of foreign financial institutions and foreign investors has resulted in greater transparency, better accounting standards, and improved corporate governance because these investors require the local market to follow global standards. Markets should focus on developing new international and domestic instruments (for example, exchange-traded funds) so that investors have a choice of investment vehicles.

What challenges does globalization pose, and how should they be addressed? Globalization has sometimes resulted in less liquidity for local markets, as trading in blue chip companies moved out of the country. Foreign money can quickly flow in and out, causing short-run volatility in the market. These issues could be addressed in two ways. First, the country could develop a plan to encourage small and medium firms to raise capital in local markets. Some companies will grow and form the future pipeline for active trading. These firms are the engines of growth for the local economy, and thus it is important to have a strategy for their growth and development.

Second, the country could make an effort to increase local savings and the local investor base in order to reduce the impact of foreign investors on portfolio flows. Investor education conducted by the stock exchanges, securities commissions, governments, and regional organizations, such as COSRA, should be an integral and central part of the capital market development strategy. Dual listings might be helpful. In Israel, for example, all the high-tech companies have gone to NASDAQ and left the Tel Aviv Stock Exchange with the smaller, less well-known, and less liquid stocks. The regulator has aligned disclosure with the United States to encourage dual listings and the return of companies to the country.

In what areas must global standards be adopted? It is necessary to adopt global standards and use the guidelines provided by international organizations, such as IOSCO and FIBV. The standards and guidelines refer to the regulation of financial markets, functioning of SROs, timely disclosure of information, accounting practices, corporate governance, and, most important, methods for enforcement of regulations. The strategy should be to strive to meet the global standards of best practice. Both regulators and market operators need to pay attention to these standards.

What are the benefits of regional alliances, and what are the best ways to structure such alliances? So far, there has been a lot of talk about partnerships and alliances, but little has actually been accomplished. This will require thinking about what countries should be included and how far this concept can be stretched.

How can trading across borders be simplified with low transaction costs? Regional harmonization could occur in several areas, including trading systems, clearance and settlement, membership, listings, SROs, and regulations.

Should there be a regional exchange or formal market linkage? If there is a regional exchange, does each country need its own stock exchange?

Technology

How will technology change the capital-raising process? Technology has resulted in several changes in the marketplace. Issuers have started using the Internet to raise capital, investors are able to access the markets much more easily, information is readily available to both institutional and retail investors, e-brokers have emerged, and the registration and filing process with the securities commission and the exchanges is becoming electronic. The region has to make sure the technological infrastructure exists in the capital markets to allow these changes to take place, so that capital markets will continue to be competitive.

How can technology in the areas of clearance and settlement and risk management be improved? The exchanges have made significant progress in updating the technology of trading systems, but clearance and settlement are the backbone of a well-functioning market, and the concerns expressed by foreign investors in this regard need to be addressed. Similarly, many markets do not have risk management systems in place and should identify and implement best practices in this area.

Will other trading systems create competition for exchanges? It is quite realistic to expect ATSs to enter some of the markets. They bring innovative technology in addition to adding value in other ways. ATSs and ECNs pose a number of issues that will need to be addressed.

Regulation

What international regulatory standards need to be adopted? IOSCO has already done a great deal of work to lay the framework for a global regulatory structure. Capital market regulators in Latin America and the Caribbean should take the necessary steps to implement these best practices. Securities commissions will need adequate human and financial resources to carry out their role. In many countries, the staff does not have sufficient training and is not familiar with global trends. It is necessary to recruit competent staff and to train current staff to carry out its responsibilities.

How should the exchanges and regulators deal with cross-border trading issues? This chapter has addressed a number of issues with regard to cross-border trading. It is important for the markets in the region to engage in the discussions taking place about these issues and make sure their viewpoint is heard. Regulators have to make cross-border trading easy and at the same time protect local investors.

How should ATSs be regulated? ATSs perform functions similar to those of an exchange, but they are not an exchange and are not typically regulated as an exchange. Exchanges sometimes might seem to be at a competitive regulatory disadvantage relative to ATSs. ATSs pose a number of regulatory issues, and the approach taken by the U.S. SEC might be a good starting point. The regulation of ATSs should be approached carefully to ensure that innovation is not stifled.

What role should SROs play in regulating capital markets? If SROs play a role in regulation, there may be conflict of interest issues, which can be more pronounced in emerging markets than in developed markets. Financial resources are also needed to carry out the SRO function, and many SROs are not able to do their job effectively because of these constraints. The alternative to SROs is to allow the securities commission to carry out all regulatory functions. However, securities commissions are not well suited to carry out all regulatory functions and can best serve in an oversight role. As Karmel shows, demutualization has made the SRO debate even more complex and the conflict of interest issues more severe (chapter 10, this volume). An option would be to consider the creation of one SRO for several markets (instead of each exchange and each clearance and settlement organization having its own SRO). However, this would create a monopoly, and there would be no other options available.

Capital market development must be supported because it plays an important role in the long-term economic growth of a country. This process is complex and will take years to implement, but it does require both a short-term and a long-term strategy. The strategy adopted will vary from country to country and region to region, depending on the unique situation of the economy and markets.

Bibliography

Asian Development Bank (ADB) and World Bank Joint Research. 1999. Managing Global Financial Integration in Asia: Emerging Lessons and Prospective Challenges. Working Paper. World Bank, Washington, D.C.

Aggarwal, Reena. 1999. Stock Market Development: Role of Securities Firms and New Products. Presentation at the World Bank workshop on Non-Bank Financial Institutions: Development and Regulation, World Bank, Washington, D.C., February 2000.

_____. 2001. Integrating Emerging Market Countries into the Global Financial System: Regulatory Infrastructure Covering Financial Markets. Presentation at the Brookings-Wharton Papers on Financial Services 4th Annual Conference, Brookings Institution, Washington, D.C., January.

Aggarwal, Reena, and Jim Angel. 1999. The Rise and Fall of the Amex Emerging Company Marketplace. *Journal of Financial Economics* 52(2):257–89.

Aggarwal, Reena, and Sandeep Dahiya. 2000. Capital Formation and the Internet. *Journal of Applied Corporate Finance* 13(1, Spring):108–13.

Aggarwal, Reena, Ian Gray, and Hal Singer. 1999. Capital Raising in the Offshore Market. *Journal of Banking and Finance* 23(8):1181–94.

Aggarwal, Reena, Carla Inclan, and Ricardo Leal. 1999. Volatility in Emerging Markets. *Journal of Financial and Quantitative Analysis* 34(1, March):33–55.

Aggarwal, Reena, and Demir Yener. 1999. Financial Fraud and Economic Collapse. Presentation at the Workshop on Economic Reform, Securities Market Development, and Fraud, World Bank and OECD, Istanbul, May.

Biagio, Bossone, and Larry Promise. *The Role of Financial Self-Regulation in Developing Economies.* The World Bank web page.

Calderon, Jorge Familiar. 2000. CNBV, Mexico. Presentation at the Alternative Market Structure Conference, Georgetown University, Washington, D.C., September.

Demirgüç-Kunt, Asli, and Vojislav Maksimovic. 1998. Law, Finance, and Firm Growth. *Journal of Finance* 53:2107–39.

Domowitz, Ian, and Ruben Lee. 1998. The Legal Basis for Stock Exchanges: The Classification and Regulation of Automated Trading Systems. Working Paper. Pennsylvania State University, March.

Dow Jones News Service. 1999. For-Profit Stock Markets Raise Regulatory Concerns, September 3.

Henry, Peter Blair. 2000a. Do Stock Market Liberalizations Cause Investment Booms? *Journal of Financial Economics* 58(1–2):301–34.

_____. 2000b. Stock Market Liberalization, Economic Reform, and Emerging Market Equity Prices. *Journal of Finance* 55(2):529–64.

International Finance Corporation (IFC). 1992. *Emerging Stock Markets Factbook 1992.* Washington, D.C.: IFC.

_____. 1995. *Emerging Stock Markets Factbook 1995.* Washington, D.C.: IFC.

_____. 2001. *Emerging Stock Markets Factbook 2001.* Washington, D.C.: IFC.

International Organization of Securities Commissions (IOSCO). 1998. *Objectives and Principles of Securities Regulation.* Madrid, Spain, September.

_____. 2000. Model for Effective Regulation. Report of the SRO Consultative Committee of the International Organization of Securities Commissions. May.

Levine, Ross. 1997. Financial Development and Economic Growth: Views and Agenda. *Journal of Economic Literature* 35:688–726.

Levine, Ross, and Sara Zervos. 1998. Stock Markets, Banks, and Economic Growth. *American Economic Review* 88:537–58.

McCaffrey, David, and David W. Hart. 1998. *Wall Street Polices Itself.* New York: Oxford University Press.

Megginson, William L., and Maria K. Boutchkova. 2000. The Impact of Privatization on Capital Market Development and Individual Share Ownership. Working Paper. University of Oklahoma.

Oesterle, David A. 1994. Comments on the SEC's Market 2000 Report: On, Among Other Things, Deference to SROs, the Mirage of Price Improvement, the Arrogation of Property Rights in Order Flow, and SEC Incrementalism. *The Journal of Corporation Law* (Spring):483–508.

Parker, Phillip. 2000. The Concept of Self-Regulation under the Federal Securities Laws. Presentation at SEC International Institute, Washington, D.C., April.

Securities Industry Association's Ad Hoc Committee on Regulatory Implications of Demutualization. 2000. *Reinventing Self-Regulation.* New York: Securities Industry Association, January.

Soo, J. Kim. 1993. Government Intervention and Regulation in Emerging Stock Markets: A Case Study of the Korean Stock Exchange. *ICSID Review — Foreign Investment Law Journal* 8(1, Spring):53–91.

Strahota, Robert. 2000. Key Principles of Securities Regulation for Emerging Markets. Presentation at SEC International Institute, Washington, D.C., April.

Sundel, Michael B., and Lystra G. Blake. 1991. Good Concept, Bad Executions: The Regulation and Self-Regulation of Automated Trading Systems in United States Futures Markets. *Northwestern University Law Review* 85(3):748–91.

World Bank. 2002. World Development Indicators 2002. CD-ROM. World Bank, Washington, D.C.

Zarb, Frank G. 2000. Building the Global Digital Stock Market. Speech given at the National Press Club, June 13. www.nasdaqnews.com/views/.

■CHAPTER 3

Internet Technology and the Development of Securities Markets

Georg Wittich
Ethiopis Tafara
Robert J. Peterson

Information is the lifeblood of modern capital markets. When information flows freely, investors invest their money more readily, established companies find the capital they need to expand, and entrepreneurs attract the cash needed to turn their ideas into reality. However, when the flow of information is constricted—or where the veracity of the available information is called into question—the flow of capital generally dries up. Investors refuse to make an investment where they do not understand the risks. In turn, larger companies find capital costly, given that the more sophisticated investors willing to take a chance purchasing these companies' securities demand a greater return on their investment to compensate for the opacity of information concerning risk. Meanwhile, smaller companies, with their untried ideas and unproven products, find it almost impossible to raise funds through capital markets.

The Internet is revolutionizing the securities industry because, at its heart, the Internet is about the flow of information. The Internet allows virtually anyone, anywhere to send and receive large volumes of information almost instantaneously and at little cost. As such, the Internet has the potential to significantly "level the playing field" among many traditional market participants.

In theory, the Internet can enable retail investors to receive the same level of detailed and timely information that in the past was available only to institutional investors and professional securities analysts. Institutional investors and professional analysts have access to even more sources of information about the companies and industries they cover. At the same time, the Internet offers dramatically lower transaction costs associated with accessing and investing in modern capital markets. The high costs traditionally associated with distributing prospectus information to potential investors can be reduced significantly, affording smaller companies and entrepreneurs greater access to public capital markets. Likewise, the brokerage expenses retail investors are charged when purchasing and selling securities can be lowered through the use of automated Internet-based ordering systems. This potential may attract even more individual investors to the market, who in the past may have been dissuaded by high brokerage fees.

The Internet holds particular promise for developing markets, many of which face some of the same hurdles faced by retail investors, small companies, and entrepreneurs. High transaction costs and a dearth of information can stall the development of a capital market. The Internet has the potential to reduce these transaction costs, while providing investors with the information necessary to instill confidence in their investments.

Regulatory Policy and the Internet

It is indisputable that the Internet has flourished because of the ingenuity and drive of the private sector. However, it is also apparent that without some type of government mediating role and law enforcement oversight a great part of the Internet's potential for capital markets may be wasted. In short, use of the Internet for securities activity requires a certain degree of regulatory attention. Otherwise, retail investors might avoid its use, thus defeating the potential benefits the Internet promises.

Keeping a regulatory eye on the operation of online brokerage systems will increase the likelihood that the systems operate properly and that the privacy of those using the systems is maintained. Similarly, securities activity via the Internet will have limited appeal unless regulators insist that electronic disclosure by issuers be tamper-proof, timely, and accurate. Uncertain laws and regulations regarding Internet transactions—for example, contract rights, liability, and intellectual property rights—also might deter investors, issuers, and brokers alike from realizing the potential benefits of the Internet.

There are more insidious dangers to securities activity via the Internet that derive from the nature of the medium. The Internet enables almost anyone, anywhere to send and receive information quickly and cheaply. However, if a sufficient amount of false or misleading information is posted via the Internet, investors will begin to doubt all such information, whether provided by fraudsters or honest issuers. Similarly, if the information available through the Internet is not timely and complete, investors will soon discount such information. In each case, the Internet's promise of free-flowing information is diluted or undermined.

Yet, regulatory vigilance should take into account that, while the medium used to buy and sell securities may change, the principles of securities regulation do not. As in a paper-based environment, securities regulations, when applied to the Internet medium, must ensure that the market is fair and transparent and that investors receive timely and accurate information. However, regulations must be structured in such a way so as not to constrain new technological developments or limit Internet innovations that may prove invaluable to all market participants in the future.

This chapter offers a general description of the early lessons many capital market regulators have learned regarding regulation of securities activities on the Internet. In particular, the chapter focuses on those areas that recently have seen the greatest growth and innovation and to which regulators have given the most attention—the use of the Internet by investors, exchanges, issuers, and market intermediaries and specific areas of concern, such as system capacity, resilience, and security, liability for hyperlinks and information contained on websites, the growth of day trading, and the unique enforcement concerns posed by Internet chat rooms and information stored by Internet service providers (ISPs). Ways in which securities regulators can use the Internet to better protect investors and promote market efficiency and transparency are also described.

The chapter finds that the most significant lesson past experience offers is that the fundamental principles of securities regulation do not change, regardless of the medium used to buy, sell, and market securities (IOSCO 1998b). Well-designed securities regulations protect investors; ensure that securities markets are fair, efficient, and transparent; and minimize systemic risk (IOSCO 1998a). They focus on delivering meaningful, complete, and timely information to investors so that they can make informed investment decisions. Regulations that focus on what information is made available to investors—rather than the manner in which that information is delivered—not only better achieve these goals, but also better promote technological advancements that themselves may better protect investors; enhance market fairness, efficiency, and transparency; and reduce systemic risk.

Likewise, the growing use of the Internet in securities transactions underscores the need for greater enforcement cooperation among securities regulators and law enforcement agencies of all countries. As investors increasingly rely on the Internet to access global capital markets, wrongdoers and scam artists also increasingly use the Internet to prey on those investors, frequently from different jurisdic-

tions. Developing markets, many of which only recently have established comprehensive securities regulatory regimes, should ensure that their regulators have far-
reaching powers to cooperate internationally in the interest of ensuring that the
cross-border aspects of this new technology do not facilitate circumvention of their
regulatory objectives.

The Internet and Capital Markets

Characteristics of the Internet

The rapid acceptance of Internet and Internet-related technologies reflects the
technology-driven nature of securities markets (table 3-1). Internet technology lends
itself to securities activity. Indeed, the typically "nonphysical" or "dematerialized" nature
of securities transactions makes the Internet an appealing medium for financial services, and its breadth, low cost, interactivity, decentralization, and flexibility extend the
reach of the financial services industry considerably.

Table 3-1 ▌ **Growth of the Internet Worldwide, 2000–02**

Region	Population online in 2000 (millions)[a]	Online as percentage of total population in 2000[b]	Population online in 2002 (millions)[c]	Online as percentage of total population in 2002[d]	Percentage increase from 2000 to 2002
World	407	6.8	544	9.0	33.7
Africa	3	0.4	4	0.5	33.3
Asia/Pacific	105	3.0	157	4.5	49.5
Europe	113	14.1	171	21.6	51.3
Middle East	2	1.1	5	2.8	150.0
United States/Canada	167	53.9	181	58.0	8.4
Latin America	17	3.2	25	4.9	47.1

[a] Nua.com November 2000 Internet Survey (http://www.nua.ie), cited in Ashfaq Ishaq, "On the Global Digital
Divide." *Finance and Development* 38:1 (September) (available at http://www.imf.org/external/pubs/ft/fandd/
2001/09/ishaq.htm).
[b] Ishaq (2001).
[c] Nua.com February 2002 Internet Survey (available at http://www.nua.com/surveys/how_many_online/index.
html).
[d] Population figures are drawn from World Development Indicators database, World Bank, April 2002 (available at http://www.worldbank.org/data/databytopic/POP.pdf).

Breadth

A common characteristic of Internet-based technology is widespread and almost in-stantaneous communication with other users. The Internet is accessible by any per-son with a computer and an account with an ISP. It is currently estimated that ap-proximately 544 million people worldwide access the Internet.[1] As table 3-1 indicates, the Internet increasingly is being used by people in developing economies as well as by those in developed markets. Consequently, the Internet offers the financial services industry a number of uses. It permits the industry to disseminate information to a wide audience. It also can be used to dispense investment advice, to make offers for the purchase or sale of securities, and to effect transactions.

Low Cost

Internet use is cheap. Dissemination of information is inexpensive, and the informa-tion can reach a broad domestic and international audience in seconds. Software pro-grams available on the Internet make it possible to produce websites quickly and eas-ily. The cost of access consists of no more than the telecommunication cost involved in connecting to a local ISP and the ISP's fee. No special equipment is required, other than a personal computer, browser software, and a modem connection to the ISP. The overall low cost of access and dissemination contributes to the enormous amount of information made available to investors via the Internet.

Interactivity

The Internet provides its users with an interactive form of communication. Graphics, audio, and written communication media are combined on the Internet to create in-formative and appealing websites and messages. Moreover, this form of communica-tion will become increasingly interactive as technologies such as voice recognition and virtual reality are improved. Interactive features that, for example, grant the option of paying or sending in trading orders electronically allow investors to effectuate invest-ment decisions instantly and take advantage of opportunities in a timely manner.

---

[1] For current statistics on regional and global Internet use, see http://www.nua.ie/surveys/how_many_online/index.html.

Hyperlinks

The Internet allows website sponsors to establish electronic links, known as "hyper-text" or "hyperlinks," which allow for the interconnection of information and materials within (internal hyperlinks) and between (external hyperlinks) websites (Gavis 1998). Hyperlinks allow viewers to move quickly and easily through documents to find the desired information, creating proximity between information sources that is not available in the paper context. This rapid, cross-referencing mechanism provides readers with a unique and valuable information-gathering tool.

Decentralization

The Internet is an "open" network without a central location from which it emanates or from which it can be controlled. It is a highly decentralized system, comprised of millions of computers and subsystems. This is in contrast to more costly and less accessible proprietary networks and commercial online networks, which are "closed" systems owned and operated by an entity responsible for maintaining and controlling its network.[2]

Flexibility

The Internet is a flexible medium that gives the industry control over the content of its websites. Unlike television and newspaper advertisements, information on websites can be easily and inexpensively erased or updated within minutes. New functions and services can be added easily.

The Internet and Its Impact on Capital Markets

Rapid advances in Internet-related technologies are changing the structure and nature of securities business, as investors and securities industry professionals both come to rely on the Internet in their daily business (see table 3-2). This section discusses the current uses of the Internet being made by the various market participants.

---

[2] In proprietary and commercial online networks, members typically pay a monthly fee to access the network. France's Minitel and America Online in the United States are examples of commercial, proprietary networks. Although these networks are extremely large (each with millions of members), they are distinguished from the Internet because they are centrally managed and controlled. Certain Internet networks that restrict access through the use of encryption technology or passwords are, in effect, "closed" networks.

Table 3-2 | **Electronic Finance in Selected Countries, 1999**

Income group/economy	Online banking (customers as percentage of bank customers)	Online brokerage (transactions as percentage of brokerage transactions)	E-money (number of merchant terminals per 100,000 people)
Industrial country average	8.5	28	434
Australia	4	22	10
Belgium	4	20	
Denmark	6	38	1,192
France	2	18	1
Germany	12	32	73
Italy	1	16	7
Japan		32	
Netherlands	15	40	1,898
Norway	8	25	1,059
Sweden	31	55	418
United Kingdom	6	26	3
United States	6	56	35
Emerging market average	4.9	27	27
Argentina	3		
Brazil	5	6	1
Mexico	3	41	2
Average of all economies	6.9	28	317

Source: Claessens, Glaessner, and Klingebiel (2001).

Internet Use by Investors

Particularly in developed capital markets, investors increasingly use the Internet to open and maintain online accounts and to place trading orders. Through the Internet, investors are able to obtain information about public issuers, receive general warnings regarding securities fraud, review the disciplinary histories of financial service providers, and lodge complaints. Moreover, investors rely on the Internet to review research concerning market data, issuers, and ratings and to chart historical data (Choncron, Grandjean, and Huve-Allard 2000). Internet discussion sites, chat rooms, and newsgroups have become common fora in which investors discuss investment strategies and company performance.[3]

---

[3] See Testimony of G. Philip Rutledge before the United States Senate Permanent Subcommittee on Investigations of the Committee on Governmental Affairs (March 23, 1999) (Westlaw Ref. 1999 WL 8085977), *25–26; and Cella and Stark (1997).

An important new development is the increasing investor interest in mobile telephony and interactive television as a means of trading and obtaining information. Mobile telephony that relies on wireless application protocol (WAP) technology enables users to access the Internet directly through cellular telephones. Data transmission speed using current WAP technology is slow, although speed likely will increase remarkably as the technology matures. While the greater interest has been securities trading and banking services, mobile telephony technology potentially could be used to open accounts.

Internet Use by Issuers and Market Intermediaries

Internet use by issuers likewise has grown rapidly. Issuers use the Internet to disseminate all kinds of information, including financial, product, transfer agent, security price, and ratings information. Issuers also use the Internet to communicate directly with shareholders, investors, and analysts. Issuers in a number of jurisdictions are developing systems to allow for online proxy voting and online shareholder and director meetings (Johnson 2002). In addition, many issuers and broker-dealers increasingly are conducting securities offerings online and relying on the Internet and electronic mail to solicit prospective investors.[4]

Market intermediaries (broker-dealers, underwriters, investment advisers, and other entities and professionals empowered to make investment decisions for others) also are exploiting the potential of the Internet. Traditional brokers are developing online services.[5] A number of discount brokerage firms only provide services over the Internet. Generally, intermediaries use the Internet to market and advertise, to present market and portfolio information, and to meet their disclosure and reporting obligations. Intermediaries also provide investment advice, including software-based advice programs, over the Internet (IOSCO 2001).

Many brokers have devised ways to allow their clients to conduct after-hours trading via the Internet and to allow for automatic processing of Internet orders and real-time routing of those orders. Others have established trading platforms on their

---

[4] See "Born in the USA," *Investors Chronicle* (June 7, 2002); "Online Brokerages: Keeping Apace of Cyberspace," Special Study by Commissioner Laura S. Unger (U.S. Securities and Exchange Commission, 1999), 17, at http://www.sec.gov/pdf/cybrtrnd.pdf; Joseph Weber and Peter Elstrom, "Transforming the Art of the Deal," *Businessweek* 3639 (July 26, 1999), 96.

[5] See IOSCO (2001). See French Online Brokers Association (at http://www.brokers-on-line.org/chiffres/default.htm) regarding the increased use of online services by French broker-dealers.

websites that allow investors to trade shares not listed on a stock exchange. More re-cently, some brokers have begun to conduct electronic initial public offering (IPO) dis-tributions whereby they accept customers' electronic indications of interest in IPOs. Certain intermediaries also conduct online auctions on behalf of issuers and take bids over the Internet, permitting issuers to more accurately price their securities in an IPO.[6]

Internet Use by Exchanges

The past few years have witnessed an increase in the use of the Internet by conven-tional securities exchanges to disseminate information to the public and to advertise products and services. Most notably, the Internet is being utilized as a means for in-vestors to route orders to a market, either directly or through an intermediary. The Internet and Internet-related technology are also behind the advent of "direct trad-ing," as evidenced by issuer and third-party electronic bulletin boards. An issuer bul-letin market is essentially a forum for investors to advertise offers of securities. A third-party bulletin market is similar to an issuer bulletin market, except that it is es-tablished and maintained by someone other than the issuer. On either type of mar-ket, transactions between buyers and sellers are effected wholly independently of the bulletin market.[7] These bulletin markets have the potential to decrease transaction costs. They also may be an effective means of facilitating transactions in the securities of emerging companies, which often do not have liquid markets.[8]

An additional development is the emergence of closed Internet markets. These websites trade contracts among members—generally a group of companies

---

[6] "Initial Public Offerings: Dutch Auctions Give Firms New Path to Public Markets," *Investor's Business Daily*, A-8 (Feb. 8, 2001).

[7] A securities transaction on an electronic bulletin system is often carried out as follows. A prospective buyer or seller posts a message on the bulletin system. Normally, investors are required to input an indication of interest to purchase or sell the security at a certain price, the trading amount, and contact information. Then another investor who sees the information on the bulletin system contacts the buyer or seller. The two parties negotiate over the Internet or phone and, after agreeing on the terms, exchange funds and securities independently of the issuer and its transfer agent. The appropriate documentation is then submitted to the issuer's transfer agent in order to transfer record own-ership from the seller to the buyer. In some jurisdictions, to avoid triggering various regulatory requirements, the is-suer or third party does not play any role in effecting the transactions and does not receive compensation for creat-ing or maintaining the system. In addition, the issuer or third party does not participate in any purchase or sale negotiations; does not provide advice as to whether an investor should buy or sell the security; and does not receive, transfer, or hold funds or securities as part of its operation of the system. The issuer may be required to keep records of all quotes entered into the system and make them available on request to the regulator and any market on which the securities are listed.

[8] The securities of emerging companies generally are not traded actively in an organized market (regulated exchanges or organized over-the-counter markets) and often do not satisfy the listing requirements of those markets.

engaged in the same type of activity (for example, energy suppliers)—where access to the website is restricted to these members.[9]

Internet Use by Securities Regulators

Securities regulators use the Internet to educate investors and ensure regulatory transparency. In particular, regulators use the Internet to do the following:

- Provide a database of registrant filings that is readily accessible by investors
- Advise investors regarding the risks of various investments and types of trading
- Warn investors against types of fraud
- List registered issuers and intermediaries (including registered representatives)
- Post new regulations and solicit public comment on proposed regulations
- Receive investor complaints
- Post litigation and press releases
- Assist investors' research by providing hyperlinks to websites of self-regulatory and international organizations
- Post decisions in enforcement matters
- Provide a list of websites identified as advertising fraudulent schemes or unlicensed activity.

Regulators likewise spend considerable resources monitoring Internet securities activity. Many have established Internet surveillance programs with staff trained to detect and investigate securities fraud conducted via the Internet. Regulators have organized international sessions to discuss surveillance techniques and trends in Internet fraud.

Today, instead of simply monitoring the medium, regulators use the Internet as a tool for international enforcement and cooperation. It can serve as a source of information regarding foreign individuals or entities whose activity is subject to investigation. For example, many regulators list firms and individuals against whom enforcement or disciplinary actions have been taken. Frequently, the registration or licensing

---

[9] See, for example, the U.K. Power Exchange (http://www.UKPX.com), a United Kingdom–based online market for trading spot and futures contracts in electricity.

status of firms and individuals is also available via these regulators' websites.[10] These sources of information can be of substantial assistance to a foreign regulator developing an investigative record in a matter involving cross-border misconduct.

Impact of the Internet on Securities Regulation

The Internet is changing the way market participants communicate and do business. However, Internet communication and business may not fit neatly within the parameters of statutes, regulations, and directives originally intended for an environment based on telephone and paper.

The three fundamental objectives of securities regulation are to protect investors, to ensure that markets are fair and efficient, and to reduce systemic risk (IOSCO 1998a). The success and health of securities markets depend on protecting investors against misleading, manipulative, or fraudulent practices. Regulatory requirements that provide the best protection against fraudulent and manipulative practices are those that call for providing investors with full, timely, and clear disclosure of information material. Market fairness is also fundamental to protecting investors. Unfair treatment of investors ultimately leads to a loss in investor confidence and undermines the strength of the market. Finally, although regulators cannot be expected to prevent the financial failure of market intermediaries, regulation should aim to reduce the risk of failure. To this end, market intermediaries should be subject to adequate and ongoing capital and other prudential requirements.

In promoting or responding to securities activity via the Internet, regulators need, in the first instance, to determine whether their current regulatory framework adequately addresses Internet use. Most securities regulators have been able to address the securities industry's use of the Internet without needing to revise their regulatory regimes. Indeed, these regulators simply clarify the application of existing domestic regulatory requirements to Internet activity through guidance and interpretive releases.

Some overarching observations can be made about the manner in which regulators in developed markets have applied existing regulatory requirements to Inter-

---

[10] See, for example, http://www.sec.gov/edgar/searchedgar/webusers.htm (the U.S. SEC's "EDGAR" online database); http://www.asic.gov.au/asic/asic_srchlodg.nsf (the Australian Securities and Investments Commission's online database); http://www.cob.fr/frset.asp?rbrq=sophie (the French Commission des Opérations de Bourse's "SOPHIE" database); and http://www.bafin.de/datenbanken.htm (the German Bundesanstalt für Finanzdienstleistungsaufsicht's database).

net activity. With regard to Internet prospectuses, regulators have insisted on the importance of satisfying the objectives of existing prospectus requirements, that is, allowing investors to make informed decisions about securities offers. At the same time, regulators generally allow for the delivery of disclosure documents via the Internet, provided there is proof that the recipients have Internet access and there is electronic evidence of the delivery of the disclosure documents.[11] Record-keeping requirements established by regulators appear to be largely the same for Internet-based and non-Internet-based securities activities.[12]

However, in a number of countries, regulators have found that certain uses of the Internet require the enactment of new laws or the amendment of existing laws. For example, in some jurisdictions, it is not possible, under the existing law, to hold shareholder and directors' meetings, disseminate voting information, or vote by proxy via the Internet. In other jurisdictions, company laws require physical meetings to be held. Some company laws require paper-based prospectuses, contract notes, and statements of account. In addition, some laws require proxy voting to be effected in person. In light of these restrictions, several developed markets are considering new or amended legislation to facilitate use of the Internet for voting and holding shareholder meetings.

Regulators in most of the developed markets, through guidance or interpretive releases, also have clarified the circumstances leading to their exercise of regulatory authority over cross-border securities activity. Generally, these statements indicate that asserting regulatory jurisdiction revolves primarily around the readily identifiable and constant set of factors developed by the International Organization of Securities Commissions (IOSCO) in 1998.[13] In this regard, IOSCO recommends that the assertion of regulatory jurisdiction (the imposition of licensing, registration, and other requirements) be predicated on conditions. The first is that the offeror of securities or services be located in a regulator's own jurisdiction. The second is that the offer of securities or services has a significant effect on residents or markets in a regulator's jurisdiction. In determining whether the offer meets the second test, regulators consider whether, among other things, the following hold:

---

[11] See, for example, Ontario Securities Commission (1999); and U.S. Securities and Exchange Commission, "Use of Electronic Media for Delivery Purposes," Final Rule, Release No. 33-7289, 34-37183, IC-21946, 17 CFR Parts 200, 228, 229, 230, 232, 239, 240, 270 and 274, (May 9, 1996) (available at http://www.sec.gov/rules/final/33-7289.txt).

[12] *IOSCO Internet Report I*, Annex, supra note 1.

[13] See *IOSCO Internet Report I*, supra note 1. IOSCO Internet Report I did not address the circumstances under which regulators would assert enforcement jurisdiction.

- The offer targets residents of the regulator's jurisdiction.
- The offeror accepts orders from or provides services to residents of the regulator's jurisdiction.
- The offeror uses e-mail or other media to push the information to residents of the regulator's jurisdiction.

Conversely, regulators could find the second test was not met if, among other things:

- The offeror clearly states to whom the Internet offer is directed, rather than appearing to extend the offer into any jurisdiction.
- The offeror provides a statement on its website listing the jurisdictions in which it is (or is not) authorized to offer or sell its securities or services.
- The offeror takes precautions that are reasonably designed to prevent sales to residents in the regulator's jurisdiction, screening addresses and other residency information of respondents (IOSCO 1998b).

Going Forward: Addressing Regulatory Challenges Posed by the Internet

The Internet has had a significant influence on securities trading, and the most recent regulatory challenges with which regulators have had to grapple are a measure of the medium's impact. In 2001, IOSCO examined a number of these challenges, including system capacity, resilience, and security; liability for Internet communications; Internet discussion sites; and the role of ISPs with respect to combating Internet fraud (IOSCO 2001).

As market participants increasingly use the Internet to route orders and place trades, the technological capacity, resilience, and security of online brokerage systems become of greater moment. Online brokers need to ensure that increased volume or periodic spikes in message traffic do not overwhelm their systems. As Internet servers reach their maximum capacity, investors may encounter delays in accessing online brokers, and brokers may have difficulty routing customer orders to the designated market for execution in a timely manner. Accordingly, it may be opportune and relevant for regulators to consider assessing online brokers' interest in ensuring the technological adequacy of their Internet-based trading systems.

As websites progressively become the medium of choice for communicating with investors, and as Internet use becomes more prevalent, issuers and intermediaries have raised a number of questions regarding the scope of their liability for Internet communications. In particular, issuers and intermediaries have asked about the scope of their liability for hyperlinks to websites containing third-party information and their liability for maintaining websites during registered offerings. Likewise, depending on the legal regime, an opinion concerning a security given via an Internet discussion site (IDS) could qualify as "investment advice" and thus subject the site to regulation as an investment adviser, generating understandable consternation among companies providing IDS facilities. Finally, ISPs frequently are unaware of the nature of Internet-related securities fraud or the types of information securities regulators seek from them when prosecuting such fraud.

The following sections, which summarize IOSCO's findings, are illustrative of the interaction among the Internet, the securities industry, and regulation.

System Capacity, Resilience, and Security

The Internet's ability to instantaneously reach a large number of market participants has reduced costs for the securities industry. As a consequence of these advantages, broker-dealers now encourage investors to trade online (box 3-1). This development has led to significant growth in the number of online securities accounts. However,

---

Box 3-1 | **Progress in the Use of the Internet**

In the United States in 2000, there were 11.7 million online investors, nearly double the number of online investors in 1999. In 2000, these investors made more than 1 million trades per day and held $1.08 trillion in assets in online brokerage accounts.

In Canada, a study conducted by the Toronto Stock Exchange in the spring of 2000 found that four in 10 Canadian investors spend more than 10 hours per month reviewing investment material online, while checking stock and mutual fund prices on the Internet every day.

IDC, a technology consulting firm, estimates that Latin America will have 75 million Internet users by 2005, with the number of individuals in Latin America accessing the Internet increasing by 40 percent per year between 2000 and 2005. Online trade in Latin America is expected to be worth $72 billion by this time.

Several Latin American nations recently have enlisted the Internet as a tool against corruption. Mexico, Argentina, and the Dominican Republic post information about public officials' personal assets on the Internet to encourage honesty, while Mexico and Chile have started processing government contracts online to encourage transparency and discourage bribery.

The number of online securities accounts in Europe is projected to grow to 10.5 million by 2003, from 3.74 million during the beginning of 2001.

Source: Toronto Stock Exchange and World Investor Link (2000).

rapid growth of online trading can push the boundaries of a broker-dealer's online system capacity and test system resilience, particularly during rapidly changing market conditions. In addition, such rapid growth can challenge the integrity of these systems by providing a gateway for security breaches and other types of fraud.

Broker-dealers and other market participants that are coming to rely on the Internet or who encourage their customers to use Internet-based services must be able to handle increased trading volume, including possible sudden spikes in use resulting from a large number of clients trying to access these Internet-based systems at times of market volatility. It is also important for a trading system to remain operational when significant components of the system have failed. System resilience is especially important for online brokers that have limited backup options (such as trading via the telephone) in the event their systems fail during critical times. Robust security is of the utmost importance, particularly where details of client assets or the assets themselves might be vulnerable to unauthorized access.

Given that the Internet involves technology that evolves rapidly and constantly, regulators are loathe to impose requirements that mandate specific technology. Such a prescriptive approach could result in online trading systems that are inappropriate or outdated. Instead, regulators usually have provided guidance or policy statements interpreting the application of existing rules in relation to system capacity, resilience, and security. In general, regulators have urged broker-dealers to assess continually their vulnerabilities to various sources of risk by, among other things, establishing capacity estimates; developing backup technology systems and procedures for handling system capacity problems; implementing procedures for maintaining data integrity whether stored, in transit, or displayed on clients' screens; and instituting controls to maintain the integrity of software source code.[14]

As a general caveat, regulators should take into account that broker-dealers have an interest in properly addressing risks relating to system capacity, resilience, and security. A broker-dealer's business will be significantly undermined if the public perceives its systems as having capacity, resilience, or security flaws and if brokers that only provide an online service are aware that loss of public confidence in their facilities would be lethal to their business.

---

[14] Hong Kong Securities and Futures Commission (2000); "Communication DI/30396 of 21 April 2000" Commissione Nazionale per le Societa e la Borsa of Italy (English version available at http://www.consob.it/produzione/docum/english/Regulations/fr_30396e.htm); The Netherlands Authority for the Financial Markets, "Further Regulation on the Supervision of Securities Trade 1999," Nadere Regeling, 1999 (English version available at http://www.autoriteit-fm.nl/Uploads/rulebook.pdf), as supplemented in February 2001 by "Policy Document 99-0003" (available at http://www.autoriteit-fm.nl/Uploads/Beleidsnotitie99-0003.pdf); and U.S. Securities and Exchange Commission (2001).

Websites and Liability for Hyperlinked Information and Communications

Securities laws impose liability for statements made to investors that contain a material falsehood or omit to state a material fact necessary to make the disclosure not misleading. Issuers and intermediaries are responsible for the accuracy of statements they make, sponsor, or endorse, regardless of the medium of communication they use. However, in the Internet realm, the question naturally arises as to whether issuers and intermediaries should be held liable for false or misleading information contained on websites to which they have hyperlinks.

For example, a broker-dealer may wish to include on its website hyperlinks to other sites that it believes might provide useful research tools for investors. Links to well-known business news websites or information clearinghouses can provide invaluable assistance to investors deciding which securities to buy. At the same time, the broker-dealer probably has no intention of scrutinizing these websites in any detailed legal fashion. However, an investor using the website could assume that the linked website was prepared by or at least authorized by the broker-dealer. If one of these linked websites contains an untrue statement that the investor relies on when purchasing a security, should the broker-dealer be held liable? And if the broker-dealer is deemed liable, will this not simply deter broker-dealers from providing investors and the public with convenient links to potentially useful news and research websites?

In general, attribution depends on whether the issuer was involved in the preparation of the hyperlinked information or has endorsed or adopted the information. One approach regulators may use to determine attribution in a way that promotes full and accurate disclosure, without unnecessarily deterring website operators from including useful hyperlinks, would be to consider certain factors in determining whether an issuer or intermediary has prepared, endorsed, or adopted hyperlinked information. Such factors may include the following:

- The context of the hyperlink—what the website operator says about the hyperlink (that is, whether there is a disclaimer about the hyperlink or a statement endorsing the information)
- Whether there is a clear and prominent indication that the viewer is leaving the market participant's website
- Whether there is framing and inlining (so-called inverse hyperlinking) that may lead a reasonable user to believe that the hyperlinked site is part of the originating operator's website
- Whether the market participant has paid or otherwise compensated the third party for posting the information

- The effort of markets and intermediaries to direct investors to certain hyper-links but not others.

Liability for Internet communications during the offering process is of special regulatory concern. When an issuer is engaged in a registered public offering, both the issuer and intermediaries participating in the offering face restrictions on the communications they can make to potential investors. That an issuer is engaged in a public offering may affect what may be presented on its website or what may be the subject of a hyperlink. Laws also limit certain communications during an offering so as not to influence investors with materials outside the prospectus.[15] Although regulators should be aware that issuers and intermediaries could use the Internet in novel ways to communicate with investors, the regulators may want to ensure that issuers and intermediaries consider carefully the content of the information available on their websites or hyperlinks during the offering process. Likewise, issuers and intermediaries should be aware that regulators could construe hyperlinks and the content of websites as illegal communications during the offering process.

Day Trading

Day trading has only recently become a topic requiring the attention of securities regulators. Day trading is popular because it allows the trader to take advantage of market inefficiencies and volatility. For a long time, day trading was the province of professional traders, banks, and investment firms. However, the Internet and significant developments in the order-routing capacities of financial service providers led to an environment that made day trading feasible and attractive for retail investors.

The high risk of loss of capital is the reason why investor protection is the primary regulatory concern with respect to day trading. As soon as day trading became available to retail investors, it became apparent that, when undertaken without sound knowledge of markets and trading conditions and without sufficient capital, it could potentially result in serious financial difficulties for the investor (see, for exam-

---

[15] In many jurisdictions, such as the United States, the first stage of the public offering process is the prefiling period. During this period, no written or oral offers of the security are permitted and no activities (written or otherwise) may be undertaken by the issuer that might arouse investor interest in the securities. During the offering period (which generally commences once the prospectus has been filed with the regulator and ends once the regulator declares a prospectus effective), the issuer and underwriters may solicit indications of investor interest, but may not sell any securities. Any written solicitation efforts during this period must be made by means of a preliminary prospectus that complies with the applicable securities laws. Finally, during the sales period, offers and sales may only be made using the final prospectus, a copy of which must be delivered to each investor before or at the same time as the written sale confirmation.

ple, Kong 2000, Buckman 2000, and Hale 1999). Dangers for inexperienced investors lurk not only in competition with professional traders but also in the high cost of repeated trading. These costs include transaction costs and other costs associated with repeatedly entering and closing positions.

Regulators facing an Internet-inspired increase in day trading can address the issue through a range of measures aimed at increasing investor education as well as establishing specific regulatory requirements for day trading accounts designed to better disclose the risks and costs day traders face. Regulators may require, for example, that day trading providers inform investors that:

- Day trading requires in-depth knowledge of the securities markets, trading techniques and strategies, and financial instruments.
- Individuals attempting to benefit from day trading must compete with professional and financially powerful market participants.
- Day trading may involve high costs due to the commission fees charged, and day traders may be unable to execute trades immediately because of possible system capacity problems.
- Options and futures transactions may lead to losses exceeding the margin provided, and the trader might face losses much greater than the amount of the initial investment.[16]

Regulators may require that providers inform investors about specific transaction costs and the conditions and costs for using or ceasing to use technical facilities or trading centers. In addition, providers may be required to supply users with a

---

[16] The U.S. SEC's Office of Compliance Inspections and Examinations conducted an examination of 47 registered broker-dealers providing day trading facilities to the general public (day trading firms) during October 1, 1998 through September 30, 1999. Although the examinations did not reveal widespread fraud, at several firms, examiners found indications of potentially serious securities law violations warranting referrals to the SEC's enforcement staff. These violations related to net capital, margin, and lending disclosure. At most firms, however, the examinations revealed less serious concerns, but indicated that many firms need to take steps to improve their compliance with net capital, short selling, and supervision rules. Firms at which examiners found deficiencies generally were issued deficiency letters, and corrective action was required. Although the deficiencies found are not unique to day trading firms, SEC staff believe that the nature of day trading itself—frequent, fast, and risky trading—makes compliance with securities laws difficult to achieve without an automated compliance infrastructure. In addition, while disclosure of the risks of day trading is not explicitly required by current SEC or self-regulatory organization rules, the examinations revealed that, as of the time of the examinations, many firms did not provide their customers with information concerning such risks. However, recent reviews of the advertising and disclosure of day trading firms indicate improved practices—many firms are using more balanced advertising and providing potential customers with better information concerning the risks of day trading. See U.S. Securities and Exchange Commission (2000).

monthly statement of all the costs and losses the user has incurred, broken down in a manner enabling the customer to see what portion of these losses are due to transaction costs (Bundesanstalt für Finanzdienstleistungsaufsicht 2000).

Some jurisdictions also impose "suitability" or "appropriateness" requirements for day traders, as well as limits on margin accounts. Suitability requirements may include restricting day trading to persons who have prior knowledge of investments, have a high level of risk tolerance, or trade only for themselves. Under this approach, regulators may require that the day trading provider make a threshold determination that day trading is generally appropriate for the customer, basing its assessment on the experience, objectives, and financial situation of the customer.

Internet Discussion Sites

A great deal of information and opinions about securities investment is available through Internet discussion sites, chat rooms, mailing lists, and similar multi-user mechanisms that enable people to send messages and information to one another. IDSs can provide investors with a number of benefits. However, regulators should also recognize that, because the Internet facilitates the rapid dissemination of information, IDSs could be a cheap and effective way for disseminating false or misleading information about securities and securities markets. In particular, an IDS could deliberately disseminate information to manipulate the price of a particular security. For example, fraudsters have used IDSs to manipulate the market in a particular stock or as part of a traditional pump and dump scheme. In some jurisdictions, an IDS facility might qualify as an investment adviser under the broad definition of the law.[17] In these jurisdictions, IDSs could be subject to the requirements imposed on investment advisers. Generally, this would require IDSs to meet licensing requirements relating to qualifications, fitness, integrity, and experience; disclose any conflicts of interest; and provide advice that is reasonable under the circumstances and tailored to the client's needs.

Given the unusual nature of IDSs, regulators could, instead, exempt IDSs from regulation as investment advisers, subject to certain disclosure, record keeping, and

---

[17] In certain jurisdictions, a person or entity is providing "financial product advice" if he, she, or it offers "a recommendation or a statement of opinion, or a report of either of those things, that (a) is intended to influence a person or persons in making a decision in relation to a particular financial product or class of financial products, or an interest in a particular financial product or class of financial products; or (b) could reasonably be regarded as being intended to have such an influence." (Australian Corporation Act of 2001, § 766B [1]) An earlier version of Australia's corporations law defined an "investment adviser" as someone who makes available to the public advice, reports, and analysis about securities with system, repetition, and continuity (Australian Corporation Law, § 77[1]).

self-regulatory requirements. In jurisdictions explicitly exempting IDSs from such regulation, IDSs frequently must still disclose to persons viewing or making a posting that
neither the IDS nor persons making postings are registered or licensed investment
advisers. Regulators also frequently require warnings that persons viewing postings
should consider consulting a licensed adviser before investing in a security discussed
at the site and a statement encouraging investors to contact the securities regulator
if the person viewing postings suspects that any posting is inaccurate, based on inside
information, or likely to mislead or deceive viewers.

In addition, regulators may require IDS operators to do the following:

- Monitor for misleading or deceptive postings or postings likely to be part of
  a scheme to defraud investors or manipulate the market
- Withdraw immediately the rights of access of a person making postings that
  appear to be part of a scheme to defraud investors or manipulate the market
- Notify the regulator within a reasonable time of any suspicious posting, complaints about suspicious postings, and the identity of persons making such
  postings
- Confirm and maintain for a certain period of time the identity of persons
  making postings
- Archive and maintain postings for a certain period of time.

In those jurisdictions where securities-related IDSs do not fall under the definition of investment advisers, some jurisdictions rely on Internet surveillance and
enforcement actions to protect investors against the types of fraud and market manipulation that sometimes occur on electronic bulletin boards and chat rooms. The
elements of such Internet surveillance and enforcement programs frequently include
the following (IOSCO 2001):

- Teams of investigators who regularly surf the Internet and visit IDSs to iden-
  tify fraudulent or misleading postings
- Automated search engines that review postings for fraudulent or misleading
  IDSs and electronic complaint centers to which IDS users may forward con-
  cerns regarding suspicious postings
- Prominent and successful enforcement actions focusing on securities fraud or
  market manipulation via IDSs
- Dialogue with the IDS industry to assist law enforcement.

Internet Service Providers

ISPs are in the business of connecting people to the Internet through dial-up telephone connections, digital subscriber lines (DSLs), co-axle cable, or other means. Once connected, an ISP subscriber's computer becomes part of the Internet, allowing it to access information available on websites and to interact with other connected parties via e-mail, chat rooms, and bulletin boards.

Because of the growing use of the Internet to commit securities fraud and manipulate markets for securities, regulators increasingly need to obtain information from ISPs about subscribers and their communications. Fraud-related "spam" (unsolicited bulk e-mail sent to thousands of Internet addresses at once) frequently is routed through e-mail addresses located in other jurisdictions. When the misconduct emanates from another jurisdiction, securities regulators often must cooperate with their foreign counterparts to obtain the necessary information. Successful cooperation therefore depends on whether regulators have access to information maintained by ISPs.

In order to determine if securities fraud has taken place and who has committed the fraud, regulators frequently need access to subscriber data as well as traffic data. However, not all ISPs maintain subscriber data and/or traffic data, and many ISPs that do maintain such information keep it for short periods of time. Therefore, regulators are confronted with the challenge of ensuring that ISPs maintain subscriber data and certain traffic data and that such data are made available to regulators when necessary. To do so, regulators may pursue one or more of several options, including (IOSCO 2001):

- Engaging in a dialogue with ISPs and ISP associations to identify the type of information regulators frequently require to investigate fraud and seeking the voluntary assistance of ISPs to collect and retain this type of information
- Pursuing legislative or regulatory initiatives that oblige ISPs to maintain records relevant to the investigation and prosecution of securities fraud via the Internet
- Seeking statutory powers enabling the regulator to compel relevant data from ISPs and to share such information with foreign counterparts
- Seeking amendments to privacy laws that allow regulators investigating Internet fraud to access data maintained by ISPs
- Exploring the possibility of invoking the assistance of another domestic authority that can compel relevant data from ISPs in the context of a foreign or domestic investigation of illegal securities activities

- Having qualified technical personnel and adequate resources to keep pace with technological development
- Ensuring system integrity in retrieving and storing data from ISPs for use in proceedings, including contracting agreements to allow transmission of non-public information.

Conclusion

The Internet has the potential to level the advantages that large markets, large issuers, and large investors traditionally have held over their smaller counterparts. If this potential is properly recognized and seized, the Internet could offer great benefits to the financial markets of developing economies. However, taking advantage of the Internet's potential is not a straightforward proposition. Internet-related technologies are new, and the securities regulators of developed markets have only recently come to grips with some of the regulatory complexities. At the same time, the first tentative steps regulators have made down this path offer distinct lessons for developing market regulators.

Almost all of the 19 jurisdictions that IOSCO's Internet Task Force recently surveyed have, through guidance or interpretive releases, clarified their regulatory authority in the area of Internet technology. Regulators in developing markets likewise should clarify their authority as soon as possible, in order to create the legal infrastructure their markets will need in order to operate most efficiently. Fortunately, the lessons learned so far by other regulators—contained in IOSCO's two Internet reports—offer valuable guidance on how developing market regulators could prioritize the Internet-related issues they confront.

The first lesson regulators have already learned about the Internet as it pertains to securities regulation is that the fundamentals have not changed. Securities markets are about accurate and timely information. Allocating capital and risk in an efficient manner requires that information flow freely among all those involved in the market—investors, issuers, intermediaries, clearance and settlement entities, and regulators. Securities regulation in an Internet world differs from traditional securities regulation only in that the volume and speed of free-flowing information are much greater than in the past. Securities regulators must still ensure that the information flowing in this environment is not contaminated with falsehoods or inaccuracies. Likewise, regulators must deter unscrupulous individuals from preying on investors through the Internet.

However, because the Internet contains many unique characteristics—in particular, its accessibility and low cost—regulating securities markets in the Internet Age will demand of regulators several new skills. As IOSCO's recent study illustrates, regulators will need to factor in Internet capacity, resiliency, and security concerns when analyzing the systemic risks their markets and market participants face. Regulators will also need to decide how public Internet fora, such as Internet discussion sites—which are, essentially, enormous global public squares where strangers meet to discuss the day's concerns—fit within the ambit of existing securities laws and regulations. Likewise, although regulators concerned about systemic stability have always paid attention to widespread market speculation, Internet-facilitated day trading has combined concerns over speculation with issues of consumer education, hidden transaction charges, and fears over growing personal bankruptcy. Securities law enforcement personnel will need to learn new technical skills to track fraudsters through ISP addresses in much the same way that they currently track ill-gotten proceeds through bank account numbers. At the same time, securities regulators themselves will need to forge new relationships with ISPs, just as they have done with the financial industry, if they wish to have ready access to the types of information they will need in order to prosecute securities fraud.

Finally, perhaps the most important lesson developing market regulators can take from the experiences of other regulators is that cooperation among regulators is a necessity if regulators hope to succeed at the vital tasks with which they are charged. In the rapidly shrinking Internet world—where investors, issuers, and intermediaries can cross borders with ease—wrongdoers and fraudsters also can easily cross these jurisdictional boundaries to prey on investors and undermine the integrity of securities markets. Where scam artists set up shop in one jurisdiction while preying on investors elsewhere, regulators will have to exchange information and assist each other in their investigations in order to protect the integrity of all markets.

As several studies have indicated, Internet use in Latin America is poised to grow exponentially. Latin American governments, some of which only recently have begun developing robust securities regulations, will be thrown into the middle of an Internet revolution in capital markets. This revolution offers Latin America the opportunity to take advantage of technology to develop advanced capital markets that, in the past, would have been impossible outside a few large cities in Europe, Asia, and North America. However, doing so will require Latin American regulators to combine this new technology not only with the requisite physical infrastructure, but also with an appropriate regulatory infrastructure. One hopes that the lessons offered by other jurisdictions will serve as a guide to future success.

Bibliography

Australian Bureau of Statistics. 2000. *Use of the Internet by Householders*. Canberra, November.

Buckman, Rebecca. 2000. The Rise and Collapse of a Day Trader. *The Asian Wall Street Journal,* February 29, p. 19.

Bundesanstalt für Finanzdienstleistungsaufsicht (formerly, Bundesaufsichtsamt für den Wertpapierhandel). 2000. *Guideline on Day Trading*. Frankfurt, August. http://www.bawe.de/down/rle00_01e.pdf.

Cameron, Doug. 2001. Online Broking Rises in Europe. *The Financial Times,* February 22, p. 27.

Cella, Joseph J. III, and John Reed Stark. 1997. SEC Enforcement and the Internet: Meeting the Challenge of the Next Millennium. *Business Lawyer* 52 (May):815.

Choncron, Monique, Hervé Grandjean, and Marianne Huve-Allard. 2000. *Les porteurs de valeurs mobilières en 2000*. ParisBourseSBF SA, June. http://www.bourse-de-paris.fr/centredoc/pdf/valmob2000.pdf.

Claessens, Stijn, Thomas Glaessner, and Daniela Klingebiel. 2001. *E-Finance in Emerging Markets: Is Leapfrogging Possible?* Financial Sector Discussion Paper 7. Washington, D.C.: World Bank.

Commissione Nazionale per le Societa e la Borsa of Italy. 2000. Letter sent by Italian Consob to Abi, Assosim, Unionsim, Assogestioni, Assofiduciaria, Assoreti, Anasf, the National Council of Stockbrokers and A.I.F.I., regarding online trading and rules of conduct, April 21.

French Online Brokers Association. http://www.brokers-on-line.org/chiffres/default.htm.

Gavis, Alexander C. 1998. Hyperlinks in Mutual Fund Advertising. *Wallstreetlawyer.com* 1(8):3–7. Reprinted in *Securities Law and the Internet: Doing Business in a Rapidly Changing Marketplace,* co-chairs B. Becker, S. J. Schulte, and M. C. Wallach. Practising Law Institute.

Hale, Brian. 1999. Cleaning Up The 'Devil's Den.' *Sydney Morning Herald,* August 2, p. 37.

Hong Kong Securities and Futures Commission. 2000. *A Consultation Paper on the Regulation of Online Trading of Securities and Futures*. Hong Kong; December. http://www.hksfc.org.hk/eng/bills/html/consultation/online.doc.

International Organization of Securities Commissions (IOSCO). 1998a. *Objectives and Principles of Securities Regulation*. Madrid, September. http://www.iosco.org/download/pdf/1998-objectives-eng.pdf.

_____. 1998b. *Securities Activity on the Internet*. Madrid, September. http://www.iosco.org/download/pdf/1998-internet_security.pdf.

_____. 2001. *Securities Activity on the Internet II*. Madrid, June.

Investor's Business Daily. 2001. Initial Public Offerings: Dutch Auctions Give Firms New Path to Public Markets. (February 8), p. A-8.

Investor's Chronicle. 2002. Born in the USA (June 7).

Johnson, Tom. 2002. Shareholder Proxy Votes May Soon Go Electronic. *Reuters English News Service* 12:50:00 (July 9).

Kong, Dolores. 2000. Amateur Hour May Be Over Volatile Market Narrows Number of Day Traders Who Suffered Heavy Losses. *The Boston Globe*, October 15, p. G1.

Ontario Securities Commission. 1999. *Delivery of Documents by Electronic Means*. Notice of Policy under the Securities Act, National Policy 11-201 (December 15). www.osc.gov.on.ca/en/Regulation/Rulemaking/Policies/11-201_19991215.html.

Rutledge, G. Philip. 1999. Testimony before the Permanent Subcommittee on Investigations of the Committee on Governmental Affairs, March 23. United States Senate.

Scheeres, Julia. 2001. The Net as Corruption Disruption. *Wired*, March 26.

Toronto Stock Exchange and World Investor Link. 2000. *The Canadian Shareowner Study 2000*. Toronto Stock Exchange.

U.S. Bancorp Piper Jaffray Equity Research. 2000. *Online Financial Service Update*. (October).

U.S. Securities and Exchange Commission. 1999. *Online Brokerages: Keeping Apace of Cyberspace*. Washington, D.C.: U.S. Securities and Exchange Commission.

_____. 2000. *Special Study: Report of Examinations of Day-Trading Broker-Dealers*. Washington, D.C.: U.S. Securities and Exchange Commission, February 25. http://www.sec.gov/news/studies/daytrading.htm.

_____. 2001. *Examinations of Broker-Dealers Offering Online Trading: Summary of Findings and Recommendations.* Washington, D.C., U.S. Securities and Exchange Commission, January 25. http://www.sec.gov/news/studies/online.htm.

Weber, Joseph, and Peter Elstrom. 1999. Transforming the Art of the Deal. *Business Week* 3639 (July 26):96.

Yankee Group. 1999. An *e-Infrastructure for a Leading e-Economy: Report on the Enhancement of the Financial Infrastructure in Hong Kong.* Boston, Mass., September.

CHAPTER 4

The Impact of the Macroeconomic Environment on Capital Markets in Emerging Latin American Economies

Valeriano F. Garcia
Luis Alberto Giorgio

From the era when rich Florentine merchants risked their purse and life to finance their princes until the current period of Internet banking, financial intermediation has been cursed as responsible for the downfall of the rich or hailed as the solution for the poor. Both claims are indeed false, but recent history has shown that, when gone awry, financial intermediation may be the Achilles' heel of the modern economic system. Modern history has shown that there is no development without vibrant capital markets.

Macroeconomic variables and the design and implementation of macroeconomic policy influence the main functions of financial markets, which are the intermediation of risks and terms. Capital markets and banks have attracted the attention of intellectuals and policymakers. In Latin America and the Caribbean, policymakers have placed great expectations in the power of banks. Thus, they have created large public sector development banks and myriad small specialty banks. The underlying assumption has been that public banks play not only a catalytic role but also a development function in correcting what some analysts assume are market failures.

In the past decade, many public banks have been dismantled after they failed to stand up to challenges, created a large fiscal burden, and distributed subsidies in a nontransparent way. More importantly, they did not provide medium- and long-term financing and did not allocate funds to competitive, export-oriented firms. By contrast, in some other regions, for example Europe, public sector financial intermediaries operate in the context of more open and integrated economies and allocate funds giving priority to borrowing firms based on their competitiveness in external markets. Developed countries have used the same public sector approach in promoting the idea that the government has to create a market for public debt in order to establish benchmarks and nurture the development of private issues. This approach and a long-term view have indeed been a successful model in many developed countries.

However, in Latin America and the Caribbean, once the market is initially set up through government debt, it is used as an instrument for running an unsustainable public deficit with significant negative effects on the development of capital markets. Under these circumstances, the private sector, which was supposed to be the final beneficiary, can never compete with the high interest rates and public guarantee of official debt. Consequently, a natural tendency prevails for crowding out the private sector because the public sector is seen as providing high returns with low risks.

Researchers have studied the legal design of financial markets, the relation-ship between financial market development and the macroeconomic environment, financial reform, and other structural factors (King and Levine 1993; La Porta and others 1997; Beck and others 2000; Henry 2000; Bekaert, Harvey, and Lundblad 2001). In general, there is consensus on the fact that financial markets tend to develop as income per capita grows and financial reform progresses.

The purpose of this chapter is to provide policymakers and financial experts with an overview of relevant issues related to the impact of macroeconomic policy and structural factors, such as institutional arrangements, on the development of capital markets in emerging economies, with particular emphasis on Latin America. The chapter analyzes the constraints imposed by exogenous macroeconomic factors on the effectiveness of capital market performance. The chapter highlights the negative impact of financial regulations giving ineffective preferred status to banking over capital market investment and financing instruments. It begins with a broad approach in analyzing the traditional moral hazard issues derived from financial policies and banking regulations. The analysis evaluates the main trends prevailing in the institutional framework affecting capital markets and summarizes the main lessons from the Latin American experiences.

Macroeconomic and Structural Constraints to Capital Market Development in Latin America

Capital markets intermediate funds across economic units and time preferences. They allow separation between those economic agents that produce surpluses and save from those that produce deficits and invest. In addition, by creating a menu of options, capital markets cater to different risk and time preference profiles. For example, the time profile of investors' demand for funding usually exceeds that of savers.

Prices represent a critical variable in determining scarcity and signaling where the resource flow should go. The interaction between supply and demand sets the price signals for traded assets in capital markets. If these signals are efficient, production and growth should be maximized. In theory, in developed capital markets, all available information is embedded in the prices of individual stocks. In a world where information is a scarce resource, this function is by no means trivial.

The macroeconomic environment and the quality of macroeconomic policies are interrelated with the functions of capital markets. When capital markets are affected by macroeconomic instability, their microeconomic functions are impaired. At the same time, some microeconomic distortions have macroeconomic implications; for example, subsidized credit may have fiscal and monetary implications. Moreover, many countries with macroeconomic stability have underdeveloped capital markets. This is the case in some countries in the region, where the lack of efficient market infrastructure or the small size of the market does not allow for capital market development. Therefore, taken separately, macroeconomic stability and an adequate structural environment are necessary but not sufficient conditions for the development of capital markets.

From a macroeconomic perspective, there is significant interaction between economic growth and financial depth. Some countries have achieved economic growth with strong debt markets and weak equity markets (for example, Germany and Japan); for others (including the United States), the opposite is true. It is generally accepted that countries with high growth rates have either well-developed or developing capital markets. There is less agreement regarding causality.

The functions of capital markets are quite important, but they may be critical or accessory depending on the existence of bad or good substitutes. Garcia (1987) puts forward the hypothesis that changes in the demand for or supply of money will cause changes in the availability of credit. Garcia analyzes and accepts, with a high degree of confidence, the hypothesis that private sector credit was a significant variable in the aggregate production function of Argentina in 1946–70. Exogenous movements in the real quantity of private sector credit significantly affected Argentina's gross domestic product (GDP).

Can the results for Argentina be generalized? The situation in Mexico after the "tequila" crisis seems to contradict them. After 1995, Mexico's banking system practically shut down. No meaningful credit flowed to the private sector. Nevertheless, after the sharp 1995 downturn, the country recovered and experienced high growth. How could it produce high growth with a closed banking system? A significant part of the explanation relies on the commercial credit provided by U.S. business firms to their subsidiaries and to large Mexican firms. Subsequently, the North American Free Trade Agreement (NAFTA) generated growth in foreign investment and external demand, which substantially helped the Mexican economy. This was a one-shot event and should not be generalized to other countries. Mexico will need to rebuild its financial markets or fully integrate itself into the U.S. financial market in order to make its growth sustainable. However, the Mexican experience shows that in emerging markets, where short-term borrowing is usually the bulk of financing, commercial credit is significantly relevant and may be a good substitute for short-term banking loans.

In most countries in Latin America, equity markets are quite underdeveloped. However, Brazil has sophisticated stock exchanges. For example, the São Paulo stock exchange, Bovespa, and the Bolsa de Mercadorias & Futuros (BM&F), which specializes in derivatives, are at the world frontier in technological advances. Electronic trading comprises 90 percent of Bovespa's trades and 55 percent of its traded value. BM&F has recently incorporated the Global Trading System, an advanced electronic trading platform with international capability. However, although Bovespa's market capitalization was 33 percent of Brazil's GDP during 1996–2000, about half of that capitalization consisted of the 10 largest companies, and relatively few medium enterprises entered the market (IMF 2001). There is still a wide gap between Brazil's technological advance in managing and administering its stock exchanges and the narrow use of those platforms by the majority of its medium and even large enterprises.

Why are capital markets, in general, and stock markets, in particular, underdeveloped in most Latin American and Caribbean countries? What have been the most important constraints to the development of capital markets in emerging economies? Here we focus on the constraints imposed by the following macroeconomic and structural factors, which could be considered exogenous to the microeconomic design of capital markets and the performance of its participants: poor macroeconomic policy; negative externalities produced by banking industry regulations; and structural constraints, such as lack of efficient institutional infrastructure, minimum size of the market, and poorly designed financial and nonfinancial reforms.

Poor Macroeconomic Policy

A well-organized and vibrant capital market cannot co-exist with a weak macroeconomic setup and much less with an explosive fiscal deficit or inconsistent policy mix. Among its functions, a capital market intermediates risks over time. Expectations about the value of macroeconomic variables are difficult to build under high and/or volatile inflation; real exchange rate volatility; noncredible exchange rate regimes; inconsistent monetary cum fiscal policy; distortionary and/or high tax rates; and directed and subsidized credit.

The concepts of risk and uncertainty converge when no probabilities of occurrence can be assigned to a state of nature. Under macroeconomic instability, the difference between risk and uncertainty becomes elusive because the instability impinges on the capabilities of economic agents to assign probabilities of occurrence to uncertain states of nature. Consequently, the savings rate, a significant input for the growth of financial intermediation, is impaired.

In many emerging markets, macroeconomic instability arises from excessive government debt financing that crowds out the private sector from both debt and equity markets. Government paper is generally preferred to private paper because all market participants know the issuer; the liquidity of government paper is usually higher than that of any other instrument. The government has the power to tax as well as the ability to print money and only defaults under crisis conditions.

Recent experience in Argentina illustrates how poor and inconsistent macroeconomic policies can significantly affect domestic capital markets. During the 1990s, and after two decades of macroeconomic instability that ended in hyperinflation, Argentina re-engineered its financial institutions. In 1991, the country implemented a currency board, fixing the peso and the dollar on a one-to-one basis. Within the 10-year period during which Argentina kept its currency board, the U.S. dollar appreciated substantially and Argentina's main trading partner, Brazil, devalued its currency by about 40 percent in real terms. Consequently, Argentina's real exchange rate appreciated substantially, and this disequilibrium required significant productivity gains, coupled with robust fiscal policy, to keep the economy competitive. Instead, toward the end of the period, the country increased its public sector deficit, which it financed by issuing debt.

Given the inflexibility of prices to downward pressure, the adjustment to lower nominal income had to be done through quantities and real income took a dive. The recession led to double-digit unemployment rates. To repair the fiscal gap, the government increased taxes. The recession deepened and fiscal revenues declined. The government responded to the higher fiscal deficit by reducing expenditures and financing with higher debt issues. The reduction in expenditures worsened the recession, the country's debt became very risky, and interest rates on its public debt soared.

By late 2001, the government defaulted on its external debt, which also affected domestic creditors, mainly banks and pension funds. It forced a swap of its high-yielding debt for new debt that was guaranteed with future fiscal revenues, yielding only 7 percent. Banks were paying much higher rates on their funding, so in order to help the placement of government debt, the Central Bank put a cap on the interest rate. Under these circumstances, internal savings were pulled out of the formal financial system, the demand for dollars increased significantly, and a full-fledged currency crisis was triggered. The time-inconsistent macroeconomic policy, the insolvency of the banking industry caused by public sector default and the private sector's lack of ability to repay loans, and weak political leadership led to a run on the banks and the collapse of the banking system.

During the "convertibility decade," Argentina strengthened its financial system by (i) requiring banks to hold capital ratios much higher than those demanded by the Basle accord; (ii) imposing high loan-loss provisions and strict international accounting standards; (iii) actively favoring the entrance of large foreign banks; (iv) requiring that banks issue subordinated debt in the form of bonds; (v) demanding that banks be rated by international rating agencies; and (vi) imposing reserve requirements higher than 20 percent on liquid deposits not withstanding their initial time structure. The lack of a lender of last resort was addressed by buying the option to borrow liquidity from international banks through contingent credit lines that would be triggered in the case of a currency run.

Argentina's trade policies were not efficiently designed—they promoted only partial openness and integration with the rest of the world—but on all aspects related to its financial system, the country "went by the book." However, one year later, the banking system was on the brink of complete insolvency, and the capital market was reduced to minimum activity. The meltdown was instantaneous because of the size of the economic shock resulting from the accumulation of disequilibria related to time-inconsistent macroeconomic policies.

The lesson from this episode is that microeconomic reform in the capital market sector is a necessary but not sufficient condition. If macroeconomic policies generate large disequilibria that may lead to a real and financial systemic implosion, even a strong financial system may collapse.

In Argentina, the financial and economic crisis mainly affected access to financing for small and medium enterprises (SMEs). However, SMEs had been suffering the brunt of the problems long before the financial meltdown. They had been paying a high risk premium imbedded in their interest rates. It is always the case that, in this type of economic and banking crisis, SMEs suffer more than large corporations because SMEs lack financial resources. Large firms have the capability of hedging their exposure to exchange rate depreciation, bypassing exchange rate controls, and obtaining commercial credit when banking credit dries up.

Several factors affected the competitiveness of all firms, including the appreciation of the real exchange rate, the lack of structural reforms in the labor sector, the heavy burden imposed by the taxing scheme, and the poorly designed privatization

process. In addition, trade reforms that were meant to strengthen commercial relations with Mercosur countries, particularly Brazil, exposed domestic firms to uneven
competition.

Another lesson from the Argentine episode relates to the deleterious influence on capital markets of the combination of systematic fiscal imbalances, financing
through debt issuing, and lack of strong private sector growth supported by significant
improvements in productivity. Firms were impaired because they were not able to
compete beyond Mercosur's markets, to generate a sustainable flow of funds to support further investment, or to demand resources through financial and capital markets.

Even during the exuberant period of the currency board and the substantial
strengthening of the banking system, the Argentine stock exchange languished. The
number of listed instruments declined steadily from 178 in 1989 to 129 in 1999 (IMF
2001). The number of listing companies also decreased. The pension reform provided
funds that were mainly used for government debt and bank deposits. The stronger
companies relocated and chose to list in foreign stock exchanges, resulting in a reduction in liquidity.

The decline of the Buenos Aires Stock Exchange (BASE) during the 1990s
can be directly related to the government's debt finance overcrowding of the private
sector and the lack of a long-term strategy for capital market development. During
1996–2000, on average, 86 percent of net primary issues dealt through BASE were
fixed-income instruments and, of those, 76 percent were government issues. The
overwhelming presence of the government is more dramatic in relation to liquidity.
More than 90 percent of trade was done on the treasury's fixed-income products,
and there was no strategy to reduce the government deficit and create more room
for private sector funding in the capital market.

Negative Externalities Derived from Tax Schemes and Financial Policies

There is a tendency for the share of equity markets to increase relative to banking
markets as per capita income increases. This relation also holds in cross-section analysis. However, there is no causal relationship in this trend. In mature markets, such as
the United States, bank debt and equity financing are roughly 50 percent; in other developed country markets, such as Germany, debt takes the bulk of financing. This trend
has not occurred in most of the countries in Latin America and the Caribbean because they have developed debt markets related to bank financing without realizing
that, at the same time, they have been imposing strong negative externalities on the
equity market.

The literature has come to the tentative conclusion that banking credit and equity finance are complementary. From the point of view of the business firm, the Modigliani-Miller theorem asserts that, under somewhat restrictive assumptions, the firm is indifferent between financing with debt or with equity (Modigliani and Miller 1958). The firm may use both to diversify its source of funding. However, in Latin America, most business enterprises use internal savings and debt, mainly borrowing from banks, as the means of financing. We argue that this behavior is mainly the result of incentives derived from government-imposed distortions through tax schemes, which is also the case regarding the behavior of the savings-surplus economic units, whose choice is equally biased by distortions favoring deposits over equity as financial assets.

Furthermore, there are other matters, not directly related to government intervention, that favor the development of the banking sector vis-à-vis the stock market. For example, although they have lower transaction costs, equity markets require more sophisticated investors than debt markets do. In the financial system, the depositor does not have to choose a portfolio. In the equity market, the saver has to make a portfolio choice. In the banking system, deposits are not tied to a specific asset; they are tied to a portfolio chosen by the bank managers. Banks are true intermediaries because they make decisions on the portfolio without consulting the clients.

Tax Distortions

Emerging economies have characterized themselves by low rates of internal savings and cyclical, severe constraints on access to international financing. In addition, tax regulations have distorted financing incentives, encouraging debt taking and debt providing. Government tax distortions against equity are generally strong on both the demand for and supply of funding.

From the point of view of the firm seeking funds (debt taking), the cost of debt financing (interest) is indeed considered a cost by the fiscal authorities. If the same firm uses equity markets, it has to pay a return on the new capital, which will not be considered a cost. From the point of view of the surplus economic units providing funds, income tax schemes in emerging markets discriminate against capital gains from equity holding, compared with the benefits of deposits in the financial system. Indeed, when the developed world had the same income per capita as today's emerging economies, its marginal income tax rates were lower than the rates that now appear in Latin American and Caribbean countries. It is common for emerging economies to tax corporations at a rate of about one-third of their income.

Financial Policy Distortions

Monetary authorities implement monetary and financial policies using instruments such as fractional reserve requirements on deposits, lender of last resort facilities, and deposit insurance schemes for bank deposits. When employed in stable and competitive financial environments (for example, in the United States), these instruments do not impose constraints on the development of capital markets. By contrast, in most Latin American and Caribbean economies, these instruments severely affect the flow of funds into the market.

Fractional reserve requirements. Central banks use legal restrictions to grant banks the ability to use part of their liabilities (demand deposits) as a means of payment. This preference differentiates banking institutions from other financial intermediaries. If banks were not required to hold 100 percent reserve requirements over quasi-money, the system would create something unique to the banking sector, that is, it would transform money into credit.

When receiving any kind of deposit, banks are required to hold only a fraction of those reserves; the rest can be lent. This has important implications because it creates a multiplier, incrementing credit (and money) by a multiple of the monetary base. Initially, the banking system can create real debt (credit) without the corresponding real savings. Therefore, the system of fractional reserve requirements implies a subsidy to the banking sector. This subsidy encourages the artificial expansion of the banking system and negatively affects the development of the equity market. In the long run, it reduces the effectiveness of both the debt and equity markets. The level of fractional reserve requirements is an inverse measure of the regulatory subsidy to the banking system.

During the 1930s, a group of economists—mostly, but not solely, affiliated with the University of Chicago[1]—launched a proposal for an alternative banking reform—the 100 percent reserve plan.[2] They suggested basing the financial system on equity, raising reserve requirements on sight deposits to 100 percent, thereby separating the creation of money from the creation of credit. Elimination of the subsidy by raising reserve requirements on sight deposits to 100 percent would imply a drastic

---

[1] This plan was formulated in the 1930s; it was associated with Hart, Simons, Mints, and (later) Milton Friedman.
[2] Simons (1947) cites the Bank Charter Act of 1844 for the Bank of England (known as The Peel's Act) as the original source of the Chicago plan. This separated the Bank of England into money issuing and lending departments and implemented the proposal of Ricardo's "Plan for the Establishment of a National Bank" (1824).

change in the banking system. Traditionally, the lending function of banks was based on equity rather than on debt. The Chicago plan for banking reform would move banks closer to the major world nonbank financial intermediaries associated with large firms, such as General Electric, General Motors, and other financial giants. These entities have shown more resilience and less vulnerability than banks have.

Garcia, Maino, and Fretes-Cibils (1998) argue that fractional reserve requirements can actually do more than just multiply. In any ordinary business, the nature of liabilities is no different from that of assets. The authors show that in the case of a fractional reserve banking business, the nature of assets is different from that of liabilities: assets are credits, whereas liabilities are money. Due to the system of fractional reserves, banks create money (credit) by means of credit (money) and, vice versa, eliminating credit (money) eliminates money (credit). In this system, money and credit are thus inextricably interwoven.

Coupled with other factors, such as poor macroeconomic policy and weak corporate governance, the fractional reserve requirement scheme could create a contagious effect on the banking system, promoting a crisis, affecting the availability of savings to be invested in capital markets, and reducing demand for resources due to the lack of projects to be financed. Most economies in Latin America have gone through this sequence of events, confronting costly and lengthy banking crises. For example, in Argentina in 1980–82, the cost of the crisis was 16.6 percent of GDP; in Chile in 1981–88, it was 45.5 percent of GDP; in Mexico in 1994–95, it was 9.6 percent of GDP; and in Uruguay in 1981–85, it was 41.7 percent of GDP.

The lender of last resort and the deposit insurance facilities. The central bank has the function of lender of last resort, which allows the monetary authority to lend to a bank whenever the market is not willing or able to do it. This should be a short-term, high-interest-rate, liquidity facility that complements the role of the interbank lending market. If the lender of last resort function were used as a substitute for the interbank lending market, it would create a preference for the banking system over capital markets, allowing banks to rely on a source of liquidity not available to other financial institutions.

The lender of last resort function of the central bank and the deposit insurance schemes are natural consequences of the system of fractional reserve requirements. Because of fractional reserve requirements, the banking system is subject to systemic risk. Under fractional reserve requirements, banks lend a multiple of their reserves; consequently, they can never have the necessary liquidity to sustain a run on deposits, and some sort of liquidity support has to be put in place.

The high leverage liability structure of the banking industry could allow the development of liquidity problems in solvent banks, through a contagion effect. The failure of one bank could induce depositors of other banks to believe that their institutions are also weak, thus promoting a sudden withdrawal of funds and creating liquidity problems in the system. If the increase in interest rates paid to retain deposits is translated into higher interest rates paid by borrowers, then an insolvency situation could emerge, and the failure of the first institution could spread to a second one and eventually to the rest of the system. Under these circumstances, deposit insurance could minimize such externalities, but, unfortunately, it has other important side effects, in particular, the moral hazard problem.

In many countries, the government subsidizes deposit insurance. Government-sponsored deposit insurance has been a widespread practice in Latin America. Most countries in the region have had banking crises in the past two decades, and the government has always bailed out depositors and, many times, shareholders. This policy inhibits market discipline and precludes the investors and supervisory authorities from using this instrument to improve the efficiency of financial markets.

The experience of Paraguay in the mid-1990s provides an example of the banking industry's preferred status regarding regulations and government support. Paraguay, like most small countries in Latin America, relied on banks to tap resources to finance all types of business concerns, with stock exchanges playing almost no role. This was mainly the consequence of the banking crisis resolution schemes used in the country. During the early 1990s, the country liberalized its banking sector, allowing the entrance of new entities. Many new banks and nonbank financial companies had low capitalization and inexperienced management. A system of loan risk classification was introduced, but never enforced. A banking crisis erupted in 1995, when two large banks were unable to meet their clearing debts. The central bank intervened and took over the management of these two banks. By mid-1995, the central bank had intervened and taken over the management of four banks and six finance companies.

Further investigation by the Superintendence of Banks revealed that more banks and finance companies had been involved in fraudulent operations and mismanagement. They had false records and loans related to their owners. Most of the banking system was working with deposits and loans that bypassed taxes and regulations. In fact, there was a huge informal financing market. The banking crisis put all this out in the open. The central bank guaranteed all the deposits and bought the bad portfolios of distressed banks in 1996. The technology used by the monetary authorities to manage the crisis created moral hazard problems; financial investment in the banking system was fully protected, and bank loans could be rescheduled or borrowers bailed out. Apart from the lack of other requisites to allow capital market development, the experience of Paraguay points to the moral hazard problem as a major constraint.

Structural Constraints

Emerging economies face significant challenges regarding the development of capital markets. Some challenges are derived from inefficient institutional infrastructure that must be changed through legal reforms; others arise from the small size of the markets, the solution to which could require financial and commercial integration processes. In addition, during the 1990s, most Latin American and Caribbean countries undertook structural reforms that downsized the scope of government as entrepreneur by means of privatization and, in some cases, restructuring the role of government in social security. In developed countries, such as the United Kingdom and Italy, this process contributed to the reinforcement of capital markets. This was not the case in Latin America due to the lack of efficient institutional infrastructure, the small size of the market, and the weak impact of structural reforms.

Lack of Efficient Institutional Infrastructure

According to La Porta and others (1996), institutional variables explain the growth of equity markets. The authors find that factors such as the rule of law, minority rights, and one share, one vote are relevant for stock market development. Institutional factors are highly correlated with stock market liquidity. Demirgüç-Kunt and Levine (1996a) find that countries with transparent regulations and properly enforced legal rules tend to have large and more-liquid stock markets. The institutional infrastructure of capital markets has several equally essential pillars:

- A strong legal framework characterized by short and reliable judicial processes with full enforcement and by trust in civil and commercial litigation
- Effective accounting standards, robust corporate governance, and well-designed and enforced prudential regulations
- Timely and reliable economic and business information that the market processes and evaluates
- Severe protection of the rights of minority shareholders.

When some or all of the pillars do not exist or are poorly designed, the lack of efficient institutional infrastructure imposes significant constraints on the development of the markets. India may be a case in point on the importance of tradition and institutions in promoting the development of capital markets. One of the poorest countries in the world, India has higher market capitalization than many developed countries. Its regulations are indeed quite cumbersome, but it has inherited the "common-law" framework from the British. India's market capitalization is almost 60 percent of GDP. It ranks 23rd in the world in terms of percentage of GDP and 16th in terms of the ratio of trade value to GDP. The country relies more on equity than on banking debt financing: the private sector banking debt is 25 percent of GDP. The huge Bombay Stock Exchange allows prices to adjust and, for example, signaled the market about episodes of fraud and default on some private issues in China in 2000.[3] Naturally, Indian companies are small, but this is precisely what is worth pointing out. The preference for direct finance is not only high, but also growing, and more companies are accessing the equity markets rather than bank financing.

By contrast, in Guatemala in 1998–99, there were several episodes of fraud and default on some private issues, which provide an example of inadequate regulation (the second pillar). The self-regulated stock exchange in Guatemala began its operations in 1987, handling mainly government debt and a small amount of private debt. At that time, and in order to avoid an inflationary process, the central bank switched to a more restrictive stance on monetary policy. This caused a huge increment in interest rates, and some businesses could not honor their debt issues. Some companies actively issued debt in the parallel (informal) stock market and disappeared. All this caused an outcry for government intervention.

When the crisis erupted, self-regulation meant very little, as regulation and official intervention were limited to a simple registry of companies wishing to tap the capital market through the exchange. The registry was weak and had no infrastructure (no computers and little personnel), and there was conflict of interest with brokers who had a stake in the listed businesses. The capital market had no regulations regarding prospectuses and investment funds and no accounting standards.

The case of Guatemala shows that in the design of an efficient institutional infrastructure an adequate balance must be kept between self-regulation and the enforcement of good accounting standards, strong corporate governance, and well-designed prudential regulations.

Minimum Size of the Market

Can small economies with good macroeconomic policies, no externalities produced by banking industry regulations, and efficient institutional infrastructure have solid cap-

---

[3] The data are for December 2000, as described in Standard and Poor's (2001).

ital markets? Even in large economies, like Brazil and Mexico, the viability of equity markets is questionable.[4] In the advanced industrial countries, financial integration through the removal of regulatory barriers has led to massive cross-border mergers. This process has revealed that even large developed economies have domestic inefficiencies and a lot to be gained from economies of scope and scale.

Among other constraints, regulatory institutions in small economies must enforce rules over enterprises that have state-of-the-art technology and highly trained human capital. The regulatory agencies face severe budget constraints and cannot pay salaries at market levels, causing frequent rotation in human resources and significantly increasing the costs of the learning process.

It may well be that the only common characteristic of small economies is that they are small. Some of them are open, while others are closed. Some, like Honduras, have underdeveloped capital markets, but others, like Panama, are financial centers. All of them may be subject to large exogenous shocks, but for some this may be due to crises in neighboring countries, and for others it may be due to changes in the prices of their main exports or imports. These sources of instability require different strategies and pose different challenges.

Small economies tend to have higher income variability than larger countries. Nonetheless, even if variability is not good per se, variable income associated with a relatively high rate of growth is better than stability associated with stagnation. High variability and high rate of growth are not antinomies. Some small economies have high productivity and a high rate of growth; others have low productivity and a low rate of growth.

Research on small economies has come to the fore because of the renewed interest of international financial institutions. Bossone, Honohan, and Long (2001) identify a few common characteristics of small economies. For example, they are prone to lumpiness (that is, investment may not come in small doses), and they have incomplete financial systems (minimum scale preludes the organization of some financial services industries). These small systems are more costly to regulate because regulation has fixed costs.

There is no unanimity regarding the issue of small economies. In fact, there is a growing view in the economic literature that small and even micro economies may not face such big problems and challenges. Easterly and Kraay (2001) find that, after controlling for a range of factors, microstates have on average higher income and productivity levels than small states and do not grow more slowly than large states.

---

[4] Brazil has one of the largest derivatives markets in the world, but its equity market is relatively small.

No matter how unsettled the issue may be, small economies can overcome any drawback that they may have in relation to capital markets. Of course, many small economies cannot overcome the fact that they are subject to terms of trade shocks due to the specialized nature of their economies, but they could use readily available, sophisticated financial instruments to smooth income flows. For example, few small economies have implemented fiscal stabilization funds. The techniques related to setting up these funds are now standard, and there is rich experience with the oil stabilization funds implemented in larger countries. Small economies should weigh the advantages of integrating with the rest of the world in addition to or instead of integrating, as they normally do, with small neighbors that face the same problems and basically qualify for the same risks.

Weak Impact of Structural Reforms

During the 1990s, most emerging economies implemented structural reforms, in particular regarding the privatization of public enterprises and social security schemes. Most countries in the region sold their public sector firms to foreign investors that used the financial resources available in developed capital markets. The need for future private sector financing arising from these privatization processes was supposed to be satisfied mainly by the reduction of government deficits and increase in internal savings. The latter were derived from the transformation of pay-as-you-go pension fund systems with individual capitalization accounts administered by private companies and external resources.

To have a significant impact on capital markets, these structural reforms must be part of a comprehensive strategy to transform the performance of the economy by increasing productivity, improving competitiveness, and allowing sustainable realization of operational cash flows of private firms. The wealth effect derived from the reform process should also have positive effects on savings, closing the gap between the additional demand for funds and the corresponding supply of financial resources.

In Latin American and Caribbean economies, policymakers have not designed and implemented such an integrated strategy in a systematic and consistent form. Political "engineering" of the reforms would need strong leadership and long-term government commitment in order to confront strong opposition from group interests, such as labor unions. In general, neither the leadership nor the commitment has been available at the same time in the region.

Fundamental objectives of the privatization of state-owned assets are to increase efficiency, reduce the government's financial burden, and spur the growth of the securities market. The securities market objective depends on the existence of other requisites for capital market development, for example, transparency and the protection of investors.

As a matter of fact, privatization of companies worldwide has contributed to the growth of stock markets both in terms of capitalization and trading volume. However, many of these positive outcomes have not significantly touched Latin America, where capitalization of companies listed in the stock exchange and trading volume have languished, particularly in the past 10 years.

Chile initiated and pioneered social security reforms during the early 1980s in order to develop capital markets, among other goals. The Chilean model substituted a pay-as-you-go system with individual capitalization accounts administered by private companies. Other countries in Latin America replicated the Chilean experience with some changes. The most popular variant was based on a three-pillar system consisting of a pay-as-you-go minimum funded from the general budget, individual accounts funded by employers and employee contributions, and voluntary contributions. The reform was intended to provide sustainable retirement benefits, creating a link between contributions and benefits. It was also expected to prop up capital markets by increasing the savings rate, which would provide long-term resources to the country's business sector. However, the regulation of these forced savings favored fixed-income instruments, that is, government debt. Inasmuch as government debt was involved, the pay-as-you-go system returned through the back door.

Social security reform has had a positive but modest impact on capital markets. Even in Chile, where market capitalization is high, a large amount of funds is invested in government bonds. Local businesses have not been able to issue sufficient instruments, and the pension fund administrators have been authorized to invest a small share on foreign stock exchanges.

It is not clear whether mandatory contributions to contractual savings plans have increased national savings. Research shows mixed results. There are several theoretical reasons to expect savings to increase. Impavido, Musalem, and Vittas (2001) argue that mandatory contributions to contractual savings plans could increase the national savings rate if some members of the population do not have sufficient access to credit. Under these conditions, they would be forced to save more because they would not be able to smooth out their consumption over their life cycle. In addition, the national savings rate could increase if governments do not take these funds as a captive source of finance. If this forced saving relaxes the government budget constraint and funds additional government expenditure, there might be no increment in net national savings. Moreover, if this takeover of retirement funds by the government occurs, all the arguments relative to the growth impact of contractual savings may not hold.

For example, in the case of the 1994 pension reform in Argentina, regulators established that pension funds could invest up to 50 percent in government bonds. That ceiling was always reached. By the end of 2001, the Argentine treasury was in crisis and increased the investment ceiling to 100 percent. In fact, the reform forced pension administrations to hold almost all their assets in government bonds. Moreover, the government also required pensions to accept a government debt swap.

In order to allow for higher diversification of risk, Mercosur shares (basically Brazilian shares) were eligible for investment on the same footing as local shares. Experience has shown that country risk in Argentina and Brazil is highly correlated, and, consequently, the diversification effect was almost nil.

Assuming that contractual savings increase the national savings rate and are allowed to invest abroad up to 100 percent, could pension reform help develop domestic capital markets? There is in fact an increment in domestic savings, and contractual savings do not pump up local government expenditures; pension funds invested in foreign markets can have a positive, but indirect, effect on domestic capital markets. The wealth effect that may be generated by the discounted expected return on the foreign investment would probably have a beneficial impact on growth and, consequently, on the domestic business environment and capital markets.

In contrast to recent reforms in the Latin American and Eastern European pension systems, some developed countries with highly developed capital markets are characterized by thousands of employer-based funds. In the United States alone, there are more than 700,000 funds; in the United Kingdom more than 200,000; and in Australia, more than 100,000.

Institutional Setup: Where Are We Heading?

A safe and sound macroeconomic environment is a necessary, but not sufficient, condition for capital market development. An adequate institutional setup is another important feature for such development to occur. This institutional architecture should balance the need for strict regulations to strengthen corporate governance and low transaction costs.

Businesses looking to tap resources from the public should be subject to strict regulation to protect investors. In this line of thought, regulations should, among other things, substantially strengthen corporate governance. Rules should prevent managers from acting in their own vested interest, avoiding insider control and agency problems; introduce transparent procedures regarding mergers and acquisitions; enact and enforce accounting standards; request timely disclosure of income statements and balance sheets; reinforce external independent audits and protection of minority share-holders; and encourage independence of market analysts.

At the same time, from the demand side, an increase in regulations implies higher transaction costs. Also, when looking at the relation between transaction costs and the number of firms deciding to go to the market to tap resources, naturally, the lower the transaction cost, the higher the number of businesses willing to go public.

These two sides of the same problem can be reconciled. Everything else being constant, the supply schedule for capital is upward sloping and the demand schedule is downward sloping with respect to price. Any change in regulations increasing the transaction cost of going public for the sake of increasing investors' confidence and protection would cause the demand for public funds to shift to the left. It would also shift to the right the supply schedule for capital. The end result of this regulatory change would indeed be a price reduction, that is, a fall in the cost of capital. However, whatever happens to the quantities would depend on the relative elasticity between the supply and demand schedules. If the general public and institutional investors are keen regarding being protected, and firms do not see the regulatory change as affect-ing their transaction costs, the price reduction will be accompanied by an increment in the quantity of capital intermediated in the capital market. If the enterprises see the regulatory change as imposing significant costs, the market will shrink.

Some Recent Trends

External factors derived from global trends that developed during the 1990s could af-fect the design and implementation of an adequate institutional setup. Deregulation, globalization, institutionalization, dematerialization, and the sophistication of financial products are giving capital markets, even in developed economies, a new framework. In addition, the tailored approach to stock exchange listing is a promising trend for facilitating the participation of particular business segments in the market.

Deregulation

The 1990s will be heralded as the deregulation decade. The banking debt flows of the 1970s and the dry season of the 1980s were followed by the capital flows revolution of the 1990s. During this 10-year span, most developing countries' regulatory frame-works allowed for more openness, transparency, and simplicity. The goal was a more competitive and market-friendly environment. This trend affected stock exchanges through the privatization of mega public sector corporations. In addition, developing countries welcomed foreign direct and portfolio investment, which also benefited stock markets.

Globalization

Globalization is the direct result of the information technology revolution. It is affect-ing all areas of the world in general and the economic environment in particular. The world-class stock exchanges have greatly benefited from this phenomenon, while many small domestic exchanges have languished.

The integration of stock exchanges within and across countries has facilitated business by increasing liquidity, reducing intermediation costs, and providing better services and more timely business information to a wider customer base. Large busi-ness concerns have received direct benefits, and SMEs have probably benefited, but in a more indirect way. As more relatively large concerns open their capital, there is a dissemination or cultural effect about the benefits of raising capital in the stock ex-change. This may be particularly important in countries where not even large business concerns have a tradition of opening capital.

Large enterprises and conglomerates have benefited from the reduction in cost due to the integration and globalization of capital markets. An example is the suc-cessful development of NOREX (the Nordic Exchange), which includes Denmark, Nor-way, and Sweden. Other alliances include the Paris, Amsterdam, and Brussels stock exchanges (Euronext), and the London, Milan, Frankfurt, Zurich, and Madrid stock ex-changes. In the United States, the New York Stock Exchange is guiding the construction of the Global Equity Market (GEM), which will create an electronic market that will be open 24 hours a day. The over-the-counter NASDAQ has worldwide reach. And there has been integration within countries; for example, all the Spanish regional bourses (Bil-bao, Valencia, Barcelona, and Madrid) have the same platform. Brazil has seven regional stock exchanges that provide information, marketing, training, and technical assistance to corporations and investors. Two of them—Bovespa in São Paulo and BVRJ in Rio de Janeiro—were bitter rivals; they have merged, and the former specializes in shares and the latter in fixed-income instruments. The new arrangement has been successful, and Bovespa is part of the GEM. Brazil has incorporated the modern system of trading, in-cluding the home broker doing business with shares through the Internet.

Institutionalization

The number of individuals investing directly in capital markets has increased significantly, but is still dwarfed by the numbers in pensions, insurance and mutual funds, and special investment funds. In fact, a large part of the current capital flows are savings channeled by institutional investors.

Dematerialization

The information revolution has led to technological innovation in the way documents are created and processed. Capital markets have not remained absent from this process; there is a plethora of electronic documents and processes for registering, ordering, clearing, settling, and custody of many types of transactions. This new technology has led to a huge reduction in transaction costs. In the world of emerging capital markets, the legal profession has somewhat lagged behind these new developments; the challenge is to bring it up to date.

Derivatives and Sophisticated Financial Engineering

The use of asset-backed instruments and advances in financial software to deal with options, futures, and all types of swaps have led to the development of complicated financial deals that cater to different risk preferences. The large size of financial markets has led to the creation of specialized exchanges, although their products can also be found in over-the-counter markets. The financial risk sometimes involved, as shown by the demise of long-term capital, has led to regulatory challenges. However, the capacity of regulators tends to lag behind the dynamic innovation in financial markets.

The Tailored Approach to Stock Exchange Listing

Initial public offerings, capital increases of existing companies, and mergers and acquisitions constitute the crucial factors that make a vibrant and growing capital market. Stock markets in emerging countries must be able to find innovative ways to attract new companies and facilitate growth. To encourage initial public offerings, some new stock exchanges have substantially lessened listing requirements for particular business segments. The idea is to reduce transaction costs for high-growth firms looking for venture capital. Since 1997, about 500 firms have been listed in Frankfurt's Neuer

Markt and in the Paris, Bruxelles, and Amsterdam Nouveau Marche. The last to join the group in 1999 was Milan's Novo Mercato.

The EuroNM is a network of European stock exchanges associated with traditional bourses. These exchanges target the financing of medium enterprises searching for venture capital, primarily in the innovative high-tech industries. The idea is to replicate the U.S. market, which is rich in venture capital financing. It is widely accepted that venture capital has made a significant contribution to the economic success and leadership of the United States.

Brazil has followed that lead with a novel three-tier regulatory framework. The Brazilian approach is interesting because it caters to the risk preferences of different capital market actors. The first tier, the Novo Mercado, imposes a significant regulatory burden and high transaction costs on corporations seeking funds from the market. In this tier, only companies committed to the highest standard of accounting norms, disclosure, and corporate governance are allowed to list. Such companies ensure the maximum protection of minority shareholders, granting full voting rights for all shares based on the principle of one share, one vote.

Companies in the Novo Mercado have to disclose a wealth of information, including quarterly statements in Portuguese and English, audit reports, cash flow statements and projections, transactions with related parties, and trading of shares by managers and controlling shareholders. The change in controlling interest has to be done through a tender offer to all shareholders. Retail distribution of new shares is required, as is the issue of a full prospectus complying with international standards. There is a minimum "lock-up period" for controlling shareholders and many other rules regarding arbitration of disputes, surveillance, and enforcement of regulations by Bovespa.

The second tier is special corporate governance level 2. Companies in this segment must comply with all the requirements of the Novo Mercado, but they may continue to issue nonvoting shares (the so-called preferred shares). Currently, 52 companies meet the conditions required by this level, holding almost 60 percent of the Bovespa market capitalization.

The third tier, corporate governance level 3, caters to those corporations that would not list if the regulatory burden were very costly and demanding. It is the place for more risk-inclined investors because it does not require companies to comply with the strict standards of the Novo Mercado.

The Amman Stock Exchange (ASE) is another successful stock market that followed a split approach to regulation. Jordan is one of the developing countries that have a tradition of equity financing. The ASE, created recently as a result or restructuring of other market institutions, has also developed three listing tiers. To list in the first floor, companies have to pass the test of strict regulations. The companies have to have reported profits in the last three years; have given out cash dividends or bonus shares at least once over the last three years; guarantee a minimum of liquidity; and publish detailed balance and income statements. The next two tiers have declining regulatory requirements, catering to more risk-inclined investors and reducing the transaction costs for SMEs.

Lessons and Policy Implications

The development of capital markets in Latin American and Caribbean economies faces significant challenges. Countries need to combine sound macroeconomic policies, local structural reforms within a long-term strategy with a regional dimension, and international trends affecting local capital markets.

The accelerated pace of technological advances as well as globalization may allow Latin American and Caribbean countries to leapfrog and avoid several of the intermediary steps toward capital market development that developed economies had to take—for instance, taking advantage of dematerialization, promoting common and regional technological bases for trading, and utilizing Internet technology. However, lessons from the past and errors in macroeconomic and structural policies should guide some fundamental recommendations, which should be implemented with a consistent and patient long-term view.

Figure 4-1 shows the complexity of government policies as well as their interaction and impact on several variables. Over time, and if implemented efficiently, government policies should favor capital market development, attract external and internal savings, and foster private projects. This section lists policy recommendations for overcoming challenges, promoting efficient intermediation of funds in the region, and attracting domestic and external savings.

Avoid Unsustainable Fiscal and Macroeconomic Imbalances

Many financial crises have been caused by macroeconomic imbalances, which tend to come to a sudden resolution with enormous costs, affecting the availability of domestic and external savings to be invested in capital markets, and reducing the demand for resources due to the lack of projects to be financed. These crises have had staggering costs. For example, in the past 20 years, Argentina has had three major banking crises,

Figure 4-1	How Macroeconomic and Structural Constraints Affect the Development of Capital Markets

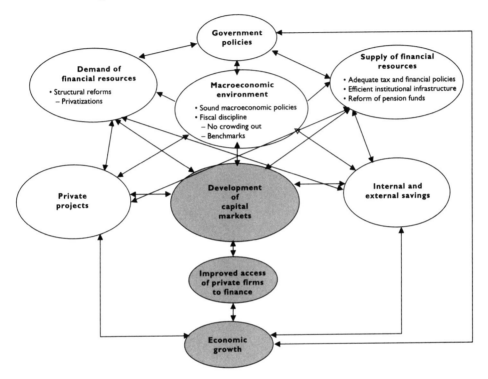

and its capital markets and exchanges have suffered in each. In 1982–83, the real value of bank deposits and credit declined by almost 60 percent, and 20 percent of the banks were liquidated. In the second major crisis, in 1995, the nominal and real quantity of money was reduced by 20 percent in four months. To put this into perspective, it is noteworthy to recall that in the general economic depression of the 1930s, the U.S. money supply contracted by 33 percent in a three-year period. In Argentina's third crisis, which is still evolving, huge nominal and real devaluation has led to a dramatic and general meltdown of the country's economic and financial structure.

During the early 1980s, Chile and Mexico experienced macroeconomic shocks and capital market debacles. The consequence was that both countries reluctantly nationalized their financial systems and have only slowly been able to shed these unwanted investments. Mexico did a poor job in privatization and permitted the buildup of unsustainable reserve losses. The country's massive depreciation led to a crisis in its financial system that is still not fully resolved.

Avoid Taxes and Regulations That Distort Markets in Favor of Bank Debt Financing

Most countries have tax systems that favor bank debt finance over equity. On the supply side, depositors do not pay taxes on the interest they receive on bank deposits. If instead of holding bank deposits, they hold equity or business debt, they have to pay taxes on those returns. On the demand side, a firm that obtains bank credit can include it as a cost of capital and reduce its tax payment. If the same firm taps the stock exchange, it cannot include any dividends as a cost of capital. In addition, minimum reserve requirements, lender of last resort facilities, and deposit insurance schemes create subsidies and preferred status for the banking industry against capital markets. Separation of the functions of banks as payment system administrators and savings-investment intermediaries (that is, the narrow banking approach) could minimize the negative impact of bank debt financing on equity financing.

Avoid Crowding Out by the Government

Governments have a critical responsibility in creating the framework for capital market development. For example, the government could adopt crucial steps for the establishment of a yield curve as a benchmark, thus promoting fiscal discipline. However, more often than not, governments in developing countries end up making the markets that they have created a captive source of funds. The high-benchmark, risk-adjusted interest rate displaces private instruments. The new capital markets give the government the opportunity to increase expenditures because it has a new venue where more financing can be found. The only way to avoid this trap is by having the government run fiscal balanced budgets.

Segment the Stock Exchanges

The segmentation of stock exchanges must be designed to give breathing room to small and medium enterprises and accommodate investors' risk preferences. As Bottazzi and Da Rin (2000) point out, the opening of EuroNM is not simply a source of finance, but also an institution that can select and support entrepreneurs and promising projects. Innovative entrepreneurial firms are typically credit constrained. They do not possess assets that can be used as collateral because they mainly rely on intangibles. They cannot self-finance because they often need years of costly research and development before they can generate significant revenues. Nor are they able to bank on their reputation, being young and not yet established. Even when they can access bank credit, entrepreneurial start-ups pay high interest rates. Hence, financing constraints constitute a powerful barrier to entrepreneurship.

The lesson is that the legal framework should cater to the individual country. Settlement, clearing, custody, and all the necessary steps should be included in a custom fit that does not overwhelm small and emerging markets with too many regulatory burdens. It would be impossible to enforce too many regulations, and such a situation would promote the creation of a parallel, nonregulated, informal credit market. Fraud would be more common, and the informal market would be costly because of the implied risks.

For example, public offering law should follow general principles and contain some basic, transparent, and simple requirements in order not to stifle the market. Minimum capital should not be an important constraint. India's success in developing its stock exchange may be due in part to the common-law tradition it inherited from the British, but also to the fact that India's public offering law does not discriminate against medium enterprises. Minimum subscribed capital to initiate a public issue is about $2 million and is reduced to about $1 million for information technology companies.

Make Information Transparency an Important Policy Goal

Transparency is a necessary condition for market discipline to operate. Firms benefit from low-cost access to capital markets, including a low regulatory burden. Requirements to frequently publish cash flows and company statements should be strictly enforced. Publications should clearly state whether such reports have been audited and by whom. The publication requirements should not impose large costs; in this respect, the Internet is an excellent option. This set of policies will enhance the role of market discipline in the performance of capital markets.

Information is not a free good, but enhancing the flow of information may be the most cost-efficient measure for the development of capital markets. The government has a crucial role in designing the rules and enforcing them, keeping at the same time a delicate balance between the costs and benefits of self-regulation and over-regulation.

It is in the interest of market participants and the government to minimize the tension between transaction costs derived from regulations and the need to ensure investors the availability of transparent information. Transparency does more than just improve market efficiency by reducing price disparities; it is also crucial for the success of good governance practices and a major enforcement instrument. The market can indeed be an excellent enforcement mechanism. For this to happen, information has to be transparent (readily available at little cost), full (detailed and complete), reliable (accounting in compliance with minimum standards), and timely. Transparent, full, reliable, and timely information is directly related to market-based regulations and discipline. This is especially crucial in situations were there is weak enforcement. In fact, forbearing and general lack of strict enforcement of rules and regulations seem to be the rule in many underdeveloped countries. This is particularly the case if the government has the leading regulating role.

Capital markets could better rely on self-regulatory bodies. This is particularly important now that capital markets are becoming increasingly more sophisticated. Different types of businesses are flourishing under complicated financial arrangements. Most of the time, financial innovations are ahead of government regulations and regulators.

Bibliography

Beck, T., A. Demirgüç-Kunt, R. Levine, and V. Maksimovic. 2000. *Financial Structure and Economic Development: Firm, Industry, and Country Evidence.* In Demirgüç-Kunt and Levine (eds.).

Bekaert, G., C. Harvey, and C. Lundblad. 2001. *Does Financial Liberalization Spur Growth?* Columbia Business School, Duke University and Indiana University, April 20.

Bencivenga, V. R., B. D. Smith, and R. M. Starr. 1996. Equity Markets, Transactions Cost, and Capital Accumulation: An Illustration. *The World Bank Economic Review* 10(2).

Bossone, G., P. Honohan, and M. Long. 2001. Policy for Small Financial Systems. Background paper for the workshop "Small Financial Systems: Many Small Problems or a Big One?" World Bank, Washington, D.C.

Bottazzi, L., and M. Da Rin. 2000. Euro NM and the Financing of European Innovative Firms. Mimeo, Univesritá Bocconi and Universitá di Torino. July 11.

Boyd, J., and B. Smith. 1996. The Coevolution of the Real and Financial Sectors in the Growth Process. *The World Bank Economic Review* 10(2).

Dermigüç-Kunt, A., and R. Levine. 1996a. Stock Market Development and Financial Intermediaries: Stylized Facts, *The World Bank Economic Review* 10(2):291–321.

_____. 1996b. Stock Markets, Corporate Finance, and Economic Growth: An Over-
view. *The World Bank Economic Review* 10(2):223–39.

Easterly, W., and A. Kraay. 2001. Small States, Small Problems? From the conference
"Small Financial Systems: Many Small Problems or a Big One?" World Bank,
Washington, D.C.

Garcia, V. F. 1987. *A Critical Inquiry into Argentine Economic History 1946–1970*. New
York: Garland Publishing Co.

Garcia, Valeriano F., Rodolfo Maino, and Vicente Fretes-Cibils. 1998. The Chicago Proposal and Islamic Banking: What Do They Have in Common? Paper presented
at the 76th Annual Meeting of the Western Economic Association, San Francisco, Calif., July.

Garcia-Herrero, A. 1997. Banking Crises in Latin America in the 1990s: Lessons from
Argentina, Paraguay, and Venezuela. IMF Working Paper WP/97/140. Washington, D.C., International Monetary Fund, October.

Goldsmith, R. W. 1969. *Financial Structure and Development*. New Haven, Conn.: Yale
University Press.

Gurley, J., and E. Shaw. 1955. Financial Aspects of Economic Development. *American
Economic Review* pp. 515–38.

_____. 1960. *Money in the Theory of Finance*. Washington, D.C.: Brookings Institution.

Henry, P. B. 2000. Stock Market Liberalization, Economic Reform, and Emerging Market Equity Prices. *Journal of Finance* 55(2):529–64.

Impavido, G., A. Musalem, and D. Vittas. 2001. Contractual Savings in Countries with a
Small Financial Sector. Mimeo. World Bank, Washington, D.C.

International Monetary Fund (IMF). 2001. World Economic and Financial Surveys. *World
Economic Outlook*. Washington, D.C., October.

King, R. G., and R. Levine. 1993. Finance and Growth: Schumpeter Might Be Right. *Quarterly Journal of Economics* 108(3):717–37.

Kotlikoff, L. 1999. The World Bank's Approach and the Right Approach to Pension Reform. Mimeo. World Bank, Washington, D.C.

La Porta, R., F. Lopez-de-Silanes, A. Shleifer, and R. Vishny. 1996. Law and Finance. NBER
Working Paper 5661. National Bureau of Economic Research, Cambridge, Mass.

_____. 1997. Legal Determinants of External Finance. *Journal of Finance* 52 (July): 1131–50.

Levine, R., and S. Zervos. 1998. Stock Markets, Banks, and Economic Growth. *American Economic Review* 88(2):537–58.

McKinnon, R. I. 1973. *Money and Capital in Economic Development.* Washington, D.C.: Brookings Institution.

Megginson, W., and J. Netter. 2001. From State to Market: A Survey of Empirical Studies on Privatization. *Journal of Economic Literature* 39 (June).

Miller, M. 1991. *Financial Innovations and Market Volatility.* Cambridge.

Modigliani, F., and M. Miller. 1958. The Cost of Capital, Corporation Finance, and the Theory of Investment. *American Economic Review* 48(3):261–97.

Rajan, R., and L. Zingales. 1998. Financial Dependence and Growth. *American Economic Review* 88(3).

Shaw, E. S. 1973. *Financial Deepening in Economic Development.* New York: Oxford University Press.

Simons, Henry C. 1947. *Economic Policy for a Free Society.* Chicago: University of Chicago.

Sjaastad, L. 1996. Preventing Banking Sector Distress and Crises in Latin America. In S. K. Bery and V. Garcia, (eds.), World Bank, Proceedings of a conference held in Washington, D.C.

Vittas, D. 2000. Pension Reform and Capital Market Development, "Feasibility" and "Impact" Preconditions. Development Research Group, World Bank, Washington, D.C.

◼CHAPTER 5

Institutional Investors
and Capital Market Development

Karen Goldstein Rossotto

Institutional investors play an increasingly important role in the world's capital markets. These investors—primarily pension funds, insurance companies, open-end investment companies (mutual funds), and closed-end investment companies—professionally manage pooled assets on behalf of their beneficiaries, policyholders, and shareholders.[1] Within the financial system, institutional investors act as the holders and managers of individual savings and wealth, as well as high-volume traders, new sources of capital financing, and influential shareholders.

Over the past half-century, total assets under institutional management have grown tremendously, although to different degrees across regions and countries. The U.S. institutional sector, one of the earliest to develop, accounts for a substantial percentage of U.S. financial assets. Institutional investors have also become a major force in the markets of other industrial economies, notably the high-income members of the Organisation for Economic Co-operation and Development (OECD). Although pension fund and insurance company assets account for the majority of institutional assets in OECD countries, the mutual fund industry has recently become particularly important, most notably in the United States, but also in other mature markets.

The establishment of institutional investors in OECD countries has occurred for a number of interdependent reasons. A favorable economy, the need for retirement support and investment diversification, tax incentives, increased investor confidence through regulation and education, and improved distribution techniques created demand for institutional investment products. In addition, deregulation and competition, effective corporate governance, and the integrated nature of the OECD economies created an ample supply of financial assets in which institutions could invest. Further-

---

[1] Other institutional investors include banks, trade unions, endowment funds, and generally any firm or individual that trades large volumes of securities. For the purposes of this chapter, the term "institutional investor" encompasses both institutional money managers (for example, investment advisers) as well as the institutional portfolios they administer.

more, the increased presence of both domestic and international institutional investors benefited local capital markets, with domestic institutions having additional desirable features for overall economic development.

Capital markets in Latin America and the Caribbean have recently experienced steady growth in their institutional investor sectors due to pension reforms and other deliberate government efforts. However, a number of the conditions necessary for further sector development either do not exist or are relatively new and have not yet demonstrated positive effects. Moreover, in spite of institutional growth, capital markets in Latin America and the Caribbean remain underdeveloped.

This chapter explores how the experience of the United States and other OECD countries provides policy guidance on how governments and policymakers may encourage further growth of domestic institutional investors in Latin America and the Caribbean and also capitalize on the sector's potential benefits to the region's markets. The chapter provides an overview of the current status of institutional investors in the United States, other OECD countries, and Latin America and the Caribbean. It discusses why capital markets are important and how domestic institutional investors may contribute to their development. It describes the factors that contributed to the growth of domestic institutional investors in the United States and other OECD markets, identifies the impediments to further sector growth in Latin America and the Caribbean, and suggests policies to reduce these impediments.

Overview of the Institutional Investor Sector

United States

The United States maintains both a highly developed institutional investor sector and highly developed capital markets. U.S. institutional assets totaled more than $18 trillion in 1999, or more than 207 percent of gross domestic product (GDP). Pension funds, with more than $8 trillion under management, account for the largest share of U.S. institutional assets (37 percent). Mutual fund assets experienced the sharpest growth over the past 10 years, rising from $915 billion in 1990 to $4 trillion in 1999 and increasing their share of U.S. institutional assets from 14 to 26 percent (OECD 2000).[2] Insurance companies, with assets of $2.8 trillion, account for 23 per-

---

[2] A significant factor accounting for the rise in mutual fund assets in the United States is their increasing use as investment vehicles for other institutional investors, particularly for retirement plans. In 2000, U.S. institutional assets represented 45 percent of all mutual fund assets (ICI 2001).

cent of U.S. institutional assets. Within the capital markets, pension funds and mutual funds control almost half of all U.S. equities and account for the majority of total U.S. daily trading volume, while insurance companies tend to own more bonds than equities (ICI 2001; Conference Board 2000).

Other OECD Countries

Institutional investors have also become the dominant holders of financial assets in other OECD countries. With increased savings through institutions, and general asset appreciation, institutional assets in OECD countries increased more than 12 percent on average in 1990–98 (OECD 2000). After the United States, the United Kingdom maintains the next-largest institutional sector, with assets of $3 trillion in 1998 (203 percent of GDP); followed by France, with $1.7 trillion in institutional assets (107 percent of GDP); Germany, with $1.6 trillion (66 percent of GDP); Japan, with $1.5 trillion (91 percent of GDP); and Italy, with about $1 trillion (79 percent of GDP).[3] However, the significance of different types of institutions, and the markets they invest in, is not uniform across OECD countries. With the exceptions of the United States and the United Kingdom, insurance companies play a dominant role in many OECD markets. Pension fund assets, although also significant, are concentrated in two countries, the United Kingdom and the Netherlands (OECD 2000). Mutual funds have generally experienced tremendous growth throughout the OECD. In the capital markets, only institutions in the United Kingdom, the United States, and Australia invest predominantly in equity securities; throughout the remainder of the OECD, institutional investor portfolios consist largely of fixed-income assets (OECD 2000).

Latin America and the Caribbean

Over the past decade, assets under institutional management in a number of Latin American and Caribbean markets experienced significant growth. However, on a regional basis, the sector remains underdeveloped relative to its potential. Using the OECD countries as a benchmark, figure 5-1 shows that the institutional assets of some Latin American countries comprise a substantially smaller percentage of GDP relative to more mature economies, thus suggesting that Latin American and Caribbean economies could sustain larger institutional sectors. A notable exception is Chile's institutional sector, which comprises more than 50 percent of GDP. With well-developed

---

[3]Other developed institutional markets are Canada, the Netherlands, Korea, Spain, and Switzerland.

Figure 5-1	**Institutional Assets in Selected Countries, 1999** *(Percentage of GDP)*

Source: OECD (2000); World Bank (2001); ICI (2001).

pension and insurance industries, Chile's institutional and capital market growth has been attributed to the initiation of a mandatory private pension system in 1981, the earliest in the region (Yermo 2000).

Within the region, the level of development varies among different types of institutional investors. Although pension fund development lags behind that of Chile throughout the remainder of Latin America and the Caribbean, pensions currently dominate the region's institutional sector. Brazil and Chile account for the majority of the region's pension assets. Brazil's pension system began with employer-sponsored plans in the 1970s and continues to consist primarily of defined-benefit employer programs, while private pension plans serve primarily to complement the social security system (Yermo 2000). The Dominican Republic, Panama, and Mexico have also had employer-sponsored pension plans over the past few decades.

Other Latin American and Caribbean countries introduced pension funds following social security privatization programs, based on the Chilean model, in the 1990s. These programs, implemented in Peru in 1993—followed by Argentina, Colombia, Uruguay, Bolivia, Mexico, and El Salvador—led to a shift away from pay-as-you-go public pension systems to fully funded, defined-contribution systems that require employee contributions to individual retirement accounts managed by private investment funds. In the Caribbean countries alone, private pension funds and other contractual savings account for 15 to 25 percent of total institutional assets (World Bank and CGCED 1998) and have relatively broad coverage in countries such as the Bahamas, Trinidad and Tobago, and Jamaica.

Insurance companies within Latin America and the Caribbean are less significant than pension funds, as shown in table 5-1, although the insurance companies have begun to foster diversity of coverage and competition (S&P 2001b). Insurance premiums as a percentage of GDP—a measure typically used to show the importance of insurance within an economy—are less than 2 percent on average in Latin America and the Caribbean,[4] compared with 8 to 13 percent in the OECD (ASSAL 2001; S&P 2001b). Six countries account for the majority of premiums in Latin America: Brazil, Mexico, Argentina, Chile, Colombia, and Venezuela (ASSAL 2001). In Barbados, Trinidad and Tobago, the Bahamas, and Jamaica, the life insurance sector is more developed than in Latin America. For example, in the mid-1990s, premiums in the Bahamas accounted for 2.8 percent of GDP, and in Jamaica they constituted 8.5 percent of GDP. A recent World Bank report credits the growth of insurance in the Caribbean largely to tax loopholes that made life insurance attractive savings and cash management vehicles. The report also notes, however, that the insurance industry in these countries is hurt by low asset returns and lack of domestic long-term investments (World Bank and CGCED 1998).

The mutual fund sector in Latin America and the Caribbean is growing rapidly, but still has great potential for further development. The sector consists of two types of funds: domestic funds that are primarily owned and administered by commercial banks and funds directed toward foreign investors. Foreign funds are administered by foreign investment companies and handled separately from those directed toward domestic investors. Thus, the development of domestic funds is integrally related to the banking industry (Yermo 2000). In a number of countries, mutual fund assets have increased sharply over the past few years. In some cases, such as Mexico, regulatory reforms have incited mutual fund growth (box 5-1). In Peru, which experienced a 37 percent growth in mutual fund assets in 2000, positive economic developments and low interest rates offered on traditional banking products have prompted mutual fund demand (AFM 2002). In spite of recent growth, the region's mutual fund sector remains relatively concentrated. In Peru, for example, the sector is made up of nine fixed-income funds, accounting for 81 percent of total sector assets, along with seven money market funds and six equity funds. The region's mutual funds are

---

[4] The insurance industry in Latin America and the Caribbean currently consists of two sectors—life insurance and general insurance. In some countries, there is a large discrepancy in the amount of premiums for each sector, averaging generally 3 to 1 within the region (Yermo 2000). References to insurance companies in this chapter refer to the sector as a whole.

Table 5-1 | Financial Assets and Market Share by Type of Investor in Selected Countries, 1995–2000

Assets	1995	1996	1997	1998	1999	2000
Argentina						
Billions of U.S. dollars						
Insurance companies	2.1	2.7	3.7	4.66	5.7	6.99
Mutual funds	.63	1.9	5.25	6.93	6.99	7.66
Pension funds	2.5	5.3	8.83	11.52	16.79	20.38
Total	5.2	9.81	17.7	23.12	29.48	35.03
Percent						
Insurance companies	40.2	27.2	20.6	20.1	19.3	20.0
Mutual funds	12.0	19.0	30.0	30.0	23.7	21.8
Pension funds	47.7	53.9	49.8	49.8	57.0	58.2
Brazil						
Billions of U.S. dollars						
Insurance companies	7.17	10.7	12.5	13	11.3	151.1
Mutual funds	63.64	103.8	108.6	118.7	117.8	74.8
Pension funds	62.69	73.5	83.4	82	71.2	
Total	133.5	187.9	204.5	213.7	200.3	
Percent						
Insurance companies	5.4	5.7	6.1	6.1	5.6	
Mutual funds	47.7	55.2	53.1	55.5	58.8	
Pension funds	47.0	39.1	40.8	38.4	36.0	
Chile						
Billions of U.S. dollars						
Insurance companies	7.12	8.49	9.87	10.48	10.28	12.23
Mutual funds	2.84	2.93	4.55	2.91	4.09	4.43
Pension funds	25.14	27.20	30.53	30.81	34.5	35.89
Total	35	38.6	44.95	44.2	48.87	52.55
Percent						
Insurance companies	20.4	22.0	22.0	23.7	21.0	23.3
Mutual funds	8.0	7.6	10.1	6.6	8.4	8.4
Pension funds	71.7	70.5	67.9	69.7	70.6	68.3
Mexico						
Billions of U.S. dollars						
Insurance companies	3.5	4.9	5.9	6.2	8.9	10.7
Mutual funds	7.6	10	13.5	14	19.5	19

Pension funds	.615	5.80	11.5	17		
Total	20	26	39.9	46.7		
Percent						
Insurance companies	29.5	23.9	22.3	22.9		
Mutual funds	67.5	53.8	48.9	40.7		
Pension funds	3.0	22.3	28.8	36.4		

Peru

Billions of U.S. dollars

Insurance companies	0.25	0.31	0.35	0.41	0.5	0.66
Mutual funds[a]	0.15	0.01	0.62	0.33	0.5	0.68
Pension funds	0.95	0.58	1.51	1.73	2.41	2.75
Total	1.35	0.89	2.48	2.47	'3.4	4.1

Percent

Insurance companies	18.4	34.2	14.2	16.7	14.6	16.0
Mutual funds	11.1	0.6	24.9	13.3	14.7	16.6
Pension funds	70.5	65.2	60.9	70.0	70.8	67.1

Italy

Percent

Insurance companies	146.1 (46.3%)	120.3 (50.3%)	151.8 (38.4%)	184.9 (28%)	204 (28.5%)	222.8 (32.3%)
Mutual funds	130 (41.2%)	79.9 (33.4%)	209.4 (52.9%)	439.7 (66.5%)	478.5 (66.9%)	418.9 (60.7%)
Pension funds	39.2 (12.4%)	39 (16.3%)	34.4 (8.7%)	36.3 (5.5%)	33.2 (4.6%)	48.1 (7%)
Total	315.3	239.2	395.6	660.9	715.7	689.8

United Kingdom

Percent

Insurance companies	1,021.6 (48.3%)	817.1 (47.2%)	1,213.5 (48.2%)	1,384.1 (49.4%)	1,587.1 (49.8%)	N/A
Mutual funds	201.3 (9.5%)	154.5 (8.9%)	235.7 (9.4%)	283.7 (10.1%)	371 (11.7%)	376.8
Pension funds	893.2 (42.2%)	759.7 (43.9%)	1,066.6 (42.4%)	1,136.5 (40.5%)	1,226.3 (38.5%)	N/A
Total	2,116.1	1,731.3	2,515.8	2,804.3	3,184.4	N/A

United States

Percent

Insurance companies	3,016.3 (26.7%)	2,803.9 (28.5%)	3,358.3 (25.1%)	3,648.6 (23.6%)	3,943.8 (22.3%)	4,007.3 (22.1%)
Mutual funds	3,526.3 (31.2%)	2,811.5 (28.6%)	4,468.2 (33.4%)	5,525.2 (35.8%)	6,846.3 (38.7%)	7,269.1 (40%)
Pension funds	4,745.7 (42.1%)	4,226.7 (42.9%)	5,563.6 (41.6%)	6,258.7 (40.6%)	6,900.8 (39%)	6,876.8 (37.9%)
Total	11,288.3	9,842.1	13,390.1	15,432.5	17,690.9	18,153.2

Source: OECD (2000); ICI (2001); ASSAL (2001); FIAP (2002); AFM (2002).

[a] Derived by author from various sources.

N/A Not available.

Box 5-1 | **Structural Reforms in Mexico**

In April 2001, the Mexican Congress passed wide-ranging reform laws governing the financial sector, including the Credit Institution Law, Financial Groups Law, National Savings and Public Bank Services Law, Securities Market Law, National Banking and Securities Commission Law, Mutual Funds Law, and the General Law on Ancillary Activities and Organizations of Credit. The purpose of these reforms is to eliminate legal hurdles and inconsistencies within the financial sector and to grant more authority to the country's banking and securities market regulatory authority, the Comisión Nacional Bancaria y de Valores (CNBV).

These reforms are being fleshed out by secondary CNBV regulations, which will provide guidance on issues such as how to effect prompt corrective actions and rules for public disclosure. New regulations have already made it possible for independent fund managers to offer equity funds denominated in foreign currencies and are expected to provide for the introduction of mutual fund distributors. This would allow funds to be sold anywhere, including retail stores and cell phone service outlets. Currently, banks are the primary mutual fund distributors.

Other developments involve the decision of more corporations and state and municipal governments to issue debt securities, whereas investment now is concentrated in federal government securities, and the decision of banks and brokers to reduce initial investment minimum requirements, some of which have gone as low as $108, compared with $54,180 a few years ago.

The reforms overall could provide greater investment diversification and make financial services more accessible to average Mexican citizens. It is also expected that Mexico's securities markets will benefit from reforms that impose clearer and more enforceable fiduciary duties on directors and create more effective rights of action for minority shareholders.

---

invested principally in fixed-income securities, and some countries have recently shifted further away from the equity markets.

The mutual fund sector in Brazil is an exception; it accounted for more than 70 percent of the region's total mutual fund assets in 1998 (Yermo 2000). As indicated in table 5-1, from 1995 to 2000, Brazilian mutual fund assets grew by more than 140 percent, to $151 billion, or 25 percent of GDP. Although Brazil has had mutual funds as long as countries such as Chile and Mexico have, Brazil's mutual fund sector was given a boost during the country's hyperinflation years when short-term, fixed-income mutual funds presented a means of preserving value (Yermo 2000). As in other Latin American and Caribbean countries, however, Brazilian equity market funds have relatively low participation because poor stock market performance and high interest rates make fixed-income funds more attractive (FEFSI 2002).

Among countries in Latin America and the Caribbean, Chile maintains the highest regional market capitalization relative to its institutional assets.[5] Due largely to

---

[5] The fact that institutional assets in some Latin American and Caribbean countries, such as Chile, Mexico, and Peru, constitute a lower percentage of GDP than their market capitalization may be due to a large amount of foreign investment in those markets. The percentages are reversed in the United States, where local institutions invest significant amounts in foreign securities.

Figure 5-2	Institutional Investor Development and Market Capitalization, 1999

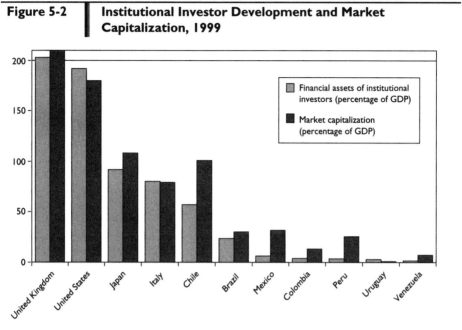

Source: OECD (2000); World Bank (2001); ICI (2001).

pension and macroeconomic reforms, Chile's market capitalization increased from $44.8 billion in 1993 to $60.5 billion in 2000, with *administradores de fondos de pensiones* (pension fund administrators) owning more than 10 percent of all Chilean equities and accounting for approximately one-quarter of all transactions in Chile's stock exchanges (Bolsa de Santiago 2001). In general, however, the region's market capitalization remains relatively low (figure 5-2). The markets also suffer from lack of liquidity, another indicator of capital market development. The region's corporate bond and equity markets are particularly illiquid, while the government debt markets are generally deeper and more liquid (S&P 2001a).

The Importance of Domestic Institutional Investors

Institutional investors contribute to local capital market development in a number of ways. In turn, well-functioning capital markets provide an efficient means of directing savings to meet the financing needs of private enterprises and governments and are increasingly viewed as a critical element for overall long-term economic growth (Levine 1997).

Enhanced Market Liquidity

The primary way institutions contribute to the ability of capital markets to affect economic growth is by creating liquidity. Liquidity exists in deep, actively traded markets where securities may be sold quickly, cheaply, and with little price impact. Liquidity is fundamental to capital market development because it allows for stock valuation, thereby reducing investment risk and the cost of capital. Liquid markets also contribute to economic growth by providing financing on favorable terms. Levine (1997) argues that if investors are able to sell their shares at any time, they are more likely to commit to longer-term and potentially more profitable investments. In this way, liquidity improves capital allocation and allows firms to rely on financing that is needed for long-term development.

In Latin America and the Caribbean, liquidity may also be a mechanism to improve the competitiveness of regional markets. In table 5-2, two common measures of liquidity—the total value of shares traded as a percentage of GDP and the turnover ratio, showing trading activity relative to market size—indicate that the region's markets are relatively illiquid compared with larger OECD markets. This has prompted larger local companies to seek cheaper and more abundant sources of capital outside Latin American and Caribbean markets. As companies delist from local exchanges, markets become less liquid and the cost of capital increases. With greater liquidity, markets may be more efficient and attractive to large local issuers. In addi-

Table 5-2 ▍ **Institutional Investor Growth and Market Liquidity**

Country	Financial assets of institutional investors (percentage of GDP)	Value traded (percentage of GDP)	Turnover ratio
Brazil	24	11.6	44.6
Chile	57	10.2	9.5
Colombia	4	0.8	3.8
Mexico	6	7.5	32.5
Peru	4	4.4	12.7
Venezuela	2	0.8	8.8
Italy	80	44.3	104
Japan	76	19.5	69.9
United Kingdom	203	82.5	66.6
United States	192	133.7	200.8

Source: World Bank (2001); S&P (2001b); SIA (2000).

tion, with high costs of local capital, small and medium enterprises may find it difficult to obtain financing and economic growth may be slowed (Gaa and others 2001).

Table 5-2 also shows that the growth of institutional investors correlates positively with the level of market liquidity. Institutions create liquidity by channeling additional savings into the markets and by actively trading in high volumes. Some institutions may create the liquidity necessary for the development of other types of investors. For example, newly established pension funds may not engage in active trading until they have accumulated sufficient financial assets (Vittas 1996), whereas mutual funds that rely on daily redemptions and the ability to mark their assets to market require a highly liquid market. In this way, pension funds may pave the way for mutual funds to enter the market.

Alternatives to Commercial Banks

Institutions also contribute to market liquidity and provide other benefits by alleviating an economy's dependence on commercial banks as savings and financing vehicles. By providing alternatives to bank deposits, institutions may create a pool of long-term financial assets available for investment, particularly through funded pension programs (Vittas 1996), and possibly increase savings as a whole (Greenough and King 1976). By channeling these savings into capital markets, institutions contribute to market growth and liquidity and transform savings into productive investments and resulting economic growth.

Institutional investors also provide alternatives to traditional bank financing through their participation in primary markets through private placements, initial public offerings, venture capital investment, and secondary market participation. Capital market financing, unlike bank financing, does not depend directly on interest rates; therefore, capital market financing may provide financing opportunities for riskier ventures and long-term projects for which bank financing may not be available (IDB 1998). As a result of the shift toward market-based financing, competitive pressures may cause banks to increase their securities activities and offer sophisticated derivatives and over-the-counter products (Gaa and others 2001).

Market Stability

Some institutional investors, particularly those with a long-term outlook, may encourage market stability. For example, pension funds, due to their nature as retirement assets and the tax penalties for early withdrawals, are more likely to remain invested during a crisis. In principle, mutual funds have the potential to aggravate stock market fluctuations because they must fulfill requests for redemption at any time. If faced with a significant amount of requests, a fund may be forced to sell a substantial amount of securities to meet redemptions (Kaminsky, Lyons, and Schmukler 2000). However, diversified funds may hold greater amounts of equity and other higher-risk investments to abate the effects of local stock market volatility (Rea 1996). As mutual funds manage increasing amounts of retirement assets, they have begun to take on a longer-term outlook and, like pension funds, are more likely to weather a crisis and remain invested.

Domestic institutions may also potentially diffuse adverse market effects caused by foreign investors. Foreign investment may benefit local capital markets and economies through an influx of liquidity and capital. However, in illiquid and concentrated markets, such as those in Latin America and the Caribbean, a sudden liquidation of a large foreign investor's shares could destabilize the local market. Domestic investors may negate the effect of foreign investors by holding local securities, thereby minimizing the percentage of a single investor's holdings in a single security. Furthermore, because domestic institutions hold other locally listed shares, they may be sensitive to the effects of a market disruption on their own portfolios, whereas a foreign investor would not.

Product Innovation and Market Modernization

As competition within the institutional investor sector develops, the need for better performance and sophisticated investment objectives leads institutions to develop innovative products and investment strategies. For example, in response to competitive pressures, mutual funds have developed more cost-efficient products (for example, indexed and money market funds) and products that may reduce tax implications (for example, exchange-traded funds). Institutions also contribute to market efficiency by acting as short-term lenders and arbitrage traders.

Because institutional investors require liquid markets that can accommodate sophisticated products, the markets are compelled to modernize (U.S. SEC 1992). For example, in an effort to attract institutional trading in the 1970s, U.S. securities markets implemented new trading mechanisms to absorb large blocs typical of institutional trades (U.S. SEC 1994). Institutional investors are also pushing for technology-driven market developments, such as enhanced access to information, and for faster, cheaper trade execution through electronic trading systems, such as electronic communication networks.[6] Furthermore, to facilitate local diversification, institutional in-

---

[6] An electronic communication network is a computerized trading network that displays and matches buy orders with sell orders in NASDAQ stocks. Electronic communication networks may provide faster trade execution and potential price improvement over market-maker quotes.

vestors may demand easier cross-border trading and efficient clearance and settlement procedures (Dowers, Gomez-Acebo, and Masci 2000). For example, in the European Union, 20 to 30 clearing and settlement firms, with differing settlement cycles,
impose high transaction costs on cross-border transactions. With a single currency
and increased cross-border trading, institutional investors are pressing for cheaper transaction costs through consolidation.

The product innovations prompted by institutions can also have broader economic and social benefits. In the United States, pension funds' demand for long-term,
low-risk, fixed-income securities contributed to the growth of mortgage-backed securities in the 1970s (Vittas 1996). Through securitization, the mortgage market attracted additional capital and provided the benefits of risk pooling to mortgage issuers. In countries such as Mexico, where housing finance depends on government
funding and mandatory wage contributions to pension funds earmarked for housing,
securitization can alleviate these pressures and contribute to the availability of mortgages (IMF 2001).

Improved Corporate Accountability

As influential shareholders, institutional investors have the ability to monitor and exert
pressure for improvements in corporate governance and the accountability of managers. Although shareholders may choose an exit option and simply sell their shares in
response to an unfavorable event or corporate policy, they may also choose to remain
invested and voice their concerns by exercising greater control over companies in
which they maintain a significant voting stake. Furthermore, through their economic
power in the markets, institutional investors encourage good corporate governance by
investing in companies on that basis. Institutions may also use their influence to compel regulatory efforts to enhance issuer transparency and information disclosure, to
prohibit abuses and misconduct, and to promote policies on behalf of shareholders.

Factors Leading to the Development of a Domestic Institutional Investor Sector

As intermediaries, institutional investors' growth is dependent on two variables: the
demand by individuals for institutional products and a sufficient supply of financial assets in which institutions can invest. In the United States and other OECD countries,
a number of factors have affected these variables, as shown in figure 5-3, leading to
the development of the institutional sector. Although taken alone, each of these fac-

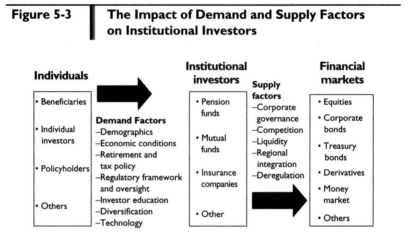

Figure 5-3 | **The Impact of Demand and Supply Factors on Institutional Investors**

tors would have had little impact; they instead worked in a mutually reinforcing fashion to create a favorable environment for growth.

Demand Factors

Favorable Economic Conditions

Although this chapter asserts that institutional investors contribute to economic growth, a base amount of domestic wealth drives initial institutional demand. As the sector develops, its benefits for the markets and the economy create momentum for further institutional development. As markets move toward efficiency, they involve a greater number of market participants or stakeholders whose interests in a well-functioning market system create the conditions for further institutional growth.

As outlined in box 5-2, during periods of strong economic growth in the United States, institutional products became more popular as individual wealth increased. In 1980–99 in particular, high corporate profit growth, low inflation, a bull market, and relatively low interest rates contributed to institutional demand (ICI 2001). However, measures to increase investor confidence in the markets and tax incentives for investment in private pension plans prompted the channeling of individual savings into institutional investments as opposed to alternative savings vehicles.

Demand for Private Pension Funds

As life expectancies in industrial economies have increased and populations have shifted to include a greater proportion of older people, governments have been com-

Box 5-2	Growth of the Institutional Investor in the United States

1900–40. Equities play a minor role in corporate financing. Few pension plans exist, and those that do invest primarily in unmarketable "book reserves" of sponsoring corporations. In the 1920s, restrictions against corporations owning stock of other corporations are lifted, and the transfer of funds from individuals to institutions begins. The modern mutual fund is created to provide small investors access to the period's boom market, and pension funds begin to invest in equities and government bonds. Institutional equity holdings remain insignificant and contribute little to market liquidity due to the lack of new issues and institutional buy-and-hold policies (U.S. SEC 1971).

1940–70. Institutions become a major force in U.S. markets, as young, less wealthy individuals favor life insurance and pension fund investments. Savers become more yield conscious and move cash out of bank accounts and away from conservative, long-term investments and into mutual funds. Pension funds hold the majority of institutionally held equity, decreasing investments in government bonds, but continuing to trade infrequently, avoid private placements, and concentrate holdings in large, well-known NYSE-listed stocks. Insurance companies, limited to investments in bonds, mortgages, and other fixed-income assets by state law, develop separate accounts free of state restrictions and begin to increase their equity holdings (U.S. SEC 1971).

1970–90. Pension funds and mutual funds reach new heights, while individual direct stock holdings fall (relatively). Rising interest rates and a rising stock market lead corporations to issue more equity. Money market mutual funds explode as interest rates rise while payments on bank deposits remain capped by regulation. Index funds first appear as the growing stock market outpaces actively invested fund returns. Institutions increase their use of derivatives products such as index options and futures. Through relaxed investment restrictions, pension funds increase financing of smaller, riskier ventures through high-yield securities, venture funds, and private equity funding. Institutions continue to hold large, primarily well-known equities, leaving financing of new and small enterprises unfulfilled (U.S. SEC 1992; Gremillion 2000; ICI 2001).

1990–2001. Mutual fund assets increase sevenfold, reaching $7 trillion. Mutual fund growth is due to investment by households attracted by equity funds' high returns and relatively low minimum investment. Mutual funds also become an important component of household retirement accounts. Investment by other institutional investors, particularly retirement plans, and fund performance also contribute to mutual fund asset growth. International funds, increased business use of money market funds for cash management, and the growing importance of defined-contribution pension plans also contribute to overall mutual fund demand (ICI 2001).

pelled to evaluate the sufficiency of their pension resources. In the United States, the demand for private pension plans first occurred when families could not meet the needs of older people who had suddenly fallen into poverty during the Great Depression (Munnell 1982). Beginning in the 1970s, an aging population coupled with decreasing birth rates strained the social security system, and the demand for private pension investments increased. In other OECD countries, aging populations have placed pressure on pay-as-you-go retirement systems and increased the need for alternative ways to ensure retirement benefits.

Another significant influence on the development of private pension plans in the United States has been the underlying tax advantages. Corporate pension plans were first made exempt from federal income tax in 1926, but became a significant source of retirement support in the 1970s after the Employee Retirement Income Security Act of 1974 (ERISA) was enacted.[7] ERISA created new disclosure and funding requirements for employee retirement plans and raised fiduciary standards governing their management. ERISA also allowed otherwise uncovered employees to take advantage of retirement-related tax benefits through the creation of individual retirement accounts (IRAs). In 1978, defined-contribution 401(k) plans were created, allowing employees to make pretax payments into a self-directed investment, such as mutual funds, that may be supplemented with employer contributions. After further tax reform was enacted in 1981 to broaden pension fund participation to small business employees, many employers chose to provide defined-contribution rather than traditional defined-benefit plans. By 2000, 35 percent of mutual fund assets represented retirement savings, and more than 42 million 401(k) accounts contained a combined $1.8 trillion in assets (ICI 2001).

Other countries that maintain defined-contribution schemes or a close variant also tend to have significant institutional investor sectors. For example, Canada encourages pension savings by providing tax advantages for retirement income invested directly in mutual funds. In countries that maintain predominantly pay-as-you-go systems, such as Germany and France, where pension fund assets account for only a small percentage of GDP, institutional investors play a less important role in the market overall (OECD 2000). Countries with a strong private pension fund system, such as the United States, the United Kingdom, and Canada, are experiencing declining government borrowing needs, while private sector borrowing of corporate bonds, commercial paper, and asset-backed securities have grown in relative importance (Gaa and others 2001).

Institutions' Ability to Diversify

In addition to tax incentives, institutional investors have offered investors the ability to diversify their portfolio holdings over a broad range of domestic and foreign stocks. In particular, mutual funds with low minimum investment requirements allow individ-

---

[7] 29 U.S.C. 1001–1461 (1994).

Box 5-3	Evolution of Chile's Pension System

Pension reform in the majority of Latin American and Caribbean countries occurred in the 1990s, and the full benefits from those reforms have yet to be realized. Chile, as the regional pioneer of pension reform in 1981, illustrates how private pension funds may benefit local capital markets as they mature.

In the pre-reform, pay-as-you-go system, the government used retirement assets as a means for financing its activities by investing them in the government bond market. After adoption of pension reform in 1981, pension fund composition remained highly restricted, with the majority of assets invested in risk-free securities, such as government bonds. As capital markets developed, pension funds started to invest in mortgage bonds and corporate bonds (Vives 1999). The growth of the corporate bond market served to attract foreign capital, further deepening the market.

Beginning in 1990, restrictions against pension fund investments in foreign securities were gradually lifted. Investments in venture capital and infrastructure funds were permitted in 1993, and equity restrictions were lifted in 1995. Since the lifting of these restrictions, pension funds have had a significant effect on Chile's capital markets. Currently, pension fund administrators own more than 10 percent of all Chilean equities and are responsible for about one-quarter of all transactions in Chile's stock exchanges. Chile's market capitalization grew over 30 percent from 1993 to 2000 (Bolsa de Santiago 2001). Pension funds also facilitated the development of credit rating agencies, stabilized prices, developed innovative products, and invested in infrastructure funds (Vives 1999).

uals to enjoy a professionally managed, diversified portfolio that otherwise would be unobtainable through direct holdings. Mutual funds have served as the primary vehicle for foreign stock purchases, allowing global diversification in the 1990s through an increased number of international equity funds (ICI 2001).

A Sound Regulatory/Legal Framework and Oversight

A sound regulatory and legal framework has increased investor confidence in the capital markets and boosted demand for institutional products as long-term investment options. The regulatory scheme governing U.S. mutual funds and other investment companies demonstrates how regulation focused on investor protection, while not hindering innovation, has allowed the fund industry to flourish. These regulations play a particularly important role as mutual funds increasingly serve as the investment vehicle for retirement assets. Chile and other countries in Latin America and the Caribbean with recently reformed pension schemes have adopted a similar structure for the management of retirement assets by private investment funds, such as mutual funds (box 5-3).

Mutual funds in the United States are subject to a comprehensive system of regulation administered by the U.S. Securities and Exchange Commission (SEC). The Investment Company Act of 1940 is the principal statute governing mutual funds and other investment companies.[8] Reflecting recognition of the role of investment companies in channeling savings into the capital markets, the act imposes detailed restrictions on investment companies to ensure they operate for the benefit of their shareholders and not in the interests of their managers and corporate insiders. Specifically, the act prohibits self-dealing, prescribes fairness in pricing investment company securities for sale or redemption, ensures the safekeeping of fund assets, restricts leveraging of company assets, and sets forth a corporate governance scheme in which independent directors serve as fund watchdogs. Detailed disclosures are required in a prospectus outlining the investment company's investment objectives, shareholder costs, and financial condition. The financial disclosure is governed by a well-established set of principles under Generally Accepted Accounting Principles (GAAP) in the United States.

The Investment Company Act was adopted with considerable cooperation from the mutual fund industry, demonstrating its commitment to sound industry practices and recognition that institutional growth depends on household demand (U.S. SEC 1992). The act also has built-in flexibility, enabling the SEC to accommodate industry innovations by exempting a company from regulation under the act if an exemption is in the public interest, is consistent with the protection of investors, and meets certain other standards.

In addition to being the holders and managers of savings, investment companies are also issuers and active traders in the securities markets and thus subject to the laws governing these activities. Other institutional investors also rely on these laws to ensure the market continues to function well and that investor confidence remains high. To protect the integrity of the markets, the Securities Exchange Act of 1934 prohibits unfair and inequitable trading practices, such as insider trading and market manipulation, and sets forth a system of self-regulation to monitor market operations, subject to SEC oversight.[9] The market governing bodies, or self-regulatory organizations, must register with the SEC and receive SEC approval of their rules. Self-regulation is cost-effective because it promotes efficient rules and eases the burden of expensive oversight from the SEC.

The laws governing market activities also rely on a system of disclosure to further confidence in the markets. The Securities Act of 1933 governs securities issuers by requiring that securities be registered with the SEC before being offered to

---

[8] 15 U.S.C. § 80a-1 (1994).
[9] 15 U.S.C. § 78a (1994).

the public and that companies disclose fair and accurate information to enable investors to allocate capital efficiently.[10] Under the Securities Exchange Act, companies are subject to quarterly and annual reporting obligations of their financial condition after they have issued securities and at any other time a material change occurs that may affect their securities while they are traded in the secondary markets.

The SEC fosters investor confidence through enforcement of these laws. Enforcement is conducted through on-site compliance and inspection programs and by investigating and prosecuting incidences of fraud and other regulatory breaches. To perform these functions, the SEC's resources include trained personnel and technology to monitor the markets. The SEC is funded through the federal government budgetary process, although it does collect fees on securities registrations, transactions, and filings.

Increased Market Exposure and Education

Investor demand for institutional products has also increased through market exposure. With the advent of private pension funds, a large segment of the population in the United States became exposed to and familiar with the markets, thus creating an "investment culture" and increasing individuals' desire for further investment. An investment culture was furthered in the 1970s with the advent of money market funds, which served as bank account substitutes when deposit account interest rates remained artificially capped through government regulation.

Largely through mutual fund and other industry trade associations, the institutional sector in the United States has been instrumental in educating investors and thereby providing them with the tools to understand mutual fund prospectuses and to spot fraud when it occurs. Investor education, along with the pressures of competition, has encouraged the industry's general adherence to high operating standards and allowed innovation through investment creativity and investor confidence. Investor confidence is evidenced by the fact that, despite several brief disruptions in the U.S. equity markets since 1940, mutual funds investing in these markets have not experienced mass redemptions, but rather a consistent growth in shareholder investment (Rea and Marcis 1996).

Distribution and Technological Developments

Technological advances in communications and information distribution have enabled institutional investors to operate at much lower cost. These developments are par-

---

[10] 15 U.S.C. § 77a (1994).

ticularly relevant to mutual funds, which rely on household demand. In the United States before 1970, high fees and advertising restrictions created an expensive distribution system for mutual fund shares. Regulatory flexibility and technology led to the creation of new, more cost-efficient, and effective distribution channels through mail, direct marketing, and third parties in the form of fund supermarkets. In some countries, technology has provided additional distribution channels for mutual fund shares, such as automatic teller machines and the Internet.

Technology has accelerated the trend toward the integration of brokerage, investment management, insurance, and banking services into single entities or complexes, creating efficiencies through economies of scale and the retention of a customer base. Through complexes, mutual funds began offering specialized products to appeal to different investors, such as those tailored to market capitalization, industry sectors, and foreign markets. Technology has also allowed institutions to operate in locations remote from their clients and facilitated cross-border flows, leading to increasing globalization and easier international portfolio diversification (Gaa and others 2001).

Supply Factors

Assets under institutional management in the United States have grown through access to a vast, integrated economy with a GDP of more than $10 trillion. Although the United States consists of 50 separate states with differences in corporate, tax, and securities laws, a constitutional prohibition on interference with interstate commerce enables transactions from state to state to flow easily. With the exception of insurance companies, state laws have affected institutional investors primarily through state registration requirements that have slowly been eliminated in favor of a federal registration and oversight system. U.S. equity markets, although previously fragmented, now essentially operate as a national market system, which has led to significant improvements in market operations (U.S. SEC 1994).[11] U.S. markets operate through a consolidated clearance and settlement system and have a sophisticated distribution system for mutual fund shares that allows funds to market their shares to parts of the country that may be experiencing greater economic prosperity relative to others (Gaa and others 2001).

---

[11] In 1975, the U.S. Congress mandated a national market system for the U.S. securities markets through the Securities Exchange Act of 1934. The purpose of the national market system was to ensure efficient execution of securities transactions, fair competition among broker-dealers and markets, and best execution of investors' orders. The markets established a consolidated quotation system and transaction tape and an intermarket trading system to link markets for listed securities (U.S. SEC 1994).

Table 5-3	Growth of Institutional Investors in the European Union Following Integration

(Institutional investor assets as a percentage of GDP)

Country	1992	1999	Percentage change
United Kingdom	131.2	226.7	72.8
Germany	34.0	76.8	123.5
Italy	21.8	96.9	344.5
Netherlands	131.5	212.8	61.8
Greece	3.0	40.1	1236
Spain	21.9	65.4	198.0
Portugal	18.3	50.8	177.6

Source: OECD (2000).

By contrast, institutional investors in the European Union, with a combined GDP of $9 trillion, suffered from disparate regulations before integrating their markets in the 1990s. As a result, institutions faced costly barriers to accessing the capital pools of member states. The United States maintains 57 percent of the world's mutual fund assets, compared with 28 percent for Europe. Europe has by far the largest number of funds due to the number of national markets and distribution channels; however, fund size in Europe has remained static, whereas in the United States it has doubled (Zurstrassen 1998). The economies of scale achieved in the United States can increase competition in performance and fee levels, thereby drawing even more investment to the market.

With the implementation of a common European currency, however, issuers have begun listing their companies on fewer exchanges, thus increasing market liquidity (Gaa and others 2001). Integration has led to cross-border exchange, recently advanced through the merger of the Paris, Amsterdam, and Brussels bourses to form Euronext. Integration has also furthered plans toward a consolidated clearance and settlement system (Gaa and others 2001). As shown in table 5-3, European Union integration has had a positive effect on the development of the institutional sector, particularly among the less wealthy member countries, such as Greece and Portugal, which have reaped considerable advantages since its implementation (box 5-4).

Good Corporate Governance

Corporate governance involves a set of relationships among a company's management, board, and shareholders and concerns the tensions that arise from the separa-

---

Box 5-4 | **Capital Market Integration in the European Union**

In 2000, the European Union appointed the "Group of Wise Men," chaired by Alexandre Lam-falussy, to review issues surrounding securities market regulation. The group's final report, the Lamfalussy report, acknowledges that a single European Union securities market is expected to bring about key economic benefits to all member states and sets forth an implementation plan.

The development of an integrated European securities market has been hindered for several interconnected reasons, including the absence of clear Europe-wide regulations on a large number of issues, such as prospectuses and market abuse; an inefficient regulatory system; inconsistent application of existing rules; and the inadequate development of funded pension schemes in most member states.

To accelerate the integration process, the report recommends a new four-level regulatory approach and the prioritization of goals that are believed obtainable in the near future. These goals include:

- A single prospectus for issuers
- Modernization of listing requirements and a clear distinction between listing and trading
- Modernization and expansion of investment rules for investment funds (investment companies) and pension funds
- Adoption of International Accounting Standards
- A single passport for recognized stock markets.

---

tion of ownership and control. Good corporate governance provides incentives for the board and management to pursue objectives that are in the best interests of the company and shareholders and facilitates effective monitoring, thereby encouraging firms to use resources more efficiently (OECD 1999).

Corporate governance has long been a key policy issue in the United States and in Europe, where the development and implementation of principles of good corporate governance have been a priority. It has more recently become a significant issue in Asia. In Korea, for example, traditional corporate institutions are characterized by large groups of related, family-controlled companies. Weak corporate governance and the influences of these groups, or *chaebol,* on the national economy have led to the structural defects surrounding the country's economic crisis in 1997. Corporate governance was one of the first sets of financial sector reform efforts after the crisis (Kyu-sung 2000).

The role of institutional investors as monitors of the companies they own is growing in the OECD countries, although they follow various models of governance. In the United States, governance is focused on the role of equity shareholders and provides a system of proxy voting and minority shareholder protections. Until recently, institutional investors often have chosen to simply sell their shares in response to an undesirable corporate event. Institutional activism has increased, partially due to the increased liquidity costs of selling shares in large portfolios and the fact that alternative investments may be limited. Other OECD countries, particularly more bank-oriented markets, effect management discipline less through the market and more through representative stakeholder interests on corporate boards.

Deregulation and the Prudent Investor Rule

Deregulation has had a substantial effect on the growth of institutional investors by lowering the cost of securities transactions. As their economic power in the markets has increased, institutions frequently have been the catalysts for reform. For example, institutions were instrumental in dismantling the fixed commission structure for securities trades in the U.S. markets. This event, which took place on May 1, 1975, or "May Day," resulted in the introduction of discount brokerage, greater price competition, and lower transaction fees (U.S. SEC 1994). As trading costs were reduced, market volume and liquidity went up. Facing the loss of commission fees, securities firms became more innovative in designing new pooled-investment products (U.S. SEC 1992). Similar to the United States, deregulation of the London Stock Exchange in 1986 with a "big bang" was intended to reduce the transaction costs of institutional investors, increase market liquidity, and enhance London's role as an international financial center (Poser 1991).

In addition to deregulation, institutions have also had access to a wide supply of potential investments through liberal portfolio investment requirements. Under ERISA, pension funds are managed in accordance with a standard known as the prudent investor rule, which allows plan fiduciaries to invest securities in the best interests of the overall portfolio. Under this standard, fiduciaries have considerable latitude in their investment choices and are able to diversify assets in accordance with modern portfolio theory.[12] Thus, ERISA allows pension funds the ability to invest in U.S. and non-U.S. equities, private equity, and high-risk investments, limited only by fiduciary prudence and certain ERISA compliance rules. To protect against self-dealing by plan sponsors, each individual with discretion over plan assets can be held liable as a fiduciary and face stiff civil and criminal penalties. In Europe, only a few countries, such as the United Kingdom and the Netherlands, operate pension investment schemes in accor-

---

[12] The prudent investor rule is a revised and updated version of the common-law "prudent man" standard governing the activities of investment trustees and other financial fiduciaries. The prudent man rule dictated that each investment be evaluated individually in terms of risk and potential return. Under the prudent investor standard, fund managers were judged on the prudence of the portfolio as a whole, thus allowing them to make riskier investments without fear that a single poorly performing investment would result in charges of fund mismanagement. Under ERISA, the prudent man standard has also been interpreted to hold fund fiduciaries to the level of skill of a professional money manager in making investment decisions or a "prudent expert."

dance with the prudent investor principle, whereas pension funds in the majority of the other European countries, including Germany, France, and Denmark, are subject to considerable restrictions on foreign and equity investments (Blommestein 1997).

Similar to pension funds, U.S. mutual fund portfolio managers enjoy investment discretion, subject to their fiduciary obligations to act in the best interests of the fund and the requirement that they invest fund assets in accordance with disclosed investment guidelines. However, U.S. insurance companies are regulated under state law and are subject to significant investment restrictions. To protect policyholders, state law requires that 90 percent of insurance company assets be invested in low-risk, low-return portfolios to ensure capital preservation. To circumvent these restrictions, in the late 1960s, insurance companies developed separate accounts free of state regulation, thus enabling them to invest under a fiduciary standard. As a result, insurance companies' share of equity investment and trading in the United States increased substantially (U.S. SEC 1971).

An additional benefit of allowing investment discretion has been the increased availability of risk capital in the United States. In 1979, the U.S. Department of Labor opened the door for pension funds to invest in venture capital by clarifying that portfolio diversification was a factor in determining the prudence of individual investments under ERISA. As a result, institutional investors became the principal source of funding for the U.S. venture capital industry. In addition to pension funds, investment by U.S. commercial banks also increased the availability of risk capital. Until recently, U.S. commercial banks were prohibited from investing in the securities markets under the Glass-Steagall Act. However, in 1958, the U.S. government introduced the Small Business Investment Company (SBIC) program specifically to increase the supply of risk capital. The program encourages the creation of funds to finance small enterprises; to comply, banks have created separate SBICs that act as venture funds (Strahota 1996).

Increasing Competition within the Institutional Sector

Competition among institutional investors resulted in greater efficiencies and innovation within the sector. In the United States, a number of developments, such as the advent of IRAs, increased disintermediation, the greater mobility of investible funds, and a general shift by institutions toward increased equity investment, eroded the traditional differences among institutional investors and heightened the degree of competition across the sector (U.S. Senate Finance Committee 1973). In response to competitive pressures, fund managers have become more performance and cost conscious, and product demand has increased. Portfolio investors have become more aggressive, engaging in short selling or other speculative techniques typical of more aggressive mutual funds. The strong demand for mutual funds has led to an expansion in the types of funds offered.

Competition within the sector, particularly for management of pension fund assets, has led to structural innovations, such as the creation of insurance company separate accounts. Under the quantitative restrictions of state laws, insurance companies do not need to maintain professional staff to engage in investment activities. After separate accounts were established, insurance companies hired and trained skilled portfolio managers, securities analysts, traders, researchers, and support personnel to support investment operations (Greenough and King 1976).

Impediments to Further Growth of Institutional Investors in Latin America and the Caribbean

In Latin America and the Caribbean, government efforts to promote the growth of domestic institutional investors through pension and market-related reforms have bolstered the importance of the sector in the region's capital markets. However, the region has certain impediments to further sector growth. Although the United States and other OECD countries cannot be generalized to Latin America and the Caribbean, their experience may provide guidance as to what factors are needed to foster further development of domestic institutional investors in the region.

Macroeconomic Policies

Throughout Latin America and the Caribbean, volatile macroeconomic conditions and regulatory uncertainty have impeded long-term capital formation by institutional investors and thus hindered financial innovation (IDB 1998). For example, investors in hedged fixed-income products in Brazil suffered extreme losses when the real was devalued in 1999. As a result, Brazilian fixed-income funds tend to remain in short-term, conservative investments, while continually high interest rates and portfolio restrictions have deterred greater equity investment (FEFSI 2002).

Demographics and Pension Reforms

Although Latin America and the Caribbean have not faced the same demographic pressures as the OECD countries, pension reform has been necessary to address the region's mismanaged pay-as-you-go programs. Pension reform has played a strategic role in governments' overall development policies (Schmidt-Hebbel 1999). Led by

Chile, the replacement of public pay-as-you-go systems with privately managed, fully funded pension systems has led to a prevalence of private defined-contribution systems within the region. However, with the exception of Chile, most countries' pension reforms are relatively recent, and their benefits are not yet fully realized.

Without further reforms to establish the other conditions necessary for institutional investor growth, pension reform alone will likely have little impact. For example, defined-contribution plans will be less effective at encouraging long-term savings without stable macroeconomic conditions (Uthoff 2000). Regulatory frameworks that limit the scope of pension fund investments influence the development of efficient and innovative capital markets.

Availability of Capital

A sufficient amount of capital is a prerequisite for a well-functioning, liquid market. Therefore, the smaller markets of Latin America and the Caribbean are at a disadvantage relative to more liquid foreign markets. Furthermore, the fact that large local companies are able to finance their activities in foreign markets adds to the problem of a lack of adequate capital for a local market to provide funding for small and medium enterprises (SMEs). Many SMEs must rely on their own resources or other local credit sources (Gaa and others 2001).

Dependence on the infusion of foreign capital to increase market liquidity has proved an unreliable strategy because foreign capital flows can be quickly cut off in periods of crisis, thus further disrupting local markets. The history of financial instability in Latin America and the Caribbean has resulted in households being reluctant to hold their assets in the formal financial markets. In a vulnerable environment, some middle- and upper-income households may invest their savings outside domestic markets (World Bank and CGCED 1998); others may meet their liquidity needs by holding cash (Rojas-Suárez and Wiesbrod 1996).

Lack of a Sound Regulatory Framework and Effective Supervision

To protect fund affiliates, Latin American and Caribbean countries with defined-contribution plans restrict the investment of pension fund portfolio assets in foreign or equity securities (Vives 1999). Because these regulations tend to create uniform investment portfolios, the institutional benefits of innovation, increased efficiencies, and diversification are not realized in the capital markets. For example, in Mexico, pension funds may not invest in equities, so their portfolios consist almost entirely of fixed-income securities. Other investments with broader social benefits are also prohibited, such as investments in infrastructure projects, venture capital financing, and securitized instruments (Vives 1999). With limited fund investment options, there is little development of local skilled portfolio managers and other securities professionals. Moreover, the lack of options for professional investors creates a culture linked to "safe" government securities; later, when more instruments are available, such a culture may not be easy to overcome.

Furthermore, with rampant delisting from local exchanges, in some cases securities regulators lose a source of funding. Regulators may lack the technical and administrative capacities for effective regulation because low wage levels and high turnover undermine the local technical capacity for supervision and regulation of the markets.

Weak Corporate Governance

Empirical studies show that development of a country's capital markets depends on the quality of its corporate governance rules (Gilson 2000; La Porta and others 1997). In large part, the growth of local securities markets in Latin America and the Caribbean has suffered from poor corporate governance. The mistreatment of minority shareholders and weak investor protection under local legal and regulatory frameworks have discouraged investors in the region's local securities markets (Lubrano 2001).

As in Asia, company ownership and management in Latin America and the Caribbean are often concentrated in families, and the development of legislation that protects the interests of minority shareholders has been met with some resistance. In Brazil, the concentrated ownership structure acts as an impediment to the development of stronger measures to protect minority shareholders. This in turn has had a chilling effect on the development of Brazil's capital markets (Coutinho and Rabelo 2001). The growth of the institutional investor sector in Latin America and the Caribbean, particularly pension funds that are significant shareholders in some of the region's largest companies, should have a positive impact on the future of corporate governance in the region.

Policy Recommendations

Long-term Government Commitment to Sound Macroeconomic Policies

As a precondition for all other factors to have an impact, Latin American and Caribbean governments must demonstrate a long-term commitment to a sound macroeconomic environment of low inflation and positive interest rates in order to restore trust and stability in their capital markets. This commitment should be part of an over-all plan to exercise conservative fiscal policy. By decreasing debt, governments will face less pressure to finance their activities through pension fund investment in govern-ment bonds, thus allowing capital to shift to the corporate bond and equity markets. Financial stability will also enable the government to establish credibility as a debt is-suer and thereby extend a legitimate long-term yield curve as a benchmark for other debt markets. Without decreased fiscal pressure, government will be constrained to devise a regulatory framework that is shaped to accommodate its needs, rather than one that is aimed at further sector growth through innovation and greater efficiency.

Movement toward Regional Market Integration

To offset problems of capital scarcity and low liquidity in attracting institutional in-vestors to Latin American and Caribbean capital markets, governments in the region should consider measures to facilitate easier cross-border transactions and move-ment toward regional integration. The fact that institutional investors in the United States had access to a vast, integrated area played a significant role in facilitating the growth of a domestic institutional sector. Institutions in the European Union are ex-periencing similar benefits. Both these markets can provide guidance to Latin Amer-ica and the Caribbean in terms of benefits and implementation.

   Although markets in the region have moved to facilitate cross-border trans-actions through regional entities, such as the Caribbean Community (CARICOM) and the Latin America Integration Association (LAIA), other measures may be taken to assist institutional investors specifically. For example, the European Union has taken steps to establish a common market for mutual fund–like investments. In 1985, the European Union passed the Undertakings on Collective Investments in Transferable Securities directive, permitting investment companies that register in one European country to sell shares in other European countries. This mutual fund "passport" was intended to assist in allowing funds to cross borders more easily. In addition, the European Commission has taken the initiative on pension reform at the European Union level to create a single market for these investments.

   To facilitate integration, local markets in Latin America and the Caribbean should continue to move toward adopting high standards of reporting and disclosure that apply across borders, such as the GAAP in the United States and the Interna-tional Accounting Standards. The adoption of fundamental principles of securities regulation offered by international organizations such as the International Organization of Securities Commissions (IOSCO) and the Council of Securities Regulators of the Americas (COSRA) seem fundamental. Furthermore, Latin American and Caribbean capital markets must establish and maintain technological capabilities that facilitate cross-border transactions, such as electronic trading platforms and efficient and uniform clearance and settlement systems (Dowers, Gomez-Acebo, and Masci 2000).

Because investors seek the lowest-cost and most liquid markets, in implementing measures toward integration, governments should take action to preserve the viability of the national market and, in particular, foster local institutional investors. Local asset managers are best able to facilitate local financing through their knowledge of the language and markets. A foreign portfolio manager might not understand the implications of a piece of market information and respond wrongly. For this reason, to attract investors to a national market and develop a local institutional base, the market must be made more attractive. One way to do this is to develop the corporate bond market as described above to allow pension fund assets to broaden their investment base beyond government securities. Rather than being based on a desire for diversification, an investor's decision to invest in bonds is typically based on interest and exchange rates and therefore is more likely to be made in the local market (Gaa and others 2001).

Small and Medium Enterprises

Integration may be a concern for SMEs that are unable to obtain financing abroad. SMEs voiced a similar concern at the initiation of integration of the European Union, although they appear to have benefited from integration developments in the European Union. One way to create a financing mechanism for SMEs would be to tap the capital reserves of banks, which play an important role in the economies of Latin America and the Caribbean. To encourage banks to lend to SMEs, a program similar to the U.S. SBIC program could be adopted under which banks would set up separate units to lend money. An alternative would be to minimize the costs associated with listing to new and smaller firms, such as occurs on the NASDAQ market and more recent similar markets, such as the Italian Nuovo Mercato, German Neuer Markt, and Brazilian Novo Mercado.[13] Given the importance of SMEs in Latin America and the Caribbean, this measure is associated with high development impact.

---

[13] See Takacs and Korcsmaros (this volume) for more on these markets.

A Regulatory Framework Based on the Prudent Investor Rule

Regulatory restrictions on the composition of pension funds should be gradually eliminated to allow portfolio managers the flexibility to make innovative investment decisions, create new products, and diversify their portfolios to allow greater risk taking.
However, because Latin America and the Caribbean does not have an established fiduciary culture and enforcement resources are limited, certain regulatory protections
need to remain in place to establish investor confidence in the sector. For example,
when regulations are loosened, disclosure requirements become increasingly important as a means for clients to monitor fiduciary activities (Frankel 1995). Information
material to investors' decisions, such as financial status and past performance, is one
of the most important means of promoting market integrity, transparency, and sector
confidence.

Investors must be able to rely on reported financial information. If investors
cannot distinguish between accurate and inaccurate financial information, they will discount all reported information. Because delivering information to investors is easy, but
delivering credible information is hard, financial statements must be certified by independent external auditors who, as intermediaries of information, place their reputations on the line (Black 2001).

Many countries in the region have recognized the necessity of adopting high
standards of accounting and auditing of internationally acceptable quality. Continued
commitment to these high standards of reporting and disclosure is critical to the
growth of the institutional investor sector and capital markets overall.

Governments must make a commitment to regulatory reform in the area of
entrenched collective interests. Entrenchment practices not only hurt market integrity,
but also discourage local professionals within the sector from developing portfolio
management skills, thereby increasing the sector's dependence on foreign expertise.
As markets develop and transparency and competition increase, institutional investors
will realize that adherence to fiduciary obligations and trust are of value to clients, and
the demand for these services will dictate the institutional market.

Good Corporate Governance

There is no single model of good corporate governance. Governance systems are affected by factors such as the larger economic context and the legal, regulatory, and
institutional environment (OECD 1999). However, in general, good corporate governance requires an examination of company structure to ensure that conflicts of in-

terest are either disclosed or prohibited and that shareholder costs are clearly and accurately disclosed. For example, in the mutual fund sector, the role of the fund sponsor should be separated from that of the portfolio manager and members, and certain members of the board of directors of the fund should act independently, free of conflicts with the underlying company.

To encourage institutions to act on behalf of their beneficiaries when participating in proxy voting, policymakers in Latin America and the Caribbean should develop and implement corporate governance systems in line with the principles outlined by the OECD, which include the protection of shareholders' rights, the equitable treatment of shareholders, the rights of stakeholders, the responsibilities of the board, and disclosure and transparency. Recent developments suggest that corporate governance has become a higher priority than it was in the past for policymakers in the region. In 2000, for example, Mexico published the Mexican Code of Best Corporate Practices, which appears to be fully consistent with these principles (Consejo Coordinador Empresarial 2000).

Investor Education Programs

Latin America and the Caribbean lacks a pervasive investment culture oriented toward domestic capital markets, and it has no tradition of looking to these markets as a viable source of financing. With fundamental investor protections in place, investors must become informed of the benefits and risks associated with committing their funds, particularly long-term funds, in the domestic capital market. To meet their investment goals, investors in the region must become better able to evaluate the information they receive so that they may make informed decisions. Moreover, knowledgeable investors are better able to detect securities fraud and may further a culture of compliance within the industry by investing only with firms that provide ethical services. Efforts toward investor education must come from both regulatory and industry initiatives, such as sector trade associations, that recognize that markets exist by the grace of investors.

Conclusion

In examining the development of the domestic institutional investor sector in the United States and other countries, it is clear that certain common elements contributed to sector growth. Favorable economic conditions, increasing need for retirement support, tax incentives, and investor confidence through regulation created demand for institutional investment products. To fulfill this demand, institutional investors required a sufficient capital base to support their growth and create capital market liquidity. Because the United States is a large, fully integrated economy, institutions do not face costly interstate barriers in distributing their shares and investing their assets. Similarly, market integration efforts in the European Union have resulted in benefits to its members' institutional sectors. Technological developments, deregulation, effective corporate governance, competition, and the ability to diversify and innovate have helped to increase the supply of available capital. Because pension funds are the largest institutional investors in OECD economies, an overriding element in institutional investor growth is pension-related reforms, particularly the movement from pay-as-you-go to defined-contribution systems.

In Latin American and Caribbean economies, many of the factors that spurred domestic sector growth in the United States and other OECD countries are not present or are not yet effective. One reason is that macroeconomic instability has adversely affected investor confidence in the markets as savings vehicles. Although Latin American and Caribbean countries have stimulated demand for a domestic institutional sector through government efforts, such as pension reforms, the sector remains underdeveloped primarily because of a lack of investible capital and correspondingly illiquid securities markets. However, since the majority of pension reform was relatively recent, benefits may not yet have been realized. Regulatory frameworks throughout the region are too rigid or fragmented to allow for the innovation and competition required to spur institutional investor growth. Corporate governance frameworks also remain weak.

Institutional investors can have a tremendous impact on the growth and structure of capital markets. Latin America and the Caribbean should focus on this key area to further local market development. As alternatives to commercial banks, institutions can channel savings into the markets to provide an additional source of capital financing. Institutions also provide necessary liquidity to allow for transparency, valuation, and, as a result, further market growth. Institutions promote market stability by providing liquidity, long-term investment, and corporate monitoring and by encouraging market modernization and innovation. In addition, institutions in Latin America and the Caribbean may promote the competitiveness of local markets and issuers.

Through long-term government commitment to macroeconomic reforms and the creation of a regional integrated market, the countries of Latin America and the Caribbean may further develop their domestic institutional sectors. To ensure the availability of local capital for SMEs, governments should maintain a local institutional investor base and healthy capital markets. To facilitate the movement of savings into the capital markets, a balanced regulatory framework must provide investor protections to increase demand for investment products. As liquidity and transparency increase, some regulations may be slowly relaxed to allow innovation and competition. It will be crucial to implement high standards of disclosure, fiduciary obligations, and investor protections provided through a strong corporate governance framework and investor education.

Although each of the factors discussed can play a role in the development of institutional investors and capital markets, ultimately, their development is a dynamic process. Policymakers must be committed to continually seeking to modernize the regulatory framework to address the needs of investors and the industry.

Bibliography

Asociación de Supervisores de Seguros de América Latina (ASSAL). 2001. *Annual Statistical Yearbook.* Santiago, Chile, http://www.assalweb.org/english/html/anuario/fr_anuario.html.

Associación de Fondos Mútuos (AFM). 2002. Country Report: Peru. http://www.fefsi.org/.

Black, Bernard S. 2001. The Legal and Institutional Preconditions for Strong Securities Markets. *UCLA Law Review* 48:781.

Blommestein, Hans J. 1997. Institutional Investors, Pension Reform, and Emerging Securities Markets. Paper for presentation at the IDB Conference on the Development of Securities Markets in Emerging Markets: Obstacles and Pre-Conditions for Success. Office of the Chief Economist, Working Paper 359. Inter-American Development Bank, Washington, D.C.

Bolsa de Santiago. 2001. *Data presented at the U.S. Securities and Exchange Commission.* International Institute for Securities Market Development. Washington, D.C., April 23–May 4.

Canute, James. 2002. New Market Aims to Deliver Island Vision: Caribbean Securities Exchange Opens with Two Stocks, but Has High Hopes. *Financial Times* (London), January 2, p. 17.

Coffee, John. 1991. Liquidity versus Control: The Institutional Investor as Corporate Monitor. *Columbia Law Review* 91:1277.

Conference Board, Inc. 2000. *The Institutional Investment Report* (formerly *The Brancato Report*). New York: The Conference Board, Inc.

Consejo Coordinador Empresarial. 2000. *The Mexican Code of Best Corporate Practices.* September 21, http://www.cce.org.mx/publicaciones/varios/corporativas.pdf.

Coutinho, Luciano, and Flavio Marcilio Rabelo. 2001. Corporate Governance in Brazil. Paper presented at the Policy Dialogue Meeting on Corporate Governance in Developing Countries and Emerging Economies. OECD Development Centre and the European Bank for Reconstruction and Development, Paris, April 23–24.

Demarigny, Fabrice. 2000. One Year After the Euro: What Type of Regulation for the European Financial Market? *Futures and Derivatives Law Report* 19(10, January):11.

Dowers, Kenroy, Felipe Gomez-Acebo, and Pietro Masci. 2000. Making Capital Markets Viable in Latin America and the Caribbean. *Inter-American Development Bank Review* 3, (December).

Eisenberg, Meyer. 2001. Establishing Corporate Governance in Emerging Markets. Presented at the U.S. Securities and Exchange Commission International Institute for Securities Market Development, Washington, D.C., May 2.

Federación Internacional de Administradoras de Fondos de Pensiones (FIAP). 2002. http://www.fiap.cl/.

Fédération Européenne des Fonds et Sociétés d'Investissement (FEFSI). 2002. Brazil Country Report. http://www.fefsi.org/.

Frankel, Tamar. 1995. Fiduciary Duties as Default Rules. *Oregon Law Review* 74:1209.

Gaa, Charles, Robert Ogrodnick, Peter Thurlow, and Stephen A. Lumpkin. 2001. Future Prospects for National Financial Markets and Trading Centers. *Financial Market Trends* (OECD) 78(1, March):37–72.

Gilson, Ronald. 2000. Transparency, Corporate Governance, and Capital Markets. Paper presented at the Latin American Corporate Governance Roundtable. Sponsored by the São Paulo Stock Exchange, São Paulo, Brazil, April 26–28, http://www.oecd.org/pdf/M00001500/M00015375.pdf.

Greenough, William C., and Francis P. King. 1976. *Pension Plans and Public Policy.* New York: Columbia University Press.

Gremillion, Lee. 2000. *A Purely American Invention, The U.S. Open-End Mutual Fund Industry*. Wellesley Hills, Mass.: The National Investment Company Service Association.

Inter-American Development Bank (IDB). 1998. Financial Market Development: Issues, Strategies, and Inter-American Development Bank Group Activities. Sustainable Development Department, Inter-American Development Bank, Washington, D.C., March.

International Monetary Fund (IMF). 2001. *Mexico: Financial System Stability Assessment*. IMF Country Report 01/192. International Monetary Fund, Washington, D.C., October.

International Organization of Securities Commissions (IOSCO). 1998. *Objectives and Principles of Securities Regulation*. IOSCO Public Document 82. September.

Investment Company Institute (ICI). 2001. *Mutual Fund Fact Book*. Washington, D.C.: Investment Company Institute.

Kaminsky, Graciela, Richard Lyons, and Sergio Schmukler. 2000. Mutual Fund Investment in Emerging Markets: An Overview. Working Paper 2529. World Bank, Washington, D.C.

Kyu-sung, Lee. 2000. The Importance of Corporate Governance. *The Korea Herald*. May 13.

La Porta, Rafael, Florencio Lopez-de-Silanes, Andrei Shleifer, and Robert W. Vishny. 1997. Legal Determinants of External Finance. *Journal of Finance* 52:1131–50.

Lamfalussy Group. 2001. Final Report of the Committee of Wise Men on the Regulation of European Securities Markets. Lamfalussy Group, Brussels, February 15.

Levine, Ross. 1997. Stock Markets, Economic Development, and Capital Control Liberalization. *Investment Company Institute Perspective* 3(5, December):1–7. http://www.ici.org/pdf/per03-05.pdf.

Lubrano, Mike. 2001. Corporate Governance: An International and Mexican Perspective. *United States-Mexico Law Journal* 9(Spring):117–22.

Munnell, Alicia H. 1982. *The Economics of Private Pensions*. Washington, D.C.: Brookings Institution.

Norman, Peter. 2001. EU in Pact on Harmonized Fund Regulation. *Financial Times* (London), March 2, p. 2.

Organisation for Economic Co-operation and Development (OECD). 1999. *Principles of Corporate Governance*. Paris: OECD, April 16. http://www.oecd.org (under "corporate governance").

———. 2000. *Institutional Investors Statistical Yearbook*. Paris: OECD.

Poser, Norman S. 1991. *International Securities Regulation: London's "Big Bang" and the European Securities Markets*. Boston, Mass.: Little, Brown and Company.

Rea, John. 1996. U.S. Emerging Market Funds: Hot Money or Stable Source of Investment Capital? *Investment Company Institute Perspective* 2(6, December):1–14. http://www.ici.org/pdf/per02-06.pdf.

Rea, John, and Richard Marcis. 1996. Mutual Fund Shareholder Activity during U.S. Stock Market Cycles, 1944–95. *Investment Company Institute Perspective* 2(2, March):1–16. http://www.ici.org/pdf/per02-02.pdf.

Reid, Brian. 2000. The 1990s: A Decade of Expansion and Change in the U.S. Mutual Fund Industry. *Investment Company Institute Perspective* 6(3, July):1–20.

Rojas-Suárez, Liliana, and Steven Wiesbrod. 1996. Building Stability in Latin American Financial Markets. Working Paper 320. Inter-American Development Bank, Washington, D.C., February.

Schmidt-Hebbel, Klaus. 1999. *Latin America's Pension Revolution: A Review of Approaches and Experience*. Prepared for the Annual Bank Conference on Development Economics, World Bank, Washington, D.C., April 28–30.

Securities Industry Association (SIA). 2000. *Securities Industry Fact Book*. New York.

Standard & Poor's (S&P). 2001a. *Emerging Markets Factbook*. New York: MacGraw-Hill.

———. 2001b. *Five Markets Dominate Developing Latin American Insurance Industry*. New York, July 25.

Strahota, Robert D. 1996. Securities Regulation in Emerging Markets: Some Issues and Suggested Answers. Paper prepared for the U.S. Securities and Exchange Commission, International Institute for Securities Market Development, Washington, D.C., April 29.

U.S. Securities and Exchange Commission (SEC). 1938–40. *Investment Trusts and Investment Companies. Report of the Securities and Exchange Commission to Congress Pursuant to Section 30 of the Public Utility Holding Company Act of 1935*, Washington, D.C.

———. 1971. *Institutional Investor Study*. 92d Congress, 1st Session, House Document 92-64. Washington, D.C., March 10.

_____. 1992. *Protecting Investors: A Half-Century of Investment Company Regulation.* Division of Investment Management, U.S. Securities and Exchange Commission, Washington, D.C., May.

_____. 1994. *Market 2000: An Examination of Current Equity Market Developments.* Division of Market Regulation, U.S. Securities and Exchange Commission, Washington, D.C., January.

U.S. Senate Finance Committee. 1973. The Role of Institutional Investors in the Stock Market (Briefing Material prepared by Staff for the Use of the Subcommittee on Financial Markets). U.S. Senate Finance Committee, Washington, D.C., July 24.

Uthoff, Andras. 2000. Pension Reform in Chile. In Larry Sawers, Daniel Schydlowsky, and David Nickerson (eds.), *Emerging Financial Markets in the Global Economy.* World Scientific Publishing Co. http://www.wspc.com.sg/books/economics/4076. html.

Vittas, Dimitri. 1996. *Pension Funds and Capital Markets: Investment Regulation, Financial Innovation, and Governance. Public Policy for the Private Sector.* Viewpoint Note 71. Washington, D.C.: World Bank.

_____. 1998. Institutional Investors and Securities Markets: Which Comes First? Paper presented at the Annual Bank Conference on Development Economics, Latin America and the Caribbean. World Bank, San Salvador, El Salvador, June 28–30.

Vives, Antonio. 1999. Pension Funds in Infrastructure Project Finance: Regulations and Instrument Design. Sustainable Development Department Technical Paper Series IFM-119. Infrastructure and Financial Markets, Inter-American Development Bank, Washington, D.C.

World Bank. 2001. *World Development Indicators.* Washington, D.C.: World Bank.

World Bank and the Caribbean Centre for Monetary Studies (CGCED). 1998. *Wider Caribbean Financial Sector Review, Increasing Competitiveness and Financial Resource Management for Economic Growth.* FY98 Agenda Report. Washington, D.C.: World Bank.

Yermo, Juan. 2000. Institutional Investors in Latin America: Recent Trends and Regulatory Challenges. *Institutional Investors in Latin America,* pp. 23–119 Paris: OECD.

Zurstrassen, Patrick. 1998. The European Investment Funds Industry in 1997. *Institutional Investors in the New Financial Landscape.* Paris: OECD.

PART III

ISSUES IN THE IMPLEMENTATION OF CAPITAL MARKET STRATEGIES

CHAPTER 6

Promoting Regional Capital Market Integration

Ruben Lee

The term integration in the context of the capital markets has been used to mean different things. It can refer to an environment where (1) identical securities are traded at essentially the same price across the markets in a region after adjustment for foreign exchange rates (Wellons 1997); (2) investors can buy and sell securities in the region's markets without restriction (Lemmen 1998); (3) all types of participants in the capital markets can offer their services throughout the region without restriction; or (4) capital markets are not fragmented, a term that itself is full of ambiguity (Lee 1999). These four attributes of an environment are closely linked, but not identical. This report focuses on the first and third. The first stresses that in an integrated market, the costs of trading should be the same throughout the region and implicitly as low as possible. The third attribute emphasizes that there should be no restrictions stopping market participants from undertaking their business activities wherever they wish in a region.

Although the phrase "regional capital market integration" implies the need for some form of cooperation between market participants or jurisdictions, it does not require it. Indeed, as will be discussed, competition both between market participants and between regulatory regimes can have an enormously positive effect on bringing about such integration. The term region is used here loosely to refer to a set of nations bound by trade or other links or to a single nation with a federal system that allows its states, provinces, or other subnational jurisdictions to pursue different laws and policies (Wellons 1997).

There are several reasons why the capital markets are currently in a state of rapid change, including the following:

- Consolidation and globalization among capital market participants, especially investment banks and issuers, but progressively investors and exchanges

- Intense competition between all types of capital market participants, including exchanges, new trading mechanisms, investment banks, brokers, issuers, and investors
- Increased demand for capital market instruments at the retail and institutional levels and for equities and bonds
- The growing importance of funded and private pension schemes as a result of demographic trends in many of the developed markets
- The move from national to sector allocation of investments, spurred in Europe by the introduction of the euro
- Increased supply of capital by companies on a borderless basis, partly as a result of large privatization schemes and partly by new entrepreneurial companies
- The demutualization of exchanges into for-profit companies
- Rapid technological advancement, including the Internet, e-business, wireless technology, and new software for market participants
- A desire to price explicitly the risks of trading and, if possible, to reduce them
- Deregulation and liberalization in some of the world's capital markets.

These trends are creating intense pressures on all markets, including emerging ones, to lower cross-border transaction costs of all types, to allow market participants to deliver services across borders, and to reduce all the many forms of risks inherent in the international trading process. Although it is possible to further all these goals at the domestic level, the potential gains of doing so at the regional level are significantly larger. Therefore, the advancement of regional capital market integration has become widely perceived as critically important, and not just by market participants. Interest in promoting regional capital market integration has been taken up at the highest political levels, most evidently by the economics and finance ministers in the European Union.

If the gains of capital market integration are larger at the regional level than at the domestic level, would they not be correspondingly larger at the global level? Although this chapter does not provide a broad answer to this question, two partial responses may be given. First, if global integration were better than regional integration, one way of reaching the global goal would be through a series of regional goals. Second, many of the activities that promote regional capital market integration are simply infeasible right now at the global level.

The chapter presents some practical recommendations for enhancing regional capital market integration. It concentrates on the equity markets and not debt markets;

however, many of the issues relevant for regional integration of the equity markets are also relevant for regional integration of the debt markets. Finally, many attempts at achieving regional capital market integration have not been well documented, so much of the information that is available comes from secondary sources.

Benefits, Costs, and Barriers

The European Union has made the most extended and extensive examination of the costs and benefits of and barriers to regional capital market integration. Following its initial report in 1966, the European Commission has issued a report every 10 years or so, focusing on the merits of regional capital market integration and on how it can be achieved.[1]

On July 17, 2000, for the first time, the issue changed from one that was primarily of concern to European bureaucrats to one that was seen as critically important at the highest political level, namely by the economic and finance ministers of the European Union. On that date, they established a "Committee of Wise Men" to determine why the capital markets in Europe were not yet integrated and what to do in order to achieve this (Committee of Wise Men 2000). The committee was established because it was recognized both that there were significant impediments limiting the integration of the European capital markets and that great gains could be achieved by such integration.

Benefits and Costs

The integration of a region's capital markets should lead to several benefits. Integration should lower prices for all financial services because competition lowers transaction costs and allows larger regional firms to exploit economies of scale and scope. These effects will be evident in all forms of intermediation, investment, and other capital market activities. More efficient, more liquid, and broader securities markets will likely have increased turnover. Integration will generate innovative financial products and services. All sectors of the capital markets industry will undergo an industrial transformation. Integration will provide cheaper financing for companies, given lower transaction costs. Capital will be allocated more efficiently because savings will flow

---

[1] See European Economic Community Commission (1966); Commission of the European Communities (1977, 1978, 1980, 1988); Commission of the European Union (1999).

more easily and cheaply to investment, and barriers to investment will be dismantled. Lower transaction costs will imply higher returns on investments. Investors who previously faced restricted opportunities will be able to diversify their investments to a greater extent and take advantage of enhanced risk-return frontiers. The improved macroeconomic performance of the region's economy will produce higher economic growth, with positive effects on employment and productivity, possibly resulting in more inward investment. Higher returns should also lower pension costs, with an attendant reduction in labor costs and enhancement of competitiveness. These benefits should obtain broad political support because they should be widely shared by the region's citizens, small and medium-size businesses, and large companies.

However, regional capital market integration may also lead to a number of costs. For example, protected industries will lose out and will lobby hard to resist the effects of regional capital market integration. Some individual companies will lose out if they prove not to be competitive in the integrated market. Furthermore, transition costs may have to be borne by some market participants; for example, there may be large unanticipated regulatory costs. Finally, regional integration may lead to unanticipated protectionism if the process is captured by vested interests.

A Positive Example: Competition between European Stock Exchanges

Integration of the capital markets has had dramatic and positive effects on competition between national stock exchanges in Europe since 1986. This integration has sharply reduced the costs of trading, enhanced the quality and quantity of services offered by exchanges, and increased the number and diversity of trading mechanisms available to market participants. Pagano (1997) provides a good summary of this integration process.[2]

Until 1985, European equity markets still worked according to a blueprint laid out in the 19th century. Continental Europe featured call auction markets with open outcry dealing, where publicly licensed, single-capacity intermediaries conveyed the orders of their customers and were compensated via statutorily fixed commissions. In London, dealers, called "jobbers," who received the customers' orders via single-capacity brokers, managed stock trading, and the members of the exchange fixed commissions. In all countries, stock exchanges were closed-membership organizations,

---

[2] The next four paragraphs are copied with permission, and also some small amendments, from Pagano (1997). See also Pagano and Roëll (1990).

with high barriers to potential entrants. Each exchange operated in isolation from the others, sheltered from competition by national regulations and especially by barriers to capital mobility and high costs of telecommunication.

These obstacles started to wither away in the mid-1980s. European integration led to increasing capital mobility, and technology made telecommunications cheaper and more effective. At the same time, institutional investors stepped up their participation in international equity markets, and their hunger for international diversification led to a rapid increase in cross-border trading. In the past decade, the microstructure of European equity markets has changed dramatically. Trading costs have been reduced, and the variety of trading mechanisms has increased substantially. Most European blue chip stocks are now simultaneously traded in continuous auction (or order-driven) systems and in dealer (or quote-driven) markets, not to mention the hybrid systems that have emerged in some exchanges. The pressure on trading costs and the proliferation of alternative trading mechanisms are both due to an unprecedented wave of competition among European exchanges.

In this ongoing competitive struggle, the balance between contending forces has shifted considerably. The London exchange, which started the competition with the inception of the SEAQ International (SEAQ-I) quote-driven trading system in 1986, was initially able to attract large trading volumes from continental exchanges. In the late 1980s, London appeared to be on its way to becoming the main marketplace for all the blue chip European stocks. But in those same years, the main continental exchanges underwent a radical restructuring of their trading mechanisms and regulations, introducing continuous, electronic order-driven systems, liberalizing access to their membership, and reducing transaction taxes. This strategy allowed them to stage a formidable comeback in the early 1990s. The London dealers' share of trading volume in continental stocks declined considerably. And even the London market for British stocks began to face the competitive pressure of order-driven trading systems, such as the London-based Tradepoint system, modeled on the continental electronic auction markets, and EUROCAC, a new segment of the French Bourse specializing in British and other continental stocks. As a result, after much controversy, the London Stock Exchange replaced its quote-driven SEAQ system with an order-driven system similar to those used in continental exchanges, while retaining its traditional dealer market for large trades.

The proliferation of trading systems offers investors greater variety in the modes of execution of their orders and exerts competitive pressure on trading costs. The wider choice is beneficial for all types of investors. Auction markets offer cheap execution to investors who want to trade small amounts, as well as to large traders who are willing to wait for their orders to be executed gradually. Direct access by institutional investors to the limit order books of electronic markets is becoming more widespread. Dealer markets are increasingly confined to providing immediate execution to block traders who need protection against execution risk. The lower trading costs also benefit issuing companies, since the reduction in trading costs is reflected in higher issue prices for equities, and hence in a reduced cost of equity capital for public companies. This has induced more companies to go public, including new entrepreneurial companies. Pagano (1997) worries that the adverse effects of fragmentation and a lack of transparency might reduce these benefits to some extent. However, his concerns have been disputed.[3]

The Relationship between Financial Markets and Growth

There is a growing body of academic work that shows a positive relationship between the development of financial markets and growth, as discussed by the Committee of Wise Men (2000). To the extent that regional capital market integration furthers growth in financial markets, it may therefore spur economic growth.

Levine (1997) studies the relationship between financial development and economic growth and concludes that most theoretical reasoning and empirical evidence indicate that development of the financial system plays an important role in the growth process. This contrasts with the view that the financial system is essentially irrelevant to economic growth and industrialization. Levine also argues that there is even evidence that the level of financial development is a good predictor of future rates of economic growth, capital accumulation, and technological change. Moreover, cross-country, case study, industry-level, and firm-level analyses document extensive periods when financial development (or lack of it) affects the speed and pattern of economic development. Levine notes that theory suggests that financial instruments, markets, and institutions arise to mitigate the effects of information and transaction costs. How well financial systems reduce information and transaction costs positively influences savings rates, investment decisions, technological innovation, and long-run growth rates.

Levine, Loayza, and Beck (2000) evaluate the nature of the effect of financial intermediary development on economic growth. The econometric approaches they

---

[3] For discussions of fragmentation, see Cohen and others (1986, ch. 8), Lee (1999, ch. 13), Schwartz (1988, ch. 9), Schwartz (1991), and U.S. SEC (1994).

employ confirm the same fact, namely that the exogenous component of financial intermediary development is positively associated with economic growth. The authors provide evidence that cross-country differences in the legal rights of creditors, the efficiency of contract enforcement, and accounting system standards help explain cross-country differences in the level of financial intermediary development, which in turn positively affects economic growth.

Beck, Levine, and Loayza (2000) study the effects of financial development on economic growth and the sources of economic growth. They focus on how development of financial intermediaries influences savings rates, physical capital accumulation, and total factor productivity growth. Their findings do not confirm a relationship between financial intermediary development and either physical capital accumulation or private savings rates. However, the findings indicate a significant positive link between financial intermediary development and growth in both real per capita gross domestic product and total factor productivity.

Levine and Zervos (1996) investigate the empirical link between stock market development and long-run growth. Their data suggest that stock market development is positively associated with economic growth. Moreover, instrumental variable procedures indicate a strong connection between the predetermined component of stock market development and economic growth in the long run. Levine and Zervos (1998) investigate whether well-functioning stock markets promote long-run economic growth. They study whether measures of stock market liquidity—including size, volatility, and integration with world capital markets—are correlated with current and future rates of economic growth, capital accumulation, productivity improvements, and savings rates. They find evidence that stock market liquidity, as measured both by the value of stock trading relative to the size of the market and by the value of trading relative to the size of the economy, is positively and significantly correlated with current and future rates of economic growth, capital accumulation, and productivity growth.

Rajan and Zingales (1998) examine whether financial development facilitates economic growth by scrutinizing one rationale for such a relationship, namely that financial development reduces the costs of external finance to firms. They study whether industrial sectors that are relatively more in need of external finance develop disproportionately faster in countries with more developed financial markets and find this to be true in a large sample of countries in the 1980s. The results suggest that financial development may play a beneficial role in the development of new firms and that the existence of a well-developed financial market may be a source of comparative advantage for a country or region with industries that are more dependent on external finance.

Barriers

A wide array of barriers may hinder regional capital market integration. Such barriers include the following:

- Currency convertibility
- Domestic or regional monopolistic or oligopolistic practices
- Multiple regulators
- Legislative and regulatory impediments
- High transaction costs
- Taxation
- Accounting differences
- Lack of information
- History and culture.

Law and Regulation

Compared with local legislators and regulators, can regional legislative and regulatory initiatives better promote regional capital market integration? The reason for phrasing the question in this manner is to highlight the fact that, contrary to common belief, many regional initiatives have significant costs associated with them, as well as potential benefits. In order to assess the merits of a proposed regional initiative, it is vital to assess both its anticipated costs as well as its proposed benefits.

At the broadest level, regional legislative and regulatory initiatives normally seek to enhance the delivery of the three key objectives of regulation, as identified by the International Organization of Securities Commissions (IOSCO), namely protecting investors; ensuring that markets are fair, efficient, and transparent; and reducing systemic risk (IOSCO 1998). Delivery of these objectives may be improved in three important ways. The first is by lowering the direct costs of operating multiple regulators that market participants bear. The second is by reducing the indirect costs that multiple regulators impose on market participants by dint of the fact that they have to comply with many different regulatory regimes. The third is by enhancing competition at a regional level between the various types of participants in the capital markets, most importantly by reducing barriers to such competition.

This section discusses the costs and benefits of four types of legislative and regulatory initiatives aimed at promoting regional capital market integration: sharing information between the regulators of different jurisdictions in a region; harmonizing

regulation between jurisdictions; establishing a system of mutual reliance between regulators in a region; and creating a legal environment in which mutual recognition between regulators, and home country control, is accepted and enforced. Each of these
four initiatives is progressively more ambitious than the last in terms of its anticipated
benefits, and each has potentially more costs associated with it.

Information Sharing

One area where regulators have sought to cooperate at a regional level is in sharing
information about both surveillance and enforcement actions against market participants and in resolving crises in a market or at a particular firm. Information-sharing
arrangements may be especially valuable in examining a firm or market that operates
in more than one jurisdiction.

     Typically, regulatory information-sharing arrangements do not have any formal
legal backing; they are established via a memorandum of understanding (MOU) that
specifies the types of information the participating regulators are willing to share and
the circumstances in which they will do so. The IOSCO has prepared guidelines on the
types of core information that market authorities may need to obtain and should be
prepared to share during periods of crisis in markets or firms (IOSCO 1997).

     However, the existence of an information-sharing MOU between regulators
does not mean that appropriate information will actually be shared (Lee 1993). The
effectiveness of MOUs in general, and of information sharing in particular, depends on
the extent to which the parties to such agreements are willing to work together. If
the aims of the regulators are congruent, then both institutions are likely to comply
with the agreement. The pursuit of fraud, for example, is likely to be a key goal of many
regulators. However, if the exchange of information would impinge on other objectives of one or more of the regulators, the effectiveness of the MOU could be in
doubt. This may, for example, be a problem when there is competition between different national markets. A regulatory agency in one jurisdiction could believe that
handing over certain information to a regulatory agency in another jurisdiction might
harm the prospects of the financial center. In such circumstances, it is debatable
whether an MOU, if one had been signed, would make any difference as to whether
the information were released by the first regulator.

Harmonization and Mutual Reliance

A conceptually simple way of reducing the costs that arise when jurisdictions have different regulations—and when capital market participants operating across boundaries

have to comply with many jurisdictions' regulations—is to harmonize the regulations across jurisdictions. Any organization operating across jurisdictions—be it an issuer, investor, intermediary, or exchange—should thereby incur lower regulatory costs in complying with harmonized regulations than if it had to comply with different regulations across jurisdictions.

Canada is an example of a set of jurisdictions that is promoting regulatory harmonization.[4] Securities regulation in Canada falls within the jurisdiction of the provinces and territories, rather than being a federal matter. Each province and territory has its own securities regulator, and there are 13 regulators operating with differing sets of rules and policies. This regulatory fragmentation is inefficient and costly for market participants, as they have to deal with the differences between jurisdictions.

Many capital market participants in Canada believe that transforming all the provincial securities' and territories' regulators into a single national securities commission would produce a more cost-efficient and effective system of regulation than the current fragmented one. However, nearly all accept that it would be politically unrealistic to do so, following three failed attempts over the past three decades. Instead, the securities regulators have sought to create a virtual national securities commission, which has been defined as a system of securities regulation administered by the various jurisdictions in such a way that the public is offered a level of efficiency and consistency that might be expected of administration by a single jurisdiction. The Canadian virtual securities commission is being developed via an informal body composed of the entire provincial and territorial securities regulators. The aim of the Canadian Securities Administrators (CSA) is precisely to harmonize legislation, regulatory standards, and policies and to coordinate the activities of the capital market regulatory authorities in the various jurisdictions.

In addition to this harmonization, the CSA is constructing a regulatory framework based on mutual reliance between provincial and territorial regulators. Mutual reliance, in this context, means that when a market participant, such as an issuer or a registrant, needs a regulatory response from more than one jurisdiction, participating commissions are willing to rely on the analysis and recommendations made by the staff of commissions in other provinces. For example, if a company wishes to issue securities in more than one jurisdiction in Canada, the issuer need deal with only one principal regulator, usually the one in the jurisdiction where the company is located. That securities commission analyzes the prospectus, provides comments to the issuer,

---

[4] The discussion about Canada draws heavily on Brown (1999) and McGlaughlin (2000).

and makes appropriate recommendations. The participating securities commissions of the other jurisdictions then agree that they will accept and rely on the recommendations of the commission in the principal jurisdiction. It should be stressed, however, that in this mutual reliance framework, each participating regulator retains the ultimate power and responsibility for regulatory decisions in its jurisdiction.

A similar initiative in the European Union that has sought to enhance the harmonization of regulatory regimes in different jurisdictions is the Forum of European Securities Commissions (FESCO), a body composed of the regulatory authorities in the European Economic Area.[5] It seeks to develop standards that complement the legal framework established by the European Directives or that cover areas where no European law exists. Each FESCO member is committed to implementing these standards in its home jurisdiction. The key areas where FESCO hopes to contribute to greater regional cooperation are in surveillance and enforcement.

The intended benefits of both the CSA and FESCO are similar. They can reduce duplication of effort, free resources for other regulatory matters, enhance consistency of analysis and decisions, and simplify and speed up regulatory rulings. They also have the strength of the participation of all the regulators in their respective regions—including some that have traditionally been sensitive to issues of jurisdiction—and the flexibility to respond to local sensitivities.

Both the CSA and FESCO face similar problems. Both work by consensus, which means that the harmonization of policies and rules takes a long time. The consensual process also means that individual jurisdictions may be able to insist on anticompetitive harmonized rules in order to protect their national interests. Both bodies lack legal powers of enforcement, and their recommendations are not binding. The implementation of decisions in the different jurisdictions depends on the regulatory powers granted to each respective regulator, and these differ widely. Other relevant areas of law and policy vary between local jurisdictions, and these can limit the effectiveness of the regulatory harmonization achieved. There is still a regulator in each local or national jurisdiction in the region, which has to be paid for by market participants. Finally, and most importantly, harmonization is unnecessary if mutual recognition and home country (or jurisdiction) control are implemented. This is because mutual recognition and home country control mean that individual firms only have to comply with the single regulatory structure in their home country; thus, there is no need to lower the costs of having to comply with multiple regulators by harmonization.

---

[5] See FESCO at http://www.europefesco.org/.

Mutual Recognition and Home Country Control

The most ambitious legislative and regulatory approach that has been used to promote regional capital market integration has been the combined use of minimum harmonization, mutual recognition, and home country control, developed in the European Union. The central goal of this program is simple, but also powerful: to enhance competition in the European Union's regional capital market by allowing market participants from any single country in the European Union to offer their services throughout the European Union and to do so with only a single regulatory authorization from their home country. Given the importance of the European Union's legislative structure governing the capital markets as a potential model for Latin America and the Caribbean, three aspects of it are outlined here: the primary legal foundation supporting the approach, some secondary pieces of legislation implementing it, and a range of problems to which it has given rise.

Legal Foundation[6]

The legal foundation for the European Union is laid out in the Treaty of Rome, which establishes the fundamental European freedoms of movement and of establishment.[7] The freedom of movement of services gives nationals who are established in one country (or member state) the right to provide services in other member states. The freedom of establishment allows a natural or legal person (namely an individual or a firm) from one member state to set up and manage a firm in another member state, under the conditions for the nationals of the second member state. A third and critical element of the treaty is that competition should not be inhibited in an inappropriate manner. These legal rights can be upheld via judicial review in the European Court. The European legal and judicial structure applies to those European Union countries with a tradition of common law and to those countries with a tradition of civil law.

The freedoms of movement and establishment are not completely without limits. Member states are allowed to impose restrictions on both these freedoms on various grounds, including that of public policy. In addition, the European Court has recognized a series of mandatory requirements that member states may impose in the absence of European Union rules, even if such impositions obstruct the exercise

---

[6] This section draws on Lee (1996).
[7] Treaties Establishing the European Economic Community (Treaty of Rome, 1957).

of the European freedoms.[8] These mandatory requirements include ensuring the effectiveness of fiscal supervision, the fairness of commercial transactions, and the defense of the consumer.

Following the passing of the Single European Act, the Treaty of Rome was amended to mandate the European Commission to draft a program of secondary legislation to bring about what is called the Single Market. The aim of this is to make the European Union "an area without internal frontiers in which the free movement of goods, persons, services and capital is ensured."[9] Although these freedoms were already guaranteed in the original treaty, the Single European Act was passed for several reasons. Among these were that it was believed that reliance on appeals to the European Court to uphold the treaty would be costly, time consuming, and unpredictable and that the many technical and other barriers that were seen as restricting the European freedoms could best be removed by direct secondary legislation.

Secondary Legislation

Although the process by which secondary legislation is passed in the European Union is complicated, certain elements of it have important implications for the nature of the law that is adopted and indeed have critically affected the legislation intended to promote the integration of the European capital markets. The basic and initial elements of the co-decision procedure normally now employed are as follows.

The European Commission initiates secondary legislation, making a proposal to the Council of Ministers of all the member states. The European Parliament then delivers an opinion on the proposal to the council. The council then discusses the proposal, and amendments to it, before voting on it, typically using a qualified majority scheme in which different member states have different numbers of votes, with the larger countries having more votes than the smaller countries. If the proposal is accepted, it is again communicated to the European Parliament, which then votes to accept or reject the proposal. Once a proposal is finally passed into European law, following further European Union institutional procedures, it then has to be transposed or, equivalently, implemented into national law in each of the member states. This means that each member state has to take the European Union proposal and adopt an appropriate form of it via its national parliament into its own law. If a member states does not do this, or does not then follow the law, the European Commission

---

[8] Rewe Zentral AG v. Bundesmonopolverwaltung für Branntwein.
[9] Article 8a, Treaty of Rome (1957).

can ask the European Court to review that member state's actions so as to enforce the European Union legislation.

Three linked strategies have been employed to achieve the Single Market for financial services: the harmonization between member states of the minimum standards for the prudential supervision of financial institutions; the mutual recognition by each member state of the competence of the supervisory bodies in each other member state for the governance of these minimum standards; and the assignment of the supervision of a financial institution to the home country of that financial institution, in those areas that have been harmonized between member states.

These strategies have been used in a wide range of secondary legislation to promote the Single Market for financial services. Among the issues addressed have been the admission of stocks to an official stock exchange quotation;[10] the particulars that should be published for securities admitted to an official stock exchange listing;[11] the contents of public offer prospectuses;[12] the information that companies admitted to an official stock exchange listing should publish on a regular basis;[13] the criteria for determining when the purchase or sale of a major shareholding in a listed company should be disclosed;[14] the standards for pooled investment vehicles, termed undertakings for collective investment in transferable securities;[15] insider dealing;[16] and the minimum capital requirements that banks and securities firms must have in order to obtain a passport to operate their securities trading businesses throughout the European Union.[17] Cooperation between securities regulators for dealing with cross-border practices and trading is only lightly covered by relevant legislation, and the investigative powers of national authorities and sanctions are not defined at the European Union level.

One important piece of secondary legislation in the European Union, the Investment Services Directive (ISD), allows firms that provide investment services, such as broker-dealers, to obtain what is called a European passport. This passport gives investment service firms the right, under certain circumstances, to provide their services without restriction throughout the European Union.[18] The ISD details the conditions under which the three-pronged approaches of minimum harmonization, mu-

---

[10] Council Directives 79/279/EEC and 82/148/EEC.
[11] Council Directives 80/390/EEC, 82/148/EEC, 87/345/EEC, and 90/211/EEC.
[12] Council Directive 89/298/EEC.
[13] Council Directive 82/121/EEC.
[14] Council Directive 88/627/EEC.
[15] Council Directives 85/611/EEC and 88/220/EEC.
[16] Council Directive 89/592/EEC.
[17] Council Directive 93/6/EEC.
[18] Council Directive 93/22/EEC.

tual recognition, and home country control for the provision of investment services are to operate. It specifies how, once an investment firm is appropriately authorized in its home member state, the firm must be allowed to offer its services in all other member states without the need for further authorization. Member states must permit investment firms to become members of, or be given access to, all regulated markets, as defined in the ISD, in their jurisdictions. National restrictions on the number of members of regulated markets must also be eliminated.

The ISD identifies a range of activities denoted as investment services and lays out various criteria that member states' competent authorities must require a firm to satisfy, both in its initial authorization and in its ongoing operations, before the firm can obtain the European passport. These include that the firm's directors be sufficiently experienced; that it have appropriate measures for administrative and accounting procedures for safeguarding clients' securities and funds and for record keeping; that it avoid any conflicts of interest in its operations or that, if such conflicts do arise, it provide for the fair management of them; and that its employees act fairly and honestly.

There are several so-called general good provisions in the ISD that allow a member state to justify the application of national regulations that restrict the fundamental European freedoms. In particular, a member state may justify the establishment of particular rules of conduct for investment firms in the general good, if such rules protect the stability and sound operation of the financial system or if they protect investors. The ISD also allows member states to create restrictive rules governing the form and content of advertising by investment firms, again in the interest of the general good.

In certain circumstances, the ISD allows a member state to require that all trades by residents or established investors be concentrated in a regulated market. If a member state applies the concentration principle, however, it is obliged to give the market participants to whom the principle applies the right not to comply with the principle and thereby to have their transactions executed away from a regulated market. Member states must allow a regulated market from another member state to establish automated trading facilities in their jurisdiction, without any additional regulatory approval other than the recognition the regulated market received in its home member state.

Problems

There are many problems in the European Union's legislative and regulatory structure for the European capital markets, which mean that its intended goals are not being achieved.[19] These problems are not just theoretical. As noted above, they have been deemed so important that the European Union's Council of Economic and Finance Ministers has appointed a so-called Committee of Wise Men with three broad mandates: to assess the current conditions for implementation of the regulation of the securities markets in the European Union; to assess how the mechanism for regulating the securities markets in the European Union can best respond to developments under way on securities markets; and, in order to eliminate barriers and obstacles, to propose scenarios for adapting current practices to ensure greater convergence and cooperation in day-to-day implementation, taking into account new developments in the market. This section discusses five major sets of problems with the European Union's legislative and regulatory structure for European capital markets.

Lack of competition. The underlying goal of the Single Market program in European capital markets is one of economic liberalism: the essence of the freedoms of movement and of establishment is that they are pro-competitive. However, the Single Market program has actually been used to obstruct competition, primarily by national authorities attempting to protect their own financial markets.

This may occur when directives are first being created and passed into law. Many attempts, for example, were made to create in the ISD a legislative tool to limit competition between the trading markets of the European Union, all in the name of enhancing fairness and investor protection. The lack of transparency in the agendas, discussions, and procedures meant that important discussions concerning the substance of the ISD remained confidential and that the way to influence the decision-making process was through informal lobbying and privileged access. The political process of negotiation and the qualified majority-voting scheme also allowed protectionist tendencies to flourish.

Once passed, there are many ways in which European Union secondary legislation may allow a member state to establish national law in a manner that suits its own markets, but not those of other member states. The ISD, for example, may be used to support anticompetitive behavior through the implementation of the conduct of business rules for investment firms. The establishment of such rules is one of the areas of supervision that remain the responsibility of a host member state, rather than the home member state of an investment firm. Given that there is no statutory definition of what the general good means, interpretation of the phrase has to rely on the European Court and its judgments. Five principles have been developed to de-

---

[19] See Committee of Wise Men (2000), Lee (1996), and Steil (1996).

cide when use of the general good, and similarly the public policy clauses in the treaty and the mandatory requirements recognized by the European Court, may justify the establishment of rules that restrict fundamental European freedoms. The principles may be denoted as nonharmonization, nondiscrimination, nonduplication, objective justification, and proportionality (Katz 1992; Van Gerven 1990).

When these criteria are satisfied, the European Court has accepted that the protection of consumers may justify national measures that restrict fundamental European freedoms. In the insurance sector, for example, the court has found that restrictive rules could be implemented because insurance was a "particularly sensitive area from the point of view of the protection of the consumer both as a policy holder and as an insured person."[20] The sensitivity was said to arise because consumers have to enter a long-term relationship with their insurers, because the timing of execution of an insurance contract is uncertain, and because consumers may not have enough information to be able to gauge the long-term financial soundness of their insurers. The court did, however, recognize that the application of restrictive national laws to large and sophisticated institutions might not be justifiable on the grounds of the general good.[21]

Member states can frustrate the liberalizing intentions of the Single Market program via both the implementation and enforcement processes. Member states might take extended periods of time to implement directives into national law and, once implemented, sometimes might not enforce them.

One of the lessons that can be learned from the European Union experience is that, where it has encouraged regulatory competition, this has led to better and cheaper regulation. Despite worries that there might be a race to the bottom in terms of regulatory regimes, with regulators attempting to deliver lighter and lighter supervision at the expense of desired regulatory goals, this has not occurred. It is not a strategy that attracts private sector market participants.

Lack of a theory of harmonization. Despite the centrality of the notion of harmonization to the stated goals of the European Union Single Market program, neither the commission nor the other European institutions have constructed a credible set of criteria to decide what should be harmonized at the European Union level and what should be left for member states to regulate. The need for such a theory is simple and compelling. Without it, not only will any decision as to what to harmonize be arbitrary, but also there will be no reason why any act of harmonization should be expected

---

[20] Commission v. Germany.
[21] Buet, R., and Educational Business Services SARL v. Ministère Public.

to have beneficial effects. This is particularly evident in the legislation governing the capital markets, where the lack of a theory of harmonization has meant that many laws have been passed, although the need for them is questionable. The merits of competition among trading systems, listing requirements, and prospectus requirements, for example, all debatably outweigh the need for the harmonization that has been attempted.

Lack of harmonization and home country control. Despite the stated goal of harmonization in the European Union Single Market program, there are many ways in which member states continue to impose differing regulations on the same activities. This applies to all types of capital market participants, including issuers, investors, intermediaries, and exchanges. For example, the European Union passport for issuers is still not a reality—companies wishing to raise capital in many European Union jurisdictions are obliged to comply with different or additional requirements in order to gain the approval of local regulatory authorities. There is no agreed definition of a public offer of securities, with the result that a similar issue of securities is classified as a private placement in some member states and not in others.

Rules on the disclosure of price-sensitive and relevant market and company information also differ between member states. Professional investors are often subject to multiple sets of conduct of business rules. There is still no legally agreed definition of what constitutes a professional investor, despite some recent progress. Retail investors are faced with different sets of consumer rules with varying levels of consumer protection. There is no agreed definition of market manipulation. Effective functioning of cross-border clearing and settlement is still impeded by legal differences in the treatment of collateral. Investment firms now have a European passport, but are often subject to multiple conduct of business rules.

The effective lack of harmonization and of home country control in the European Union means that market participants still have to obtain appropriate regulatory authorization from most of the European Union countries in which they operate with the attendant costs this entails.

Ineffectiveness of the European Court. Reliance on the European Court to resolve problems with national implementation and enforcement of European Union legislation is ineffective. The court's workings are too slow, and it does not have the expertise necessary to evaluate the rapidly changing trading mechanisms and products of the financial markets. Furthermore, the commission has shown a reluctance to use the European Court to combat recalcitrant member states for several reasons: the likelihood that the court's rulings will not be enforced and that this in turn may undermine the standing of the court; ambiguities in some of the legislation; lack of commission resources; and a low number of complaints.

Ambiguity, rigidity, and slowness. The necessity of obtaining a political consensus in the voting structure of the European Council of Ministers when negotiating new legislation can lead to the adoption of ambiguous texts or texts with a level of harmonization so minimal that no real integration is achieved. Reasons for this may be the lack of transparency in the procedure by which negotiations are conducted and the arbitrariness of the political process. The ISD, for example, does not give sufficient clarity about whose conduct of business rules should apply to wholesale business. The same provisions are often interpreted and applied by member states in a different manner. Without legal clarity, efficient delivery mechanisms cannot guarantee equivalent implementation.

European Union legislation is time-consuming, difficult to achieve, and, once obtained, difficult to change. Even when political problems do not arise, it takes three years on average to agree to a directive. Such a timescale means that legislation cannot keep pace with the capital markets, given their complexity and the speed at which they are developing. There is no rapid mechanism in place to update community directives to new market developments, and, importantly, the Single Market program relies too much on legislation for determining detailed rules.

Cooperative Initiatives in Market Infrastructure

This section describes and assesses key types of cooperative initiatives in the provision of market infrastructure that can be used to promote regional capital market integration. Attention is focused on examining and evaluating projects between organizations that deliver the following seven market infrastructure functions: listing, information dissemination, order routing, trading, clearing via a central counterparty, settlement, and marketing. In addition, the section provides some general comments on the success and failure of linkages and cooperative efforts at regional market integration.

The discussion concentrates on cooperative projects between market infrastructure providers because these are frequently projects that affect the public interest, that are large in nature, and that governments and regulators seek both to instigate and supervise. However, competition, rather than cooperation, between all types of market participants, including infrastructure providers, is one of the most powerful drivers toward regional capital market integration. Private self-interest is normally sufficient to promote such competition, as long as there are no regulatory barriers impeding it.

Listing

There are many reasons why a company may choose to obtain a listing outside its home country:[22]

- To obtain cheap financing
- To improve liquidity for its shares[23]
- To enhance or improve its corporate visibility and status
- To support the implementation of corporate strategies
- To alleviate market segmentation
- To develop a broad shareholder base
- To obtain good analyst coverage of its stock
- To obtain high standards of regulation
- To reduce political risk.

Historically, once a company satisfied an exchange's listing requirements, namely certain minimum initial and ongoing standards for investor protection, the company was said to be listed on the exchange, and its shares would be traded on the exchange's trading system. This is still the situation in many jurisdictions. However, in some jurisdictions, a distinction has arisen between a security being admitted to listing and to trading. In these jurisdictions, admission to listing refers only to the process of being listed in accordance with the relevant legislation, namely satisfying the minimum initial and ongoing requirements, under the supervision of a designated listing authority. Such an authority may be an exchange, as was normally the case in the past, or it may be a regulator distinct from any exchange. Admission to trading, in contrast, refers to the process by which an exchange or other form of trading system chooses to let a particular security be traded on its dealing mechanism. This is not a regulatory decision and remains the responsibility of exchanges and trading systems. In the jurisdictions where this distinction has arisen, an exchange can admit securities to trading while not being in charge of admitting them for listing. In a regional context, a key question concerns whether an exchange in one jurisdiction can admit securities for trading that are admitted for listing in another jurisdiction.

Most of the benefits to a company of listing abroad can be obtained in a regional environment in which listing authorities (exchanges or nonexchange regula-

---

[22] Baker and Johnson (1990); LSE (1999); NYSE (1999); and Pagano, Roëll, and Zechner (2000).
[23] Foerster and Karolyi (1998); Smith and Sofianos (1997); Domowitz, Glen, and Madhavan (1998a, 1998b).

tors) compete with each other to attract listings and in which the providers of trad-ing systems (exchanges or other forms of organization) compete with each other to attract trading. Nevertheless, there have been various cooperative attempts at pro-moting cross-listing and/or cross-trading, most of which have failed.

The most ambitious cooperative attempt at allowing companies listed on one exchange in a region to be listed and traded on other exchanges in the region was a project called EuroList, which was proposed in 1990 by the Federation of Stock Ex-changes of the European Community (now called the Federation of European Stock Exchanges). The aim of EuroList was to allow the largest European companies to be officially and simultaneously listed, and thus traded, on all stock exchanges in the Eu-ropean Union. It was thought that this would be advantageous to issuers because they would gain a European status by being showcased on such a list and to investors, thanks to multiple market access and, it was hoped, increased liquidity. Investors would also be able to trade on their national stock exchange. It was anticipated that com-panies would be required to pay a listing fee for multiple listings, in addition to their national listing fee, and that each country would choose the domestic companies that it wished to quote on the European list. Prices of multiple-listed issues would be quoted in their domestic currency, in the currency of the national exchange on which they were quoted, and possibly also in European currency units. A central element of the project involved the creation of a network that would enable a company to give information to the domestic exchange on which it was listed, which could in turn then transmit the information instantly to the other exchanges on which the company's shares were listed.

For several reasons, the Eurolist project was never implemented. It was seen by the London Stock Exchange (LSE) as an attempt by the continental European stock exchanges (particularly those in France, Belgium, and Italy) to buttress their positions against the perceived success of the LSE in attracting trading in continental European stocks. Another reason why the project failed was that there was little de-mand for it by the major European corporations.

Information Dissemination

Information dissemination is the act of transmitting pre- and post-trade data about quotes and trades, respectively, to market participants.[24] In a regional context—specif-ically, when there are multiple arenas in which trading may be undertaken—a key

---

[24] This discussion is drawn from Lee (1999, pp. 121–28).

question arises as to whether and how information about quotes and trades should be consolidated. The jurisdiction that has been most aggressive in mandating the publication and consolidation of prices and quotes is the United States, via its National Market System (NMS). The concept of the NMS may be viewed both as a set of objectives that Congress ordered the Securities and Exchange Commission (SEC) to pursue and as the institutions that have been established in order to deliver these objectives.[25] The U.S. Congress found that it is in the public interest and appropriate for the protection of investors and the maintenance of fair and orderly markets to ensure the following:

- Economically efficient execution of securities transactions
- Fair competition among brokers and dealers, among exchange markets, and between exchange markets and other markets
- The availability to brokers, dealers, and investors of information with respect to securities quotations and transactions
- The practicability of brokers executing investors' orders in the best market, and the opportunity, consistent with the [above] provisions, for investors' orders to be executed without the participation of a dealer.[26]

The SEC initially passed three key rules to implement the NMS goals with regard to the dissemination of price and quote information: the last-sale rule, the quote rule, and the display rule. The last-sale rule requires that a report be published of all trades in national market securities.[27] Such securities include all exchange-listed stocks and the largest NASDAQ stocks.[28] The price and volume of the transaction and the marketplace where each transaction is executed must be reported. No vendor may be prohibited from retransmitting the data available from a transaction reporting plan, provided the vendor pays the appropriate fees.

The firm quotation or quote rule requires each broker or dealer to communicate promptly to its exchange its best bids and offers and associated quotation sizes for all relevant securities. It also requires that each exchange make available to quotation vendors the highest bid and the lowest offer for the relevant securities, plus the quotation size or aggregate quotation size.[29] The aggregate quotation size is the sum

---

[25] The SEC has imposed many obligations on exchanges and other market participants to implement the price and quote dissemination elements of the NMS that are not discussed here.

[26] Section 11(A), SEA (1934).

[27] Section 240.11Aa3-1, C.F.R.

[28] Those aspects of the NMS that refer to NASDAQ stocks are for the most part ignored in the rest of this section.

[29] Section 240.11Ac1-1, C.F.R.

of the quotation sizes of all responsible brokers and dealers. Each exchange must also be able to identify and disclose to other members of that exchange the brokers or dealers making the relevant quotes. A series of important amendments to the quote rule have been made in order to improve the handling and execution of customer orders by brokers and dealers.[30] These concern so-called electronic communications networks and alternative trading systems.

The third key rule created to implement the NMS, the display rule, requires that if a vendor disseminates last-sale data for securities subject to mandatory trade reporting, it must distribute the consolidated price, consolidated volume, and identifier indicating the market center where trades occur.[31] Similarly, a vendor disseminating quotation information must distribute consolidated quotation information including the best bid and offer for such a security, the quotation size or aggregate quotation size associated with the best bid and offer, and identifiers indicating the market centers that reported these quotes or a quotation montage from all other reporting centers.

The consolidated price and volume is the price and volume of the most recent transaction from all reporting market centers. The best bid and offer for listed securities is the highest bid or lowest offer quoted by any reporting center, with bids and offers of equal values ranked first by size and then by time for exchange-listed securities. A quotation montage shows best bids and offers from all reporting market centers.

Two key institutions were developed to coordinate information dissemination in the NMS: the Consolidated Quotation System (CQS) and the Consolidated Tape Association (CTA). The CQS was established to implement the firm quotation rule.[32] It is a mechanism for making available to data vendors information about the bid and offer quotations and associated volumes for eligible securities from the markets that participate in the NMS. The bid and ask quotes from all the exchanges are combined to obtain a consolidated best bid and offer. The CQS disseminates both the best bid and offer and all the quotes provided by all the participants. The source of each quote and the relevant exchange or market maker are also identified.

An operating committee composed of one representative from each plan participant, namely each exchange and the National Association of Securities Dealers (NASD), administers the CQS. Each participant has one vote on the committee, and amendments to the CQS plan require unanimity. The participants share in the income and expenses associated with publishing the quotation information. Any net income

---

[30] U.S. SEC Release No. 34-37619 (August 29, 1996).
[31] 240.11Ac1-2, C.F.R.
[32] See CQS (December 1995).

from the sale of the CQS information is divided proportionally among the different exchanges according to their relative annual shares. The annual share of an exchange for any calendar year is essentially the total number of last-sale prices of the network's eligible securities reported by the participant divided by the total number of reported last sales. The CTA was established to consolidate the last-sale reporting of all trades in exchange-listed securities.[33] Trade reports by participants must be made promptly so that, under normal conditions, not less than 90 percent of such prices must be reported within one and a half minutes. A committee similar to the one running the CQS undertakes the administration of the CTA.

There has been much controversy about the merits of consolidating price and quote information in the United States.[34] The proponents of mandatory price and quote transparency believe, in essence, that it promotes almost all the key goals that regulation of the securities markets should seek to deliver. The goals include investor protection, fairness, competition, market efficiency, liquidity, market integrity, and investor confidence. The proponents therefore argue that mandatory price and quote transparency should be a fundamental and universal cornerstone of the regulation of exchanges and markets. Others have argued, in contrast, that such a policy may be inappropriate in that it does not recognize that there may be a significant trade-off in the attainment of different regulatory goals. In particular, they claim that mandatory transparency can compromise the delivery of the two key goals of efficiency and liquidity. Private incentives as opposed to regulatory fiat are thought best to lead to the level of transparency that most effectively delivers these goals. More practically, each exchange has a strong incentive to publish appropriate amounts of information about prices and quotes, and data vendors have a strong incentive to consolidate by themselves all relevant information about such prices and quotes.

A further lesson of the American experience for regional attempts at consolidating price and quote information is that it is an extremely political exercise that takes a long time to realize.

Order Routing

Order routing is the act of delivering orders from their originators, such as investors and financial intermediaries, to an order execution mechanism or trading system. Hand, cart, telephone, telex, fax, Internet, and other information distribution mecha-

---

[33] See CTA (12/1995). It started operating on April 30, 1976.
[34] This paragraph is drawn from the discussion in Lee (1999, pp. 255–71).

nisms may deliver orders. The longest-running regional integrated order-routing facil-ity has been the Intermarket Trading System (ITS), developed in the United States, again at the prompting of the Congress and the SEC.

The goal of the ITS is to provide an intermarket communications linkage by which a member of one exchange may trade with a member from another exchange, provided that the first exchange furnishes continuous two-sided quotes in the secu-rity.[35] Operation of the ITS presupposes the existence of a mechanism such as the CQS to disseminate quotes in the market, as market participants must be able to see which exchange is quoting the best price in the security in which they are interested. A member of a participating market wishing to trade at a price quoted on another market can send a commitment to trade to the other market. A commitment to trade is a firm order that is good for a prespecified period of either one or two min-utes. If the quote is still available at the market to which the commitment to trade is sent, or if a better price is available, and if the market rules permit an execution at that price, the market must accept the commitment and execute the order. If the commitment is not accepted within the specified time frame, it is automatically can-celed. Partial executions may occur. All the exchanges and NASDAQ participate in the system.

In the mid-1980s, five order-routing linkages between various securities ex-changes in the United States and elsewhere were proposed.[36] Of these, three were linkages between a U.S. exchange and a Canadian exchange, and the other two were between a U.S. stock exchange and the LSE. Only three of the proposed linkages were actually established, and all of them subsequently failed. The most ambitious was between the American Stock Exchange (Amex) and the Toronto Stock Exchange (TSE). It was between two primary markets, intended to involve trading in different currencies, and joined two trading floors with many dissimilar trading procedures, in-cluding different market-making systems, different priority rules for the execution of orders, and somewhat different concepts of agency and principal transactions. Among the anticipated benefits of the link were that it would give investors in both countries an opportunity to obtain the best prices in either country for dually listed stocks, faster executions, more cost-effectiveness, and greater liquidity.

The linkage started with a pilot scheme that allowed orders to be sent from the floor of the TSE to the floor of the Amex for execution. Although it was also in-

---

[35] The ITS arose as a result of Section 11A(a)(3.(B) of the act and SEC Rule 11Aa3-2. Since its inception, it has been amended many times.

[36] This discussion is taken from Lee (1999, pp. 73–76).

tended to facilitate a northbound flow of orders from the Amex to the TSE, this was delayed because the TSE did not initially have the ability to provide a currency transaction at the same time as a northbound stock trade was executed through the linkage. Each exchange displayed on its trading floor the quotes distributed by the other exchange in the linkage stocks. Quotes on the Amex were in U.S. dollars, while those in Toronto were at first in Canadian dollars. Orders were transmitted between the two trading floors using the existing automated routing systems of the two exchanges. Initially, only marketable limit orders were sent over the linkage. These were orders for which the price was equal to, or better than, the quote then being displayed at the receiving exchange. Such orders were treated as immediate or cancel orders, to be promptly executed or canceled depending on whether they were marketable when received by the relevant market maker at the receiving exchange. Agency orders were guaranteed an execution up to a minimum amount of shares. It was planned to accommodate away from the market orders, namely orders whose prices were worse than the best available quote at the receiving exchange, at a later date. The linkage was initially available only for dual-listed stocks, namely stocks traded on both the Amex and the TSE. Transactions were cleared and settled through an interface between the American National Securities Clearing Corporation and the Canadian Depository Service.

The Amex/TSE link began operating on September 24, 1985. Six stocks were listed on the link to begin; this number later increased to 20. It was perceived as obtaining a minimal order flow, most of which was between the specialists on the floors of the two exchanges. The average ratio of southbound to northbound transactions was approximately 5:1. A TSE report noted that although such a ratio might be "interpreted as a loss of market share by the TSE to Amex . . . any such interpretation should take into account that some southbound order flow may have been a result of offsets for TSE trades. As such, a trade on the Amex may not necessarily take away an opportunity for a trade on the TSE but take place only because a trade was done on the TSE." The linkage was discontinued at the end of 1988 as being uneconomical to run.

The value of cooperative order-routing systems has been controversial. On the one hand, the ITS has been seen by some in the United States as an essential element of the NMS and as a means of ensuring that competition between markets is enhanced by ensuring that orders are always routed to the trading system that has the best quote. On the other hand, it has been viewed both as harmful—in that it encourages quote matching—and as anticompetitive—in that it preserves a function for stock exchange floor members and does not threaten the central role of specialists, precisely when new technology can disintermediate such intermediaries.[37] Two common criticisms of cooperative, as opposed to privately established, order-routing systems are that there is little demand for them and that market participants themselves have the best incentive to deliver good order-routing systems because they can attract more business by doing so.

Trading

A trading system or order execution mechanism lies at the heart of any market. There are many ways in which operators of trading systems in different countries might cooperate to promote regional market integration. Four cooperative ventures that have been attempted are NOREX in Scandinavia; BRVM in West Africa; Euronext in France, Italy, and the Netherlands; and iX in Germany and the United Kingdom.

NOREX

The Nordic Exchange (NOREX) Alliance is a cooperative venture between independent exchanges to form a common marketplace for trading in financial instruments.[38] The objective is to create a single market covering a wide range of products with participation from exchanges and other stakeholders from countries in the Nordic and Baltic area. NOREX was initiated with a letter of intent between the Stockholm and Copenhagen stock exchanges signed in June 1997. In January 1998, final cooperation agreements were signed between the two exchanges, and on June 21, 1999, Danish stocks listed on the Copenhagen Stock Exchange began trading on the Swedish technology platform. On October 17, 2000, the Oslo Stock Exchange Board approved the agreements to form the basis for it to join NOREX. There is an open invitation to the Helsinki Stock Exchange to become a partner in the NOREX alliance, and discussions have also been held with the Baltic exchanges.

The central elements of the alliance are as follows. Participating exchanges use one trading system: the OM Technology SAXESS platform. The regulatory functions of listing companies and supervision of trading and membership are retained by each national exchange; however, the general rules and regulations have been harmonized. The alliance is based on cross-membership of the exchanges for intermedi-

---

37 Joel Seligman, quoted in Cox and Michael (1987, p. 848).
38 This section draws on Copenhagen Stock Exchange, http://www.xcse.dk/uk/nyt/norex/10marketeff.asp?n=6; Oslo Stock Exchange, http://www.ose.no/; and NOREX, http://www.nordic exchanges.com/index.asp.

aries. A security only needs to be listed on one of the exchanges in the alliance to be traded on the system. The price structure at the different participating exchanges will gradually be harmonized for listing, membership, and trading.

The anticipated advantages of NOREX are as follows. It makes it cheaper and easier for member firms of the participating exchanges to access a wider range of shares than is currently possible, given that access to participating markets is via a single connection. It is hoped that the combined market offered by NOREX will stimulate increased activity and attract new market participants, who do not currently consider the separate markets to be large enough to be worth investment. Individually, the Nordic exchanges are relatively small; however, together they comprise Europe's fifth-largest equity market. It is hoped this will enhance turnover and liquidity and raise the profile of shares listed on the participating exchanges. Listed companies will no longer find it necessary to arrange separate listings of their shares on international stock exchanges.

Two simple lessons are evident from the NOREX example. First, it is possible to agree on and successfully implement a cooperative regional project between exchanges in a relatively short time. Second, and although it is difficult to measure this formally, the shared culture of the Scandinavian countries has been a significant factor in the success of the venture.

BRVM

On November 14, 1973, the seven French-speaking member countries of the West African Economic and Monetary Union (UEMOA)—Benin, Burkina Faso, Côte d'Ivoire, Mali, Niger, Senegal, and Togo (more recently, Guinea-Bissau joined the union)—signed a treaty concerning the creation of a regional financial market.[39] On December 17, 1993, the monetary authorities mandated the UEMOA central bank (Banque Centrale des États de l'Afrique de l'Ouest) to lead the project. After extensive negotiations between member countries, a regulator called the Regional Council for Public Savings and Financial Markets (Conseil Régional de l'Épargne Publique et des Marchés Financiers) was formed in October 1997. On September 16, 1998, the Bourse Régionale des Valeurs Mobilières (BRVM, regional stock exchange) opened. The BRVM has branches in each of the UEMOA member countries and its headquarters in Abidjan, Côte d'Ivoire. Although the bourse is majority owned by the private sector, the member governments have 13.5 percent of the capital.

---

[39] This section draws on BRVM (2000); BRVM, www.brvm.org; M. Bendi (March 12, 1999), and other informal sources.

Trading on the BRVM is computerized, with satellite links, which allow brokers to transmit orders from any of the member countries to the central site in Abidjan, to check and interact with the order book, and to see information about the market and the central depository. The exchange has 15 brokerage firms. Trading takes place on three days of the week, and all orders are filled at a price set at a fixing once a day. Trades are cleared and settled at the Dépositaire Central/Banque de Règlement S.A. Initially, 35 companies were quoted on the BRVM. Current capitalization is just over 827 billion CFA ($1.13 billion).[40] The average value of all transactions at each trading session of the exchange from October to December 2000 was 215 million CFA ($295,000). If this level of transactions were continued for the whole year, the amount turned over would be 33.54 billion CFA ($45.6 million) a year. This would represent about 4 percent of the total capitalization of the exchange, a relatively low amount of turnover.

Three lessons may be learned from the experience of the development of the BRVM. First, it can take a very long time to build a regionally integrated exchange. Second, the fact that a regionally integrated exchange is built does not mean that it will be used or that it will integrate the markets. Third, the sustainability of any regional project must be carefully assessed before the project is undertaken. Private sector market participants, as opposed to regulators, central banks, or other public institutions, normally have the best incentive to determine whether the expenditure on a particular integration scheme for market infrastructure is worthwhile, especially when they are spending their own money.

Euronext

On September 22, 2000, Euronext was created from a merger of the Amsterdam Exchanges, Brussels Exchanges, and Paris Bourse.[41] The three exchanges agreed to take the following stakes in Euronext: Paris Bourse, 60 percent; Amsterdam Exchanges, 32 percent; and Brussels Exchanges, 8 percent. Euronext will continue to operate three subsidiary holding companies in its three member countries, each of which will continue to hold an exchange license for the local capital market. Euronext is providing a unified order-driven trading platform based on the French system, NSC, and a single set of trading rules; a central counterpart, netting, and clearinghouse for all trades

---

[40] The exchange rate for December 1999 was US$1 = CFA 735.28. See Mbendi, http://www.mbendi.co.za/ cyexch. htm.
[41] This section draws on Euronext, http://www.euronext.com/en/, and Euronext (2000).

executed on Euronext via Clearnet; and a unified settlement and custody platform with Euroclear. Takeover rules will continue to be imposed domestically.

Listed companies will remain listed on their current exchanges, but listing requirements will be harmonized, all shares will be traded on the single integrated trading platform, and each listed security will be accessible to all members of Euronext, regardless of the nationality of the issuer or the member. Companies seeking a listing on Euronext can choose to do so in any one of the three member financial centers. By choosing their entry point, they will automatically choose their home country as far as regulation is concerned. Although companies could consider more than one listing agreement with Euronext in different financial centers, this would provide them with no added value, as there would be only one order book for their equities regardless of the number of listings on Euronext. The jurisdiction of a listing agreement determines the regulator to which Euronext's market surveillance department reports, concerning irregularities in trading in the securities issued by a company.

The regulators in the three member countries have agreed that a market participant licensed in one country will automatically receive a passport to operate in the other Euronext countries. Market participants will be subject to the supervision of the regulator of the country in which they are granted their main license. The Euronext entry point chosen by a market participant will determine the jurisdiction governing the membership agreement concluded between Euronext and the market participant.

The main reason that Euronext was created was to reduce costs by using a simpler structure rather than attempting to negotiate complex linkage agreements between the three different partner exchanges. In addition, it would provide a simple and flexible regulatory environment for listed companies, members, and the exchanges. Euronext anticipates making cost savings amounting to €50 million a year, mainly from savings in information technology. It also hopes to achieve enhanced liquidity, transparency, and price discovery resulting from the creation of a single order book.

Several lessons may be drawn from the Euronext experience. First, it is possible to merge large exchanges from several countries, each of which has a strong tradition of national sovereignty and ambition for creating a local financial center. Second, in order to achieve such a merger, it is essential to have the goodwill of all the regulatory authorities involved. Third, clarity and simplicity both in ownership structures of markets and in regulatory environments are attractive propositions to market participants.

iX

On May 3, 2000, Deutsche Bourse and the LSE announced that they had agreed to merge to create a new exchange, called iX-international exchanges plc (iX).[42] The plan was that LSE shareholders, in aggregate, and Deutsche Bourse were each to own 50 percent of the shares in iX. The new exchange would be headquartered in London and have two main subsidiaries in London and Frankfurt. The London-based market would be a pan-European blue chip market subject to U.K. regulation. The Frankfurt-based market, which was to be developed in association with NASDAQ, would be a pan-European high-growth market subject to German regulation. Other elements of the merger proposal concerned Eurex, the futures exchange of Deutsche Bourse, and various issues concerning clearing and settlement.

　　Existing listed companies on either of the two merging exchanges would not be required by iX to give up their home country listing in order to be admitted to trading on iX's markets or to adopt a particular currency in which to raise capital, state their accounts, or pay dividends. Newly admitted companies could choose to be listed through the regulatory authority of their choosing. iX would operate a single electronic trading platform based on the German Xetra technology for all its cash markets and offer support to users in mitigating the costs of technical migration. iX would also adopt common market models and a consistent regulatory approach and offer facilities for trading in equities from other European markets.

　　It was anticipated that the merged organization could better provide a single management, a single trading platform with international remote access, and a single pricing model, than could the two exchanges apart. In addition, the size of the combined exchange was seen as a major advantage in the competition between European exchanges. iX would be the leading European exchange in terms of volume and value of equity trading. On a combined basis, the two exchanges accounted for just over half of European equity traded volume in the 12 months prior to March 31, 2000, with 41 percent of Europe's top 300 companies having their primary listing on either the Frankfurt or London exchange. Through Eurex, the group would have an 80 percent economic interest in the world's leading derivatives exchange.

　　It was also argued that the merger would create significant value for shareholders and significant benefits for customers, including private client brokers, dealers, investors, and issuers. iX was expected to deliver operating cost savings, excluding any

---

[42] This section draws on Deutsche Bourse and LSE (2000); Hilton and Lascelles (2000); and Lee (2000).

possible impact on combined revenues as a result of the merger, of approximately £50 million a year, commencing on January 1, 2002. These savings would come in part from a reduction in the complexity of information technology operations for iX.

Following much criticism of the merger proposal, and also an unanticipated hostile bid for the LSE by the OM Group, which operated the Swedish exchanges, the proposed merger was abandoned. Among the criticisms of the merger were the following:

- It was not cost-efficient.
- The distinction between iX (for Europe's top companies) and the iX-NASDAQ joint venture (for pan-European high-growth companies) would lead to conflict.
- Management's valuation of the LSE implied in the iX proposal was thought to be too low.
- It had an unworkable split regulatory regime.
- The merger was dictated by political compromise at the market level rather than economic interests.
- The merger was not sensitive to national politics.

Central Counterparty Clearing

The key role of a central counterparty (CCP) in clearing is to minimize the credit and market risk faced by market participants when settling their transactions.[43] It can do this in two main ways: by the process of novation, namely by placing itself as an intermediate counterpart between all buyers and sellers and acting to guarantee trades, and by providing a netting system, so as to reduce the total number of financial obligations requiring settlement, thereby further minimizing risk. These two functions may lead to various other benefits, including the preservation of market participants' anonymity; the reduction in collateral that market participants need to support their trading activity, which in turn allows them to take larger positions, possibly increasing the liquidity of the market; the simplification of risk management; the standardization of processing and operational procedures, thus lowering costs; and a reduction in systemic risk. Of course, establishing and operating a CCP also have a range of associated costs.

---

[43] See, for example, DTCC (2000) and Scott-Quinn and Walmsley (1999). Hobson (2000) provides a good discussion of the costs and benefits of merging CCPs and CSDs.

Not all markets need a CCP—cost-benefit analysis would be required to make such an assessment—and not all markets have one. For example, while most futures markets typically have a CCP, not all cash markets do. But even for those countries that do have them, there is no consensus about what the optimal structure of CCPs should be across countries. This section presents three issues relating to how CCPs might cooperatively seek to promote regional capital market integration: consolidation, cooperation, and the link between CCPs, for example, between the Chicago Mercantile Exchange and the Singapore International Monetary Exchange.

Consolidation

The reasons for consolidating CCPs across countries in a region are essentially the same as those for establishing one in a single jurisdiction, except that the net gains of doing so may be greater for regional consolidation. In addition, spreading costs across a larger base of trading activity might lead to economies of scale in administration and the use and development of technology. Exploiting the correlation between underlying markets might lead to better risk management. And the merged CCP might reduce operational costs by establishing links with multiple trading mechanisms, settlement organizations, and other market participants, including investors, dealers, and custodians.

The issue of whether and how CCPs should be integrated at a regional level is being most actively considered in Europe. Following the creation of Euronext, clearing for all three of its constituent exchanges will go through a single legal entity, Euronext's French subsidiary, Clearnet S.A. The clearing divisions of the Amsterdam Exchanges and Brussels Exchanges are thus transferring their assets and liabilities to Clearnet S.A. The three exchanges have agreed that the French jurisdiction should govern the guaranteeing of all transactions.

However, there is a debate about whether and how Clearnet and the other two large CCPs in Europe—Eurex Clearing in Germany and the London Clearing House in the United Kingdom—should be linked or merged. Clearnet, Eurex Clearing, and the London Clearing House have all explored the possibility of different merger combinations. A group of the largest investment banks in Europe, which are also among the largest users and owners of all three CCPs, has recently formed an association called the European Securities Forum, which, among other initiatives, is arguing for the creation of a single CCP to support the equity markets in Europe. At one stage in late 2000, the European Securities Forum even contemplated creating its own pan-European CCP if Clearnet, Eurex, and the London Clearing House did not agree to merge. This idea was subsequently retracted. The Depository Trust and Clearing Corporation (DTCC), the single American organization that acts as a CCP for all cash securities, has also indicated its interest in playing a role in this linkage or consolidation process. As yet, however, no resolution has been reached as to the best regional industrial model.

Cooperation

There are many ways in which CCPs may cooperate with each other to promote regional capital market integration. The DTCC (2000) has identified some of these, several of which may operate simultaneously. For example, dialogue can be valuable as a means of sharing basic expertise and developing common industry positions on common problems. CCPs may cooperate through shared standards on communications, messaging, technology, and operating standards and systems. Collateral optimization arrangements, such as agreements on cross-guarantees, cross-collateralization, and cross-margining, would allow one CCP to take account of relevant margins, collateral, and positions held in another. Shared technology investment could reduce development costs if similar platforms were adopted. And business policies and plans could lead to harmonization of policies and procedures. These forms of cooperation may in theory bring about similar benefits to those obtainable from a merger; however, in practice, maintaining the necessary level of cooperation would be difficult.

The DTCC has noted that three business models could facilitate these forms of cooperation. First, an integrating clearer could act as a clearinghouse and CCP for other CCPs, enabling trade and settlement novation and netting across a region served by different types of asset-specific (such as equities or futures) CCPs and national CCPs. Second, a joint venture could arise, for example, among major CCPs to provide common services, such as operational processing or the development and management of technology. Third, an application system provider (ASP) could remotely deliver and maintain technology. This could occur if a large CCP delivered technology to a smaller one or if a joint venture were established to deliver technology to a number of CCPs.

Chicago Mercantile Exchange–Singapore International Monetary Exchange Link

One of the few instances of CCPs cooperating has been in the futures markets with the mutual offset arrangement agreed between the Chicago Mercantile Exchange (CME) and the Singapore International Monetary Exchange (SIMEX) on September 7,

1984.[44] This arrangement allows a trader taking a position on one exchange to reverse the position on the other exchange. A trade executed on SIMEX by a CME clearing member, for example, can be transferred to the CME's account at the SIMEX clearing organization, which in turn results in the establishment of an identical position on the CME for the CME clearing member. CME traders can thus effectively use SIMEX as an extension of the CME trading floor after the CME has closed. An analogous arrangement allows SIMEX traders to use the CME while SIMEX is closed.

The primary reason why the CME established the link was as a weapon to help it compete internationally against the London International Financial Futures Exchange (LIFFE), which was then battling against the CME to establish itself as the dominant forum for trading eurodollar contracts. Given LIFFE's perceived advantage in being closer to the Asian time zone than the CME, a link with SIMEX was viewed as providing a valuable foothold for the CME in the Far East. The CME also identified several benefits of the link for its members and their clients. The advantages noted for Futures Commission Merchants were that it gave them the ability to offer clients something closer to 24-hour trading at low cost and that it reduced the costs and risks they incurred in trading on a foreign market. CME member firms also gained the ability to increase business by acting as an executing agent for those SIMEX member firms that wished to have their trades cleared through the CME. The benefits of the link anticipated for members' clients were as follows: they gained the ability to manage the risk of potential price movements overnight; the link expanded the number of trading hours available for active traders; it reduced transaction costs by requiring only a single margin structure; it assured clients the ability to offset a position taken on SIMEX on what they knew to be a liquid market, namely the CME; and it gave clients reassurance because their positions, whether initiated in Singapore or on the CME, could be held in Chicago on the books of the CME.

The link was initially agreed for a 10-year period in 1984. Although the contractual details of the scheme were not released, there was apparently no financial aspect to the original CME/SIMEX agreement. The CME thus saw the main goals of the linkage to be to increase order flow to its members and to forestall LIFFE's attempts to trade eurodollar contracts. The mutual offset system succeeded in doing this, as LIFFE's share of trading volume dwindled, following the opening of the link, until LIFFE finally delisted its Eurodollar contract in 1996. When the CME/SIMEX mutual offset agreement was renegotiated in 1994, a financial element to the contract was established. In particular, if one exchange was a net transferor of contracts to the other ex-

---

[44] The discussion of the CME-SIMEX linkage is taken from Lee (1999, pp. 76–77).

change, the first exchange agreed to pay a prespecified fee per contract to the other exchange.

The main tactical benefit of establishing the link for Singapore was to build a financial center to rival Hong Kong. The link gave SIMEX access to a contract for which there was already a pool of liquidity in the United States with a reputable exchange and for which demand had already been identified. It thus gave the new exchange a good chance at being successful.

Two key lessons may be taken from this form of cooperation between the CME and SIMEX. First, private incentives may be sufficient to promote a link between CCPs that enhances regional capital market integration. Second, mutually beneficial cooperation is possible between CCPs in countries with strong notions of sovereignty and different regulatory structures.

Settlement

A custodial agent called a depository normally undertakes the settlement of matched securities transactions via a book-entry system. Until recently, there has normally been a single depository in each jurisdiction, called a central securities depository (CSD). CSDs may provide a range of services in addition to pure settlement services, including confirmation and the handling of the money side of settlement procedures. CSDs can also provide facilities for borrowing and lending securities in order to ensure that, if market participants do not have either the securities or the money necessary to settle the transactions on which they have agreed, they can borrow either the securities or the money against appropriate collateral. As with CCPs, there is no consensus on how best to achieve regional capital integration for settlement institutions, and it has again been in Europe that the most intense discussion about this issue has recently been conducted, given the commonly accepted belief that there are too many CSDs in Europe. This section describes six different cooperative models for how the industry might be configured to enhance regional market integration.[45]

RegionClear

The simplest conceptual solution would be to create a single regional settlement facility that would replace all CSDs and international CSDs in a region and allow traders and investors to settle trades in all markets, securities, and currencies in the same way

---

[45] A key source for the descriptions in this section is various issues of *Global Custodian*.

and through the same organization. However, the establishment of such a RegionClear is commonly agreed to be impractical for several reasons. It would be too expensive to build and would require large write-offs by the existing systems. User fees would be prohibitively expensive. Countries would be unlikely to eliminate the legal, tax, currency, and regulatory barriers that would hinder the effective functioning of the system. Custodian banks and domestic CSDs would resist development of such a facility. Any failure of the system, or fraud or default within it, would have serious repercussions throughout the markets. And finally, as a regional monopoly, it might lack the spur of competition.

Central Processing Unit

The central processing unit model is similar to the notion of an ASP. Essentially, CSDs would outsource their securities processing functions to a single computer utility or a string of regional utilities using common software. By leaving safekeeping and settlement functions in the hands of custodians and CSDs, a central processing unit could standardize, accelerate, and make settlement less expensive without provoking political resistance. However, it would be costly and complex to build and would not make settlement between markets more efficient. This model is also now regarded as unworkable.

European Clearinghouse

Cedel (although the model relates primarily to settlement rather than to clearing) proposed a so-called European clearinghouse model. The intention was to merge an international CSD with a CSD to obtain a nucleus for settlement activities in Europe with an open and flexible structure. Other depositories and clearing organizations could then integrate with the European clearinghouse by merging, outsourcing their securities processing services, or establishing electronic delivery versus payment links. While these options allow each national CSD the flexibility of joining the European clearinghouse, they also give rise to complexity that is difficult to manage.

Three main benefits were anticipated from the model. First, costs could be reduced via the economies of scale of combining markets and adopting a common technology. Second, by pooling the assets of customers in one entity, it would be easier for customers both to assess more quickly which assets were available and to use them for trading activities and asset optimization activities, including lending and the collateralization of payments. This would both reduce costs for customers and provide increased opportunities for revenue. Third, counterparts would be able to settle their securities transactions through a common interface using standardized access, thus reducing the risks associated with cross-border settlement.

Hub and Spokes

Euroclear promoted a hub and spokes model in 1999, although it was subsequently discarded (Euroclear 1999). The proposal had two key aims. First, it would transform Euroclear into the main point of entry to every European CSD for international fund managers, custodian banks, and broker-dealers. Second, it would allow Euroclear to act as a central information-processing unit for local banks and broker-dealers doing business with international counterparts through their local CSDs. In addition to its role of linking the spokes, the hub was intended to serve as the primary cross-border settlement provider for global intermediaries. This business would require a high concentration of both assets and counterparts to guarantee the greatest possible settlement efficiency, facilitated by integrated credit and collateral management and enhanced custody services.

The spokes were to settle high-volume, domestic, retail-driven securities transactions, which could include the domestic transactions of global capital market participants. The spokes would have the prime relationship with their respective domestic markets and, therefore, be responsible for the supply and quality of securities information to the whole system. They would also have a key role in securities issuance and communications with issuers, registrars, and tax authorities. The spokes would act as the primary depositories for securities issued by domestic issuers. They also would provide their participants with settlement and custody services in foreign securities through their linkages with the hub.

The hub and spokes model was anticipated to have a number of benefits. It would be a single interface for each market participant to a single settlement infrastructure covering the European capital markets. It would generate cost savings for users from the availability of the single settlement feed. It would provide a gateway to non-European capital markets and counterparts. It would foster timely and efficient relationships with local markets (including issuers, registrars, and tax authorities). High settlement efficiency would yield a reduction in credit and collateral needs and financing costs. The model would have low setup and operating costs. And it would have reduced overall settlement risk. Among the criticisms of the proposal, some thought it would diminish the perceived value of the national European CSDs; that the high-profit institutional business would be handled by the hub, while the national CSDs (the spokes) would be left with the low-profit retail business; and that the cost savings were overestimated.

Eurolinks

The European Central Securities Depositories Association (1999) and Crest put forth the Eurolinks model. Essentially, it advocates direct bilateral links between independent CSDs in order to give customers of one CSD access to the securities in another. Each CSD would provide its customers with a single point of entry that would allow them to hold and transfer securities issued in any other CSD participating in the network using their local CSD's software and connectivity. This would avoid the need to develop an expensive network of custodial relationships or open settlement memberships at multiple CSDs.

Several main advantages were anticipated. First, the links would be cheaper and could be put in place more quickly than those that result from mergers or more formal alliances. Second, the establishment of Eurolinks would allow a degree of competition between clearers. Third, technology was developing fast enough to make Eurolinks possible. Fourth, differences in regulations, taxes, and settlement practices would not hinder the usefulness of the model. Fifth, standardization would reduce complexity and cost for CSDs and their members. And sixth, genuine cross-border delivery versus payment links would reduce cross-border settlement risk. Firms would benefit because Eurolinks would reduce their overheads by limiting the number of interfaces they require for different CSDs, bring their holdings and transactions within the single legal framework of their chosen CSD, and take advantage of their existing investment in software and connectivity by using their local CSD to settle foreign securities and mobilize cross-border collateral.

However, there were some shortcomings with the Eurolinks approach. Interdepository links between domestic CSDs would solve bilateral problems rather than multilateral, multicurrency problems. Preserving national CSDs would make it harder to obtain economies of scale. The approach ignores the banking and value-added services that some market participants believe are necessary to attract major cross-border investors. Finally, it is difficult to fashion flexible and effective links between markets at different levels of development.

CCP Linkage

Crest and Clearstream proposed this model prior to the aborted iX merger. The advantage of the CCP linkage model was that international trades by customers of each domestic CSD would be cleared through the CSD country's domestic CCP. Only the net balances between the CCPs would need to be settled internationally via national CSDs. Although the cost of these net cross-border trades could be high, there would be only a small number of them, and thus the unit cost of settling international trades would be sharply reduced.

Marketing

The marketing of any market is a critical element of its success. Two forms of regional cooperation in such marketing are examined here: Euro.NM, which aimed to band together several continental European high-technology markets, and the creation of some new indices by Euronext.

Euro.NM

In 1998, the stock exchanges in France, the Netherlands, and Belgium set up an alliance called Euro.NM to market their growth company boards. The aim was to create a network of European stock exchanges that would provide high-growth companies with access to the international investment community, within an accessible and well-regulated market structure. The central elements of Euro.NM were common admission criteria, geared specifically to provide growing companies with a route from their domestic investment community to an international one; combined marketing; harmonized membership, trading, and disclosure standards; and a proposed cross-market electronic trading facility.

At its height, Euro.NM was composed of five separate markets: Le Nouveau Marché from Paris, EURO.NM Belgium from Belgium, the Neuer Markt from Frankfurt, the Nuovo Mercato from Milan, and NMAX from Amsterdam. The dominance of Euro.NM by Deutsche Bourse's Neuer Markt, in terms of the number and capitalization of its listed companies, put a strain on the alliance, and Deutsche Bourse was repeatedly reported as considering leaving the alliance. With the commencement of Euronext, Euro.NM was phased out at the end of 2000.

Euronext Indices

The development of a market index is one way of attracting investor interest to a regional market. Euronext is a typical example. It is constructing four new indices to promote its market. The Euronext 100 is composed of the 100 largest officially listed securities in the Euronext stock market. It represents approximately 87 percent of Euronext's total market capitalization and reflects trends in blue chip securities in the Euronext region. The Next 150 index is composed of the 150 largest companies on the basis of market capitalization not represented in the Euronext 100 index. The Next Economy index allows market participants to follow trends in the new economy sector. And the Prime index improves the visibility of high-quality companies in traditional sectors.

General Comments

Of the many attempts at cooperation between market infrastructure institutions that have been proposed, few have been implemented; of those that have been realized, most have failed.[46] There are many ways in which such institutions can effect a linkage, joint venture, or merger with each other. Any subset of the various functions undertaken by them can be shared, including marketing, listing, order routing, information dissemination, order execution, matching, clearing, and settlement. There are also different contractual procedures by which shared delivery of these services can be implemented. For example, one market structure institution could purchase services from another such institution, both might agree to subcontract delivery to a third party, or one might buy the other. Given their diversity, a general comparison of market linkages and other joint projects between market structure institutions would not be useful, let alone feasible. However, four important and closely associated aspects of such schemes are common to many of them—costs, technology, governance, and credible contractual commitments.

Costs

A prime aim of any market structure institution in entering a linkage, joint venture, or merger is normally to reduce costs. The relevant costs are not simply those incurred by the institution itself, but also those borne by all its patrons.[47] The term patron is used here in broad terms to include, among others, the institution's owners, members, controllers, management, and consumers.

Cost savings can arise from many sources. For example, an exchange may establish an order-routing mechanism or joint clearing arrangement with another exchange in order to offer some of its products to members of the other exchange, without requiring them either to buy a seat on its market or to deal through a local intermediary. This may allow traders who are not members of the first exchange

---

[46] This discussion draws on Lee (1999, pp. 61–65).
[47] This use of the term "patron" comes from Hansmann (1980).

cheaper access to its products than would otherwise be available. The presumed cost advantage of an exchange-sponsored linkage may, however, be less than anticipated. If an individual firm at one exchange does enough business at another exchange, it may pay the firm to establish its own dedicated link to the second exchange, rather than deal via an exchange-sponsored linkage. If a sufficient number of firms do this, the exchange-sponsored linkage will not attract enough order flow to cover its costs. Similarly, if a larger firm that has direct access to both markets buys the firms trading on one exchange that has a linkage with another exchange, the trading firms may have no need for a link between the two exchanges because internal linkages will be sufficient.

Two or more cooperating market structure institutions may realize many other types of efficiencies. Economies of scale may be available to both, if their shared costs in joint facilities are less than the sum of their separate costs would be. This may occur in investment not only in physical facilities but also in such intangible items as marketing, education, and product development. A link between two markets that operate sequentially in different time zones may reduce the risks incurred by market participants. The ability of traders with positions at one exchange to liquidate their positions on the other exchange, for example, means that they will face lower timing risks than if they were not able to liquidate their positions on the second market and had to wait until the first one was open again to do so. Linkages between CCPs may reduce the costs of maintaining offsetting positions on both CCPs, such as the need to pay two margin requirements. A linkage may also allow cooperating exchanges to benefit from a network externality associated with the attraction of order flow. If the linked exchanges are able to combine the order flows they receive for similar products in a manner that is unavailable without a linkage between them, they may together be able to achieve a more liquid market than either would be able to realize separately.

When considering what the cost savings might be from a cooperative project between market infrastructure institutions, it is vital to conduct a full cost-benefit analysis. Without such an assessment, it would be easy to overestimate the potential gains from such projects, a mistake that has frequently occurred in practice.

Mergers can also be extremely costly both in terms of transition expenses and the amount of management time needed to make them successful. Indeed, it is well known that mergers are typically not cost-effective for shareholders. Mergers may also be costly and hard to complete successfully if the negotiating parties are evenly balanced in economic strength; if significant differences exist in their business, operational, or technical models; if their respective shareholders have competing economic interests; or if they have overlapping capabilities or different organizational cultures or governance structures (DTCC 2000). Bilateral cooperative arrangements can also be costly because they multiply in number and in complexity.

Technology

A second critical element common to most cooperative initiatives between market infrastructure institutions is the central role that technology plays in their development. Its significance is unsurprising, given its importance as one of the primary sources of costs incurred by such entities. Five simple aspects of technology development have proved important in past projects:

- Building appropriate technology for market infrastructure projects frequently takes longer and is more expensive than is initially anticipated.
- A ready-made technology package may be cheaper and more efficient than developing a new one for a single project.
- A good time to consider embarking on a cooperative project is when the useful life of a particularly important technological aspect of market infrastructure is coming to an end.
- Changes in technology should normally not be the prime motivation for attempting a cooperative venture to deliver regional capital market integration.
- Rapidly shrinking costs of computing and communications technology and the ever-increasing power and sophistication of software being developed are strong factors against the need for a cooperative solution to market infrastructure barriers to regional capital market integration.

Governance

The third important element common to most cooperative market infrastructure projects is the pivotal influence that governance has on their development and success. Linkages, joint ventures, and mergers are never neutral in terms of their effects on the various patrons of the participating organizations. As a result, one or more constituencies at the institutions potentially cooperating in a joint initiative frequently fear that it, or they, may be worse off if such a project were established. The governance structures of the collaborating institutions determine how any benefits obtained by the scheme will be distributed and whether those constituencies that believe their interests might be harmed have the power to change or obstruct its implementation.

For example, the adoption of the technology necessary to implement an exchange linkage may be associated with a reform in an exchange's operating structure and typically with the elimination of floor trading. In such circumstances, conflict may arise between traders based on the floor of the exchange, who are typically relatively small in capitalization, and the larger firms, which have offices in many locations and are members of many exchanges. Floor members may worry about the possibility of business either moving from the floor to the electronic system, on which they believe they will lose their privileges, or, worse, migrating to the other exchanges participating in the linkage. In contrast, the institutional members of the exchange may believe that significant benefits will accrue to them.

Sometimes the resolution of such conflicts is in favor of those members whose welfare is most closely linked to the functioning of the exchange, namely the floor traders, rather than the other groups whose interests are not so integrated with those of the exchange. This often occurs when the governance structure of the relevant exchange grants each member only one vote and when the exchange has a relatively large number of floor members. In other circumstances, the larger, wealthier members triumph, normally because they are required to fund the necessary investments for modernization of the exchange. Sometimes the wealthier members can succeed in buying off the resistance of the smaller members by reimbursing them for the future losses they believe they will incur.

Joint ventures may give rise to conflict both within a particular institution participating in such a scheme and between the institutions supposedly working together on the project. The resolution of these conflicts may be dependent not only on the contractual agreements signed between the relevant parties but also on their relative commercial power.

Notwithstanding the ever-present potential for conflict, there are several ways in which tension between cooperating capital market institutions may be reduced. The simplest occurs where the ownership configurations of the participating institutions are exactly the same. In such circumstances, the success of the link is solely dependent on whether the combined trading volume of both of them increases as a result of the link. The benefits of growth in trading volume that occurs at either institution will accrue to the same people, namely the shareholders of both institutions, and there are thus no concerns about the distribution of benefits obtained as a result of the link.

A similar instance may arise if their members dominate both the governance structures of the linking organizations and if there is a large overlap in membership between the participating organizations. For example, if the member firms of two potentially cooperating exchanges are indifferent about where they conduct their business, they will not be concerned about movements in trading volumes between the exchanges, and the intensity of competition between the cooperating exchanges will again be attenuated. This often occurs when the regional exchanges in a country merge to form a single linked exchange, as has taken place, for example, in Australia, France, Italy, and Switzerland. Conflict between cooperating exchanges may also be diminished if the exchanges operate in different time zones because the possibility of their members competing may appear less.

Credible Contractual Commitments

A fourth noteworthy aspect of cooperative market infrastructure projects is the difficulty of creating credible contractual commitments between the cooperating partners. To achieve this, not only do such agreements have to be initially beneficial for the participants, they have to continue to be so even in a changing environment. If material circumstances vary, as often occurs, one or more of the participating entities may decide that the original contractual agreement is no longer appropriate. It would normally be difficult for the other participating organizations to insist that the dissenting institution honor its original agreement. The costs of enforcing such contracts are typically too high to warrant a legal attempt to do so, particularly in an international environment. More importantly, even if a participating entity could be forced into an action it perceived as unfavorable, the market participants the entity represents could not be compelled to use it. There is thus little point in forcing an unwilling organization to continue honoring an initial participation agreement without the active support of its customers.

One of the benefits of a merger over a cooperative venture is precisely that contracts do not have to be fully specified in a merger, as they do between cooperating but distinct institutions. Internal incentives are normally sufficient for the different components of a merged entity to work together, even in changing circumstances.

A Strategy for Latin America and the Caribbean

This section proposes a two-stage strategy to promote capital market integration in Latin America and the Caribbean. The first stage should be to develop and implement an institutional mechanism that can both pose and answer some initial key questions that need to be addressed in order to promote capital market integration. The second stage should be to implement the results of the first stage. Only summary aspects of the second stage of the strategy are described here, not least because its development requires that the first stage be completed. It is vital to stress at the outset that the strategy is critically important for the development of the region, that it will be difficult but very worthwhile to achieve, and that it will require support at the highest political levels.

Key Questions

In preparing a broad strategy of this nature, it is crucial that the key questions it needs to address be specified in advance. If this is not done, it is likely both that the strategy will become unfocused and that its output will not be useful. It is recommended that the strategy deliver answers to four broad sets of questions relating to the benefits of integration, the determination of the region or regions to which the strategy should apply, the barriers to integration, and the method by which the barriers should be removed.

Benefits of Integration

What are the benefits of regional capital market integration? Answering this question is important to obtain support for the whole process of regional capital market integration. The benefits integration can bring need to be analyzed and widely disseminated. Among the benefits that should be identified are lower prices for all financial services; more efficient, more liquid, and broader securities markets; innovative financial products and services; an industrial transformation of all sectors of the capital markets industry; cheaper financing for companies; more efficient allocation of capital; higher returns on investments; enhanced risk-return frontiers; and improved macroeconomic performance.

Determination of the Region

What parts of the entire region of Latin America and the Caribbean should be covered by the strategy? If the region is taken to include the whole of Latin America and the Caribbean, it will be difficult for the strategy to deliver more than high-level proposals, which are unlikely to be implemented. The smaller the number of countries in the designated region, the more likely the strategy will be successful, but the less important will be any agreement that is reached. Other factors affecting the choice of region might include the cultural affinity between the different countries and the potential benefits that could be obtained by more enhanced capital market integration in the region. It might be appropriate to work on several options, or groups of countries, simultaneously.

Barriers to Integration

What are the barriers to integration and, of these, which have the most detrimental effects? This requires answering two key subsidiary questions. Where are the costs of trading on a regional basis unnecessarily high? And are there any restrictions on market participants' ability to undertake their business activities wherever they wish in the region? Areas where these barriers might arise include the convertibility of currencies, domestic or regional monopolistic or oligopolistic practices, the existence and cost of multiple regulators, legislative and regulatory impediments, transaction costs, taxation, accounting, lack of information about aspects of capital markets across a region, and issues related to the region's history and culture.[48]

Removal of Barriers

How can the barriers to regional capital market integration be removed? What are the costs and difficulties in attempting to remove these barriers, and which barriers would it be most beneficial to remove? Answers to these questions will determine how the second stage of the strategy should be implemented. Among the major alternatives for removing the barriers to regional capital market integration that will need to be considered are removing unnecessary legislative and regulatory barriers to regional competition, stopping monopolistic and oligopolistic practices, developing regional cooperative market infrastructure projects by the private sector, establishing a mutual reliance scheme between regulators, establishing home country control, and harmonizing regulation.

At this stage, it is important to emphasize the merits of competition. Regulatory differences can create significant costs, especially if market participants have to comply with rules from multiple jurisdictions. However, neither the harmonization of laws nor of regulations is essential for regional capital market integration. Further-

---

[48] Some barriers to regional capital integration in Latin America are noted in Pieper and Vogel (1997).

more, the process of harmonization is frequently used as a protectionist anticompetitive device.

Institutional Framework

This section contains recommendations for the institutional framework that should be
created in order to best address the questions noted above. Two aspects of the framework are described: some attributes it should have and its institutional structure.

Attributes

For the strategy to have a practical chance of success, it will require the following
characteristics:

- High-level political support
- Ambitious but realistic targets
- Widespread legitimacy
- Initial and continuing momentum
- Adequate financing
- Flexibility.

Structure

The best institutional framework would be to establish a Committee of Wise Men
composed of no more than 10 members, with an appropriate mandate to promote
regional capital market integration. This committee should be established in an appropriate forum by the highest political levels possible, ideally at the level of the minister of finance or economics. It is crucial that the members of the committee be of
the highest possible reputation in the region's financial markets, that they come from
throughout the region, that they be willing to work hard on the committee, and that
they be representative of different constituencies in the markets. The mandate of the
committee should be to pose and answer the key questions noted above.

  The Committee of Wise Men would have the following benefits: a reputation
for independence and expertise that is difficult to match in other institutional contexts; its own agenda and recommendations, without fear of political consequences;
independence from capture by any particular constituency; and the ability to be flexible and work fast. It is recommended that the committee employ the following procedures and attributes:

- A formal process of publication, consultation, and justification of its findings and resolutions
- Permanent staff
- An ambitious and publicly stated timescale for the delivery of its final report and other reports published on a regular basis
- Expertise
- Independence
- A plan to market the results of its deliberations and conclusions.

Roles of Interested Parties

It is anticipated that the key types of parties interested in the promotion of regional capital market integration should play the following roles in the strategy. The Inter-American Development Bank should mobilize support for the strategy at the highest political levels throughout Latin America and the Caribbean, allow its president to sit on the Committee of Wise Men, liaise with other relevant international financial institutions, fund the strategy, and be a neutral sponsor to facilitate the implementation of the strategy. In particular, this could mean providing appropriate expert staff for the workings of the committee.

National governments should support the initiative at the highest political level, use their influence to have the highest-quality people sit on the committee, and make available to the committee whatever resources it reasonably needs, possibly including funding.

Regional organizations interested in the capital markets—such as the Council of Securities Regulators of the Americas and the Federación Iberoamericana de Bolsas de Valores—and national regulators and private sector participants would play an essential role in the successful implementation of the strategy. They should be involved at all stages in the committee's work: delivering advice, submissions, and information to the committee; answering questions raised by the committee and, where appropriate, garnering support for the project; and disseminating the results of the committee's findings to other market participants and the wider public.

The press should be contacted right from the outset of the strategy, as it could play a vital role both in disseminating information about the project and in garnering support for it. This would require that the committee hold appropriate press conferences and briefings and that all relevant information be circulated efficiently to the press.

Conclusions

This chapter has provided a summary of the costs and benefits of, and barriers to, regional capital market integration. It has evaluated the manner in which legislative and regulatory initiatives may or may not further regional capital market integration. It has described and assessed key types of cooperative initiatives in the provision of market infrastructure to promote regional capital market integration. And it has proposed a strategy to promote capital market integration in Latin America and the Caribbean.

The promotion of regional capital market integration is critically important for regional development, and its importance is becoming progressively more widely accepted, not only by market participants but also at the highest political levels. Regional capital market integration requires two key elements: lower cross-border transaction costs and the ability of market participants to deliver their services across borders without restrictions. Although it is possible to further these goals at a domestic level, the potential gains of doing so at a regional level are significantly larger.

Bibliography

Baker, H. Kent, and Martha Johnson. 1990. A Survey of Management Views on Exchange Listing. *Quarterly Journal of Business Economics* 29(4):3–20.

Beck, Thorsten, Ross Levine, and Norman Loayza. 2000. Finance and the Sources of Growth. *Journal of Financial Economics* (58):261–300.

Bourse Régionale des Valeurs Mobilières (BRVM). 2000. *Revue trimestrielle: 1 octobre 1999–31 decembre 1999* (5).

Brown Q. C., David A. 1999. *After MacKay, Re Aligning Financial Services Regulation: A Framework for Market Regulation in Canada.* Securities Superconference, Toronto, Canada, February 24.

Cochrane, James L., James E. Shapiro, and Jean E. Tobin. 1995. Foreign Equities and U.S. Investors: Breaking Down the Barriers Separating Supply and Demand. NYSE Working Paper 95-04. New York Stock Exchange, December 8.

Cohen, K. J., S. F. Maier, R. A. Schwartz, and D. K. Whitcomb. 1986. *The Microstructure of Securities Markets.* Englewood Cliffs, N.J.: Prentice-Hall.

Commission of the European Communities. 1977. *Advantages and Disadvantages of an Integrated Market Compared with a Fragmented Market.* Studies, Competition—Approximation of Legislation Series (Schmidt Report) 30.

_____. 1978. *Control of Securities Markets in the European Economic Community.* Studies, Competition—Approximation of Legislation Series 31 (Wymeersch Report I).

_____. 1979. *Supervision of the Securities Markets in the Member States of the European Community—Individual Country Studies: Part I Belgium, Federal Republic of Germany, Denmark, Ireland, France.* Studies, Competition—Approximation of Legislation Series 32 (Wymeersch Report II).

_____. 1980. *Supervision of the Securities Markets in the Member States of the European Community—Reports on the National Systems of Control: Part II UK, Italy, Luxembourg, Netherlands.* Studies, Competition—Approximation of Legislation Series 33 (Wymeersch Report III).

_____. 1988. *The Costs of Non Europe: Report of the Cecchini Committee.* Luxembourg: Office of Official Publications.

Commission of the European Union. 1999. *Financial Services: Implementing the Framework for Financial Markets: Action Plan.* Communication of the Commission COM 232 (May 11).

Committee of Wise Men. 2000. *Initial Report of the Committee of Wise Men on the Regulation of European Securities Markets.* Brussels, November 9.

Council of Securities Regulators of the Americas. 1995. *Principles of Effective Market Oversight.* (May).

Cox, Charles C., and Douglas C. Michael. 1987. The Market for Markets: The Development of International Securities Markets and Commodities Trading. *The Catholic University Law Review* 36(Summer): 833–62.

Depository Trust and Clearing Corporation (DTCC). 2000. *Central Counterparts: Development, Cooperation, and Consolidation—A White Paper on the Future of CCPs.* (October).

Deutsche Bourse and London Stock Exchange (LSE). 2000. *iX–international exchanges. Merger of Deutsche Bourse and London Stock Exchange: Information Document.* (July 15).

Domowitz, Ian, Jack Glen, and Ananth Madhavan. 1998a. International Cross-listing, Market Segmentation, and Foreign Ownership Restrictions: The Case of Mexico. In Richard Levich (ed.), *Emerging Market Capital Flows.* Kluwer Publishing.

_____. 1998b. International Cross-listing and Order Flow Migration: Evidence from an Emerging Market. *Journal of Finance* 53:2001–27.

Euroclear. 1999. The Hub and Spokes Clearance and Settlement Model: The Pan-European Settlement Solution for Efficient and Competitive Capital Markets. Brussels, May.

Euronext. 2000. *Comprehensive Paper.*

European Central Securities Depositories Association. 1999. *Eurolinks: Delivering the Future.*

European Economic Community Commission. 1966. *The Development of a European Capital Market: Report of a Group of Experts Appointed by the EEC Commission.* (Segré Report). Brussels.

Foerster, Stephen R., and G. Andrew Karolyi. 1998. Multimarket Trading and Liquidity: A Transaction Data Analysis of Canada-U.S. Interlistings. Working Paper 98-12. Charles A. Dice Center for Research in Financial Economics, Fisher College of Business, Ohio State University.

Hansmann, Henry B. 1980. The Role of Nonprofit Enterprise. *Yale Law Journal* 89: 835–98.

_____. 2000. *The Ownership of Enterprise.* Cambridge, Mass.: Harvard University Press.

Hilton, Andrew, and David Lascelles. 2000. *iX: Better or Just Bigger?* Paper 46 Center for the Study of Financial Innovation, August.

Hobson, Dominic. 2000. Market Infrastructure: Assertions versus Arithmetic. *Global Custodian* (Winter): 66–78.

International Organization of Securities Commissions (IOSCO). 1997. *Guidance on Information Sharing.* November.

_____. 1998. *Objectives and Principles of Securities Regulation.* September.

Katz, Sherman E. 1992. The Second Banking Directive, the General Good, and the United Kingdom Banking 1987 Act. Diploma in Law Thesis, University of Oxford, Oxford.

Lee, Ruben M. G. 1993. *Enforcement Issues in Securities Markets.* IOSCO Annual Conference, Mexico City, October.

_____. 1996. Supervising EC Capital Markets: Do We Need a European SEC? In Richard M. Buxbaum, Gérard Hertig, Alain Hirsch, and Klaus J. Hopt (eds.), *European Economic Business Law: Legal and Economic Analyses on Integration and Harmonization.* Berlin and New York: Walter de Gruyter.

_____. 1999. *What Is an Exchange? The Automation, Management, and Regulation of Financial Markets*. Oxford: Oxford University Press.

_____. 2000. LSE's Catalogue of Errors. *Financial News*, September 4.

Lemmen, Jan. 1998. *Integrating Financial Markets in the European Union*. Cheltenham, U.K.: Edward Elgar.

Levine, Ross. 1997. Financial Development and Economic Growth: Views and Agenda. *Journal of Economic Literature* 35(June):688–726.

Levine, Ross, Norman Loayza, and Thorsten Beck. 2000. Financial Intermediation and Growth: Causality and Causes. *Journal of Monetary Economics* 46(August): 31–77.

Levine, Ross, and Sara Zervos. 1996. Stock Markets Development and Long-Run Growth. *The World Bank Economic Review* 10(2):323–39.

_____. 1998. Stock Markets, Banks and Economic Growth. *American Economic Review* 88(June):537–58.

London Stock Exchange (LSE). 1999. *Listing Shares in London*.

McGlaughlin, Grant E. 2000. The Virtual National Securities Commission: Reality or Oxymoron? *The Material Change Report* 9(1, January).

Miller, Darius. 1999. The Market Reaction to International Cross-listings: Evidence from Depository Receipts. *Journal of Financial Economics* 51:103–23.

New York Stock Exchange (NYSE). 1999. *An International Marketplace*.

Pagano, Marco. 1997. The Changing Microstructure of European Equity Markets. Center for Studies in Economics and Finance, Working Paper 4. Dipartimento di Scienze Economiche, Università degli Studi di Salerno, April.

Pagano, Marco, and Ailsa Roëll. 1990. Trading Systems in European Stock Exchanges: Current Performance and Policy Options. *Economic Policy* (October):65–115.

Pagano, Marco, Ailsa Roëll, and Josef Zechner. 2000. *The Geography of Equity Listing: Why Do European Companies List Abroad?* Center for Studies in Economics and Finance, Working Paper 28. Dipartimento di Scienze Economiche, Università degli Studi di Salerno, December.

Pieper, Paul B., and Robert C. Vogel. 1997. *Stock Market Integration in Latin America*. CAER Discussion Paper. IMCC, October.

Promethée Distler, Catherine. 1993. *Stock Exchanges Integration in Europe: Commission Pull or Customer Push.* REDES note 21, Layer 2, no. 21 (December).

Pulatkonak, Melek, and G. Sofianos. 1999. *The Distribution in Global Trading of NYSE Listed Non U.S. Stocks.* New York Stock Exchange. Working Paper 99-03.

Rajan, Raghuram G., and Luigi Zingales. 1998. Financial Dependence and Growth. *American Economic Review* 88 (June):559–86.

Schwartz, R. A. 1988. *Equity Markets: Structure, Trading, and Performance.* New York: Harper and Row.

Schwartz, R. A., assisted by L. M. Cohen. 1991. *Reshaping the Equity Markets: A Guide for the 1990s.* New York: Harper and Row.

Scott-Quinn, Brian, and Julian Walmsley. 1999. *New Frontiers in Clearing and Settlement.* International Securities Market Association.

Smith, K., and G. Sofianos. 1997. *The Impact of a NYSE Listing on the Global Trading of Non U.S. Stocks.* New York Stock Exchange. Working Paper 97-02.

Steil, Benn. 1996. Equity Trading IV: The ISD and the Regulation of European Market Structure. In B. Steil and others (eds.), *The European Equity Market: The State of the Union and an Agenda for the Millennium.* London: European Capital Markets Institute, Royal Institute of International Affairs.

———. 1998. *Regional Financial Market Integration: Learning from the European Experience.* Royal Institute of International Affairs, London.

U.S. Securities and Exchange Commission (SEC). 1994. *Market 2000: An Examination of Current Equity Market Developments.* Washington, D.C.: Division of Market Regulation, U.S. Securities and Exchange Commission, January.

Van Gerven, Walter. 1990. The Second Banking Directive and the Case-law of the Court of Justice. *Yearbook of European Law.* 10

Wellons, Phillip A. 1997. *Integration of Stock Exchanges in Regions in Europe, Asia, Canada and the U.S.* CAER Discussion Paper 14 (April).

World Bank. 1997. Preparing Capital Markets for Financial Integration. In *Private Capital Flows to Developing Countries: The Road to Financial Integration.* World Bank Policy Research Report. New York: Oxford University Press, September.

■CHAPTER 7

Accounting and Auditing Standards

Pietro Masci
Ivan Sotomayor

Information disclosure plays an essential role in capital market development and in the valuation of assets by market operators and agents—investors as well as research analysts and rating agencies—according to the risk-reward paradigm. This function is regarded as a form of market discipline.[1] That is, bondholders, depositors, and stockholders use information disclosure to evaluate changes in the firms' risk and the actions of their management, shareholders, or other players to undertake corrective measures to control the risk level. However, to achieve market discipline, financial markets need essential information that allows market operators and agents to understand the performance and risk-reward functions of going concerns and decide a course of action. Confidence in capital markets begins with the quality of financial information, that is, its timeliness, accuracy, and availability to the various market players.

Disclosure of information according to agreed parameters, which makes it easily accessible and understandable, allows investors to make decisions and in turn serves the overall objective of allocating resources. Thus, generally accepted accounting and auditing standards permit widespread participation in capital market activity, build the confidence of participants, and create the conditions for growth and the appropriate allocation of capital. The effective implementation of accounting standards in a given country is one of the factors that enhance disclosure of information. Moreover, the convergence and ultimate harmonization of the standards will facilitate the integration of capital markets and the cross-border flows of capital and foreign direct investment.

In December 2001, Enron Corp, one of the largest companies in the United States, filed for Chapter 11 protection from creditors under the U.S. bankruptcy code.

---

[1] Market discipline is a relatively new concept in the financial literature. It constitutes one of the three pillars of the new Basle Capital Accord (the so-called Basle 2).

The filing followed large losses in the previous quarters, repeated restatements of earnings, revelations of partnerships that kept debt off the balance sheet, and inquiries from the U.S. Securities and Exchange Commission (SEC). The Enron case shows that failures of the information disclosure systems can have a devastating impact even in a well-developed financial system. Therefore, it emphasizes the need for continuous oversight of a complex capital market system that requires the intervention of various players and stakeholders.

Even before the Enron debacle, economic and financial crisis broke out in emerging economies in the late 1990s. Crises began in 1998 in Asia and spread to other regions of the world, showing the need for reliable and transparent accounting and financial reporting to support sound decisionmaking by investors, lenders, and regulatory authorities. In 1998, the G-7 finance ministers and central bank governors committed to endeavor to ensure that private sector institutions in their countries complied with internationally agreed principles, standards, and codes of best practices. The ministers and governors called on all countries that participate in global capital markets to equally commit to comply with the internationally agreed codes and standards. In the international context, the objective was to achieve financial stability as a global public good.

Financial Information, Accounting, and the Capital Market

Investors as well as lenders have a clear interest in the value of the businesses in which they invest. Assuming efficient markets, a firm's value is defined as the present value of expected future net cash flows discounted at the appropriate risk-adjusted rate of return. Within this framework, the firm's performance as reported in its financial statements is important, but does not constitute the only input for the so-called fundamental analysis that establishes the value of the firm. The Financial Accounting Standards Board (FASB) confirms this conceptual framework when it declares that financial statements should help investors and creditors in making correct decisions and "in assessing the amounts, timing and uncertainty" of future cash flows.[2] Therefore, there must be a time association between financial performance and net future cash flows as well as a more direct association between security prices and financial performance. Fundamental analysis plays a crucial role in that it entails the use of in-

---

[2] FASB Statement of Financial Accounting Concepts, No. 1, 1978.

formation and disclosure in current and past financial statements in conjunction with macroeconomics and sector data to arrive at the firm's intrinsic value.

The difference between the intrinsic value and the current market value drives the activity of the stock market, indicates the reward expected for investing in the security, and ultimately drives the economic allocation of resources. However, if Fama's (1970, 1991) statement that "security prices fully reflect all available information" is correct, the reward from fundamental analysis, and therefore from accounting, would be greatly reduced, possibly leading to the collapse of markets because there would be little incentive to gather costly information, and trade and liquidity would disappear (Grossman and Stiglitz 1980). Therefore, the knowledge of an informationally efficient capital market is enormously relevant for investors, regulators, and standard setters. In an efficient market, theoretically, the choice between disclosure in the footnotes and full disclosure in the financial statement does not have a relevant impact on the price of securities. Conversely, inefficient markets would require fundamental analysis and accounting standards.

After many years of studies and research and thousands of articles and papers, financial economists have not settled the issue about whether financial markets are efficient (for example, the efficient markets hypothesis). What has become relevant, however, is not the absolute concept of market efficiency, but rather the relative concept of efficiency. For example, a particular market might be efficient relative to other markets or to a certain type of information.

In the context of relative efficiency, numerous studies have been undertaken to analyze the link between accounting and capital markets. Ball and Brown (1968) study the impact of accounting numbers on capital markets; Ball and Kothari (1991) analyze the impact of earnings announcements on security prices; Ball (1972) looks at the impact of changes in accounting methods on security prices. The various studies show that capital markets are informationally inefficient and prices would take years before they would fully reflect all available information. The research has demonstrated that historical cost reporting and financial statement numbers—including quarterly earnings—reflect information that influences security prices although it is not necessarily timely. This suggests that accounting, while relevant, does not constitute a monopoly source of information. This is confirmed by studies showing that prices lead accounting earnings (Collins and others 1994). It also allows the conclusion that, even in an ideal efficient market, fundamental analysis plays a crucial role in guiding knowledge about what drives value. The research demonstrates that fundamental valuation—a function that goes beyond accounting—relies heavily, but not exclusively, on accounting as an instrument to compile and comprehend information and can yield satisfactory rewards in an inefficient market. Financial statements and quarterly reports are inadequate, on a stand-alone basis, to anticipate the firm's expected revenues and therefore the prediction of future earnings. Information embedded in prices cannot be understood without the input of additional forward-looking considerations, which are the prerogative of the research analyst and of the market in general. At the same time, one of the basic principles of accounting, that is, the revenue recognition principle, makes financial statements unlikely to provide timely indicators of market value, which only valuation models can offer.

Recent events, from Enron to Tyco to WorldCom, that have shaken U.S. capital markets and investors' confidence, further confirm the limitations of capital markets and demonstrate how the misuse of accounting has a significant impact on stock prices and valuation. However, these events also illustrate that accounting is an instrument for organizing information according to certain rules; accounting is not, per se, responsible for financial disclosure. The crucial issue remains corporate governance and management selection and oversight. According to Jensen and Meckling (1976) and Watts and Zimmerman (1978, 1979, 1983, 1986), accounting and auditing, in addition to helping to perform the valuation function, contribute to enhancing corporate governance by improving the accuracy of management disclosure, monitoring its behavior, and reducing corruption and agency costs. In dealing with an organization, agency problems exist, that is, the relationship is a contract under which one or more persons, the principals, engage another person, the agent, to perform some service on their behalf that involves delegation of some decisionmaking authority. Therefore, shareholders may want to link managerial compensation to shareholders' value as expressed by the stock price. However, shareholders also need to monitor management, which could manipulate accounting values, policies, and procedures to influence stock price performance.[3] As the market is not perfectly efficient and accounting manipulation can affect the stock price, the proper functioning of accounting and auditing is essential to ensure that representations are not fraudulent, deceptive, or likely to compromise the health of the firm.

Accurate and transparent financial statements provide a practical form of contract verification among managers, owners, and lenders. Disclosure and accounting information as well as auditing are expected to ensure that asymmetric information between managers, owners, and investors is eliminated so that research analysts and investors have adequate information to monitor the performance of managers

---

[3] For instance, bonus plans in favor of management increase the probability of selecting corporate accounting procedures that shift accounting earnings from the future to the current period.

Figure 7-1	Accounting, Corporate Governance, and Capital Markets: Players and Links

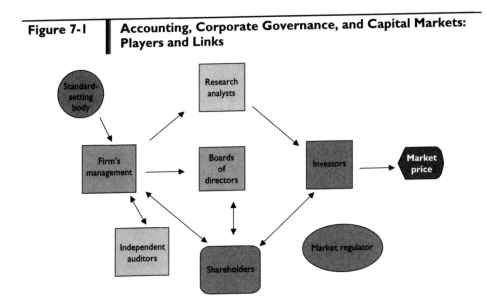

and assess the fair value of the firm. Timely disclosure has substantial merit regardless of whether the market is efficient. Timely disclosure links the relevance of accurate accounting and standards to governance and ultimately to investors' confidence, which is essential for capital market development. Figure 7-1 shows how accounting, corporate governance, and capital markets interact and how accounting and auditing standards are instrumental to the functioning of corporate governance and to the determination of price and fair market value, which is the task of capital markets.

Given the relevance of generally accepted accounting and auditing standards and practices, should there be a uniform set of global accounting standards or diversity? Should the standards be developed internationally, or should the long-tested U.S. Generally Accepted Accounting Principles (GAAP) be the standards? Should standards be different across nations, given their cultural, political, and legal differences? How can countries incorporate into their legal systems the harmonization of standards? How should they deal with their existing legal national accounting rules? How would different levels of efficiency of domestic capital markets affect the nature of international standards? Who would be responsible for (and finance) the introduction of accounting standards in emerging countries?

The responses to these questions need to be tackled because accounting constitutes a mechanism for the public good of financial stability and development. The responses should also address the progress and advances made and steps under way by the two major existing standard-setting bodies to achieve a common accounting language.

Implementation of Accounting Standards for the Public Good

The financial crises of the 1980s and particularly those of the 1990s have prompted the financial literature to develop a line of reasoning that characterizes financial stability as a global public good because financial instability is a public bad. Financial instability spreads across countries and creates devastating economic and political costs, which, in many cases, are borne by the lower segments of the population.[4] The reasoning, developed from the point of view of instability as a public bad, goes as follows: markets are not perfect, and market failure exists due to information asymmetries and leads to financial instability, which constitutes a public bad that in turn creates externalities in terms of spillovers (for example, contagion) of crises that spread from one country to another, generating cost and redistribution impacts. These externalities do not have a market price or a pecuniary equivalent. Under these circumstances, there is underprovisioning of the global good, financial stability, thereby creating externalities and costs.

Following this rationale, a series of instruments or mechanisms have been designed to promote financial stability.[5] The promulgation of international standards—defined as minimally accepted practice that countries should meet in various areas, such as fiscal, monetary, banking, and securities supervision; auditing and accounting; bankruptcy; and corporate governance—is crucial for upgrading financial systems and achieving financial stability. Accounting standards constitute a critical device that supposedly would allow all economic agents to share a high level of information, thus realizing the economist's dream of perfect competition. Truthful, timely, and transparent reporting and auditing according to commonly agreed standards would certainly favor financial stability as well as the correct functioning of markets and would provide large benefits to the entire society.

---

[4] The Bank for International Settlements (BIS 1997) estimated that the cost of banking crises was 2–3 percent of gross domestic product (GDP) in the case of the savings and loans crises in the United States in 1980s and 55 percent of GDP in the case of the banking crises in Argentina during 1980–82.

[5] According to Wyplosz (1999), the primary mechanisms for promoting financial stability are adequate macroeconomic and structural policies, a legal framework that recognizes and protects property rights, efficient and deep financial markets, regulation and supervision, and monitoring of capital flows.

The economic crisis in Mexico in 1994 shows why accounting rules and practices constitute a relevant tool for financial stability. At that time, Mexican accounting rules permitted banks to recognize as past due amounts only those payments that were past due and not the outstanding loan balance. In addition, it was also widespread practice to roll over loans as well as to lend money to distressed creditors to make interest payments. These two accounting practices created severe underestimation of problem loans that were in excess of shareholders' equity.

The case of Mexico is just one example that shows the importance of effective accounting standards and monitoring by an auditing committee and the need for adoption of common global standards that are universally understood. Increased globalization of financial markets will require uniformity of standards for disclosure and release of information to pave the road for financial stability as a global public good. However, this abstract notion has to be powerful enough to convince emerging economies that effective accounting standards would help them not only to achieve financial stability but also to produce the political will and support and economic incentives to undertake reforms. A motivating factor is that financial crises are extremely expensive and create poverty and other negative outputs.

As a given country makes decisions about the effective implementation of accounting standards, the authorities of that country will have to take into consideration the domestic political economy in selecting the appropriate set of standards. With respect to the latter, the authorities must select from among competing accounting conventions—the U.S. GAAP, the International Accounting Standards (IAS), and national standards. This plurality has an impact on transparency because a single event can have two or more accounting interpretations and therefore can lead to different conclusions. This, in turn, involves a type of transaction cost, in adjusting the two accounting languages and making them comparable and acceptable to a wide range of market operators and agents. In other words, it represents the cost of transparency, given the different accounting methods. The use of competitive methods increases the cost of capital for those companies willing to undergo the reconciliation exercise. For example, some countries do not permit companies to use IAS without a reconciliation to domestic generally accepted accounting principles and may also discourage other companies from going the same route to tap capital markets for financing investments and innovation.

Evidently, the equilibrium of diverse sets of accounting standards is not efficient. Therefore, it should be helpful to explore the differences between the sets of standards and the actions under way for harmonization among standards and convergence.

United States, International, and National Accounting Standards and Principles

FASB and the International Accounting Standards Board (IASB) are the prominent standard-setting bodies.[6] Developments over the past few years show that, while each of the standard-setting bodies intends to preserve the validity of its choices, FASB and IASB are working together to resolve differences in standards and provide the global business community with a common language.

In appearance, U.S. GAAP and IAS are similar, thanks to the efforts of the respective standard-setting bodies in eliminating differences. In reality, once the standards are applied within the context of national customs and policies, substantial differences remain. However, the IASB constitution envisions a partnership between IASB and national bodies working together to achieve the convergence of accounting standards worldwide. The convergence between U.S. GAAP and IAS continues to move at an accelerated pace, with FASB and IASB working in concert. For instance, it is becoming customary that when IASB decides to review a particular practice on its agenda, FASB immediately does the same.

FASB's objective for participating in international activities is to increase international comparability and the quality of standards used in the United States. FASB pursues that objective in cooperation with national standard setters and in particular with IASB. FASB believes that the ideal outcome of cooperative international accounting standard-setting efforts would be the worldwide use of a single set of high-quality accounting standards for both domestic and cross-border financial reporting (FASB 1998). While U.S. GAAP and IAS represent the main contenders, many emerging and nonemerging markets have their own solid accounting systems ruled by an independent body that follows the so-called local or national GAAP.

---

[6] FASB is a private, independent, nonprofit body, based in Connecticut, led by members of the accounting profession and industry, responsible for establishing and interpreting general accounting principles. The mission of FASB is to establish and improve standards of financial accounting and reporting for the guidance and education of the public, including issuers, auditors, and users of financial information. Accounting standards are critical to the free enterprise system, the depth and liquidity of capital markets, and their efficiency. The information that results when the standards are applied is used to help allocate scarce capital resources and to provide a basis of corporate accountability. FASB was formed in 1973.

IASB is an independent, privately funded accounting standard setter based in London. IASB members come from nine countries and have a variety of functional backgrounds. IASB is committed to developing, in the public interest, a single set of high-quality, understandable, and enforceable global accounting standards that require transparent and comparable information in general-purpose financial statements. IASB cooperates with national accounting standard setters to achieve convergence in accounting standards around the world. It was founded in 2001.

In March 2002, the European Parliament ruled that all companies listed on the European exchanges, approximately 7,000, must present their financial statements using IAS no later than December 31, 2005. Currently, the U.S. SEC—which has a crucial interest in the process of disclosure and in the integrity of the accounting system—does not accept the presentation of financial statements using IAS and requires conversion to U.S. GAAP.[7] Approximately 50 foreign issuers listed on the U.S. exchanges must present such reconciliation. The new requirement of the European Parliament will affect approximately 600 European companies listed on the U.S. exchanges, which will have to file according to U.S. GAAP as required by the SEC. It is clear that the new ruling will put pressure on both standard setters to converge their systems as soon as possible.

Differences between U.S. and International Accounting Standards

Resolution of the differences between the two sets of standards is complicated by philosophical, cultural, and political factors, such as the debate involving the fact that FASB uses a methodology based on rules, while IASB uses a methodology based on principles.[8] Some proponents argue about the superiority of U.S. GAAP as a standard due to the fact that IAS allows much more room for interpretation. However, opponents point out that the voluminous and detailed FASB guides were not enough to prevent the Enron disaster. The debate on whether Enron violated the 3 percent guideline of EITF 90-15, which defines control of special-purpose entities (SPEs) and the consolidation requirement, is regarded as meaningless.[9] In fact, under IAS, control is not defined quantitatively, but rather looks at the ability to exercise operating control, execution, and decisionmaking over the SPE.

---

[7] In February 2000, the U.S. SEC issued a Concept Release (the first stage in a proposed change in its Rules), which discussed the use of IAS in U.S. capital markets. The release solicited comments regarding the quality of IAS and raised questions regarding what supporting infrastructure would be necessary in an environment where issuers and auditors often are multinational organizations, providing financial information in many countries. The release sought to identify what important concerns would be raised by acceptance of IAS standards; it asked for comments on whether the Commission should modify its current requirement that all financial statements be reconciled to U.S. GAAP.

[8] Standards based on principles would require more flexibility, but a much stronger audit function.

[9] The guidelines require that only up to 3 percent of the SPE be owned by an outside investor to avoid classification of the SPE as a subsidiary, thus, forcing the entity to include the SPE's financial position and results of operations in its financial statement. The Emerging Issues Task Force (EITF) was formed in 1984 in response to the recommendations of FASB's task force for timely financial reporting guidelines and FASB's invitation to comment on those recommendations.

In testimony before the U.S. Congress in March 2002, the SEC chairman supported standards based on principles (Pitt 2002). This indicated that the SEC would use its power as regulator to insure that FASB, as the standard setter in the United States, would start using the methodology based on principles instead of the complex and detailed methodology based on rules.

In some instances, elimination of the differences between U.S. GAAP and IAS would require replacing some of the existing standards with completely new standards. Both FASB and IASB are focused on issuing quality standards and not just attempting to converge the standards. For example, both bodies allow the use of smoothing to determine the value of pension plan assets. This technique allows smoothing out the peaks and valleys of the securities market in recognizing the value of the investments. It was impossible to decide which was the appropriate methodology allowed under both standards IAS 19 and FAS 87, and the replacement of both standards seems the right course of action.[10]

In other circumstances, the cooperation and influence of one standard-setting body could favor the standard-setting process of the other, as was the case in the treatment of stock options. IASB has taken the position that stock options must be recorded as an expense. In 1993, FASB took the same initial position while drafting FAS 123 Accounting for Stock Based Compensation, but in its final version, the standard was changed due to lobbying by business interests and politicians. The standard ended up in a compromise, which opted for a disclosure in the footnotes of the financial statement rather than the recognition of stock options as an expense as suggested by FASB's initial position.

IASB likewise is under pressure by political and business interests that may undermine its capability as an independent standard-setting body. In the process of convergence, it is essential that the accounting standard-setting bodies, national and international, build in mechanisms that assure independence in the face of pressures exercised by various interest groups. This is crucial for ensuring that the capital market agents and operators have confidence in the pronouncements of the standard-setting body.

---

[10] Both standards allow the use of the asset-smoothing method as an alternative means by which a defined-benefit pension plan measures its assets for funding and expense purposes. It spreads the impact of investment gains and losses over several years rather than incurring the impact in a single year as in the case of the market asset method. The resulting smoothed asset value must be within plus or minus 20 percent of market assets.

Characteristics and Applications

IASB and FASB have a mandate to operate in different environments (international and national, respectively), respond to diverse needs, and apply distinct standard-setting structures and processes. The difference between the two sets of standards is inevitable, but, if financial statements presented under IAS are to be considered appropriate for cross-border filings, it is essential that IAS satisfy the need of the world financial markets for high-quality financial information. In this respect, U.S. GAAP has a longer history of use and records and has been repeatedly tested in the largest and most efficient capital market in the world.

Most of the controversy and debate surrounding the comparability of financial statements prepared under IAS and U.S. GAAP revolve around four main themes. First, although IAS and U.S. GAAP are broadly similar and, in many cases, the use of IAS can provide results that are analogous to those obtained by using U.S. GAAP, the existence of alternatives creates the potential for different results. For example, under *IAS 23 Borrowing Costs*, the allowed alternative treatment requires capitalization of borrowing costs incurred in the purchase, construction, or production of certain assets in a manner similar to that of *FAS 34 Capitalization of Interest Costs*. However, IAS 23 benchmark treatment requires that borrowing costs be expensed, which constitutes an alternative treatment with respect to U.S. GAAP. The existence of different alternative treatments and benchmarks creates a potential for noncomparability of financial statements.

Second, some experts argue that IAS is too broad and general and cannot guarantee that similar accounting methods are applied in similar circumstances or that similar results are consistently achieved. Arguably, this is true in some instances, although in others, IAS is equally as effective as or more effective than U.S. GAAP. For example, both *IAS 2 Inventories* and *Accounting and Research Bulletin No 43: Restatement and Revision of Accounting Research Bulletins* provide broad, general guidelines on cost-flow assumptions in estimating the cost of inventories. However, with regard to accounting for the inventories of service providers, IAS 2 provides more detailed guidance than the does U.S. GAAP.

Third, in some circumstances, IAS and U.S. GAAP standards are identical, but the lack of implementation guidance by IAS creates differences when applying the standards. For example, *IAS 33 Earnings per Share* and its U.S. GAAP counterpart, *FAS 128 Earnings per Share*, resulted from a team effort between IASB and FASB. However, FAS 128 implementation guidance is more detailed for some of the calculations required for determining earnings per share, as is the case in determining the impact of different types of contingencies related to contingent issuable shares. Consequently, there may be different results in the calculation of earnings per share between entities following IAS 33 and FASB 128.

Fourth, the difference in reported results between IAS and U.S. GAAP may be even more difficult to compare as more countries adopt IAS as their national standard. The lack of consistency in the application and enforcement of the standard in some jurisdictions will make it difficult to compare an IAS-based financial statement of an entity in Germany with a comparable IAS-based financial statement of an entity in Japan and, clearly, almost impossible to compare with a U.S. GAAP-based financial statement.

Agendas

At the top of IASB's agenda is the Improvements Project, which was undertaken following a request from the International Organization of Securities Commissions (IOSCO), the European Commission, and national standards setters such as FASB and includes several changes, both large and small, in 14 international standards. The purpose is to eliminate alternatives, redundancies, and conflicts in existing standards and align IAS with U.S. GAAP in areas such as accounting for foreign exchange and investment in subsidiaries that are not consolidated. In other areas, a dramatic divergence continues to exist in standards such as the last in, first out inventory method, which is allowed under U.S. GAAP but not under IAS.

The Improvements Project has also eliminated extraordinary items. Although in appearance this area seems to have significant differences between U.S. GAAP and IAS, in reality, the differences are minimal because not many transactions are treated as extraordinary items. In the United States, reporting an extraordinary item has become an ordinary occurrence. FASB did not totally eliminate this category, but instead decided to rescind one of the principal sources of extraordinary items, that is, the early extinguishment of debt. When *FAS 4 Reporting Gains and Losses from Extinguishment of Debt* was issued, it constituted an extraordinary item. Now, with all the innovations in the financial market, most companies have greater flexibility on how to retire their debt, and it is not considered an extraordinary item.

After debate among various stakeholders, FASB eliminated the standard that allowed use of the pooling-of-interest method for business combinations effective with acquisitions in 2001. The IASB also has a project on its agenda to do the same in 2002.

Innovation coupled with the need to create global standards has generated the necessity for FASB and IASB to reevaluate accounting standards. In addition, the creation of accounting standards is not static; rather, it has to be continually adapted to new commercial and financial transactions in a global environment.

The Impact of Standard Setting on Quality Control in Latin America and the Caribbean

Some emerging market countries have benefited by adopting either IAS or U.S. GAAP as their national accounting standards. This is especially true for those countries that had no national standards or whose national accounting standards did not provide adequate transparency.

In Latin America and the Caribbean, the adoption and convergence of the national standard-setting bodies to one of the existing standards have been mixed (see table 7-1):

- Two countries, Canada and Mexico, have convergence to IAS on their agendas. Canada's policy is to conform to IAS unless there is a fundamental disagreement or circumstances that warrant a different approach. In Mexico, Bulletin A-8 requires the use of IAS in the absence of a Mexican standard.
- Brazil and Uruguay issue national GAAP standards influenced by IAS. Argentina issues its own national standards and has announced that, in the future, it plans to base most, but not all, of its standards on IAS.
- Peru, Costa Rica, Honduras, the Dominican Republic, Panama, Guatemala, Ecuador, El Salvador, Nicaragua, and Haiti have adopted IAS in their entirety as the national accounting standards.
- Chile and Venezuela follow their own national GAAP and, in the absence of a national standard, require the use of IAS. Colombia also follows its own national standard, which is influenced by U.S. GAAP.
- Bolivia and Paraguay follow their own national GAAP, and there is no indication that they will adopt or converge to IAS.

The diversity of the standard-setting process in Latin America makes difficult, if not impossible, the comparison of financial statements prepared under the national GAAP with IAS or U.S. GAAP. The difficulty of the comparison includes those countries

Table 7-1 | National Accounting Standards and Quality Assurance Policies

Country	National professional organization	Estimated number of public accountants	National accounting standard	System quality control
United States	American Association of Certified Public Accountants (AICPA)	480,000	U.S. GAAP Convergence Project to IAS	Yes
Barbados	Institute of Chartered Accountants of Barbados (ICAB)		IAS fully adopted as benchmark	
Jamaica	Institute of Chartered Accountants of Jamaica		Examining the possibility of adopting IAS	
Brazil	Conselho Federal de Contabilidade	340,000	Brazilian GAAP influenced by IAS	In-process
Argentina	Fed. Argentina de Consejos Prof. de C.E. Fed. Argentina de Graduados en C.E.	80,000	Argentinean GAAP. Plan to base future standard setting mostly on IAS	No
Canada	Canadian Institute of Chartered Accountants	65,000	Canadian GAAP Convergence Project to IAS	Yes
Mexico	Instituto Mexicano de Contadores Públicos	27,000	Mexican GAAP Convergence Project to IAS	In-process
Colombia	CONFECOP INCPC	60,000	Colombian GAAP influenced by U.S. GAAP	No
Venezuela	Fed. de Colegios de Contadores Públicos	36,000	Venezuelan GAAP, in absence follow IAS, Mexican GAAP, U.S. GAAP in this order	No
Peru	Fed. de Colegios de Contadores Públicos	24,000	IAS in absence of IAS follow U.S. GAAP	Evaluation in process
Chile	Colegio de Contadores	8,800	Chilean GAAP in absence follow IAS	No

Country	Organization	Members	Standards	Adopted
Puerto Rico	Colegio de Contadores Públicos Autorizados	3,500	U.S. GAAP	Yes
Uruguay	Colegio de Contadores, Economistas y Adm.	3,500	Uruguayan GAAP influenced by IAS	No
Costa Rica	Colegio de Contadores Públicos	3,100	IAS	No
Paraguay	Colegio de Contadores	12,000	Paraguayan GAAP	No
Bolivia	Colegio de Auditores Colegio de Contadores	7,680	Bolivian GAAP	No
Honduras	Colegio de Profesionales Universitarios Colegio Peritos Mercantiles y Contadores	7,300	IAS	No
Dominican Republic	Instituto de Contadores Públicos Autorizados	6,000	IAS	No
Panama	Colegio de Contadores Públicos Autorizados Asociacion de Contadores Públicos	5,500	IAS	Evaluation in process
Guatemala	Instituto de Contadores Públicos y Auditores	4,000	IAS	No
Ecuador	Federación Nacional de Contadores	3,000	IAS	No
El Salvador	Asociación de Contadores Públicos Corporación de Contadores	3,000	IAS	No
Nicaragua	Colegio de Contadores Públicos	500	IAS	No
Haiti	Ordre des Comptables Professionnels Agrees	400	IAS	No
Trinidad and Tobago			IAS are adopted as national standards	
Total		**1,180,280**		

Source: Authors' calculations.

adopting IAS mainly due to the lack of consistency in the application of the standards and leniency of local regulatory enforcement of the standards.

Is a quality control system for firms in the practice of accounting and auditing necessary in Latin America and the Caribbean? A properly designed quality control system, which adapts to the culture and local practices of each country, is a requirement if the country wants to achieve the following:

- Raise the professional level of its professionals
- Improve the quality of audits
- Ensure that financial information is transparent, timely, and relevant
- Provide international and national investors with information that is useful in making business and economic decisions
- Reduce the cost of capital, which in turn will promote economic progress and innovation.

The adoption of a quality control system by the individual countries would enforce consistency in the application of the standard, which, if coupled with local regulatory enforcement, would permit the comparison of financial statements prepared for those enterprises in the countries that have adopted IAS or U.S. GAAP.

To implement quality in the preparation of financial statements, a country's system of quality control must first create the enabling conditions and controls to assure integrity of the system through consistent application of the standards, mandatory continued education, and independent supervision and enforcement of the system (see figure 7-2).

In Latin America and the Caribbean, the accounting and professional practice rules are enacted under a diverse set of mechanisms, which makes harmonization in the region difficult, but not impossible. Some countries enact the rules through the legislative process, while others have delegated the process to the country's regulators and professional accounting organizations. For example, a country in Central America adopted IAS as its accounting standard and enacted it into law by authority delegated to the government accounting regulator. A small, interested group of accountants challenged the enactment on grounds of a constitutional technicality in the form of the enactment, rather than in the substance of the law. In an around-the-problem solution, the government opted for giving autonomy to its regulators, the Superintendent of Banks, the Securities Exchange Commission, and the Insurance Commission, which require and enforce the use of IAS for financial statements filed by the agencies under their jurisdictions and represent approximately 90 percent of

Figure 7-2 | System of Quality Control for Audits

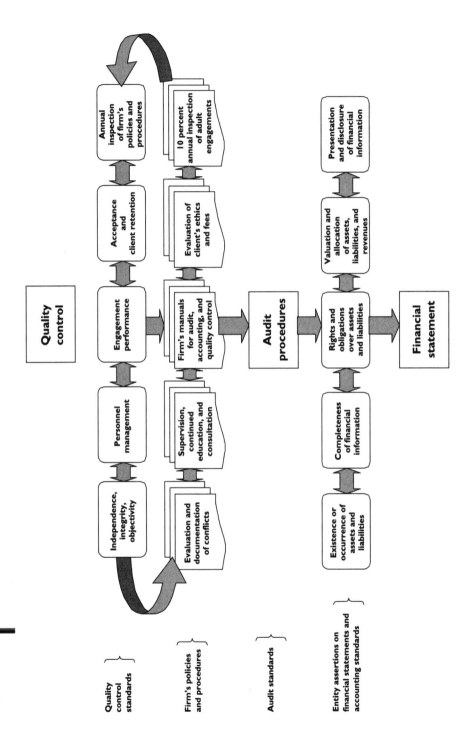

| Figure 7-3 | Enabling Conditions for Quality |

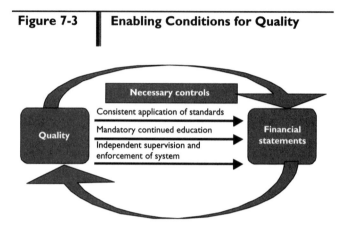

all filings. Thus, it is clear that Latin America and the Caribbean will have to implement enabling conditions and controls through a different mechanism in a coordinated effort with regulators.

A quality control system for accounting firms in private practice consists of the application of the quality control standards against which the structural organization of the firm and its established policies and procedures will be benchmarked. Such a system should be implemented to reasonably assure that professional accounting, auditing, and ethical standards are observed in the firms' business practices.

Figure 7-3 shows the flow of a system of quality control for an audit in which the quality control standards are applied against the firm's policies, and the auditing procedures test management's assertions on the financial statements and the consistent application of the accounting standards.

In those countries that have not adopted IAS or U.S. GAAP in their entirety, a reconciliation of the financial statements prepared under the countries' GAAPs to IAS and U.S. GAAP should be required for entities listed in the local exchange, banks, insurance companies, investment funds, and, in general, all entities of public interest. Table 7-2 presents a synopsis of the major differences between U.S. GAAP and IAS.

Policy Considerations and the Role of Multilateral Financial Institutions

This chapter has shown how healthy development of the financial sector—and of capital markets in particular—depends on disclosure and timely information. The

Table 7-2 | Areas of Major Differences between IAS and U.S. GAAP

Area of difference	IAS	U.S. GAAP
Stock compensation	No accrual and no disclosure of fair values[a]	The fair value of the stock option is recorded as expense or disclosed. The FMV of shares and the appreciation rights of the shares given to employees must be recorded as expense
Business combinations	The pooling-of-interest is allowed if the acquirer cannot be identified[a]	All combinations must be accounted under the purchase method
Goodwill	Amortized over a period of 20 years and also subject to the asset impairment test[a]	Generally is not amortized, but is subject to the asset impairment test
Research & development—acquisitions in process	Must be amortized	Recorded as an expense
Financial statement consolidation	Control test (could be with voting rights less than 50 percent)	Control test (majority of voting rights—over 50 percent)
Asset impairment	Is recognized if the discounted present value of future cash flows is bellow the asset's book value	Is recognized only if the future cash flows (not discounted) are bellow the asset's book value
Provision for liabilities of uncertain timing and amount	Once comprehensive standards exist, discounting is required	No general standard in effect. Some provisions are not discounted
Issuance of convertible debt	The proceeds from issuance are divided between liability and equity	The proceeds are recorded entirely as a liability

(Table continues on next page.)

Table 7-2 | Areas of Major Differences between IAS and U.S. GAAP *(continued)*

Area of difference	IAS	U.S. GAAP
Hyperinflation	General price-level adjustment of subsidiary's financial statements is required and gain or loss of net monetary position is recorded in net income	Remeasure of subsidiary using parent's functional currency
Discontinued operations: Expectation for future operating losses	No accrual	Accrual
Direct initial costs for lessors	Amortize or expense over the term of the lease[a]	Recognized as an expense
Foreign exchange differences on monetary transactions	Sometimes is added to the cost basis of the asset[a]	Always recorded in net income
Segment reporting	Business segments are lines of business and geographical areas. Must report using consolidated GAAP. Segment definition	Segments are components for which information is reported to management and can use whatever GAAP is used for internal purposes. No segment definition
Property, plant, and equipment	Revaluation is allowed	Revaluation is not allowed
Investment in property	Can use either fair value or cost model	Only cost model is allowed
Correction of errors	Either restate or include cumulative effect in earnings[a]	Restate

Accounting changes—nonrequired	Either restate or include cumulative effect in earnings[a]	Restate
Financial statement formats	Specific line items are required	SEC regulations require specific formats but not under FASB
Comprehensive income	Reporting not required[a]	Reporting required
Statement of cash flows	Interest received and paid could be recorded as operating, investing, or financing	Interest received and paid is recorded as operating
Construction contracts for which the percentage of completion cannot be determined	Cost recovery method	Completed contract method
Capitalization of interest on constructed assets	Optional	Required
Preferred shares—mandatory redemption	Recorded as liability	Split between liabilities and equity
Investment in joint ventures—incorporated	Equity method or proportionate consolidation	Equity method
Change in value on investments with not readily available market	Either in equity with recycling or in earnings[a]	In equity with recycling
Special-purpose entities (SPEs)	Must be consolidated if controlled	Qualifying SPEs are not consolidated

[a] The IASB currently has a convergence project with U.S. GAAP.

application of accounting standards in financial reporting constitutes a fundamental instrument for achieving the goal of releasing information according to the criteria of accuracy, completeness, and comparability. These requisites allow the market to function and grow, introducing more effective market discipline, which results in proper valuation of business entities according to the risk-reward trade-offs.

Latin American and Caribbean countries are at a crossroads; if the countries in the region want to develop their financial markets, they must embrace the process of transparency and disclosure. It is likely that in the long run, through cooperation among national and international standard-setting bodies, the two relevant bodies of standards, that is, IAS and U.S. GAAP, will converge. Nevertheless, Latin American and Caribbean countries should aggressively pursue the political decision to effectively implement appropriate and internationally accepted accounting and auditing standards and prepare themselves for the process of harmonization and globalization. Implementation requires more than just passing legislation. Making accounting standards a part of the routine of the local business community entails considerable efforts through setting up independent regulatory bodies, ensuring effective enforcement, providing training and education, and implementing quality control systems. It represents a long-term, continuous exercise that demands patience, commitment, and oversight.

Any change in a country's legal and regulatory system requires coping with the political, cultural, and social realities of that country. However, internationally accepted accounting standards have specific characteristics that facilitate their adoption and effective implementation. More than other standards, they are self-contained and stand alone, in that their application does not require that the domestic legal system necessarily be changed. This is the so-called interdependence of rule under which the rules have to be inserted and understood in the context of other legal concepts of the domestic system. The autonomy feature of the accounting standards facilitates their introduction in national systems as the rules embodied in the international standards make only limited reference to legal terms and concepts existing in the recipient legal system. In addition, accounting standards are a crucial component of financial stability and therefore have important characteristics and benefits that go beyond an individual country.

It should be highlighted, however, that no matter how good and sophisticated the rules and practices that are put in place, the system's success ultimately depends on the set of incentives that are designed around various stakeholders whose ultimate interest is the preservation of an efficient capital market system.

The system also depends on the institutional settings that mold the behavior of the various players. In addition, policymakers must have a long-term view and be aware that results will not come quickly and that there is a continuous need for over-sight in introducing changes and adjustments. These are the hard lessons of recent ex-periences in the capital markets in the United States.

Just as it is recognized that accounting is a mechanism for the public good of financial stability, it is also recognized that the effective implementation of accounting and auditing standards provides benefits at more than just the country level. Against this background of financial stability as an international or regional public good, the World Bank and the Inter-American Development Bank, in the context of their work on financial sector reform, provide advice (in the form of best or good practices) and financing to support countries introducing mechanisms, such as accounting and audit-ing standards, that favor financial stability and financial sector development.

The International Monetary Fund and the World Bank have been conducting Reports on the Observance of Standards and Codes (ROSCs) that analyze country compliance with selected international standards, including those related to account-ing and auditing. The accounting and auditing module of a ROSC assesses the status of the accounting practices in a given country and prepares a specific report for the government. The report helps to guide policy discussions with the relevant national authorities and is used by rating agencies in their country assessments and by the pri-vate sector for risk analysis. As countries undergo ROSC assessments, the demand for assistance in accounting and auditing standards will increase.

The Multilateral Investment Program (MIF) of the Inter-American Develop-ment Bank has launched a complementary program as part of its Cluster Action Plan. The program is aimed at supporting the competitiveness of Latin American and Carib-bean countries through the adoption of internationally accepted standards and the pro-vision of financial support to countries and/or accounting associations that want to move ahead in the areas of application of the standards, training, and quality control. Projects in the accounting cluster will share the same technical theme and development goals and can be managed and monitored as a group. This will promote the effective use of MIF resources, generating economies of scale and facilitating the sharing of proj-ect information and experiences that will yield important lessons. Moreover, these operations will provide valuable demonstration effects through the dissemination of results from projects that promote the implementation and harmonization of interna-tional accounting and auditing standards. In addition, clustering these projects offers a high potential for a catalytic impact that will encourage learning and sustainable out-comes across the region. Finally, MIF financing, coming partly coming from so-called non-borrowing countries and partly from recipient countries, is particularly appropriate be-cause of the nature of the program and the fact that the effective implementation of accounting and auditing standards and practice constitutes a public good whose benefits are not confined to the country that is undertaking the implementation.

Bibliography

American Institute of Certified Public Accountants (AICPA). http://www.aicpa.org/.

Ball, R. 1972. Changes in Accounting Techniques and Stock Prices. *Journal of Accounting Research* Supplement 10:1–38.

Ball, R., and P. Brown. 1968. An Empirical Evaluation of Accounting Income Numbers. *Journal of Accounting Research* 6:159–77.

Ball, R., and S. Kothari. 1991. Security Returns Around Earnings Announcements. *The Accounting Review* 66:718–38.

Bank for International Settlements (BIS). 1997. *Draghi Report. Financial Stability in Emerging Market Economies.* Basle, Switzerland.

Collins, D., S. Kothari, J. Shaken, and R. Sloan. 1994. Lack of Timeliness Versus Noise as Explanations for Low Contemporaneous Return Earnings Association. *Journal of Accounting and Economics* 18:289–324.

Crockett, Andrew. 1997. Why Is Financial Stability a Goal of Public Policy? In Federal Reserve Bank of Kansas City, *Maintaining Financial Stability in a Global Economy.* Kansas City.

Di Piazza, Samuel A., and G. Robert Eccles. 2002. *Building Public Trust. The Future of Corporate Reporting.* New York: John Wiley and Sons.

Fama, Eugene. 1970. Efficient Capital Markets: A Review of Theory and Empirical Work. *Journal of Finance* 25:383–417.

_____. 1991. Efficient Capital Markets II. *Journal of Finance* 46:1575–617.

Financial Accounting Standards Board (FASB). http://www.fasb.org.

_____. 1998. *International Accounting Standard Setting: A Vision for the Future.* FASB's Special Report. Norwalk, Conn.: Financial Accounting Standards Board.

Grossman, S., and Joseph Stiglitz. 1980. On the Impossibility of Informationally Efficient Markets. *American Economic Review* 70:573–85.

Herdman, Robert K. 2002. *The Roles of the SEC and the FASB in Establishing GAAP.* Testimony of the chief accountant, U.S. Securities and Exchange Commission before the House Subcommittee on Capital Markets, Insurance, and Government-Sponsored Enterprises, Committee on Financial Services, May 14.

Inter-American Development Bank and Multilateral Investment Program (IDB-MIF). http://www.iadb.org/mif.

International Accounting Standards Board (IASB). http://www.iasb.org.uk/.

_____. 2002. *Improvements to International Accounting Standards.* London.

International Federation of Accountants (IFAC). http://ifac.org.

Jensen, Michael. 2000. *A Theory of the Firm.* Cambridge, Mass.: Harvard University Press.

Jensen, Michael, and William Meckling. 1976. Theory of the Firm: Managerial Behavior, Agency Costs, and Ownership Structure. *Journal of Financial Economics* 3:305–60.

Kaul, Inge, Isabelle Grunberg, and Marc Stern (eds.). 1999. *Global Public Goods.* New York: United Nations Development Programme (UNDP).

Kothari, S. P. 2002. *Capital Markets Research in Accounting.* Cambridge, Mass.: Massachusetts Institute of Technology, Sloan School of Management.

La Porta, Rafael, Florencio Lopez-de-Silanes, Andrei Shleifer, and Robert Vishny. 1998. Law and Finance. *Journal of Political Economy* 106 (December).

Litan, E. Robert, and J. Peter Wallison. 2000. *The GAAP Gap-Corporate Disclosure in the Internet Age.* Washington, D.C.: American Enterprise Institute-Brookings Joint Center for Regulatory Studies.

Lo, Andrew W., and A. Craig MacKinlay. 2002. *A Non-Random Walk Down Wall Street.* Princeton, N.J.: Princeton University Press.

Nobles, W. Christopher (ed.). 2001. *Introducing GAAP 2001.* Andersen, BDO, Deloitte Touche Tohmatsu, Ernst & Young, Grant Thornton, KPMG, Price Waterhouse Coopers.

Pistor, Katharina. 2000. *The Standardization of Law and Its Effect on Developing Economies.* G-24 Discussion Papers. New York: United Nations and Harvard University Center for International Development.

Pitt, Harvey L. 2002. *Accounting and Investor Protection Issues Raised by Enron and Other Public Companies.* Testimony of the chairman U.S. Securities and Exchange Commission, before the Committee on Banking, Housing, and Urban Affairs, United States Senate, March 21.

Saudagaran, Shahrokh M. 2001. *International Accounting. A User Perspective.* South Western College Publishing, Thomson Learning.

Shiller, Robert. 2002. Celebrity CEOs Share the Blame for Street Scandals. *The Wall Street Journal,* June 6.

Staking, Kim, and Alison Schultz (eds.). 1999. *Financial Disclosure.* Inter-American Development Bank.

Sunder, Shyam. 2001. *Knowing What Others Know: Common Knowledge, Accounting, and Capital Markets.* Working Paper AC-08. School of Management Yale University.

U.S. Securities and Exchange Commission (SEC). http://www.sec.gov/.

Watts, R., and J. Zimmerman. 1978. Towards a Positive Theory of the Determination of Accounting Standards. *The Accounting Review* 53:112–34.

_____. 1979. The Demand and Supply of Accounting Theories: The Market for Excuses. *The Accounting Review* 54:273–305.

_____. 1983. Agency Problems Auditing and the Theory for the Firm: Some Evidence. *Journal of Law and Economics* 26:613–34.

_____. 1986. *Positive Accounting Theory.* Englewood Cliffs, N.J.: Prentice Hall.

World Bank. 2001. *Global Public Policies and Programs—Implications for Financing and Evaluation.* Proceedings from a World Bank Workshop. Washington, D.C.: Operations Evaluation Department.

Wyplosz, C. 1999. *International Financial Stability.* In Inge Kaul, Isabelle Grunberg, and Marc Stern (eds.), *Global Public Goods.* New York: United Nations Development Programme (UNDP).

CHAPTER 8

Enhancing Market Infrastructure in Emerging Economies

Andrew Hook

In today's competitive capital markets, improvement of capital market infrastructure should be an integral part of any capital market reform or modernization program. Capital market infrastructure constitutes the set of systems, procedures, processes, and regulations that assure the trading, settlement, and clearing of capital market transactions. Compliance with evolving international standards—whether for clearing, settlement, or custody of securities—is necessary in order to assure investors that appropriate care is being taken of their investments. In a number of countries, the public sector is taking a proactive attitude by participating in international forums and encouraging the implementation of legislation, rules, and other measures to reduce the risks and inefficiencies associated with financial sector infrastructure. In addition, strong and effective competition among markets, financial sector participants, and specialized institutions is further driving institutions to develop and/or upgrade capital and financial market infrastructure that will make the country more competitive. The results of these actions from various sides are shorter settlement cycles, increased reliance on technology, and a premium on liquidity.

Prompted by high-profile disruptions of capital markets and by the public sector's emphasis on financial stability, investors in many countries are directly or indirectly taking the condition of capital market infrastructure into account in deciding in which markets to invest. Issuers are shifting their activity to the most liquid markets to reduce costs, and less liquid capital markets are losing some of their most actively traded securities and business. Without improvements in clearing, settlement, and tools for liquidity management, it will be difficult for many capital markets to flourish in the years ahead.

Although financial sector infrastructure is complex, its basic function is simple: to assure that trades of securities and derivatives are carried out promptly and without error in an orderly manner. The best type of infrastructure is virtually invisible to the investor—like the plumbing in the house—in that the investor never needs to think about what is happening or how it works. The clearing or preparation for settlement of securities and funds is reasonably simple, but it becomes more complex due to the variety of intermediaries. The settlement or actual exchange of value of securities or contracts and funds is equally simple but becomes complex due to the number of intermediaries and the interaction of securities and payment systems.

Under these circumstances, a major benefit of including financial infrastructure in capital market reform is that it improves the competitiveness of the overall market and, in particular, cross-border investors. However, even if other markets offer settlement at T+1 (where T+1 denotes trade date plus one, and T+0 is the same day of the trade), the movement of funds across borders could take longer than T+1. For example, the move to T+1 in the United States and Canada will likely be for domestic transactions only. Some in the industry also believe that the move to T+1 could create liquidity problems because international investors may have to pre-fund to ensure timely cross-border flows. If other markets offer straight-through processing (STP), some investors may well make this a decisive factor in determining where to invest. A market that requires less liquidity on the part of investors, in terms of positioning funds or credit for settlement, will be more attractive than one requiring more. An up-to-date infrastructure that complies with international standards and best practices is much more likely to attract a critical mass of investors than one that does not.

An additional benefit from including financial infrastructure in capital market reform is that it provides a vehicle for mobilizing marketwide support for the reform. A comprehensive strategy of capital market reform that includes infrastructure could improve the framework for decisionmaking, identify more viable alternative approaches, add another dimension to the reform effort, and more confidently develop a long-term perspective.

This chapter focuses on some of the issues that policymakers have to face in building market infrastructure in emerging economies. The underlying idea is that developing or upgrading capital market infrastructure is a key ingredient for effective capital market development. Designing and operating infrastructure that performs with a minimum of errors and delays and that can interact with other financial and information systems is a major challenge for policymakers in emerging economies and in Latin America and the Caribbean in particular. At the same time, policymakers have to regard this particular activity as part of the larger strategy for capital market development and provide the right incentives for the private sector to be part of this initiative.

Framework for Enhancing Financial Sector Infrastructure

In the past, policymakers tended to view financial sector infrastructure as a minor issue that could be left to technicians, but this is no longer the case. The growing relationships and linkages among capital markets worldwide mean that national policymakers must consider and define a public sector role in financial sector infrastructure and that they must recognize and address the strong competitive forces affecting markets and infrastructure. International financial institutions and organizations, such as the International Organization of Securities Commissions (IOSCO), the Bank for International Settlements (BIS), the International Monetary Fund (IMF), and the World Bank, as well as private sector entities, are developing standards and best practices for clearing and settlement that cannot be ignored. Infrastructure is now one crucial element in a capital market's overall competitiveness, and weaknesses in clearing and settlement can jeopardize the successful development of a capital market. This section introduces some of the key policy issues relevant for market infrastructure.

Efficiency

A fundamental challenge for market infrastructure is to ensure proper management of risks in the process of trading and settlement. There are several types of risk in this process, including principal risk, replacement cost risk, and liquidity risk, which arise from the possibility that the counterpart to a trade fails. Operational risk and legal risk may also give rise to principal risk, replacement cost risk, and liquidity risk. Operational risks arise from deficiencies in systems, human error, and management processes. Legal risk arises when the legal or regulatory regime does not fully support a clearance and settlement system, its rules, or the application of the rules designed to enforce the rights of system operators, participants, and their customers. Systemic risk is the risk that one participant that fails to meet its settlement obligations can cause other participants to subsequently default on their obligations.

Financial sector infrastructure is important because all participants in capital markets depend on its smooth and efficient functioning. It represents the intersection of the diverse and heterogeneous participants. It is composed of the institutions, mechanisms, rules, and laws that govern the clearing, settlement, and custody of capital market trades. Without a well-functioning infrastructure, capital markets could not flourish. Functions covered include registry of ownership, custody, communication of information, and instructions concerning changes in the status of securities. The infrastructure brings together participants in the capital markets to differing degrees. For issuers, the infrastructure provides the support for issuing equity, debt, and derivative instruments. For investors, including banks, market makers, brokers, institutional investors, nonbank investors, and individuals, infrastructure supports their trading activity and provides custody and related information services. For brokers and securities dealers, infrastructure supports the clearing and settlement of their own and their customers' trades in equity, debt, and derivatives.

Institutional Specialization

The institutional infrastructure framework for capital markets differs from market to market, but typically there are a number of specialized institutions responsible for different services. The key post-trade functions are clearing, settlement, and custody. Clearing involves preparation for settlement, including matching and instructions for delivering securities and/or funds. Settlement is the actual exchange of securities for funds or contracts for funds. In both cases, there can be significant economies of scale. In this context, over the years, participants in the markets have developed specialized institutions for different parts of the infrastructure. All or some of the participants in the market often own these institutions.

Stock exchanges, clearinghouses, central securities depositories (CSDs), and central counterparts are among the specialized institutions providing clearing and settlement services to the capital markets. Historically, a department of a stock exchange often carried out clearing and settlement functions. This department would be responsible for the execution of the securities side of the settlement. Another department or part of the stock exchange often oversaw the financial settlement of securities trades. Over time, these functions could be separated from the stock exchange and operated as autonomous organizations.[1]

Globally, CSDs continue to play a key role in securities clearing and settlement. The major trends are toward immobilization and dematerialization of securities, more timely and detailed information for custodians, more automation of services and linkages, or mechanisms to provide delivery versus payment. The U.S. Securities and Exchange Commission (SEC) Rule 17f-7 and similar rules that other regulatory bodies have issued, including IOSCO and regional securities organizations, show the tendency to move CSDs worldwide toward a set of best practices. In a number of

---

[1] The demutualization of exchanges to facilitate more rapid and innovative decisionmaking has represented one of the most important trends in the 1990s. In the mutual form, stock exchanges have often been slow to respond to competition and to adopt new structures and technologies. The new privately owned exchanges, however, pose a whole new set of regulatory and risk issues. See Karmel (this volume) on demutualization and capital market development.

countries, central banks are recognizing the marketwide importance of delivery versus payment (DVP) for securities markets, and some central banks are providing services that can reduce overall settlement risk.[2]

Central Counterparts

In the interests of reducing risk and increasing efficiency, exchanges have introduced
central counterparts in securities settlement. Traditionally, derivatives clearinghouses
have used central counterparts, as in the case of the Chicago derivatives exchanges.
Recently, institutions outside the United States have considered, and in some cases
adopted, central counterpart structures. A central counterpart in a typical case becomes the counterpart for each trade and maintains risk measures in order to limit
settlement and counterpart risk. This type of model can provide advantages for participants, in terms of capital requirements, and offers the advantage of anonymity for
traders. It can also present participants with a new set of risks, which may be difficult
to manage. For example, under this new framework, custodians, who traditionally
have maintained an agency relationship with securities clearinghouses, may now take
on a principal relationship vis-à-vis the clearinghouse. This changes the entire risk profile of the custody business, which could drive institutions to exit the business.

Cross-border Linkages

Cross-border linkages between central securities depositories are still relatively limited in number and usage; however, Europe and other parts of the world are paying
increased attention to them. A variety of custodian banks, commercial banks, and securities firms support cross-border securities functions on a company basis. If central
securities depositories or central counterparts were to extend their services, in particular to provide more real-time information on the settlement process, this could
improve efficiency. It also could represent competition for the financial institutions currently providing these services to institutional investors and other clients.

     Several recent developments underline the growing importance of cross-
border linkages of securities markets and infrastructure: the formation of a Central
Counterpart Group (CCP-12), the Group of 30 review of global clearance and settlement, and the Committee on Payments and Settlement Systems (CPSS)/IOSCO
recommendations on securities settlement systems. In 2001, 12 of the world's lead-

---

[2] Delivery versus payment refers to the extent to which market participants can safely exchange funds for securities.

ing clearing organizations formed a new association, CCP-12, dedicated to improving global clearing, netting, and central counterpart services.[3] Three specialist working groups will focus on collateral management, linkages, and risk management and best practices. Also in 2001, the Group of 30 formed a high-level committee to undertake a comprehensive review of clearance and settlement arrangements in global capital markets. The study will identify potential vulnerabilities in global clearing and settlement infrastructure and recommend steps to ensure its continued safe and efficient operation, with special emphasis on cross-border activity. Finally, the CPSS/IOSCO recommendations identify cross-border issues as a high priority for future work.

Role of Public Policy

Over the past five years, public policy, technology, and institutional organization and competition have been driving change in financial sector infrastructure. Changes in these areas are likely to shape the future evolution of markets and to play a critical role in the success or failure of developing capital markets. Renewed attention by officials on financial stability worldwide is leading to more emphasis on international standards and best practices, which are enforced in part through international institutions such as the IMF and World Bank and in part by the markets and investors. Box 8-1 presents an example of an ongoing initiative to develop modern recommendations for security clearance and settlement systems.

The public sector has been playing an important role in shaping the development of market infrastructure by emphasizing safety and reliability issues and, more recently, competition policy. With financial sector liberalization, privatization, and deregulation, capital markets around the world have grown in volume, and the authorities have recognized the importance of market-friendly measures to reduce and limit risks associated with capital markets. The rapid growth of cross-border transactions has underlined the importance of consistent and effective risk measures in a wide range of markets and countries. Key factors in public policy are:

- Increased international coordination on standards and best practices for financial markets and tighter risk controls

---

[3] As of mid-2001, membership included the Australian Stock Exchange Limited (ASX), the Brazilian Clearing and Depository Corporation (CBLS), the Canadian Depository for Securities Limited (CSD), Clearnet, the Depository Trust and Clearing Corporation, Eurex Clearing AG, Hong Kong Exchanges and Clearing Limited (HKEx), S. D. Indeval Mexico, London Clearing House (LCH), the Options Clearing Corporation (OCC), Singapore Exchange Limited (SGX)/ the Central Depository (Pte) Limited, Tokyo Stock Exchange (TSE), and the Chicago Mercantile Exchange Inc. (CME).

Box 8-1 | **Recommendations for Securities Settlement Systems**

In 2001, a task force established by the Committee on Payments and Settlement Systems and the Technical Committee of the International Organization of Securities Commissions jointly issued *Recommendations for Securities Settlement Systems*. The recommendations build on and extend the Group of 30's recommendations published in 1989. The task force was composed of 28 central bankers and securities regulators from 18 countries. A consultative report was circulated, and input was received from central bankers and securities regulators who together represented about 30 countries, as well as from representatives of the International Monetary Fund and World Bank.

The report presents 19 recommendations on key functions in securities settlement, including legal, pre-settlement, settlement, operational, and custody issues. The work builds on and is complementary to other international initiatives that focus on strengthening financial infrastructure. The emphasis is not prescriptive; it allows for significant flexibility in the implementation of the recommendations. As in the Core Principles for Systemically Important Payment Systems, participants are expected to be responsible for identifying and managing their own risks within a system where such risks are well defined.

These recommendations identify essential elements of securities settlement from a public sector perspective and provide officially endorsed standards for promoting improvements in the safety and efficiency of securities settlement systems. Recognizing the institutional diversity and country differences in securities systems, the recommendations focus on functions rather than specific types of institutions. While the recommendations themselves are fairly general, additional explanations and questions are provided to assist in their implementation. National authorities are responsible for the actual implementation of the recommendations.

- More emphasis on competition policy, particularly in the European Union for securities clearing and settlement
- A shift to settlement at T+1 in the United States, which is scheduled for 2004 and likely to be introduced in other securities markets.

Core Principles

In the past five years, international initiatives sponsored by international institutions and associations have complemented national initiatives to strengthen the regulatory framework. Although the Group of 30 recommendations on clearing and settlement date from the late 1980s, in many cases serious efforts were not undertaken to implement these principles until the late 1990s. A wide range of international institutions and associations are now developing best practices, core principles, and standards for various aspects of financial sector infrastructure. The institutions include the IMF, the World Bank, the BIS, IOSCO, the Group of 30, and various private sector international associations, such as the International Federation of Stock Exchanges (FIBV) and the International Society of Securities Administrators (ISSA).[4]

The approach has generally emphasized principles and objectives governing capital markets rather than dictating specific measures or means to achieve these goals. In a particular country, the private sector is asked to develop the means of achieving the stated goals, and the authorities must agree that the means are appropriate and adequate. At the international level, for example, the CPSS of the BIS is taking a similar approach to reducing foreign exchange risk associated with independent settlement of the two legs of a typical foreign exchange transaction. A group of private sector financial institutions has been developing a multicurrency settlement system (continuous linked settlement, CLS) to reduce these risks.

Technology as a Key Driver

Securities market infrastructure is becoming even more dependent on information technology (IT) and telecommunications, and the supporting systems are becoming more complex. Competitive issues and the evolution of the regulatory framework are shaping the changes. In general, regulators have sought to remain neutral with regard to any specific technology, in part to avoid commercial bias. While this objective will remain crucial, the deepening interdependence of market infrastructure and technology will underline the importance of a good understanding of existing and evolving technologies supporting the markets. This interdependence is also driving regulatory concerns about operational risk and the importance of adequate contingency planning.

Key areas for technology in market infrastructure include STP, standards for messages and information, delivery versus payment, real-time information, translation, and action capabilities and optimization for collateral management and similar systems.

After a long period of relatively little change in traditional capital market infrastructure, competitive, technology, and regulatory forces are reshaping the infrastructure. The traditional structure was characterized by mutually owned service utilities that tended toward vertical integration of trading, clearing, and settlement. Derivatives exchanges tended to be operated independently of equity exchanges. Technology was important, but largely viewed as supportive and developed in-house.

Competition, deregulation, and new capabilities provided by technology are causing market participants and organizations to review the allocation of infrastructure functions and business activities from a strategic perspective. Third-party vendors

---

[4] See FIBV (1999), International Securities Services Association (2000), and Guadamillas and Keppler (2001).

and IT and consulting companies are developing alternatives to in-house securities processing. Fund managers, broker-dealers, custodian and subcustodian banks, investment banks, institutional investors, and others are questioning how deeply they want to be involved in IT support functions.

Global Developments to Upgrade Capital Market Infrastructure

Globally, financial sector infrastructure is experiencing a period of transition. Changes in the institutional and regulatory frameworks and stiff competition, nationally and internationally, are transforming financial sector infrastructure in most of the major economies. For many years, until recently, the infrastructure was characterized by national regulation and mutual ownership of exchanges and various related functions by participants or a subset of participants. This model has supported a tremendous increase in capital market activity over the past 10–15 years.

During this period, competition among exchanges was limited, as each focused on its own business and listed securities. First, to the extent that there was integration, it was vertical, including functions relating to one market. Competition existed between exchanges in the United States and through American Depository Receipts, but in general there was a home market for securities listed on a particular exchange. This structure started to erode a few years ago, marked by the success of Eurex in winning business away from the London Stock Exchange. A second factor was the formation of electronic communications networks, which challenged the dominant positions of established exchanges.

Rapid changes in technology enabled a whole range of securities trading and processing functions to be delivered at relatively low prices. The combination of innovative technology and strong and large competitive financial institutions meant that no exchange was beyond threat, particularly if that exchange was not keeping up with the new developments in technology. In this world of rapid change, the old corporate form of mutualization and cooperatives did not allow for rapid decisionmaking, precisely at a time when it was urgently needed. The third characteristic of the transitional period is the demutualization of exchanges to allow more rapid decisionmaking and strategic thinking.

In payment systems, real-time gross settlement (RTGS) systems are increasingly being implemented as the core system in national markets, while new types of hybrid payment systems are evolving. RTGS systems are becoming the large-value payment transfer system of choice for central banks, as such systems are being implemented in countries throughout the world. In the context of evolving technology and internationally endorsed core principles, more standardized RTGS systems are being developed for small and medium-size financial sectors. Hybrid payment systems, which retain elements of netting, but which are almost functionally equivalent to RTGS systems, are also being developed. These systems enhance the risk management of deferred net settlement systems and seek to economize on the need for liquidity for settlement purposes. One such system, EAD, has been developed in Germany, while the Clearing House Inter-Bank Payments System (CHIPS) is also moving toward a real-time hybrid net settlement system.

The adoption of the Target payment system in Europe for the euro is the first case of an extensive cross-border payment system, although there have been several privately operated systems on a smaller scale. The Target system, introduced in 1999, makes use of a system of cross-collateral held at the central banks in order to facilitate liquidity management. The major private sector initiative, the CLS system, is progressing with the formation of a bank and clearing organization, but the pilot has yet to be undertaken. The CLS is designed to settle both legs of foreign exchange transactions for the major currencies so as to reduce or eliminate the principal risk that currently exists for most transactions.

Derivatives exchanges are likely to be an integral part of the new financial infrastructure, as they have been developing rapidly, taking advantage of the new technologies. Although a few of the older style open outcry pits continue, particularly in Chicago, the systems of choice are electronic trading systems. Eurex has demonstrated the potency of electronic exchanges, and this is clearly the direction of the future. To the extent that derivatives exchanges are successful, and many are, there will be an incentive for other clearing and settlement institutions to tap into this flow of business through mergers, acquisitions, or strategic partnerships.

In the United States, the SEC has decided to reduce settlement risk by mandating that the settlement period for securities should be shortened to T+1 from T+3. This decision will have a major impact on financial sector infrastructure over the next five years, requiring major adjustments in most firms' internal operations as well as measures common to the entire market. Estimates of the cost for preparation for T+1 for the financial sector in the United States range from $8 billion to $9 billion, as new systems are introduced throughout the industry. The switch over is currently scheduled for mid-2004. Institutions and authorities in other countries are already examining the implications for their own markets, with the likelihood that a similar T+1 settlement period will be introduced in many of them.

The shift to a T+1 settlement period involves the whole market and the examination of each step in transaction processing to reduce the time and chance of errors. Participants at each level of the market—fund managers, brokers, and custodians—must be involved, as well as the clearing and settlement institutions. In addition, specialized service providers are offering to support market participants who want to outsource various parts of the transaction cycle. The scale and scope of changes required in IT are such that the overall institutional infrastructure is likely to change over the next five years. Not every firm will want to be heavily involved in the IT upgrading and changes that will be required, but IT firms or firms specializing in aspects of IT and market infrastructure will be looking for business opportunities.

A good example of the way in which cross-border standards are being developed for capital market infrastructure can be seen in Rule 17f-7 of the U.S. SEC, which became effective on July 2, 2001. This rule requires global custodians to provide U.S. investment funds with an analysis of risks for each non-U.S. depository that they use. The rule identifies key risk areas but does not dictate what and how the risks must be limited or managed. The rule has led not only custodian banks, but also central securities depositories and some private sector entities, to evaluate depository risks in the context of consistent definitions and measures of risk. Other regulatory bodies, such as the Financial Services Authority in the United Kingdom, are also developing guidelines for their institutions that use foreign depositories.

In the United States, electronic communication networks and industry efforts to streamline the transaction cycle for securities have also raised competition issues. Two groups of institutions, the Global Straight through Processing Association (GSTPA) and Omgeo, are competing to automate the transaction chain to support a T+1 settlement period. Omgeo is a venture between Thompson Financial and the Depository Trust and Clearing Corporation (DTCC). The U.S. SEC has required interoperability for Omgeo to avoid undue control over access to the network by DTCC.[5] While it is too early to predict the shape of the final market infrastructure that will result from the competition, it is certain that the evolving competition policy of U.S. regulators will influence the infrastructure.

The move toward STP is having a major impact on market infrastructure in the United States, and other markets are moving in this direction. All aspects of capital markets in the United States are being affected, and 90 percent of the cost of moving to T+1 is expected to be dedicated to achieving STP. In the pre-settlement environment, three areas must be covered: a matching engine, information management, and performance measurement tools. Interim solutions will be needed to deal with the various languages in current use, including Financial Information Exchange

---

[5] Omgeo is primarily focused on the U.S. market and GSTPA on the cross-border market. While both focus on institutional delivery, they are not involved in clearing and settlement or the exchange of the trader.

(FIX), Extensible Markup Language (XML), and SWIFT. The use of performance tools and benchmarking by asset managers will put pressure on settlement and clearing providers. In the United States, the Securities Industry Association estimates cost savings related to STP and T+1 settlement to be $2.7 billion per year, while SWIFT puts the global savings at $12 billion.[6] Translating these estimates to concrete cost savings for institutions will be a major challenge.

In this proliferation of technologies and solutions, standardized solutions or platforms for clearing and settlement have been slow to emerge. As more agreements are reached internationally on best practices, regulatory standards, and linkages, more comprehensive medium and small-size IT solutions will be possible. In the area of payment systems, for example, models for small but scalable RTGS systems are developing. The complexity and central importance of RTGS systems mean that totally off-the-shelf solutions do not make sense; however, with existing technology and experience, such systems are much more standardized than they were even a few years ago. Such platforms are likely to develop in the next few years for securities markets as well.

This strategic review is clearly evident in the United States, as institutions prepare for the shortening of the settlement period to T+1. Only the largest financial institutions and those specifically specialized in securities processing will certainly remain in the securities processing business; even some of these will modify their strategies in order to optimize over a range of related securities functions, including custody, securities lending, and collateral management. Fund managers and smaller custodians and subcustodians are more likely to look at outsourcing and alternative service providers. For example, stiff competition among fund managers for clients may lead these managers to focus more in-house resources on the competition for clients and less on securities processing and related issues.

In the United States, GSTPA and Omgeo are competing for transaction processing to support T+1, and other companies are focusing on other parts of the transaction cycle.[7] While this work may not have an immediate impact on clearing and settlement in other parts of the world, including Latin America and the Caribbean, it will have an impact in the longer term. Institutions in Canada, for example, are already gearing up for the switch to T+1 at the same time as in the United States, and institutions in Mexico are likely to have a similar response. A coordinated shift in these countries to T+1 will strengthen these markets and provide a reliable base for further expansion.

---

[6] Further information can be found at www.sia.com and www.swift.com.
[7] For further information, see gstpa.org and omgeo.com.

Even for markets that do not expect to change to T+1 at the same time as the United States, the new technologies and standards should provide means of speeding up the settlement process and improving reliability. In fact, the challenge for this shift in the United States is considerably larger than in many other countries because of the scale and scope of activities and the diversity of participants in the U.S. capital markets. Some markets outside the United States already have a capability of settling in T+1, and consequently this shift in the United States may open new possibilities for other markets willing to think and act strategically.

Perhaps even more than in the United States, securities processing and market infrastructure in Europe are in a period of structural change, driven by technology and likely to be shaped by regulatory policies. Although national clearing and settlement systems in Europe are efficient and well functioning, cross-border transactions carry high costs relative to national costs. Consolidation of securities processing has already started in Europe, with the formation of Euronext, which is bringing together markets in Belgium, France, and the Netherlands. At present, the attention of the exchanges, central securities depositories, and other institutions, such as the ICSDs, are focused on developments in Europe. Once the consolidation has occurred, the surviving institutions can be expected to compete globally with market infrastructure in other countries.

Nonetheless, major differences of opinion on the type of consolidation or integration remain in Europe concerning the advantages of horizontal or vertical integration. The London Stock Exchange is making a case for the benefits of horizontal integration, possibly with a Europe-wide clearing and settlement platform, while the Deutsche Bourse seems to be arguing more for vertical integration similar to what currently exists in Germany.[8] The issue is a complex one, not least because of competitive forces and regulatory concerns. The European Union has already launched a review of competition in securities clearing and settlement in Europe, and this is very likely to have an impact on the range of possible solutions on a Europe-wide basis. At this point, it is impossible to predict what sort of solution or integration will result, in part due to the large number of strong competitors. These include Euroclear, Clearstream, as well as SWIFT, the exchanges themselves and the clearinghouses, large financial institutions, and central securities depositories. The only thing that is certain about the process is that it will take considerable time, from a political, regulatory, and strategic perspective and from an IT perspective.

---

[8] In vertical integration, the different layers of infrastructure, depository, clearing, and settlement are owned and operated by local parties, as a type of silo. In horizontal integration, for settlement, for example, the settlement system operates across different markets and is owned and operated by one set of owners.

In addition to the establishment of Euronext, which illustrates an incremental approach to consolidation or integration of market infrastructure, institutions in Scandinavia are exploring regional solutions for market infrastructure. Swedish and Danish institutions are leading a collaboration of Scandinavian stock exchanges and central securities depositories to develop common platforms and linkages among the markets.[9] Political, regulatory, and technology differences persist, however, and it will take some time for the four markets to become fully integrated. A key element of the effort in Scandinavia is the formation of national securities associations and similar organizations to develop and lobby for necessary changes in legislation and regulation.

In Asia and other areas of the world, the focus in market infrastructure continues to be primarily at the national or country level. Institutions are focusing on the implementation of the Group of 30 recommendations on securities clearing and settlement, including delivery versus payment, T+3 as a settlement period, same-day funds, and a central securities depository. Malaysia is an example of a pro-active strategy where a major set of reforms for the securities market as a whole has been implemented. The overarching goal is to strengthen investor confidence in the market's operation, drawing heavily on best practices internationally and in other countries. The Kuala Lumpur Stock Exchange is to offer institutional settlement service for clearing and settlement. Clearing membership is being extended to include resident custodian banks and institutional investors, and DVP has been introduced.

Capital Market Infrastructure in Latin America and the Caribbean

National goals of encouraging foreign investment and maintaining or increasing liquidity and market size in the face of strong international competition drive the development of capital market infrastructure in Latin America and the Caribbean. For instance, in Brazil, both the private and public sectors are moving along these lines.

Capital markets in developed countries increasingly attract large companies based in Latin America and the Caribbean that are seeking to raise funds. American Depository Receipts, for example, are siphoning liquidity from the region. Furthermore, mergers and acquisitions of companies making up a large part of the float (ac-

---

[9] Information on the Norex alliance (Copenhagen Stock Exchange, Iceland Stock Exchange, Stockholmsborsen, and Oslo Bors) can be found at www.norex.com. Finland is currently taking a different approach, seeking linkages with systems within the European Union.

tively traded shares) and outside companies are reducing the size of markets in the region, which is affecting Argentina, for example.

In these circumstances, many markets in Latin America and the Caribbean are actively undertaking modernization and reform projects. These initiatives extend from the largest markets to the smallest and include Brazil, Mexico, Colombia, Peru, Panama, Costa Rica, and Jamaica. The main emphasis has been on improving existing infrastructure, largely at the national level. Initiatives are continuing in parallel in Central America and the Caribbean to develop regional market infrastructure. Although some exchanges and CSDs have linkages with other institutions in other countries, usage of these linkages is still limited and individual financial institutions with branches in many countries continue to play a key role in cross-border clearing and settlement.

While the initiatives vary from country to country, a number of elements are common, including introduction of international standards (G-30, IOSCO, and CPSS), DVP settlement, central bank participation, same-day funds finality, immobilization and dematerialization, and measures to assure liquidity and guarantee funds. International and regional institutions and organizations—the IMF, the World Bank, BIS, IOSCO, the Inter-American Development Bank, the Centro de Estudios Monetarios Latinoamericano (CEMLA), and the Council of Securities Regulators of the Americas (COSRA)— have been extending their work in standards and best practices for capital markets.[10]

Increased emphasis on the importance of delivery versus payment for settlement and on the advantage of either real-time or same-day finality has led to more central bank participation in capital market infrastructure improvements. This can be seen in the cases of Brazil, Colombia, and Mexico. This section reviews recent developments in capital market infrastructure in Latin America and the Caribbean, particularly in Brazil and Mexico and, to a more limited extent, in other countries. With well-designed account structures and risk controls, central bank provision of all or part of the financial settlement can be effective in reducing risk.

While the shift toward immobilization and dematerialization has been uneven from country to country, the general trend is clear; in most cases, the key market institutions are promoting dematerialization. Mexico in 1984 and Brazil in 1990 prohibited the issuance of bearer securities, initiating a shift toward more efficiency. There is also some progress in the registration of securities, although in some markets the registration process continues to go on after the settlement, undermining final legal transfer of ownership. In some cases, securities cannot be traded until after the registration, which can take days after the securities settlement.

---

[10] Further information can be found at the following websites: www.imf.org, www.bis.org, www.iosco.org, www.iadb. org, and www.cemla.org.

Brazil and Mexico

Large numbers of participants, diverse groups of financial institutions, complex legal and regulatory histories, and relatively large market capitalization and trading volumes characterize capital market infrastructure in Brazil and Mexico. Strategies for modernization and reform of the infrastructure are strongly influenced by unique factors in each country and not easily transferred to other markets. One common feature that will be relevant in other markets is the close cooperation between market participants, private sector institutions, and regulatory bodies, including the central bank. In these complex and diverse markets, coordination and cooperation between market participants and relevant public sector bodies are essential to carry out significant reforms and improvements of capital market infrastructure. At the same time, issues of risks and risk management, IT, telecommunications, and international standards will have direct relevance to reforms in other countries.

In the case of Brazil, capital market infrastructure is complex and sophisticated, reflecting its institutional evolution and development of underlying capital markets. Initially, market participants emphasized technical efficiency, reducing error rates, and automating the transaction cycle. In most cases, securities are dematerialized, with the remainder being immobilized.[11] Four areas concerning the infrastructure merit further attention:

- Institutionalized cooperation within groups of financial institutions and across groups
- Consolidation of entities providing services and support to the market
- Sophisticated IT platforms and solutions for securities processing
- Current introduction of an RTGS payment system and a set of changes so that the securities processing systems will meet current and evolving international standards and best practices.

In Brazil, the five major financial trade associations have been an essential part of the development of capital market infrastructure. In part this reflects a concerted effort by financial institutions in the past to survive and even flourish during periods of extremely high inflation. These associations have established key clearing and settlement institutions—the Brazilian Clearing and Depository Corporation (CBLC), for equities; the Center for Custody and Financial Settlement of Securities (CETIP), for

---

[11] The issuance of bearer securities was prohibited in Brazil in 1990.

other private sector and some government securities; and the Special System for Settlement and Custody (SELIC), for government securities—that play a role in the ongoing operation of the systems.[12] For example, the National Association of Open Market Institutions (ANDIMA) is responsible for furnishing hardware computer systems and skilled personnel for the SELIC system, which is owned by the central bank. With the high degree of diversity, competition, and business in Brazilian capital markets, this institutionalization of a cooperative approach to clearing and settlement has contributed to the streamlining of market infrastructure.

The past 10 years have seen considerable consolidation in market infrastructure in Brazil. Ten years ago, there were eight stock exchanges in the country, but the merger of the São Paulo Stock Exchange (Bovespa) with the Rio de Janeiro Stock Exchange at the beginning of 2000 leaves Bovespa as the only stock exchange in the country. Bovespa is a nonprofit organization owned by its members and is a key owner of the CBLC. Furthermore, the vast majority of derivatives transactions in Brazil are cleared and settled through the Commodities and Futures Exchange (BM&F). This exchange uses CETIP for financial settlements and provides its own clearing and custodian functions.

In spite of highly efficient technical securities processing, the lack of a payment system with same-day finality made the introduction of DVP difficult and did not support same-day finality for payments, as recommended by the Group of 30. In 2001 the country began introducing new arrangements for securities clearing and settlement and for payment systems, which are due to be completed in 2002. The central bank's launching of an RTGS system will support DVP for equities and other securities and will introduce same-day finality for payments. The new RTGS systems will support CBLC and CETIP settlement directly in accounts at the central bank. CETIP will establish a clearinghouse and will join CBLC in becoming a central counterpart for all trades that it clears and settles. These new systems will include a range of risk control measures in line with international standards and best practices.

The private and public sectors in Mexico are actively modernizing capital market structure in terms of risk management, efficiency, and liquidity. As in the case of Canadian markets, close attention is focused on developments in the United States, in particular on the shift to a T+1 settlement period. S.D. Indeval is the only company in Mexico authorized to operate as a securities depository.[13] It was incorporated as a private corporation in 1987 and provides custody, administration, and transfer of securities, as well as clearing and settlement.

---

[12] See www.cblc.com.br, www.cetip.com.br, bacen.gov.br, and bcb.gov.br.
[13] Indeval's annual report and other information are available at indeval.com.mx.

The market capitalization of securities held in S.D. Indeval was $321 billion at the end of 2000, with the equity market making up $179 billion; government securities, $111 billion; and bank securities, $31 billion. Daily turnover in 2000 was $63 million on average. The bulk of the turnover was for bank and government securities, that is, $39 million and $24 million, respectively, while daily equities turnover was only $324,000. Institutional trading drives the transactions in fixed-rate instruments, in contrast to equities where institutions do not play a large direct role.

All Mexican securities are held in registered form since S.D. Indeval acts as a central registrar, with assets held under the participant's name in a segregated account designated as belonging to third parties.[14] Registration of securities is executed simultaneously with settlement in S.D. Indeval. Securities are centrally immobilized in the depository. S.D. Indeval is promoting dematerialization for all securities. At present, government securities are dematerialized and held by Banco de México and settled through S.D. Indeval.

S.D. Indeval keeps abreast of international developments in capital market infrastructure through participation in international initiatives and national projects. The depository is a member of the Global Equity Market (GEM), a project to connect eight stock markets in 10 different countries, with the goal of performing settlement on a global basis. The depository is working with the Mexican Stock Exchange to develop this strategic project for the market. S.D. Indeval has also joined the CCP-12 group of central counterparts that is focusing on settlement issues.

S.D. Indeval is developing central counterpart capabilities as a way to reduce the use of credit and funding for settlement, increase liquidity, reduce default rates, and create a more robust guarantee fund to back settlements. Before the capabilities can be activated, however, the governing laws must be modified, and the depository is working to encourage the necessary changes. Finally, S.D. Indeval has launched a project aimed at encouraging STP, which is seen as essential for shifting to a shorter settlement period and maintaining consistent practices internationally.

Developments in Other Countries in Latin America and the Caribbean

Argentina

In the Southern Cone, large-scale modernization of payments and securities systems has been achieved in Argentina, while market infrastructure in Chile, although well functioning, has several areas that could be strengthened, relating to payment systems

---

[14] Bearer securities were prohibited in Mexico in 1984.

and same-day finality. Uruguay is about to launch reforms and establish the basic infrastructure for capital markets. Peru has implemented reforms and modernization, and Colombia has made significant progress. Several other countries, including Bolivia, Ecuador, and Venezuela, have started initiatives.

In the late 1990s, the Central Bank of Argentina, working with the private sector, developed a new regulatory framework for payment systems and launched an RTGS, the Electronic Payment Means (MEP). An interbank payment system committee was formed to support ongoing payment system reform. Other structural changes include the consolidation and privatization of low-value automated clearinghouses across the country and the development of large-value automated clearinghouses (ACHs).

The Mercado de Valores de Buenos Aires (Merval) maintains and operates the main clearing and settlement system for transactions for equity and corporate debt.[15] There is a single clearing and settlement system, which operates on a multilateral net settlement basis, similar to model 3 of the BIS approach to delivery versus payment. There is a separate clearing and settlement system for the settlement of certain short-term government securities, CRYL, or Central de Registración y Liquidación de Instrumentos de Endeudamiento Público. The central bank is operating this system initially, but it is expected to become part of a single settlement system for all securities in Argentina.

The government in Argentina has mandated that the financial markets establish a single clearinghouse to settle all over-the-counter trades on a DVP basis. The private sector has started work on this clearinghouse, which has been named Argenclear. The architecture for the system has been developed, but operations have not yet started. Argenclear's operations will be limited to securities registered and traded in the Mercado Electrónico Abierto (MAE), an institutionally oriented market for fixed-rate instruments.

Chile

Market infrastructure in Chile has recorded many years of smooth functioning in payments and securities markets; however, the use of checks, even cashiers checks, means that risk management has been different than in many other countries. In the early 1980s, the Central Bank of Chile made it clear that the development of market infrastructure, including payment systems, was the responsibility of the private sector. Since then, the banking system has developed an efficient countrywide check-clearing process. However, there are no payment instruments with real-time finality, and same-

---

[15] Further information is available at cajaval.sba.com.ar.

day finality depends, at least indirectly, on the central bank's guarantee of a certain type of check. This system has worked smoothly, but in light of the emerging importance of real-time gross settlement systems, the central bank is currently moving toward the establishment of such a system.

On the securities side, the Depósito Central de Valores (DCV) is the only depository in Chile and administers all forms of securities.[16] All stock exchange transactions for fixed-income instruments and stocks are cleared and settled through the depository. The settlement periods are T+3 for equities, T+2 for fixed-income instruments, and T for money market instruments. A little over one-third of securities held in DCV at the end of 2000 (a total of $67 billion) were in dematerialized form. There are two types of settlement, bilateral and multilateral (among brokers only). Bilateral settlement is on a DVP basis using certified checks, while multilateral settlement is not on a DVP basis. Multilateral settlement only covers equity trades among brokers and is relatively small compared with overall trading volume, but contains counterpart risk.

Peru

In Peru, the private and public sectors have taken a number of steps in recent years to improve market infrastructure. In 1998, the central bank established the Payment System Inter-bank Commission (CISPA) to spearhead change in payment systems. CISPA has provided a forum for developing a consensus on payment system reform. The central bank has recently introduced an RTGS system and is working with CISPA to introduce an electronic clearinghouse to streamline the large number of checks currently being used.

During the 1990s, capital markets in Peru underwent significant development, with the passage and implementation of securities market legislation. The Securities Market Law of 1996 presents the principles that govern the functions of securities markets in Peru. The country has passed legislation for a CSD and an independent private company, CAVALI.[17] This company started providing depository services in 1997, and the securities commission approved internal regulations in 2000.

Andean Countries

Among the Andean countries, Colombia has done the most to improve market infrastructure, although other countries are developing initiatives. Ecuador is working on

---

[16] DCV's website is www.dcv.cl.
[17] Further information on CAVALI can be found at www.cavali.com.pe.

a clearing and settlement platform for government securities, and Bolivia has legislation in place to support modern infrastructure. The Bolivian Stock Exchange is working with CAVALI in Peru to develop depository and settlement services. Modernization of market infrastructure is still in the early stages in Venezuela.

Colombia

Colombia illustrates how a comprehensive strategy for modernizing and reforming market infrastructure can be put in place. A critical element of this strategy is a cooperative marketwide approach with market participants, the CSD, stock exchanges, the central bank, and securities regulators playing key roles. The traditional institutional arrangement was similar to that in other countries in the region: a CSD with no linkages to the payment system, continued use of checks for some financial settlements, multiple stock exchanges (three), bearer securities and no or limited dematerialization, no central counterpart, and decentralized risk management for over-the-counter trades.

In the case of Colombia, the CSD, DECEVAL (Depósito Centralizado de Valores de Colombia) has been playing a key role in the improvement of market infrastructure.[18] Strong planning and implementation capability support the initiative, and recognition that institutional and regulatory changes take time has helped. DECEVAL has developed both short- and long-term strategies, planning for 2003 a central counterpart, collateral management system, and improved information services for the market. These plans are developed in consultation with market participants, regulators, and other stakeholders and approved by the board of directors of DECEVAL.

The president of the stock exchange has led the board, which included the vice presidents of treasury and operations of the most prominent banking entities in the financial sector. By tradition and practice, the board focuses on market development and not on private or individually driven initiatives. In addition, the superintendence also plays an important role in reviewing decisions, reports, and pronouncements of the General Assembly.

Following the consolidation of the three Colombian stock exchanges in 2001, a new settlement process is to be introduced. Linkages between the CSD (DECEVAL), settlement systems, the trading systems of the stock exchange, and the payment system of the central bank will become operational and will support a gross settlement model 1 for all securities except equities.[19] These will continue to follow a model

---

[18] DECEVAL's website is www.deceval.com.

[19] Information on the central bank's payment system can be found at www.banrep.gov.co.

2 settlement, with gross settlement of securities and net settlement of funds. Investors will have the option of choosing the DVP settlement or the free-of-payment settlement. DECEVAL will oversee the DVP settlement, and securities will be transferred directly from the seller's account to that of the purchaser. Funds and securities will be immediately available for retransfer on receipt. Initially, equities transfers will be executed on a free-of-payment basis, with the stock exchange continuing to operate the overall settlement for equities, which account for only 5 percent of the total market.

Other elements in the strategy include DECEVAL's promotion of the dematerialization of all securities in Colombia. Although a large part of securities in the country are still held outside DECEVAL, the intent is to dematerialize all securities and have these deposited with DECEVAL. Mechanisms to support securities lending and collateral management are also being developed, and investors will have access to real-time information concerning clearing and settlement through an Internet application. Off-site processing capability is also being developed for the new clearing and settlement systems.

Central America

In Central America, market infrastructure is less developed than in most South American markets, as capital markets remain limited in size and dominated by money market and fixed-rate instruments. CSDs have been introduced in most countries, although these institutions are still relatively new. Considerable progress has been made on both the regulatory and institutional sides in Costa Rica and Panama, while the depository in Nicaragua is developing a new clearing and settlement system.

A new securities law has recently been passed in Panama, and the internal regulations for LatinClear, the CSD, were approved by the regulatory authority in 2001. These deal with issues such as immobilization and dematerialization.[20] LatinClear has introduced a DVP mechanism with settlement at the National Bank of Panama (equivalent to the central bank). Checks are no longer used for financial settlement. To achieve DVP, securities are blocked on the trade date, but plans are in place to reduce the settlement period, currently T+3, and thus the period of time between the delivery of securities and the receipt of funds (asset commitment risk).

In most other countries in Central America, modernization of market infrastructure is in an early phase. Checks continue to be the most frequently used non-cash payment instrument, although an RTGS has been established in Costa Rica. A

---

[20] Information on developments in Panama can be found at www.latinclear.com.pa.

natural next step for check systems would be an ACH, but the lack of an appropriate legal and regulatory framework has delayed the introduction of ACHs in the case of El Salvador, for example. The appropriate legal and regulatory framework is an obstacle for modernization, in particular in regards to electronic payments, dematerialization, and registration of securities. In many countries, efforts to pass appropriate legislation are being undertaken, but the process is slow.

In the securities markets, clearing and settlement tend to be on a decentralized basis. The establishment of CSDs in the region is relatively new, and, in a number of countries, the depository functions are the responsibility of a department of the stock exchange. As in the case of payments, the lack of updated securities laws has been a serious obstacle to progress in a number of countries. New securities laws are being passed, however, as in the case of Honduras in 2001 and the Dominican Republic. With this foundation, modernization should be able to move ahead.

A regional initiative by financial institutions in Costa Rica, El Salvador, Guatemala, Honduras, Nicaragua, and Panama is under way to develop a common clearing and settlement platform that will be used in all these countries and a central depository with branches in each country. The Inter-American Development Bank and the Banco Centroamericano de Integración Económica (BCIE) are providing support for this initiative, which is being designed to meet international standards. Initially, each country will have its own central security depository, and these will be linked to carry out the proposed functions and communications. The BCIE has been undertaking feasibility studies with private sector consultants. The new platform is expected to build on technology developed for a real-time electronic funds transfer system, which is sponsored by the BCIE. Implementation is expected to start in 2002.

Caribbean Countries

In recent years, considerable progress has been made in modernizing market infrastructure in the Caribbean in terms of supporting legislation, launching new institutions (CSDs), and preparing for a regionally integrated capital market. Jamaica has been leading the efforts, both in terms of developing its own market infrastructure and encouraging the regional initiative. In 1998, the Jamaica Central Securities Depository Limited (JCSD) started operations as a wholly owned subsidiary of the Jamaica Stock Exchange (JSE).[21] That same year, the JSE launched its own automated clearing and settlement platform. CSDs have recently been established in Barbados, Bermuda,

---

[21] An annual report and other information on the JCSD can be found at www.jamstockex.com.

and Trinidad and Tobago and are being developed in the Bahamas and the Dominican Republic.

Starting in 1989, there has been a series of actions taken to support the development of a single capital market in the Caribbean. This has involved plans and work in three areas: establishment of a regional stock exchange; establishment of a common, automated clearing and settlement platform; and establishment of depositories in all markets. In 1989, the Jamaican government presented the Caribbean Common Market with a proposal for a Caribbean Stock Exchange in the form of a merger of exchanges in Jamaica, Barbados, and Trinidad and Tobago. In 1996, the Bahamas and the Dominican Republic were included in this plan.

In 1991, the stock exchanges of Jamaica, Barbados, and Trinidad and Tobago began cross-listing and cross-trading programs. Currently there are four companies participating in these programs. The JSE and Trinidad and Tobago exchanges also allow simultaneous trading. General interest in the creation of a regional exchange waned for several years, but recently has been renewed.

Conclusion: Strategies for Accelerating the Development of Capital Market Infrastructure in Latin America and the Caribbean

Efficient, safe, and well-functioning infrastructure is an integral part of any successful capital market. Without such an infrastructure, a capital market will not be able to compete with other markets that have achieved international standards with the effective use of current technology. As a growing number of investors turn to cross-border opportunities, observance of best practices and policies promoted by international financial institutions will become essential for individual capital markets to compete for business.

Capital market infrastructure has been evolving and is currently entering a new phase, with a new set of rules and objectives. In the earlier phase, the emphasis was on drafting and enacting appropriate legislation; establishing appropriate institutions, such as clearinghouses or central security depositories; and reaching a settlement period of T+3 and delivery versus payment for settlement. As these first initiatives are being completed, the need to move to the next phase of infrastructure development is becoming evident.

The next phase, which is currently under way, extends the standards and practices from the exchange of documents and instruments to the end users, intermediaries, and issuers. In this phase, market participants are also taking additional measures to economize on liquidity, while still controlling risk. Key elements of this new phase are:

- T+1 settlement period, or even T+0
- Straight-through processing
- Linkages and/or mergers between clearing and settlement institutions
- Closer linkages of securities and derivatives clearing and settlement with payment systems.

Under these circumstances, policymakers need to closely monitor the elements mentioned above, as well as the ongoing implementation of international standards and best practice in clearing and settlement. Faced with strong international competition for attracting resources, policymakers need to identify and promote the general interest of their own market and infrastructure and to counter narrow interest group positions that can undermine the viability of the overall market.

In addition, policymakers will need to devote more attention to the technology aspects of infrastructure, as these will determine in large part the success of a particular market in achieving a T+1 settlement with limited risk. It will be important to keep options open for modifications and changes in technology and its application and to avoid locking into solutions that can quickly become obsolete. Monitoring developments in technology as markets move to T+1 or even T+0 will be an important part of policymakers' decisionmaking process.

To be successful in developing capital market infrastructure, policymakers need to provide a vision, exercise good management, and obtain funding. In the past, market infrastructure was seen as an afterthought, something left to a few specialists, but it is now recognized that successful modernization requires attention and decisions from top managers. Investments at the market and institution level can be very costly, as shown by the estimated cost of shifting to T+1 in the United States, which is $8 billion to $9 billion. For individual institutions, capital investments are significant, and once the new systems are in place, further rapid changes tend to be prohibitively expensive. Senior management needs to make sure that regulatory requirements are met and the new infrastructure is strategically well placed for linkages, mergers, or acquisitions.

Vision

Vision is a necessary requisite to take into account the configuration of institutions, regulations, competition, and technologies in selecting the best set of alternatives for the modernization and success of a particular market infrastructure. This requires an excellent understanding not only of conditions in the market in question but also of relevant worldwide developments that could influence an effective solution. Some of the industry and company initiatives impose a standard for transactions processing in the United States with an emphasis on straight-through processing. Some of the industry work on establishing standards for transactions processing in the United States will support market infrastructure development in other countries. The experience of Euronext in consolidating the three markets and infrastructure in Belgium, France, and the Netherlands should also be relevant in other countries. Partnerships or other business arrangements with experienced companies can save time and cost in the modernization effort.

In these partnership and technology issues, vision is needed to inform final decisions. The IT and financial sectors are very competitive, meaning that many solutions do not succeed. Identifying the needs of a market, its participants, and infrastructure is as essential as evaluating the partners and the business plan and understanding current and future demand for services. The partnership between Morgan Stanley and OM (a Swedish technology and financial sector company) to provide a Europe-wide securities platform for retail trades is an example of a partnership that has been facing difficult times because of the market slump. Other partnerships could be with consulting firms, particularly those specializing in securities processing, and/or technology companies.

Similar to asset managers, some custodian banks are outsourcing securities processing, a move that may be appropriate in Latin America and the Caribbean. This could be at the level of an individual institution or a marketwide institution, such as a CSD or clearinghouse. This approach may make sense for regional markets with shared clearing and settlement capabilities. One innovative approach is that of Bolivia, which is working with CAVALI, the CSD in Peru, in developing its own CSD. The plan is to have the settlement done on a remote site, in Lima, by CAVALI. This would allow the existing capabilities in Peru to be more fully utilized and would save Bolivia the expense of building an entirely new system. The resolution of legal and regulatory issues is clearly essential for this type of arrangement. It is precisely for this reason that the experience in Bolivia and Peru should be valuable for other markets in the region.

Two regional initiatives are already under way in Central America and the Caribbean, and others could be undertaken for the Andean markets or the Southern Cone. The existing efforts deserve close attention, as they may initiate viable models for other regions. Currently, the tendency seems to be toward a common clearing and settlement platform, but with a depository in each country. To the extent that a company issues equity or other securities in its own country and that there is a legal basis for holding the securities in the country, it may make sense to continue to have depositories in each country, but with functions limited largely to custody. However, this is by no means the only possible outcome, as depositories could take on a wider range of functions, possibly cutting into the business of custodian banks. The point here is not to predict necessary outcomes, but to highlight the importance of monitoring developments in areas such as regional integration and IT.

Vision should be built on good, timely, relevant, and accurate information on a range of activities in IT, regulation, and institutional development. Strategic partners can be essential. In this context, international and regional institutions and associations can play an essential role by streamlining the flows of information and assuring more targeted dissemination. Activities in these areas can also help raise awareness of problems and issues for key parties that are not direct stakeholders in the market infrastructure. Some of the public sector institutions and organizations are IOSCO, CPSS of the BIS, the IMF, the World Bank, and the Inter-American Development Bank. At a regional level, COSRA and CEMLA have an important role to play, particularly in the implementation of best practices within the region. Various private sector associations, such as the American Association of Central Securities Depositories, also can play an important role in this process.

Management

Good management is essential for successful modernization of market infrastructure to translate the vision into strategies and action and to achieve concrete results. The large number of institutions involved, the multidisciplinary nature of market infrastructure, the importance to financial institutions active in clearing and settlement, the potentially high costs of investment, and the difficulty in visualizing opportunity costs make good management absolutely essential for successful modernization initiatives. The indispensable characteristics for management in this area are not different from those needed in any other large-scale business, although the diversity of stakeholders is probably wider than in other cases.

One of the challenges for management is to obtain the participation and commitment of all relevant stakeholders. Failure to reach a consensus among various stakeholders can jeopardize the initiative, even after considerable investment and work. It is also essential to have the active participation of financial sector supervisors, including the central bank and securities commissions. The safety and soundness of financial markets are a central objective of regulators, and the infrastructure needs to meet the requirements of supervisors. This can involve supervisory review of the modernization initiative at different phases. In some cases, in Brazil or Colombia, for example, the public sector may take a more active leadership role in the modernization effort. Where changes in legislation are required, this can be an effective approach.

In the past few years, supervisors and international financial institutions have devoted more attention to governance and its importance for safety and soundness. Governance is also crucial for the quality of decisionmaking. The responsibilities, composition, and powers of the boards of directors of market institutions are particularly important. A broader composition of board members is one way of taking the views of different sectors into account in deciding about modernization plans, and in shaping and implementing them. It is likely, for example, that the presence of central bank officials on the board of directors overseeing securities market reform, as in the case of Mexico, leads to better results for the initiative. The composition, powers, and terms of reference for the board of directors of the CSD in Colombia are most likely one reason for the success of the modernization initiative in that country.

Funding

Without adequate funding, no modernization can move ahead. In fact, both the vision and management functions are essential in order to obtain funding. Various development institutions, including the World Bank, the Inter-American Development Bank, the Banco Centroamericano de Integración Económico, and the Corporación Andino de Fomento, might be able to provide financial support and funding for market modernization. Funding may also come from market participants, demutualization, or the securities processing institutions.

The *Final Report of the Committee of Wise Men on the Regulation of European Securities Markets* addresses issues relating to the integration of securities markets in multiple jurisdictions.[22] The report aims at promoting efficiency, consistency, and fairness in securities markets. Recognizing the costs of fragmentation of markets, infrastructure, and regulation, the report presents recommendations for promoting a more integrated regulatory and supervisory structure. While the details of the recommendations may not be directly relevant for other regions, the underlying market, competitive, and institutional issues are likely to be similar. Thus, this report and its repercussions should be useful for other initiatives seeking to integrate or harmonize securities markets in other parts of the world.

---

[22] Committee of Wise Men (2001); www.europa.eu.int.

The report stresses that further restructuring of clearing and settlement is needed in Europe, in particular to achieve reasonable efficiencies. This restructuring is seen as primarily the responsibility of the private sector. However, inasmuch as an efficient clearing system is a public good, the report indicates that, in the absence of adequate private sector progress, "a clear public policy orientation would be needed to move forward." This is also the direction that Latin American and Caribbean countries should pursue.

Bibliography

Committee of Wise Men, Chairman Alexandre Lamfalussy. 2001. *Final Report of the Committee of Wise Men on the Regulation of European Securities Markets.* Brussels, February 15. (www.europa.eu.int).

Committee on the Global Financial System. 1999. Implications *of Repo Markets for Central Banks.* Report of a Working Group, Bank for International Settlements. Basle, Switzerland. (www.bis.org).

Committee on Payment and Settlement Systems (CPSS). 1992. *Delivery versus Payment in Securities Settlement Systems,* Bank for International Settlements. Basle, Switzerland. (www.bis.org).

_____. 2001. *Core Principles for Systemically Important Payment Systems, Report of the Task Force on Payment System Principles and Practices.* Basle, Switzerland. (www. bis.org).

Committee on Payment and Settlement Systems (CPSS) and International Organization of Securities Commissions (IOSCO). 1997. *Disclosure Framework for Securities Settlement Systems.* Bank for International Settlements, Basle, Switzerland. (www.bis.org).

_____. 2001. *Recommendations for Securities Settlement Systems,* November. Basle, Switzerland. (www.bis.org).

Council of Securities Regulators of the Americas (COSRA). 1996. *Principles of Clearance and Settlement,* Comissão de Valores Mobiliarios, Rio de Janeiro, Brazil.

Depository Trust and Clearing Corporation (DTCC). 2000. *Central Counterparts: Development, Cooperation, and Consolidation,* October. (www.dtcc.com).

Depository Trust and Clearing Corporation (DTCC) and Government Securities Clearing Corporation (BSCC). 2001. *Real-time Trade Matching (RTTM) for NSCC-Eligible Fixed Income Securities: Business Overview.* August. (www.dtcc.com).

Earle, Dennis, and Margaret Koonz. 1999. *Linking the Capital Markets of Transitional Economies*, National Securities Clearing Corporation (NSCC June 15).

European Central Bank. 1998. *Assessment of EU Securities Settlement Systems against the Standards for Their Use in ESCB Credit Operations*, Frankfurt, Germany (www. ecb.int).

Forum of European Securities Commissions (FESCO). 2002. *Proposed Standards for Alternative Trading Systems, Paper for Final Consultation*, January, Paris, France. (www.europefesco.org).

Group of Thirty. 1988. *Clearance and Settlement Systems in the World's Securities Markets*. Washington, D.C. (www.group30.org).

Guadamillas, Mario, and Robert Keppler. 2001. Securities Clearance and Settlement Systems, A Guide to Best Practices. Policy Research Working Paper 2581. World Bank, Washington, D.C., April.

International Federation of Stock Exchanges (FIBV). 1999. *FIBV Clearing and Settlement Best Practices Report 1999*. September 1999. (www.fibv.com).

International Organization of Securities Commissions (IOSCO). 1998. *Objectives and Principles of Securities Regulation*. Montreal Canada. (www.iosco.org).

International Securities Services Association. 2000. *Recommendations*. Switzerland, June.

■CHAPTER 9

Demutualization of Exchanges as a Strategy for Capital Market Regulatory Reform

Roberta S. Karmel

Demutualization is the process of transforming an exchange from a cooperative or mutual form of business organization to a for-profit, shareholder-owned corporation. In some cases, where the exchange is not privately owned, there is a privatization or corporatization involved along the way to making the exchange a for-profit share-holder corporation. Traditionally, stock exchanges were member-managed, nonprofit cooperative organizations. Either members owned the exchange or the chamber of commerce or some other government entity owned it, but in any event, profits from exchange trading were returned to exchange members in the form of lower access fees or trading profits.

Many stock exchanges around the world have demutualized or are in the process of doing so, while other exchanges are considering whether to demutualize. In 1999, of 52 exchanges present at a meeting of the Federation Internationale des Bourses des Valeurs (FIBV), 15 had demutualized, 14 had member approval to de-mutualize, and 15 were actively contemplating demutualization (IOSCO 2000). De-mutualization is a recent movement. The first stock exchange to demutualize was the Stockholm Stock Exchange in 1993. By the middle of 2001, demutualized exchanges included the Australian Stock Exchange, the Hong Kong Stock and Futures Exchanges, the Singapore Stock Exchange, the Bogotá Stock Exchange, the Amsterdam Stock Exchange, the London Stock Exchange, the Paris Bourse, the Deutsche Bourse, the Toronto Stock Exchange, the Chicago Mercantile Exchange (CME), and the NASDAQ Stock Market.[1] However, not all demutualizations occurred in exchanges in mature

---

[1] Hughes (2001) and "The Hunt for Liquidity," *The Economist*, July 28, 2001, p. 65.

capital markets; the Philippines Stock Exchange is in the process of demutualizing and the Kuala Lumpur Exchange is planning to do so in the future.

As evident in the increasing trend toward demutualization, many exchanges have opted for this structure primarily for strategic reasons. Until recently, trading at most exchanges was floor based, with a limited number of members having access to the floor. Today, exchange trading is electronic, with some notable exceptions. This shift from floor-based to electronic trading is part of the demutualization story because liquidity no longer exists in a physical location, and it is no longer in the best interests of an exchange to be dominated by floor members. Rather, an electronic exchange may wish to put its terminals and screens in as many locations as possible. The most obvious consequence of demutualization is a change in an exchange's governance structure. The need to change governance in response to technological and competitive pressures is an important driver of demutualization.

Another change accompanying demutualization is regulatory readjustment. A traditional aspect of stock exchanges is self-regulation. When an exchange becomes a for-profit, shareholder-owned corporation, in the context of competitive markets, questions are raised as to whether all of the previous regulatory responsibilities remain appropriately in a self-regulatory framework or whether some responsibilities should be shifted to government regulators. Therefore, demutualization has prompted reform, or at least reexamination, of securities regulation, although the circumstances of demutualization and regulatory reform are not the same in all countries.

The objective of this chapter is to present the story behind demutualization and examine the key factors driving this trend. The chapter demonstrates that there are significant public policy, governance, regulatory, and strategic ramifications for exchanges and jurisdictions that opt to demutualize. Furthermore, the chapter identifies the relevance for emerging economies, the regulatory implications of this trend, and possible responses within an overall regulatory framework. Although demutualization is not a panacea for emerging economies trying to jumpstart their capital markets, it is a policy alternative that is relevant given the confluence of pertinent factors.

Overview

The International Organization of Securities Commissions (IOSCO 2000) points out that a key regulatory issue is whether for-profit exchanges, which compete with other exchanges and electronic networks, will undermine the commitment of resources and capabilities that a stock exchange needs to effectively fulfill its regulatory and public interest responsibilities. Traditionally, exchanges have engaged in self-regulation, which generally is more efficient and cost-effective than government regulation. In addition, self-regulation involves those subject to regulation as participants in the regulatory process, making the imposition of regulatory controls more palatable. Whether the change from a nonprofit mutual form of organization to a for-profit corporate form makes self-regulation more problematic is an interesting question, which can be broken down into a number of issues. First, what conflicts of interest are created or increased where a for-profit entity also performs exchange regulatory functions, especially securities listing, secondary market regulation, and member regulation? Second, is there a need to impose a special regime on exchanges to protect the public interest, such as particular corporate governance arrangements or rules with respect to share ownership? Third, will a for-profit exchange be run with more regard for its financial viability than its regulatory effectiveness?

Although demutualization raises these issues, the answers become even more difficult when an exchange makes a public offering of securities and then self-lists on its own board. Although the decisions to demutualize and go public are separate, most exchanges that have demutualized contemplate a public offering at an appropriate future time. Therefore, as an exchange considers whether to demutualize, the government regulator dealing with the problems that the transaction entails should probably look ahead to the exchange becoming a public company in resolving the regulatory problems involved.

Different jurisdictions have approached these issues from the perspective of their own legal, regulatory, and corporate finance systems. IOSCO tries to identify common approaches. It considers the corporate governance requirements mandating the appointment of public directors—that is, directors who are not engaged in the securities business—and the public good of an exchange, not merely the good of members or stockholders (IOSCO 2000). Such public directors can help solve conflict of interest problems and ensure the fair and efficient functioning of the exchange. Exchanges have a public interest responsibility because they provide liquidity and price discovery facilities to aid capital formation. In a demutualized environment, IOSCO (2000) suggests evaluating the need for some greater regulatory oversight of exchange managers. Furthermore, consideration needs to be given to placing restrictions on who may become shareholders and who may control exchanges as shareholders.

The funding of the regulatory activities of a demutualized exchange is an important public interest concern. In particular, the demutualization process should pay attention to cross-subsidization of for-profit activities using cash flows from regulatory activities, uneconomic pricing, allocation of regulatory costs, and financial viability (IOSCO 2000). The desirability of exchange expansion into new businesses needs to be carefully considered from a conflict of interest perspective.

Drivers for Demutualization

Competition from other exchanges—including nontraditional trading markets, such as electronic communications networks (ECNs) and alternative trading systems (ATSs)—constitutes the primary driver for demutualization. Competition has put pressure on trading profits at a time when trading volumes have increased, but technology has made trading more efficient. In order to compete with ECNs, traditional exchanges have had to better align their governance and business strategies to satisfy institutional and retail customers rather than the short-term interests of their members. In Latin America, bank members of stock exchanges are important providers of finance, and they wish to maintain this role. It has been asserted that outsider-owned, as opposed to member-owned, exchanges are more efficient as members' business interests become more diverse and as exchanges face more competition (Hart and Moore 1996).

In addition to the competitive pressure to become more efficient and customer focused, the move from floor trading to electronic trading requires significant capital. It also changes the value of exchange memberships. There is no longer a physical need to limit the number of exchange members, and it is in the interest of exchanges to place their trading terminals in as many places as possible. Once customers have direct access to screens, exchange memberships have diminished economic value. Demutualization can buy out the vested interests of traders, shift power to other firms, and at the same time raise capital for modernization of trading. However, these generalizations need some qualification. The National Association of Security Dealers (NASD) has never had a trading floor, but its subsidiary, NASDAQ, has demutualized. The New York Stock Exchange (NYSE) continues to have one, and it may demutualize in the future.

Another important driver for demutualization has been globalization and the perceived need of exchanges to affiliate with exchanges in other countries in order to survive. This has been a particularly important factor in Europe. The advent of a common currency and the European Central Bank have led many observers to believe that there are too many exchanges in Europe and that some consolidation will occur.[2] Elsewhere, smaller exchanges have consolidated on a national level; mergers

---

[2] "The Battle of the Bourses," *The Economist*, May 5, 2001, p. 517.

and affiliations in Europe are beginning to occur on a cross-border level.[3] Even in the absence of a common currency, Latin American exchanges may decide to demutualize and consolidate. They will need to consider competition with U.S. exchanges for trading Latin American securities listed on the NYSE or NASDAQ. Once an exchange has common stock, it has a currency that can be used for acquisitions, mergers, and joint ventures.

Exchanges have set forth various reasons for their demutualization initiatives, and these statements are informative. The CME has identified five objectives of its demutualization as follows:[4]

- Improve governance and managerial structure. According to the CME, the traditional distinctions between the exchange's activities and the activities of its members and clearing members were becoming increasingly blurred. Members and clearing members decided their affairs, but some of them competed directly with the CME by developing off-exchange products and business and by joining alternative market initiatives. The board of CME believed that demutualization would enable management to reduce the impact of these conflicts, by creating a governance and management structure that would be more agile and swift in responding to competition. It would also increase CME's enterprise value for the benefit of its equity owners. Management of the demutualized entity could make decisions regarding listing contracts electronically, changing clearing and transaction fees when appropriate, or expanding existing product and service offerings.
- Ameliorate the financial decisionmaking model. Commercial decisionmaking was expected to diminish members' political influence. Commercial pricing of services and the profit-making objective would ensure that resources were allocated to those business initiatives and ventures that enhanced, or had the potential to enhance, stockholder value.
- Create a catalyst for pursuing new business strategies. To capitalize on the potential of financial innovation and demand for new risk management and

---

[3] For example, until the last decade, Australia had six stock exchanges, formed between 1859 and 1889, the legacy of a federal system in which there were rivalries between the states. The threat of international competition, however, led these six exchanges to merge into the Australian Stock Exchange in 1987. See Humphry (1995). The Nordic stock market alliance includes the Stockholm, Copenhagen, and Oslo stock exchanges. See "Oslo Wants to Join Nordic Stock Market," *Alliance*, Finanstidningen 6, August 25, 1999, WL 10643741. In Latin America, the exchanges in Colombia merged.

[4] *Amendment No. 5 to Form S-4 Registration Statement*, April 25, 2000, available at http://www.sec.gov/Archives/edgar/data/1103945/0000950131-00-002795.txt.

derivative products, a demutualized CME would be able to attract outside investment, further expand its current technology platforms, and broaden its product and service offerings.

- Unlock members' equity values. Over the years, many retired CME owners experienced substantial declines in their seat values and turned to income from leasing. These owners became generally less interested in member opportunity on the floor. They became more interested in maintaining their asset values and deriving income from them and became more like traditional stockholders than exchange members. Demutualization would unlock equity value and provide shareholder returns.

- Provide a signal and a currency for working with strategic partners. Technology firms, as well as firms interested in acquiring an equity stake in the CME, prefer to work with a demutualized corporation, rather than a member-owned mutual organization. Demutualization and conversion of memberships into shares were expected to create a valuable currency for strategic alliances.

The board of directors of NASDAQ believed that it was in the interest of both its shareholders and the investing public for NASDAQ shares to be publicly traded and widely held through an initial public offering (IPO).[5] As a for-profit, stock-based company governed by the market's leading participants, NASDAQ would be more agile, flexible, and effective in responding to industry and market conditions. Public ownership would have two main advantages. First, an IPO and the capital it provides would allow NASDAQ to continue to improve its market and compete effectively with domestic and international competitors, facilitating the sale of its remaining equity ownership, and creating a liquid acquisition currency for NASDAQ. Second, an IPO would provide a valuation benchmark and liquidity for current investors and allow NASDAQ to control the development of the trading market for its stock. NASDAQ's interests would be aligned with those of key participants. NASDAQ would have both an initial infusion of capital and easier ongoing access to funding.

Some non-U.S. exchanges have demutualized for somewhat different reasons, although competitive pressures and the resulting need to effect governance changes are a common theme. The Stockholm Stock Exchange demutualized to effect privatization of the exchange and reform of securities regulation, in part to compete with OM Gruppen AB (OM), which began to trade derivatives, a product Swedish stock exchanges were forbidden to trade. The Stockholm Stock Exchange had no owners

---

[5] *Nasdaq to Become a Public Company,* available at http://www.nasdaqnews.com/news/pr2001/ne_section01_140.html.

as such, but operated as a not-for-profit mutual organization regulated by the chamber of commerce. It had no right to build up capital, and the fees it charged members and issuers could not exceed its costs (Ryden 1997). Members could trade seats, which could not be purchased or sold. Although the exchange was a legal monopoly, trading volume was low due to a turnover tax, which sent the primary market in many issues to London. Then, in the late 1980s and 1990s, the political climate changed, and the turnover tax and currency control were repealed. This led to a decision to privatize the exchange and modernize trading.

The Australian Stock Exchange also was demutualized in response to technological change and international competition. A member of the exchange developed an electronic crossing system, and another organization started a bulletin board type of trading network for unlisted securities (Humphry 1995). In addition to developing new trading platforms and mechanisms, the exchange determined that it had to be more responsive to the needs of market users, particularly investors and issuers, and to that end it was no longer appropriate for individual stockbrokers to control the exchange.

In 1987, when the Australian exchanges combined, 627 out of 693 members were natural persons, that is, individuals (Donnan 1999). In 1993, the Australian Stock Exchange proposed that individual membership be abolished and that membership be confined to corporations, but this proposal failed.[6] Therefore, the exchange formed the Governance Task Force of board members and senior exchange management and a panel of stockbrokers from each state. The exchange commissioned an independent consultant to prepare a report—the Hogan, Stokes Report—on the future of exchange corporate governance (Hogan, Stokes Pty Limited 1996). Although the Australian Stock Exchange was not a legal mutual society, it was a company limited by guarantee with no shares and thus had the essential feature of mutual, collective ownership. The exchange was prohibited from paying profits or income to members, and the surplus was applied toward promoting the objects of the exchange (Donnan 1999). Members had a guarantee liability of at least $1,000 in the event of a winding up, in addition to the exchange's power to impose levies and fees.

To the extent that competition or regulation did not control market power, mutual governance had the potential to give stockbroker members of the exchange control of the price, quality, and range of services it produced (Hogan, Stokes Pty Lim-

---

[6] Although individuals were offered $25,000 to surrender membership, and a resolution to change to corporate membership achieved the support of 69 percent of the members, the resolution failed because 75 percent of the vote was required.

ited 1996). However, according to the Hogan, Stokes Report, in a more competitive climate, the value of mutual ownership as a means of controlling market power would be diminished.[7] Furthermore, it would be more difficult for a mutual as opposed to a corporate organization to make contentious business decisions under the time pressures created by competition. The Hogan, Stokes Report therefore recommended changing to a corporate structure to enable the Australian Stock Exchange to operate more effectively as a business under growing competitive pressure and to reduce the potential for growing inequities among the owners of a mutual. The report also recommended listing corporatized exchange shares on the Australian Stock Exchange.

The Amsterdam Stock Exchange merged with the Amsterdam options and futures exchanges and then demutualized in order to strengthen its commercial thrust in the face of increased international competition.[8] It believed that it was necessary to organize the Amsterdam exchanges as a business in order to change their culture from a civil service type of organization to one primarily driven by business objectives (Hogan, Stokes Pty Limited 1996). These changes paved the way for the subsequent merger with the Paris and Brussels stock exchanges.

Issues Related to Demutualization

Demutualization creates a number of issues and trade-offs, most of which are linked with the self-regulatory nature of stock exchanges and the ensuing conflicts of interest.

Conflicts of Interest

One of the more contentious issues under discussion is the future of self-regulation. Questions concerning the ability of exchanges to enforce their regulations against members and listed companies have focused on the conflicts of interest involved, but demutualization raises these questions in a new context. The issue is whether a commercial entity carrying on the business of running an exchange and seeking to protect and promote its business can continue to support the integrity and efficiency of the trading markets by setting and enforcing appropriate regulations in the public interest (IOSCO 2000). It can be argued that there would be conflicts of interests between shareholders and members in a demutualized exchange environment that

---

[7] Hogan, Stokes Pty Limited (1996).
[8] Prospectus, AEX, February 20, 1997, p. 16.

would diminish the ability of exchanges to engage in effective self-regulation. A potentially serious conflict is the regulation of an ATS market by an exchange that functions as a self-regulatory organization (SRO). These conflicts could become manifest in discrimination through sanctions imposed in disciplinary proceedings, unfairness in not being permitted to participate in particular activities, or discrimination with respect to fees charged.

In the United States, stock exchanges engage in self-regulation in four areas: listed company governance and disclosure; surveillance and discipline of their markets and specialists, floor brokers, and market makers; member firm financial and operational compliance; and fair and equitable treatment of customers. Commodities' exchanges are not engaged in issuer corporate governance regulation, but they regulate their markets and members. Both the NYSE and NASD run arbitration facilities for disputes between members and disputes between members and customers, but customer reparations proceedings against commodities intermediaries can be prosecuted before the Commodity Futures Trading Commission (CFTC). In other countries, exchanges also act as SROs and conduct some or all of these functions in conjunction with public oversight. In many countries, exchanges have been responsible for enforcing public disclosure by listed issuers.

NYSE listing requirements go back to the nineteenth century and stem from a concern about the quality of the securities sold on the exchange. These requirements were intended to facilitate an efficient, continuous auction market by setting minimum numerical standards for capitalization, number of shares, and shareholders, by establishing disclosure requirements, and by specifying certain shareholder protection or corporate governance mechanisms (Michael 1992). The NYSE developed these requirements because it recognized that standards were good for its business and could give the exchange a competitive advantage. When NASDAQ was organized as an electronic market, it also established listing qualifications in order to preserve and improve the quality of and public confidence in its market.[9]

If the NYSE and NASDAQ become public companies, it will perhaps be anomalous for them to negotiate listing agreements with themselves and then supervise continuing compliance with such agreements. For this reason, when the Stockholm and Australian stock exchanges went public, government regulators were assigned the task of overseeing disclosure by the exchange to shareholders.[10] On the other hand, exchanges will continue to have a motivation to market themselves as lists of quality

---

[9] See NASD Rules 4300, 4310, NASD Manual (CCH), pp. 5271–79.
[10] In the United States, however, the Securities and Exchange Commission already has this authority.

issuers. It has also been argued in some circles that the benefits of increased capital mobility would be better realized through regulatory decentralization—that is, more self-regulation—than through greater centralization by way of more government regulation. Under a decentralized model, exchanges should be the primary writers and enforcers of rules relating to disclosure by listed companies, standards of conduct for member broker-dealers, and market structure (Mahoney 1997; Karmel 2001).

When an exchange becomes a for-profit public company, some new conflicts could call into question its regulatory role with regard to issuer corporate governance. If an exchange enters or considers entering a joint venture with a listed company, the exchange might be tempted to underregulate that company. Conversely, an exchange could behave in a discriminatory way toward a competitor. For example, Instinet, a direct competitor of the NYSE and NASDAQ, is now a public issuer.[11] It may be concerned about whether it will be treated on an equal footing with other listed companies.

Demutualization also raises several corporate governance questions related to contests for corporate control. Demutualized exchanges tend to have corporate governance provisions to prevent shareholders from having more than a specified percentage stock ownership, thus preventing them from taking complete control over the exchange. Would such an issuer continue vigorously to enforce corporate governance standards preventing companies from adopting certain poison pills in response to a hostile takeover bid without shareholder approval?[12]

Exchange regulation of broker-dealers has its roots in efforts to assure the creditworthiness of exchange members. This continues to be a significant issue and an important aspect of SRO regulation. When exchanges go public, it is likely that clearing member firms and listed companies will be large stockholders. This will give them an incentive to maintain high standards of financial and operational capabilities for member firms in order to maintain the quality of the exchange's brand. The changing nature of ownership may create some new conflicts of interest, but others will be resolved because market makers and floor members will have a diminished role in exchange governance and will be less able to exert political influence on the exchange's board.

The incentive of exchanges to police their markets for manipulation, and their effectiveness in doing so, would probably be greater following a public offering than it

---

[11] On May 9, 2001, Instinet, a Delaware limited liability company, converted into a Delaware corporation, Instinet Group Incorporated. On May 18, 2001, Instinet Group Incorporated announced that its shares commenced trading on the NASDAQ stock market under the symbol "INET" after its registration statement relating to the initial public offering of 32 million newly issued shares of common stock was declared effective by the SEC. Instinet Group Inc. Prospectus filed pursuant to Rule 424 on May 18, 2001, available at http://www.investor.instinet.com/edgar.cfm.

[12] See NYSE Listed Company Manual, §§ 308, 312.03 (1999), available at http://www.nyse.com/listed/listed.html.

is today. There would be fewer conflicts of interest in policing the markets if ownership of these SROs were spread beyond those concerned with making markets. Nevertheless, some rearrangement of regulatory responsibilities might be appropriate in connection with demutualization. For example, in the United States and Europe, insider trading enforcement is a government responsibility. But in jurisdictions where this continues to be an SRO responsibility, would a for-profit exchange be a vigorous enforcer, especially if businessmen and academics viewed insider trading as normal?

Self-regulation of the broker-customer relationship is another issue. Although just and equitable principles of trade have long been a basis for policing sales practices in the United States, aggressive government oversight and the threat of civil liability in actions by customers prod SRO effectiveness. Although exchanges are concerned about their reputations as fair marketplaces, aggressive enforcement is costly, and the fair treatment of customers by members in such areas as suitability and sales practices is only indirectly related to the fairness of an exchange's marketplace. A for-profit marketplace might not be interested in devoting its resources to funding a rigorous enforcement program in this area, or it might decide to make enforcement penalties a source of its funding. Therefore changes in government oversight of the broker-dealer customer relationship might be required.

Regulatory Solutions

A variety of regulatory solutions can respond to the conflict of interest issues raised by an exchange's demutualization. All of these solutions involve rebalancing government and self-regulatory standard setting and enforcement. The ability of an exchange to continue to enforce listing standards, including disclosure standards for public companies, is of great importance in countries where government regulators do not determine what disclosure and other obligations public companies owe shareholders. Other types of regulatory challenges are generated with regard to SRO regulation of members and markets, especially if demutualization is coincident with a switch from floor to electronic trading.

Listing Standards

When the Australian Stock Exchange demutualized and self-listed, Australian law was changed so that the Australian Securities and Investment Commission would act as the listing authority for the Australian Stock Exchange, but the exchange continues to act as the listing authority for all other issuers (Segal 2001). By contrast, coincident with the demutualization and public offering by the London Stock Exchange, authority over listings and disclosure obligations of listed companies was transferred to the Financial Services Authority, the government regulator.[13]

In the United States, listing standards have long been an SRO function. The Securities and Exchange Commission (SEC) has regulated a public company's disclosure obligations since 1933. These obligations include making annual and other periodic reports as well as disclosures in connection with securities offerings. Stock exchanges also impose continuous disclosure obligations on listed companies.

Initially, the NYSE was concerned with financial disclosure, but this emphasis precipitated several corporate governance listing standards (Lowenthal 1933). An annual stockholders' meeting, the first corporate governance standard, was imposed as a term within the listing agreement and was eventually linked to annual reporting requirements (Michael 1992). By 1900, listing agreements required companies to distribute annual reports to their stockholders (Cooke 1969). By 1909, those reports had to be distributed prior to the stockholders' annual meeting (Michael 1992). By 1914, agreements required that a listed company must notify the exchange of any change in the rights of stockholders or in the redemption of preferred stock. By 1917, agreements provided for the disclosure of a semiannual income statement and balance sheet. In 1926, the NYSE adopted a one share, one vote listing standard (Seligman 1986). Finally, with the enactment of the Securities Exchange Act of 1934 (the Exchange Act), the policies of the NYSE regarding independent audits became a matter of federal law.[14] The value of the NYSE's listing requirements was demonstrated by the fact that Congress closely tracked the NYSE disclosure requirements when it drafted the Exchange Act (Pritchard 1999).

NASDAQ listing requirements have a somewhat different history, rooted in blue-sky merit regulation.[15] Most state securities laws traditionally provided an exemption from their securities registration requirements to issuers that were listed on a national securities exchange. This was known as the blue chip exemption. Some states also provided an exemption for certain over-the-counter securities (U.S. Congress 1986). In 1985, NASDAQ initiated its first corporate governance listing standard in an effort to secure blue-sky exemptions in a greater number of states (Michael 1992). This was part of a campaign for broader exemptions from state registration so

---

[13] See About Us, http://www.londonstockexchange.com/about/about_05.asp (September 5, 2001).

[14] Items 25 and 26 of Schedule A to the Securities Act of 1933 (Securities Act), 15 U.S.C. §§ 77aa(25) and (26).

[15] A merit regulator has the authority to prevent an issuer from selling securities in the state because the offering or the issuer's capital structure is substantively unfair or presents excessive risk to investors.

that securities listed on NASDAQ or designated as "national market system securities" would be exempt from state blue-sky registration requirements.[16]

Corporate governance in the United States is primarily a matter of state corporation law.[17] Therefore, exchange listing standards have been critical in the development of national corporate governance standards. The SEC has used disclosure requirements for their prophylactic effect of regulating corporate governance. In addition, the SEC has broad powers under the Exchange Act to regulate exchanges and securities traded in the national market system. It has used this power to persuade exchanges to mandate audit committees with a majority of independent directors for listed companies.[18] Nevertheless, when the SEC tested the limits of its authority in dictating corporate governance standards for listed companies, attempting to enforce a one share, one vote exchange listing standard, the D.C. Circuit Court held this was beyond the SEC's power.[19]

NASDAQ has demutualized, but not yet made a public offering of its shares. The NYSE's plans to demutualize have been on hold for a few years. The decisions to demutualize and to go public and list are separate. A regulatory rebalancing between SRO listing requirements and governmental oversight of listing standards may not become essential until an exchange self-lists. In any event, NASDAQ was not required to address this issue in connection with its demutualization. Another aspect of this problem is the development of ATSs. If markets of the future are competing ECNs instead of floor-based exchanges, which serve as a price discovery mechanism for listed companies, listing may diminish in importance and exchanges may not have the same leverage to enforce listing standards as they have had in the past. New power to formulate and enforce corporate governance standards may then have to be given to SROs or government regulators.

---

[16] Exchange Act Rule 11Aa-2-1, 17 C.F.R. §240.11Aa-2-1. The controversy concerning the merit of NASDAQ listing standards in contrast to the standards of national securities exchanges was settled by the National Securities Markets Improvement Act of 1996, Pub. Law 104-290, 110 Stat. 3416 (1996), which preempted state regulation of the securities registration and offering process for "covered securities." This means merit review is not applicable to nationally traded securities, including NASDAQ listed securities. Securities Act, §18(a)(3), 15 U.S.C. §77r(a)(3).

[17] Schreiber v. Burlington Northern, Inc. 472 U.S. 1 (1977); Santa Fe Industries, Inc. v. Green, 430 U.S. 462 (1977); Cort. v. Ash, 422 U.S. 66, 84 (1975).

[18] Self-Regulatory Organizations; Order Approving Proposed Rule Change by the New York Stock Exchange, Inc. Amending the Exchange's Audit Committee Requirements and Notice of Filing and Order Granting Accelerated Approval of Amendments No. 1 and 2 Thereto, Exchange Act Release No. 42233, 64 Fed. Reg. 71529 (December 21, 1999). New SEC disclosure rules complement these requirements. See Audit Committee Disclosure, Exchange Act Release No. 42266, 64 Fed. Reg. 73389 (December 30, 1999).

[19] Business Roundtable v. SEC, 905 F.2d 406 (D.C.Cir. 1990).

Oversight of Markets and Members

A movement toward the displacement of self-regulation by government regulation of exchange markets and members has been taking place in Europe, not only because of exchange demutualizations, but also as the result of European Union directives requiring government agencies or designated SROs to enforce capital market standards.

In the United States, the Securities Industry Association (SIA) has given thoughtful consideration to how self-regulation should function in a demutualized exchange environment. The SIA's Ad Hoc Committee on the Regulatory Implications of De-Mutualization has determined guiding principles for analyzing an appropriate SRO structure and has suggested six models for future regulation of the securities industry (SIA 2000). The SIA's Ad Hoc Committee's guidelines for evaluating regulatory options state that any regulatory structure should foster investor protection; preserve fair competition; eliminate inefficiencies; encourage expert regulation; promote reasonable and fair regulatory costs; foster due process; and encourage industry participation and self-regulation. The six models the committee put forward are status quo; multiple exchanges with separate boards and information barriers for their regulatory arms (NASDR model); multiple SROs with firms designated to a single SRO for examination purposes (DEA model); one SRO for member firms, markets regulate their own trading (hybrid model); all-purpose single SRO (single SRO model); and single regulatory organization (SEC-only model).

The SIA's Ad Hoc Committee endorsed the hybrid model in which there would be a central SRO responsible for firm oversight and cross-market issues, including rules generally applicable to all markets.[20] Individual market SROs would then be responsible for market-specific rules, including rules regarding trading and listing. Cross-market rules would include front running, manipulation, free riding and withholding rules, sales practice regulation, industry admission standards, financial responsibility requirements, training and supervision, and record keeping. Arguments in favor of the hybrid model are that this model would improve regulation, decrease regulatory costs, preserve the synergy between markets and market-specific oversight, foster competition, and continue self-regulation. On March 22, 2000, the SIA board of directors endorsed the hybrid model.[21] One reason for this endorsement is that the

---

[20] Securities Industry Association, Reinventing Self-regulation—Recommendations Regarding Self-regulatory Structure (last modified March 23, 2000) http://www.sia.com/demutualization/htmv/recommendations-regarding-self.html.
[21] Securities Industry Association press release, *Securities Industry Board Endorses "Hybrid" Model to Enhance Benefits of Self-Regulation for Investors,* (last modified March 22, 2000) http://www.sia.com/html/pr993.html.

securities industry would like to avoid duplication of examinations and inconsistent regulation. In that connection, the white paper advocates a single, independent arbitration forum.

The NASD has come out in favor of a single SRO model, and the chairman of the SEC briefly embraced this model,[22] but the NYSE has opposed it.[23] The SEC does not have the statutory authority to impose corporate governance requirements on listed companies, and neither would a freestanding single SRO.[24] Although the SEC might find it convenient to oversee a sole self-regulator, the SEC might be tempted to make it an arm of the government, rather than a true self-regulator. Yet, SROs do not afford those they discipline the protections of persons who are investigated or prosecuted by government officials.[25] These problems might not emerge in Latin America, where there is only one dominant exchange in a particular country, but similar problems could emerge in countries that have more than one exchange, where ATSs develop in competition with exchanges or where there are cross-border mergers or alliances.

In the United States, one of the goals of the Exchange Act is "fair competition among brokers and dealers, among exchange markets, and between exchange markets and markets other than exchange markets."[26] For the SEC to suppress or eliminate competition among SROs could be contrary to this goal because an important function of an exchange is self-regulation.[27] However, an ATS regulated as a member of an exchange could complain of unfair competition and yet find it uneconomical to become a full-service SRO. Furthermore, although the benefits of regulatory competition are often touted, regulatory competition can be unseemly and destructive of public confidence in the regulators. Given the serious fissures within the U.S. securities industry at the present time, the hybrid model seems the most likely solution to self-regulation after demutualization.

One of the many difficulties with any new SRO structure is adequate funding. Currently, U.S. SROs rely on four primary sources for their funding: regulatory fees and assessments paid by SRO members, transaction service fees, listing fees, and market information fees (SIA 2000). The continued viability of these fees in rapidly chang-

---

[22] Garten (1999); Schroeder (1999); *The Wall Street Journal* (1999); NASD (1999).

[23] Fried (1999); testimony of Richard A. Grasso before the Senate Banking Committee, September 28, 1999, available at 1999 WL 27594853.

[24] Business Roundtable v. SEC, supra note 58.

[25] See, for example, in the matter of Stephen J. Gluckman, Exchange Act Release No. 41628, 70 SEC DOC. 323 (July 20, 1999).

[26] Exchange Act, § 11A(a)(1)(C)(ii), 15 U.S.C. § 78k-1(C)(ii).

[27] Exchange Act § 6(b).

ing market conditions is unclear. The SEC has issued a complex and provocative release on some of these fees, and however uncomfortable the SEC may be with establishing fees for market users, this is an issue that will not disappear.[28] Clearly, rigorous, expert, and fair regulation is not possible unless SRO regulation is adequately funded. But after demutualization, subsidizing general broker-dealer enforcement activities through fees other than regulatory assessments of members may prove difficult. The exchanges could try to make fines and penalties a profit stream, and this would raise a variety of new questions and problems. This suggests that the U.S. securities industry is likely to focus on the costs of duplicative self-regulation (SIA 2000). Any Latin American exchange considering demutualization would need to analyze how it currently pays for regulation of its markets and members and whether these funding sources would still be available after demutualization.

Demutualization Experiences

No two demutualizations have proceeded exactly the same way, due to differences in legal, political, and corporate finance systems across countries and the range of strategies that exchanges have followed. Review of the various exchange demutualizations can provide valuable lessons and models for Latin American countries.

The demutualization of the Stockholm Stock Exchange, the first to take place, accomplished many of the goals the Swedish authorities envisioned, but had some unexpected developments. The demutualization in Australia involved a common-law federal system, in which the stock exchange had considerable self-regulatory powers. This demutualization also was successful, but the Australian competition authority thwarted some of the objectives of the demutualized exchange. The demutualization in Amsterdam coincided with a rearrangement of government and self-regulatory responsibilities and was followed by a merger of the Paris, Amsterdam, and Brussels exchanges.

Sweden

In 1989, the Swedish government formed a committee to study the stock market; in 1992, it passed a new stock exchange law based on the committee's recommendations. With these political and legal changes, there was a pioneering transformation of

---

[28] Regulation of Market Fees and Revenues, Exchange Act Release No. 42208, 64 Fed. Reg. 70613 (December 9, 1999).

the Stockholm Stock Exchange, which occurred in three steps: modernization of trading, privatization of the exchange, and internationalization of the market (Ryden 1997). These changes took place in the context of a political shift from a socialist to a more market-oriented government, the aftermath of the 1987 stock market crash, and a financial crisis in the Swedish banking system.

In 1986, the Stockholm Stock Exchange decided to develop an automated electronic trading system with order matching, which was successfully implemented in 1990 (Ryden 1997). This development was in part a response to competition from OM, which started operations in 1985 as a clearinghouse and options exchange in Swedish stocks. It did business as a brokerage firm limited company, however, because derivatives trading on exchanges had been forbidden since 1919. In 1991, the merger of the Bank Inspection Board, the Private Insurance Supervisory Service, and the Swedish Accounting Standards Board formed the Swedish Financial Supervisory Authority.[29] The 1992 Securities Exchange and Clearing Operations Act then abolished the monopoly of the Stockholm Stock Exchange and provided for the authorization as an exchange by the Financial Supervisory Authority of "any undertaking which conducts business operations with the aim of establishing regular trading in financial instruments."[30] Both the Stockholm Stock Exchange and OM became so authorized and licensed as exchanges when the act became effective in 1993. Since then, several additional firms have been licensed as marketplaces.[31]

Coincident with the adoption of the 1992 Securities Exchange and Operations Act, demutualization of the Stockholm Stock Exchange took place in 1992–93 as part of a decision to become a public joint stock corporation. Because the 1992 law ended the exchange's legal monopoly, it was felt that in order to compete efficiently in an international environment, the exchange needed economic incentives and a business attitude (Ryden 1997). In addition, since the exchange had been operating as a government-sanctioned enterprise, its transformation to a joint stock company was viewed as a privatization in keeping with the new, more market-oriented government.

Shares were sold to listed issuers and exchange members but were not freely tradable for one year (Ryden 1997). Once the shares were transferable, no restrictions were imposed on ownership. Appointments to the old exchange board of 22 members were influenced by the Swedish government and represented various so-

---

[29] Finans–Inspektionen, Annual Report 1997, p. 4. This authority is accountable to the Ministry of Finance and is responsible for exercising supervision over companies in the financial sector. It also monitors compliance with the act prohibiting insider trading passed in 1991. Insider Act, SFS 1990: 1342.

[30] Securities Exchange and Clearing Operations Act, ch. 1, §§ 1, 3, SFS 1992: 543.

[31] "Brewery First Company on Northern Exchange," *Svenska Dagbladet*, July 31, 1998, 1998 WL 8510230.

cial interests—political parties, labor unions, members, issuers, and investors. The new board had nine members elected by the shareholders. Transparency and free access to the market, including remote memberships, were part of an international strategy.

Since OM was a listed company, it was entitled to be an initial subscriber to shares in the Stockholm Stock Exchange and took advantage of this opportunity. Thereafter, OM increased its share ownership to 20 percent and in 1998 proposed a merger between OM and the Stockholm Stock Exchange. This was a controversial proposal that succeeded because the Ministry of Finance believed a merger of the cash and derivatives markets would be beneficial to the Swedish capital market. In order to satisfy opponents of the merger, the Swedish government became a shareholder of both the Stockholm Stock Exchange and OM. At the time the merger was completed, in January 1998, the Swedish government owned 6.3 percent of shares in the combined entities and had announced an expectation of becoming a 10 percent owner, allowing it to block measures.[32] In addition, new legislation was passed increasing the supervision of exchanges by the Financial Supervisory Authority.

This new law gave the Financial Supervisory Authority the power to vet owners (more than 10 percent stockholders) and managers of exchanges, similar to the licensing of persons associated with banks and brokerages. The authority was given direct supervision of public disclosure by OM and the Stockholm Stock Exchange. The Financial Supervisory Authority was given the right to initiate disciplinary proceedings in cases concerning companies with a qualified holding in an exchange.

Equity markets are important in Sweden. In the late 1990s, one of every two Swedes owned shares, either directly or indirectly (Stockholm Stock Exchange 1997). At the end of 1997, Stockholm had the eighth-largest market capitalization in Europe, which was 127 percent of gross national product.[33] The merger of the Stockholm Stock Exchange and OM consolidated equities and derivatives exchanges in a single business, including foreign exchange commodities, bonds, and derivatives instruments based on them, now called the Stockholm Exchanges (OM Gruppen 1997). The combined exchanges also have been consolidating internationally, especially in the Nordic region. In 1997, a clearing link was established between OM and the Finnish derivatives exchange. On February 14, 1997, the Swedish and Norwegian derivatives markets were united via the world's first electronic trading and clearing link between independent exchanges. On June 21, 1999, Sweden and Denmark launched the first

---

[32] OM and Stockholms Fondbörse, Information Relating to the Merger of OM Gruppen and Stockholms Fondbörse 12 (translation of excerpts from the Swedish prospectus, dated December 19, 1997).
[33] Stockholm Stock Exchange (1997); http://www.fese.be/allmarkets/htm.

cross-border joint equities trading system, called Norex, designed to raise liquidity in the Scandinavian markets (Stone 1999).

The innovative demutualization conducted by the Stockholm Stock Exchange was responsive to the entrepreneurial competitive threat to the exchange's franchise by OM, but OM eventually acquired the exchange. Yet, this series of events enabled the Stockholm Stock Exchange to modernize its business operations and governance structure. In addition, the Swedish government was able to privatize ownership of the exchange, but put into place a more comprehensive and stringent regulatory system than had previously been the case. After demutualization, however, when OM attempted to take over the London Stock Exchange, its bid was rejected, perhaps demonstrating the limits of hostile takeovers by publicly owned exchanges (Cowell 2001).

Australia

On October 18, 1996, the stockbrokers at the Australian Stock Exchange overwhelmingly backed a plan to demutualize the exchange. All current members became entitled to shares in the new corporation.[34] In order to effectuate this plan, however, new legislation was required. The legislation was passed in record time, in a period when public share ownership in Australia was growing and the Australian government was engaged in a campaign to privatize noncore assets.[35] The statute provided a mechanism for the conversion of the Australian Stock Exchange from a mutual organization to a public company; expanded the regulatory and public interest responsibilities of securities exchanges as SROs, as well as the exchange's accountability to the Australian Securities and Investments Commission (ASIC); separated stockbrokers' rights to trade on an exchange from shareholders' rights; imposed a 5 percent limit on shareholdings in the Australian Stock Exchange; allowed a securities exchange to self-list on its own exchange; and provided for the supervision of any such self-listing by the ASIC (Donnan 1999). The Australian stock exchange then demutualized and on October 14, 1998, listed on its own board.[36] This prompted some to argue that the ASIC should assume regulation not only of the listed Australian Stock Exchange but also of all listed companies.[37]

---

[34] Victoria Tait, "ASX Members Vote for Corporation," *Sydney Morning Herald*, October 19, 1996, p. 89.
[35] Elizabeth Robinson, "Privatisation Sharecroppers to Shareholders," *Financial Times*, October 27, 1997, p. 4; "Law Allowing Demutualization ASX Passes in Near Record," *AAP Newsfeed*, November 19, 1997.
[36] Gwen Robinson, "ASX Shares Likely to Start Above A 3.50," *Financial Times*, October 14, 1998, p. 18.
[37] Trevor Sykes, "ASIC Should Assume ASX Powers," *Australian Financial Review*, October 17, 1998, p. 14.

Thereafter, ASX Ltd., the parent company of the Australian Stock Exchange, proposed to take over the Sydney Futures Exchange,[38] but then found itself in a bidding war for the futures exchange with Computershare Ltd., a share registry and software firm.[39] This threat to the Australian Stock Exchange's monopoly and plans for the future were complicated further by the submission of their merger plan to the Australian Competition and Consumer Commission (ACCC), which considered it to be anticompetitive.[40] The ACCC response, coupled with an increased bid from Computershare, has all but removed any hopes of an alliance between the two exchanges.[41] The key issue raised before the ACCC was whether a securities exchange should be protected and fostered as a national capital market champion or just another entity competing in the marketplace like the companies that use it to raise capital.[42]

According to a survey released by the Australian Stock Exchange in February 2000, demutualization and privatization dramatically increased share ownership among Australians.[43] From 1998 to 2000, the number of people in the share market nearly doubled, and Australia could boast of the highest participation of adults in the share market in the world, with 53 percent of Australians owning shares (including direct and indirect share ownership) as compared with 48 percent share ownership in the United States.[44] Factors contributing to this dramatic increase included increased media publicity about winning fast profits in the share market,[45] easier access to markets, and reduced trading costs through Internet trading; the privatization of former government enterprises; the demutualization of ASX and the major life insurance companies;[46] the increase in superannuation; and the presence of a bull market.[47] Despite obvious optimism, commentators were concerned that there was an undue concentration of investment in too few companies and encouraged investors to diversify.[48]

---

[38] Australian Stock, "Futures Exchange to Merge," *National Post*, April 28, 1999; 1999 WL 13671786.

[39] "Bidding War Breaks out Over SFE," *Independent Business Weekly* 18, May 26, 1999; 1999 WL 12566164.

[40] Ian Harper, "Let's Face Reality: Go Global," *Australian Financial Review*, July 21, 1999; 1999 WL 19334887; Eli Greenblat, "Fels Warning as SFE Ruling Delayed," *The Age*, July 22, 1999; 1999 WL 21179820.

[41] Stephen Bartholomeusz, "Why There's No Futures for The Bourse," *Sydney Morning Herald*, July 30, 1999; 1999 WL 21601567.

[42] "Mapping the Futures of Exchanges," *Australian Financial Review*, July 31, 1999, p. 20; 1999 WL 19335693.

[43] "Ownership of Shares In Australia Increases to 53% of Adults," *Asian Wall Street Journal*, February 9, 2000, p. 17; Leanne Bland, "Your Eggs in One Basket? May As Well Back A Horse," *Sydney Morning Herald*, February 9, 2000, p. 6.

[44] Leanne Bland, "A Share of the Action," *Sydney Morning Herald*, February 12, 2000, p. 128; 2000 WL 231110; "Share Revolution Must Put Stock in Diversity," *Australian Financial Review*, February 12, 2000, p. 20; 2000 WL 3977215.

[45] Henry Bosch, "To Market, To Market," *Shares Magazine*, April 1, 2000, p. 144; 2000 WL 2104638.

[46] "Share Revolution Must Put Stock in Diversity," *Australian Financial Review*, February 12, 2000, p. 20; Leanne Bland, "A Share of the Action," *Sydney Morning Herald*, February 12, 2000, p. 128.

[47] Henry Bosch, "To Market, To Market," *Shares Magazine*, April 1, 2000, p. 144.

[48] "Share Revolution Must Put Stock in Diversity," *Australian Financial Review*, February 12, 2000, p. 20.

Amsterdam

Amsterdam has the world's oldest organized stock exchange, dating back to the early seventeenth century. Until recently, it had a floor and a specialist system with some similarities to the NYSE agency auction system. In the late 1990s, however, the winds of change buffeted the Amsterdam Stock Exchange and caused it to give up its floor and adopt an electronic trading system, affiliate with the Amsterdam options exchange and the Amsterdam futures exchange, demutualize, and then affiliate with the Paris and Brussels stock exchanges in the Euronext project. In addition, over the past 15 years, Amsterdam went from a regulatory regime, which was almost entirely conducted by exchanges as SROs, to one in which a new government-designated and -supervised SRO assumed many regulatory responsibilities.

Prior to the mid-1980s, most securities regulation in the Netherlands was self-regulatory. The minister of finance supervised the stock exchange under a 1914 law, but government regulation was not on a day-to-day basis. In 1988, the Securities Board of the Netherlands was created to supervise the securities markets and securities exchanges. This board is an independent body, removed from both the government and the private sector. It was created in response to various scandals in the markets in the mid-1980s to oversee the Amsterdam Stock Exchange, the European Options Exchange, and the financial futures market. In the early 1990s, securities reform legislation was passed, giving the minister of finance clear authority to supervise the Securities Board. These reforms were prompted in part by the need to designate a supervisory body in connection with the implementation of European Union securities law directives. However, the loss of the Amsterdam Stock Exchange's market share in Dutch securities to London in the early 1990s prompted more far-reaching business and regulatory changes.

On January 1, 1997, the European Options Exchange and the Amsterdam Stock Exchange merged. The merger included the settlement systems and depositories of these organizations. The activities of the futures market were then included. The Amsterdam Exchange demutualized, selling half its shares to former exchange members and placing the remainder with institutional members and listed companies. In connection with these transactions, the Amsterdam Exchange gave up its floor for the trading of equities, changed the role of the "hoeckman," whose role was to provide quotes to supplement the order-driven market, and began recruiting international brokerage houses for remote membership.

After the Amsterdam Exchange demutualized, it merged with the Paris and Brussels stock exchanges to form Euronext, which began operations in September

2000. Initially, the Paris Bourse owned 60 percent of Euronext; the Amsterdam Exchange, 32 percent; and the Brussels Exchange, 8 percent.[49] Euronext was formed as a Dutch company; it uses a French trading platform and offers a central counterpart and netting and clearinghouse for trade execution via Clearnet. Issuers continue to be listed on their home exchanges but trade on a single integrated trading platform with harmonized listing requirements. It is anticipated that national regulators will agree to a common rulebook.[50]

Lessons for Latin America and the Caribbean

Each of the case studies discussed above contains possible lessons for Latin American exchanges. In Sweden, demutualization was an important part of a process of converting a government-controlled entity in a socialist state into a business-oriented stock exchange, which repatriated trading in Swedish equities from London to Stockholm. With recapitalization and the proceeds from a public offering, the Stockholm Stock Exchange was able to act as a leader in structuring affiliations with other Scandinavian exchanges. The Stockholm Stock Exchange proved an easy takeover target for OM, but OM's bid for the London Stock Exchange was a failure. These experiences show the importance of determining whether a demutualized exchange should become a public company and whether there should be limitations on the percentage of voting stock any single shareholder should be permitted to hold.

The Australian Stock Exchange demutualization was part of an effort to internationalize this exchange and make it a leader in Asia. This involved adopting new legislation at the federal level in a strongly federalist legal system and the modernization of exchange membership and governance. Yet, when the exchange attempted to expand its business interests from equities trading to include financial futures trading, the competition authorities thwarted it. This experience demonstrates the need to focus on whether an exchange should make a public offering as well as demutualize and to determine what use can and should be made of the proceeds from any public offering.

The Amsterdam Stock Exchange demutualization is an example of how an old and well-established exchange was forced by legal and economic circumstances

---

[49] "Paris, Amsterdam and Brussels Bourses to Approve Merger Terms," *Wall Street Journal Europe*, July 4, 2000; 2000 WL *Wall Street Journal Europe* 21065465.

[50] http://www.euronext.com/en/euronext/implementation.

to give up its floor, change its governance and regulatory oversight, and affiliate with two other European exchanges, one larger, one smaller. The Amsterdam experience may be of particular relevance to some Latin American exchanges, which may be too small to remain national champions, especially when confronted with competition from U.S. exchanges.

Conclusion

To date, there is not a body of evidence from which to argue that demutualization of an exchange will increase the number of issuers choosing to list there or improve the exchange's liquidity. Nevertheless, an examination of the process of demutualization demonstrates that it can be a prod for securities law reform, regulatory change, and corporate governance reform of the exchange. In particular, demutualization can be used as a vehicle for achieving greater transparency, accountability, and responsibility at the exchange, three of the four core governance standards necessary to attract private capital.[51] The fourth standard, fairness to shareholders, should be an objective of the demutualized exchange, regardless of whether it chooses to go public. If the leading exchange in a country sets an example of good governance, it is in a better position to encourage good governance in its listed companies.

Stock exchange demutualization also gives government securities regulators the opportunity to examine the balance between government regulation and self-regulation and to make adjustments to the legal regime for securities law disclosure and trading as may be necessary and appropriate. This may result in an increase in government regulatory authority, but it may also lead to devolution of authority to the private sector in the form of improved self-regulation or other accountability mechanisms. One observer has argued that much self-regulation is wholly consistent with profit-maximizing behavior (Steil 2002). Yet, since the fundamental purpose of securities regulation is to protect investors, there is a limit as to how effective a regulator a for-profit organization can be.

It should be stressed that, although demutualization is a response to many of the technological, economic, and political forces to which exchanges are subject in today's world, it is first and primarily a change in the exchange's governance. It generally is part of a process of transforming an exchange from a member-controlled organization, governed by committees seeking consensus, to an organization led by pro-

---

[51] Holly J. Gregory, "The Globalization of Corporate Governance," *Director's Monthly*, August 2001, p. 9.

fessional managers and staff with a board of directors that includes independent public directors not associated with a securities firm. This enables the exchange to focus on customer needs and make decisions more expeditiously. It also enables an exchange to modernize its technology and plan acquisitions and affiliations to strengthen its business.

Bibliography

Bradley, Caroline. 2001. Demutualization of Financial Exchanges: Business as Usual? *N.W.J. Int'l L. & Bus* 21(657).

Coffee, John C. Jr. The Coming Competition among Securities Markets: What Strategies Will Dominate? Working Paper 192. http://www.law.columbia.edu/lawec/.

Cooke, Gilbert W. 1969. *The Stock Markets*. Cambridge, Mass.: Schenkman Publishing.

Cowell, Alan. 2001. The London Stock Exchange Says It Will Go Public in July. *The New York Times*. May 25. p. W-1.

Donnan, Frank. 1999. Self-Regulation and Demutualization of the Australian Stock Exchange. *Australian Journal of Corporate Law*. 1(10).

Fried, Lisa L. 1999. Plans Debated for Stock Markets' For-Profit Conversion. *New York Law Journal*, September 30, p. 5.

Garten, Jeffrey E. 1999. Manager's Journal: How to Keep NYSE's Stock High. *The Wall Street Journal*, September 13, p. A44.

Hart, Oliver, and John Moore. 1996. The Governance of Exchanges: Members' Cooperatives Versus Outside Ownership. *Oxford Review of Economic Policy* 12(4).

Hogan, Stokes Pty Limited. 1996. *Report on Future Governance of the Australian Stock Exchange*. (July) [Hogan, Stokes Report].

Hughes, Pamela S. 2001. Exchange Demutualizations. APEC Financial Regulators Training Initiative Regional Seminar, August 13–14. Asian Development Bank.

Humphry, Richard G. 1995. The Future Structure of Securities Markets. *Asx Perspective*, 4th quarter, p. 9

IOSCO Technical Committee. 2000. Discussion Paper on Stock Exchange Demutualization, December. http://www.iosco.org/docs-public2000-stock-exchange-demutualization.html.

Kahan, Marcel. 1997. Some Problems with Stock Exchange-Based Securities Regulation. *Virginia Law Review* 83(1509).

Karmel, Roberta S. 2001. The Future of Corporate Governance Listing Requirements, *SMU L. Rev* 54(325).

_____. 2002. Turning Seats Into Shares: Causes and Implications of Demutualization of Stock and Futures Exchanges. *Hastings L. J.* 54(367).

Karmel, Roberta S. (ed.). Forthcoming. *Demutualization of Stock Exchanges—Problems, Solutions, and Case Studies.* Manila: Asian Development Bank.

Lowenthal, Max. 1933. The Stock Exchange and Protective Committee Securities. *Columbia Law Review* 33(8): 1298.

Mahoney, Paul G. 1997. The Exchange as Regulator., *Virginia Law Review* 83(1453).

Michael, Douglas C. 1992. Untenable Status of Corporate Governance Listing Standards under the Securities Exchange Act. *Business Law* 47, p. 1461.

National Association of Security Dealers (NASD). 1999. NASD's Frank Zarb Asks Securities Industry to Embrace Change. Press Release. http://www.nasd.com/news/02/ne_section99.html (last modified June 23, 1999)

OM Gruppen. 1997. *OM Annual Report.*

Pritchard, A. C. 1999. Markets as Monitors: A Proposal to Replace Class Actions with Exchanges as Securities Fraud Enforcers. *Virginia Law Review* 85(925):1008.

Ryden, Bengt. 1997. The Privatization of Stock Exchanges: The Case of Stockholm Stock Exchange. *ISE Review* (July-September).

Schroeder, Michael. 1999. Levitt Studies Plan for Single Market Regulator. *The Wall Street Journal*, September 21, p. C1.

Securities Industry Association (SIA). 2000. Reinventing Self-Regulation: White Paper for the Security Industry Association's Ad Hoc Committee on Regulatory Implications of De-Mutualization, January 5 (SIA White Paper). Available at http://www.sia.com/demutualization.

Segal, Jillian. 2001. Demutualization and Privatization of Exchanges, 26th IOSCO Annual Conference, Panel 5, Stockholm, Sweden, June 28.

Seligman, Joel. 1986. Equal Protection in Shareholder Voting Rights: The One Share, One Vote Controversy. *George Washington Law Review* 54(687):694–98.

Steil, Benn. 2002. Changes in the Ownership and Governance of Stock Exchanges: Causes and Consequences. In *Brookings-Wharton Papers on Financial Services*. Washington, D.C.: Brookings Institution.

Stockholm Stock Exchange. 1997. *Annual Report*.

Stone, Rod. 1999. Swedish, Danish Bourse Link Starts Well; More Links Seen, *Dow Jones International News Service*. June 21, *available at* wl djinsplus.

U.S. Congress. 1986. Ad Hoc Subcommittee on Merit Regulation of the State Regulation of Securities Committee. Report on State Merit Regulation of Securities Offerings. *Business Law* (41)785, 787.

The Wall Street Journal. 1999. Levitt Studies Plan for Single Market Regulator. September 21, p. C1.

CHAPTER 10

Developing Bond Markets: A Comprehensive View

Clemente del Valle

Bond markets provide the means to fulfill mid- and long-term funding needs. Developed bond markets help to reduce financial risks in the overall economy, provide the government with a noninflationary source of finance, create a well-balanced financial environment, and promote economic growth. Due to the importance of these markets, governments must take the lead in developing them by creating a domestic government securities market and providing an adequate framework for developing corporate bond markets. Indeed, government bond markets are the foundation for domestic bond markets.

From an inter-American perspective, the level of bond market development varies across countries, which can be categorized in three groups. The first one, the developed group, includes Canada and the United States; both countries have well-developed capital and bond markets where the government obtains all its funding needs via the issuance of fixed-rate and local-denominated currency bonds. Second, the developing group includes Argentina, Brazil, Chile, Colombia, and Mexico; these countries have achieved substantial progress in developing bond markets, especially government securities markets, but the process is far from complete. Third, the predeveloping group includes the rest of the Latin American countries, which are mostly small economies where the size of the financial system does not support the infrastructure required to develop a bond market or countries that have not yet begun the process of developing a bond market. Table 10-1 shows the relative size of the government securities market with respect to the domestic and international bond markets in selected developed and emerging countries.

Government bond markets form the base of the entire bond market. Table 10-1 also shows that most of the developed countries fund their financial needs in their domestic markets, while Latin American countries require access to international

Table 10-1 | **Size of the Government Securities Market**
| *(Outstanding debt securities, September 2001)*

Country	Domestic markets		International markets	
	Total debt (billions of U.S. dollars)	Government securities (percent)	Total debt (billions of U.S. dollars)	Government securities (percent)
Argentina	30	90.4	87	85.1
Brazil	269	85.0	63	51.7
Canada	563	69.9	206	49.6
Chile	31	60.3	5	9.3
Colombia			13	83.6
France	1,091	60.7	375	7.3
Germany	1,656	43.3	1,003	1.9
Italy	1,314	75.3	261	27.6
Japan	6,343	75.3	277	6.1
Mexico	81	83.3	65	46.3
Peru	4	45.9	0	
Spain	365	75.9	174	21.2
United Kingdom	939	45.2	599	1.1
United States	15,057	55.7	2,126	29.4
Uruguay			3	89.3
Venezuela			12	56.3

Source: BIS.

sources (multilateral banks and international capital markets) to finance their needs. Thus, the first challenge that Latin American countries face in the capital markets framework is to develop sound domestic government securities markets and to respond to their growing financing needs. To achieve this goal, countries must tackle important challenges at the micro level. The main challenges are to develop sound money markets, increase competition among market participants, provide liquidity and transparency to secondary markets, expand the investor base, provide a sound regulatory framework, establish a regular and transparent primary market system, and strengthen government debt management capacity (human resources and information technology).

The challenges and the initial achievements are clear. What seems to be lacking in many of these countries is government awareness that, by having a more systematic and comprehensive vision of the requirements of developing bond markets, the countries could be more successful and expedient in achieving this very impor-

tant goal. In fact, like any other major project that involves many institutions and policies, developing vibrant capital markets, and bond markets in particular, requires a
sound framework, the right inputs, and proper management. Therefore, due to the importance of bond markets in building a sound capital market, governments should
take the lead in developing a comprehensive framework. Moreover, bond markets are
one of the principal means for achieving a developed and sound domestic capital
market. Thus, governments, through their ministries of finance, are not only developers, but also issuers. Policymakers must address important questions about the sequence of development, the essential initiatives, and the role of the government.

This chapter provides general policy guidelines and recommendations for
market development. The main goal of the chapter is to convey the simple but important message that it is essential for policymakers to work on bond market development as a comprehensive and dynamic process. It is clear that the government,
through the ministry of finance or in some cases the central bank or the securities
regulatory agency, must lead the development process. A developed bond market di-
versifies the risks of the entire economy and leads to a more competitive economic
and financial environment, which is especially important in Latin America because the
region's lack of competitiveness has historically hampered economic growth. Thus, it
appears clear that bond market development and, more generally, capital market development will lead the region to more sustainable economic growth. In addition, the
chapter provides a succinct description of what Latin American countries have done
and the biggest challenges ahead.[1]

A Comprehensive View

Governments pursue economic growth and development by their policies and actions. Well-developed capital markets provide benefits for the entire economy and
are thus an essential tool for growth. A sound domestic capital market reduces risks
and interest rates, leads to lower volatility and higher diversification, and establishes a
long-term horizon for investments. The money market is usually the first step in the
development of a sound domestic bond market, followed by the government securities market, the corporate bond market, and finally the derivatives market. This se-

---

[1] The chapter relies heavily on World Bank and IMF (2001), World Bank (2001), and our experience as bond and capital market developers and debt managers.

quence has not always been followed; sometimes the level of competition, the grade of macroeconomic stability, or the investor base modifies it. Although the four types of markets follow a sequence, they have a close relationship, and one helps to build or improve the other. For example, the money market helps to provide liquidity toward development of the government bond market, supports the short-term process of building the yield curve, and reduces the costs of government securities. The government bond market provides short-term bonds and standardized issues to the money market, ensuring the supply of instruments to maintain a proper level of liquidity. Both the money and government bond markets help to build the private sector bond market by providing infrastructure, tools for price discovery, and hedging mechanisms. The corporate bond market expands investors' options and leads to a more balanced domestic financial architecture, reinforcing the development of the entire bond market. The derivatives market arises as a consequence of the need for participants to hedge their risks; its creation leads to low interest rates and better financial management practices. The benefits of that market spill over to the other three markets and reinforce their development. The links among markets show not only the crucial role of capital markets as a tool for economic development, but also the importance of governments taking the links into account when designing economic policies. Figure 10-1 shows the correlation between development and deepening of capital markets; the size of each circle shows the relative significance of the market it represents.

Since capital markets are a means for promoting economic development, government needs to take a capital market developer's role and create and promote a government securities market. The developer's role has two dimensions: (a) government bond issuer and (b) regulator and developer for private market participants. Therefore, it appears clear that the government, through the ministry of finance (issuer and market developer), has to lead the development process. In some countries, this leadership could be passed on to the securities regulator, especially when development moves away from the government bond market into the other markets. It is important to note that, particularly in small economies, central banks play a key role because they have some financial and market knowledge and capacity and need efficient money markets to support their monetary policy operation. If the government does not issue or is not capable of issuing bonds, the central bank must assume the developer role (for example, as in Chile), so that, in some cases, central banks are the only issuers of short-term instruments in the money markets.

Success lies in building a close partnership between the finance ministry, the regulators, and the central bank. The partnership is extremely important at the be-

| Figure 10-1 | **Depth of Domestic Capital Markets and Per Capita GDP, Selected Countries, December 2000** |

Source: IDB based on FIBV, OECD, and BIS.

ginning of the process, when they have to design a comprehensive and strategic plan for capital and bond market development. The ministry of finance has to coordinate with government agencies and bodies to ensure that the development process and the government's policies are consistent over time. This is especially important because in some stages of the process conflicts could arise; for example, the tax authority may want to raise more revenues from the financial system, and the monetary and economic authorities might aim at the bond market development process. Therefore, the ministry of finance must ensure the proper sequencing, make better use of the different synergies, and coordinate relevant agencies. Institutional weaknesses arise as a consequence of lack of coordination; therefore, from the early stages of the process, it is essential to establish proper management in order to achieve a comprehensive development process. The ministry of finance, as a leader of the process, should build a dialogue with the market participants to get feedback on its actions and policies. The developer and coordinator must have the comprehensive perspective of the complex network of market components and their interactions in order to design policies and initiatives. In fact, it is fundamental that investors, infrastructure, regulation, supply, government agencies, intermediaries, and other market players have a role in the strategic market development plan.

Prerequisites for Market Development

Development of the government bond market is a long-term, dynamic process. Building and establishing a credible market for government securities must be viewed as a key component of the country's development strategy. It should be noted that not all the mature economies have a similar strategy, either because the government has not run budget deficits requiring funding or because the country is not large enough to support the necessary infrastructure (see box 10-1). There are two main prerequisites for developing medium- and longer-term government securities markets: a certain level of macroeconomic stability and a liberalized and stable financial system supported by competition. In addition, in order to develop a corporate bond market, it is essential to pass a bankruptcy law that clearly delimits rights and obligations. Therefore, at first, efforts must be aimed at achieving these basic prerequisites, which will then be complemented by others, such as a credible and stable government and a sound legal and regulatory framework.

The Macroeconomic Framework

A sound and credible macroeconomic framework includes sustainable fiscal policy, stable monetary conditions, and a credible and transparent exchange rate regime.

Fiscal Policy

In the context of government securities market development, the government must be able to communicate to the market that fiscal policy is on a sustainable path and under control. Therefore, it is important that investors perceive the ability of the government not only to manage expenditures and debts but also to collect taxes; otherwise, a higher risk of default will be perceived, and the cost of the government debt will rise. A credible budget and control system for expenditures plays a key role in fiscal policy. High real interest rates are one of the common effects of an economy with a government incapable of implementing discipline on the fiscal side and constitute a major impediment for extending the yield curve and developing a liquid nominal bond market.

Monetary Conditions

Stable monetary conditions are closely related to fiscal policy because fiscal deficits financed by the central bank through monetary issues generate inflation. Inflationary

Box 10-1	Small Economies and Bond Markets

Some countries have not developed a domestic bond market because they do not carry fiscal deficits or the size of their economy is not big enough to support the infrastructure required to develop a bond market. This is relevant in Latin America, where many countries have small and nondeveloped economies. In these cases, governments must carefully analyze the necessity of developing a bond market. The authorities have to explore what other mechanisms of funding might prove more efficient. Some alternative funding channels are private placements, access to international markets, and regional solutions.

Other schemes could include syndicated lending, multilateral organizations lending, bilateral loans, or combinations of these alternatives. It is clear that Latin American economies rely on external sources to finance their needs. In fact, except for Brazil, Costa Rica, Chile, and Jamaica, the external debt is greater than the domestic one in every Latin American country. This could increase government exposure to foreign exchange risk that could become unsustainable in the medium term.

In many cases, the activities undertaken are more the consequence of an improvised funding mechanism than a strategic funding policy. A particularly interesting possible solution for countries with small financial systems is a regional market. Merging different small markets in a bigger regional one would create scale economies that could support the required infrastructure and resources that markets require. However, this type of initiative requires macroeconomic and financial harmonization among participants, which is especially difficult to accomplish among developing countries. The lack of compatibility among financial and macroeconomic country schemes constitutes a major barrier for market integration.

External Debt as a Percentage of GDP, December 2000

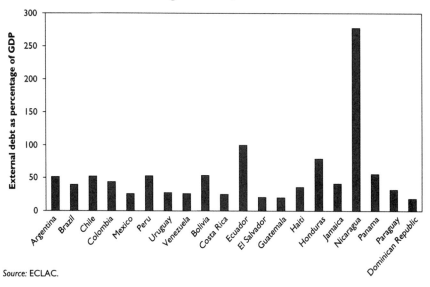

Source: ECLAC.

expectations discourage investors from allocating resources to government bonds, increase the cost of funds, and shorten the maturity of issues. A credible commitment to contain inflation is an essential step in developing a securities market; therefore, an independent and well-managed central bank is necessary to complement fiscal policy. Likewise, sound fiscal policy must complement the monetary authority's efforts to contain inflation.

Exchange Rate Regime

Exchange rate and capital account policies have a direct impact on government bond yields, reflecting exchange rate and default premiums. Inadequate policies increase both volatility and interest rates. Volatility has a negative impact not only on developing long-term government bonds but also on secondary market liquidity, especially where no complementary markets exist to hedge the risk of price movements. Capital account deregulation needs to be carefully considered because unrestricted capital movements could expose the economy to risks of contagion from external crises. Sound monetary and fiscal policies combined with good management of debt and reserves can lessen these risks. An unstable macroeconomic framework not only constitutes an impediment to capital market development but also destroys efforts and achievements in that direction.

Financial Sector Reform and Stability

Investors' concerns about the banking system adversely affect the government's efforts to develop the market. Moreover, lack of financially healthy intermediaries will cause secondary market liquidity to fall. Therefore, with a banking system in crisis, it is not possible to develop a government securities market, because markets—such as the repo and interbank markets—are closely related to both government securities and the financial market and cannot function properly with an unsound banking system. Financial system reform—liberalization and stabilization—must address information infrastructure, sound supervision and regulation, interest rate liberalization, and competition.

Information Infrastructure

Information disclosure plays a key role in building market credibility, not only because investors are reluctant to deal without properly disclosed information but also because disclosure leads to transparence and best practices. Well-established and transparent accounting and auditing methods help the monetary authority and the market in supervising the financial system. Moreover, it is important that the monetary authority collects and processes all information in order to ensure the proper disclosure of the information that the market needs.

Supervision and Regulation

Banking regulation must be designed according to international standards. Prudential regulations—including lending standards, capital adequacy, and asset diversification—must be addressed to gradually reach the standards of the Bank for International Settlements (BIS). In addition, the supervisory authority must gain enforcement power; otherwise, control will be downgraded to a monitoring function without intervention. A sound financial system reinforces investor confidence and facilitates the development of new products, such as mutual funds. In order to prevent systemic risks, a safety net should support banks that are experiencing temporary liquidity (but not solvency) problems.

Interest Rate Liberalization

Removing interest rate and portfolio limits from the banking system and the financial sector as a whole is necessary to build a sound financial system. This form of liberalization leads to better pricing and allocation of assets and liabilities. In order to develop the government securities market, liberalization must be complemented by regulations and reforms not only to improve loan foreclosure and corporate bankruptcy but also to reach international standards of prudential regulation.

Competition

A more competitive environment spreads benefits over the entire market and helps the development of the process. The entry of international financial service providers is an interesting move toward banking and financial sector reform, but should be carefully analyzed, especially during the first stages, in order to avoid damage to local players.

In some countries, the banking system is the center of the financial system, and, in an environment of limited competition and weak supervision, banks may be less interested in supporting the disintermediation implied by developing bond markets. In addition, if the system operates under a flexible regime where banks dominate the asset management industry (for example, mutual funds and pension funds) and the brokerage firms, this lack of interest could become a major impediment to developing domestic debt markets.

The Situation in Latin America

Currently in Latin America, bond markets are unevenly developed because of structural and economic differences in the level of development across countries. To a large extent, differences in the key prerequisites described above explain the differences in achievement. For example, larger economies in the region may find it easier to support development of their debt markets. For instance, the second group of countries (Argentina, Brazil, Chile, Colombia, and Mexico) achieved a level of macroeconomic stability during the first half of the 1990s.[2] For the financial sector, the 1990s were also characterized by reforms, such as the liberalization of markets and the inflow of foreign direct investment to the financial system. The latter was prompted in some countries by the Mexican crisis, which exposed deficiencies in corporate governance and weaknesses in the regulatory framework of the financial system. The second half of the 1990s was characterized by developments in the bond markets, which were favored by lower levels of inflation, sounder financial systems, and relatively more stable macroeconomic environment. In fact, low inflation allowed these governments to extend bond maturities and issue fixed-rate instruments. It is important to set aside the case of Chile, which implemented reforms long before any other Latin American country and, in certain areas of capital market development, is more advanced. However, in the case of bond markets in Chile, most fixed-income securities (central bank and corporate sector securities) are inflation indexed, which has represented a major impediment for more active and deeper markets.

Brazil and Mexico have been exposed to currency and macroeconomic crises during the past decade. However, since the crisis of 1995 and the North American Free Trade Agreement (NAFTA), Mexico has been consolidating key reforms in the macro and financial sectors. For example, after the 1994–95 crisis, the government encouraged international banks to participate in the domestic financial market, leading to privatization and consolidation of the banking system. Due to better macroeconomic and financial practices, Mexico was upgraded to investment grade. This positive environment, combined with a more proactive debt management strategy to develop the local debt

---

[2] Chile gained macroeconomic stability much earlier due to the reforms implemented during the 1980s. The recent currency devaluation in Argentina has introduced a high degree of macroeconomic instability in that country.

markets, has proved to be quite effective. The Mexican authorities have been able to extend the average maturity of the debt portfolio, increase its duration with the introduction of the 5- and 10-year nominal fixed-rate bonds, and improve liquidity because of increased fungibility and the reopening and introduction of market makers in 2000.

Since its devaluation in 1999, Brazil has experimented with high levels of volatility in the key financial variables. Although the country has achieved important results in terms of consolidating a sounder macroeconomic framework, volatility continues to be high and Brazil's real interest rates are among the highest in the world. This environment represents a major constraint for further development of the local debt markets and has forced the government to offer indexed instruments (to the foreign exchange rate and the overnight interest rate) in order to extend maturities and maintain control of refinancing risk and the cost of debt in the short term. Therefore, reducing real interest rates and realizing further stability in the financial variables should be key priorities for the government going forward.

Colombia implemented important reforms in the macro and financial sectors, combined with a relatively well-organized strategy, which proved effective in building the market. Colombia is one of the few countries in the region that has been able to establish a liquid 10-year benchmark for nominal bonds. Since 1997/98, deterioration in Colombia's fiscal situation has brought a more complicated debt overhang, which is seriously endangering the process of development. However, lower real interest rates have contributed to partially offset the problem of accelerated growth in the stock of government debt.

Argentina had built a stable macroeconomic framework during the 1990s, which contributed to development of the local debt markets. However, the unsustainable fiscal deficit carried over during the past few years has led the country to default and devaluation, creating an unstable macroeconomic environment aggravated by a broken financial system.

The situation in the third group of countries is substantially different. Costa Rica, Uruguay, and Venezuela are in some ways the more advanced markets within this group, given the more proactive role of their governments in supporting bond market development, which is still in its early stages. In Peru, relatively small net financing needs and the country's explicit decision, until recently, not to engage in active financing in the local *soles* market explain the limited development of the local debt markets. In addition, the real sector relies on dollar-denominated loans. In the case of Panama, the economy is fully dollarized and the country has been a financial center for a long time. These special conditions have enabled the government to rely primarily on international sources (capital markets and international organizations) and to a lesser degree on local sources.

Figure 10-2 | **Sequence of Development**

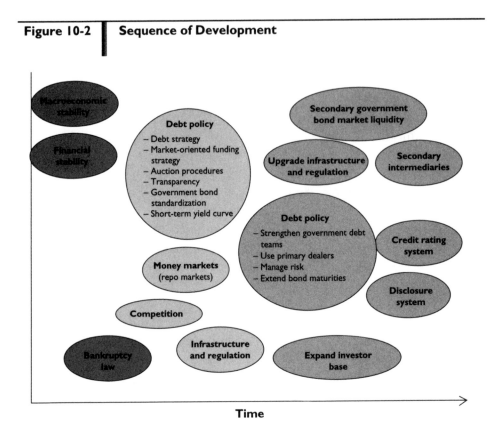

Time

Sequence of Development

The sequence of development of the government bond market has three main stages: prerequisites, expansion, and maturity. The strength of the financial sector, the size of the economy, and the investor base exert a substantial impact on developing the market, and could modify the dynamics of these stages. Moreover, these stages are not watertight compartments; the development process must be regarded as a flexible framework in which the stages coexist at different points in time. Policymakers have to keep in mind that, in general, corporate market development will tend to follow the government securities process, and the former is built on the latter. It is essential to begin with a comprehensive view because initiatives designed for the government securities market will affect on the corporate bond market and ultimately the capital market. Figure 10-2 provides an illustration of the policies involved during the three main stages of development of the government bond market.

Expansion

During the second stage, governments have to deal with various challenges and undertake four essential initiatives: building the money markets (repo markets); designing and implementing a market-oriented funding strategy; establishing a basic and safe
market infrastructure and regulatory framework; and promoting and improving competition. The ministry of finance and the monetary authority must coordinate efforts
to develop money markets and liquid repo markets in particular; the former will provide instruments, such as treasury bills, and the latter will conduct monetary policy.
The ministry of finance must design a debt strategy that includes better auction procedures, transparent government securities operations, standardization of instruments,
and development of a short-term yield curve. However, the most important initiative
is government movement away from captive sources of funding and implementation
of a market-oriented funding strategy.

At this stage, banks and money market funds are essential players that support
the achievements of the first two initiatives. The legal framework has to be adapted to
meet market-oriented legal requirements. Complex infrastructure is not needed at this
time, but it must provide a safe environment. One of the actions that has to be implemented at this stage is to encourage and promote competition among the participants
in the market, establishing the pillars of a more diversified base of investors. This will
be especially challenging in those economies where the banking industry is vertically
and horizontally integrated. Some Latin American countries have allowed international
banks to enter their domestic markets, bringing know-how in treasury management
and competition. In fact, some long-term initiatives to diversify the investor base and
market participants, such as pension fund reform, which takes years to implement,
could be initiated in the early stages; the same could apply to mutual funds. In any case,
the results of these initiatives will be seen in the mid and long term.

Maturity

The last stage of the development process presents new challenges. Lengthening the
maturity of government securities by issuing fixed interest rates or indexed bonds is
one of these challenges. Government debt managers are vital at this stage, and the
government has to ensure that the "debt team" has the needed resources to implement a debt management strategy with special focus on managing risks properly.

The key step in the third stage, to ensure and promote liquidity in secondary
government securities markets, will require market infrastructure and regulation. In

fact, secondary market liquidity is the most complex goal because it is extremely sensitive to a wide combination of factors, such as the existence of standardized and fungible instruments, diversified investors, safe and efficient infrastructure, conducive regulation, a well-balanced tax regime, and sound monetary and fiscal policies. A credible and sound framework of market regulation and supervision needs to be in place to avoid loss of confidence by the investors due to abuses by intermediaries and issuers. Moreover, settlement and depository systems have to be upgraded, and government bonds need to be fully dematerialized in order to achieve delivery versus payment (DVP) standards. In addition, credit rating and disclosure systems have to be designed and put in place to satisfy specific corporate bond market necessities. At this stage, the government needs to carefully analyze the use of primary dealers as market makers and the role of intermediaries in the secondary market. Another major challenge during this stage is to develop and expand the investor base, promoting long-term investors such as institutional investors, including pension and insurance funds.

The Government Bond Market

Bond markets are the link between issuers and investors with medium- and long-term financing and investment needs. The government bond market is the backbone of most fixed-income securities markets, not only in developed countries but also in developing ones (World Bank and IMF 2001). The benefits of such markets are wide and can be viewed from both macro and microeconomic perspectives.

Benefits of Developing a Government Bond Market

From a macroeconomic point of view, the government securities market provides a benchmark yield curve, which helps not only to determine the prices of the assets in the economy and improve the transmission conduit of monetary policy but also to make comparisons among countries. This market is a suitable channel for funding domestic fiscal deficits without using the central bank and, as a consequence, for reducing the potential damage to monetary policy. Moreover, the behavior of the cost of funding constitutes a market test for government policy. Taking into account the close relationship between monetary policy and securities markets, the government bond market strengthens the transmission of monetary policy through the use of indirect monetary policy instruments in order to achieve, for example, inflation targets. Another important advantage is that the government bond market reduces foreign currency issues and dependence on international bond markets. In fact, if it is combined with sound debt management policy, the domestic bond market reduces exposure to financial risks. Moreover, a market-oriented funding policy based on a liquid government securities market will reduce debt service costs over the medium to long term. It is only by having a less risky portfolio and lower real costs that governments can achieve more sustainable growth in their debt portfolio.

From a microeconomic and market architecture perspective, the government securities market leads to the development of financial infrastructure, products, and services, creating a competitive environment that helps to build long-term financial sustainability. If properly developed, the securities market could change the financial architecture of a country from a bank-oriented system to a bipolar system with a significant capital market component aimed at more harmonious financial development. In addition, the government bond market helps develop legal, information, and institutional infrastructure that benefits the entire financial system. Finally, some financial products, such as derivatives, repos, and money market instruments, which help to manage risks for the overall economy and improve financial stability, can only be introduced after the government securities market is either developed or being developed.

Money Markets and Monetary Policy

Government cash transactions and movements have a significant impact on the money supply, not only because governments are the largest participants of the banking system in most economies but also because they deposit their cash in the central bank in order to avoid credit counterparty risks. Since uncertain government cash movements are an unpredictable source of liquidity for central banks and could force the monetary authority to tighten conditions for banks, sound cash management practices are essential. And proper cash management practices support the efforts of the central bank to stabilize inflation and develop money markets.

Banking systems need to manage liquidity and risks, and both can be addressed through government securities, which bear zero risk and are the most liquid instruments in almost every market. After short-term interest rate liberalization, the development of short-term government securities and money markets can grow simultaneously and reinforce each other. A sound money market is a necessary condition for the government bond market because it provides liquidity for those securities. This market not only makes government securities cheaper and less risky to warehouse but also funds trading portfolios of securities, which is essential for the effective involvement of market intermediaries in developing secondary markets (for example, market makers).

In recent years, monetary operations have been implemented more and more through indirect monetary instruments, such as open market operations. Indirect instruments improve the efficiency of monetary policy by allocating financial resources on a market basis. In order to develop a money market, the role of the central bank is essential, thus encouraging participants to manage risks actively and trade in that market.

The monetary authority can do this by lengthening the reserve compliance period, excluding interbank transactions from reserve requirements, adopting a costly accommodation policy, and maintaining the daily level or excess reserves close to that desired by the banks (World Bank and IMF 2001).

When markets are thin, the ministry of finance and the monetary authority can use the same short-term instruments, the former to fund short-term cash flow needs and the latter to implement indirect monetary policy. In these cases, information becomes very important, and it must be ensured that funds raised by the monetary authority will not be used to provide funding to the treasury. In other circumstances, when the treasury bill market is developed, bills issued by the central bank might fragment the market.

Once again, the discussion shows that coordination between the ministry of finance and the central bank is both essential and unavoidable. The former has to make known its intentions to raise funds and provide a daily forecast of its revenues and expenditures; the latter must provide information about money market conditions and the best time for tapping the market with issues.

Government Securities Issuance Strategy and the Primary Markets

The government bond issuance process has a direct impact on government securities market development. This process is an essential component of the debt management strategy, and both must be viewed as means to achieve a major end: securities market development. A sound debt management strategy sets some of the groundwork on which the credibility of the market is built. Commitment to market practices and transparency combined with a market funding policy implies a long-term view of market development. In addition, an adequate regulatory framework is important in order to support market development.

A market-oriented strategy shows commitment to market practices, reinforced during the first stages when, in the short term, the cost of funding may increase compared with other sources of funding. It is essential that governments move away from captive sources of funding. In the medium term, the government can concentrate on building a sovereign yield curve, issuing simple and standardized government secu-rities, avoiding market fragmentation, and providing enough liquidity for each issue. In the early stages, the authorities may need to issue inflation-linked or floating-rate securi-ties to obtain longer maturities, particularly in countries that have recently experienced poor macroeconomic management (high inflation, debt restructuring, or unsustainable deficits) or that could face significant refinancing risk due to the size of their debt.

The most common type of government bond benchmarks in developed markets are those issued at fixed interest rates; the benchmark maturities usually are 2–3, 5, and 10 years. Treasury bills issued as zero-coupon instruments dominate the short-term portion of the yield curve. Some Latin American countries have reached an interesting level of development in benchmark issues. Colombian authorities have established a 10-year fixed-interest-rate bond benchmark, extending the average life of the debt portfolio (box 10-2). Chile has achieved an extended range of maturities, reaching 30-year maturity. However, given that the instruments are indexed to the inflation rate and the issues are not very liquid, the market is not active; therefore, the yield does not necessarily constitute a true benchmark. The limited liquidity of the market could lead to higher interest rates as a result of liquidity premiums. Brazil has been issuing indexed bonds (to the overnight rate, the inflation rate, or the U.S. dol-lar) to reach longer maturities, but this strategy diminishes the country's rollover risk and brings other risks, such as interest rate and currency risks. In fact, the government carries all the risks and still pays high real interest rates, while the bondholder basi-cally only assumes the sovereign credit risk. This practice has not been conducive to sustainable market development.

Another important component of a sound debt issuance strategy is access to primary markets. The main objectives for implementing an effective securities sale method are to increase competition in the primary market and to efficiently deliver securities to investors.

It is important that the legal framework supports government actions and reinforces market development. The most common sales procedure in mature mar-kets is by auction, but early-stage syndication is also useful because it ensures the allocation of the issue and minimizes placement risks. Primary dealers could play a key role in the government's funding strategy because their principal goals are to promote investment in government securities and to ensure activity in the govern-ment bond market. Some rules of the game must be established in order to regulate rights, limits, and obligations. Some of the benefits of using primary dealers are that they provide liquidity, the government can reach different types of investors, and pri-mary dealers can facilitate the shift to a market-based funding environment. However,

Box 10-2	Government Debt Strategy in Colombia

Since 2000, the Colombian Debt Office has focused on two main goals: development of the domestic government securities markets and extension of the sovereign yield curve. In 2001, the government implemented its first domestic debt swap, which supported these goals. Colombia exchanged 52 issues due in 2001, 2002, and 2003 for 3 issues due in 2001, 2004, and 2006. The swap was successful not only because it diminished market fragmentation but also because it extended the average life of the domestic debt portfolio from 3.4 to 4.5 years. The amount exchanged was almost three times higher than that previously estimated. In fact, because the swap diminished the cost of funding and provided more liquid instruments, international analysts rated the transaction very highly. One of the major achievements of the last two years is that the government developed a 10-year fixed-rate bond benchmark, moving away from indexed inflation bonds. Moreover, this strategy is helping to create a long-term investment culture, which is needed to extend the investment horizon of the entire economy.

The country has also made efforts to establish a liquid yield curve composed of 1-, 2-, 3-, 5-, 7-, 8-, and 10-year bonds. The figure below shows not only that the debt team has extended the average life of the debt portfolio and diminished its rollover risk but also that it has lowered the cost of access to the market. The use of primary dealers has helped in implementing the strategy. Moreover, in the past (1998 and 1999), the country had to rely on higher interest rates to extend the average life of the debt; in 2000, 2001, and 2002, Colombia both extended its portfolio average life and diminished interest rates. In large part, the explanation lies in the serious slowdown of the economy (one of the worst in many decades) and the negative expectations of the market participants for the future recovery. However, the proactive debt management strategy has taken advantage of the situation to improve the structure and cost of the debt portfolio. Much has been done and much remains to be accomplished. One of the main challenges for the future is to define a clear commitment to a market-oriented funding strategy, moving away from captive sources of funding.

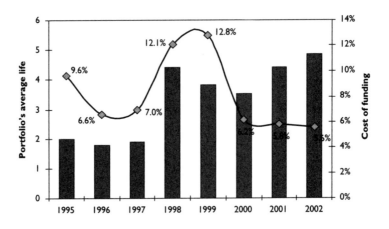

Source: Colombian Ministry of Finance.

Table 10-2 ▌ Access to the Market, by Type of Auction

Auction, country	Calendar of issues	Participation
Uniform price		
Argentina	Yes	Financial intermediaries
Chile	Yes	Financial intermediaries and institutional investors
Colombia	Yes	Primary dealers
Peru	Yes	Stock brokers
Multiple price		
Costa Rica	Yes	Stock brokers
Honduras	No	Everyone
Jamaica	Yes	Everyone
Panama	Annual	Stock brokers
Uruguay	No	Financial intermediaries
Venezuela	Yes	Financial intermediaries
Both methods		
Brazil	Yes	Financial intermediaries
Mexico	Quarterly	Financial intermediaries

Source: World Bank (2001).

the disadvantages of primary dealers are collusion in countries with small financial sectors (World Bank and IMF 2001); limited competition, particularly in small markets; and limited development in cases of scarce liquidity due to lack of repos and other hedging instruments.

The authorities must ensure fulfillment of the required conditions that primary dealers need to operate as market makers in the secondary market. At the same time, the government needs to have the capacity to properly monitor the performance of the primary dealers to avoid market manipulations or artificial activity. The government must carefully analyze the benefits and risks associated with the primary dealer system in order to determine its usefulness. Transparency and information disclosure are also important components of a sound debt management strategy. This includes providing information about funding needs and costs, debt structure and strategies, the issues calendar, expenditures, and revenues. Finally, it is important that the government develops a dynamic interaction with private and public market participants to obtain feedback on its actions and build internal capacity to better read and follow the market. Table 10-2 shows the types of auctions that selected Latin American governments are implementing as well as the countries that work with primary dealers.

Another important fact in the case of Latin America is that, after achieving a higher level of development of their markets, countries introduce primary dealers. Argentina and Colombia introduced primary dealers in 1997, followed by Mexico in 2000. Several countries based their dealers' scheme on the experience of Spain in the late 1980s. That country successfully used primary dealers to promote its government securities, increase competition among participants, and lead the banking sector to the disintermediation process.

Investor Base for Government Securities

A diversified investor base is essential to create and develop a government securities market. In the early stages of development, both developed and developing countries have historically relied on coercion and regulation to raise funds, for example, by establishing that banks must meet their reserve requirements by holding government securities. The consequence of these practices is that market participants cannot reach an optimal portfolio, producing an opportunity cost for their investors' assets and inducing some moral hazard within the government. While most developed countries have implemented reforms toward eliminating such distortions, few developing countries have introduced reforms to change the situation. The commitment to market-oriented funding strategies is especially threatened when government faces deteriorated fiscal conditions that could prompt the return to the use of captive sources of funding.

Commercial banks are one of the major investors in government securities, particularly at the early stages of market development. They allocate resources in government bonds not only to meet reserve and liquidity requirements but also to manage short-term liquidity, provide collateral for repo transactions, obtain stable interest income, and hedge interest rate positions. However, a more permanent, strong presence in the government securities market could indicate that those banks are weak in doing their job, which is lending.[3] When banks are the dominant player in the market and limited competition exists, some resistance could arise against developing a government bond market because it would lead to a disintermediation process that would threaten the banks' traditional business. Government action becomes essential in those markets where banks are the owners of related financial business, such as in-

---

[3] This behavior can also be seen in countries that have recently gone through a financial crisis and/or an economic recession. These situations could induce a credit crunch due to the high credit risk perceived by banks and the high cost of maintaining prudential reserves.

surance, brokerages, and mutual funds. The government, as the developer of the market, is the only one in position to offset the stated resistance by setting rules to encourage disintermediation from bank deposits to capital market instruments and promoting competition among participants. One way to do this is by presenting a large enough business perspective to the new players and strong moral suasion, which only public sector authorities can exercise. In Latin American countries, the banking industry dominates the financial system, and that is especially difficult to change in small economies. In Costa Rica, for example, one or two banks dominate the system, and a more competitive environment would be difficult to establish due to the lack of economies of scale and the political resistance to reforming public sector banks.

Mutual funds represent a significant source of demand for short- and mid-term segments of government securities markets. The fact that these funds are created for special investment purposes explains why they do not necessarily have diversified portfolios. In order to develop the mutual fund industry, it is important to increase competition, removing barriers to entry to the financial sector and allowing international institutions to enter domestic markets. In addition, a sound regulatory framework must be built to develop mutual funds, which should include investor protection, market integrity, high standards of disclosure of information, and a clear separation between managers and depository institutions. It is imperative to avoid any regulatory arbitrage, especially between the regulatory frameworks for banks and mutual funds. Mutual funds constitute an excellent means for reaching out to retail investors. However, mutual funds require the network of commercial banks to distribute their products, which may lead to conflicts of interest between both market participants that government has to address by creating a more competitive environment. Brazil constitutes a showcase, where the mutual fund industry has experimented with a major increase in the savings channeled by these institutions. This growth can be partially explained by the tax benefit that the funds receive with respect to the tax applied to financial transactions; that is, investments made by mutual funds do not pay the transaction tax. Therefore, economic agents, including other institutional investors (banks, pension funds, and insurance companies), directed an important part of their investments through mutual funds. Now that the industry has reached a certain level of development, an interesting problem has arisen from the tax distortion; that is, the concentration of the investor base has affected the liquidity of the market as fewer participants are managing a greater part of the resources.

Pension funds and insurance companies provide a strong demand for fixed-income securities. Institutional investors benefit capital market development by introducing financial innovation, transparency, corporate governance, competition, efficient financial practices, and market integrity (see Vittas 1998, 2000). Government securities can fulfill the need for long-term, fixed-interest, and low credit risk instruments. In countries where equity markets are well developed, institutional investors usually allocate a substantial portion of their portfolios in those markets, but where they have not developed, pension funds and insurance companies invest heavily in bonds. In addition, where the bond market is well developed, institutional investors prefer nongovernmental fixed-income securities, while in nondeveloped bond markets, pension funds and insurance companies invest heavily in government bonds. Finally, it is important to note that institutional investors and securities markets complement and improve each other, thus generating a virtuous circle. Chile was the first Latin American country that implemented pension reform. Other countries that have implemented similar schemes are Argentina, Colombia, Mexico, Peru, and Uruguay. Due to their professionalism, these new market participants have introduced better risk management and better market practices to Latin American countries. The main challenge going forward is to avoid a high level of concentration in industry as a result of the high concentration in the financial system due to economies of scale or barriers to entry.

Retail investors constitute a nonvolatile source of funding, but the problem of reaching out to this clientele has to do with high processing and distribution costs. However, the use of new technologies, such as the Internet, may open new opportunities to sell government securities directly to retail investors efficiently and at low cost.

Nonfinancial corporations do not tend to invest in government securities. Although they use these securities to manage liquidity and hedge risks, they are not long-term investors. Despite this circumstance, nonfinancial corporations can contribute to the development of money markets by investing directly in treasury bills and short-term government bonds or indirectly via money market funds.

Foreign investors are important participants in emerging markets and could be heavy investors in domestic government bonds. They not only add liquidity to the market but also help extend the yield curve of government securities. Foreign investors demand high-quality and cheap financial services and credible and safe infrastructure. And, because they are especially sensitive to market movements and their portfolios are actively managed, foreign investors can add volatility to the market. This could aggravate a delicate financial situation and, because emerging markets are perceived as one asset class, foreign investors could spread a contagion effect to countries with sound economic fundamentals. However, economies with more stable and sound macro conditions will be better equipped to make the participation of foreign investors in local markets a win-win situation.

Figure 10-3	The Investor Base in Selected Latin American Countries, December 2000 *(Percentage of assets)*

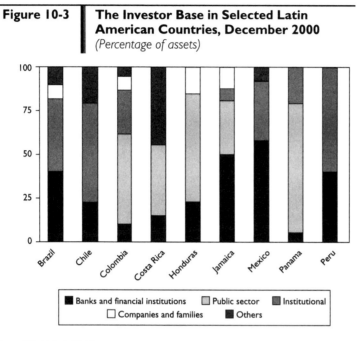

Banks and financial institutions | Public sector | Institutional
Companies and families | Others

Source: World Bank (2001).

A broad investor base implies several benefits for developing a government securities market, including but not limited to market stability, financial innovation, increased liquidity, and lower costs of funding. The government must lead the process of expanding its investor base through developing an environment that attracts diverse investors. The banking disintermediation process deserves special attention because banks do not have great incentives to expand the investor base and disintermediate their activities. Therefore, regulation and competition become essential tools to achieve that goal.

Figure 10-3 shows that countries like Colombia, Costa Rica, Honduras, Jamaica, and Panama rely heavily on public sector investments that constitute a captive source of funding. For example, in Colombia, financial surpluses from state companies and agencies must be invested in government securities, including the public sector social security fund, and this captive investor represents around 50 percent of the total demand for government bonds. In addition, the majority of Latin American countries still directly or indirectly require that banking reserves be met exclusively by government securities.

Secondary Markets and Infrastructure

A liquid secondary market for government securities requires the involvement and commitment of several market participants. Developing a liquid secondary market calls for not only sound infrastructure but also an adequate regulatory framework. Sound infrastructure involves trading systems and procedures, market intermediaries, related markets, and settlement and depository systems.

Spot trade is the main form of transaction in secondary markets, and governments must ensure that those trades can be executed and settled safely. It is important that government securities be perceived as liquid instruments. Therefore, these securities have to have low transaction costs, widely available and continuous pricing, wide access to trading systems and intermediaries that provide immediate execution, safe and rapid settlement of transactions, and efficient custodial and safe-keeping services (World Bank and IMF 2001).

One way to provide liquidity to the secondary market is by using intermediaries in the government bond market. Market makers need to hedge risks; otherwise, the cost of carrying an inventory of government bonds increases. Thus, derivatives markets help and complement development of the government securities market. In addition, the existence of dealer-brokers can improve market liquidity by helping market makers execute transactions and the price discovery process.

Government bonds have historically been traded in over-the-counter (OTC) markets, where dealers, large investors, or dealer-brokers close the trades by telephone and confirm the deal by fax. Table 10-3 shows the different markets in which

Table 10-3	Government Bond Trading by Type of Market (Percent)	
Country	Stock exchanges	Over-the-counter markets
Argentina	15	85
Brazil	20	80
Colombia	16	84
Costa Rica	100	
Honduras	100	
Mexico		Most of them
Panama	2	98
Peru	100	
Venezuela		Most of them

Source: World Bank (2001).

government securities are traded; it shows that most government bonds are traded in OTC markets, especially in countries that have reached a certain level of development.

To provide liquidity in the early stages of market development, the authorities can require that specific market participants trade government securities in specific places. Trading and information systems that facilitate efficient completion of transactions are essential for effective secondary market infrastructure. In the early stages, markets are thin and illiquid, but liquidity can be gained by implementing short trading sessions (that is, periodic markets); when markets are more liquid, they can move to continuous trading. In the more developed stages, market volumes and activity grow, and electronic trading systems may provide the lowest cost for trades and the possibility of selling and distributing government securities to final investors. Therefore, the government has to remove entry barriers to the market for corporations that own those trading systems. Brazil has developed one of the first transactional electronic systems for trading government securities in the region, using part of the infrastructure of the Rio de Janeiro Stock Exchange, but creating a new organization with a different governance structure in which banks are the major players. In Colombia in 1998, the central bank introduced an electronic trading platform for the dealer community and, more recently, the Colombia Stock Exchange introduced another electronic trading platform aimed at providing a platform for dealers to trade with their institutional clients (the second tier).

The settlement system is one of the key aspects in developing a securities market. Dematerialized bonds not only help the settlement process because they can be processed quickly and cheaply but also provide protection to investors because they cannot be destroyed or lost. Therefore, one of the first steps in improving settlement procedures must be to change paper government securities for dematerialized ones. Moreover, a key decision in settlement design is to determine the gap between trade execution and settlement. The gap is related to the infrastructure of the settlement system; the shorter the gap between execution and settlement, the lower the risks. Nevertheless, in order to reinforce the view that government instruments are very liquid, some government securities, such as treasury bills, can be settled in shorter periods (that is, T+1) than other government bonds can.

To reach DVP transactions, it is necessary to provide a settlement system that supports large-value trades. Thus, it is preferable for members of the depository system to have accounts at the central bank, which can be credited and debited in order to ensure settlement of both the securities and payment sides of the trade. In order to provide transparency and security, a separate clearing and settlement agency or corporation is required. In OTC markets, those functions work bilaterally, and each participant assumes the credit risk of the counterpart. In the early stages of development, the collection of settlement orders can be implemented by unsophisticated methods, such as telephone or fax, but always ensuring validation, encryption, and authentication.

The custody of government securities can be carried out through the central bank; other options are private companies, partly private companies, and/or a separate government agency. In any case, due to the fact that depository activity is a centralized business, the authorities must ensure nonmonopoly practices, transparency, competition, and wide access to the custody agent. According to table 10-4, there is no clear trend in depository arrangements among the selected group of Latin American countries. The table also shows that those countries that have reached a certain level of development operate only with dematerialized securities. Argentina, Brazil, Chile, Colombia, and Mexico began the dematerialization of securities relatively early. Other countries, like Costa Rica, are currently in the process of introducing the electronic book entry system.

International investors prefer to deal with just one custody agent, which assures better liquidity management practices. At a later stage, efforts must be oriented toward linking domestic custody systems with cross-border depository houses, such as Clearstream or EUROCLEAR, especially in those markets where foreign investors have a large presence.

The design of infrastructure plays a key role in developing secondary government securities markets. Therefore, it is important that policymakers view the design in

Table 10-4 | **Depository Services and Dematerialized Securities**

	Dematerialized (percent)	Depository
Argentina	100	Independent company
Brazil	100	Central bank
Chile	99	Independent company
Colombia	100	Central bank
Costa Rica	0	Stock exchange
Ecuador	0	Independent company
Honduras	90	Central bank
Mexico	100	Independent company
Panama	28	Stock exchange
Peru	100	Stock exchange
Uruguay	44	Central bank

Source: World Bank (2001).

perspective, analyzing its impact in three market dimensions: capital markets as a whole, the government securities market, and secondary markets for government bonds.

Regulatory Framework and Information

A sound legal and regulatory framework is a requisite for market development. Therefore, the first stage of development must address legal reform. The government securities market and the corporate bond market have in common most of the rules of the secondary market, except those related to information requirements because the government does not have to meet disclosure standards. Most countries regulate and supervise the market through a securities regulatory agency, although that body is not the only one that controls and regulates the market. Other government agencies and bodies, such as the central bank and the ministry of finance, are involved in the process and need to coordinate their activities. In any case, the legal framework has to achieve three main goals: ensure transparent and efficient markets, reduce systemic risks, and provide protection for investors.

During the early stages, the government acts as a regulator, using legislation to set the stage for the market. The congress has to pass bills that include but are not limited to a securities law, a public offering framework, a bankruptcy law, the role of the central bank, and the role of the securities regulatory agency. The principal objective of these laws is to establish the rules for the market, including enforcement power of the central bank and securities regulatory agency, basic practices for disclosure of material information, legal resources against market participants, and liabilities for organizations that manage third-party investment accounts.

The legal framework has to be consistent with a market-oriented funding strategy. The ministry of finance, or the government body or agency that borrows funds, has to be empowered with clear borrowing powers. In general, legislatures establish annual borrowing limits, but this practice needs to be reconsidered because it could limit a proactive debt management scheme.[4] In that sense, it is preferable that congress establishes net borrowing limits rather than gross ones.

The regulatory framework of the market should be transparent and efficient, discouraging and sanctioning improper trading practices, including insider trading, use of clients' trading information, fraud, and market manipulation. Since treasury bonds

---

[4] If legislatures establish borrowing limits, they may threaten the capacity of the ministry of finance to implement debt swaps and other forms of debt management.

are generally traded in OTC markets, the authority should have access to trading records in order to investigate compliance with the rules.

Another important goal of market regulation is to minimize systemic risks, which can be addressed by introducing capital requirements and risk-control systems to market participants. Capital adequacy has to be carefully considered because non-uniformity of capital requirements within the same class of securities market actors could increase systemic and credit risks, but different capital requirements across different classes of market participants could create incentives for self-regulation. Capital adequacy must address liquidity and price and credit risk not only for the assets of the intermediaries but also for third-party assets. Margin requirement surveillance is also important for managing risks. In order to minimize systemic risks, the government authority is essential because it generally determines and supervises the margin requirements, capital adequacy, risk control systems, and settlement operations of dealers engaged in the government market. In some countries, part of the authority has been granted to the central bank; however, a clear definition of responsibility will need to be established with the supervisors of the different types of dealers (banks and brokerage firms) in order to avoid conflicts, excessive controls, or gray areas.

In ruling and supervising the secondary market, the securities regulatory agency is not on its own: the central bank is a relevant participant. Self-regulatory organizations help the authorities not only in supervising and implementing rules but also in creating, faster than governments, new regulations in response to new financial products.

Finally, regulation must be consistent among financial industries in order to avoid regulatory arbitrages. Two interesting Latin American examples are Mexico and Peru. In the mid-1990s in Mexico, separate agencies regulated banks and mutual funds, which reformed and improved at different speeds. Consequently, banks, which were more rigorously regulated and supervised, but owned and managed the mutual funds, allocated their funds to their clients through those vehicles in order to avoid the restrictions on banking. During the Mexican and Asian crises, many of the funds were exposed to large losses that came as a surprise to the investors because there was limited transparency and weak supervision. Since then, regulation and supervision have been strengthened, but the credibility of mutual funds suffered enormously and has made renewed development of this institutional investor more difficult. A similar situation occurred in Peru in the late 1990s, when the local securities exchange commission had two formal roles: supervisor and market developer. In this case, under the flag of being a market developer, the commission allowed lax regulation in terms of establishing clear "Chinese Walls" on the management of funds; this affected the financial industry's credibility during the recent international crisis.

Private Sector

The development of corporate bond markets will come, in general, after the development of government securities markets and will require three specific elements: a credit rating system, a disclosure system, and bankruptcy laws. With the exception of those in the United States, secondary corporate bond markets are not very liquid; the main activity of the private sector bond market is focused on the primary market. The size of the corporate bond market differs noticeably among developed and developing countries: in the latter, the private sector bond market rarely exceeds 10 percent of gross domestic product, while in the former, the market generally exceeds that figure, reaching the highest in the United States (70.2 percent of gross domestic product).[5] There are two main classes of corporate bond issuers: major issuers and minor issuers. Major issuers are financially strong, issue low-risk and uniform bonds, have large and stable issues, regularly access the market in a nonopportunistic manner, and are well known by the investor community. Minor issuers are those that access the market irregularly and at opportunistic times, have heterogeneous bonds that are not frequently traded in secondary markets, and usually reach certain types of investors with specific investment needs.

Benefits of the Corporate Bond Market

From a macroeconomic point of view, the corporate bond market benefits not only the private sector but the entire economy as well. Corporate finance managers have to decide how to finance their companies, and they know that an adequate mix of debt and equity is essential for sustainable growth. They must choose between loans and bonds. Although both vehicles have advantages, bonds are more cost-effective for long-term, large-scale, and opportunistic financing. From a broad perspective, corporate bond markets do the following: provide long-term investment products for long-term savings, improve the supply of long-term funds for long-term investment needs, lead to financial innovation in order to meet the specific needs of investors and borrowers, provide lower funding costs by capturing a liquidity premium, relocate capital more efficiently, and diffuse stresses on the banking sector by diversifying credit risks across the economy. Private sector fixed-income securities not only contribute to the disintermediation process mitigating financial risks but also reduce interest rate, foreign exchange, and refunding risks by issuing long-term, fixed-rate local currency bonds.

---

[5] Data for December 1998 from World Bank and IMF (2001, table 12.4).

An underdeveloped and dysfunctional corporate bond market can have widespread consequences that produce an impact not only on the corporate sector but on the whole economic system. The absence of private sector fixed-income securities complicates diversification of assets, leading to inefficient portfolio investments. Other negative effects are that companies may be forced to build an unbalanced structure of funding, financing their needs through international corporate bond markets and exposing the economy and themselves to foreign exchange risks.

Current Trends

Two main trends are supporting development of the corporate bond market: (a) disintermediation and (b) deregulation and privatization. The latter is related in most cases to the increasing incapacity of governments to finance major infrastructure projects, utilities, and housing. In addition, due to the pursuit of economic efficiency, government companies and infrastructure activities have shifted from the public sector to the private one. These changes have been implemented by privatization and deregulation processes. Given the large sizes and long development periods of infrastructure projects, the corporate bond market is the proper place to finance those projects, although many of them are financed by syndicated loans from commercial banks, particularly in the early stages of the projects. From 1990 to 1997, it is estimated that in developing countries, 10 to 20 percent of infrastructure projects were financed by debt securities.[6] By contrast, in many developing countries, privatized companies are becoming the most outstanding issuers of private sector bonds. Given that housing is one of the government's major socioeconomic priorities, efforts have to be aimed at developing a mortgage market. Disintermediation through securitization is the right procedure for promoting and developing the mortgage market, not only because it leads banks toward a higher lending capacity, but also because housing is an engine of economic growth (box 10-3). The size of residential mortgage markets varies throughout the developed countries, but these markets are clearly underdeveloped in emerging economies, in many cases due to limited standardization of the mortgage loan market. In any case, governments have to assess, design, and implement the development of an efficient corporate bond market.

Development of the government bond market constitutes a sort of prerequisite for development of a private sector fixed-income securities market. The exis-

---

[6] World Bank and IMF (2001, p. 368).

Box 10-3	Structured Products

Structured products are collateralized securities that in general adopt the form of bonds. During the last few years, the industry of structured products has grown significantly as a consequence of risk disintermediation through securitization. The most prominent sector in the structured products industry is the mortgage bond sector, particularly in the United States, where at the end of 2001 the mortgage securities market reached $3.6 billion in debt outstanding. Mortgage bonds are securities backed by a pool of mortgages, and the United States has the greatest mortgage securities market in the world. In the United States, government-sponsored enterprises promote and back mortgage securities, with the implicit or explicit guarantee of the federal government (for example, Fannie Mae and Ginnie Mae). As a consequence of collateral guarantees and diversification, these securities are highly rated, and their spreads over treasury bonds are low.

Moreover, a properly developed mortgage securities market can be an engine of disintermediation, stimulating the securitization process, leading to better management of risks, improving the use of capital, and reducing interest rates. In countries that do not carry fiscal deficits and that do not issue government bonds, mortgage bonds can be an imperfect but valid substitute for treasury bonds by creating a benchmark yield curve based on mortgage bonds. Latin America has a great potential to develop mortgage markets, given that the macroeconomic framework is becoming more stable and there is a huge housing deficit. The region has not achieved significant advances in real estate finance, except for Chile, where mortgage products purchased by pension funds represented 17 percent of gross domestic product in 2000 and funded 66 percent of the mortgage needs. Recently, Colombia introduced a mortgage securitization scheme based on the long-established mortgage loan industry in the country.

Other interesting structured products are those that use credit enhancements to allow corporations and subnational governments to be rated better than the sovereign, and this is especially important in emerging markets. There are many forms of credit enhancements, including over-collateralization, insurance policies against political and exchange risks, special-purpose vehicles, sinking funds, asset collateralization, multilateral organization guarantees, and offshore trusts. During the past decade, many Latin American issuers adopted these types of products in order to be rated higher than their sovereigns. An interesting example is the province of Salta in Argentina, which sold its oil revenues to an offshore trust that issued a 15-year fixed-rate bullet bond. The oil revenues that the province sold to the trust backed these bonds. Despite the fact that the bond was over-collateralized, the structure also had an insurance policy against exchange risks that covered 31 months of debt service and a six-month interest reserve fund. Standard & Poor's assigned an investment grade to that structured product, while the Argentine government was internationally rated as a noninvestment-grade country. It is important to note that after the Argentine default, the Salta Hydrocarbon Royalty Trust honored its debt service in time and form.

Source: Particular Issues in Developing Corporate Bond Markets.

tence of a stock market is another main requisite for developing the corporate bond market. Three aspects that do not stem from the existence of a government bond market are particularly important: disclosure systems, credit rating systems, and bankruptcy laws. Every bond issuer has to disclose objective, relevant, and timely information not only about itself but also about its securities. It is important to establish sound standards of information aimed at reaching the international ones, which include international accounting and auditing standards. In addition, improvement in corporate governance promotes transparency and helps disclosure standards. The credit rating system represents an important complement of the disclosure system. Credit rating agencies encourage transparency, increase information flows, and improve accounting and auditing practices. These companies provide an independent and objective view of instruments and their issuers. A low credit rating implies that the issuer might not afford debt services properly; therefore, these ratings have a direct impact on corporate bond interest rates because the lower the rating, the higher the interest rate. That aspect constitutes an incentive for companies to improve both their financial structures and operations. The government can promote credit rating agencies establishing that certain investors, such as pension funds, can only buy rated instruments. It is important to note that competition among credit agencies is essential. Finally, a bankruptcy law is vital for developing the corporate bond market, defining the boundary of the investor's legal ability to force a bankrupt issuer to service obligations and procedures to reach that limit. In addition, it is important to have an efficient mechanism for the bond issuer to recover investments and determine the priority or subordination of an investor's right to that of other creditors.

Regulatory Framework and Information

An important goal of the legal framework is to ensure a transparent and efficient market, discouraging and sanctioning improper trading practices. Information disclosure requirements are especially important for corporate bonds, not only in primary markets but also in secondary ones. The regulation has to enforce that corporations release relevant information expeditiously, reaching all market participants at the same time to avoid inside information practices. In order to build sound information disclosure procedures, it is desirable that countries adopt international standards of information disclosure not only in terms of prospects for primary markets but also in periodic informative disclosures. Credit rating agencies are especially important for the corporate bond market because they have a direct relationship with companies and provide an independent view that ensures investors a good credit risk assessment.

Another main objective of market regulation is investor protection, which could be achieved by means of a sound legal framework and transparent information disclosure. A sound investor protection framework includes bankruptcy law, which is especially important for corporate bonds in order to determine rights and obligations of market participants; best execution of trades; separate treatment and management of intermediary and client assets; acquisition of licenses for brokers and advisors to operate, but not introduction of barriers to new participants because competition reinforces professionalism among brokers and advisors; and legal resources against market participants and efficient conflict resolution, which means that investors can initiate legal actions against brokers, dealers, corporate issuers, clearinghouses, and even the government itself to exert their bondholder rights.

Linkages between Markets

Government securities markets and corporate bond markets have strong linkages not only between them but with other markets as well. Therefore, a comprehensive approach must be taken in the design and implementation of initiatives. In this process, the government has two roles: first as regulator and developer and second as bond issuer. It is important that authorities keep in mind the global perspective in reconciling their funding needs with their role as developer. Essential linkages between these two markets take place via many channels: government benchmark issues, intermediary experience, the investor base, infrastructure, disclosure practices, regulatory framework, and the experience of the authorities. In addition, fixed-income markets are closely related to other markets, such as the derivatives and money markets. Government bonds are the principal source of price discovery in other markets, and the short-term yield curve is especially important to ensure money market efficiency. The government bond market is so important for the corporate bond market that some countries, like Hong Kong and Singapore, have taken the initiative of issuing government bonds even when they do not carry fiscal deficits. Of course, this is an expensive proposition that not many countries can afford to implement.

Impediments for Development

Governments can hinder the corporate bond market instead of promoting it by crowding out the market and setting statutory restrictions. Given that government securities are risk free, they are the preferred choice of many investors. Recurrent deficits combined with market-oriented funding policies could lead to crowding out the corporate bond market. In that scenario, private bond issuers would not find investors for their bonds, or would have to issue bonds with high interest rates. Other crowding out practices are the use of captive sources of funds and the issue of government bonds with special benefits, such as tax exemptions. And statutory restrictions are usually imposed on products and/or market participants. These restrictions have seemingly sustainable objectives, but they usually hide their real purposes and negative impacts. For instance, the restrictions protect the interests of certain market participants (for example, pension funds), the existing tax base, and inefficient bureaucracies. At some point, development of the fixed-income market would threaten banks, which would lose a share of their intermediation business; therefore, banks might use their political influence to establish certain types of statutory restrictions. Statutory restrictions could be introduced or not removed because of the government's lack of capacity to collect taxes or because of its inefficient bureaucratic system.

A Virtuous Circle

In a virtuous scheme, the government, as both issuer and developer, establishes the base for corporate bond market development by implementing a comprehensive strategy of market development. The virtuous circle begins with a sound sovereign issuer and regulator committed to overall market development that sets the base for the corporate bond market by issuing benchmark bonds, improving infrastructure, building a sound legal framework, and sharing more developed intermediaries and investors. In addition, new hedging and collateral options arise with the government bond market. The process of developing the private sector fixed-income securities market leads to better priced and more liquid corporate bonds, technological and financial innovation, and possibly private benchmarks that reduce the government's role. The benefits of the corporate bond market—namely, sustainable and balanced corporate debt structures, a more diversified financial system, less systemic risks, better shock absorbability, and more efficient capital allocation—reinforce government finances, corporate governance, and economic efficiency in general, closing the circle and strengthening the entire economy.

A Vicious Circle

In a negative scenario, the government can hinder the market by running unsustainable deficits or by not being proactive, and thus starting a vicious circle. The government hinders market development by crowding out the market, carrying recurrent deficits, and using captive sources of funding or, in some cases, by not funding needs or taking recourse to external financing. Crowding out could cause higher interest rates, limit the investor base, and make the legal and tax frameworks inadequate. Pressured by the need for substantial funding, the government might act in a selfish manner, not sharing infrastructure or the investor base. Moreover, captive sources of funds draw demand away from the private sector and lead to additional market distortions. This would seriously affect the corporate bond market, forcing the private sector to rely exclusively on the banking system or international bond markets to finance its needs and leading to nonoptimal debt structures, high interest rates, and asset concentration. This situation perpetuates an unsound and inefficient financial system, decreasing private sector investment. Finally, the unstable financial system, unsustainable fiscal deficits, and negative effects on corporate governance and economic efficiency would slow economic growth and hold back further development.

Primary and Secondary Markets

At the early stage of government bond market development, primary markets are essential. At a later stage, the only way to consolidate a regular and efficient primary market is by developing an active secondary government securities market. The secondary market not only serves as a basis for pricing corporate bonds and further government securities but also provides hedging tools for market participants and helps develop the required infrastructure.

As a regulator, the government has to provide the legal framework for primary and secondary markets. Secondary market regulation—which is designed and controlled by the same government body, in general, the national securities agency—should aim to be the same for both corporate and government securities, but the scheme in the primary market is very different. The government is a self-regulated issuer, not only because regulation is its inherent duty but also because primary market government securities are in general not regulated by the national securities agency. Thus, the ministry of finance is the regulator and the issuer of the primary government bond market. Therefore, the ministry of finance is the key actor, and it has to not only coordinate the issues but also make sure there is proper disclosure of information on government finances and the debt policy. As issuer, the ministry of finance has to ensure that the congress has passed the required authorizations to borrow funds and the rights to act as market regulator. Moreover, the congress has to delegate to the ministry of finance the power to borrow money.

The government and the private sector should share the infrastructure and regulatory framework of the secondary market, but there are two important considerations. First, except in the United States, where corporate bonds are liquid instruments, corporate bond markets enjoy limited activity in secondary markets (figure 10-4). Second, governments are generally exempt from disclosure requirements, but they have to provide transparent and timely information to the market in order

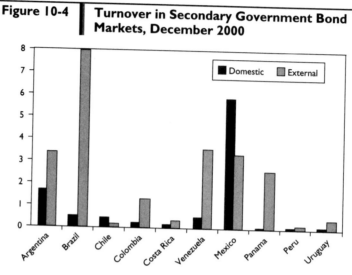

Figure 10-4 | **Turnover in Secondary Government Bond Markets, December 2000**

Source: World Bank survey.

to build confidence in their debt strategy. Legally and constitutionally, in most cases, the government has an obligation to society to be transparent and disclose all necessary information on important activities that the government carries out. Moreover, the business infrastructure built to support secondary markets of government securities is an essential component in facilitating the development of primary corporate bond markets. Without that infrastructure, the costs involved in supporting a corporate bond market structure would be higher than the profits. For example, in the intermediary market, illiquid corporate bond markets cannot be supported without an active secondary government bond market because the profits from trading government bonds and the hedging tools that it provides compensate the costs and risks of the illiquid private sector bond market. Investors benefit from the corporate bond market because it leads to more diversified portfolios with a better risk-return relationship due to the higher yields of private sector bonds.

Taxation Policy

Taxation policies have a major impact on securities and financial market development. As tax systems are more rigid than other systems, it is important for regulators to implement a coordinated approach between financial and tax policymakers in order to design the tax system for financial and capital markets.

In developing countries, tax authorities usually attempt to take advantage of the financial system structure to collect revenues by imposing taxes on that sector, although these tax policies are at odds with the objective of developing the capital market. If bond market development is a national objective, tax policies and regulations must be suitable to achieve that goal without damaging efficient tax practices. In addition to the lack of capacity of some governments to collect taxes, particularly in developing countries, poor and improvised tax policies hamper the development of certain financial instruments and markets.

Tax incentives have been used in developed and developing countries either to promote the use of some financial instruments or to encourage the development of a sector or market. Some governments have provided tax exemptions to bonds in order to extend maturities. In any case, regulators have to keep in mind that tax policies affect not only financial instruments and their development but also consumption behavior, as well as savings and investment decisions. As a first step, authorities must pursue tax neutrality by avoiding tax fragmentation, tax loopholes, and tax avoidance opportunities (World Bank and IMF 2001). Therefore, an efficient taxation system should be based on tax neutrality, simplicity, and fairness.

Conclusion

Domestic capital markets are one of the most important means for development, and the bond market, especially the government bond market, is the backbone of capital markets. In fact, the government securities market is a key foundation of domestic capital markets, and its expansion has to be addressed in a comprehensive way. Moreover, policymakers have to keep in mind that it is a long-term process that requires vision and a strategic plan. Government agencies and bodies have to be independent but coordinated. The ministry of finance is usually the one that leads, implements, and coordinates the process of developing domestic government bond markets.

Countries in Latin America and the Caribbean face substantial development challenges. Some countries have made significant advances in developing their markets, but the process is far from complete. Other countries that have not initiated the process due to their economic size must evaluate the convenience of such effort. The challenges are common and range from designing a comprehensive plan to developing the market, setting higher information standards, implementing more transparent practices, increasing the liquidity of secondary markets, expanding the investor base, strengthening government debt management, promoting competition among market participants, and implementing a monetary policy conducive to money market development.

The region's bond markets are seriously threatened. Argentina has defaulted its debt, producing the highest default in the history of the world. Brazil's government bonds are facing higher spreads over U.S. treasury bonds, and most of its debt is indexed to the dollar or the overnight rate, revealing a great market risk to investors. Colombia has done well in achieving its goals in recent years, but its constant fiscal deficits could complicate debt management and cause permanent damage to the progress. Chile has a relatively sound position, but the turbulence in South America affects the country and its capital market. The regional crises have not yet affected Mexico, but as emerging markets are perceived as one asset class, the country has to reinforce its commitment to sound market practices and consolidation of the market development process. The rest of the countries face similar or more complicated problems and must explore alternatives for market development, including regional solutions.

The process of bond market development requires a long-term view and a firm commitment to market practices, especially during the first stages when governments are usually tempted to return to old behavior. Policymakers have to be fully convinced that the benefits of their efforts are much higher than the costs and that market development will positively affect the entire economy.

Bibliography

Bank for International Settlements (BIS). 1996. *Changing Financial Systems in Small Open Economies.* Policy Paper 1. Basle, Switzerland.

_____. *Statistical Tables on Securities.* Available at www.bis.org.

Economic Commission for Latin America and the Caribbean (ECLAC). 2001. *Statistical Yearbook for Latin America and the Caribbean.* Available at www.cepal.org.

Iberoamerican Federation of Stock Exchanges (FIABV). 2000. *Statistical Summary.* Available at www.fiabv.org.

_____. *2000 Statistics.* Available at www.world-exchanges.org.

Rodriguez, Gerardo. 2001. *Development of the Domestic Debt Market in Mexico.* World Bank Regional Government Bond Market Workshop. Rio de Janeiro (June 11).

Sardenbergs, Rubens. 2002. *VI Seminar of Risk Management*. São Paulo, Brazil (May).

Sharpe, William F., Gordon J. Alexander, and Jeffery V. Bailey. 1995. *Investments*. New York: Prentice Hall.

Standard and Poor's. 2002. *Local and Regional Government*.

_____. 1999. *Public Finance Criteria*.

_____. 2000. *Global Credit Rating Criteria*.

Vittas, Dimitri. 1998. Institutional Investors and Securities Markets: Which Comes First? In J. Burki and G. Perry, eds., *Banks and Capital Markets*. Annual World Bank Conference on Development in Latin America and the Caribbean. Washington, D.C.: World Bank.

_____. 2000. *Pension Reform and Capital Markets Development*. Development Research Group, World Bank, Washington, D.C.

Vives, Antonio. 2002. Financial and Capital Markets Development in Latin America and Caribbean. Presentation at the Inter-American Development Bank, Washington, D.C. (May).

World Bank. 2001. *Regional Snapshot, Rio de Janeiro*. Working paper. World Bank, Washington, D.C.

World Bank and International Monetary Fund (IMF). 2001. *Developing Government Bond Markets: A Handbook*. Washington, D.C.: World Bank.

■CHAPTER 11

Designing a Derivatives Complement to Cash Markets in Developing Countries

Andrea M. Corcoran
Ronald B. Hobson
Gregory J. Kuserk
Karen K. Wuertz
Derek West

Futures markets are centuries old. The value of forward pricing for reducing price risks to producers and consumers was recognized in Holland in the 1600s and in Japan in the 18th century. Over-the-counter (OTC) derivatives in the United States date from cotton-linked bonds issued during the Civil War. For at least the past 150 years, futures contracts on agricultural commodities have permitted participants in agricultural markets in the United States to reduce their exposure to price changes by establishing positions in the futures markets opposite their cash market positions or obligations. Futures and exchange-traded options contracts on metals, financial instruments (stocks, bonds, and foreign currencies), and energy products were developed following rate deregulation in the respective underlying markets. Experience demonstrated that, if properly managed, such deregulation provided the same opportunities to financial institutions and corporations facing uncertain price exposure in these markets to use futures and options for risk management, as had the former markets for agricultural and physical commodities. Similar deregulatory developments outside the United States also led to demand for effective risk management markets. The Futures Industry Association's (2001) statistics on volume of trading show that most non-U.S. derivatives markets have developed since the mid-1980s, with substantial growth in the 1990s (see table 11-1). In the late 1980s and 1990s, almost every mature market added a financial derivatives market on sovereign debt and the local stock index. This fact has led policymakers interested in developing and enhancing capital markets to explore whether and how they should treat derivatives when

Table 11-1 | **Annual Volume of Futures Contracts Traded, by Exchange, 1999–2000**

Exchange	2000 contract volume	1999 contract volume	Change in 2000	Percentage change in 2000
Eurex	289,952,183	244,686,104	45,266,079	18.50
Liffe, U.K.	105,712,717	97,689,714	8,023,003	8.21
BM&F, Brazil	80,073,865	52,797,466	27,276,399	51.66
Paris Bourse SA	62,968,563	35,129,074	27,839,489	79.25
London Metal Exchange	61,413,076	57,563,009	3,850,067	6.69
Tokyo Commodity Exchange	50,851,882	48,442,161	2,409,721	4.97
Euronext Brussels Derivative Market (formerly BELFOX)	30,299,351	5,711,482	24,587,869	430.50
Sydney Futures Exchange	28,923,442	27,183,166	1,740,276	6.40
SIMEX, Singapore	26,804,964	24,480,004	2,324,960	9.50
International Petroleum Exchange	24,938,224	22,442,222	2,496,002	11.12
Central Japan Commodity Exchange (formerly Chubu Commodity Exchange)	21,328,867	1,327,024	20,001,843	1507.27
Tokyo Grain Exchange	20,778,338	18,018,443	2,759,895	15.32
Korea Stock Exchange	19,666,518	17,200,349	2,466,169	14.34
OM Stockholm Exchange	18,993,709	21,063,746	(2,070,037)	(9.83)
Tokyo International Financial Futures Exchange (TIFFE)	17,089,946	14,658,415	2,431,531	16.59
Tokyo Stock Exchange	14,254,348	13,023,411	1,230,937	9.45
South African Futures Exchange (SAFEX)	9,182,243	9,064,389	117,854	1.30
Osaka Securities Exchange	8,707,853	10,540,224	(1,832,371)	(17.38)
Montreal Exchange	7,766,687	7,931,831	(165,144)	(2.08)
Kanmon Commodity Exchange	6,431,820	4,693,896	1,737,924	37.03
Osaka Mercantile Exchange	5,142,913	5,352,572	(209,659)	(3.92)
Italian Derivatives Market of the Italian Stock Exchange	4,620,568	5,099,456	(478,888)	(9.39)
Hong Kong Exchanges & Clearing-Derivatives Unit (HKFE & HKSE)	4,521,926	5,563,358	(1,041,432)	(18.72)
Meff Renta Variable, Spain	4,183,028	5,101,588	(918,560)	(18.01)
Shanghai Futures Exchange	4,129,521	3,134,268	995,253	31.75
Korea Futures Exchange	2,959,974	945,403	2,014,571	213.09
Amsterdam Exchanges	2,704,999	2,941,296	(236,297)	(8.03)
Kansai Commodity Exchange	2,447,652	2,442,440	5,212	0.21

Table 11-1 | **Annual Volume of Futures Contracts Traded, by Exchange, 1999–2000** (continued)

Exchange	2000 contract volume	1999 contract volume	Change in 2000	Percentage change in 2000
Winnipeg Commodity Exchange	2,391,565	2,086,909	304,656	14.60
Budapest Commodity Exchange	2,174,480	1,588,047	586,433	36.93
Taiwan Futures Exchange	1,926,789	1,077,672	849,117	78.79
Budapest Stock Exchange	1,402,378	1,814,078	(411,700)	(22.69)
Yokohama Commodity Exchange	1,384,995	895,705	489,290	54.63
Meff Renta FIJA, Spain	1,094,922	3,639,648	(2,544,726)	(69.92)
FUTOP Clearing Centre, Denmark	1,029,369	1,135,288	(105,919)	(9.33)
Oslo Stock Exchange	1,024,266	875,530	148,736	16.99
Helsinki Exchanges (formerly Finnish Options Market Exchange)	874,862	1,101,616	(226,754)	(20.58)
New Zealand Exchange	794,502	825,546	(31,044)	(3.76)
Wiener Borse	658,877	802,582	(143,705)	(17.91)
Kuala Lumpur Options & Financial Futures Exchange	366,942	436,678	(69,736)	(15.97)
Commodity and Monetary Exchange of Malaysia	353,434	416,775	(63,341)	(15.20)
Mercado a Término de Buenos Aires	179,547	171,708	7,839	4.57
Agricultural Futures Markets Amsterdam	96,242	111,886	(15,644)	(13.98)
Mercado Italiano dei Futures	1,966	209,610	(207,644)	(99.06)
Toronto Futures Exchange	0	382,149	(382,149)	(100.00)
Total	952,604,313	781,797,938	170,806,375	21.85

Source: Futures Industry Association (2001).

engaging in specific capital market development projects or otherwise assisting countries in addressing their risk management needs.

This chapter examines the requirements for identifying products and conditions that will support the development of a traditionally structured financial derivatives market in a developing country.[1] Although the discussion is of general applicability, where possible, the examples are drawn with Latin American jurisdictions in

---

[1] All derivatives, regardless of whether the underlying reference price is based on a commodity or a financial instrument, are financial instruments, and many design issues are generic. Most examples in this discussion, however, are drawn from derivatives based on financial assets.

mind. Based on World Bank figures, Latin American countries are among the five lead-ing producers of the following commodities: sugar, the soybean complex, maize, cop-per, aluminum, iron, nickel, and oil. Seventeen Latin American and Caribbean countries depend on commodities for more than 50 percent (ranging from 56 to 91 percent in 1997) of their export earnings. Many Latin American jurisdictions are moving to de-velop benchmark sovereign debt markets. In each case, derivatives can be explored as a potential means to enhance management of price volatility and improve the func-tioning of the cash market (World Bank 1999). In addition to a likely product, how-ever, an accommodating macroeconomic environment, sound legal system, and well-functioning cash market are ordinarily preconditions for successful derivatives market development, and such markets more often evolve than are created (see the appen-dix for the experience of Brazil).

Identifying Development Needs, a Product, and an Approach

In general, derivatives are distinguished from other financial instruments because their primary use is for shifting market risk as opposed to raising capital. The basic types of financial instruments that typically are included in the term "derivatives" are futures, options, swaps, and combinations of the foregoing. The common feature shared by all types is that they are contractual arrangements for providing opposite, but otherwise identical, market exposures to both contract parties. Derivatives can be based on cur-rencies, interest rates, securities, physical commodities, or indexes representing values of groups of such instruments and assets. In recent years, derivatives with a value de-pendent on variables such as weather and crop yields have been developed.[2]

In addition to the direct benefits of hedging to commercial producers, con-sumers, lenders, and other middlemen, others involved in the production and dis-tribution of commodities and financial instruments benefit from the availability of continuous, well-publicized prices discovered in exchange-based derivatives markets. Indeed, wholesale (and sometimes retail) transaction prices in industries or sectors that produce or distribute goods or assets traded on active futures markets are often based on the prices discovered in those overlying derivatives markets.[3]

---

[2] Insurance policies covering weather phenomena and crop yields have existed for some time. The primary distinc-tion between derivatives and insurance is that insurance payoffs generally depend on the loss incurred on the part of the insured. Derivatives payoffs are tied exclusively to changes in the underlying variable.

[3] For example, although much of the world's copper production is in Latin America, the world price is denominated in dollars and based on London Metal Exchange/Commodity Exchange prices.

As the discussion proceeds, it will become clear that developed (and developing) capital markets can facilitate the establishment of derivatives markets of all types. In fact, the relationship between derivatives markets and capital markets is symbiotic. By providing a means of managing the risks associated with capital (and commodity) market transactions, derivatives markets complement and improve overall market structure in that they can do the following:

- Support market-making activities
- Render the underlying financial and other markets more accessible and hence potentially more efficient
- Reduce volatility in the pricing of commodities or financial instruments
- Promote better management of production and procurement by permitting risk shifting and facilitating price discovery
- Provide incentives for centralizing delivery facilities and grading and standardizing products
- Reduce the cost of financing commercial transactions.

For example, in Mexico, as an alternative to long-standing policies that guaranteed minimum prices, the government began to offer farmers and their associations the opportunity to purchase price insurance. Although the program was launched as a way of reducing farmers' income risk, improved credit access was an unanticipated benefit because banks apparently were more willing to lend to program participants (World Bank and IMF 2001). Mexico has tried several times to establish a futures market in financial instruments and is optimistic that its current initiatives in that regard will be successful.

Market users and the economy as a whole can benefit from properly overseen noncommercial speculative activity that is essential to the functioning of exchange-traded derivatives markets. Beyond providing market users with valued liquidity, which in turn complements market price discovery, such speculative activity can contribute to greater price stability in the markets underlying the derivatives by permitting hedgers to lock in favorable prices and by rendering the price more transparent and efficient. A market purely of commercials, which are entirely involved in trading for their own business-related interests, may not obtain the same results because commercials may have narrow interests that may not produce sufficient trading for an efficient price. Furthermore, as demonstrated by some of the alleged activity in the California cash energy markets, protection against manipulative activities is essential for proper price formation. That being said, because the price discovery and risk-shifting functions served by futures markets can be effective tools for dealing with the volatility common to emerging market economies, the development of futures markets in such economies can assist in better management of expected revenues in countries dependent on export commodities and otherwise enhance commercial markets. For example, the ability to neutralize and price interest rate risk in an organized derivatives market may make a jurisdiction's own sovereign debt more attractive.

In this regard, the primary example of a successful derivatives market in Latin America is in Brazil, where the derivatives market evolved from a cash commercial market. The Bolsa de Mercadorias & Futuros (BM&F) in Brazil originated from the bottom up through the evolving activities of cash market participants. The market has profited from price volatility, survived macroeconomic instability, and learned from its mistakes (see the appendix). In Brazil, the regulatory framework for derivatives products is changing, with new legislation adopted this year providing additional powers to the securities regulator to regulate the market in financial as well as equity-based derivatives and to enhance the scheme of central bank supervision of institutions engaging in derivatives transactions. Brazil is also unique in that a number of the transactions that occur at the BM&F are not typical of most futures markets; they are more tailored counterparty transactions that are guaranteed by the exchange.

Although this chapter focuses on the development of exchange-traded derivatives, in the past three decades, OTC options and swaps (and in some markets, more customized exchange offerings) have increasingly been part of the mix of derivatives instruments available to market participants. Many of the benefits associated with these bilateral contracts, which can be tailored precisely to specific risks, are similar to those associated with futures contracts traded on an exchange. That is, they allow users to manage price risk. However, OTC transactions differ from futures in that they permit users to fine-tune their risk management activities and consequent hedges to a greater degree than is easily accomplished with the more standardized contracts generally thought necessary to support most traditional exchange trading. Substantial standardization is viewed as essential to the functioning of the exchange markets because a contract entered into between A and B is intended to be offset with a transaction between A and C. Identity of contract terms makes the contracts fungible. In contrast, an interest rate swap is a financial transaction between two specific counterparties who agree to exchange, at specified intervals and for a set term, streams of payments based on specified interest rates calculated on an agreed notional principal amount. Typically, one party will agree to pay the other party a stream of payments based on a fixed interest rate, while the latter party agrees to pay the former party a stream of payments based on a variable interest rate, although there are other models. Of course, the flexibility of OTC derivatives is not obtained without cost. Because such transactions traditionally are not standardized and hence not fungible, OTC derivatives positions reduce basis risk, but usually are difficult to adjust or offset once established, as one must return to the original counterparty to do so and market conditions may not favor renegotiation.[4]

The challenge of developing exchange-traded derivatives markets, which can permit effective risk transfer and, by centralizing demand, foster better price discovery, is to combine liquidity and hedging utility—that is, to balance the standardization necessary for trading with a design that limits basis risk or the differential between the price of the exchange-standardized product and the actual cash commodity (Martel 2001). Not all jurisdictions can support exchange markets, and for those which cannot, variants of more tailored OTC solutions for risk management may be desirable if properly designed, understood, and monitored.[5]

Designing Derivatives Contracts and Markets

Policymakers who seek to design or encourage the design and development of successful derivatives markets must combine an analysis of demand for a product with development of an appropriate infrastructure, oversight framework, and supportive economic environment. The design might be based on a top-down, bottom-up, or hybrid development approach. Figure 11-1 illustrates the traditional view of the evolution of derivatives markets. The best approach depends on the status of the preconditions in the jurisdiction seeking to develop a market. This section discusses some of the product development issues policymakers should consider.

The Underlying Cash Market

In theory, any financial asset can serve as the basis for an exchange-traded derivatives contract. In practice, however, relatively few financial assets have served successfully as

---

[4] Basis refers to the difference between the spot or cash price of a commodity and the price of the nearest futures contract for the same or a related commodity. Today, in some jurisdictions, there are arrangements for clearing OTC transactions, and exchange products have used flexible, tailored structures or limited auctions, to some extent blurring the early distinctions between exchange and OTC products. Master agreements, which facilitate netting, are intended to accomplish the netting of payments and obligations that is required by law and exchange rules through a central counterparty. These arrangements still depend on agreement as to the closeout price.

[5] For an excellent discussion of the evolution of markets and how private cash markets and forward markets can be precursors for successful exchange futures markets or cleared OTC markets, see Kroszner (1999). Successful markets are more likely to evolve over time when fostered by the right conditions than to be created out of whole cloth (Martel 2001).

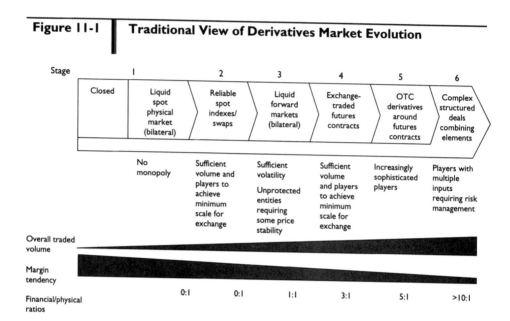

Figure 11-1 | Traditional View of Derivatives Market Evolution

the basis for such contracts, with even fewer leading to overwhelming success.[6] While many factors related to the assets and markets for them play a role in the ultimate success of a derivatives contract, derivative designers usually focus on the attributes of the assets and the liquidity of the underlying cash market to gauge the potential success of derivatives contracts.

Ability to Standardize

Policymakers considering a derivatives market need to understand at the outset that exchange contract design involves an exercise in trade-offs (table 11-2). This is because ideally a contract should minimize basis risk, which increases the transaction costs of hedging; but at the same time a contract should maximize liquidity. To maximize liquidity and minimize credit risk, some standardization is essential. Numerous factors play a role in the balancing act necessary to provide precision without sacrificing liquidity and efficient credit management. Some of these may be beyond the

---

[6] Even in the United States, as many as 80 percent of contracts proposed never result in a functioning market. It is often the second contract developed that is successful; in the case of the Chicago Board of Trade's development of financial futures, the initial government agency contract did not succeed, but the later bond contract did. The Chicago Mercantile Exchange has had a similar experience with contract development.

Table 11-2	Trade-off between Futures and Forwards or Exchange and OTC Designs Generally	
Characteristic	**Forwards**	**Futures**
Counterpart credit risk	High	Low
Contract terms	Flexible	Inflexible
Delivery expected	Yes	No
Timing flexibility	No	Yes
Regulation	Low	High
Liquidity requirements	Low	High
Capital requirements	High	Low

control of the developer. In terms of selecting the potential financial assets on which to develop highly standardized and liquid contracts, those assets that are homogeneous and freely available in large quantities serve as the best candidates. This has been clearly observed in the history of agricultural markets, where the most successful futures and options markets have been for widely available, highly standardized commodities such as corn, soybeans, coffee, and sugar.[7]

Homogeneity and Contract Design

As with agricultural markets, homogeneity in financial assets often plays an important role in the success of a derivatives contract. Capital market assets are essentially defined by the credit risk of the issuer, or assets backing the issue, and the term structure of the individual issues. The similarity of credit risks and term structures of individual issues within a class define the homogeneity of a particular class of instruments. For example, in comparing national government-issued debt versus corporate debt within a particular country, the government debt tends to be more homogeneous than the corporate debt in terms of credit risk because the issuer is constant across the debt. In addition, governments often issue debt at regular intervals and of similar maturities, which leads to homogeneity in term structure.

While national government debt typically represents the largest pool of homogeneous capital market assets in an economy, and is the most likely candidate as a reference price for financial derivatives, corporate debt, although less homogeneous,

---

[7] For example, the attempt to establish cattle futures markets in some Latin American jurisdictions has experienced difficulty because they do not use feedlots for developing a sufficiently standardized product to permit reliable delivery and pricing.

can also serve as a viable base for derivatives contracts. Corporate debt tends to vary widely in terms of the credit risks of the issuers, the term structure of the instruments, and the regularity with which debt is issued. As such, corporate debt is often a less attractive candidate in its raw form for establishing liquid markets in standardized derivatives contracts. In addition, thin supplies of corporate debt often characterize Latin American markets, as companies tend to raise funds through bank borrowing rather than issuing debt securities.

There are two approaches for dealing with the limited supply and heterogeneous nature of corporate debt (or other similar products). The first approach, which involves a cash market solution, is to pool or convert heterogeneous debt into homogeneous debt. Through securitization, assets having similar attributes can be pooled into vehicles on which new securities are issued. In this way, small supplies of somewhat homogeneous assets can be pooled together to create a larger supply of assets. Similarly, quite different assets can be pooled together to create similar instruments. In this case, pooling and securitization transcend diversification in the pool of assets to create homogeneous securities out of heterogeneous ones. Government or private guarantees attached to securitized instruments can further enhance the homogeneity of the instruments.[8]

The second approach to dealing with a heterogeneous class of financial assets is to tailor an OTC product precisely to the expected risk management use. But this chapter focuses on the exchange solution. A hybrid solution would be to establish an auction for more tailored solutions. This approach typically involves the creation of customized OTC derivatives contracts, where the derivatives contract can be tailored to reflect the idiosyncrasies of the underlying instrument. The advantage of this approach is that basis risk can be reduced to very low levels. The downside, however, is that liquidity risk rises as customers in this market are reliant on the derivatives contract issuer to make a market in the instrument. A possible third option would be to organize an automated bidding process seeking bids from several offerors to price a specific OTC risk management solution.

Characteristics of the Underlying Market

Three characteristics typically are of importance in assessing the suitability of the underlying markets: price volatility, market size, and participatory structure. Above all

---

[8] For example, mortgage-backed securities issued by U.S. government-sponsored entities have to date been less successful than government bond contracts.

other characteristics, price volatility is the most important prerequisite for a commodity or asset market for which a complementary derivatives market is being developed. Volatility creates a demand for risk management that is translatable into demand for effective derivatives contracts and, thereby, supports liquidity in a market for such contracts. This in turn renders the market an effective venue for risk transfer. Price volatility by its nature creates a commercial risk for those investing in and issuing capital market instruments. Thus, to the extent that price volatility is high, there will be a greater need to hedge price risk and therefore to use risk transfer instruments. At the same time, price volatility generates speculative activity that in turn creates risk transfers for commercial users that seek to use derivatives contracts to render their own price risk less volatile, thereby permitting better management of their businesses. In essence, price volatility is the engine that drives derivatives markets.[9] Where volatility is low, other means of managing risk may be available or the attendant transaction costs will not warrant risk management activity.

Price support programs that have been implemented for many physical commodities around the world (for example, agricultural products) can affect the design and viability of derivatives contracts based on those commodities. To the extent the price support program obviates producers' price risk, a derivatives contract to manage that price risk is not necessary and likely would be unviable if proposed by a market operator. However, even in the case of a commodity covered by a price support system, a derivatives contract designed to meet the needs of processors and users of that commodity may nonetheless be viable if the price risks of these traders are not addressed by the price support system. In complex markets, such as the petroleum market, where a group of producers forms an imperfect cartel that attempts to manipulate the supply of the commodity, the price volatility that results both from the cartel's manipulation of the supply and the limitations on its ability to control the supply is sufficient to support an active derivatives market. Furthermore, the market transparency that is achieved through the operation of the derivatives market is used by both cartel and noncartel members in making decisions concerning their operations.

The overall size of the cash market is also an important consideration in assessing the potential viability of a derivatives contract. When assessing the size of a market, two characteristics should be considered: the outstanding supply of the financial asset and the volume or turnover in the market. Ideally, derivatives contracts should be based on an asset that is issued in large quantities and actively traded in a

---

[9] For example, in the United States, no financial or foreign exchange products were traded until the domestic deregulation of interest and exchange rates (Rudder Associates 2000).

liquid cash market. Such conditions are conducive to transparent markets and can ensure a source of asset supply essential to avoiding squeezes where the derivatives contract relies on delivery at contract expiration. As volume or turnover drops, even a large outstanding supply of the asset may not be adequate to overcome potential congestion or manipulation in the derivatives contract. This factor is especially important in Latin America, where many cash markets are not fully developed, are broadly dispersed, or lack depth. Too small a supply of an asset may render it susceptible to manipulation even where the volume of trading is typically high.

Related to market size is the organization of the underlying market, such as that for financial assets.[10] Often market organization affects trading volume and the supply of financial assets. In terms of market organization, the number of issuers, concentration of issuers, and patterns of issuance and investment are the most important attributes to consider. For example, there may be one or many issuers of debt instrument derivatives, depending on how the class of underlying cash instruments is delimited. For government debt, there usually is a sole issuer of the underlying asset. In such a case, important considerations include whether the issuer is a reliable source of supply for the asset and, if it is, whether the issuer can be expected to manipulate the price of the asset.[11] Where there are many issuers, control of supply is of less concern, although heterogeneity of the asset may adversely affect its potential risk management uses.

In addition to the overall number of issuers, the concentration among issuers may also be of concern. As with having a small number of issuers, a high concentration among issuers would raise concerns over potential disruptions in the supply and pricing of the underlying assets. Thus, derivatives contracts on assets for which there is low market concentration will be less susceptible to manipulative threats and may lead to more viable derivatives contracts than on assets with high levels of issuer concentration.

Finally, it is important to take into consideration the patterns of issuance and investment. Successful derivatives contracts usually rely on a regular, reliable source of assets. Such a source serves several purposes. First, a steady supply leads to a more efficient cash market so that investors can readily ascertain the value of their investments. This, in turn, aids in the pricing of derivatives contracts. Second, a steady sup-

---

[10] While cash settlement can be a technique for avoiding congestion, market size may also be an issue in finding a means to price the settlement of cash-settled futures.

[11] IOSCO (2002a) includes an instructive appendix on the rate of economic growth; size and structure of the bond market; liquidity ratios; benchmark/government securities; legal, regulatory, and tax framework; corporate bonds; issuers and investors; macroeconomic policies; and market microstructure based on responses from several countries, including Argentina, Brazil, El Salvador, Peru, and Trinidad and Tobago.

ply of assets ensures that ample supplies of the assets are available when delivery obligations on derivatives contracts must be met. The same adverse effects can originate on the demand as on the supply side of the equation. That is, periodic episodes of high demand could tie up the supply of the assets, and investors could try to lock up available deliverable supplies, thereby effectively reducing the overall supply of the settlement instrument.[12] Thus, in choosing assets on which to base derivatives contracts, the best candidates are those assets with predictable patterns of issuance and demand, and where the source of supply is not subject to manipulation. If market developers are able to demonstrate a successful pricing track record, this should increase interest in a market and result in enhanced liquidity.

Potential Alternative Hedging or Risk Management Tools

The decision to base a derivatives contract on a given commodity or asset must be based on the demand for and supply of such contracts. Examining the cash market for the attributes (volatility, size, homogeneity, and structure) is akin to assessing the potential demand for the contract. The companion question that also must be asked is whether other mechanisms exist that can satisfy that demand.[13] The early history of financial futures and options market development in the United States suggests that attempts to duplicate or even improve on existing active derivatives markets, including nonindigenous markets that reflect the world price for a product, are doomed to failure. The attempted development of a cattle futures market in Argentina provides an excellent example of the case in point: an existing forward pricing system, through providing risk exposure protection and merchandising opportunities, satisfied the hedging needs of the cattle industry and remained viable as a contemporaneous futures experiment failed. Technology may permit development of average pricing for cash markets, which also could undercut the need to develop more formal risk management to smooth pricing for users and producers. With experience, derivatives exchanges have focused on the development of unique contracts based on assets that cannot be hedged otherwise.

---

[12] For example, Fenchurch attempted to corner the supply of 10-year treasury notes through the repo market, thus forcing the shorts to deliver more valuable treasury notes and thereby increasing the costs of delivery pursuant to the conventions of the Board of Trade contract (CFTC 1996). Under those contracts, which represent a basket of securities, several notes would qualify as deliverable. Use of the product, however, is based on the expectation that shorts will deliver the "cheapest to deliver" at the end of the delivery period.

[13] Common impediments to derivatives market development are the inability to develop speculative (intermediary) interest, objections from the cash market, the fear of cash market participants that the product will exacerbate rather than moderate volatility, and alternative venues or means of risk management.

Commercial Terms

Because of the critical role that commercial participation plays in the ultimate viability of a derivatives contract, an overriding consideration in the design of such contracts is the incorporation of terms and conditions that reflect commercial cash market practices. This is generally not a challenge in the case of a bilateral, counterparty contract. Where such contracts are individually negotiated between two parties, only the business practices of the contracting counterparties need be considered. For a contract that is to be standardized and widely traded, however, there likely exists a range of practices that may be specified. The choice of these may be relevant not only to assuring the success of the contract, but also to preventing manipulation and ensuring price convergence at expiration.

It is, in fact, the quest for standardization that gives rise to the trade-off between pricing specificity and deliverable supply in designing exchange-listed derivatives contracts. One way of addressing this problem is to design a contract that permits delivery of a range or "basket" of issues and maturities that at the same time provides for price adjustments (or a formula that calculates such adjustments) that reflect cash market valuation differentials.[14] The key to this approach is the specification of futures price delivery adjustments that are responsive to changes in cash market fundamentals. This has proved to be difficult in the context of agricultural futures markets, but less so for financial futures and options.

An alternative way of addressing the pricing/supply issue is to incorporate a cash settlement feature into the contract in lieu of a physical delivery requirement. This, of course, eliminates any deliverable supply and convergence concerns and allows the contract designer to be more specific regarding the asset to be priced via the derivatives contract. However, cash settlement raises considerations similar to those surrounding delivery, owing to the need for a reliable cash market reference price on which to base the settlement price. In addition to the timeliness and public availability of the pricing information used to calculate the reference price, a viable cash settlement procedure presupposes a liquid cash market with a low potential for price manipulation or distortion or other controls to ensure the integrity of pricing. The pricing methodology should be transparent, with clear criteria for its calculation. These steps should prevent tampering or leaking material information to market participant insiders (Tokyo Communiqué 1997; IOSCO 1998).

---

[14] The Chicago Board of Trade bond contract is based on a basket with the convention that in the event of delivery the "cheapest to deliver" issue will be the deliverable.

Trading Facility Structure

A wide range of derivatives trading facilities exists around the world today, and, based on the historical trading experience of each, no specific combination of attributes appears to be optimal from the standpoint of market activity. There are active markets that use an electronic trading platform exclusively, and there are active markets that still use the open outcry (continuous auction) method. Likewise, not all successful derivatives markets use pure continuous auctions; some use market-maker systems, while others use other price discovery methods, such as periodic calls, price indications, or single price auctions. Like the contractual product, the market structure must take into account the likely level of liquidity, the cash market for the product that provides the reference value, the type of market participants, and the desired level of transparency.

An additional aspect of the operability of exchange-traded models that is difficult to assess in advance and yet critical to long-run success is the attraction of users, including speculative capital. New electronic technology makes it economic to operate markets that have limited volume and smaller contracts, or that represent niche interests, thereby providing more flexibility to market and contract designers than existed when "bricks and mortar" markets were the rule. However, the participation of commercial interests alone may not be sufficient to support active trading using a traditional exchange format, as trading interest is essential to the ability to offset contracts. Of course, over time, sufficient market liquidity may evolve. Furthermore, in emerging or created markets, it may be necessary to identify and develop users. For example, in the United States, small farmers usually sell their crops forward and use futures markets through specialist intermediaries that may be cooperative organizations, farm management organizations, grain elevators, or storage facilities or through facilities arranged through lenders. In some jurisdictions, the government (or the private sector) organizes collective purchasing entities that export commodities, and these entities undertake risk management, passing on some of the price benefits to the underlying producer. These arrangements reflect that the use of derivatives markets requires some expertise that, where unavailable, must be developed.

In addition, to permit effective offsetting of risk, particularly if commercials tend to operate from one side of the market, other sources of liquidity may be required.[15] Such liquidity requires the more or less continuous presence and potential

---

[15] The recent failure of a number of so-called business-to-business market models is an example of this problem. Exchanges usually interview potential users of the market when designing contracts. With the new electronic technology, some cash markets (for example, chemicals) participants, having developed a cash market, have requested the assistance of an existing futures exchange to provide a risk management market to ensure the necessary liquidity and back-office support necessary for such a market to succeed.

participation of speculators who are capable of assuming significant positions. A portion of this interest may come from local financial firms (or so-called intermediaries) willing to make a market on the exchange—which may be easier to organize than nonfinancial commercials—and the remainder must come from outside the market. Attraction of such users requires that the culture of the jurisdiction seeking to develop a market be supportive of speculative activity.

A more recent way to provide liquidity is to permit commercials, which have an active cash market, to seek an organized electronic derivatives market to host their product. The host brings with it a liquidity facility and committed users and permits the commercial interest to develop trading liquidity from local traders or investors or market makers already doing business on the facility. Although fungibility is considered a necessary component of a contract that would attract such interest, it is often not sufficient.[16] There also must be an arbitrage or profit potential and traders with an appetite to take as well as transfer risk.[17] Even in the experience of the United States, a country that is especially rich in speculative capital, many more contracts fail than succeed on account of the absence of profit potential.

Characteristically, organized derivatives markets (as opposed to OTC and alternative markets) are highly transparent. This is because making pricing transparent is part of their purpose and permits the liquidity essential to anonymous risk shifting. When price and market information is revealed in a timely manner, market participants are able to assess the quality of prices they obtain on transactions. Where the quality of price fills (the price at which the contract is executed) is low, a participant may elect to seek higher-quality venues. Where these do not exist, entrepreneurs will be encouraged to improve the market or establish better ones. Thus, there should be a tendency for participants to gather in markets offering the fairest prices, thereby concentrating liquidity and enhancing the efficiency of the market.[18] In the absence of transparency, or where price negotiations are between counterparties of similar expertise, knowledge, and market power, market participants may remain in illiquid, inefficient markets for extended periods of time because of the search costs involved in seeking out better markets and prices. Such markets may prove deficient for risk management purposes. Transparency ensures that derivatives markets can function

---

[16] The cleared OTC contracts at BM&F may be an exception.

[17] New types of arrangements are now being contemplated that would couple the tailoring possible on the front end that is characteristic of OTC markets, with the credit support of a central counterparty or other guarantee arrangements previously characteristic of exchange markets. Market developers should consider what combination of front end (trading) and back end (credit) would most likely support their risk management needs.

[18] The dissemination of ticker or prices traditionally has been a significant source of revenue for futures markets.

properly, are readily achievable electronically, and should be strongly supported by the relevant market authorities and regulators.

Regulatory Implications of Market Structure and Contract Design

The importance of contract design is underscored by the fact that international regulators of derivatives markets have incorporated many of the principles relating to standardization of terms and the relationship to the underlying market discussed herein into their frameworks. For example, the U.S. Commodity Futures Trading Commission (CFTC) relies on its Guideline No. 1, a checklist of contract design principles, in evaluating new futures and options contracts and in reviewing changes to existing contracts.

This type of contract review or oversight is not limited to the United States, but is fairly common to regulated derivatives markets generally—as the terms and conditions of contracts are viewed as rules that must be either approved or subject to a nonobjection process—for antitrust protection and price integrity purposes.[19] Some jurisdictions combine these two means of oversight by permitting a certification process subject to regulatory power to amend or otherwise affect the contract if the certification that the contract meets relevant criteria and does not violate existing law is incorrect.

More generically, in 1997, futures and options regulators from around the world met in Tokyo and reached an international consensus on regulatory concerns related to physical derivatives markets of finite supply. The meeting was prompted by Sumitomo's manipulation of the copper market.[20] At the end of the meeting convened by authorities from Japan, the United Kingdom, and the United States, the participants issued the Tokyo Communiqué, which, among other things, endorsed two guidance papers. One paper was on best practices for the design and/or review of commodity derivatives contracts, and the other was on market surveillance and information sharing relative to derivatives markets. This guidance represents the first occasion on which regulators responsible for overseeing commodity derivatives markets favorably considered international standards for the supervision of such markets and underscored the essential elements of well-designed contracts, the relationship be-

---

[19] CFTC (1999a) addresses Australia, Canada (Ontario and Quebec), France, Germany, Italy, Singapore, Spain, Switzerland, and the United Kingdom.
[20] Australia, Brazil, Canada (Grain Commission), France, Germany, Hong Kong, Hungary, Italy, Japan (Ministry of Agriculture, Forestry, and Fisheries and Ministry of International Trade and Industry), Korea, Malaysia, the Netherlands, Singapore, South Africa, the United Kingdom, and the United States.

tween contract design and surveillance needs, and, in particular, the need for reliable and deliverable supply. In September 1998, the Technical Committee of the International Organization of Securities Commissions (IOSCO)[21] adopted versions of these guidance papers related to financial derivatives contracts in addition to physical commodity futures, pointing out that even cash-settled contracts must be based on reliable pricing sources.[22]

Regulatory Infrastructure: Preconditions for Successful, Well-Functioning Markets

When policymakers assess how to advise developing markets about designing successful derivatives markets, it may seem difficult to decide which comes first, the necessary regulatory infrastructure or a product. In fact, if the market, user, and local economic conditions will not support an indigenous exchange from a business perspective (as opposed to an OTC market or use of offshore markets or other alternatives), the existence of the infrastructure needed for successful capital markets will not change that result.

For example, Brazil has one of the largest, most successful exchanges in the world. Nonetheless, the coffee contract traded on the BM&F, which is approximately one-third the size of the U.S. contract equivalent, traded adjusted for size 167,401 (CSCE equivalents) to the coffee, sugar, and cocoa exchange's annual volume of 2,199,371 for the same year (2001). Chile has tried several times to offer an equity index product and has one of the most fiscally responsible Latin American systems, but the market has not yet succeeded. In this connection, it is worthwhile for countries desiring to add derivatives to their capital market structure to compare their development experiences. See, for example, Corcoran (2000) and table 11-3 on derivatives markets in Mexico and South America.

In the past, in the United States and many other jurisdictions, most derivatives markets evolved from cash markets. The regulatory requirements applicable to such markets also evolved, taking account of the rules market members developed for themselves. Nonetheless, although private regulation of markets through contract is possible in jurisdictions that honor contract obligations, like other markets for financial

---

[21] IOSCO is the international standard setter for financial markets and comprises 110 jurisdictions in various stages of development.

[22] The Tokyo Communiqué (1997) cites the following elements of contract design: accountability, economic utility, correlation with cash market, settlement and delivery reliability, responsiveness, and transparency. See also IOSCO (1998).

Table 11-3 | Derivatives Markets in Latin America, 2001

Country	Exchange	Average daily volume	Annual volume	Contract types	Specialized futures law
Argentina	Mercado a Término de Buenos Aires, S.A.	970 contracts	232,105 contracts	Futures and options on wheat, sunflowers, corn, and soybeans	Yes
Argentina	Rosaria Futures Exchange	425 contracts	102,176 contracts	Futures and options on wheat, sunflower, corn, Rosafe Soybean index, and Rosafe Meat index	Yes
Argentina	Mercado de Valores de Buenos Aires S.A.	838 contracts (August–December 1999)	83,813 contracts (August–December 1999)	Futures and options MERVAL stock index and M.AR stock index	Yes
Brazil	Bolsa de Mercadorias & Futuros	December 1999 value: $8,286,329,000	41,841,726 contracts	Registers swaps and flexible options (performed in OTC markets); futures and options on debt, equity indexes, foreign exchange, gold, and agricultural commodities	No. Derivatives are regulated pursuant to the securities law regime
Brazil	The São Paulo Stock Exchange	Not applicable	Not applicable	Options on individual equities	No. Derivatives are regulated pursuant to the securities law regime
Chile	Santiago Stock Exchange	0	0	Equity index, U.S. dollar and interest rate futures; options on individual equities	Yes. Specific requirements are included within the securities laws

(Table continues on next page.)

Table 11-3 ▌ Derivatives Markets in Latin America, 2001 *(continued)*

Country	Exchange	Average daily volume	Annual volume	Contract types	Specialized futures law
Mexico	MexDer	2,452 contracts	619,352 contracts	Futures on 91-day Cetes, U.S. dollar, equity index, 28-day inter-bank interest rate, and individual equities	There are no special-ized laws, but the Ministry of Finance, the Mexican Central Bank, and the National Banking and Securities Commission have issued specialized regulations
Peru	Lima Stock Exchange	Not applicable	Not applicable	Equity, bonds, and short-term instruments	No, but derivatives trading is permitted under the securities laws
Peru	Lima Commodity Exchange	Not applicable	Not applicable	Agricultural, livestock, fishing, mining, and industrial commodities	No, but derivatives trading is permitted under the securities laws
Venezuela	Cámara de Compensación de Opciones y Futuros	Not applicable	Not applicable	Equities, dollar, and interest rate futures	Yes

Source: CFTC (2001).

instruments, futures markets benefit from an appropriate regulatory and legal infra-structure and from regulatory support. Moreover, in some circumstances, because the markets involve pricing contracts among members who otherwise would be com-petitors, a government predicate is essential to avoid conflict with fair trading or an-titrust laws.

IOSCO (1998, 2002b) points out that the basic objectives of securities reg-ulation—customer protection; fair, efficient, and transparent markets; and reduction of systemic risk—apply equally to derivatives. Such objectives also generally are the ob-jectives of market participants, creating an identity of interests between regulating authorities and users of the markets. Typically, even the markets that are self-regulated realize that to prosper they must provide fundamental assurances that the rules of the game are fair and will be equitably applied and that obligations undertaken or fi-duciary responsibilities assumed will be enforced. Where local law enforces exchange and clearing rules, more specific law may not be necessary for a market to develop. However, if the desire is to attract the largest potential user base, international ac-ceptance of the market, or international credit enhancements, then the regulatory framework becomes critical to pursuit of that strategy. In Brazil, for example, self-regulation was deemed insufficient to address the manipulation of the futures market by Naji Robert Nahas; similar reasons were cited for establishment of the U.K. Finan-cial Services Authority (FSA), that is, that self-regulation without regulatory backbone was insufficient.

An additional argument for appropriate infrastructure is that futures market regulation begins by assuming that pricing in exchange derivatives markets has com-mercial uses and, therefore, is of relevance to the real economy. A principal purpose of the regulation of these markets is to protect price integrity and prevent cash mar-ket distortions. It is critical that derivatives markets are protected from manipulation of prices and market abuses. Such abuses prevent the appropriate functioning of the market and its risk management uses (hedging, facilitating financing, improving the management of production, and distribution). Such abuses also may compromise the cash market that developing market authorities are hoping to improve. If the deriva-tives prices are related to indigenous commodities or assets, the regulatory authority can be called on to provide confidence that the derivatives price achieved in the mar-ket is not distorting cash prices.

Reliable, continuous functioning is critical to such markets; it permits reliable shifting of risks rather than exacerbation of risk. If the risk of transacting in the mar-ket and shifting risk is greater than holding the risk, obviously the market will not be used. Derivatives markets only shift risk, that is, transfer it from one group to another.

They do not eliminate risk; the resulting transferred risks must also be managed. Developers who promise elimination of risks do a disservice to potential users. Finally, risks of distortion arising from development of derivatives markets will be greater where cash markets are thin or derivatives are based on decentralized or fledgling cash markets. In such environments, it may be useful to study whether some combination approach to risk management is preferable to establishment of an indigenous derivatives market.[23]

The optimal regulatory framework should be designed to ensure reliable hedging for economic exposures and price discovery. It must therefore ensure that the contracts that are traded in the market are valid and enforceable and that the trading rules (which may be incorporated in an electronic algorithm) are equitably enforced and fair. Furthermore, because derivatives markets depend on credit enhancement arrangements to balance the leverage essential for their functioning, the regulatory framework must fulfill two tasks. First, it must manage the risk of the leverage that is an essential aspect of the provision of liquidity. Second, it must support the type of credit enhancement mechanisms embedded in the markets, including their operability notwithstanding the default of any participant.

Achieving these purposes generally requires legislative support. Therefore, the development of derivatives markets assumes applicability of the rule of law; a framework for qualifying markets, market intermediaries, and products; and regulatory oversight to constrain manipulation, tie speculation to financial capacity, and otherwise ensure the proper functioning of the market for risk-shifting purposes. As new markets have emerged, privatized, and matured, a regulatory system or framework usually has developed contemporaneously, often drawing on private contractual arrangements already affecting market operations.[24] For example, the growth of futures trading in the United States exploded after the creation of the CFTC. Regulation, to be helpful, also must provide confidence that government interests will not unduly tamper with the market, a particular concern in some emerging markets.[25]

This section examines some of the regulatory and legal preconditions for the development of a successful derivatives market, in particular, legal certainty, transparency, fair governance, risk management, and appropriate oversight.

---

[23] For example, in China, when speculation was uncoupled from cash markets and financial capacity, such markets were considered potentially harmful to the cash markets on which they were based.

[24] Today more than 40 non-U.S. futures markets interactively report volume to the U.S. Futures Industry Association. All of these markets are supported by regulatory systems. The new Commodity Futures Modernization Act of 2000 permits new markets to adopt a more rigorous regulatory regime than necessarily required, and some market operators have done so.

[25] In China, it was sometimes perceived that the price controls led to a market in speculation on government actions rather than a hedging/price discovery market.

Legal Certainty

Ordinarily, derivatives markets permit trading of contracts representing a potential property interest in an underlying asset, anonymous transacting, and leverage by substituting a common counterparty for individual counterparties.[26] Legal support for such arrangements ordinarily is necessary. Such support reinforces confidence in the reliable and continuous functioning of the market and credit enhancement features, which are crucial for anonymous transacting and sound clearing arrangements for leveraged risk transfer contracts.[27]

The desirable legal framework includes laws of general application (regarding property, contracts, torts, general commercial law, banking, and insolvency) and laws of special application specifically directed to the operation of the market (laws and regulations regarding the legal relationships between customers, brokers, exchanges, clearing corporations, and settlement banks; the property and contractual rights and interests held through the market; and the insolvency of a market participant).[28] As these markets depend on the rules and contract terms of the product, regulation or legislation should support certainty that these terms, contractual arrangements, and rules are enforceable.

The legal framework should do the following:

- Protect the claims of users to the value of their positions, related delivery rights, and the conclusion of transactions
- Include provisions that address and support the property rights to or interests in margins posted with the market, market positions, and the accrued value of positions taken (until disbursed or offset) by market users, brokers, and the clearinghouse or common counterparty, including provisions that address the credit enhancer's collateral interest in cash or securities posted as margin, the disposition of margin in the event of a participant's default, and the relative priority of the clearinghouse (which represents the market) and other claimants, such as market participants and third parties

---

[26] Portions of this section on legal certainty and the following on transparency have been adapted to address development issues with permission from Corcoran (2002).

[27] Markets whose business is interrupted for financial reasons (such as the Hang Seng Index in 1987 in Hong Kong, and the default in the New Zealand market in 1986) or market abuse (London Fox in 1994) may take several years to recover.

[28] For a general list of types of laws critical to a robust framework for the successful operation of securities markets, see IOSCO (1998, 2002b).

- Prefer the operation and integrity of the system and permit the payment and collection of profits and losses, notwithstanding the failure of a single participant by isolating the failure to the individual party and protecting the system for guaranteeing transactions as a whole
- Make transparent to participants the applicable laws and rules under which it operates.[29]

Transparency

Transparency, that is, price transparency and transparency of contracts and rules, in addition to promoting legal certainty, is an independent requisite.

Price Transparency

The following may influence prices:[30]

- Market conditions
- Who can participate in the market
- The depth of the market
- The taking of large interests by a market participant
- Whether those interests are commercial or speculative
- How and when price and volume information is disseminated.

The more information that is available on the market and the price formation process, the more timely that information is, and the more reliable it is, the more efficient and bona fide the prices formed in that market are likely to be. Although few

---

[29] As used here, "markets" refers both to an exchange and to other arrangements whereby buying and selling interests can be brought together. Differential levels of transparency and regulation or oversight may apply to transactions that are undertaken bilaterally between professional counterparties, through alternative trading systems, or on organized or regulated markets (Forum of European Securities Commissions 2000; CFTC 1999b). Among other things, a market participant needs to know the type of market venue (and level of oversight) in which its transaction will occur. Even in new electronic markets where participants may be referred to as subscribers or users, the terms of the contract traded, the trading algorithm, and the terms for settling transactions constitute the contract between the subscriber and the market in ordinary circumstances and in the event of default. In such markets, however, these terms may be expressed solely as contractual terms rather than as rules.

[30] The influence on prices will depend on the market. Prices may be formed outside the market and be reported to the market; prices may be the product of a continuous or a noncontinuous auction; orders may be fully visible or fully or partially hidden; participants may be identified or anonymous; participants may be limited to particular categories of experience, commercial interest, or credit; bids and offers and sales prices may or may not be available; volume and daily turnover may or may not be available; and information on large holdings of open interest may or may not be available.

regulators require dissemination of prices in real time, in fact, market participation is facilitated by real time access to such prices and in most cases direct users of the market demand such access. Information on the depth of the market and the configuration of bids and offers also promotes confidence in prices achieved and avoids surprises regarding settlement prices and liquidity.

Depending on the structure of the market, less liquid markets can use market makers, single price auctions, or average price mechanisms without necessarily adversely affecting the purity of price discovery and the effectiveness of hedges. In fact, many markets provide special treatments for large orders or permit only partial quantities to be disclosed as part of an electronic bidding process to promote liquidity or moderate the price changes introduced by large transactions.

In any case, price transparency, in addition to permitting price discovery and facilitating hedging, assists in maintaining the liquidity necessary to offset expeditiously contracts or to liquidate positions under normal trading conditions and in volatile markets or in the event of customer or firm defaults.[31] This, in turn, permits preventing the accrual of losses caused by price changes and ensures that risk shifting is possible by permitting hedges to be adjusted in a timely way.

Because centering all price information maximizes the liquidity and operability of the markets, in some jurisdictions, all trading interest in exchange-related financial contracts, even those taken over the counter, must be reported to exchange markets.[32] Off-market trades are reported to prevent so-called free riding, to ensure that market-quoted prices are representative and that interests moving into and off markets do not have a destabilizing effect. These measures are intended to promote best execution, help maintain continuous liquidity, and prevent market abuse.[33] Added transparency of exposures may be especially helpful in smaller markets in promoting efficiency and reducing spreads.

Some transparency issues are unique to the fair operation of derivatives markets, in particular, futures markets. For example, in the case of contracts based on commodity reference prices, basis risk is the risk arising from a difference in price between the standardized traded commodity or contract deliverable and the commodity being held or produced by the party seeking risk management services. In order to design a

---

[31] There is significant anecdotal evidence that in times of uncertainty, trading volume migrates from off-exchange (less transparent) to on-exchange (more transparent) venues. Some examples are the trading that moved to the Intercontinental Exchange (ICE) and the New York Mercantile Exchange in the wake of the collapse of Enron and the trading of large institutions during the 1987 market crash.

[32] See, for example, the information regarding Brazil in CFTC (1999b).

[33] Other jurisdictions (such as the United Kingdom) also obtain transaction information. In some jurisdictions, retail customers must transact in an exchange venue to permit regulators to be sure that appropriate customer protections are applied.

hedge that properly takes account of this basis risk, the ability to make an analysis of the terms of the futures contract regarding the deliverable commodity in relation to the reliable availability of (or a substitute cash settlement price for) the deliverable commodity is necessary (Tokyo Communiqué 1997; IOSCO 1998). As cash and OTC markets continue to evolve, more transparency may be brought to other trading venues, and this in turn may enhance the capacity to design futures markets. In any event, many derivatives markets make available substantial information on the cash market that sets the reference price for the derivative and, where there is physical delivery, on the status of deliverable supplies.[34] Traders are interested in market participation as a whole. This information assists users in deciding how to use the market and in assessing liquidity and is publicly available in certain jurisdictions.[35]

The practices of the market regarding the price at which positions are carried also may assist or adversely affect market users. If original trade prices are preserved and not adjusted or marked to market at least when positions are rolled forward, losses may be hidden, and this may lead to market failure.[36] If customer positions are reported and margined net of each other, then losses may be disguised to the credit provider. Simultaneously, holding open positions on both the long and short side can disguise losses and real open interest. This can adversely affect the market as a pricing mechanism.[37] An advantage of a centralized clearing function and the attendant daily mark-to-market is that it disciplines the accumulation of credit risk and provides information on actual positions and their relative risk.

Transparency of Contract Terms and Market Rules

Contractual clarity is important because a futures market is a financial market in property interests that are themselves contract rights. A contract for future settlement is

---

[34] Access to reliable delivery mechanisms and/or storage mechanisms can be an issue in developing economies. In some countries, delivery for many commodities is not centralized, and elevators or storage facilities may not be subject to oversight (World Bank 1999).

[35] After the Sumitomo crisis, the London Metal Exchange acted to make large exposure information more transparent, and the Osaka Futures Exchange makes the 10 largest positions available to the public. The CFTC Commitment of Traders Reports are the most visited part of its website at http://www.cftc.gov/cftc/cftccotreports.htm. These reports contain aggregated commercial and speculative interest figures by contract.

[36] This issue apparently helped to disguise losses in the copper market in the Sumitomo and Codelco cases (Securities and Investments Board 1996).

[37] For example, the CFTC required a purchase and sale statement for each transaction and disclosure of the practice of taking positions on opposite sides of the market. Although usually less significant than in equity markets, accounting rule differences also can lead to misunderstandings as to whether the criteria for access to the market are met. In addition, poor risk management practices by a market can have inequitable effects. If some participants are allowed to limit liability for personal trading, the risk of that trading may unexpectedly be transferred to other participants.

valued using a cash market or calculated reference price. The settlement can be a cash payment of differences in value and/or physical delivery of the reference product for contracts held to expiration. Like any other contract, in order to know its value, market users need to know the contract terms and conditions. Knowing these enables users to determine whether the contract is likely to be favorable, how to price it, and the consequences in the event of default. At the same time, a futures contract is a financial instrument. Therefore, the characteristics and degree (and quality) of regulation (and/or self-regulation) of the market on which it is offered as well as the costs, conditions, and rules of trading must be accessible if users are to be capable of determining the contract's functionality and properly pricing it.

The terms and conditions of a futures contract ordinarily are included in the rules of the market in the case of membership exchanges and in the user or subscriber agreement in other markets. Direct market participants, whether acting in a proprietary capacity or as an intermediary, ordinarily agree as a condition of market access to be bound not only by all the present terms and conditions of the contract and trading rules but also by any changes in those terms or rules.[38] Customers of intermediaries, who have an indirect relationship to the market, generally also must agree to take positions subject to the rules of the marketplace or the contractual conditions of trading. From a commonsense perspective, the ability to transfer risk by locking in a price requires both price integrity and an understanding of how the contract terms are intended to work; that is, contractual settlement arrangements, the pricing algorithm in the case of electronic markets, and how these relate to the cash market. Therefore, regulators should support measures that help to fulfill users' interest in the accessibility and fair and equitable execution of market rules, including contract terms. Indeed, the enforceability of the contract can be tied to the process chosen by the regulator to permit the listing of the contracts for trading.

Governance, Accountability, and Independence

Fair and Equitable Treatment

Not only legal certainty but also certainty in the fair application of rules is critical to derivatives markets. Inconsistently applied or differentially applied rules could affect both the pricing function and the hedging function of the market. Indeed, contract terms, including forms of margining, cannot readily be changed midterm for any given

---

[38] Contract terms that affect price ordinarily should not be changed (or changeable) prior to the expiration of a contract.

contract because this could have an external effect on pricing—which is why indexes must be calibrated to address the effects of substitutions. Fair governance of the market and equitable application and consistent enforcement of the rules are critical irrespective of the structure of the market and of whether the market is a mutual or for-profit model. However, as the structure of a market can affect its efficiency and reliability, structure must be taken into consideration when finding an appropriate product and in matching the governance to the trading structure. For example, established cash markets with expert commercials or financial intermediaries may lend themselves to self-regulation, whereas newer created markets may not.

In ensuring fair treatment of nonmember participants in organized exchange derivatives markets, the same issues arise as in public companies: adequate disclosure about financial integrity and hence viability of the market, prohibition of self-dealing or conflicts of interest, and fair governance or representation of relevant stakeholders. Some additional issues, such as fair treatment of orders, are important. The applicable rules—that is, the regulatory and legal infrastructure or custom and practice—must be designed to overcome any concern that members or insiders may act to the detriment of nonmembers and other users. In this regard, regulatory authorities usually provide that customer orders must be fairly treated, that professional traders cannot front run or otherwise take advantage of customer orders, and that the market environment must otherwise be fair. In fact, provisions that protect outside stakeholders and customers should protect market insiders as well because confidence in continuation of the market is in their self-interest. In the United States, futures markets are required to enforce their own rules and the terms and conditions of contracts fairly and equitably, subject to government oversight. Other jurisdictions have accorded markets more or less legal or quasi-government responsibility consistent with the experience of market operators and the jurisdiction of such markets. Because success is linked to the perception of fairness, market insiders have the incentives to make the market operate in a fair way, and rules and oversight can and should be structured to enhance these incentives.

Avoidance of Conflicts

Like ensuring fair pricing, a principal function of government oversight is ensuring fair operation of the market, so that self-regulation by market operators ensures consistent and equitable rule (or contract) enforcement. Such oversight, for example, should prevent anticompetitive activity by market insiders and ensure that conflicts of interest are avoided. Typically, regulatory authorities review, or have the capacity to review or alter, exchange rules and procedures expressly to ensure that they are fair and equitable and consistent with statutory or legal requirements relating to open and efficient markets. A culture of fairness is an objective of financial market regulation and a precondition of market confidence (IOSCO 2002b).

In order to address the concern that the governing boards of exchanges may act in their own self-interest in exercising their self-regulatory responsibilities, such boards often are required by law to reflect the various interests of market participants, including end-user interests (IOSCO 2000). Ideally, relevant law would restrict members or exchange supervisors, who have the obligation to maintain orderly markets, from voting on proposed exchange emergency actions or other market interventions where they have a financial interest in the outcome. This protects the functionalities of market surveillance related to maintaining an orderly market, addressing delivery congestion, or handling a financial emergency and maintains confidence in the market by ensuring such oversight measures are not misused.

Creditworthiness and Fitness

To ensure that users are not disadvantaged, the framework should provide for appropriate dispute resolution mechanisms. Because customers or users of the market do not have direct access, they are dependent on intermediaries or others with direct access; therefore, the framework should provide for the fitness and propriety of market operators, intermediaries that act for customers and custodians of customer funds, the protection of funds and positions committed to their accounts, and the creditworthiness of users that have direct access. To prevent so-called excessive speculation, users should be required to have a financial stake in their positions.

Confidence in Regulation

Users need to have confidence in the regulators, their independence from the political process, and their accountability for their performance. This is especially true in emerging markets, where sometimes there is the perception that the rules are changed to the advantage of domestic users when market instability occurs. Just as users must have confidence in the rules of the market's fair application, confidence in the regulatory regime will enhance the public's confidence in the market and the potential for outside participation.

Risk Management

An essential component of futures regulation and derivatives market functionality is to ensure that the credit enhancement mechanism permits financially sound, anonymous conclusion of derivatives transactions and limits excessive speculation. Anonymous transacting requires reliable credit enhancement and clearing mechanisms. There are several models for these, but most active derivatives markets use central counter-party clearing. The basic risk management features that require regulatory or statutory support are described here.[39]

Market Risk and Margin

Margin is the stake in a transaction and security against its completion. As such, margin is viewed as essential to exchange markets, but may be insufficient to address market risk for a number of reasons. Margin is backward looking. It is calculated using variables that are estimates or projections. In addition, margins must be set at levels that permit economic use of the market for hedging purposes. Therefore, it is unlikely that margin would, could, or ever should cover all outlier price moves. There must be no question that, absent collusion, margin can be used as good collateral; in many cases, building such confidence will require both a fair governance framework and special legislation.[40] The appropriateness of margin and access to margin by the credit facility (brokers and the clearinghouse) must be indisputable as a matter of law and as a matter of fact.

On most U.S. futures markets, for example, performance bond margin (that is, standing maintenance or clearing margin) is only intended to cover at least 95 percent of historical observations (of specified durations) of one-day price moves. In practice, most exchanges look at six months, three months, and one month of price data, as well as five- and 10-year data, current events, and implied option volatilities in setting margin levels. For example, the price moves in U.S. markets on October 19, 1987, October 20, 1987, or October 13, 1989, exceeded standing margin many times. That being said, changes in price equivalent to the current margin requirement have occurred on only a small percentage of days since October 1987. Projecting market

---

[39] Portions of this section have been adapted with permission from Corcoran (1994).

[40] For example, formerly in Germany, margin posted on futures contracts was not collectable because the contracts potentially violated wagering laws. In the United States, there are special bankruptcy provisions that provide that payment of margin is not a preferential transfer (see Sec. 548 [d] of Title 11 of the U.S. Code). The Settlement Finality Directive in the European Union accomplishes the same objectives.

risk and concomitant credit risk is the same exercise in OTC markets, but is more difficult in that the prices for esoteric instruments, or long-dated instruments, may be more difficult to derive in the absence of disseminated prices and in light of the complexity of such instruments. Quotations may be less useful as a measure of risk because of the need to negotiate reversals of transactions with the original counterparty, possibly after a change in circumstances.

Portfolio systems for measuring appropriate margin, based on the overall risk of a combination of futures and options positions, are used globally by many futures markets.[41] However, these systems can be vulnerable to dramatic change based on changes in volatility. This is because not only are projections of market risk uncertain, but also implied volatility can only be estimated. In addition, options prices are unstable as they move toward expiration or where their intrinsic value is deep out of the money. Therefore, regulatory and market authorities, as well as policymakers, should ensure that margin is complemented by other risk management measures.

Credit Risk and Clearing Member Requirements

Credit risk is the risk of counterparty default. Because exchange markets are symmetric, market and credit risk are related and exist irrespective of the direction in which the price is moving.[42] As a consequence, two-way collateral usually is required, that is, both counterparties to each transaction are required to post margin.[43] Such margin is considered, and commonly called, a performance bond because it guarantees each counterparty's commitment to make daily settlement to the clearing organization of any losses resulting from price movements.

On many futures exchange markets, the clearing organization substitutes its credit for that of individual counterparties and manages the accumulation of risk by the daily or more frequent payment and collection of variation margin on each futures position. The clearing organization usually uses a one-day measure of market risk

---

[41] The Standard Portfolio Analysis of Risk Margining (SPAN) system, approved by the Commission for use at the Chicago Mercantile Exchange on November 21, 1988, is a proprietary model based on Black Scholes used by all futures markets in the United States. Many other markets have adopted this model, although the markets can specify parameters unique to conditions in their case. Interestingly, the SPAN system produces substantially similar results to the Theoretical Intermarket Margining System, the Cox-Rubinstein model employed by the Chicago Board Options Exchange, and the Options Clearing Corporation. The U.S. Securities Exchange Commission first approved this system on a pilot basis for setting certain capital charges. See Securities and Exchange Act Release No. 34-33761 (59 Fed. Reg. 13275, March 21, 1994).

[42] Acknowledging this relationship is fundamental to the design of credit support facilities for futures markets.

[43] In Brazil, certain counterparty contracts that are settled and guaranteed by the BM&F are supported by two-way exchange collateral requirements.

because clearing members are required to settle at least daily in cash all losses on house and customer positions, thereby permitting the clearing organization to distribute daily gains in cash on all house and customer positions so that, in theory, the value of each futures contract is reset at zero on a daily basis. Standing margin is intended to cover the credit risk to the clearing organization that its clearing members will not make daily settlement, that is, pay variation margin.[44]

Standing margin is set based on an assumption that any position could be liquidated or the credit risk offset within that one-day window. Therefore, market risk is priced daily, and credit risk is effectively removed from the system on a daily (or more frequent) basis. Daily variation settlement is intended to ensure that gains are not permitted to accumulate against a counterparty whose capacity to pay may change over time based on market events, a change in its business fortunes, or because of its other exposures. Measuring the risk that is thus removed from the system (which estimates the replacement cost of the contract) is a straightforward process because such risk is valued based on actual prices, and reduction of this risk is a concern of market participants and operators as well as regulatory authorities. The more liquid the market, the more controlled this risk is.

Most futures regulation requires profits and losses to be settled daily or more frequently because credit is not evaluated on a transaction-by-transaction basis. The payment of daily variation is intended to avoid situations where accrued losses go unnoticed or losses exceed financial capacity and posted collateral. The cash flow to support variation payments also can be provided by drawing on lines of credit and other guarantees. Regulators and policymakers should require markets and common counterparties to have adequate procedures for addressing market risk and related and unrelated credit risk, including adequate funding liquidity arrangements. Regulators also should be concerned that market users not insulate themselves from responsibility for their proprietary trading by the use of limited risk vehicles. If guarantees or automatic deductions are used, as in the case of some electronic markets, pre-prescribed credit limits or automatic filters also may be desirable.

Some markets use automatic trading halts when prices hit a specified limit to permit collection of margin purportedly to protect the conclusion of settlement and financial integrity. However, economists believe these types of price limits may interfere with the hedging efficacy of the markets because cash market prices are not sim-

---

[44] Standing margin is a deposit in the nature of collateral. It collateralizes the obligation to pay variation margin. It could thus be regarded as a measure of the likely replacement cost to liquidate or repurchase the position. Standing margin is generally posted in highly liquid securities or cash equivalents. Variation margin is the payment of daily profits and collection of losses that must be paid in cash.

ilarly restricted. In principle, such limits do permit the markets to digest extreme price information and protect overall liquidity in the market and thus may be appropriate in markets that are less deep and liquid.

Capital-based Position Limits

Credit risk may also be addressed by imposition of capital-based position limits by either the market itself or clearing firms or organizations. Such limits ordinarily impose higher levels of margin above a predetermined level of exposure. The limits address the fact that the risk of default or credit risk is asymmetric even if market risk is neutral because the likelihood of nonperformance on a net position is greater where a member is carrying a concentrated exposure to a particular customer or in a particular contract. U.S. futures clearing organizations assume no risk to the market, which may be the preferred clearing model from the perspective of clearing members. Regulatory oversight encourages self-regulatory management of the risks assumed.

Segregation

The use of segregation as a form of risk management varies across jurisdictions. In some (for example, Japan), it is impossible to impose a trust on cash, so segregation can only be maintained for customer securities. In some, commercials can opt out of segregation. And in some jurisdictions, segregation is only an accounting entry coupled with a priority in bankruptcy. In the United States, although recent amendments provide more flexibility, segregation has been viewed as a market as well as a customer protection and, therefore, opting out has not been permitted. In any case, segregation does not provide complete protection of either customer funds or the market. A customer default that exceeds the capital of the carrying firm can result in a shortfall of requisite funds to repay the firm's obligations to customers if customer margin is held as a pool rather than identified with specific customers at the clearinghouse, as is typically the case.

In practical terms, segregation is a means of distinguishing customer property held by a broker from the broker's own property. Legally, segregation is the requirement that all money, securities, and property deposited by customers of a broker with respect to a futures position, and the accruals thereon, be accounted for separately and treated by the broker and any depository and clearing or settlement system as belonging to the customer. Required segregation is a common risk management and customer protection feature of derivatives regulation because segregation is intended fully to secure the broker's obligations to its customers, including the accruals on their positions and, as such, is an important protection against the credit risk that the broker will default on the payment of profits owed to its customers.[45] Segregation also can assist in managing of market risk and in isolating risk in the event a firm defaults.[46]

When segregation is maintained not only by the carrying broker firm but also by each depository of customer funds, in the event of broker insolvency, customer funds and positions will be readily identifiable. In some jurisdictions, such funds are held in actual trust; in others, they are treated as if held in a statutory trust and thereby insulated from a broker's creditors in the event the broker fails or a customer default implicates the broker's capital. In the event of a firm disruption caused by proprietary trading, segregation and daily settlement can prevent the accrual of losses in the failed firm as segregation facilitates the movement of positions from one firm to another, thereby permitting solvent customers to preserve their positions and continue to support daily settlements on those positions notwithstanding the insolvency of their carrying firm. The movement of positions isolates the disruption, and possibly expanded financial failure that could occur if such customers discontinued payments to the failed intermediary, and thereby reduces risks to clearing organizations, their members, and the market as a whole.

Segregation protects customers not only from a disturbance due to the proprietary trading of their carrying firm (assuming no fraud or conversion) but also from a destabilizing run on the firm by customers demanding that their accounts be disbursed or transferred. Segregation is easier to calculate than capital, and, thus, segregation compliance is a good measure of the capacity of a firm to fulfill obligations to its customers and the market. In some markets, customer positions are directly held at the clearinghouse. This also protects customer funds, but makes the clearinghouse directly accountable to the customers, which, while less risky for customers of individual brokers, may compromise the liquidity of the market in a marketwide disturbance. Segregation and similar types of arrangements to protect customer positions and isolate risks require legal support to be effective.[47]

---

[45] The variation margin payments required in United States markets facilitate such collateralization of customer claims. As most brokers cannot cover these accruals out of capital, the system facilitates the securing of accruals by requiring the passing of the necessary cash to do so. When the London Metal Exchange first listed financial contracts, it required segregation of such accruals, in part because of this feature.

[46] See the Windsor Declaration by the representatives of regulatory bodies from 16 countries responsible for supervising the activities of the world's major futures and options markets, made in May 1995, available at http://www.cftc.gov/oia/oiawindsordeclaration.htm.

[47] However, in Spain and Finland, customers are direct participants in clearing (Corcoran and Ervin 1987).

Capital

Capital requirements in derivatives markets generally secure overnight exposure on futures positions, that is, the risk that the price will move in an amount greater than the standing margin (or secured risk) before the prior day's variation is collected. As such, the capital requirement is designed to ensure a high level of liquidity or market staying power, that is, to ensure that obligations can be met as they become due. Regulatory minimum capital requirements generally would not be sufficient to cover outlier events, an extended period of accumulated losses, or multiple failures or to act as a substitute for vigilant risk management controls at member firms and exchanges. Regulation should assume that capital requirements, even assuming "haircuts" (adjustment of collateral value to reflect the market risk of converting it to use), must be supplemented by other risk management measures, such as stress testing, to ensure that available financial resources are adequate to cover actual and projected risks and are sufficiently liquid to be readily accessible.

For example, in the United States, at its simplest, the minimum regulatory capital requirement is stated as a measure of customer business (that is, the greater of 4 percent of funds segregated on behalf of customers for domestic and foreign transactions or $250,000). A firm capitalized at $250,000 of capital thus could carry accounts for customers with net liquidating equities totaling $6,250,000. Assuming a margin level of 10 percent, positions with notional values of more than $60 million could be carried by that firm. Of course, regulatory capital requirements must be met with assets that are haircut to reflect the potential cost and time to liquidate positions. Proprietary futures and written options positions are charged to capital at between 100 and 200 percent of clearing margin, depending on whether the firm taking the charge is a clearing member, a nonclearing member, or a nonmember firm. Therefore, proprietary positions in exchange-traded derivatives subject to regulation in the United States are valued for capital purposes based on the same model as that used for margin calculation, that is, a model that uses options pricing theory, nets specified positions, uses proprietary formulas and assumptions for estimating and measuring volatilities, and gives certain hedge and spread concessions. In the United States, all unsecured receivables must be discounted 100 percent.

To the extent that portfolio margins are imprecise or backward-looking estimates, the capital requirement derived from margins shares these features.[48] Various

---

[48] These risk management measures have proved themselves over time. But in modern circumstances, where trading and clearing are decoupled, new or different models to ensure completion of transactions may be used (CPSS/IOSCO 2001).

measures of capital can be used, but the guidelines for risk management remain the same. That is, assets should be discounted to reflect the cost of liquefying them in time to support funding of variation and settlement necessary for the market clearing function performed by the central counterparty. And capital should take into account unsecured liabilities and be sufficient to carry the volume of business and risk undertaken.[49]

Other Measures

In futures markets, transaction costs must be limited if hedging tools are to be economic; the time horizon for the quantification of risks secured by margin, daily settlement, and capital is short; and the exchange systems' projections of risk are estimates at best. Risk management controls and supervision of exposures by exchange compliance staff and personnel independent of traders are critical to maintaining financial integrity. Requirements for and oversight of these functions should be a self-regulatory as well as regulatory concern. This puts a premium on mandated self-regulatory financial surveillance responsibilities coupled with such oversight. Regulators should reinforce the commercial incentive to promote the integrity of the system by requiring market participants to be financially accountable and by promoting clearing arrangements that reinforce these incentives. These could include required shareholdings, provision of specified/collateralized guarantees, bonding or insurance, or security deposited with a third-party clearer. In some electronic markets, funds are directly deducted from users.

Some of the other risk management measures or features of the exchange marketplace that address the quantification and management of risk are transparency, price limits (or circuit breakers), large trader position reports, and delivery period position limits. These measures are directed at maintaining market integrity from the perspective of both price and financial integrity. Typically, in most mature jurisdictions, regulation supports these types of measures or other measures intended to protect the pricing process from market abuses associated with concentrations of market power.[50]

Surveillance, Enforcement, and Market Oversight

In addition to appropriate contract design, credit criteria for access and risk management, and fair governance, derivatives markets require effective oversight because

---

[49] Futures markets also ordinarily require self-cleared proprietary trading to be guaranteed by a parent if done on its behalf, so that firms can limit liability to the central counterparty's common bond arrangements, but not for their own trading.

[50] In developing markets, reference also should be made to available guidance on clearing and settlement. See CPSS/IOSCO (2001) and Corcoran (1994).

they ordinarily operate by rules that are largely self-enforced. Furthermore, effectively designed surveillance can compensate for smaller markets and contracts designed on underlying markets that are not optimal. As stated more generally in IOSCO (1998; 2002b):

- The regulator should have comprehensive inspection, investigation, and surveillance powers.
- The regulator should have comprehensive enforcement powers.
- The regulatory system should ensure effective and credible use of inspection, investigation, surveillance, and enforcement powers and implementation of an effective compliance program.

Market Surveillance

Derivatives markets essentially are secondary markets for transferring risk. Surveillance of the market is especially important because it ensures that the trading and credit enhancement facilities of the derivatives market function and complement the protections of contract design. In turn, it ensures that market abuses do not distort prices, otherwise impair the risk shifting and price discovery functions, adversely affect cash market prices, or permit the accumulation of excessive exposures.

The components of effective surveillance have been set forth in the Tokyo Communiqué (1997), in which derivatives regulators from 16 different national jurisdictions set forth best practice guidance for derivatives regulators on components of market surveillance and information sharing. These include the following:

- A framework for undertaking market surveillance
- Access to and collection of information on a routine and nonroutine basis, which permits analysis of the composition of the market, including information on concentrations of positions and cash markets related to the derivative
- Analysis of information, based on collection of information that permits timely action
- Analysis of market abuse, the power to investigate abuse, and clarity as to what constitutes congestion, provision of false information, or manipulative activities
- Intervention powers to address disorderly conditions and clarity as to when such powers can be exercised
- Disciplinary sanctions against members of the market and power to address abuses of nonmembers

- Ability to cooperate with other authorities to carry out supervisory responsibilities.[51]

Surveillance helps maintain an appropriately functioning market and, therefore, contributes not only to market integrity and customer protection but also to market success.

Enforcement

IOSCO (2002b) notes, "The complex character of securities transactions and the sophistication of fraudulent schemes require strong and rigorous enforcement of securities laws. The case can be made *a fortiori* for derivatives markets where customers of the markets may be vulnerable to misconduct by intermediaries and others if unsophisticated or to failures of integrity that can adversely affect the market's intended use. Policymakers should assure that the regulator or other competent government authority is provided with comprehensive investigative and enforcement powers including:

- Regulatory and investigative powers to obtain data, information, documents statements, and records from persons involved in the relevant conduct or who may have information relevant to the inquiry
- Power to seek orders and/or take other action to ensure compliance with those regulatory, administrative, and investigation powers
- Power to impose administrative sanctions and/or seek orders from courts or tribunals
- Power to initiate or to refer matters for criminal prosecution
- Power to order the suspension of trading in securities or to take other appropriate action and
- Where enforcement action is able to be taken, the power to enter into enforceable settlements and to accept binding undertakings."[52]

---

[51] The detailed articulation of this surveillance guidance includes specific types of information that should be accessible and can be used by designers of regulatory systems in ensuring that market authorities have relevant supervisory powers. Although this list was developed primarily for physical delivery markets of finite supply, its tenets were cited by IOSCO in 1998 as a menu to be consulted in overseeing financial derivatives markets.

[52] IOSCO (1998) Principle 8. Enforcement of Securities Regulation, pp. 15–16.

Information Sharing

Given the increasingly international nature of contemporary derivatives markets, regulators have concluded that it is vital for the enforcement authority to be effective in
cross-border situations. Many cash markets span more than one jurisdiction, and, typically, these markets have international trading interests. Accordingly, IOSCO (2002b)
recognizes that "the regulator should strive to ensure that it or another authority in
its jurisdiction has the necessary authority to obtain information, including statements
and documents, that may be relevant to investigating and prosecuting potential violations of laws and regulations relating to securities transactions and that such information can be shared directly with other regulators or indirectly through authorities in
their jurisdictions for use in investigations and prosecutions of securities violations," including those that cross borders.[53]

Market Oversight and Self-Regulation

Development Issues

This chapter assumes that the nature of derivatives markets is that they tend to grow
best in a legal and regulatory framework that supports existing commercial practices.
Experience demonstrates that financial markets have succeeded best where there
was a culture of honoring commercial obligations and an enthusiasm for trading activities. Mandated self-regulation is a feature of U.S. market regulatory systems for financial markets at least in part as a result of these observations. Such self-regulation
is required as part of a framework intended to ensure that markets enforce their
rules or contractual arrangements fairly and equitably and have market and financial
integrity programs in place. Mandated self-regulation is not unlike rendering private
companies increasingly subject to requirements to maintain internal and operational
controls.

But self-regulation will not work without an effective oversight framework,
both because the public may lack confidence in its fairness and evenhandedness and
because of the potential market power that derivatives markets have. Self-regulation

---

[53] IOSCO (1998, p. 17). Twenty-six countries have signed a special arrangement commonly known as the Boca Declaration to permit requests for information on related exposures in different markets. See http://www.cftc.gov/oia/
oiabocadec0398.htm and IOSCO (1998).

gets its credibility from the government framework and from the fact that the government protects the public interest in the prices determined in the marketplace. However, self-regulation may not work in jurisdictions where there is no tradition of markets or trading expertise. When self-regulation may not be appropriate, policymakers in some jurisdictions have created the market as a public entity and then with experience ceded responsibility for its operation (for example, in Italy). With for-profit markets, regulators and policymakers are reassessing what is the appropriate balance of self-regulation and government oversight. As a result, in the United States, so-called independent self-regulatory authorities (with statutory powers) have solicited certain compliance responsibilities formerly undertaken by exchanges.

Consideration of what elements of self-regulation might be appropriate should at least be of interest to policymakers and market developers, especially in a bottom-up development situation. This is because self-regulators typically combine private and government interests, efficiently supplementing government regulation.

IOSCO views the use of self-regulatory organizations (SROs) within statutory oversight frameworks as permissible but optional. As stated in IOSCO (2002b), SROs can be a valuable component to the regulator in achieving the objectives of securities regulation. IOSCO recommends an inquiry into how use of SROs with direct responsibilities in their areas of competency can be appropriate, given the size and complexity of a particular jurisdiction's markets, in assisting regulators to meet their regulatory objectives. In fact, industry representation and self-regulation are integral parts of most regulatory schemes, affecting derivatives markets, at least where there is a history of forward markets. Where the government itself is developing a market, the use of self-regulatory expertise may be less feasible or may have to be imported from another marketplace or a specialist provider. Derivatives markets depend on the frontline, day-to-day and, in some cases, minute-to-minute operational oversight that usually is more readily achieved by self-regulatory than government authorities. Therefore, the authorities should carefully consider a framework that permits the use of the self-regulatory governance systems that are in place or that might evolve over time.

Where a derivatives market is not imposed, but grows out of an existing well-developed cash market, it is important to take into account participants that have intimate knowledge of the market, including how to maximize regulatory benefits (orderly markets, customer protection, and reduction of systemic risk) while minimizing business costs. Where commercials and financial institutions have intimate knowledge of the market, this knowledge can be exploited to support a self-regulatory complement to regulatory oversight, which is perceived as appropriate and reasonable by both regulated individuals and market users. This perception, in turn, results in greater

acceptance by the market participants operating within the self-regulatory framework. Moreover, the closeness of overseers to the marketplace ensures that the
rules for commerce in that particular market are continually and quickly adapted to
the evolution in trade.[54] The challenge is to get the right balance.

Objectives of Self-Regulation

The broad objectives of self-regulation are the same as those identified for government regulation of financial markets in IOSCO (2002b): to preserve market integrity
(fair, efficient, and transparent markets), to preserve financial integrity (reduce systemic
risk), and to protect investors. Many forms of self-regulation currently exist for financial markets to achieve these objectives. Increasingly, there is a trend for self-regulation to be provided by specialists that have been delegated quasi-government functions and not by the markets themselves. However, a multitude of models—industry
self-regulatory organizations, self-regulatory exchange frameworks, and private associations—define and encourage adherence to standards of best practice among their
participants. Self-regulation may focus on oversight of the market itself, qualification
standards for market intermediation, and oversight of the business conduct of intermediaries, including their relationship with client market users. A single SRO may perform these areas of responsibility, or they may be divided or shared among SROs
within a given country or market sector.

Powers of Self-regulators

SROs usually draw their powers by statute or by delegation from a regulatory authority. These powers may include vetting and authorizing individuals, making rules,
enforcing rules, exercising a disciplinary function, sharing information with other self-
regulators and regulators, and intervening to maintain orderly markets. The role of
self-regulation varies across countries, market sectors, and developed and emerging
markets. Where its role is significant, it almost invariably has a demonstrated track
record of responsible behavior under the oversight of statutory regulators.

---

[54] In the United States, futures and securities exchanges were the first regulators in the industry, long before the federal government required them to regulate themselves. These futures and securities exchange markets have a long
history of voluntary regulation. The exchanges adopted rules of conduct governing members and member organizations and recognized from the beginning that self-regulation was necessary in order to maintain orderly markets and
promote public confidence in those markets.

From the perspective of both developing and mature markets, the use of SROs can meet several objectives:

- Expand regulatory resources
- Enhance regulatory expertise
- Provide the immediacy of frontline monitoring
- Create a culture of acceptance of regulated markets and responsibility for orderly markets
- Counterbalance excessive government intervention.

Oversight, Expertise, and Coverage

Specialized Knowledge

SROs may offer considerable depth and expertise regarding market operations and practices and may be able to respond more quickly and flexibly than the government authority to changing market conditions.

Industry Motivation

Self-policing systems and the general concept of self-regulation work because, when they are properly administered and governed, there should be a business incentive to operate a fair, financially sound, and competitive marketplace. Reputation and competition are powerful motivating forces for sustained proper behavior, especially in today's global environment where market participants have virtually immediate, 24-hour access to a range of competing markets and products. Reputation risk also motivates government regulators. The ability to share the responsibility for oversight can reduce this risk by making the market as well as the regulator accountable for its fair operation. Incorporating self-regulation into the regulatory framework can result in better regulation by supplementing and enforcing the statutory regulator. Self-regulation takes advantage of entities directly involved in the regulated activity that have more detailed knowledge of its operational or technical aspects. Making use of self-regulators with statutory responsibilities to oversee markets and industry professionals is akin to requiring firms to have supervisory programs and internal controls. It makes the industry responsible for itself, which can be a powerful factor in jurisdictions where stakeholders complain of self-regulatory failures.

Contractual Relationship

The contractual relationship that an SRO has with the individuals and entities it regulates can cross national boundaries, reaching where statutory powers may not. IOSCO (2002b) states that SROs should observe ethical standards that go beyond government regulations.

Transparency and Accountability

Properly designed and representative SROs can reinforce good governance standards. Policymakers should ensure that SRO compliance programs are transparent and accountable and that SROs follow professional standards of behavior on matters including confidentiality and procedural fairness. The inclusion of both public representatives and industry professionals on an SRO's governing body could provide the foundation for an open organization. In some jurisdictions, SROs prepare regulatory plans that are submitted to their statutory regulator and made available to the public. These regulatory plans describe the SRO's regulatory objectives, what the SRO intends to do in the next year, how it will do it, and what it will cost.

Coordination and Information Sharing

As the markets become more globalized, coordination of market oversight becomes more important. Coordination occurs among SROs and between SROs and regulators. SROs provide an excellent forum for bringing together various interests on regulatory issues. Coordination and information sharing must be a priority among policymakers and markets in order to address cross-market issues and potential market abuse or systemic risk concerns that may affect more than one market.

Increasing Acceptance of a Culture of Regulation

In the optimal model, self-regulators are subject to oversight, so that the exercise of self-regulatory responsibilities within the regulatory framework fosters a culture of compliance. The regulator can use the self-regulator to develop, implement, and enforce rules that govern its activities; to conserve government resources; and to ensure workable rules to provide greater flexibility in resolving complex problems.

Oversight of Functions

Effective self-regulation must be defined within the context of government oversight, which is an essential element in the self-regulatory structure. Government oversight of SRO activities ensures that, among other things, all interests are given the proper consideration and voice in all regulatory activities, and self-regulators do not act in an anticompetitive way by positing standards that are inappropriate or create inappropriate barriers to entry. That self-regulation is subject to oversight provides a system of checks and balances. The governing statute should clearly delineate the respective roles of the statutory regulators and the SROs.

In addition to the natural checks and balances of market forces, the oversight framework should address the potential for conflicts of interest to occur where industry participants may favor their interests over those of the investing public. The statutory regulator can, and should, verify that the processes and programs executed by the SROs are, in fact, effective in meeting the established regulatory objectives through spot-checking or other types of periodic review.

In most cases, statutory regulators perform inspections of SROs and evaluate their performance of regulatory responsibilities. SROs may also be required to report regularly on compliance with the statutory requirements and provide special reports, if needed. Because government regulators ultimately retain jurisdiction over the activities of an SRO, statutory regulators may be willing to delegate responsibilities to SROs where the requisite expertise and governance protections exist (see Principle 7 in IOSCO 1998).

Relationship with the Regulator

Because derivatives markets, in particular, require direct surveillance, self-regulation is a valuable augmentation of regulatory powers and capability. Regulators in Latin America have found that a regulatory framework can warrant establishing SROs where no self-regulatory organizations exist. At the same time, the securities regulators recognize that government oversight of self-regulatory organizations is critical to guard against the potential conflicts between industry self-interest and the public interest. The Council of Securities Regulators of the Americas (COSRA) offers eight principles of market oversight (see box 11-1).[55] In any event, the statutory regula-

---

[55] Self-regulation, subject to appropriate government oversight, can provide an effective means for overseeing the activities of market intermediaries and market operators. An illustration of effective market oversight can be found in the U.S. futures industry. Since the National Futures Association began operations in 1982, trading volume has increased by 284 percent, while customer complaints have dropped by 72 percent.

Box 11-1 | **COSRA's Principles of Effective Market Oversight**

Authorization, Responsibility, and Accountability

- Market operators and market intermediaries should be required to receive authorization from the government authority before they may lawfully engage in the securities or futures business. The government authority should impose appropriate conditions before granting such authorization, such as an obligation to comply with applicable laws, regulations, and rules and demonstration of the absence of past misconduct.
- The goal of an effective market oversight system is fair, honest, and orderly markets. To achieve this goal, a regulatory system requires a mechanism for imposing responsibility and accountability on market operators and market intermediaries.
- The government authority should consider creating a regulatory system where market operators or market intermediaries exercise direct oversight responsibility over their respective areas of competence, subject to appropriate government supervision and to the extent appropriate to the size and complexity of the markets.
- The government authority should require a self-regulatory organization to meet appropriate conditions before allowing the organization to exercise its authority. Moreover, once the self-regulatory organization is operating, the government authority should assure itself that the exercise of this power results in fair and consistent enforcement of applicable securities and futures laws, regulations, and appropriate self-regulatory organization rules.
- The government authority and/or self-regulatory organization should develop enforceable standards, including standards of business conduct for market intermediaries, based on high standards of commercial honor, just and equitable principles of trade, and standards of financial integrity.
- Where a government authority allows market operators or market intermediaries to exercise oversight authority in a system of self-regulation, the government authority should retain direct authority over all market operators and market intermediaries, to be exercised at its discretion.

Monitoring for Compliance

- An effective market oversight system must have a mechanism for monitoring compliance with laws, regulations, and self-regulatory organization rules.

Enforcement

- An effective market oversight system requires a strong enforcement program. An enforcement program safeguards the integrity of the marketplace by deterring market participants from violating laws, regulations, and self-regulatory organization rules, by providing an effective mechanism for compliance, and by enhancing investor confidence in the integrity of the markets and market intermediaries.

Source: http://www.cvm.gov.br/ingl/inter/cosra/inter.asp.

---

tor should step in if a self-regulatory organization shirks its responsibilities or if its members endanger customer funds or engage in fraud, manipulation, or other illegal conduct.[56]

---

[56] In the United States, an SRO can have numerous regulatory responsibilities and can be sanctioned if it does not perform them properly.

Backstop to Inappropriate Government Intervention

Involving the market in its own oversight, in some cultures and situations, may prove an effective counterweight against inappropriate government tampering because it provides an organizational factor to market interests. The general elements of self-regulation transcend distinctions based on type of financial instrument (securities or derivatives), market structure (electronic versus physical on-floor auction markets), nature of market users (institutional or retail), and nature of transactions (principal, agency, or both). Specific elements must be tailored to the goals, objectives, and needs of each market and regulatory regime. Indeed, the flexibility of design of self-regulatory programs is one of the hallmarks of self-regulation and a significant benefit.

As a result of advances in technology and telecommunications, financial markets are increasingly global and trade without regard to national boundaries. The markets are increasingly integrated through market users, market intermediaries, and payment systems, and distinctions between exchange and OTC market structures are blurring. The regulatory framework must be continuously evaluated in light of the changes that are occurring and will occur. The regulatory framework cannot unduly lag behind or act an as impediment to market innovations.

Endorsement of self-regulation is an acknowledgment that, because the regulator cannot be everywhere, regulation must impose responsibility on markets and persons with access to markets directly and on intermediaries to self-monitor and have compliance functions. This enhances confidence that markets will be properly run and supervised from the perspective of customer protection, market integrity, and financial integrity. While not a substitute for the important elements of regulation specified above, self-regulation is a powerful and potentially extremely effective complement. In fact, as markets become more complex and diverse, some aspects of regulation may be privatized.

Ideally, a regulatory approach should be the ultimate goal of any regulatory structure. A regulatory approach should minimize cost burdens, maximize investor confidence and fairness in the market, and contribute to the reduction of systemic risk. If the costs of regulation outweigh the benefits, businesses can migrate to markets with lower costs. However, market abuses or failures related to insufficient regulation also deter participation and result in reduced liquidity, so the appropriate balance is critical. Properly implemented, self-regulation is not a form of deregulation, but a form of promoting strong internal and operational controls. As such, where the circumstances warrant, it is an important part of a model of efficient and broad-based regulation.

Conclusion

Policymakers confronted with the choice of determining whether to build derivatives markets to complement cash or other capital market or real economy risk management enhancements need to carefully consider the necessary preconditions for such markets and for their effective oversight. This involves assessing a number of competing matters:

- Alternative risk management methods that could be equally effective (OTC solutions, other markets, or host electronic facilities)
- The possibility of developing a standardized product in the area for which a derivative is desired
- Whether there are adequate institutions to provide liquidity
- The possibility of designing a market structure that will support the expected level of trading activity
- The infrastructure listed in box 11-2 and whether it can be put in place to ensure that the credit enhancement and trading mechanisms can function reliably and effectively.

In any case, an evaluation of the amount of volatility in underlying prices, and hence of the demand for risk management, is also essential.

Development of effective derivatives markets in and outside Latin America appears to require that a commercial need be wedded to the appropriate infrastructure and economic environment. Such an environment requires an amenable political and macroeconomic context as well as an appropriate legal framework. The appropriate framework should support the trading and credit enhancement mechanism and ensure certainty in the transfer of contracts representing the underlying value or product. Policymakers must be prepared to address the following:

- Transparency in the rules of the market, the terms of contracts offered, and prices
- Governance and accountability of market operators
- Criteria for access and handling of customer funds and trades
- Risk management, including treatment of funds and customers in the event of default
- Enforcement and investigative powers
- Market oversight.

Box 11-2 | **Infrastructure for Derivatives Markets**

The U.S. Commodity Futures Trading Commission provides specific forms for three types of contracts: physical delivery futures, cash-settled futures, and options on futures. The types of information listed below would be needed for physical delivery futures.

Commodity characteristics (grade, quality, weight class, growth, issuer, source, and rating):

- Quality differentials for non-par deliveries or lack thereof
- Delivery points by region
- Location differences for non-par deliveries
- Delivery facilities (type, number, capacity, and ownership)
- Contract size and/or trading unit
- Delivery instrument (warehouse, receipt, or shipping certificate)
- Transportation terms (free on board or other)
- Delivery procedures
- Delivery months
- Delivery period/last trading day
- Verification of delivery eligibility (inspection and certification)
- Minimum price change (relationship to cash mark)
- Daily price limit (relationship to cash price movements).

Method for estimating deliverables/supplies.

Speculative limits:

- Spot month
- Non-spot month
- Reporting level
- Aggregation rule.

Other relevant information for hedging or basing prices.

Source: http://www.cftc.gov/dea/analysis/deabackground_guide1.htm.

In considering how best to accommodate the legislative and administrative infrastructure of a jurisdiction to the aforesaid preconditions, policymakers should also consider the optimal balance between private and public rules and between regulation and self-regulation. The details of this chapter are intended to give some guidance to development experts on the considerations essential to achieve these preconditions and determine the requisite balance.

To date, the principal success in Latin America has been the market in Brazil, in which all of the essential elements set forth in this chapter were in place. Even that market, however, has experienced growing pains and makes clear that policymakers seeking to promote derivatives market risk management solutions must be prepared to explain how they took steps to address potential risks as well as the rewards of such markets in their jurisdictions.

Policymakers must not only keep each of these considerations in mind when evaluating tradable instruments, the development of liquidity, and credit enhancement in order to ensure success, they must also carefully consider the type of product to trade, the best trading structure (type of auction, algorithm, or other method of specifying trading rules), and whether it is possible to build a derivatives market where it is necessary to develop both the derivative and the cash component. This has been the case in some bond markets.

A further consideration in making these determinations is whether there are effective financial and commercial institutions in place that have the cultural and economic impetus and expertise to use a derivatives market for risk-shifting functions. One reason perhaps that the history of nonfinancial derivatives markets has been one of evolution from commercial markets is that such markets can provide users and potential users the necessary experience in risk shifting and trading. In some situations, the educational exercise of determining what types of risk management and market and/or counterparty structures make sense in a specific economy will be as important as the development of the optimal regulatory framework and choice of product.

Appendix. The Brazilian Experience

The São Paulo Commodities Exchange (BMSP) was founded in 1917 by exporters, businessmen, and commodity producers to trade primarily forward in agricultural commodities, including coffee, live cattle, and cotton. This was an unregulated market used by big commercials and food processors. In the mid-1970s, the Rio de Janeiro and São Paulo stock exchanges began trading options on equities among local participants. These ventures were successful. At that time, there was no competing American Depository Receipts market. Appendix table 11-1 summarizes basic economic and capital market indicators for Brazil.

In 1986, the Brazilian Futures Exchange of Rio de Janeiro (BM&F) began trading financial assets. In 1991, it merged with the BMSP, and in June 1997, it merged with the Brazilian Futures Exchange of Rio de Janeiro, which had been founded in 1983 using a British model. In January 2000, BM&F joined the Globex Alliance through the French electronic trading system NSC.

Appendix Table 11-1	Economic and Capital Market Indicators for Brazil, 2001
Indicator	**Value**
Macroeconomic	
Gross domestic product	
Billions of U.S. dollars	503.9
Billions of reais	1,184.80
Consumer price index increase (percent)	7.67
Balance of trade surplus (billions of U.S. dollars)	2.64
Total external debt (billions of U.S. dollars)	209.9
Exchange rate (reais per U.S. dollar)	
June 1999	1.7695
June 2000	1.8000
June 2001	2.3049
December 2001	2.3204
June 2002	2.8444
Capital market	
Stock market capitalization (billions of U.S. dollars)	185.4
Corporate debt market (billions of U.S. dollars)	16.33
Sovereign debt market (billions of U.S. dollars)	163.37
Sub-sovereign debt market (billions of U.S. dollars)	103.41
Sovereign debt rating by S&P as of September 8, 2000	
Local currency, long term	BB
Outlook	Positive
Local currency, short term	B
Foreign currency, long term	B+
Outlook	Positive
Foreign currency, short term	B

The BM&F has an in-house department that acts as a central counterpart. Clearing members must maintain minimum net working capital set by the Clearing Division, post collateral to fund the Clearing Fund, comply with the limits imposed on positions for which they are responsible, and participate in or provide a common bond against default of other members up to a specified amount. Brokers and locals also must meet minimum requirements of operational capacity and financial standing. Clearing members may impose additional limits on brokers and locals.

Brazil provides an example of a market that developed largely on a self-regulatory or private contractual plan—that is, a bottom-up market (similar to those that developed in the United States), not a top-down approach as some jurisdictions have tried to promote.

Until the devaluation of the real in 1999, Brazil accounted for more than 40 percent of Latin America's gross domestic product (GDP). The country has approximately 180 million people, or one-third of the population of Latin America. Brazil has a long history, throughout the 1970s and 1980s, of double-digit or more inflation, a trend that was sharply reversed with the implementation of the Real Plan in 1994.

Several factors have contributed to the country's success over the years:

- The preexistence of a sophisticated financial system with many banks and broker-dealers
- Cultural optimism and an appetite for risk taking
- Rapid development in the 1970s, when the savings rate grew to more than 20 percent of GDP
- Derivatives contracts that were designed around mature underlying markets
- The need for inflation/volatility hedging
- Lack of transaction taxes and other favorable fiscal policies
- Limitation of Brazilians to local markets
- Limitation on dollar-denominated debt
- A fiscal responsibility law that is difficult to repeal.

There have been failures as well in Brazil, such as the speculative bubble in futures on individual stocks that killed that market. In 1989, there was a manipulation of the Rio stock market by traders acting in concert using futures, options and wash trading, unauthorized trading, and accounts, orchestrated by a trader who previously had been sanctioned for participating in the manipulation of the U.S. silver market. This resulted in multiple broker failures, suspension of trading in futures contracts, and civil and criminal penalties for multiple parties. Significant changes were made to strengthen the system as a result of this experience, including identification of end users, reduction of the settlement period in the cash market, prohibition of cash advances, and linking surveillance between futures, options, and cash markets in securities. To date, efforts to revive a market in single stock futures have been unsuccessful, but this may change if planned securities futures products prove successful in the United States.

Prior to 2002, the central bank supervised only certain contracts on the futures markets, and the Commissão de Valores Mobiliarios (CVM) supervised contracts on equities. Jurisdiction by law for most of the financial market, including futures, has now been granted to the securities regulator, although some money market instruments and foreign exchange remain subject to the central bank's oversight.

Interestingly, by virtue of a National Monetary Council resolution, only instruments allowed by the central bank can be traded over the counter, and these are required to be registered with the Central Securities Depository or an exchange (except for those OTC products subject to CVM jurisdiction). BM&F offers a registration function and provides for transparency and security by also providing a disclosed, competitive auction market and collateral management for such OTC transactions and, where there is an active dealing market, a guarantee. A recent statistic from the market indicates that total open interest in swaps and flexible options is 4,078,074, of which 465,131 are not guaranteed.

References

CPSS/IOSCO. 2001. Recommendations for Securities Settlement Systems, CPSS/IOSCO (November). At www.bis.org.

Commodity Futures Trading Commission (CFTC). 1996. Fenchurch Capital Management.

_____. 1999a. Futures Exchange and Contract Authorization: Standards and Procedures in Selected Countries. (August). http:/www.cftc.gov/oia/oia_publications. htm

_____. 1999b. Survey on Regulation of Over-the-Counter (OTC) Derivatives, CFTC Office of International Affairs (March), at http://www.cftc.gov/oia/oia_publications. htm#Survey.

_____. 2001. Exchange-Traded Derivatives in Developing Capital Markets (March).

Corcoran, Andrea M. 1994. Prudential Regulation of OTC Derivatives: Lessons from the Exchange-Traded Sector. In G. Ferrarini, ed., *Prudential Regulation of Banks and Securities Firms*. Kluwer Law International.

_____. 2000. The Uses of New Capital Markets: Electronic Commerce and the Rules of the Game in an International Marketplace, 49 American University Law Review 581 (February): p. 585.

_____. 2002. Cross-Border Financial Transactions: 25 Questions to Consider in Making Risk Management Decisions. In G. Ferrarini, ed., *Capital Markets in the Age of the Euro*. Kluwer Law International.

Corcoran and Ervin. 1987. Maintenance of Market Strategies in Futures Broker Insolvencies: Futures Position Transfers from Troubled Firms. *Washington and Lee Law Review* 44(849, summer).

Forum of European Securities Commissions. 2000. The Regulation of Alternative Trading Systems in Europe (December).

Futures Industry Association. 2001. International Futures Volume Comparison Table for 1999 and 2000. *Exchange-Traded Derivatives in Developing Capital Markets.* Available at http://www.cftc.gov/oia/oia_publications.htm.

International Organization of Securities Commissions (IOSCO). 1998. Application of the Tokyo Communiqué to Exchange-Traded Financial Derivatives Contracts. http://www.iosco.org/docspublic/1998exchange_traded_derivatives.html (September).

_____. 2000. Stock Exchange Demutualization, Consultation Draft of the Technical Committee. Discussion Paper, IOSCO (December).

_____. 2002a. *The Development of Corporate Bond Markets in Emerging Market Countries.* Report of Emerging Markets Committee Working Group 2.

_____. 2002b. *Objectives and Principles of Securities Regulation.* IOSCO (February).

Kroszner. 1999. Can the Financial Markets Privately Regulate Risk? The Development of Derivatives Clearinghouses and Recent Over-the-Counter Innovations. *Money, Credit, and Banking* 31 (3, August).

Martel, Terrence. 2001. Continuum of Market Evolution. Presentation at Commodity Futures Trading Commission/International Finance Corporation (CFTC/IFC) Program on Developing Derivatives Markets, October 19.

Rudder Associates. 2000. *Innovations in Energy Products; Innovations in Interest Rate (and Credit) Products.* Reprinted with presentation by Gregory Huyt, Managing Director, Rudder Associates, at CFTC/IFC Program on Developing Derivatives Markets. October.

Securities and Investments Board. 1996. A Review of the Metals Market, Securities and Investments Board (August) pp. 14 and 37 (Historic Price Carries).

Tokyo Communiqué. 1997. http://www.cftc.gov/files/oia/oiatokyopt.pdf (October).

World Bank. 1999. *Dealing with Commodity Price Volatility in Developing Countries.* International Task Force on Commodity Risk Management in Developing Countries, World Bank, Washington, D.C.

World Bank and International Monetary Fund (IMF). 2001. *Developing Government Bond Markets, A Handbook.* Washington, D.C.: International Monetary Fund and World Bank.

CHAPTER 12

Access to Financing for Small and Medium Enterprises

Hannes Takacs
Kinga Korcsmaros

The recent literature contains many accounts regarding the importance of small and medium enterprises (SMEs) as a sector with significant potential for job creation, sparking economic activities in emerging economies, and as a basis for entrepreneurship and innovation. However, the literature is also replete with accounts of the significant constraints that affect the development of SMEs. The constraints are numerous and include factors that are idiosyncratic to the nature of the enterprise and factors pertinent to the environment in which they operate. Access to finance is one of the most significant factors affecting the expansion of SMEs.

Providers of finance, such as development banks, which are active in SME issues, consider access to funding an essential requirement for SMEs. Entrepreneurs also mention the relevance of the lack of access to finance as a key problem that they encounter. In a recent study, SMEs in almost all European Union member countries were asked to rank development constraints according to their importance. For most respondents, access to finance was among the three most important constraints.[1] Experts also indicated that the absolute importance of access to finance is negatively correlated with the size of the enterprise. Enterprises with 1–9 employees rank this constraint higher than other constraints, compared with enterprises with 10–49 employees (European Observatory for SMEs 2000). This finding hints at the role of the underlying growth cycle in the evolution of SMEs, where businesses usually start with their own resources, then graduate to a state where they become undercapitalized, and thus require additional funds. In developing countries, in particular, financing institutions are usually unable to meet the needs of SMEs for seed money and investment capital. Problems of high transaction costs and perceived risks, lack of collateral and

---

[1] Respondents highlighted the relevance of tax and legal issues as key factors affecting SME development.

financial data, and negative bank experience in dealing with small asset-backed borrowing are intensified in high-inflation environments.

The primary objective of this chapter is to analyze the importance of access to finance for the development of SMEs and the role capital markets can play. The chapter reviews the situation and financing issues of SMEs in general and presents examples from various regions, highlighting successful financing structures in the context of specific economic and political environments. Going beyond the issue of capital markets, the chapter focuses on the comprehensive set of factors that determine the level of access of SMEs to finance (financial and capital markets) and its constraints and the strategies, programs, and available best practices in the field. Additional SME growth factors, such as legal and tax issues, are mentioned.

A main conclusion of this chapter is that, although SMEs can access capital markets (via either equity or debt instruments), there is not a preponderance of evidence that indicates that capital markets would constitute a panacea for resolving the constraints to finance that SMEs face. Instead, the analysis should explore SME access to financial markets in general. In this context, the initial public offering (IPO), which is regarded as one of the main drivers of capital and stock market development, becomes an effective instrument for SMEs only at later stages of their growth.

Unfortunately, there is no uniform definition of SMEs that is accepted worldwide. SMEs are a heterogeneous group, even within the context of national economies. In certain economic sectors (for example, the agriculture or craft sector), SMEs might play a dominant role, whereas in others (such as financial institutions or communication), they might be less heralded. However, most of the existing definitions of SMEs state that they include micro, small, and medium-size enterprises. Many countries and regions have developed their own definitions for SMEs. As expected, the definition is significantly influenced by the importance SMEs play in a country's economy. However, given the lack of a single SME definition of global validity, it is difficult to make international comparisons. This chapter uses the European Union's official definition of SMEs, unless indicated otherwise (table 12-1).

The Importance of Small and Medium Enterprises

In many countries, the SME sector is a core element for economic growth. More than 95 percent of enterprises in the Organisation for Economic Co-operation and Development (OECD) are SMEs, and they account for approximately 60–70 percent

Table 12-1 | **The European Union's Official Definition of Small and Medium Enterprises**

Criteria	Micro	Small	Medium
Number of employees	Fewer than 10	Fewer than 50	Fewer than 250
Annual turnover or total balance sheet		Less than € 7 million Less than € 5 million	Less than € 40 million Less than € 27 million
Independence		Not more than 25 percent of the capital or voting rights held by one or more enterprises, which are not themselves SMEs	

Source: European Commission (1996).

of employment in most countries (OECD 2000). Numerous studies have been conducted on the importance of SMEs for the economy, analyzing their role in job creation, performance and efficiency, innovation, and social and political matters. Researchers have attempted to challenge the role and size of SMEs in the economy. However, most studies have confirmed the sector's strong impact on the economy.

In the OECD, the vast majority of enterprises are SMEs, and there is an ongoing trend toward the reduction in firm size. In the United States, SMEs (firms with fewer than 500 employees, according to the U.S. definition) account for more than 99 percent of businesses; in Japan, SMEs (firms with fewer than 300 employees) account for almost 99 percent of all enterprises; and in the European Union, there are almost 19 million SMEs (firms with fewer than 250 employees), representing 99.8 percent of all businesses (OECD 2000). Although the quantitative dominance of SMEs among enterprises is clear, a relatively large portion of new enterprises do not survive the first year of activity. On average, 87 percent of all European start-ups survive their first year, 68 percent survive for at least three years, and 55 percent survive to the end of the fifth year.[2]

The service sectors are generally the primary domain for SMEs, in particular, activities such as construction, wholesale trade, retail trade, and tourism. SMEs also play an important role in strategic business services, such as computer software, information processing, research and development, technical testing, marketing, business organization, and human resource development (OECD 2000). In some countries, SMEs account for a high percentage of manufacturing firms.

---

[2] European Commission (1998); http://europ.eu.int/opnews/495/en/ r3414.htm (17.05.2001)

Job Creation

The importance of SMEs for job creation is widely acknowledged. Between 1969 and 1979, 81 percent of net new jobs created were attributable to businesses with fewer than 100 employees.[3] SMEs account for approximately half the total employment in the OECD area, although differences can be observed between countries and sectors. In the European Union, SMEs provide jobs for 70 million people, thus accounting for two-thirds of total employment. In Japan, small businesses account for 78 percent of employment, and in the United States, SMEs provide employment for more than half of all private sector workers (OECD 2000).

Hallberg (2000, p. 3) argues, "While gross job creation rates are substantially higher for small firms, so are gross destruction rates. This is because small firms exhibit high birth and death rates, and many small firms fail to grow." Net job creation rates (gross job creation less gross job destruction) do not show a systematic relationship to firm size in developed countries (Davis, Haltiwanger, and Schuh 1993). Because small businesses have higher gross job creation and higher destruction rates than large enterprises, SMEs may offer less job security compared with large enterprises (Hallberg 2000). However, job destruction during recessions is usually lower for SMEs, probably because of the greater wage flexibility in small businesses; that is, small and medium entrepreneurs may accept lower wages in times of recession in order to keep their businesses (Haltiwanger 1999). Firm sizes change and businesses continuously start up and die, making it difficult indeed to prove whether SMEs generate the most jobs in an economy.

Performance and Innovation

In the OECD, in the service and manufacturing sectors, businesses with fewer than 10 employees produce approximately 20 percent of output, and those with fewer than 50 employees produce more than 40 percent of output. In the United States, enterprises with fewer than 19 employees generate 10 percent of the manufacturing output, and medium-size businesses contribute more or less the same amount (Hallberg 2000).

SMEs also tend to be more and more global. Their contribution to manufactured exports worldwide is around 25–35 percent (OECD 2000). SMEs tend to be increasingly involved in international strategic alliances and joint ventures on national and international levels. They are adopting Internet technologies and electronic commerce at an unusually fast pace, allowing them easy and fast access to global markets.

---

[3] http://www.cfib.ca/research/reports/jobengine.pdf (04.12.2001).

In developed countries, small businesses often follow a so-called "niche strategy," providing high quality, flexibility, and fast response to customer needs in order to compete with larger enterprises. Many of these small firms are innovative. However, innovations require time and resources that are more often found in larger firms. Nevertheless, approximately 30–60 percent of SMEs are characterized as innovative in the OECD. About 10 percent of small businesses conduct research and development (R&D); they often receive government financing for private sector R&D. Many of them also engage in informal R&D efforts (OECD 2000). The top 5–10 percent of all growing firms are said to be so-called "high-growth SMEs" that are exceptional performers in innovation and job creation. Usually, their job creation rates exceed those of larger companies. They are usually active in knowledge-intensive service sectors and in regions with intense economic activity and clustering. In addition to being innovative, their entrepreneurial spirit is the key to exceptional growth.

Social and Political Contributions

Small businesses represent the initial mechanism by which millions of people enter the economic and social mainstream. In many cases, micro, small, and medium enterprises are the only employment opportunity for the poor. However, microenterprises have a more direct contribution to poverty reduction than SMEs. Small business workers and owners are situated in the lower half of the income distribution; therefore, promoting their growth may lead to a more equitable distribution of income. However, it is unlikely that SME owners and employees are the poorest of the poor. In this context, Hallberg (2000, p. 5) says, "Therefore SME promotion may not be the most effective poverty alleviation instrument." She argues, "The real reason that developing country governments should be interested in microenterprises and SMEs is because they account for a large share of firms and employment—in other words, because they are there" (Hallberg 2000, p. 5). Searching for further justification to promote smallness as an instrument of poverty alleviation is not necessary, it is enough to recognize that microenterprises and SMEs are the emerging private sector in poor countries and thus form the base for private sector–led growth.

Many countries see the development and support of microenterprises and SMEs as their key to reduce poverty and increase growth. One reason is that they believe globalization threatens their local economies unless proactive steps are taken to build the competitiveness of local enterprises. The desire of governments to promote SMEs is often based on political and social considerations because SMEs are a domain of certain ethnic groups or political constituencies.

Access to Finance

This section analyzes the issues, sources, and instruments available to SME finance. First, it discusses the relevance and constraints of the SME business environment for helping SMEs access finance and provides suggestions for improvement. Factors in the business environment include a stable political system, macroeconomic stability, predictable and transparent legal and regulatory framework and enforcement, reasonable tax structures, and a sound and competitive financial sector. Second, it introduces the financial sources and institutions that provide capital to SMEs and describes and discusses the financing instruments available to SMEs.

Business Environment

The regulatory framework constitutes an important aspect of the impact of the environment on SME access to finance (OECD 2000). Regulatory burdens on SMEs originate from regulatory systems developed for larger firms, which have the capacity to benefit from economies of scale and where stability rather than flexibility is the order of the day. Smaller enterprises have less capacity to absorb unproductive expenditures because they have less capital and managerial resources at their disposal. High start-up costs (including licensing and registration requirements), complicated paperwork, high costs of settling legal claims, and long delays in court proceedings affect small enterprises much more than their larger counterparts. The lack of property rights limits SME access to foreign technologies, and the lack of antitrust legislation in many cases favors larger enterprises.

Several countries have made efforts to reduce regulatory burdens for smaller firms. So-called one-stop shops have been established, where businesses can both gather information about all relevant regulations and complete administrative formalities. For instance, in the European Union, the Business Environment Simplification Task Force, adopted in April 1999, has removed, simplified, and standardized legislation in many areas of regulation and has led to a number of instruments promoting reform of SME requirements.

Although regulatory issues in many areas have a major impact on the success and survival of SMEs, there are specific issues regarding regulations that affect the availability of financing for SMEs. Small businesses tend to rely primarily on self-financing, that is, the personal resources of owners. Regulations affect the attractiveness of starting and operating an enterprise and can influence the amount of available financial resources. They can affect the type of financial instruments available to finance new enterprises and so stand in the way of financing the start-up or expansion of enterprises. Taxation can be a heavy burden on SMEs. Therefore, many governments are introducing tax relief or tax incentives for SMEs to encourage investment and research and development. Streamlining tax-related procedures is also essential.

Sources of Finance

The provision of venture capital is crucial to SMEs. The most influential regulations for the development of venture capital or private equity markets are those of the government determining the type of investor eligible for funding venture capital funds and firms. In some countries, pension funds, insurance companies, or other institutions are not permitted to invest in venture capital because it could involve too high a risk for certain classes of investors. Some countries have regulations regarding the liabilities of parties to investment partnerships, which can result in discouraging institutional investing in venture capital funds. Although some of these regulations are useful and necessary to avoid defaults, at the same time they can limit the supply of venture capital funding for SMEs.

In many cases, the underdevelopment of stock markets, particularly secondary markets for smaller firms, stands in the way of stock markets being the major source of SME financing. Registration and listing on stock markets are often too expensive and complicated. The rules for stock exchange listing may require a minimum firm size or age, a certain level of profits, or other enterprise characteristics, which are inappropriate for many SMEs. These regulations need to be tailored in a way that qualification standards for registration are more relaxed, registration procedures simplified, and new pricing methods in place.

The banking sector remains a major source of financing for SMEs. In fact, because of inadequate venture capital resources and inaccessible stock markets, SMEs are often too dependent on bank financing. The lending practices of banks are influenced by the regulations of the financial sector. However, in many cases, banks lack the capacity to evaluate the long-term potential of SMEs or to assess the value of their intangible assets. Banks may require additional collateral, which SMEs may not possess. Banks usually require long-term track records or a minimum level of profit or turnover

as a requirement for receiving credit. Appropriate regulations, providing and distributing information to all key players and thus transparency, would improve the functioning of the credit market.

Business development services (BDS) can significantly contribute to building
the competitiveness of SMEs. Training and consultancy services in financial management, financing methods, and instruments could improve SME access to capital and
finance. However, the demand for BDS among SMEs is relatively low because SMEs
do not recognize the potential benefits of these services or cannot afford expensive
courses or trainers. The government initiatives in Taiwan are a good example of successful financial BDS for SMEs. The Taiwan government invited a group of international
experts to advise SMEs to solidify their financial structure and strengthen their conditions for financing. The experts provide objective opinions to financial institutions considering providing loans to SMEs. The SME Joint Assistance Center provides guidance
in financial management, coordinates among financial institutions in solving funding
problems, assists SMEs in training their financial managers, and compiles publications
on financial management. So far, more than 20,000 SMEs have received assistance and
guidance from the center.[4]

Financing Instruments

Enterprises require differential levels of funding at various points in their life cycle, such
as debt capital, equity financing, or some combination of the two. The combination of
financing depends on many factors, including the size of the firm, its life cycle stage,
and its growth prospects. This section shows that the mechanisms to access capital
depend on specific factors. The analysis focuses on the following factors:

- Destination of funds: equity or debt finance
- Source of funds: internal finance (own funds or retained profit) and external
  finance (private and institutional investors or lenders)
- Period of financing: short-, medium-, or long-term finance.

Table 12-2 shows the different sources of debt and equity financing. For example, in Europe, bank financing dominates the distribution of resources for SMEs
throughout their entire life cycle (table 12-3).

---

[4] See http://www.moeasmea.gov.tw/english/html (October 18, 2001).

Table 12-2 ▍ Sources of Financing for Small and Medium Enterprises

Financing source	Financing characteristics
Debt financing source	
Commercial banks	Smaller companies are likely to obtain financing after their start-up phase from commercial banks. The bank will closely examine credit rating, collateral, ability to repay the loan, nature of the business, management team, competition, industry trends, and strategy.
Commercial finance companies	Companies that cannot obtain a loan from a commercial bank turn to commercial finance companies because they usually have more flexible lending policies and they might be more willing to take risks greater than those of traditional commercial banks. These companies have higher rates than those of institutional lenders, but in many cases companies can negotiate lower rates if they are willing to make use of other chargeable services of the finance company.
Leasing companies	Leasing companies are the source of debt finance for purchasing assets. Instead of borrowing money, enterprises can "rent" money to purchase equipment in the form of either operating or capital leasing. Operating lease includes the money to purchase the asset and a service contract for a certain period of time (usually shorter than the actual useful lifetime of the asset). Operating leases can be canceled with no or a very little penalty. A capital lease differs from an operating lease in that it usually does not include a maintenance contract and involves the use of the purchased equipment over the asset's full useful life.
Government, public funding institutions, and development agencies	There are many public sector entities that offer direct capital or related assistance to SMEs. The lending strategies and conditions of these institutions differ in many ways.
Trade credit and consortiums	Suppliers often have a strong interest in the growth and development of their customers and are willing to provide favorable trade-credit terms or even direct financing to them in order to accelerate their growth. The same principle applies to the customers of a growing company who rely on the company as a key supplier. Customer-related financing often appears in consortiums.
Equity financing source	
Private investors	Private investors often provide equity capital to early-stage companies. These investors are called "angels" or "bands of angels" and are becoming increasingly important as a form of private equity financing.

(Table continues on next page)

Table 12-2 | **Sources of Financing for Small and Medium Enterprises**
| *(continued)*

Financing source	Financing characteristics
Institutional venture capital firms	Venture capital firms are formally organized pools of venture capital. They collect funds from different sources, such as private investors or large enterprises, and allocate them to young enterprises with high growth potential.
Mergers and acquisitions	Mergers and acquisitions (M&As) with "wealthy" companies can also provide an important source of capital for young growing companies. M&As are associated with several structural, legal, and tax issues.
Strategic investors and corporate venture capitalists	There are many large corporations that have established venture capital firms as subsidiaries. These venture capital firms usually look for investment opportunities within their own industries. Their goal is not only the achievement of financial return, but also a strategic objective, such as gaining access to unique technologies.
Intermediaries	Intermediaries (companies or individuals) are not a direct source of equity capital, but they usually assist growing companies in their search for capital through commercial lenders, insurance companies, personal funds, or other institutional sources as well as equity investment by private investors.

Products and Methods in Early-stage Financing

Start-up Financing/Seed Capital

Third-party financial sources require demonstration of the owner's willingness to risk investing in the business. Therefore, traditionally, entrepreneurs use their own resources, usually originating from savings, personal loans, or credit cards, to finance pre-launch expenses and initial seed investment for their business. Entrepreneurs may also obtain the initial capital from family or friends.[5] Starting in the 1990s, so-called "angel investing" has become a critical source of financing for seed and early-stage companies, and its share in providing seed capital has grown significantly. In the United States, researchers at the Center of Venture Research at the University of New Hampshire estimate that 250,000 active "angel investors" invest approximately $20 billion annu-

---

[5] Own resources or resources of family, relatives, or friends ("love money") are an extremely significant source of SME finance and can be structured as either debt or equity finance.

Table 12-3 ▌ Financing According to Life Cycle

Main source of finance	Pre-start-up	Start-up	Early growth	Expansion	Succession	Maturity
Own capital	X	x	x			
Family	X	x	x			
Banks		x	x	X	X	x
Separate SME bank units	X	x	x	X	X	x
Suppliers of substitutes, including banks		x	x	X	X	x
Regional development agencies	X	x	x			
Public funding institutions	X	x	x	X	X	x
Retained profit			x	X	X	x
Informal investors		X	x	X		
Venture capital funds		x	x	X	X	x
Institutional investors				X	X	x
Junior stock markets				X	X	x

ally in some 30,000 ventures; in comparison, in 1998, institutional venture capital funding was estimated to be around $10 billion (Sherman 2000). Business angels usually select companies with high growth potential. There are several different forms of angels or venture funds: nonprofit angel networks, pledge funds, investment clubs, CEO angels, or angels online (Sherman 2000). There are other sources of seed finance, although they might not be utilized as often as the ones mentioned above, for example, business incubators, public agencies, and customer or vendor financing.

Private Placements

Private placement constitutes an important financing strategy available to early-stage companies. It basically means the offering of securities by a small or growing company in a relatively simple and inexpensive way, as it does not have to be registered with the Securities and Exchange Commission or the appropriate authority. Private placement does not require extensive reporting, and therefore the costs are much lower than in the case of IPOs. By contrast, IPOs attract sophisticated investors who might offer certain benefits and industry knowledge to the company and permit rapid penetration into capital markets.

Commercial Lending

During their growth period, most SMEs borrow some amount of funds from a traditional bank loan source. Commercial banks provide operating lines of credit and letters of credit, which are usually categorized according to term, expected use, and amount of the loan. The selection and availability of a specific loan depend on the bank's assessment of the creditworthiness of the applicant and the nature of its industry.

Leasing, Factoring, and Government Programs

When a business does not have the collateral or credit history to qualify for traditional debt financing, it can utilize alternative debt strategies, such as leasing, factoring, or government/public funding institution programs.

Products in Growth Financing

Venture Capital

Venture capital firms are financial intermediaries that collect funds from private or industrial investors and allocate these funds to young enterprises with high growth potential. Venture capital firms invest through funds organized as either limited partnerships in which the venture capital firm is a general partner or independent companies. Often venture capital firms are affiliates or subsidiaries of commercial banks or insurance companies. Corporate ventures or direct investors are affiliates of industrial companies that make investments congruent with the strategic mission of the parent firms. Venture capital firms offer advisory services to the companies they invest in to ensure and accelerate growth. They usually hold the equity for an average period of five to seven years, depending on the business sector. The ultimate goal of the venture capital firm is to sell the equity (on the equity market or through a buyout by a larger corporation) and thus generate capital gain. In order to limit their risk, venture capital firms usually provide financing in stages. Owners of early-stage growing companies often have second thoughts about the institutional venture capital industry: they usually welcome the money and management support, but fear the loss of control and restrictions related to the transaction.

In the United States, more than 800 venture capital firms provide funding to more than 2,200 early-stage, growing companies per year. In 1999, venture capital investment was distributed among businesses as follows (Sherman 2000):

Table 12-4	Capital Managed, 1998–99 (Billions of U.S. dollars)	
Region	1998	1999
United States	332.3	400.0
Europe	79.0	92.0
Asia	29.1	38.3

Source: Dubocage (2000, p. 18).

- 20 percent for early-stage and start-ups
- 60 percent for expansion/high-growth companies
- 20 percent for pre-IPO companies, mergers and acquisitions, later-stage deals, and special situations.

Venture capital has become an important financing tool in Europe; however, private equity sources in the United States still outperform those in Europe. Table 12-4 compares equity under management in Europe, Asia, and the United States in 1998 and 1999.

The growth of the European venture capital market accelerated in the 1990s. The United Kingdom alone represents 45 percent of the European venture capital portfolio, and France and Germany are the next largest markets (Yli-Renko and Hay 1999). Despite recent growth, the venture capital market is still rather limited. Venture capital firms receive a high number of proposals, the vast majority of which remain unread or rejected. And venture capital is expensive: a typical venture capitalist demands around 40 percent of the equity in a company.

Initial Public Offering

The first public equity issue that a company makes is referred to as an initial public offering, or IPO. Many entrepreneurs consider the process of going public as the top of financial success. However, an IPO requires great strategic planning and analysis from both legal and business perspectives. As with other financing mechanisms, going public has its advantages and disadvantages (table 12-5).

Direct Public Offering

Direct public offering (DPO) is a primary market stock or debenture sale of securities from the company issuing the shares to the public. It may represent an alterna-

Table 12-5 | Advantages and Disadvantages of Going Public

Advantages	Disadvantages
Greater access to capital. An initial public offering provides a certain amount of immediate capital that can be utilized for many purposes, such as fixed assets, working capital, research and development, and repayment of existing debts.	One-time and ongoing expenses. There are many significant expenses in connection with an IPO and later on in connection with administrative and reporting requirements.
Increased market value. Due to their liquidity, available information, and ascertained value, public companies tend to be more valuable than private companies.	Volatility. The company's value is more affected by the state of the economy and the stock market.
Exit strategy. Liquidity and greater shareholder value may be achieved subject to certain restrictions. Shareholders may sell their stock in the public market over time; existing stock may also be used as collateral.	Pressure for short-term performance. The management of a public company is under constant pressure to balance short-term demands with strategies that achieve long-term goals; if the company does not meet the expectations of analysts with regard to short-term earnings, it can seriously hurt the company's long-term valuation on the market.
Equity advantages. An IPO results in an immediate increase in the company's net worth and facilitates financing due to an improved debt-equity ratio.	Sharing of financial success with shareholders.
Enhanced reputation, prestige, and public image. Public companies receive more and broader attention and with time acceptance from the investment community and customers.	Loss of privacy. A public company immediately becomes subject to periodic reporting; sensitive areas of disclosure are available to competitors, customers, and employees, such as compensation of officers and directors and the security holdings of officers, directors, and major shareholders.
Ability to attract and keep key personnel. Flexibility of employee ownership and participation.	Dilution of control. If more than 50 percent of the company's shares are sold to just a few outside individuals, the original owners could lose control of the company.
Less dilution. If conditions permit, the company may achieve a better price and less dilution in comparison to other forms of equity financing.	Compliance with complex regulations.
Opportunities for mergers and acquisitions. Going public may raise a lot of cash for acquisitions but also create liquidity that can be used to buy other companies	Risk. If an IPO is unsuccessful, the company must bear the costs.

tive to a traditional IPO. The issuer performs the underwriting structuring, filing, and selling of its offer without the underwriter and selling syndicate that is used in an IPO. DPOs are gaining popularity on the Internet, especially in the United States, due to the rise of e-commerce and online investors.

Small and Medium Enterprise Markets

Definition and Scope

The jury is still out on the accomplishments attained by stock exchanges dedicated to serve SMEs and the extent to which they have been successful in bringing SMEs to the capital market. On one side, there is support for the notion that, especially in emerging economies, stock exchanges are particularly relevant in helping medium-size indigenous firms gain access to finance and supporting local market development. On the other side, there are doubts that suggest that the very nature of SMEs makes them unsuitable to access capital markets. A related implication for the first perspective, which is being borne out by the evidence, is that large firms find international listing, such as American Depository Receipts and Global Depository Receipts, the best form of accessing capital markets. This section reviews some of the evidence and examples of stock exchanges that have been dedicated to SMEs and their different levels of success.

An SME stock market, established as either a separate or integrated market, is an exchange facility specially designed and operated for the listing and trading of the securities of small and mid-size companies. According to an International Federation of Stock Exchanges (FIBV) study on small and medium-size business markets, such a market may have multiple objectives (Schulman 1999):

- Provide a nursing ground for small and medium companies and allow them to expand until they are large enough for the main market
- Stimulate the regional economy by creating new paths for capital intermediation and motivating individuals and institutions to invest in the local economy and increase their interest in those markets
- Transform the local economy by giving local businesses the stimulus for growth and the larger perspective that comes from managing a public company
- Open the economy, enhancing the efficiency of capital transfers within the private business sector and causing local businesses and investors to think and behave more actively and globally

- Maintain the commercial viability of stock exchanges in order to survive long-term economic and market cycles and allow businesses to raise capital continuously by trading their shares.

Types of Markets

Some exchanges have established more than one SME stock market using either sector or market gap divisions with the intention of separating them by risk. The Helsinki Stock Exchange, for instance, separates its SME market by sectors: the New Market List is for young, fast-growing, and small high-tech companies; and the Investors' List (previously the OTC List and Brokers' List) is for other SMEs. The main purpose is to distinguish between higher- and slower-growing sectors. This solution usually attracts investor attention to the young, high-risk, but fast-growing companies, and so in some cases it can be rather disadvantageous for those companies that are listed on the other market, which might be neglected by investors. A market division by market capitalization usually serves to help investors distinguish between micro, early-stage, high-risk companies and established, small and medium-size, lower-risk companies.

An interesting solution for a subdivided SME market is the Deutsche Bourse's example, which represents a hybrid segmentation of both sector and market capitalization:

- SMAX, established in 1999, is a small-cap segment for micro blue chips.
- Neuer Markt (New Market), established in March 1997, is an IPO segment for high-growth companies involving admission according to the rules of the regulated market, but offering trading in the third segment (the regulated unofficial market).

Another interesting example is the Australian Stock Exchange, which, on one hand, allows the listing of small-cap stocks on its main exchange and, on the other hand, created a so-called Enterprise Market as a seed funding market in 1998. In terms of company size, it is probably one of the smallest SME markets and in many respects might not even be considered a proper market because companies do not officially list or trade on it. It is an Internet-based market that brings together companies offering investment opportunities, potential investors, and a business network of advisors. Here companies need a prospectus and operate without securities commission regulation. These businesses do not list; they simply publish their investment opportunity to the investment community. Once the business succeeds in attracting an investor, it begins private negotiations with the potential investor. The negotiation is done face-to-face, but the establishment of the market is online.

Benefits

A notable aspect of the establishment of SME markets is the issue of competition with other sources of financing. Some exchanges face competition from private equity or other forms of financing available for SMEs, but at the same time, many exchanges see private equity as the seed round of financing. For the latter exchanges, the SME market is either a funding option at a later funding stage or an actual exit strategy for private equity and thus complementary to other forms of financing. In fact, a well-functioning SME market helps exchanges, investors, the SMEs, and the economy in the following ways (Schulman 1999):

- SME markets serve as a breeding ground for new listing on the main market.
- A wider range of equity investment vehicles helps establish better sector strategies and enhances investors' opportunities.
- The economy benefits from the link that SME markets provide for the capital flow from local and foreign investors into SMEs.

According to Schulman's (1999) study, as perceived by exchanges, listing shares present the following advantages for SMEs:

- Accelerate the future development of the company
- Make it easier to attract and keep talented employees by making share option incentives easier to implement
- Ease tax burdens (in some countries, the inheritance of private companies can often be a problem for families)
- Diversify funding sources and thus provide financial flexibility
- Improve the profile and commercial visibility of the company.

Special Characteristics

The design of SME markets depends on several factors, such as the political and economic environment, available exchange systems, and the legal and regulatory framework. The majority of SME markets have easier market admittance rules than the main markets. The listing requirements for SME markets are usually lower in the following:

- Market capitalization
- Percentage of free-floating shares
- Number of shareholders needed
- Minimum number of shares floated
- Number of years of operation or audited accounts.

SME markets differ in their transparency requirements. Although a minimum level of transparency is required, most exchanges also believe that more stringent disclosure rules for an SME outweigh the costs because of the comfort and confidence they give to the market. As for initial investor ownership rules, some markets strive for a higher and faster distribution of initial ownership in order to increase the number of free-floating shares and thus enhance liquidity. By contrast, other markets want to ensure that the initial investors remain vested in the success of their IPO and therefore block the sell-off of insider shares.

Another important issue is the cost of listing for SMEs on their markets. Most SME markets charge an initial one-time fee (flat, scaled, or a combination) when a company first lists on the exchange and also charge an annual listing fee. An exception is Ireland's Developing Companies and Exploration Securities Market, which levies no introduction or annual fee. However, the associated costs of listing (lawyers, accountants, bankers, and notaries) are usually the most expensive part of the listing procedure.

Liquidity is another important issue for SME markets, many of which do not have minimum volume requirements for the continuance of listing. The most common requirement set by SME exchanges is the appointment of a market-maker/liquidity provider. Liquidity providers (specialists or market makers) are used for keeping bid-ask spreads low and promoting turnover. Furthermore, in some markets, it is the explicit responsibility of the liquidity provider to improve the information flow on the listed company. The use of liquidity providers is an old, proven technology: it creates advantages for issuers and investors as well as for the liquidity providers.

Beyond offering trading systems that have a positive effect on liquidity, exchanges offer several other services to their SME clients:

- Presentation and creation of media attention and publicity for the SME market and its companies at different forums

- Pre- and post-listing educational programs for issuers
- Research promotion on SMEs
- Creation of indices
- Knowledge distribution, mainly for potential investors.

New Markets in Europe

After the success of NASDAQ in attracting young, innovative, and high-growth companies, many European exchanges decided to establish similar markets. By the end of 2001, there were 20 new markets aimed at young, high-growth, and mostly technology-focused enterprises. These European markets have not been as successful as NASDAQ because many of them have failed to attract an appropriate number of issuers, and others have suffered from regulation, risk, or liquidity issues. The growth of all markets has slowed down, which most likely will affect the smaller markets that are widely considered more risky. In 2000, all markets suffered from the decline of technology stocks. In 2001, the decline halted and a slow recovery began, followed by uncertainties linked with the terrorist attacks of September 11. Table 12-6 gives an overview of the new markets in Europe as of the end of 2001 (Grant Thornton 2002).

Evaluation

Many of the exchanges established their SME markets for competitive reasons, such as marketing purposes, and not all of them operate under the explicit goal of profitability. SME markets are often viewed simultaneously as incubators for the main market and as legitimate and important capital markets in their own right.

In 2002, only 3 percent of the total SME sector and only 10 percent of medium-size companies in Europe considered flotation as an option in the foreseeable future. In fact, half of the SMEs indicated that they were not going to seek a change of ownership in the foreseeable future. Most SMEs seek a change of ownership in a period of three-to-five years and show two preferences: trade sale and passing the business to the next generation. However, for medium-size businesses, there are two options that are ranked higher relative to the overall SME sector: private equity investors are 22 percent compared with 15 percent, and flotation is 10 percent compared with 3 percent (Grant Thornton 2002).

It is somewhat difficult to prove the success of small and medium enterprise markets because only limited data are available and little evaluation has been made so far. Schulman (1999, p. 12) claims that the "responses to the FIBV's [Small and

Table 12-6 | **Small and Medium Enterprise Markets in Europe**

Country (year of establishment)	City	New market	Number of listed companies	Market cap (€)
Belgium (2000)	Brussels	NASDAQ Europe	50	8 bn
Czech Republic (1999)	Prague	Prague SE New Market	0	0
Denmark (2000)	Copenhagen	KVX Growth Market	13	1 bn
Finland (1998)	Helsinki	HEX New Markt	16	437 m
France (1996)	Paris	Nouveau Marché (Euronext)	164	15 bn
Germany (1997)	Frankfurt	Neuer Markt	327	50 bn
Greece (2001)	Athens	Athens SE (NEXA)	1	50 m
Iceland (2001)	Reykjavik	ICEX Alternative Market	3	472 m
Ireland (1997)	Dublin	Developing Companies Market	4	34 m
Italy (1999)	Milan	Nuovo Mercato	45	13 bn
Malta (2001)	Valletta	Alternative Companies List	1	28 m
Netherlands (1997)	Amsterdam	EuroNM Amsterdam (Euronext)	9	268 m
Poland (2000)	Warsaw	Warsaw SE (SiTECH/TechWIG)	21	7 bn
Slovak Republic (2000)	Bratislava	Bratislava SE New Market	0	0
Spain (2000)	Madrid	Nuevo Mercado	13	17 bn
Switzerland (1999)	Zurich	Swiss Exchange New Market	15	4 bn
Sweden (1998)	Stockholm	Stockholmsborsen New Market	22	291 m
Sweden (2000)	Stockholm	Nordic Growth Market	55	301 m
United Kingdom (1995)	London	AIM	629	19 bn
United Kingdom (1999)	London	TechMARK	246	693 bn

Source: Grant Thornton (2002).

Medium-size Business] Questionnaire strongly indicate that SMEs are benefiting from coming to the market." Another study, carried out by Grant Thornton (2002) on new markets in Europe, ranks the perceived benefits of flotation only by medium-size companies. According to this study, 41 percent named "availability of capital" as the most important benefit of being listed (see table 12-7).

Table 12-8 shows Grant Thornton's (2002) ranking of the barriers to flotation. More than 40 percent of the SMEs in the sample considered company size to be the main barrier to listing. They believed they needed to be larger to float. For many companies, floating lacks relevance, and they find the procedure far too time-consuming.

New markets have sprung up across Europe over the past few years, although some of these markets are so young that they only have a few, if any, companies listed. The most active European markets are AIM, NASDAQ Europe, Neuer Markt, Nordic Growth Market, Nouveau Marché, Nuovo Mercato, and techMARK. The indices of these markets grew steadily during 1999 when the technology and dotcom sector

Table 12-7	Benefits of Floating for Medium-Size Companies	
Benefit		**Percent**
Availability of capital		41
Acquisition opportunities		23
Higher profile		22
Cost of capital		12
Exit opportunities		11
None		11
Options granted to employees		8

Source: Grant Thornton (2002).

Table 12-8	Barriers to Floatation for Medium-Size Companies	
Barrier		**Percent**
Size of company		44
Not relevant		36
Time-consuming		20
Entry criteria		15
Equity dilution		15
Expense		15
Low market valuations		10
Lack of liquidity		9
Vetting by exchange		4

was booming in both Europe and the United States. The boom in these sectors continued, although a drop in stock values followed, until September 2000, when international markets began to lose confidence in dotcom companies and many of them went out of business.

In terms of the number of companies listed, AIM has been the most successful market for small and medium-size enterprises in Europe. It had 324 companies listed in 1999, 437 in 2000, and 580 in 2001 (for comparison purposes, NASDAQ had 4,396 listed companies during the same period). By the end of 2001, the Neuer Markt had 310 listed companies. However, the market capitalization of these companies was much higher than that of those on AIM (Grant Thornton 2002). Certain companies on the markets have an unusually high market capitalization that can lead to a distortion of the overall picture. According to Grant Thornton (2002), in terms of adjusted

Table 12-9 ▍ Market Capitalization

Market	Average market capitalization per company
Neuer Markt	88
NASDAQ Europe	54
Nouveau Marché	44
Nordic Growth Market	29
AIM	7

(not considering companies with a market capitalization of at least 10 times higher than the median) total market capitalization in 2001, Neuer Markt took first place with 29 billion euro; followed by Nouveau Marché, with 7 billion euro; Nordic Growth Market and NASDAQ Europe, each with 3 billion euro; and AIM, with 2 billion euro (Grant Thornton 2002). The average market capitalization in 2001 per company is presented in table 12-9 (Grant Thornton 2002).

In spite of the fact that NASDAQ has a very high market capitalization, its liquidity (turnover of shares as a percentage of total market capitalization) is not so much different from that of some of the new markets in Europe that are considerably smaller. Nuovo Mercato and techMARK proved to be the most liquid new markets in the past few years (Grant Thornton 2002).

Conclusion and Recommendations

The chapter has shown that there are a wide variety of perspectives on the overall role of SMEs in economic growth. SMEs are usually seen as the key to job creation, and therefore high emphasis is placed on policies that promote entrepreneurship and competitiveness and enhance SME access to finance.

In order to analyze the role of capital markets in SME financing, it is necessary to look at the broader issue of the factors affecting SME access to finance. Therefore, a more holistic perspective, which includes an examination of the relevance of other financing instruments, would appear insightful. The key policy conclusion of the chapter pertains to the differential financing needs and capacities of SMEs along their life cycle. The challenges SMEs face depend on the stage in their growth. For the specific case of capital markets, there is no firm indication that dynamic capital markets would not be the most appropriate mechanism to support SME access to capital. It is certain that both effective and dynamic capital markets and healthy and strong SMEs contribute to economic success and that one can certainly help to facilitate the other. However, while there is no certain causality between these two factors, it is understood that dynamic capital markets can serve as catalysts to create and feed the presence of active private equity and thus support enterprise development.

Under these circumstances, policymakers should avoid designing and implementing capital market solutions for an SME environment that is not ready yet for that form of financing. It would be a misplaced effort and ill-directed resources. Indeed, policymakers must understand that SMEs need appropriate support, including financing in order to grow, compete, and contribute substantially to economic growth. The financial support must be adequate to the stage of development of the SMEs.

In the early stages of their development, particularly in emerging countries, SMEs are generally less prepared to access the capital market and risk capital. However, seed capital, private placements, commercial lending, leasing, and government programs are applicable. For SMEs, and particularly medium-size enterprises, access to capital markets and risk capital might be more pertinent for those in the growth stage. At that point, venture funding, limited debt offerings, and IPOs are likely possibilities. Moreover, the existence of a capital market constitutes an incentive to investors to make the company grow so they can reap the benefits with a sale or IPO in the market. This leads to the additional consideration that, to be effective, capital market access has to be tailor made, appeal to various risk profiles, but still not compromise the basic need of transparency and disclosure. However, prior to accessing these instruments, the enhancement of institutional capacity for these enterprises has to be addressed, as well as the need to prepare these companies to appropriately access this type of financing.

The chapter has reviewed the specific barriers SMEs face to access risk capital, utilizing the case of SME stock exchanges in Europe as a reference. Although risk equity markets have not served as the primary source for SME finance in general, the example of Europe demonstrates that the barriers SMEs face could impose a serious problem for the development of high-growth companies in capital-intensive sectors. In Europe, these markets are often too small, have strict and complex regulatory requirements, and lack liquidity. Some of the great success stories are high-tech, high-growth firms in the United States that are backed by active and strong venture capital and junior public markets as well as NASDAQ. It is important to note that NASDAQ serves an international clientele: from the approximately 5,000 listed companies, more than 500 are foreign, over 140 of them are indeed European. At the same time, in spite of the wide proliferation of new markets in Europe, companies looking for finance do not have many real choices. Domestic markets generally offer the best environment for raising capital. The establishment of a pan-European supervisory and regulatory body for stock exchanges would be a first step toward their much-needed consolidation, followed by the harmonized set of trading rules for all markets and a fully integrated trading, clearing, and settlement system.

The lessons drawn from the European experience and the conclusions of the chapter are relevant for emerging Latin American and Caribbean economies. Underdeveloped stock markets in many countries, specifically secondary markets for SMEs, often limit their ability to be a major source of SME financing. Regulatory requirements can be somewhat complicated or sometimes inappropriate for small companies. Furthermore, they often result in costs that could be onerous for SMEs. In general, to enhance capital market financing of SMEs, some reform of the regulatory requirements pertinent to capital markets must be considered to make them more relevant for SMEs.

Lessons can also be drawn from the venture funds market. Comparing the venture capital markets in Europe and the United States, it is evident that the fundraising processes are quite different. The actual amount involved and the size of the funds seem to be much higher in the United States. Europe raises annually about €20 billion, compared with $84 billion in the United States. It is also clear that U.S. investors have a much greater opportunity to IPO their investment than do their European counterparts or other investors in countries with less well-developed capital markets. This naturally has a strong effect on SME finance as a whole and encourages the recycling of funds into new investments. This component, along with a simpler regulatory framework, facilitates and enhances the development and functioning of private equity and venture capital markets and thus SME access to capital. Many countries are currently reviewing the regulations that govern their private equity and venture capital markets and are considering loosening their restrictions. A good starting point would be for governments to seek an appropriate and healthy balance between the interest of investors and that of SMEs seeking finance.

The chapter has indicated that there is evidence that SMEs face major barriers to finance in general and capital markets specifically. Clearly, the timing of stock market development for SMEs is the crucial issue for making the traditional stock exchange more relevant for SMEs. In this respect, specific actions to help increase SME access to financing should be tailored to SME needs and could include harmonizing measures to improve the structural, economic, but most importantly regulatory conditions for the participation of financial intermediaries, issuers, and private and institutional investors. This would have at some stage the added positive outcome of making many local capital markets more relevant and able to attain their true potential to serve those enterprises that are at a stage to access risk capital.

Bibliography

Davis, Stephen J., John Haltiwanger, and Scott Schuh. 1993. *Small Business and Job Creation: Dissecting the Myth and Reassessing the Facts.* Working Paper 4492. National Bureau of Economic Research, Cambridge, Mass. (October).

Dubocage, E. 2000. *Financing Innovation by Venture Capital in Europe and in the USA: A Comparative and Sectoral Approach.* Paris (France): TSER.

European Commission. 1996. Recommendation. *Official Journal of Law* 107. Brussels (Belgium): European Commission (April 3).

_____. 1998. *3rd Annual Report on Small and Medium Enterprises.* Brussels (Belgium): European Commission.

European Observatory for SMEs. 2000. *Sixth Annual Report 2000, Executive Summary.* Luxembourg (Belgium): European Observatory for SMEs.

Grant Thornton. 2002. *European New Markets Guide 2002.* London (United Kingdom): Grant Thornton.

Hallberg, K. 2000. *A Market-Oriented Strategy for Small and Medium-Scale Enterprises.* Washington, D.C.: World Bank and International Finance Corporation.

Haltiwanger, John. 1999. Job Creation and Destruction: Cyclical Dynamics. In Acs Zoltan, Bo Carlsson, and Charlie Karlsson, eds., *Entrepreneurship, Small and Medium-Sized Enterprises, and the Macroeconomy.* New York: Cambridge University Press.

OECD. 2000. *Small and Medium Enterprise Outlook.* Paris (France): OECD.

Schulman, Michael Ashley. 1999. *Small and Medium Size Business Markets. An FIBV Working Committee Focus Group Study.* Paris (France): International Federation of Stock Exchanges.

Sherman, Andrew J. 2000. *Raising Capital. Get the Money You Need to Grow Your Business.* New York: Kiplinger.

Yli-Renko, Helena, and Michael Hay. 1999. European Venture Capital. An Overview. In William D. Bygrave, Michael Hay, and Jos B. Peeters, eds., *The Venture Capital Handbook.* Great Britain: Pearson Education Ltd.

CHAPTER 13

Developing Capital Markets in Latin America and the Caribbean: Ethical Issues

Osvaldo R. Agatiello

Trust and similar values, loyalty and truth-telling, are examples of what the economist would call 'externalities.' They are goods, they are commodities; they have real, practical, economic value; they increase the efficiency of the system . . . But they are not commodities for which trade on the open market is technically possible or even meaningful.
Arrow (1974, p. 23)

There are more than one reason and way to explain why every economy south of the Rio Grande is a developing one. It is obviously not a question of size because at least three Latin American countries rank among the first quintile of nations in terms of gross national product. It would only be natural that their capital markets radiated their influence on the subregions of Central America and the Caribbean, the Andean arc, and the Southern Cone, respectively. It is not a question of longevity because, at least in the case of the larger Latin American economies, most of their stock exchanges were established during the second half of the nineteenth century. But, arguably, the only two consolidated capital markets in the Western Hemisphere, in terms of both market capitalization per capita and depth, are those of the United States and Canada, and only the former exerts a commanding influence across the region.

One or two exceptions can be argued for, but even then queries of contestability (favoritism, information imperfections, and market reserves) and transparency (money laundering and other forms of underground economic activity) loom large in the collective psyche of economic agents. The impact of fractious instability in international financial and commodity markets or internal security concerns can disrupt their best intentions of nurturing built-in stabilizers of intertemporal trust, as the attention of policymakers becomes dominated by crisis management. Impaired personal security, for instance, which currently affects many urban centers across the region, is an urgent priority. Whether resulting from protracted civil wars or common crime, assassinations, kidnappings, destruction and unlawful occupation of private property, and similar violations of the public order are commanding signals in the wrong direction. Closely related to the performance of the banking, insurance, and foreign trade sectors, capital markets in Latin America and the Caribbean vie for a clientele that is too frequently pushed away by macroeconomic instability and permanently pulled away by the lure of international private bankers and other investment managers.

Is the underdevelopment of the capital markets of Latin America and the Caribbean the result of lack of appropriate rules, standards, and levels of professionalism? Would the solution lie in the introduction of corrective mechanisms—a set of practices, institutions, and structures—that have proved to work in more mature capital markets? Or is underdevelopment the result of macroeconomic distortions, so that taking care of fundamentals should suffice to foster growth? Or do cultural impediments—ethical, religious, or psychosocial—stand in the way? Looking forward, is it a question of years, decades, or generations before a substantial change for the better can realistically be expected?

This chapter suggests that the introduction of more ambitious ethical methods of analysis and reasoning can offer some practical solutions and ways forward to these conundrums. It discusses the role of ethics in the marketplace, analyzes the need to have a suitable moral framework as an underpinning to the workings of open markets, and recommends an ethical agenda for policymakers and development experts in Latin America and the Caribbean. For all their importance, the chapter does not address the gross legal violations of criminal law and judicial and administrative enforcement, like administrative and political corruption, false accounting, insider trading, or fraudulent collusions. Instead, it discusses the moral dilemmas, the gray areas of impropriety, free riding, and devious manipulation that so perniciously affect confidence and efficiency in the open markets and in civilized society.

Ethics in the Marketplace

As they do for all markets, the goods in trade (their price and quality), the sellers (their information), the buyers (their money), and the professionals (their professionalism and trustworthiness) shape capital markets. With so many actors and interests at play, the marketplace cannot be construed as either a lyceum for model ethics or a morality-free zone. The most intuitive notions of fairness and predictability—justice as regularity—may be nurtured through the workings of free markets. The business world is fundamentally cooperative, and markets foster sociability by providing the opportunity for people to work together without coercion, which in turn further spreads cooperation habits. And, as the ability to cooperate is dependent on ingrained habits, traditions, and norms, these very elements serve to build the market itself through a sort of reflexive equilibrium between the general principles and challenges posed by real-life dilemmas (Solomon 1993).

This means that market cultures are influenced by the kinds of real people who participate in them as well as their experiences, which explain, even in a world of converging standards, the peculiarities and particularities of each single market. To a large extent, operative ethics depends on learning-by-doing in the marketplace, so that trade itself serves as a teacher and sometimes a promoter of the virtues of integrity, honesty, trustworthiness, responsibility, and prudence (Etzioni 1996; McCloskey 1998). More often than not, the moral intuitions of market actors are formed not on the basis of explicit rules, but out of ethical habits and reciprocal moral obligations internalized through quotidian interaction (Fukuyama 1995). Liberal tradition claims that concepts such as fairness, impartiality, mutual respect, and reasonableness can be defined in ways not hostage to partisan agendas and that the market gives them a fair chance to become operative (Fish 1999). Indeed, honesty, integrity, reliability, and confidence—all values associated with trust—are moral concepts that express the core of normative ethics, which is to do no harm to others, respect the rights of others (be fair and just), refrain from lying or cheating (be honest), keep promises (be faithful), and obey the law (Goodpaster 1997; Kagan 1998; Mill 1998).[1]

Capital markets have a long-standing tradition of self-regulation. For example, Federal Reserve System (2002) sets out the ethical requirements for operating in the United States. Financial institutions are directed to establish their own comprehensive rules of conduct and ethical standards for the activities of their agents. Their policies and standards should specifically address conflicts of interest, confidentiality, insider trading, proper oversight, trading restrictions, internal controls, external audits, ethical training, and related matters, all in accordance with the applicable laws and regulations, industry conventions, and other established policies in the United States. Numerous professionals intervene in trading, recording and reporting, information processing,

---

[1] Diversity and multiplicity in the national and international communities pose mountainous challenges to the discipline of normative ethics. Establishing ethical "bridgeheads" with the world of economics and business, which drives the globalization process, is one of the most urgent and complex (Enderle 2002).

sales and marketing, legal and contractual, accounting and auditing, research analysis, asset management, advisory relationships, and many other activities, with varying degrees of discretionary authority. Be they accountants, attorneys, notaries, company and trust formation agents, or other licensed professionals, they are mandated to comply with the codes of ethics and professional standards that govern their respective professions as well as with the requirements of continuing ethical education in the jurisdictions where they are admitted to practice.[2] Consider the business conduct and suitability rules of the National Association of Securities Dealers for registered dealer-brokers, the American Bar Association professional responsibility rules and standards and model rules of professional conduct for attorneys and judges, and the code of professional conduct of the American Institute of Certified Public Accountants, among others. Similar guidelines and regulations apply in other capital markets, expressing a delicate balance between the punitive power of the controlling authorities and the moral voice of the professional communities.

Codes have a tradition of institutionalizing ethics into culture that dates back to the third millennium B.C. A professional code establishes standards of practice for a particular group, whether by describing appropriate existing practice or by instituting new ones. It is a higher morality in terms of gradation of moral conscience—that of voluntarily adopting a set of stricter-than-customary moral standards in order to be recognized as a full-fledged member (Ryan 1997; Davis 1997).[3]

Thus, professional careers can be viewed as social functions that carry general, group, and personal rights and obligations. On one hand, professions are a unique social product, organized and financed at great cost to society. On the other, individual professionals are required to dedicate themselves to satisfying the (legitimate) requirements of their particular clients. This creates multiple fiduciary relationships (professional-client, professional-profession, and professional-community), with conflict-

---

[2] Requirements of the latter sort are virtually nonexistent across Latin America and the Caribbean.

[3] Kohlberg (1981) suggests that moral development can be classified according to levels (pre-conventional, conventional, post-conventional), stages, behaviors, and attitudes. The pre-conventional level includes the stages of punishment and obedience and instrumental relativism. The conventional level includes the stages of social conformity and order and legality. The post-conventional level includes the stages of social contract and universal principles. The corresponding attitudes are avoiding punishment and obeying power blindly; pragmatically satisfying one's own needs; pleasing others to obtain their approval; submitting to an impartial, orderly regime of social, legal, or religious norms; defining right and wrong after rationally arriving at social utility considerations; and deciding what is just by applying individually chosen principles. Kohlberg's research shows that individuals' ethical intuitions rarely go beyond one stage above or below the average morality of their societies, that progress from one stage to the next takes several years of maturation, and that progress can be accelerated through ethical training (Colby and Kohlberg 1987). In other words, societies as much as individuals also grow (or regress) in moral terms. Within this context, at a post-conventional moral level, a social contract stage must be reached for capital markets (and democracies) to prosper.

ing values and loyalties invariably at play. And perceiving professional relationships from an integrated moral perspective sheds light on the practical nature of ethical analysis. For example, no capital market is so advanced that the nonoccurrence of insider trading, unfaithful accounting, or abuse of authority (all departures from usual professional standards, good faith, and common decency) can be taken for granted, as recent scandals have made clear in the United States, Europe, and Japan.[4] Professional cultures are formed over time, by events big and small that determine how individual agents and groups behave when not being watched. Moreover, whether the behavior of professionals is close to the ethical expectations of society largely depends on the moral framework of each given community.

A Suitable Moral Framework

The formation of professional character is a social and moral commitment to build trust that requires much more than codes of ethics and tribunals of conduct. Society delegates to the professions the responsibility to guard their segment of the public interest, with the privileges and benefits that self-government entails; and society revokes such mandate when negligence, temerity, or disorder become apparent. This retraction may be implicit in the statutory reforms that enhance accountability standards and make more rigorous the penalties for noncompliance. Examples abound, and in all cases, the moral commitment required should be understood in its modest sense, that is, not requiring supererogatory behavior that, above and beyond the call of duty, would be expected from heroes and saints rather than from ordinary market agents (Baron 1997).

   Ethics codes apply to adults who have manifold visions of the world, values, attitudes, habits, ways of processing and interpreting information, prejudices, and, usually, limited formal education in applied ethics (Sembor and Leighninger 1993). Professional ethics training normally restricts itself to discussion of the standards and practices of the respective professions rather than to the free examination of more complex ethical paradigms. There are ethics of principles, ethics of conflicts, and professional ethics, which is a subcategory of the other two. Demand grows by the day for business ethics, a kind of applied ethics, to go beyond the questions of institutions

---

[4] Smith (1979, bk. 1, ch. 11) expresses this sentiment when pointing out, "The interest of the dealers . . . is never exactly the same with that of the public, who have generally an interest to deceive and even to oppress the public, and who accordingly have, upon many occasions, both deceived and oppressed it."

and rules, and individual and organizational behavior. Business ethics is being called to foster a multi-tiered approach that encompasses the roles, responsibilities, and inter-actions of persons, organizations, and systems in a highly complex system of multiple actors and overlapping sets of rules. The fact that transactions have become more in-tricate and speedy, and that businesses interrelate more widely and deeply than ever before, cannot escape moral analysis and discussion (Enderle 2003). Moreover, in this process, it becomes necessary to separate considerations of individual or group in-terest from respect for the ethical order and its demands. For it is precisely when duty prevails over interest that morality has a *raison d'être* and an overarching role in civi-lized life (Gauthier 1986; Hausman 1989).[5] This rational decision at the individual, group, and system levels may be the single most important step toward building trust in the markets in the long run.

While social morality is interested in collective behavior (interest), religious morality is concerned with the internal dimension of individual behavior (virtue). Ra-tional morality does not disavow either, but aims at governing and interpreting altruis-tic, egoistic, or indifferent behaviors through the lens of rationality (duty). Social moral-ity is minimally expressed in the legal morality contained in positive law, especially as minutely described in criminal law. Genuinely engaging in practical ethics exercises to try to resolve moral dilemmas is a prolonged, demanding, and costly effort, which sel-dom suffices per se to control some behaviors (Etzioni 1996; Kagan 1989). This process includes recognizing moral issues through increased ethical awareness and sensitivity, sharpening analytical skills, finding ways to sort out specific disagreements, ideally af-fecting the decisions and behaviors of participants and their milieus, and eventually trusting the judgment of others (Callahan 1997; Carter 1998). This sequence is not capricious, but rather a methodology refined over the course of centuries, indepen-dent of the moral viewpoint (virtue-based, duty-based, rights-based, or interest-based), the perception and interpretation of the facts, and the loyalties involved. In the follow-ing list, the first three steps are aimed at overcoming the deeply ingrained reaction of taking refuge in neutrality or pretended tolerance to escape hard decisions:

- *Recognizing moral issues* requires specialized training, particularly when those issues—people's welfare, sentiments, characters, relationships, and obligations—go unnoticed.

---

[5] With impeccable elegance, Cicero (1913, vol. III, p. iv) warns us that "those . . . who measure everything by a stan-dard of profits and personal advantage and refuse to have these outweighed by considerations of moral rectitude are accustomed, in considering any question, to weigh the morally right against what they think the expedient; good men are not."

- *Developing moral imagination* requires a further commitment, that is, putting oneself in other people's shoes or discarding conventional wisdom, like in the case of discriminated minorities, disadvantaged economic actors, or conflicting values.
- *Honing analytical and critical skills*, by examining arguments, evidence, and logical relationships, requires exploring common grounds with others and finding reasons to rule out some behaviors and not others.
- *Finding ways to sort out disagreements* includes knowing how to live with the residues of disagreement that inevitably result from clashes of value orders, religious persuasions, interpretations of facts, and the like.
- *Affecting our decisions and behaviors and those of others*, applied ethics is interested in contributing to processes and procedures that yield rationally advanced and, above all, practical solutions for the real world.

Surely there are costs associated with strictly adhering to moral rules and processing relevant decisions through the prism of ethics, but the enforcement of property rights is not cost-free either. In both cases, the overall benefits surely exceed the costs of making them possible. Thus, moral analysis can be perceived as a means of putting ethical principles to work in order to find a just, proper, fair, and dynamic equilibrium between self-interest and the interest of others, between "us" and "them" (Hosmer 1997). The predictability and rationality that ethical analysis helps introduce becomes a practical tool for policymakers, professional associations, and market agents to nurture a virtuous circle of trust buildup.

A company or industry's voluntary introduction of new layers of accounting control, beyond statutory exigencies and generally accepted accounting principles, with the aim of proudly showing *erga omnes* its commitment to transparency and accountability, is less rare than conventional wisdom has it. For instance, the hotel industry introduced into its uniform accounting and financial reporting system the notion of RevPAR, a performance metric of the total guestroom revenue per available room per day that is applicable all over the world. This not only benefits investors and companies, but also other stakeholders, like employees, customers, and suppliers, whose interests are elevated *pari passu* by this new, overall wave of increased transparency.

Trust

The advanced capital market forces agents to care about their reputation because successful performance is inextricably linked to the ethical behaviors prescribed in a number of professional standards, such as codes of conduct and model rules. Trust in this context may be defined as the rational expectation of ethically justifiable behavior, that is, morally correct decisions based on established ethical principles of analysis and action. Trust is both result and constitutive element of decisions and actions that simultaneously take into account self-interest and the interest of others.[6] Controls and reviews, although necessary, are expensive substitutes for trust, and it is their cost that usually makes them limited in scope and depth. That is why it is customary in business to speak of "good-faith efforts" to comply with agreements, "full and fair disclosure" when dealing with information, or a "general willingness" not to take undue advantage of counterparts when conditions change, thus acknowledging that no piece of legislation, contractual clause, enforcement practice, or human intervention will be infallibly problem-free (Hosmer 1997).[7]

In addition to rules and regulations on disclosure, adequate procedures, accountability, and transparency, building up confidence requires the agency of trustworthy people. This means that professional actors in the market not only should be competent in their respective capacities but also should be aware of the trust in their activities and functions and the moral commitment to live up to such trust. Individuals, particularly professionals, frequently encounter discretionary space in their activities as, by definition, no rule can predict all outcomes. For example, the accountant, the attorney, and the market analyst regularly have to make assumptions and representations that often cannot be verified by the client at the time of making an investment decision. Or, more seriously, they may have to take actions that cannot wait for the approval of their clients.

This leads to a new level of analysis, beyond the consumption of confidence and even the individual production of confidence. If confidence were conceived as a public good in economic terms—that is, as a good from which nobody could be excluded and that could be consumed by any economic agent without reducing or impairing its consumption by others—then the production of confidence would require the collective effort of all participants in the system (Enderle 2000, 2002). Individual efforts cannot produce public goods because even the intrinsic and instrumental benefits of individual trustworthiness are of no use if there is no one to trust or to be

---

[6] For instance, corruption being "the violation of established rules for personal gain and profit," Sen (1999, p. 175) purports, "that it cannot be eradicated by inducing people to be more self-interested." This is consistent with the ethically comprehensive view of reaching a reflexive equilibrium between self-interest and the interest of others, also called the I-We paradigm (Etzioni 1997).

[7] Some will argue that this is not the realm of ethics, but an expedient way to deal with legal lacunae. However, this argument does not detract from the expectation of virtuous behavior. For instance, Cicero (1913, vol. III, pp. xiii–xiv) reminds us that "concealment consists in trying for your own profit to keep others from finding out something that you know, when it is for their interest to know it."

trusted by.[8] Trustworthiness is beneficial in a decent environment because it fosters cooperative relations, lowering the costs associated with uncertainty and ambiguity. It is not a question of altruism since "trustworthiness contributes intrinsically to self-interest via its connection to self-respect, intimacy, and identity" (Hausman 2002). Furthermore, an individual who loses trust in a close-knit social and business environment may risk losing social standing and professional identity. For example, old master dealers who authenticate, valuate, receive in consignment, or bid in auctions for major works of art on behalf of collectors (sometimes private collectors, sometimes institutional ones, like museums and art academies) seldom sign receipts or contracts with their client collectors; they know that one *faux pas* would force them out of business for good. Trust (fr. Old English *trēowe*, faithful), confidence (fr. Lat. *confidĕre*, to place faith), and credit (fr. Lat. *credĕre*, to believe) are, to paraphrase Prospero (Shakespeare 1973, *The Tempest*, act 4, sc. 1), such stuff as dreams of cooperation and reciprocity are made.

Ethics and the Law

There are many manifestations of social trust, like those associated with the expectation of reliable accounting, the ethical conduct of (ethical) business, and the pursuit of transparency in the marketplace, which are addressed in other chapters of this book. Another social form of trust is the generalized belief that government pursues the common good and that it has a monopoly of legitimate force. When this is in doubt because of perceived asymmetry in the workings of the market, the functioning of government, or unpunished acts of rebellion or common delinquency, a fiction is uncovered: the government does not have the strength and legitimacy it invokes. Asymmetries can result from government action, like some of the welfare state policies of the postwar period that redounded in the debilitation of the rule of law through their encroachment on private property rights. But, more perniciously, high and variable inflation as much as deep, protracted recessions can profoundly distort social and economic values and standards in society, impelling some sectors into desperation while enriching others. It is difficult for the public to trust government authorities and institutions, current and future, when macroeconomic or political mismanagement is the direct determinant of their predicaments. Nobody doubts that legitimacy also stems

---

[8] This runs parallel to the findings of social capital theorists. Putnam (1993), for instance, finds that both states and markets operate more efficiently in civic settings, that social context and history profoundly condition the effectiveness of institutions, that changing formal institutions can change political practice, and that most institutional history moves very, very slowly.

from a justifiable, expedient exercise of authority and that the public's impatience in this sense is increasingly loud across all latitudes (Sunstein 1996).

Rules and regulations express a society's efforts to address the issues it confronts through peacefully accepted political processes. Respect for the law also reveals respect for one's fellow citizens as "the lawbreaker arrogates for herself a privileged position outside the moral community" (Luban 1988, p. 44). Obeying the law is a *prima facie* obligation, that is, it depends on the generality and fairness of its content. But when the law becomes an instrument of interested parties in detriment to the common good, it looses its moral authority and becomes a mere vehicle of coercion, no matter how effectively it can be enforced. A peculiar, purely contextual social morality develops in these circumstances that challenges and supplants the universal rule of law as the established mechanism to process and resolve conflicts in civilized society. An example of this is the scandalous inability of many Latin American and Caribbean governments to effectively collect taxes, especially direct ones, and the correlative nonchalance of the transgressors. The historical context has to be taken into account as well. For instance, when the highest social compact of a country—its political constitution, from which all legislation logically derives—goes largely unheeded, it is a natural consequence over time that some segments of the population, or some of their activities, will not abide by positive law either and will be governed by an informal substitute. Contracts are unlikely to have unquestionable validity and predictable enforceability under such circumstances.

In the Western tradition, this discussion goes back at least to the Roman dictum *Pacta sunt servanda*, the juridical notion that the stipulations of the parties to a contract must be observed like law itself (a deal is a deal is a deal—again, the intuitive notion of justice as regularity). However, in an environment of endemic economic and political instability, the legal profession may resort to the equally ancient principle *Rebus sic stantibus* (the stipulations of the parties to a contract cease to be obligatory when facts and conditions substantially change). This principle feeds the theory of improvision, which originated in French administrative law in the 1950s and has been received with enthusiasm by the judicial doctrine of some Latin American and Caribbean countries. Extending its use beyond the narrow limits of gross inequities, this notion may nurture moral hazard as a questionable culture of "post-contractual opportunism" rapidly spreads (Milgrom and Roberts 1992).

What can be done for the ethics of free markets to prevail? The first step is the strengthening of the rule of law for all economic agents (once more, justice as regularity). This also means that the legal framework is an external limit to the market and that the moral framework, in turn, is an external limit to the legal framework (Kirzner 1993). The moral, legal, and economic orders are harmoniously interarticulated through rational processes of reasoning, based on principles that disavow coercion (justice as fairness).[9]

In times of great moral crisis, enduring changes can be implemented, as the lack of an adequate ethical framework becomes self-evident and reveals a systemic gap that needs to be addressed. The Watergate crimes and misdemeanors produced such a turning point in the early 1970s, prompting an overhaul of the required ethical training for the legal profession in the United States. The current scandals involving Enron, WorldCom, and Arthur Andersen, among others, may provide a similar opportunity for the trading and capital markets professions around the world, especially in the development of new international accounting and auditing standards and extensible business reporting languages, such as XBRL (see Masci and Sotomayor, this volume). Latin America and the Caribbean may profit immensely from this turn of events, by acquiring state-of-the-art tools and procedures to update the regulatory and technical frameworks of their capital markets, and in their quest for convergence and integration with the capital-exporting economies.

This is a peremptory priority, so that the improvements that are introduced in mature capital markets, now and in future, do not pass by the region and leave it behind. A positive influence would be that the direct democracy advanced by the marketplace would contribute to the consolidation of a political democracy able to deliver sustainable socioeconomic progress. To achieve this, the region would have to consciously and consistently pursue an ambitious ethical agenda in the coming years.

An Ethical Agenda for Latin America and the Caribbean

Speaking of Latin America and the Caribbean as a unit whole, especially in terms of financial markets, may be rather misleading. The only activity of this order in the Caribbean basin is that related to offshore banks and funds. Argentina, Brazil, Chile, and Mexico have disparate capital markets, with São Paulo being the largest (arguably larger than that of Canada) and Santiago the most consolidated one. In the rest of Latin America, trading activity is negligible in economic terms. In most cases, though, local stock and commodity exchanges enjoy significant monopoly powers and are closely related to the political apparatus.

---

[9] Much moral theoretical reasoning is modeled after methods of analysis that are legal (the Benthamite approach) or economic (the Hobbesian approach) in nature. The doctrine of law and economics aims at an integrated approach (Jamieson 1993). Perhaps, in Latin America and the Caribbean, lawyers should understand more economics, economists should understand more law, and all should understand more ethics.

Latin America and the Caribbean is a part of the world where personal trust is the currency of business. More abstract and far-reaching forms of confidence and commitment are shunned because of a history of instability and unpredictability of, and unreliability in, the legal framework, the system of justice, the rule of law, government decisions, macroeconomic policy, and everyday business practices. Naturally, this varies enormously from country to country, within countries, and across activities. Although the legal environment, as prescribed by laws and regulations and enforced (or not) by specialized government agents, especially the judiciary, affects the size and scope of capital markets, evidence shows that cultural patterns must be factored in when attempting to understand why investor protection differs so much from one country to the other and across regions (Stultz and Williamson 2002; López de Silanes 2002; Calvo 2002). And there is no question that cultures, and the ethical frameworks they inform, constantly change for better or worse.

It is increasingly clear that the procedural approach applied in developed countries for the supervision of capital markets takes for granted institutional and moral underpinnings that may not exist in much of Latin America and the Caribbean. The natural reaction is to try to institute better rules, regulations, and procedures to improve supervision. The problem is that, while it is true that legal enforcement mechanisms can provide a partial substitute for trust, the cost of promoting and ascertaining compliance, even in cases of (partially) privatized enforcement, may make transactions prohibitively expensive (Stiglitz 2001). The cost of foreign exchange, interest rate or transfer risk hedging, or the issuance of performance bonds in the region, for instance, are cases in point.

The adoption of a three-pronged methodological approach could help in this area. At the macro level, governments are responsible for the regulatory framework. Self-regulation and customs govern the meso level of industries, professional associations, and corporate governance, encompassing more specific norms. The micro level is made up of individual practitioners, investors, and other stakeholders.[10] All three

---

[10] Although easy to comprehend, the introduction of the meso level runs contrary to the intuitions of mainstream economists and political scientists, who are disinclined to communitarian devices that may restrain individual freedom in the economic and political domains. This methodological approach is essential, however, because seldom can the problems at one level be thoroughly solved exclusively with measures at another level (Enderle 2003). Resorting to legislation to improve supervision, a common policy in Latin America and the Caribbean, may not necessarily result in better compliance, where active engagement of institutions and individuals is required. This does not mean that ethical displacement may not be necessary to resolve some dilemmas. This is a technique in applied ethics that seeks a solution at a different level than the one where the problem appears (De George 1993). A vivid example was the recent introduction of legislation in the United States (the macro level) mandating higher standards of transparency and accountability in the "corporate reporting supply chain" (executives, boards, auditors, analysts, and information disseminators), thus giving a strong signal that corporate cultures (the meso level) and individual behaviors (the micro level) had to change fast. This is the basis for advocating an integrated approach in which a rational, conscientious compromise between freedom and responsibility can be achieved at all levels.

levels require discrete attention. The regulatory framework for capital markets in Latin America and the Caribbean requires strengthening at the macro level (better norms, better "normality"); a stronger legal framework would include the hardening of statutory penalties for violators. At the meso level, corporate governance rules and the role and activities of professional associations would also have to be strengthened, so that they do not limit themselves to intervening only in the most egregious violations. Finally, at the micro level, individual market actors, especially professional ones, must be made aware of their responsibilities to address the moral decisions related to honoring the trust deposited in them by their communities when exercising their functions (Enderle 2002). These are moral commitments at the individual, group, and collective levels, which require an overhaul of those practices, proclivities, and states of mind that impede transparency, contestability, and concerted action. This is a tall order indeed, but one that is amenable to education and training.

Governments have towering responsibilities in the educational process of building intertemporal trust, especially by leading through virtuous example and rejecting the pressure of interest groups that lobby for discriminatory measures, like the imposition of asymmetric foreign exchange, tax, and tariff regimes; the nationalization of private sector debts; or the nonprosecution of the financially privileged. The exemplary punishment of corporate and professional wrongdoers is part and parcel of this agenda. Because consistency is the mortar of systemic confidence, governments in Latin America and the Caribbean must acknowledge their responsibility to lead the process of ethical awakening and enhanced ethical sensitivity, especially through the requirement for ethical training at all levels. In other words, finding a suitable, sustainable social path for ethical growth as part of capital market development should rank high among their primary responsibilities of providing the public good of intertemporal trust.

Another common problem that should be addressed and overcome is the decontextualization of training in public ethics, which is generally limited to the hypothetical examination of ethical problems faced by individual actors, such as conflicts of interest, whistle-blowing, and deceit. It is essential to the success of public ethics training to add the context of the community on which ethical standards and modes of applied learning and teaching must be based. Engaged citizen participation and control are at the root of successful initiatives of this sort (Sembor and Leighninger 1993).[11]

---

[11] As Sembor and Leighninger (1993, p. 175) vigorously advocate, "[The] vision of participatory, public ethics is not a code of conduct that must be continually rewritten to suit the times, or an infallible new method of oversight and enforcement. Making public administration compatible with ethics requires a more fundamental change. Democratic civic institutions produce a professional, political, and personal transformation that brings ethics back to its roots."

Global convergence marks the trend for the articulation of ethical standards in professions that operate in the financial markets, such as research analysts, investment managers, and dealer-brokers, given the increasing interpenetration of capital markets across the world. A number of internationally accepted ethical guidelines promoting integrity, competence, and dignity within the financial community are open to the voluntary adherence of Latin American and Caribbean practitioners. Organizations like the Association for Investment Management and Research (AIMR), a professional association of more than 100,000 investment practitioners and educators in over 100 countries, help sustain the highest standards of professional conduct to operate ethically and in a manner that benefits clients and investors. This and similar initiatives that foster professionalism and accountability in market agents are the most focused path for accelerating moral awareness and sensitivity in the financial markets of Latin America and the Caribbean. AIMR members and nonmembers alike are bound to report questionable or unethical business practices of AIMR members, fostering peer control and the convergence of professional standards.[12] This addresses the meso and individual levels.

However, at the macro level, a more ambitious agenda should be pursued as a component of the still-pending second wave of structural reform in the region and even as a new conditionality requisite, the introduction of ethical assessment studies and audits as sine qua non elements for the approval of investment projects and credit operations.[13] International financial organizations could be instrumental in advancing such an initiative, creating an additional systemic stabilizer that would go a long way toward fostering greater trust in the financial markets they serve. This will require strong leadership and may it be a virtuous instance of "soft power" in which OECD economies could exercise a lasting influence for the better on emerging markets (Nye 2002). The Inter-American Development Bank, the Inter-American Investment Corporation, and the Multilateral Investment Fund, in particular, should have a pivotal role in the implementation of these initiatives across the region, working with member country governments to promote the organization of ethical education at all levels as

---

[12] Prentice (2002) strongly believes, "Centers for the study of business ethics are necessary to represent the ideals to which we aspire. But most business students will always view business ethics as hortatory rather than mandatory, as extra credit rather than required … [S]trong judicial systems administering rigorous financial laws enable companies to raise money more quickly and facilitate more efficient stock markets. Legitimate companies want laws that require accurate financial disclosure and rules that punish fraudulent firms."

[13] It is safe to predict that the beneficiaries of these measures, frequently immersed in crisis management situations, will be the first ones to oppose them, as yet a new set of hurdles to the disbursement of funds. All paths of change are fraught with risk.

well as the introduction of ethical assessment studies and audits.[14] In the long run, this could also help give rational form to the frequent demands for transparency and due process in the establishment of credit and investment conditionality.

For better or worse, as the mass media is making painfully evident on a daily basis, better regulation, enhanced supervision, self-regulation, and corporate internal and external control processes may still fail to offer sufficiently strong incentives to maximize ethical behavior. In these cases, capital markets remain a powerful, disinterested check on the actions of corporate management and administration alike, forming a court of last resort on behalf of investors and lenders (Chaplinsky 1997). In other words, in Latin America and the Caribbean as much as in the consolidated capital markets of industrial countries, beyond sound legal frameworks, responsible professional intermediation, and peer supervision, the greatest protector of investor interest in the long run may well be market freedom itself, that is, a culture of freedom and responsibility.

Conclusion

The discussion provides some answers to the questions posed in the introduction. First, the capital markets of Latin America and the Caribbean need better supervision, rules, standards, and levels of professionalism; addressing these issues is vital to fostering growth and consolidation. Second, consistently addressing macroeconomic fundamentals in a coherent manner would provide the right incentives for building trust in capital markets, although this alone would not be sufficient. Third, ethical impediments could be addressed through a mix of ethical instruction and the practice of the right values. And fourth, for permanent solutions to fully germinate, many years of persistent effort are required at the collective, group, and individual level, and inter-

---

[14] The sources for the study and discussion of business ethics are numerous and tested by time, including the publications *Business Ethics, Business Ethics Quarterly, Business and Professional Ethics Journal, Business and Society, International Journal of Value-based Management*, and *Journal of Business Ethics*. Most research centers and societies belong to universities, like the Olsson Center for Applied Ethics (established at the University of Virginia in 1966), the Center for Business Ethics (Bentley College), the Society for Business Ethics (Loyola University, Chicago), the Center for Ethics and Corporate Policy (Loyola Marymount University), the International Society of Business, Economics, and Ethics, and the Center for Ethics and Religious Values in Business (both at the University of Notre Dame). Other centers and associations are independent, such as the Ethics Resource Center (Washington, D.C.), the Institute for the Study of Business Values (Hong Kong), and the Westminster Institute for Ethics and Human Values (London). Many are oriented toward specific professions, like the Program in Ethics and Professions (Harvard University) and the Center for the Study of Ethics and Behavior in Accounting (State University of New York, Binghamton).

national cooperation could be instrumental in accomplishing discrete targets and accelerating the process.

At the national level, like all efforts in an integrated community willing to grow together, the progress of the whole is part of the progress of individuals and intermediate groups. Trust is a wager, and the size of any wager is a direct function of the resources at stake, the perception of risk in the given environment, and the expected gains.[15] "Putting suspicion to sleep," to use the felicitous phrase attributed to Thomas Paine, is harder when there is a recent, traumatic history of government, corporate, or professional deception or mismanagement from which to draw conclusions and project future outcomes.

Nevertheless, there is no civilizational stumbling block—religious, philosophical, or psychological—that cannot be resolved with concerted effort and external cooperation.[16] Latin American and Caribbean countries and markets are not scorched earth. On the contrary, those that could lead the way have vibrant, competitive export sectors, highly integrated financial systems, and a highly educated workforce willing and able to compete in the globalized marketplace. They need ever more sophisticated capital markets to help finance their socioeconomic growth in a more efficient manner, and some of them have the human capital to build now, even in the midst of unfavorable conditions in the world economy. Some remain committed to the prejudice that the countries of Latin America and the Caribbean lack the cultural fabric to develop capital markets; those individuals advance a line of reasoning that was widespread in the 1960s and 1970s, when the region was deemed not ready for democratic governance.

An abundant literature describing the social and economic requisites for democracy sprang from the seminal research of the late 1950s and provides startling empirical evidence (Lipset 1981; Camp 1996). It confirms that higher levels of wealth, industrialization, urbanization, and education are directly correlated with democratic governance and socioeconomic progress. These are not sufficient conditions, but that they are necessary nobody doubts by now.

There is also empirical evidence showing that the higher their level of education, the likelier it is for people to trust others and to trust more, to support rules

---

[15] O'Donnell (1999, p. 29) says, "Political democracy … is the only regime that is the result of an institutionalized, universalistic, and inclusive wager." A wager of trust, one might add. Also see Di Palma (1990).

[16] Quigley's theoretical and empirical analysis (1979) delved into the notion of civilizational decline in the 1970s, which can be predicated from manifestations of increased antisocial behavior (violent crime, drug abuse), family decay, low levels of social capital, a relaxation of the work ethic, and low levels of scholastic achievement. Huntington's (1996) "clash of civilizations" and religious fundamentalism have brought this discussion back to the fore.

and habits of civic behavior, and to adhere (however reservedly) to superior forms of democratic government (Power and Clark 2001; Ryan 1994). This is why the attention of policymakers, development experts, and international financial organizations, like the Inter-American Development Bank Group, should be focused toward effective governance; as recent polls show, even in a region in economic turmoil and dramatic income inequality, support for liberal democracy remains high and is likely to stay high (Latinobarómetro; Lagos 2001). There is an inescapable link between socioeconomic development and a generalized belief in the legitimacy and effectiveness of government, but the perceived benefits of democratic forms of government consistently override it (Diamond, Linz, and Lipset 1990; Garretón and Newman 2001).

The same line of reasoning can be applied to financial markets. They, too, need to join the collective enterprise of building intertemporal trust through the adoption of better legal frameworks and better standards for supervision and professional activity. Certainly, governments must refocus their efforts toward increasing their legitimacy and improving their political and socioeconomic performance. This will require sound macroeconomic decisions, effective legal and administrative action, major commitments on the part of the private sector, and considerable luck. But it is also a moral enterprise whose rewards could spill over many other areas of social interaction, helping articulate a culture of rationality and decency, the moral underpinnings of civilized life.

Twenty-four centuries ago, Aristotle suggested that a society that could not reach a practical agreement on its conception of justice—rationality cum fairness—might lack the capacity to sustain a political community (MacIntyre 1984). The discussion here further suggests that a society that cannot reach a practical agreement on its conception of political community—freedom cum responsibility—may lack the capacity to establish mature capital markets.

Bibliography

Arrow, K. J. 1974. *The Limits of Organization.* New York: Norton.

Association for Investment Management and Research (AINR). 1999. *Standards of Practice Handbook: The Code of Ethics and the Standards of Professional Conduct.* Eighth edition. Charlottesville, Va.: AIMR. (http://www.aimr.org/pdf/standards/english_code.pdf).

Baron, M. W. 1997. In *The Blackwell Encyclopedic Dictionary of Business Ethics.* Edited by P. H. Werhane and R. E. Freeman. Oxford, Eng.: Blackwell Publishers.

Bowie, N. E. 1999. *Business Ethics: A Kantian Perspective*. Malden, Mass. and Oxford: Blackwell.

Callahan, J. C. 1997. Applied Ethics. In *The Blackwell Encyclopedic Dictionary of Business Ethics*. Edited by P. H. Werhane and R. E. Freeman. Oxford, Eng.: Blackwell Publishers.

Calvo, G. A. 2002. Globalization Hazard and Delayed Reform in Emerging Markets. *Economía*, Spring, 1–29.

Camp, R. A. 1996. *Democracy in Latin America: Patterns and Cycles*. Wilmington, Del.: Scholarly Resources.

Carter, S. L. 1998. *Civility: Manners, Morals, and the Etiquette of Democracy*. New York: Basic Books.

Chaplinsky, S. 1997. Market for Corporate Control. In *The Blackwell Encyclopedic Dictionary of Business Ethics*. Edited by P. H. Werhane and R. E. Freeman. Oxford: Blackwell Publishers.

Cicero, M. T. 1913 [45–44 B.C.]. *De Officiis*. Loeb edition. Cambridge, Mass.: Harvard University Press.

Colby, A., and Kohlberg, L. 1987. *The Measurement of Moral Judgment*. Cambridge, Mass. and New York: Cambridge University Press.

Davis, M. 1997. Professional Codes. In *The Blackwell Encyclopedic Dictionary of Business Ethics*. Edited by P. H. Werhane and R. E. Freeman. Oxford: Blackwell Publishers.

De George, R. T. 1993. *Competing with Integrity in International Business*. New York: Oxford University Press.

Di Palma, G. 1990. *To Craft Democracies: An Essay on Democratic Transitions*. Berkeley, Los Angeles, Oxford: University of California Press.

Diamond, L., J. J. Linz, and S. M. Lipset. 1990. *Politics in Developing Countries: Comparing Experiences with Democracy*. Boulder, Colo. and London: Lynne Rienner Publishers.

DiPiazza, S. A. Jr., and R. G. Eccles. 2002. *Building Public Trust: The Future of Corporate Reporting*. New York, N.Y.: John Wiley & Sons.

Enderle, G. 2000. Whose Ethos for Public Goods in a Global Economy? An Exploration in International Business Ethics. *Business Ethics Quarterly*, January, 131–44.

_____. 2002. Confidence in the Financial Reporting System: Easier to Lose than to Restore. Mendoza College of Business, University of Notre Dame.

_____. 2003. Business Ethics. In *Blackwell Companion to Philosophy*. Edited by N. Bunnin and E. P. Tsui-James. Oxford, U.K.: Blackwell Publishers.

Etzioni, A. 1996. *The New Golden Rule: Community and Morality in a Democratic Society*. New York: Basic Books.

_____. 1997. Socio-economics. In *The Blackwell Encyclopedic Dictionary of Business Ethics*. Edited by P. H. Werhane and R. E. Freeman. Oxford: Blackwell Publishers.

Federal Reserve System. 2002. *Trading and Capital-markets Activities Manual*. Washington, D.C.: Board of Governors of the Federal Reserve System, Publication Services, April. (http://www.federalreserve.gov/boarddocs/supmanual/trading/trading.pdf).

Fish, S. E. 1999. *The Trouble with Principle*. Cambridge, Mass. and London: Harvard University Press.

Fukuyama, F. 1995. *Trust: The Social Virtues and the Creation of Prosperity*. New York: Free Press.

Garretón, M. A. and E. Newman. 2001. *Democracy in Latin America: (Re)Constructing Political Society*. Tokyo, New York and Paris: United Nations University Press.

Gauthier, D. P. 1986. *Morals by Agreement*. Oxford: Oxford University Press.

Goodpaster, K. E. 1997. Business Ethics. In *The Blackwell Encyclopedic Dictionary of Business Ethics*. Edited by P. H. Werhane and R. E. Freeman. Oxford: Blackwell Publishers.

Hausman, D. M. 1989. Are Markets Morally Free Zones? *Philosophy and Public Affairs* 18:317–333.

_____. 2002. Trustworthiness and Self-interest. In *Managing Ethical Risk: How Investing in Ethics Adds Value*. Edited by Cosimano, T., R. Chami, and C. Fullenkamp, *Journal of Banking and Finance*, forthcoming.

Hosmer, L. T. 1997. Trust. In *The Blackwell Encyclopedic Dictionary of Business Ethics*. Edited by P. H. Werhane and R. E. Freeman. Oxford: Blackwell Publishers.

Huntington, S. P. 1996. *The Clash of Civilizations and the Remaking of World Order*. New York: Simon & Schuster.

Jamieson, D. 1993. Method and Moral Theory. In *A Companion to Ethics*. Edited by P. Singer. Oxford: Blackwell Publishers, 476-87.

Kagan, S. 1989. *The Limits of Morality*. Oxford: Clarendon Press; New York: Oxford University Press.

———. 1998. *Normative Ethics.* Boulder, Colo.: Westview Press.

Kirzner, I. M. 1993. The Limits of the Market: The Real and the Imagined. New York University.

Kohlberg, L. 1981. *The Philosophy of Moral Development: Moral Stages and the Idea of Justice.* San Francisco, Calif.: Harper & Row.

Lagos, M. 2001. How People View Democracy: Between Stability and Crisis in Latin America. *Journal of Democracy,* 12:137–145.

Latinobarómetro: Opinión pública latinoamericana. Santiago de Chile: Corporación Latinobarómetro, since 1995 (http://www.latinobarometro.org/).

Lipset, S. M. 1981. *Political Man: The Social Bases of Politics.* 3rd edition. Baltimore, Md.: The Johns Hopkins University Press.

López de Silanes, F. 2002. The Politics of Legal Reform. *Economía,* Spring, 91–136.

Luban, D. 1988. *Lawyers and Justice: An Ethical Study.* Princeton, N.J.: Princeton University Press.

MacIntyre, A. C. 1984. *After Virtue: A Study of Moral Theory.* 2nd edition. Notre Dame, Ind.: University of Notre Dame.

McCloskey, D. N. 1998. Virtue in the Marketplace. *The Journal of Economic History,* June.

Milgrom, P., and J. Roberts. 1992. *Economics: Organization and Management.* Englewood Cliffs, N.J.: Prentice Hall.

Mill, J. S. 1998 [1863]. *Utilitarianism.* Oxford: Oxford University Press.

Nye, J. S. 2002. *The Paradox of American Power: Why the World's Only Superpower Can't Go It Alone.* Oxford and New York: Oxford University Press.

O'Donnell, G. A. 1999. Democratic Theory and Comparative Politics. Kellogg Institute for International Studies, University of Notre Dame.

Power, T. J. and M. A. Clark. 2001. Does Trust Matter? Interpersonal Trust and Democratic Values in Chile, Costa Rica, and Mexico. In *Citizen Views of Democracy in Latin America.* Edited by R. A. Camp. Pittsburgh, Penn.: University of Pittsburg Press, 51–70.

Prentice, R. 2002. Lessons Learned in Business School. *The New York Times.* August 20. Op-Ed.

Putnam, R. D., with R. Leonardi and R. Y. Nanetti. 1993. *Making Democracy Work: Civic Traditions in Modern Italy.* Princeton, N.J.: Princeton University Press.

Quigley, C. 1979. *The Evolution of Civilization: An Introduction to Historical Analysis*. Indianapolis, Ind.: Liberty Press.

Rueschemeyer, D., E. H. Stephens, and J. D. Stephens. 1992. *Capitalist Development and Democracy*. Chicago: University of Chicago Press.

Ryan, A. 1994. Capitalism, Civic Virtue, and Democracy. In *Virtue, Corruption, and Self-interest*, ed. by R. K. Matthews. Bethlehem, Pa.: Lehigh Press; London and Toronto: Associated University Presses, 148–171.

Ryan, L. V. 1997. Codes of Ethics. In *The Blackwell Encyclopedic Dictionary of Business Ethics*. Edited by P. H. Werhane and R. E. Freeman. Oxford: Blackwell Publishers.

Sembor, E. and M. E. Leighninger. 1993. Rediscovering the Public: Reconnecting Ethics and Ethos Through Democratic Civic Institutions. In *Ethical Dilemmas in Public Administration*. Edited by L. Pasquerella, A. G. Killilea and M. Vocino. Westport, Conn. and London: Praeger, 161–177.

Sen, A. K. 1999. *Development as Freedom*. New York: Alfred A. Knopf.

Shakespeare, William. 1973 [1613]. *The Complete Works*. The Alexander Texts. London and Glasgow: Collins.

Smith, A. 1979 [1776]. *An Inquiry into the Nature and Causes of the Wealth of Nations*. Cannan edition. Tokyo: Charles E. Tuttle Co.

Solomon, R. C. 1993. Business Ethics. *A Companion to Ethics*. Edited by P. Singer. Oxford: Blackwell Publishers, 354–366.

Stiglitz, J. E. 2001. Ethics, Economic Advice, and Economic Policy. Economics Department, Columbia University.

Stultz, R. M. and R. Williamson. 2002. Culture, Openness, and Finance. August. Processed.

Sunstein, C. R. 1996. *Legal Reasoning and Political Conflict*. New York and Oxford: Oxford University Press.

■CHAPTER 14

Corporate Governance and Capital Market Development: Recent Experiences in Latin America

Mike Lubrano

In the wake of the 1995 Mexico crisis and the 1997 Asian financial crisis, it has become more widely recognized that good corporate governance is a necessary condition for well-functioning financial markets. At the very core of these crises was the failure of both boards of directors and financial markets to exercise effective oversight and provide a check against the financial excesses undertaken by enterprises and their management. The corporate scandals that erupted in 2002 in the United States have further focused the thinking of policymakers, financial intermediaries, company chiefs, and the investing public on the importance of board oversight, shareholder rights, and transparency and disclosure for financial sector stability and economic growth.

The interrelationship between capital market development and corporate governance has been characterized as "neither simple nor linear; rather, it is in the nature of a complex feedback loop, a dynamic process responsive to many factors" (Jordan and Lubrano 2002). How effective capital markets are in exerting governance over corporations is in part a function of legal rules; in part a question of business culture; in part the outcome of incentives facing companies, investors, and intermediaries; and in part a question of institutional capacity. This chapter looks at a set of corporate governance initiatives driven by capital markets that have been undertaken in Latin America in recent years and tries to draw some tentative conclusions about their effectiveness.[1] In particular, it highlights one striking characteristic of recent efforts—the combination of mandatory legal rule changes and voluntary private or quasi-private mechanisms for promoting better corporate governance.

---

[1] Portions of this chapter were published in earlier form in Jordan and Lubrano (2002).

Much of the international debate (and academic literature) on corporate governance began in the United Kingdom and the United States, where, in the main, the central challenge of corporate governance is managing the principal/agent conflict between atomized owners and a cadre of professional managers. By contrast, the corporate governance problem in most emerging markets (and in particular in Latin America) revolves around the divergence of interests and power between majority and minority shareholders, with the associated risk of expropriation by the former. Of course, to the extent that the controlling shareholders place themselves in management positions for which they are not ideally qualified, the viability of the company's operations are also put at risk, with negative consequences for controllers, minority shareholders, and all other stakeholders in the enterprise.

The strength of minority rights and their ability to limit the scope for expropriation by controlling shareholders thus play an important role in investor confidence in such markets. Therein lies a key link between the development of good corporate governance and capital market development in emerging economies. Recent research supports the proposition that a better environment for corporate governance facilitates capital market development. It has been demonstrated across countries that capital market development correlates positively with the degree of shareholder protection, but there is undoubtedly more to this than simple linear causality (Beck, Levine, and Loayza 2000; La Porta and others 2000). Furthermore, although it is difficult to quantify with precision, markets with perceived shortcomings in minority shareholder protections do suffer from a "corporate governance discount" (McKinsey & Company 2002). And across firms, equity market values are higher in environments where shareholder protection is stronger (La Porta and others 2002).

In spite of the increasing awareness of these issues and interrelationships, and notwithstanding the reforms implemented by advanced industrial and emerging markets in their legal and regulatory frameworks in the past decade, corporate governance systems remain weak in many countries (including in Latin America). Each market presents a unique combination of factors (legal framework, incentives, and institutional development), and progress toward improvement will therefore require a different mix of responses. The objective of this chapter is to review recent developments at the nexus of capital markets and corporate governance in Latin America and draw some conclusions about what sorts of reform efforts are likely to be successful under what sorts of conditions, recognizing that the regional and indeed worldwide experiences thus far require that conclusions be treated as preliminary.

A Framework for Appraising Corporate Governance

The Principles of Corporate Governance published by the Organisation for Economic Co-operation and Development (OECD) in May 1999 have come to be the most broadly accepted framework for conducting analysis of corporate governance systems in both OECD and non-OECD countries. The principles were intended to provide a common point of reference and a common vocabulary rather than a detailed blueprint for helping those involved in the process of strengthening and enhancing corporate governance systems, principally for publicly traded companies.

The principles are nonbinding and do not aim at detailed prescriptions for national legislation; they represent the core elements considered essential for good corporate governance and are intended to be applied in accordance with national and company-specific circumstances. Since their publication, the principles have been the conceptual framework for a series of high-level regional roundtables of policymakers, financial intermediaries, and company chiefs in Latin America, Asia, and the transition economies.[2] The broad backing and high-level recognition given to the principles provide a unique international reference point for government policymakers, regulators, and practitioners. The principles have also served as the point of departure for various efforts to assess or "rate" the corporate governance of markets and individual companies. The principles are the basis for the methodology developed by the World Bank for assessing the quality of the corporate governance in client countries. In connection with its work to improve the corporate governance of its client companies, International Finance Corporation (IFC) has elaborated a set of matrices that present representative trajectories for improvements in company governance. Appendix table 14-1 gives the current version of the matrix for publicly listed companies.

The principles are organized around five subject areas: rights of shareholders; equitable treatment of shareholders; role of stakeholders in corporate governance; disclosure and transparency; and responsibilities of the board. What follows is a brief summary of the principles and the explanatory notes published with them.

Rights of Shareholders

The corporate governance framework should protect shareholder rights. Basic shareholder rights include the right to secure methods of ownership registration, convey

---

[2] The papers presented at the corporate governance roundtables sponsored by the OECD and World Bank Group can be downloaded from the OECD Corporate Affairs Division website (www.oecd.org/daf/corporate-affairs/).

or transfer shares, obtain relevant information on the corporation on a timely and regular basis, participate and vote in general shareholder meetings, elect members of the board, and share in the profits of the corporation.

Equitable Treatment of Shareholders

The corporate governance framework should ensure the equitable treatment of shareholders, including minority and foreign shareholders. All shareholders should have the opportunity to obtain effective redress for the violation of their rights. An important determinant of the degree to which shareholder rights are protected is whether effective methods exist to obtain redress for grievances at a reasonable cost and without excessive delay.

All shareholders of the same class should be treated equally, insider trading and abusive self-dealing should be prohibited, and members of the board and managers should be required to disclose any material interests in transactions or matters affecting the corporation.

Role of Stakeholders in Corporate Governance

A good corporate governance framework should also recognize the rights of stakeholders in addition to shareholders as established by law and encourage active cooperation between corporations and such stakeholders in creating wealth, jobs, and the sustainability of financially sound enterprises. The corporate governance framework should assure that the rights of stakeholders that are protected by law are respected. Furthermore, where law protects the interests of stakeholders, they should have the opportunity to obtain effective redress for violation of their rights. And all relevant information—a key element in ensuring that the interests of stakeholders are upheld—should be made available to all stakeholders on a timely basis.

Disclosure and Transparency

The principles focus on three aspects of disclosure: the nature of information that should be disclosed, the basis for verification of the information, and the mechanisms used to disclose information. Regarding the content, the corporate governance framework should ensure that timely and accurate disclosure is made on all material matters regarding the corporation, including the financial situation, performance, ownership, and governance of the corporation. Disclosure should include, but not be limited to, material information on the financial and operating results of the corporation, corporation objectives, major share ownership and voting rights, members of the board and key executives and their remuneration, foreseeable risk factors, material issues regarding employees and other stockholders, and governance structures and policies.

The principles state that all financial information should be prepared, audited, and disclosed in accordance with high-quality standards of accounting, financial and nonfinancial disclosure, and auditing. The principles strongly support the relevance of an annual audit that is conducted by an external auditor to provide independent and objective assurance on the way in which financial statements have been prepared and presented. Finally, the principles advocate that channels for disseminating information should provide for fair, timely, and cost-efficient access to relevant information by users.

Responsibilities of the Board

The principles assign special importance to the board of directors as the key mechanism to ensure the strategic guidance of the corporation and effectively monitor the quality of management. The board should pay special attention to its own accountability to the corporation and the shareholders. Members of the board should act on a fully informed basis, in good faith, with due diligence and care, and in the best interests of the corporation and shareholders. Box 14-1 summarizes some of the key functions of the board as presented by the principles.

The principles also emphasize that the board should exercise objective judgment on corporate affairs and, in particular, be independent of management. Examples of such key responsibilities are financial reporting, nomination, and executive and board remuneration. The responsibility of board members to exercise independent judgment where there is potential for conflicts of interest is particularly highlighted. Finally, in addition to stressing the importance of the central duties of care and loyalty, the principles emphasize that board members should devote sufficient time to their responsibilities, for which they should have access to accurate, relevant, and timely information.

Overview of Corporate Governance Reform Efforts

Improving the Legal Framework

When corporate governance issues become popular fodder for the national press, as they have in both mature and emerging markets in recent years, it is unusual for na-

---

Box 14-1 | **Functions of the Board of Directors**

The OECD principles highlight some key functions that the board should perform, including:

- Treating all stakeholders fairly
- Reviewing and guiding corporate strategy, major plans of action, risk policy, annual budgets, and business plans; setting performance objectives; monitoring implementation and corporate performance; overseeing major capital expenditures, acquisitions, and divestitures; ensuring compliance with applicable law; taking into account the interests of shareholders; selecting, compensating, monitoring, and, when necessary, replacing key executives; and overseeing succession planning
- Reviewing remuneration for key executives and boards and ensuring a formal and transparent board nomination process
- Monitoring and managing potential conflicts of interest of management, board members, and shareholders, including misuse of corporate assets and abuse in related-party transactions
- Ensuring the integrity of the corporation's accounting and financial reporting systems, including the independent audit, and seeing that appropriate systems of control are in place, in particular, systems for monitoring risk, financial control, and compliance with the law
- Monitoring the effectiveness of the governance practices under which the board operates and making changes as needed
- Overseeing the process of disclosure and communications.

---

tional legislatures to remain quiescent. In the past five years, OECD countries and emerging markets have undertaken numerous reforms of company law and capital market legislation.[3] In Latin America, high-profile amendments to the legal and regulatory framework have become law in the four major markets: Argentina, Brazil, Chile, and Mexico.[4] Similar legislation was introduced in Colombia in 2002.

Scandals, the Impetus for Reforms

The reforms of Latin American company and securities laws were typically conceived in the aftermath (or sometimes during the course) of scandals in public securities

---

[3] U.S. President Bush signed the Sarbanes-Oxley Act of 2002 on July 30, 2002 (Pub 6. No 107-204, 116 Stat. 745 [2002]). Sarbanes-Oxley introduced sweeping changes in the requirements for corporate governance of public companies listed in the United States.

[4] In Chile, December 2000 (mandatory tender offers, pension fund–nominated directors, class actions, special procedures and board committees for transactions with affiliates, and director responsibility); Argentina, June 2001 (mandatory tender offers, audit committees, and shareholder rights); Mexico, June 2001 (nonvoting shares, independent directors, and code compliance disclosure); Brazil, November 2001 (mandatory tender offers, accounting standards, board representation for minority voting and nonvoting shareholders, voting procedures, and legal authorization for arbitration).

markets involving perceived inequitable treatment of shareholders. In Chile, the managers and controllers of the power company Enersis managed to secure fully one-third of the total price paid for control of the company in return for their economic interest in the company of less than 1 percent. The shareholders of TV Azteca in Mexico took up arms after the controlling shareholder used the company as a virtual bank to finance his purchase of cellular licenses (after publicly vowing that he would never do such a thing). Investors in a series of Brazilian and Argentine companies were forced to accept "low-ball" offers from controlling shareholders who decided to delist the companies. Brazilian shareholders (most of them holders of nonvoting "preferred" shares of such companies) felt they were unfairly frozen out of transactions in which those holding a majority of the voting shares sold the control of the company at a premium over prevailing market prices.

As the cases discussed later in this chapter demonstrate, capital market participants of one sort or another have almost always undertaken supplementary private initiatives in the area of corporate governance, either simultaneously or immediately following efforts to amend the legal framework. One problem with legislated reform is its general applicability to all companies similarly situated (for example, all listed companies must comply with all legislation pertaining to corporate governance). Not surprisingly, the recent spate of Latin American legislative initiatives failed to enjoy the unanimous support of the business community. Typically, established firms with proven track records in the market or with dominant positions in the equity indexes were less enthusiastic about having to disclose additional information to shareholders or allow outsiders on their boards. Controllers fought doggedly against mandatory tender offer triggers that would force them to share control premiums with minority shareholders. During the reform debates, it became evident that many listed Latin American companies (including some blue chips) no longer thought of the public securities markets as a potential future source of capital. Rather, a fair number of such companies anticipated selling control to a larger national or, more often, international competitor (in transactions precisely like those in which the tender offer reforms were designed to apply) and thus were indifferent to the prices at which their securities traded in the markets. To the controllers of such companies, any strengthening of the tender offer regime was anathema.

Not all securities issuers or potential issuers were resistant. A handful of listed firms voluntarily amended their charters to incorporate some of the elements of the legislative reforms in advance of their passage. Several companies in Brazil negotiated tag-along rights for minority voting shares and even nonvoting shares before the legislated reforms were passed in 2001. A major Mexican company was the first firm there to adopt the Mexican code of best practices in an effort to turn around its rep-utation for trampling on minority shareholder rights. The less resistant firms typically expect heavy capital raising requirements in the short to medium term and hence are more willing to accommodate market expectations.

In the end, the final measures approved by the respective legislatures and signed into law in Latin America were more or less watered-down versions of what was initially proposed. Chile's reformers were perhaps the most successful, but even there, majority shareholders were permitted to suspend the application of the law's manda-tory tender offer provisions for three years. Mexico's legislation delegated authority for setting the parameters of the mandatory tender offer rule to the banking and securi-ties regulator, which after much delay was able to issue strong mandatory bid rules in early 2002. Brazil's comprehensive legislative initiative was the subject of extensive horse-trading in the legislature. In the end, the mandatory tender offer requirement for nonvoting shares and the provisions that would have given minority shareholders con-trol over fiscal boards had to be dropped. However, the international media attention paid to the Enron, Global Crossing, and other corporate scandals in the United States, and the subsequent responses from the legislature and the U.S. exchanges, may yet pro-vide impetus for further legal reforms in the rest of the hemisphere.

Early Results: Mixed

The promoters of the recent legislative initiatives in Latin America, and elsewhere in emerging markets, clearly hoped that by mandating greater transparency, providing shareholders with better tools to ensure equitable treatment, and beefing up judicial enforcement, the reforms would have salutary effects on the development of capital markets. In the case of the Latin American reforms, it is certainly too early to make definitive judgments about the long-term impact on access to and cost of capital, new offerings, liquidity, securities prices, or company performance. Two or three more years must pass before there is enough solid data to test the hypothesis that the reforms helped reduce the overall "governance discounts" in the respective markets and will ultimately result in more access to capital at lower cost. (One prominent analyst, how-ever, already asserts that the Brazilian legal reform shifted the balance of power in Brazilian companies positively for minority shareholders and recommended that in-vestors buy minority voting shares in Brazilian firms.[5])

---

[5] Deutsche Bank Latin America Strategy, November 5, 2001.

Short-term anecdotal information presents a mixed picture. Clearly, the supporters of reform have succeeded in focusing the attention of companies, managers and directors, institutional investors, and the general public on the importance of corporate governance to the health of the capital markets (and by extension the pension savings regimes). Although it is hard to judge just how much the legal reforms encouraged the development of private contractual arrangements, recent experience supports the conclusion that legal reforms can have the effect of accelerating the development and adoption of complementary or supplementary private contractual mechanisms.

The reforms have not been a panacea. There has been no immediate rise in equity prices that might have reflected a reduction in the governance discount as a result of passage of the reforms. Controversial delistings and changes of control accelerated during 2001 and continue today. It may be that controllers have tried to "get while the getting is good" before the legal reforms were in place (and during the grace period before Chile's mandatory tender offer regime goes into effect). Nor does the impetus created by the legal reforms for voluntary private contracting appear to be uniform. All public companies in Chile have duly constituted the conflicts committees required by the legislation, and growth companies, firms with American Depository Receipt programs (ADRs), and those with large pension fund stake holdings have begun to improve their overall practices. However, Santiago's tightly knit community of senior managers and directors has not experienced an epiphany. There has not been a general blossoming of interest in restructuring corporate boards to make them more effective watchdogs of shareholder interests. Private efforts (some with support from the government) to publish an accepted best practices code for Chilean companies have yet to demonstrate significant momentum. And the organization of an institute of corporate directors is still nascent.

Stock Exchange Listing Rules: Brazil's Novo Mercado

The New York Stock Exchange requirements for independent directors and audit committees are often cited as an example of the positive role that self-regulatory organizations in the securities markets can play in improving corporate governance standards.[6] However, before the mid-1990s, many stock markets in both OECD and emerging markets resisted calls to impose higher standards on shareholder rights or

---

[6] The New York Stock Exchange's requirements for corporate governance of listed companies will be dramatically tightened when new rules recommended by the NYSE Corporate Accountability and Listing Standards Committee (submitted to the U.S. Securities and Exchange Commission on August 15, 2002) go into force.

board composition. Not surprisingly, this resistance was grounded in a concern that list-ing rules that exceeded the minimum requirements of local company law might dis-courage new listings, particularly by start-up, founder-controlled companies. Most es-tablished listed companies were also less than anxious to change their practices. As with legislation, listing rules can suffer from the "one size fits all" problem. That is, all issuers are usually required to meet the same minimum standards, so the old guard resists.

Born of Need and Disappointment

The Novo Mercado initiative of the São Paolo Stock Exchange (Bovespa) traces its roots to the efforts to reform Brazilian company and securities legislation. The initia-tive represents a quasi-private effort to make up for the perceived shortcomings of legislative reform by creating a voluntary mechanism to encourage adherence to ap-propriate standards and providing specialized private dispute resolution. Bovespa's leadership conceived the Novo Mercado at a time when two trends particularly wor-risome for a stock exchange were evident. First, market capitalization and trading vol-umes in the public equities markets were contracting dramatically. Second, efforts to enact comprehensive corporate governance reform were encountering strong polit-ical resistance.

By the end of the 1990s, the weaknesses of the Brazilian capital market were painfully evident. In 1999 and 2000, there were no initial public offerings (IPOs), few new issues by companies already listed, and a growing number of delistings. Li-quidity was drying up for all but the largest companies as trading volumes declined. Another ongoing challenge for Bovespa was a shift of trading in shares of the largest Brazilian companies to the ADR market in New York. Although these disturbing trends were attributable to many factors, one of the more important was the perception by domestic and international investors that Brazilian companies had poor corporate governance practices and inadequate legal protections (particularly those dealing with minority shareholder rights).[7] Bovespa decided that perception called for some sort of response.[8]

The compromises that were made in the course of legislative consideration of the initial company and securities law reform bill in Brazil guided the content of the

---

[7] McKinsey Global Investor Opinion Survey 2002. The survey key findings can be accessed at www.mckinsey.com/corporategovernance.

[8] The president of Brazil's securities commission took a leading role in the effort to reform the company and securi-ties law precisely because he shared the view that, while improvements in corporate governance of Brazilian compa-nies alone would not effect a recovery of the equity market, they were a necessary condition.

Novo Mercado listing rules. Bovespa recognized that the well-understood shortcomings of existing law that the legal reforms ultimately failed to address could provide the basis for a voluntary rules-based response. Bovespa's initiative can properly be called a privatization of part of the reform process.

Different Strokes for Different Folks

The Novo Mercado is a listing segment of Bovespa for companies that choose to commit themselves to the highest standards of corporate governance by contract.[9] In addition to the Novo Mercado, Bovespa created two intermediate listing segments, Special Corporate Governance Level I and Level 2. The listing rules for Levels I and 2 also require higher corporate governance standards than existing norms, but they are not as strict as the requirements of the full Novo Mercado. Companies remain free to list under Bovespa's old rules, which simply require compliance with Brazil's (now amended) company and securities laws. Therefore, companies listed on Bovespa now have the option to choose among four listing segments, in ascending order of corporate governance standards: the old market, Level I, Level 2, and the Novo Mercado.[10]

By committing themselves to higher standards of corporate governance, companies that join the Novo Mercado hope that investors will respond by placing higher valuations on their securities, reducing the general corporate governance discount applied to Brazilian firms.[11] The creation of the Level I and Level 2 segments was a bit of an afterthought. Bovespa felt it had to offer something that would allow such companies to avoid appearing indifferent to investor concerns and that would, it hoped, encourage such issues to eventually move up to full Novo Mercado status.[12]

---

[9] www.novomercadobovespa.com.br/english/index.htm.

[10] The idea of creating a separate set of listing rules within an established stock market was taken from the German Neuer Markt. However, an important difference is that the Neuer Markt was designed for companies from the technology, media, and telecom sectors, whereas the Novo Mercado is intended for all companies wishing to demonstrate adherence to the highest standards of corporate governance, regardless of the industrial sector.

[11] The most exigent of the Novo Mercado's rules is that companies may not issue nonvoting shares. The other main rules require that public shares be offered through mechanisms that favor capital dispersion; that the company maintain a free float equivalent to 25 percent of the outstanding stock; that the same conditions provided to controlling shareholders in the transfer of the controlling bloc must be extended to all shareholders (tag-along rights); that the company be obliged to make a tender offer at an objectively determined "economic value" share price should a decision be taken to delist from the Novo Mercado; that a single one-year term for the entire board of directors be established; that the annual balance sheet be made available in accordance with accepted international accounting practices; and that quarterly reports be improved (consolidated financial statements are required).

[12] Level 2 has almost all the same rules as the Novo Mercado. The notable exception is that Level 2 companies may still issue nonvoting shares. Level I relates mainly to transparency and disclosure, rather than shareholder rights. It is doubtful whether a company's adherence to Level I shows a real improvement in its corporate governance; adoption of Level I standards are better viewed as a first step toward more substantial changes.

Novo Mercado and Level 2 companies, but not Level I companies, must settle disputes using the Market Arbitration Panel. (In anticipation of the Novo Mercado, the Brazilian legal reforms explicitly strengthened the legal standing of voluntary arbitration, making the enforcement of arbitral awards easier.) Obviously, the establishment of the Market Arbitration Panel reflects market doubts about the effectiveness of the Brazilian judiciary to deal with shareholder disputes in a fair and expeditious manner.[13]

Any Takers?

Since Bovespa launched its corporate governance initiative, several public and quasi-public entities have taken supportive action. BNDES, the Brazilian national development bank, has devised a simple formula for offering progressively lower interest rates on loans to companies that follow the requirements of Level I, Level 2, and the Novo Mercado. The pension fund and insurance company regulators allow pension funds and insurance companies to invest a larger proportion of their assets in companies listed on Level I, Level 2, or the Novo Mercado, creating another incentive for companies to move to these listing segments.

The Novo Mercado listing rules were officially launched in December 2000, but it was not until February 2002 that Companhia de Concessões Rodoviarias (CCR), a highway concession manager, became the first company to make an IPO on the Novo Mercado. As of December 15, 2002, two companies qualified for a full Novo Mercado listing. Meanwhile, 24 companies have joined Level I, and three have joined Level 2 (with several others announcing their intention to move to Level 2 in the near future). By focusing on transparency and disclosure, rather than shareholder rights, Level I was envisaged as a stepping-stone to Level 2. Certain institutional investors have begun to pressure companies to adhere to the Market Arbitration Panel, including most notably Bradesco-Templeton's Fondo de Valor e Liquidez, further encouraging companies to move up the ladder.

Ad Hoc Contracting in Brazil before and after the Reforms

Every time a company issues securities, it enters into a set of voluntary explicit and implicit contracts with investors concerning the company's governance. The company's

---

[13] The Market Arbitration Panel appears to represent a significant shift of power to shareholders and is reported to be perhaps the greatest single obstacle to persuading companies to adhere to Level 2.

charter, the terms of the securities, and any representations made in the marketing materials amount to explicit contracts, usually enforceable in law. Other understandings between issuers and investors—for example, that the company's voluntary governance practices are in line with evolving market standards and expectations—may be subtle (and less easily enforced). As investors in Latin American equity markets become more conscious of the shortcomings of governance during the debates over legal reforms, direct negotiation between investors and companies with respect to the governance practices seems to have become more common. Two Brazilian IPOs, one for ADRs issued before passage of the legal reform and another that was the first listing on the Novo Mercado, illustrate this tendency.

Issuer-Investor Negotiation over Tag-along Rights

Ultrapar is a large Brazilian liquefied petroleum gas and petrochemicals distribution company. Its total sales amounted to almost $1 billion in 2001.[14] As of March 1, 2002, its market capitalization exceeded $460 million.[15] Ultrapar decided to test the international market in 1999, offering nonvoting shares to U.S. investors through a sponsored ADR program listed on the New York Stock Exchange. The company had a solid reputation in Brazil for professional management and comparatively good treatment of shareholders. Although descendents of the founder still held the largest block of Ultrapar equity, day-to-day control of the company had long been entrusted to a cadre of professional managers, many of whom had come to hold substantial amounts of shares themselves, mostly locked in trusts set up as part of their long-term compensation packages.

Despite Ultrapar's history of good shareholder relations, during the "road show" for the ADR offering, investors expressed concerns about the prospective treatment of shareholders in the event of a sale of control of the company. Neither the company nor its underwriters seemed to have anticipated the depth of investor concerns during preparation of the offering. Given the existing control arrangement in the company (with the founder's descendents and senior management holding a majority of voting shares and a fair amount of nonvoting shares as well) and the nature of the industry, it was reasonable to expect a merger or takeover in the future, at which time a significant amount of the value of the company would be realized. Under existing Brazilian company and securities laws, there was no requirement that

---

[14] Currency is in U.S. dollars unless otherwise specified.
[15] Ultrapar's annual report is available at www.ultra.com.br.

a purchaser of a controlling interest offer to purchase the nonvoting shares, so ADR holders could be left out in the cold. The investors wanted tag-along rights, entitling them to sell their shares at the same price as the controllers and thereby secure an equal share of the control premium.

After a certain amount of back and forth among the company, its underwriters, and investors, Ultrapar's chairman verbally committed to amend the company's charter after the offering to grant all nonvoting shares tag-along rights (something he could ensure, given the combined voting power of the founder's descendents and the management team). This undertaking was apparently credible enough to permit the offering to go forward. Indeed the ADRs were successfully placed in October 1999. Investors and intermediaries felt that the company's reputation for fair dealing was sufficient collateral to assure that the chairman would honor his promise. It may also have been understood that there was something of a community of interest between the investors and the management group, since the managers would have a direct interest in a higher share price once their shares of the company were released from the trust arrangements. Ultrapar amended its charter at its next general meeting of shareholders in March 2000.

Issuer-Investor Negotiation over Conflicts of Interest

The more recent case of CCR is a similar example of investors demanding protections that go beyond those required by law. Indeed, it is an example of investors and the company agreeing to the whole gamut of protections and enforcement: the benefits of the Brazilian legal reforms; the Novo Mercado protections, including arbitration; and additional ad hoc arrangements tailored to the company's special circumstances and investor concerns.

CCR is the result of the merger of a set of Brazilian highway concession managers. Its initial shareholders were Brazilian civil engineering companies (that build highways) and a Portuguese construction contractor. The objective of its equity offering in the domestic market in early 2002 was to deleverage the company and establish a base on which to finance expansions (that is, the purchase of new concessions). The company's controllers intended to sell a large minority interest (up to 49 percent) in the company through the IPO. From the start, they committed that CCR would meet all the qualifications for Novo Mercado, including one share, one vote; tag-along rights; international accounting standards; independent directors; and arbitration of shareholder disputes. In fact, CCR proved to be the first company to achieve a Novo Mercado listing. However, given the controllers' potential conflict of interest (together they represented most of the country's highway construction industry), investors insisted on protections going beyond those of the Novo Mercado requirements. Discussions focused on special procedures for approval of contracts between the company and the controllers. CCR's management is reported to have originally offered to empower a majority of the company's independent directors to order an appraisal (fairness opinion) in the case of any transaction in excess of $1 million reais ($450,000) between the companies and affiliates. In the end, the company had to go beyond this, agreeing that any single director could demand such an independent appraisal. This provision was duly incorporated into the company's charter and was described in the final prospectus for the offering. The $300 million reais ($135 million) offering was successfully concluded in late January 2002.

Ad Hoc Contracting: Alive and Well

Ultrapar and CCR show that ad hoc contracting on corporate governance between issuers and investors is practiced in Brazil. Ultrapar's experience was well publicized in Brazil and certainly contributed to the thinking behind, and the eventual content of, Bovespa's Novo Mercado rules. Institutionalized contracting arrangements such as Novo Mercado can grow out of shared experiences with ad hoc contracting. At the same time, the CCR case demonstrates that institutional mechanisms such as Novo Mercado can complement and also be supplemented by ad hoc arrangements that take the packaged institutional arrangement as a basis on which to build an appropriate company-specific governance structure that the markets deem credible.

Voluntary Codes in Mexico

The understanding most practitioners have of a national code of best practices is that of a set of voluntary standards of corporate behavior produced by some sort of grouping of representatives from the private sector, academics, and market participants. However, in some emerging markets, the government has taken the lead role, push-starting the effort.[16] The Mexican Code of Best Corporate Practices, adopted in 2000, provides an illustration of this trajectory.[17]

---

[16] The recently issued German Corporate Governance Code was produced by a commission appointed by the German justice minister, with the government restricting its intervention in the process of drafting the code to issues of legal interpretation. The German government thus regards the German Corporate Governance Code as an act of private self-regulation (www.corporate-governance-code.de).

[17] For Mexico, see Business Coordinating Council, Codigo de Mejores Prácticas Corporativas (www.cce.org.mx).

Mexico: Push-starting a Code

In the aftermath of the Mexican banking sector collapse of 1995–96, it was apparent that the financial system had done little to promote sound corporate governance practices among securities issuers and borrowers. The evident lack of transparency and accountability in the corporate sector complicated the process of financial system resolution, contributing to the more than $100 billion cost of the rescue of Mexico's banking system. In late 1999, the Comisión Nacional Bancaria y de Valores (CNBV), Mexico's banking and securities supervisor, launched an initiative to draft a code of best practices for public companies. Mexico's Business Coordinating Council (the umbrella group including most national corporate and financial sector associations) was tapped to coordinate the private sector's contribution to the effort, and it selected well-known academics and representatives of the legal community to participate. The result was a set of fairly mild guidelines focusing largely on the quality of financial information and disclosure and on the composition and functioning of boards of directors. The code requires the boards of public companies to establish finance, compensation, and audit committees; a majority of directors on the audit committees must be independent of management and controllers. From the start of the process, it was expected that public companies would be required to disclose periodically the extent to which their practices were in compliance with the code. Soon after publication of the code, the CNBV issued a regulation requiring such periodic disclosure.

The Mexican approach contrasts importantly with what has occurred in the other large market in the region, Brazil. The Brazilian Code of Best Practice of Corporate Governance, produced by the Brazilian Institute of Corporate Governance, was instigated and produced by a strictly private entity.[18] Its aim is to set higher standards to which it encourages private companies to aspire. Independently, Brazil's securities regulator has issued the significantly more modest Recommendations for Corporate Governance, with which, as in Mexico, companies are required to comply or disclose.[19]

Prospects for Effectiveness and Enforcement

What is the significance of a voluntary code that is issued, for all intents and purposes, by the regulator? Should such a code be regarded as a legal prescription to be en-

---

[18] See www.cvm.gov.br.
[19] See www.cvm.gov.br.

forced in the courts (or through administrative action) or as an informal arrangement enforceable strictly as a reputation matter? Or should it be regarded as a mix, with ex ante characteristics of legislation, but with enforcement left mostly to private means? The ultimate answer in any particular case probably depends largely on the approaches the regulator takes to enforcement and the courts take to interpretation. Regulators that push-start the code-drafting process but do not monopolize its content (as in Mexico) may accelerate the emergence of appropriate benchmarks for good governance if the process is inclusive. However, if the regulator construes the code as akin to a law or regulation, particularly in an environment where judicial oversight of executive action is weak, then the code may come to be regarded as law. This may have important implications for compliance. In such a case, as with most laws, companies may come to regard minimum formal compliance as the goal, with perhaps negative consequences for development of more voluntary initiatives and even for the development of public discourse on the topic of corporate governance.

Disclosure Regime in Colombia

Corporate Governance Activism in Colombia: A Combined Response

Developments in Colombia are proving to be an interesting example of the interrelation between public policy efforts and voluntary initiatives with respect to sound corporate governance practices. Before the end of 2000, both the public and private sectors began to focus public attention on the shortcomings of the corporate governance regime and practices in Colombian corporations. In preparing a proposed capital markets law for presentation to Congress, the Superintendency of Securities insisted that the new legislation had to address perceived problems with the enforceability of shareholder rights, transparency, board practices, and director and controller liability.[20] At about the same time, the Confederation of Chambers of Commerce launched a corporate governance project to increase awareness by Colombian companies of market expectations, an effort joined by the Stock Exchange of Colombia, which was interested in preparing unlisted companies for the public markets, and the Pension Funds Association, representing the country's principal institutional investors.[21] Consequently, a benchmark national code project is now in its early stages, with participation from all major private sector associations.

---

[20] Interestingly, in anticipation of further private sector initiatives, the draft law included specific legal authorization for corporate governance rating agencies.

[21] Confederation of Chambers of Commerce, Corporate Governance Project (www.confecamaras.org.co).

Superintendency of Securities Resolution 275

On May 23, 2001, Colombia's Superintendency of Securities issued Resolution 275 pursuant to its power to prescribe certain rules for issuers whose securities (both debt and equity) are to be eligible for purchase by Colombia's pension funds.[22] Perhaps because of concern that too prescriptive a rule might be resisted in practice or challenged in the courts on the grounds that it went beyond the Superintendency's statutory authority, Resolution 275 does not mandate specific shareholder protection, board practice, transparency, or enforcement provisions to be included in company charters.[23] Rather, Article 3 of the resolution states that, in order for a company's securities to be eligible for purchase by pension funds, the company must have specific mechanisms in place to ensure protection of shareholder rights and equitable treatment of investors.[24] Articles 4, 5, and 6 require that these mechanisms be disclosed in some specificity to investors through the preparation, approval, and publication of a company-specific code of good governance.

In essence, Resolution 275 establishes a minimum disclosure regime for corporate governance for all Colombian listed companies (since in practice companies without access to the pension funds market are unlikely to achieve much liquidity in their shares or issue new securities). The companies themselves (and the market) are to interpret what the term "specific mechanisms" means, although companies will be hard pressed to put in place at least the minimal measures in each of the areas specifically covered by the resolution. The resolution also injects the potential for three levels of enforcement. Judicial enforcement of company charter provisions will presumably now extend to those provisions amended by, or construed in accordance with, the provisions of the new codes (which must be approved by the board of directors and presented at the shareholders meeting). The superintendency itself will play a role in ensuring that companies comply, at least in form, with the resolution—a role that may eventually lead to the use of the superintendency's disclosure oversight powers to influence the content of codes and companies' compliance with them. Finally, Resolution 275's references to enforcement seem to contemplate the adoption of arbitration mechanisms for enforcement of investor rights.

---

[22] Law 100 of 1993, Article 100, sections 3 and 4.

[23] Article 7 of the resolution does require that companies achieve at least a 20 percent public float in their shares within four years of the resolution's effectiveness.

[24] Such specific mechanisms must at a minimum cover management control and oversight, conflicts of interest, identification and disclosure of risks, the election and role of the *revisor fiscal*, special audits, internal controls, requirements for minorities to be able to call a shareholders meeting, and enforcement.

Company Responses to Resolution 275

Colombian listed companies presented their codes to shareholders at their 2002 annual general meetings, and many have made them publicly available on the company's website, through the media, and directly to pension funds. A number of companies appear to have opted for technical compliance. These companies view Resolution 275 as little more than a box-ticking exercise and recite their existing charter provisions and practices with appropriate cross reference to the resolution. Investors now have a clearer and more concise statement of the policies and practices of such companies, but the companies themselves have made no dramatic improvements in policies or practices.

Other companies seem to have embraced Resolution 275 as an opportunity to improve their governance practices and, just as importantly, to communicate their commitment to good governance to current and future investors. In a number of cases, company management (sometimes with the help of outside consultants) drafted codes organized more or less along the lines of the OECD Principles, with specific shareholder protections and transparency requirements that went beyond the requirements of current Colombian law and listing rules. Although the codes that have been made available to the public so far exhibit a diversity of style and content, some of them clearly represent a new contract between the company and its investors in key areas of corporate governance.

The code adopted by Inversura, an insurance holding company, is illustrative of the use of a Resolution 275 code by a Colombian company as a voluntary contractual and privately enforceable mechanism of corporate governance.[25] The Inversura code is organized largely along the lines of the OECD Principles (with separate chapters for shareholder rights and equitable treatment, the role and organization of the board, and stakeholders), with an additional chapter covering ethical treatment of clients, suppliers, and government officials.

In its code, Inversura's management binds the company to a number of important shareholder protections and board practices. Cumulative voting is authorized, and the company is prohibited from issuing multiple voting or nonvoting equity. At least four of the 10 board directors must be independent of management and controllers. The board is required to have audit, compensation, and governance commit-

---

[25] Inversura is not a public company; it devised its code in anticipation of its eventual entry into the public securities markets. Its code is certainly among the most shareholder friendly and board professional among Colombian companies, although others have taken similar approaches.

tees, with the audit committee dominated by independent directors. Perhaps most significantly, the code provides that disputes between shareholders and the company will be submitted to arbitration by an outside panel, in this case the Commercial Arbitration Panel of the Chamber of Commerce of Medellín.

Colombian institutional investors report that Resolution 275 has had positive effects on transparency. The resolution has helped move corporate governance issues up the public agenda and garnered a great deal of public attention. Indeed, Resolution 275 accelerated the very active collaboration of the Pension Funds Association, the Confederation of Chambers of Commerce, the Stock Exchange of Colombia, and the Superintendency of Securities in jointly promoting best practices in corporate governance throughout the country. This degree of formal voluntary cooperation among representatives of issuers, investors, intermediaries, and government is perhaps unique in an emerging market. It is probably fair to state that one reason cooperation has been possible is precisely the lack of prescription and the opening for voluntary initiative that Resolution 275 presented to the private sector.

It remains to be seen how well companies will actually comply with their new codes and how enforceable their obligation to do so will be in the longer term. The efforts that companies have expended to comply with Resolution 275 (preparation, board approval, and submission to the annual shareholders meetings) may have the unintended consequence of discouraging later amendment of the initial compliance-type codes produced by less progressive companies. It will be particularly interesting to follow the development of the initial codes over the next few years. Will there be competition among issuers to adopt more shareholder-friendly provisions? Or will a certain set of minimum standards be seen as sufficient? Will the pension funds play an active role in pushing issuers to do more? Will the market permanently bifurcate into one set of issuers that take a progressive stance and another interested only in bare compliance? What will be the experience with enforcement? Will recourse to the courts remain the ultimate tool for enforcement, or will actions by the Superintendency of Securities and arbitration take on greater importance? And what will be the contribution to capital market development? It will require at least a few years before any firm conclusions can be drawn.

Conclusions

As stated at the outset of this chapter, it is too early to determine the lessons of recent experiences with corporate governance reforms. However, the encouraging results from the initiatives in Brazil, Colombia, and elsewhere would seem to indicate that there is likely to be space in Latin America and other emerging markets for combinations of legal reforms, strictly voluntary initiatives, and intermediate forms of quasi-private legal rules enforceable by private means (such as special listing segments, ratings, other types of benchmarking, and investment disclosure regimes). Indeed, some of the most effective mechanisms may be found in these intermediate forms.

Key market characteristics that almost certainly affect the trajectory of public and private corporate governance initiatives and their prospects for effectiveness include:

- *Relative adequacy of existing practices.* Are the salient problems relatively objectively determinable (such as a lack of tag-along rights, too many nonvoting shares, application of substandard accounting rules, and uncertain rules for protection of minority shareholders in delistings) or subtle (poor audit quality; lackluster boards; and managers, boards, regulators, and investors in conflict)?
- *Number, size, and industry of public issuers.* Is there a club atmosphere among controlling shareholders and corporate executives, or are there multiple centers of entrepreneurship, competing aggressively in the financial markets (and perhaps in the political sphere as well)?
- *Number, size, and nature of principal investor groups* (institutional, pension, and international groups). How well are the investors governed? Are there distortions in their incentives or conflicts of interest that limit the extent to which they are profit maximizers?
- *Resources of the enforcement mechanisms* (courts, regulators, and existing alternative dispute resolution). What enforcement agents are realistically in the best position to see that the parties perform according to their contracts, observe standards, and comply with regulations?

Markets are idiosyncratic. Indeed, the importance (and even the presence) of the economic actors involved in public debate over reforms and private initiatives is a function of the characteristics of the market. In the interest of encouraging further examination, analysis, and debate among policymakers and practitioners, some tentative observations are offered:

- The most effective initiatives in the short-to-medium term will probably be private voluntary efforts that build on the limited legal reform efforts already undertaken.

- Ad hoc negotiations between issuers and investors will continue to be critical, and will inform the thinking that goes into future public and private innovations.
- Standardized private rulemaking (and dispute resolution), such as the Novo Mercado in Brazil, probably works best when there is general agreement on the set of objectively determinable deficiencies of the legal framework and corporate governance practices and when there are a reasonably large number of issuers and investors (such that no single issuer or investor is likely to set the standards and negotiate directly).
- Private standard setting of any type (listing rules, voluntary codes, or rating criteria) is likely to have the most immediate impact on the IPO market, as such standards provide investors with a common negotiating position.
- Dominant domestic investors, such as pension funds in small markets, may become the de facto corporate governance standard setters. However, this will depend on how well such investors are themselves governed.

There are good reasons for continued optimism about the prospects of further public and private sector initiatives in corporate governance in Latin America. One is that, as some of the cases described in this chapter demonstrate, much of the impetus for corporate governance reform in the region has been largely of domestic origin. The Enersis case in Chile burst on the scene before the Asian crisis and long before the recent corporate governance scandals erupted in the United States. In Chile and the other major Latin American markets, domestic institutional investors (particularly pension funds and mutual fund managers) are among the most important advocates for equitable treatment of shareholders, albeit often with a great deal of support from international fund managers and foreign shareholders. On the whole, Latin American governments (notably Chile, Colombia, and Brazil, but also Mexico and Argentina) were relatively quick to respond to the domestic pressures for a better governance regime. In some countries outside the region, notably in East Asia, the official response came only haltingly, and then often only at the urging of the international financial community in the wake of a crisis. Most, although not all, stock exchanges in Latin America also openly identify themselves with efforts to improve the governance of listed companies.

Another encouraging factor that bodes well for the sustainable success of the Latin American corporate governance movement is the speed with which those interested in better corporate governance have come together, both within countries and across the region as a whole. This chapter has described the timely cooperation and complementary activities of national public and private sector reformers in Brazil and Colombia. An important manifestation of cooperation across the region is the success of the Latin America Corporate Governance Roundtable of the OECD and the World Bank Group. The roundtable first brought together high-level policymakers, corporate leaders, investors, academics, and corporate governance professionals at Bovespa in 2000 for discussions organized around the framework of the OECD principles, and again at the Bolsa de Comercio de Buenos Aires in 2001 and the Bolsa Mexicana de Valores in 2002.[26] The roundtable meetings and follow-up efforts supported by the Global Corporate Governance Forum, World Bank, IFC, Inter-American Development Bank, Inter-American Investment Corporation, Corporación Andina de Fomento, and other public and private entities have made important contributions to the content and execution of several of the initiatives described in this chapter. The roundtable, the Global Corporate Governance Forum, and the IFC have supported members of the business community organizing institutes of directors. The Brazilian Institute of Corporate Governance is without a doubt the current leader in this regard. With the support of the Global Corporate Governance Forum, an association of institutes of directors from throughout the region has been established to promote sharing of resources and experiences among member organizations in Argentina, Brazil, Chile, Colombia, Mexico, and Peru.[27]

---

[26] The proceedings of the roundtable meetings are on the website of the Corporate Affairs Division of the OECD (www.oecd.org/corporate-affairs). The final meeting of the roundtable will be held in Santiago in March/April 2003.
[27] See www.gcgf.org.

Appendix Table 14-1 | Corporate Governance Progression for Listed Businesses

Attribute	Level 1. Acceptable corporate governance practices	Level 2. Extra steps to ensure good corporate governance	Level 3. Major contribution to improving corporate governance nationally	Level 4. Leadership
A. Commitment to corporate governance	The basic formalities of corporate governance are in place. The company has a well-articulated set of policies or a code of corporate governance addressing, at a minimum, the rights and treatment of shareholders, the role of the board of directors, and transparency and disclosure.	The company has a designated officer responsible for ensuring compliance with the corporate governance policies and/or code of the company and for periodic review of such code and policies. The company periodically discloses to shareholders its corporate governance policies/code and the extent to which its practices conform to voluntary codes of best practice in the country.	The company meets all applicable recommendations of the voluntary code of best practices of the country. The board has a governance committee.	The company is publicly recognized as a national leader and among the global leaders in corporate governance.
B. Structure and functioning of the board of directors	The board of directors meets regularly and deliberates independently of the executive management of the company. Board members are provided with adequate information and sufficient time for analysis and deliberation to exercise their duties of oversight and development of company direction and strategy. The board includes directors who are not executives of the company or its affiliates and not members of the controlling shareholder group.	The board includes two or more directors independent of management and controlling shareholders. The board has an audit committee with a majority of independent directors that recommends the selection of external auditors to the shareholder meetings, reviews and approves the reports of the external and internal auditors, and is responsible for overseeing implementation of audit or recommendations. Board composition (competencies/skill mix) is adequate to oversight duties. Annual evaluation is conducted.	The board has an audit committee composed entirely of independent directors. A committee of the board composed entirely of independent directors is required to approve all material transactions with affiliates of the controllers, directors, or management. Other specialized committees of the board exist to address special technical topics or potential conflicts of interest (nominating, compensation, and risk management).	The company's board is composed of a majority of independent directors.

C. Transparency and disclosure	The company's financial statements are prepared in accordance with an internationally recognized system of accounting and audited by a recognized independent auditing firm. The company has in place an appropriate system of internal controls and internal auditing that regularly interfaces with the external auditors and is responsible to the board of directors. The company complies with all disclosure requirements under applicable law, regulations, and listing rules. Investors and financial analysts are treated equally regarding information disclosure (fair disclosure).	The company publishes meaningful quarterly reports, containing segment reporting as well as results per share. Its practices go beyond local listing requirements. The company prepares and presents all financial statements and reporting in accordance with IAS or U.S. GAAP, audited by a recognized international accounting firm in accordance with international standards of auditing.		The company's financial and non-financial disclosure practices are in accordance with highest international standards. All disclosure and communications with shareholders are made available on the Internet in a timely fashion.
D. Treatment of minority shareholders	Minority shareholders are provided with adequate notice and agenda of all shareholders meetings and permitted to participate and vote at shareholders meetings. The company treats all shareholders of the same class equally with respect to voting rights, subscription rights, and transfer rights. All securities holders are treated equally regarding information disclosure (fair disclosure). Shareholders are provided with accurate and timely information regarding the number of shares of all classes held by controllers and affiliates (ownership concentration).	Effective representation of minority shareholders is provided by cumulative voting or similar mechanisms. The company has clearly articulated and enforceable policies with respect to treatment of minority shareholders in changes of control. The company has a well-understood policy and practice of full and timely disclosure to shareholders of all material transactions with affiliates of the controlling shareholders, directors, or management (conflicts of interest), and complete, timely, and accurate disclosure is made of all material shareholder agreements among controllers. The company's annual report discloses the principal risks to minority shareholders associated with the identity of the company's controlling shareholders, the degree of ownership concentration, cross-holdings among company affiliates, and any imbalances between controller voting power and overall equity position in the company.	The company has in place effective shareholder voting mechanisms (which may include super-majority requirements or "majority of minority" provisions) to protect minority shareholders against unfairly prejudiced actions of controllers when ownership is especially concentrated or controlling shareholders may have strong conflicts of interest.	The company's history of equitable treatment of shareholders evidences consistent conformance with international market expectations.

Bibliography

Beck, Thorsten, Ross Levine, and Norman Loayza. 2000. Finance and the Sources of Growth. *Journal of Financial Economics* 58, 261–300.

Jordan, Cally. 2000. "Experimentation in Capital Markets Regulation." International Organization of Securities Commissions, Montreal.

Jordan, Cally, and Mike Lubrano. 2002. *How Effective Are Capital Markets in Exerting Corporate Governance on Corporations? Financial Sector Governance: The Roles of the Public and Private Sectors.* Washington, D.C.: Brookings Press.

La Porta, Rafael, Florencio Lopez-de-Silanes, Andrei Shleifer, and Robert W. Vishny. 2000. Investor Protection and Corporate Valuation. *Journal of Financial Economics (Netherlands).* Issue 1–2 (October/November).

La Porta, Rafael, Florencio Lopez-de-Silanes, Robert W. Vishny, and Andrei Shleifer. 2002. Investor Protection and Corporate Valuation. *Journal of Finance.*

McKinsey & Company. 2002. Global Investor Opinion Survey: Key Findings, July 2002 (accessible from the Global Corporate Governance Forum: www.www.gcgf.org/docs).

CHAPTER 15

Human Capacity Development for Capital Market Professionals in Latin America and the Caribbean

Catherine Chandler-Crichlow

The process of financial sector development involves a complex mix of a number of factors, such as institutional strengthening, identification of the products and services best suited to a domestic market, and a culture of savings and asset accumulation. But no single factor is as vital to this process as the development of the human capital base needed for sustained growth in the sector. Outreville (1999) shows that there is a positive correlation between human capital development and growth in financial sectors. Furthermore, there is increasing recognition internationally that, for sustained growth in domestic economies, greater focus needs to be placed on developing the human resource base to ensure that workers and professionals have the skills, knowledge, and critical thinking abilities to be productive in the workplace (Becker 1993; OECD 1998; UNDP 1996).

Considering the diversity of natural resources, cultural groupings, political regimes, and educational systems in Latin America and the Caribbean, it is imperative that a human capital agenda be implemented that provides professionals with the skills, knowledge, and competencies they need to help achieve sustained economic growth. Capital markets in Latin America and the Caribbean span a wide spectrum, from sophisticated systems with multiple stock exchanges and active trading volumes to others that are still in an embryonic phase. In addition to the structural nuance of these capital markets, there continues to be tremendous interest by foreign investors who wish to be part of the exploration of the natural resources in Latin America and the Caribbean.

Models of human capital development in the region seem to follow a similar pattern of capital market development, with differences in the level of sophistication in approaches. In her paper on human capital development, Hunter (2000) finds that few regions have experienced the rapid economic transformation that has occurred in Latin America and the Caribbean. She links this to a surge in economic growth that has increased not only the wages and incomes of nationals but also an awareness of the need to provide more equitable educational systems to increase the skill base of potential workers in the region.

What is human capital development? Contemporary literature describes a number of elements of human capital; however, no one document provides a comprehensive picture of this process (Becker 1993; Hunter 2000; OECD 1998; Outreville 1999; UNDP 2002). This chapter uses the following definition:

> The process of creating a learning predisposition in workers and professionals in a sector, which would perpetuate a desire for continuous improvement of the skills, knowledge, and competencies they need to be marketable in the workplace.

Implicit in this definition is the notion of a combination of individual and social responsibility in human capital development. The chapter is based on the idea that there is a strong interaction between what is available in a system for individuals to use for development purposes and the individuals' commitment to a development path. Effective human capital development strategies should engender the dynamic interplay of a push strategy by the broader society and a pull strategy by the individual. The commitment of limited financial resources to the establishment of products and services for upgrading workers and professionals should respond to individuals' zest for continuous self-improvement.

The balance between general social growth and specific individual development would apply to any sector within a given system—financial services, health care, or agriculture. For countries where there are established approaches to human capital development, this balance might be readily achieved. However, it might be difficult for countries where models of and predisposition to developing human capital do not exist. Such countries need a catalyst for change, a compelling vision of sector development and its role in the broader economic development of the country. In such environments, there would be a greater onus placed on the political level to define and establish a system of good business practices. Governments therefore could play a facilitating role in harmonizing human capital and sector growth in the early phases of a sector's development. This could serve to create a strong base from which sectors evolve in a given country. This government intervention in the provision of a public good, as it were, could be done on a cooperative basis with appropriate parts of the private sector.

For the purposes of this chapter, capital markets are defined as a sector that exists in a broader social context. The chapter assumes that in a specific country, the domestic environment has implicit bureaucracies and perspectives on human development, which affect the growth of any sector in that jurisdiction. As capital markets in Latin America and the Caribbean span a broad spectrum of complexity, the chapter seeks to answer the specific question: What is the current level of investment in human capital development in the capital markets of Latin America and the Caribbean? Here investment is defined as the current infrastructure that is in place and not the financial outlay that has been made in establishing its development. While there are many facets to human capital development, the chapter focuses only on the elements of workforce development and sector governance. The indicator of workforce development used here is the availability of training programs developed by and used in the region for professionals in the capital market sector. The indicators of sector governance examined are the presence of regional and/or professional associations and sector-specific training institutions in the region.

The chapter describes two human capacity elements in three developed capital markets: Canada, the United Kingdom, and the United States. A similar analysis compares the capital markets in Latin America and the Caribbean with countries in Oceania (Australia, Fiji, New Zealand, Papua New Guinea, and Vanuatu).

A Framework for Human Capital Development

From contemporary literature, the term human capital is used to characterize the broader skills, knowledge, and abilities of individuals irrespective of the specific roles they play in a given society. This perspective focuses on the investment made to develop a literate, marketable individual who can make a contribution to the sustained growth of a country. In this chapter, the individual is defined as a professional in the capital market sector. In considering the development of workers and professionals of a given sector, there is a need to recognize that there are some areas of expertise that would be unique to that sector and in which participants in that sector need to be trained. For example, having an in-depth understanding of the dynamics of flight should be an aim of all workers and professionals in the aerospace industry, but not so for individuals in the health care field. The public places its trust in pilots, surgeons, teachers, lawyers, and other specialists because these professionals typically have developed a unique skill set beyond basic literacy. So, too, it should be with capital markets. A sector-based approach to human capital development would therefore need to reflect the unique areas of learning that are critical to participants in that field.

Figure 15-1	A Framework for Human Capital Development

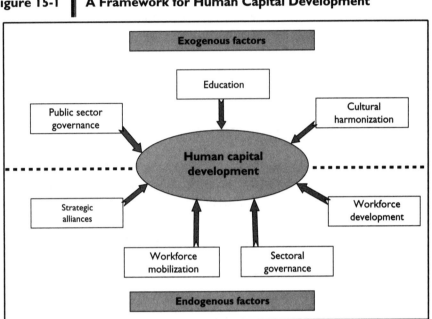

Sector-based human capital development can be envisioned as having two broad categories: endogenous factors and exogenous factors. The factors endogenous to a sector are the institutions, partnerships, associations, and specific products and services that clearly differentiate the sector from any other. The factors exogenous to a sector are those that characterize the national environment in which a sector is situated and include, but are not limited to, areas such as the domestic education system, cultural norms, and public sector governance. Figure 15-1 presents a framework for sector-based human capital development. Implicit in this model of human capital development is the notion that the process is as efficient and effective as the milieu in which it evolves. The model implies a dynamic relationship between the approaches of the private and public sectors to governance. A domestic environment that places a premium on educational opportunities for its population, cultural integration, and effective public sector governance is one that would be predisposed to implementing strong human capital development approaches. The converse of this might also be true in countries where the exogenous factors place limitations on the development of a highly skilled and knowledgeable workforce. The following elements are considered endogenous to a sector:

- Workforce development. This is the level of opportunities provided for workers/professionals in a given sector to continuously hone their skills, knowledge, and attitudes to keep pace with changes in the sector. Ideally, this would be implemented using a holistic approach that integrates the development of technical, operational, and behavioral competencies such as project management, decisionmaking, and problem solving.
- Workforce mobilization. This is the capacity developed in the system for workers and professionals to be able to move into different career paths in the same sector or across sectors, which is facilitated by the continuous skill upgrading that is provided in the workplace.
- Sector governance. This refers to the ability of a sector to organize a strong enabling infrastructure in the form of professional associations and human resource development institutions that could bring consistency, standards of conduct, a mechanism for continuous information sharing among market professionals, and continuous human capacity development in the sector.
- Strategic alliances. International agencies, educational institutions, private sector corporations, and industry associations can use collaborative strategies to leverage and integrate the investments made in the development of workers and professionals.

It is assumed here that, for sectors that are in an embryonic stage of development, workforce development and sector governance would be the first hurdles that need to be cleared in creating a competitive and efficient business environment. As these sectors become more developed, the elements of workforce mobilization and strategic alliances would become increasingly relevant. The following elements are considered exogenous to a sector:

- Public sector governance. The political infrastructure, the norms and patterns of operations in public service, and the relationship between government and private sector collaboration are some of the elements that constitute public sector governance.
- Education. The education element includes the provisions made at the national level to provide primary, secondary, and post-secondary opportunities for a population to develop the basic skills, knowledge, and attitudes needed to thrive in a given domestic environment.
- Cultural harmonization. New and innovative business strategies and government policies are aligned with the beliefs, traditions, and norms that characterize different ethnic groupings within a country.

Table 15-1 ▌ Indicators of Human Capital Development

Elements of human capital development	Indicators
Endogenous factors	
Workforce development	Presence of domestic private/public training institutions
	Investment by government in sector development programs as a percentage of gross domestic product
	Investment by businesses in a sector for developing its workforce
	Workforce participation in sector-based training programs
Workforce mobilization	Movement of workforce to different roles in the same sector
	Movement of workforce to different roles in a different sector
	Movement of workforce across different sectors
Sector governance	Number of professional associations
	Number of training associations
	Provision of standards of practice by professional associations
	Size of membership of sector associations
Strategic alliance	Alliances with domestic associations/educational institutions
	Alliances with regional associations/educational institutions
	Alliance with international associations/educational institutions
Exogenous factors	
Public sector governance	Judicial understanding of needs of the sector
	Executive understanding of needs of the sector
	Government assistance programs
Education	Government investment in formal and informal educational opportunities
	Completed years in formal primary, secondary, and tertiary educational levels
	Infrastructure for informal education
Cultural harmonization	Alignment of products and services to cultural norms
	Participation of indigenous cultural groups in the development of the sector
	Presence of strategies that would facilitate the movement of indigenous societal customs toward a business model of developed economies

The indicators in table 15-1 could be used to assess the degree to which the elements of human capital development are established in a given locale. This is not an exhaustive list, but it provides a framework for studying the sector. This model can be used to provide a profile of human capital development for any given sector irrespective of geographic or jurisdictional differences. Unfortunately, there is a paucity of information in the public domain for using this model to determine the current state of affairs of human capital development for capital markets in Latin America and the Caribbean. Therefore, this chapter provides only a snapshot of the sector in the region. Although exogenous factors play a critical role in the development of capital markets, their impacts in the politically and socially diverse context of Latin America and the Caribbean are beyond the scope of this report.

Countries with Developed Capital Markets

Developed countries benefit from an extensive history in financial sector development, a strong focus on public and private sector governance, high per capita earnings, awareness by the business community of the value of investing in the human resource base, and highly structured educational systems. For example, the OECD (1998) report on human capital investment shows that developed countries such as Belgium, Canada, Sweden, the United Kingdom, and the United States have financial service sectors in which workers have high literacy levels. The presence of these exogenous factors in sophisticated formats provides intrinsic expectations on the manner in which a sector does business and develops its workforce. Because of the size of capital markets in these countries, there are enough people to be trained to warrant the establishment of sector-specific training institutions in each country. There is also an availability of financial resources for developing professionals critical to sustaining continued growth in the sector. The OECD (1998) report also shows that Australia, Canada, New Zealand, the United Kingdom, and the United States have the highest participation levels for job-related training.

There are a number of key similarities in the developed capital markets profiled here. First, there are professional associations that provide industry standards and guidelines, training programs and conferences for continuous improvement of professionals, as well as investors in those markets. The intent in this overview is not to comment on the quality of training programs offered to the market, but to identify that in fact there exists an infrastructure to deliver these programs to professionals and investors. Second, the regulatory agencies in these countries play a pivotal role in public awareness and investor education. With the focus on safeguarding the rights of the investor, the involvement of regulatory agencies in investor education is simply good practice. A third commonality in these markets is the role of training institutes whose main products are services that target professionals in capital markets. Some of these programs are primarily skill building, while others are designed to support organizational compliance to industry and/or regulatory standards. In summary, the three markets profiled here—Canada, the United Kingdom, and the United States—all have a demonstrated commitment to human capacity development and an infrastructure established to develop professionals and investors.

Canada

Canada is a federation with 10 provinces and three territories. Its capital markets can be characterized as having a strong regulatory focus, a diversity of professional associations, and many private sector firms that specialize in skills and knowledge development programs for the sector. Table 15-2 provides a summary of key players in the sector.

A significant feature observed in this context is the fact that all of the industry associations include continuous upgrading courses for their memberships through sector-specific programs. Professionals in this environment therefore have access to a range of training and development opportunities. Regulatory agencies and stock exchanges are key contributors to investor educational programs available in the sector.

Table 15-2 | Human Capacity Development Components in Capital Markets in Canada

Regulators	Stock exchanges	Industry associations	Training institutions
• Alberta Securities Commission • British Columbia Securities Commission • Canadian Securities Institute (CSI) • The Ontario Securities Commission (OSC) • The Quebec Securities Commission	• Canadian Venture Exchange • Montreal Exchange • Toronto Stock Exchange	• Canadian Capital Markets Association • Canadian Securities Administrators (CSA) • Mutual Funds Dealers Association of Canada (MFDA) • Investment Dealers Association of Canada (IDA) • Independent Financial Brokers of Canada (IFBC)	• Investment Funds Institute of Canada (IFIC) • International Quality and Productivity Centre • RBC Capital Markets

Table 15-3 | Human Capacity Development Components in Capital Markets in the United Kingdom

Regulators	Stock exchanges	Industry associations	Training institutions
• The Financial Services Authority (FSA)	• FTSE International (London Stock Exchange) • London Stock Exchange: Daily Price Summary • Electronic Share Information • London Metal Exchange • London International Financial Futures and Options Exchange	• Association of Investment Trust Companies • Investment Management Association (IMA) • The Financial Markets Association • The Futures and Options Association (FOA)	• British Bankers' Association • BCM Training • International Quality and Productivity Centre • Intuition • J. J. Associates • Panagaea Partners • Securities Institute • Sun Microsystems

In summary, Canada has five regulatory agencies, three stock exchanges, five professional industry associations, and three institutions dedicated to providing training programs for professionals in the capital market sector. These data suggest that there is a heavy emphasis placed on development of human capital in this environment.

The United Kingdom

With one of the world's most extensive international financial centers and with the largest share of many global markets, the United Kingdom has a well-developed, stable capital market sector. Because of the presence of a range of international financial intermediaries in the British market, there is great depth of liquidity and flexibility in its financial markets. Its consolidated supervisory model is organized as the Financial Supervisory Authority, which provides increased potential for information sharing among key market participants and a more informed regulator. As in the Canadian context, in this market diverse professional associations and private sector firms specialize in skills and knowledge development programs for the sector. Table 15-3 summarizes the key players in the sector.

A significant feature observed in this context is the fact that all of the industry associations include in their mandates continuous upgrading of their membership through sector-specific programs. Professionals in this environment therefore have access to a range of training and development opportunities. Here again, the regulatory agency and stock exchanges listed offer a range of investor education programs. With more than 10 training institutions and industry associations in this market, there appears to be an even greater emphasis placed on human capital development; there are five stock exchanges and one regulator in this jurisdiction.

The United States

Like Canada, the United States is a federation, which in this case is composed of 50 states. As a major player in global markets and a hub for international capital flows, the United States has a highly structured capital market sector. Here capital markets can be characterized as having a plethora of professional associations and private sector firms that specialize in the development of skills and knowledge for the sector. The sector is regulated at a federal level by two key agencies, and stock is traded on 11 stock exchanges. Table 15-4 gives a summary of key players in the sector. It is noteworthy that all groups listed here offer some form of technical and/or operational training for professionals in the sector.

Capital Markets in Latin America and the Caribbean

Two major factors that contribute to the development of capital markets are the ability of a country to sustain high domestic savings and a national culture of wealth accumulation. These exogenous factors can also affect the ability of a country to build the infrastructure needed to implement a human capital approach that develops knowledgeable professionals and investors. Herein lies the major challenge faced in Latin America and the Caribbean. While the countries in the region may have marketable commodities such as oil, natural gas, and minerals, and while some have built strong economies from tourism, some countries are still plagued with low domestic savings rates and low per capita earnings. To reap the social benefits from their natural resources, there is therefore a strong reliance on foreign investors in local markets.

How should countries that are seeking to build stronger domestic markets balance investment in developing the institutional capital versus the human capital for the sector? The sector needs technology, a payment and settlement system, and many other essential items. There is the potential for a vicious cycle of decisionmaking on prioritizing sector development investments, a situation that is exacerbated when there is a scarcity of financial resources to support sustainable growth of the sector. The task

Table 15-4 | **Human Capacity Development Components in Capital Markets in the United States**

Regulators	Stock exchanges	Industry associations	Training institutions
• The Securities and Exchange Commission (SEC) • Commodity Futures Trading Commission (CFTC)	• New York Stock Exchange (NYSE) • NASDAQ • The Arizona Stock Exchange • Chicago Stock Exchange • Chicago Board Options Exchange • Chicago Board of Trade • Chicago Mercantile Exchange • Kansas City Board of Trade • Minneapolis Grain Exchange • Pacific Stock Exchange • Philadelphia Stock Exchange	• Bank Securities Association (BSA) • Bond Market Association • Commodity Floor Brokers and Traders Association • Futures Industry Institute • Institute of Financial Markets (IFM) • Managed Funds Association • National Association of Investors Corporation (NAIC) • National Association of Stockbrokers (NAS) • National Association of Securities Dealers (NASD) • National Investor Relations Institute (NIRI) • Securities Industry Association (SIA) • Securities Traders Association • The Bond Market Association	• Euromoney Financial Training • International Quality and Productivity Centre • Pangaea Partners

might seem daunting in Latin America and the Caribbean, considering the financial resources that would be needed in each country to establish its unique infrastructure.

There is an even greater conundrum from the human capital perspective. In the region, there is a need to engender a culture of institutional savings at the domestic level. This is no easy task given the cultural norms of investment in some countries in the region. For example, many cultures use a range of noninstitutional savings vehicles that have allowed them to become socially mobile, that is, to build homes and educate children. Indigenous savings and credit formats such as the "sou-sou" and "chaitey" in Trinidad and Tobago or the "meetings" in Barbados serve a similar role as the "consorcio" in Brazil or the "pandero" in Peru. While these models do not have the western predilection for institution building, they represent strong societal norms for asset accumulation. The extent to which domestic savings from multiple small, closed savings stocks is mobilized into larger savings flows of an institutional nature will be influenced by the extent to which the society trusts the corporate governance of those savings institutions. There is therefore a weak lure to institutional saving strategies for some of these cultures. Even with some of the more adventurous investors, the purchase of shares in profitable companies is not done for trading purposes. Rather, shares are often perceived to be priceless family heirlooms to be passed on for many generations. Unfortunately, the half-life of many of these companies is quite short, and heirs inherit ornate pieces of worthless paper. Central to the strengthening of capital markets across the region is the need for public education as well as professional development of the human resource base needed to implement the sector.

It is axiomatic that strong leadership is critical to defining and implementing a vision for capital market development. A review of the products and services offered by professional associations and training institutions serving the capital markets reveals a dearth of programs that focus on developing professionals with strong leadership and management competencies. Latin America and the Caribbean are at that stage in their growth that this component could be included in human capital models established in the region. Sustained growth of a sector would benefit from having a combination of knowledgeable professionals and a strong vision for sector improvement. Conversely, sector growth would be impeded when there is not a critical mass of knowledgeable professionals in the sector and there is not a unifying vision for the growth of that sector at a domestic or regional level. Table 15-5 summarizes the human capital components in place in Latin America and the Caribbean.

A number of key insights emerge when the data on human capital development for capital markets in Latin America and Caribbean are compared with those of the developed countries profiled in this chapter. First, investments in physical infrastructure in the form of "bricks and mortar" in the region far outweigh those allocated to developing the professional base and workforce to support the sector. It is noteworthy that for a region that currently has 16 stock exchanges that vary widely in their size, volume of trading, and the sophistication of companies traded on their exchanges, and 21 regulatory agencies, there is no single regional entity that identifies,

Table 15-5 | **Human Capacity Development Components in Capital Markets in Latin America and the Caribbean**

Regulators	Stock exchanges	Industry associations	Training institutions
Bahamas Securities Commission Banco de Guatemala Banco Central de Uruguay Bermuda Monetary Authority, Bermuda Comisión Nacional de Valores, Argentina Comisión Nacional de Valores, Costa Rica Comisión Nacional Bancaria y de Valores, Mexico Comisión Nacional de Valores, Panama Comisión Nacional de Valores, Paraguay Comisión Nacional Supervisora de Empresas y Valores, Peru Comisión Nacional de Valores, Venezuela Comisión Nacional de Bancos y Seguros, Honduras Financial Services Investment Commission, Jamaica Securities and Exchange Commission, Brazil Securities and Exchange Commission, Trinidad and Tobago Superintendencia de Bancos y Otras Instituciones Financieras, Nicaragua Superintendencia de Valores, Bolivia Superintendencia de Valores y Seguros, Chile Superintendencia de Valores, Colombia Superintendencia de Valores, El Salvador Superintendencia de Compañías, Ecuador	• Barbados Stock Exchange • Bermuda Stock Exchange • Rio de Janeiro Stock Exchange • São Paulo Stock Exchange • Cayman Islands Stock Exchange • Chile Electronic Stock Exchange • Santiago Stock Exchange • Bogotá Stock Exchange • Occidente Stock Exchange • Guayaquil Stock Exchange • Jamaica Stock Exchange • Nicaraguan Stock Exchange • Lima Stock Exchange • Trinidad and Tobago Stock Exchange • Caracas Stock Exchange • Venezuela Electronic Stock Exchange	• Centre for Latin American Monetary Studies—Western Hemisphere Payments and Securities, Clearing and Settlement Initiative • Centre for Latin American Capital Markets • Ibero-American Association of Stock Exchanges • Council of Securities Regulators of the Americas (COSRA)	None identified

coordinates, develops, and implements professional training and development programs. Conversely, in the developed countries, there appears to be a balance in the
investments made for physical infrastructure and human capital development.

Second, for Latin America and the Caribbean as well as the developed countries, the regulatory agencies with oversight responsibilities for the capital markets
have a diversity of institutional structures. Some are independent autonomous agencies; others are combined insurance and capital markets. These institutional models
bring differences in terms of levels of autonomy, industry stakeholders, as well as budgets for developing regulatory staff. With their roles in creating sound, stable markets
as well as protecting the rights of investors, it is imperative that regulators be provided with the skills, knowledge, and leadership competencies to stay one pace ahead
of developments in the markets. It should be noted that in some locations, the regulatory agency plays a pivotal role in investor education.

Third, the data show that while the developed countries have strong sector
governance in the form of professional and training associations, there is a paucity of
these frameworks in Latin America and the Caribbean. The Ibero-American Association of Stock Exchanges provides a systematic approach to understanding the needs
of professionals in the stock exchanges in Latin America. Regulators in the region are
members of the Council of Securities Regulators of the Americas (COSRA), which
has a mandate for stimulating regional dialogue on issues critical to regulators. The associations provide mechanisms for conducting research and dialogue among their
members through conferences and ongoing communication. This facilitates information sharing among professionals in the region and an ability to discuss the impact of
issues such as globalization, advances in technology, and the increasing complexity of
financial products and services on local markets. However, neither of these associations has the breadth or depth of training programs to provide sustained upgrading
of the professionals who are their members.

There is no single entity dedicated to the creation of education, training, or development programs for the region. For instance, COSRA does not have the budgetary or institutional capacity to develop, deliver, and maintain training and education
programs for regional regulators; instead it forms strategic alliances to bring training
programs to its members. For example, in June 2002, 15 leaders in capital markets regulation participated in a leadership program hosted in Toronto, Canada. This initiative
was the result of a partnership among COSRA, the Inter-American Development
Bank, and the Toronto International Leadership Centre for Financial Sector Supervision.

Some might argue that it would be more meaningful to compare Latin America and the Caribbean with another geographic area that has an equal diversity in sophistication of financial markets and history of human capital development than to

Table 15-6 | Human Capacity Development Components in Capital Markets in Oceania

Regulators	Stock exchanges	Industry associations	Training institutions
• Australian Securities and Investments Commission • Securities Commission, New Zealand • Securities Commission of Papua New Guinea	• Australian Derivatives Exchange • Australian Stock Exchange • New Zealand Futures and Options Exchange • New Zealand Stock Exchange • Sydney Futures Exchange	• Asian Securities Analysts Federation Inc. • Australasian Investor Relations Association • Securities and Derivatives Industry Association • Securities Registrars Association of Australia Inc. • Securities Industry Research Centre for Asia-Pacific (SIRCA)	• Corporation Builders • Institute of Financial Professionals of New Zealand • Securities Institute of Australia • ShareChat Education • Standard and Poor's

compare the region to developed countries. To determine whether there are major differences between comparable regions, an empirical examination of human capital development in an equally diverse region was done. Using the human development index produced by the United Nations Development Programme (1996), countries close to those of Latin America and the Caribbean were identified (for example, the human development for New Zealand is 0.927; Barbados, 0.906; Fiji, 0.853; Mexico, 0.845; Nicaragua, 0.569; and Vanuatu, 0.562). Based on these ratings, Oceania was chosen for comparison, and data on human capital development in this region are summarized in table 15-6.

Oceania comprises of fewer countries than Latin America and the Caribbean. In two countries in Oceania—Australia and New Zealand—employees in the workplace have high levels of literacy (OECD 1998). Oceania has five stock exchanges, six professional associations, and five organizations specializing in training and development programs for professionals in capital markets (table 15-6). The data suggest that there is a balanced approach to investing in the physical and human infrastructure for capital markets in Oceania.

In comparing Latin America and the Caribbean, the three developed markets, and the countries of Oceania, a key area of similarity is the role played by regulatory agencies in their proactive approach to investor education. However, all of the locations have a limited number of professional associations and training institutions that provide ongoing opportunities for development of leadership competencies in the capital market sector.

Human Capacity Development

The intrinsic need to learn could diminish when environmental factors mitigate the ability of the individual to engage in active learning. The acquisition of knowledge could be attained through formal instructional methods such as seminars, workshops, lectures, and self-paced learning materials. Alternatively, techniques such as networking and mentoring could be used in informal instructional models. Irrespective of the instructional model used, the litmus test of success in developing the human capacity of any group lies in the ability to create a synergistic integration of formal and informal strategies. This is a key consideration in defining an agenda for building the human resource capacity of capital markets in Latin America and the Caribbean. Whether the groups are investors, regulators, dealers, stockbrokers, or issuers, there is a need to consider the linguistic, cultural, and infrastructure contexts in which programs can be introduced.

An additional factor that needs to be considered in defining a human capital development agenda for a region is the phase of development of capital markets in the area or country. For example, the developed countries cited in this article are in a more advanced phase in the development of their markets, and their workforce development approaches appear to generally keep pace with market trends and evolution. Conversely, many member states of Latin America and the Caribbean are in early formative stages in the development of their domestic markets and place greater emphasis on start-up activities rather than the development of the human resources needed to sustain growth of the sector. This perhaps points to a lesson to be learned for these countries in that there should be a co-incident focus on both physical infrastructure and human capital development. A focus on workforce development and sector governance of human capital investment should help to define the needs of the region in more concrete terms.

Growth of Capital Markets

A sector model for human capacity development could be approached from two perspectives. The first would use a theoretical model of best practices and apply it to a sector at the macro level. This would allow for a top-down, systematic approach to structuring the development needs for all participants in a given sector. The second perspective would involve a flexible, needs-driven approach that reflects the nuances of the market. The latter approach is pragmatic and intrinsically situates the development of curricula in the realities of stakeholders in the region. Given the diverse stages of development of the capital markets in Latin America and the Caribbean, this latter approach seems best suited to the needs of the region.

Many benefits may be derived from having a knowledgeable professional base and an informed investor group. Three main aspects of the current status of human capacity development in Latin America and the Caribbean could impede further capital market growth: low trust in market intermediaries, limited market activity, and limited confidence in the market.

Low Trust in Market Intermediaries

Issuers or other financial intermediaries typically have a more expansive quantity and quality of knowledge of the securities being traded than the individual investor. This type of information asymmetry places the investor in a vulnerable situation and, when losses occur, might reduce trust levels between these two key participants. It is therefore critical to ensure that issuers are educated on the importance of their relationship with investors and their contribution to building stable markets.

Limited Market Activity

Informed investors are able to discern between reputable and dishonest issuers as well as to recognize that capital markets are not long-term alternatives to the deposit-taking system of banks or credit unions. In the absence of a structured public education program, the value of capital market products and services would not be understood; this could consequently limit market development at the domestic level.

Limited Confidence in the Market

Regulators play a key role in the development of capital markets when they implement regulatory guidelines to build domestic savings and investments by limiting the level of offshore investment permissible from local savings. They create attractive markets by being transparent in their requirements and by engendering transparency from companies they regulate. The confidence developed in the system through the work of regulatory agencies cannot be overstated.

The current status of human capital development and the growth in physical infrastructure of the capital markets in the region point to the need for the powers that be in Latin America and the Caribbean to strengthen the human facets of the sector. To subordinate human capacity development to investment in business infrastructure in emerging economies by default also puts a secondary emphasis on the long-term development of capital markets in the region.

A Process

The linguistic, cultural, political, and economic diversity in Latin America and the Caribbean creates a mosaic that is evident not only in its peoples but also in the financial development of the region. It is necessary to be cognizant of these differences in building an integrated model for developing the region. Such a model could best be conceptualized as a tiered curriculum that provides programs for the hierarchical levels of professions as well as cross-pollination on areas of common need across professional groups. A human capital development process would include four components.

First, it would include determining the needs of key market participants. To build an efficient capital market sector, stockbrokers, analysts, investors, regulators, policymakers, and other actors all require knowledge to make them effective. A first step would be to identify the specific themes that each group needs to help it function as a market participant. Technocrats with weak problem solving, decisionmaking, or analytical thinking competencies are no better than uninformed leaders. The real opportunity that exists in Latin America and the Caribbean is to combine strong technical and operational knowledge with strong leadership competencies. A frequent mistake in the establishment of any new sector-based curriculum is to place an inordinate emphasis on technical and operational training programs with little or no attention given to the development of behavioral competencies. A balanced curriculum would integrate the two components.

Second, human capital development would require identifying current regional resources. A key step in building a sectorwide training and development model would be to conduct an in-depth inventory of technical and operational courses in the region. This would be a step toward optimization of existing materials and the development of new curricula based on themes common across a number of professional groups. For example, regulators across the region could all benefit from programs that cover areas such as market manipulation, insider trading, or the fight against money laundering. At the domestic level, the same regulators could benefit from participating jointly with policymakers, brokers, or issuers in seminars on the impact of rapid technological change on capital flows at regional and international levels. Such materials must be developed in English, Spanish, and Portuguese to meet the needs of all countries across the region.

Third, the approach would examine the accessibility of training programs. Here an analysis would be done to identify the factors that facilitate or hinder access to training programs for members of the sector. It would also identify the training approaches currently used, including seminars, workshops, lectures, or self-study materials. A human capital development approach that provides an effective mix of program delivery strategies that include classroom and modular self-study alternatives could increase both overall access to ongoing professional development and cost efficiencies.

Fourth, the approach would require determining the sector's use of information. Never before in history has there been access to so much information from so many different media forms and on such a broad range of topics. Some proponents in the field of information management suggest that this plethora of facts is at times received with an amazing absence of analysis by the recipients of such information. Professionals need help in the process of seeking relevant information, analyzing clear and ambiguous information, and determining the potential impact of market and global trends on local markets. Assessing the information used by market participants and the strategies for making them more effective in analyzing such information would be another key step in developing a human capital approach for the sector.

Barriers

While there is a clear need for implementing a human capital development approach for Latin America and the Caribbean, three challenges need to be addressed. First is the funding process. Setting up training and development curricula for capital markets requires seed financing. A funding approach that involves a partnership among international agencies, regional governments, and the regional private sector needs to be established.

The second challenge is to strengthen regional associations. Although COSRA provides a forum for dialogue among regulators in Latin America and the Caribbean, such associations need to be strengthened to assume a more pivotal role in developing the human resource base in the region. This is a challenge because the membership does not have the financial resources needed to support the infrastructure needed by the association. In comparing the region to the developed countries or Oceania, this membership model provides a knowledgeable pool of resources through focused investment in professional groups.

The third challenge is to harmonize human capital investment in the region. Diversity in languages, political systems, social and cultural norms, risk-averse behavior of the private sector, and emphasis on developing human capital all come together in Latin America and the Caribbean to create one major barrier: bureaucracy. Yet these differences are the factors that drive the introduction of an approach to harmonizing the capital markets of the region. No one nation can provide all the training and development programs, information systems, and physical infrastructure needed to create efficient capital markets.

Enablers

Research in education shows that peer learning is one of the most powerful instructional strategies for adults. Peers are able to connect intellectually, solve problems as a group, develop plans to deal with common challenges, or be catalysts for change. It is this aspect of human capital development that could most easily be established in an emerging market. Whether professionals meet at seminars or conferences, the mutual sharing of information is a powerful process for the development of a sector. Increased dialogue among professionals across Latin America and the Caribbean would serve as an enabler toward identifying the training needs of the different groups and defining financing models for the sector.

The establishment of regional professional bodies would further enable human capital development. There are some concepts that span all professional groups in capital markets. Areas such as corporate governance, accounting standards and practices, reliance on external auditors, and intrasector information sharing should be important to all groups. Associations could also serve to reduce inconsistencies in policies and practices within a sector. The establishment of professional associations could facilitate discussion within and across professions and would provide the information base that could be used to direct the investment of limited financial resources to produce maximum benefits for the sector. Being mindful of the fact that the number of professionals in some countries might be small, consideration should be given to establishing common regional groups that would influence the standards of practice across all jurisdictions in the region.

The creation of strategic alliances would be another enabler. A proverbial maxim of not reinventing the wheel is applicable to capital markets in Latin America and the Caribbean. Although the region lacks institutions that can deliver specialized training to professions in the sector, the acquisition of such programs could be easily managed through the establishment of strategic alliances with academic institutions in the region or private sector firms from other jurisdictions. This strategy would facilitate an expedient introduction of training programs without the extensive development time required to produce new training applications.

A multilingual scope would further enable human capital development. The linguistic differences across Latin America and the Caribbean make it imperative that all training courses and seminars, professional development materials, and lectures be made available in the main languages of the region. It might be perceived that the cost of such an approach would be exorbitant. However, if a database of trainers, educators, and translators in the region were produced, these resources could be used in the development of such materials. While associations such as COSRA, the Centro de Estudios Monetarios Latinoamericanos (CEMLA), and the Asociación de Supervisores Bancarias de las Américas (ASBA) exist to provide training for specific sections of the financial sector, there appears to be merit in the need for a financial sector curriculum development committee focused on advancing the development of all aspects of financial sector development in the region.

Conclusion

With the untapped natural resources in Latin America and the Caribbean, the region maintains the potential to develop vibrant capital markets. However, this promise of financial sector growth is contingent on the design, delivery, and implementation of a holistic approach to human capital development in this area. The sector in the region is characterized by rapid advancements in the establishment of domestic capital markets, gaps in human resource infrastructure, a need to introduce standards of practice for different professional groups, and wide disparity in financial resources available to each country to develop the professionals in the sector. Thus, it is essential to implement a coordinated approach to developing the human dimension of the capital markets of Latin America and the Caribbean in order to realize their latent strength.

Bibliography

Baldwin, J.R. 1995. *Human Capital Development and Innovation: The Case of Training in Small and Medium Sized Firms*. Ottawa, Canada: Statistics Canada.

Becker, G. 1993. *Human Capital*. Chicago: University of Chicago Press.

Business 2.0. 2002. Web Guide to Stock Exchanges in the Caribbean. Business 2.0 Media Inc. http://www.business2.com/webguide/0,1660,9470,00.html.

Hunter, W. 2000. Human Capital Development in Latin America: Past Polices and Prospects for Change. A paper prepared for presentation at the conference, "Current Policy Dilemmas in Latin America's Foreign Economic Relations," Tufts University, Fletcher School of Diplomacy, Massachusetts, USA (November).

International Business Information (IBI) Directory. Chapter 5 – Latin America and the Caribbean. Information Today, Inc. http://www.infotoday.com/ibi/ibi-chapter5. htm.

Moneymile.com Directory. UK Investment Training & Education, London. http://www.moneymile.com/training/investtraining.asp.

Nemirowsky, H., and J. Wright.1996. Issues Surrounding Security Regulation in Latin America and the Caribbean. *Sustainable Development Department—Infrastructure and Financial Markets,* The Inter-American Development Bank, Washington, D.C.

OECD. 1998. *Human Capital Investment: An International Comparison.* Paris.

Outreville, J.F. 1999. Financial Development, Human Capital, and Political Stability. UNCTAD Report No. 142. Geneva.

Securities Institute (Australia): Training Courses. http://www.securities.edu.au/.

Stoll, H. R. 1998. Regulation of Financial Markets: A Focused Approach. *Multinational Finance Journal,* v 2, no 2, pp. 87–99.

The Reuters Forum. 2000. Human Capital: Are Governments Placing Market Development Above Human Development? Archived Webcast, March 29, 2000, 6:00pm.

UNDP. 1996. *Human Development Report.* New York: United Nations Development Programme.

————. 2002. Human Development Report Examines Country-by-Country Progress on Millennium Development Goals. *Human Development Report 2002.* New York: United Nations Development Programme.

PART IV

CONCLUSION

CHAPTER 16

Pragmatic Issues in Capital Market Development in Emerging Economies

Kenroy Dowers
Ruben Lee
Antonio Vives

This book is based on the assumption that a fundamental relationship exists between capital market development and economic growth. A growing body of research supports this finding and has encouraged policymakers in both emerging economies and international financial institutions to consider the development of capital markets with the expressed intention of making markets more attractive to local and foreign investors and issuers.[1] However, many capital markets in emerging economies have not developed at the pace anticipated, and financial crises continue to undermine the perception of stability in many markets.[2] A key point of departure for the book is the fact that past strategies have had limited success and new trends have caused analysts to rethink the appropriate set of strategies that would lead to viable capital markets in emerging countries.

The tasks of the book are twofold. First, it sets out to demonstrate how the following factors contribute to capital market development: the impact of globalization, technology, and regulation; market scale; and institutional investors. Second, it explores various aspects of developing capital market strategies for different types of markets in emerging economies, including bond markets, equity markets, derivatives markets, and commodity markets.

This concluding chapter focuses on the pragmatic issues that are relevant for implementing feasible capital market development strategies. It discusses key aspects of implementing a holistic approach to stimulate capital market development. In a sense,

---

[1] See Bekaert, Harvey, and Lundbald (2001); Demirgüç-Kunt and Levine (1996); Levine (1997); and Levine and Zervos (1996, 1998). For an opposing opinion, see Clayton, Jorgensen, and Kavajecz (1999).

[2] Levich (2000) concludes that while emerging financial markets have grown since 1982, they are small relative to mature markets and typically small relative to gross domestic product. He adds that these facts make emerging markets vulnerable to large inward and outward capital flows from global investors.

the chapter represents a culmination of the various ideas of the book and the real-world considerations that must be incorporated into a working strategy. For example, the notion of financial sector reform has become relevant for policymakers, and the chapter discusses the optimal sequence for reform in tandem with development in the real sector.

The book aims to provide guidance for capital market development beyond the approaches that have been offered in the past. Dowers, Gomez-Acebo, and Masci (chapter 1) interpret this changing focus, which has shifted to market participants and instruments, as part of an evolution from a first to a second wave of reforms to promote capital markets. The first wave, which took place in emerging markets in the 1990s, focused on creating a good foundation for market activity. Carmichael and Pomerleano (2002) and Levich (2000) also draw a distinction between first- and second-generation reforms.

In the first-generation reforms, a key preoccupation was the introduction of an appropriate legal and regulatory framework for the operation of stock and debt markets. This included the enactment of appropriate capital market regulation and the creation of a securities regulatory body to introduce new attitudes and behaviors among market players. Attention was directed at the delicate balance between creating a legal/regulatory environment to stimulate capital market activity and establishing safety, discipline, and soundness. Another component of the first generation of capital market reform was the emphasis on market infrastructure. Some of the visible elements of this first phase included the introduction of trading mechanisms, clearance and settlement systems, and investor education. Although the first wave of reforms pertained to the developments espoused and implemented in the 1990s, many countries are still struggling with some of these issues and should ensure that these changes are expedited, keeping in mind that the development of capital markets is part of a process that involves financial, economic, and other environmental challenges.

Second-generation strategies for capital market development presume that the foundation for capital markets in an economy has been laid, or is well under way, and that the focus is on increasing market activity and liquidity, broadening investor participation, and expanding the types of instruments that are traded. Advances in technology and increasing investor sophistication also drive second-generation reforms. Carmichael and Pomerleano (2002) identify the following issues as being core for second-generation reforms: improving corporate governance, strengthening disclosure, protecting minority shareholder rights, developing bond markets, fostering development of domestic institutional investors, and strengthening self-regulatory organizations.[3] Although we distinguish between first- and second-generation reforms, the intent is to develop an overall strategy that draws on elements categorized in both reform stages.

Lessons from Experience

This section draws some broad lessons from past experience regarding the most effective ways to promote capital market development. The lessons are divided in two groups. The first concerns the objectives that capital market development initiatives should pursue and the manner in which they should be implemented. The second group concerns policy issues that often need to be addressed in capital market development projects.

Objectives and Implementation of Development Projects

Three broad lessons concerning the objectives and implementation of capital market development projects are identified here. They concern whether there is a need for a market infrastructure and indeed a market in a particular jurisdiction, the value of ensuring that a capital market development program is consistent with reforms made throughout the entire financial sector, and the "ownership" of capital market development projects.

Market Infrastructure and Markets

A central lesson that may be drawn from past experience in capital market development is that building the infrastructure for a market in a country is not sufficient to ensure that a capital market actually operates in the country. Although this may now appear so obvious as to be self-evident, up until recently it was not. In a growing number of countries, a full market infrastructure has been constructed, but there is no real market.[4]

---

[3] Carmichael and Pomerleano (2002) also demonstrate that some key policy issues that could be associated with this second wave of reform include e-finance, the role and impact of foreign investors in equity markets, rapidly changing trading platforms, and the changing nature of financial intermediation.

[4] Within the past decade, most of the capital markets in Latin America and the Caribbean, including countries in the English-speaking Caribbean, Andean countries, and Central America, have instituted modern technology for trading clearance and settlement systems. However, there is no evidence to demonstrate that these modern systems have contributed to increase market liquidity.

The implications of this lesson for capital market development strategies are, however, more difficult to infer than at first sight appears. One critical implication is that, prior to building any particular market infrastructure, an assessment needs to be made about whether the market in question would be sustainable. Such an assessment is in general not easy to undertake for a range of reasons. There are many risk factors that may limit the development of capital markets in a particular country, some of which are within the power of the country to control, while others are not. In addition, special interests may dictate the rationale for developing the market, but do so without a broad national consensus.

Ideally, for a capital market to function efficiently, a constellation of many requirements is necessary. At a minimum, these include a relatively stable macroeconomic environment and the existence of a sufficient number of large and profitable enterprises that cannot fund their projects utilizing internally generated funds or that have surpassed their debt capacity. It is also important to have a well-functioning and efficient banking and payment system; an operating trading system; sound and competent brokers and investors; a secure clearing and settlement system; appropriate legal, regulatory, accounting, and taxation frameworks; reasonable enforcement mechanisms; and an independent regulator. In many capital markets, however, not all these requirements are present.

An example of the difficulty in assessing the viability of a particular market can be seen in considering the United Kingdom's Know-how Fund to support the development of the Budapest Stock Exchange in Hungary. An evaluation of the completed Budapest Stock Exchange project noted that its principal original objective and justification had been to ensure that the exchange was in a position to support effectively the trade in shares issued to the public through privatization (DFID, undated). The assumed dealing volumes on which the computer trading systems were planned were based on government privatization plans that appeared realistic at the time. However, the privatization program proceeded considerably more slowly than expected; as a result, the trading system operated well below its planned capacity, and turnover on the exchange was only a fraction of what was originally forecast. Although this clearly affected the viability of the exchange, it was beyond the control of the aid agency.

In similar examples in Latin America and the Caribbean, governments have led efforts to introduce an exchange, but the exchange never became a high-volume trading entity. Stock exchanges in Peru, Colombia, the English-speaking Caribbean, and Central American countries are good examples of government-led efforts. Although the rationale for these efforts is clearly understood, after the incubation period, a subsequent private sector–led phase did not materialize.

It is extremely difficult to undertake a full cost-benefit analysis when assessing whether a particular market may be viable. Capital markets may perform a wide range of economic and political functions (Lee 1998). They may offer forums for trading, investment, speculation, hedging, and arbitrage; serve as mechanisms for price discovery and information dissemination; provide vehicles for raising finance for countries and companies; help obtain effective corporate governance and facilitate changes in corporate control; and be used to implement privatization programs. They may facilitate the development of emerging and transition economies. Measuring many of these objectives is extremely difficult. In addition, the direct costs of establishing a market are shrinking as the costs of installing and operating a computerized trading system continue to decrease.

Consistency with the Entire Financial Sector Reform Process

A capital market is only one element in a complex, tightly linked network of different elements that together compose the financial sector of a country. A capital market development strategy for a country should therefore be encapsulated within, and be consistent with, a wider strategy for financial sector development in the country. A holistic approach is necessary that ensures consistency between, for example, the development of the capital and financial markets, the role of institutional investors, and the solution to social problems. A good example of the latter is the case of Chile, where the reform of the pension fund system was a key to significant growth in the liquidity of the markets in the late 1980s and 1990s. Several European countries that have linked the development of domestic capital markets to privatization, reduction of government deficits, and pension reform provide other examples.

There are many ways in which to exploit synergies between reform in other areas of a financial sector and the capital markets. For example, strategies targeting pension systems, access to housing finance, monetary and fiscal policy, the development of small and medium enterprises (SMEs), privatization, and the construction of a country's large physical infrastructure can all be opportunities to increase the viability of capital market instruments.

Institutional investors can be a good vector for corporate governance and shareholder activism. However, policy initiatives to develop institutional investors often require handling policy issues outside the realm of capital market development, such as reform of pension funds. It is important in such contexts that the policy objective of capital market development be balanced against other social objectives. While reform of a pension system can bring benefits for the capital markets, policymakers must understand that the focus of pension reform should be to increase insurance for retirement. The same can be said for public policy regarding mutual funds and insurance markets. Vittas (1998) indicates that the promotion of private pension funds and insurance companies should be pursued for their own sake and for their potential economic, fiscal, and financial benefits; such promotion should not be dependent on the prior development of securities markets.

Ownership

The concept of ownership in the context of capital market development projects is complex. It refers to the extent to which the recipients of aid, technical assistance, or other types of support for such projects, in both the private and public sectors, are interested in the project, believe that they are involved in the project, and wish to commit themselves to support the project. Given that the development of a market requires participation at many levels by both the private and public sectors in a jurisdiction, such ownership is vital for any project to succeed.

At the most extreme level, without ownership of the projects, the relevant market participants do not support the development of capital markets. One example of where this occurred was in the provision of technical assistance programs in Russia. As noted by Cadogan Financial (1999, pp. 13–14):

> . . . Long delays between an initial request for help and the inception of projects have often meant that the problem for whose solution aid had been requested had either gone away, been solved by other means, or mutated. The project nonetheless continued without variation, often with the result that the recipient ignored the consultants or that the consultants simply didn't contact their client.

Although there is no simple method to ensure the ownership of a development project by local official and private sector counterparts, a range of techniques may be used to maintain their interest and involvement. Prior to the inception of the project, all relevant parties need to be involved in the discussions regarding the goals and implementation process of the project and how its success should be evaluated. Throughout the project, an ongoing dialogue is also required, both to communicate to recipients how the project is proceeding and to ensure that counterparts have adequate input into the development of the project.

Policy Issues

Law and Enforcement

It has become widely accepted that the development of capital markets in a particular jurisdiction requires the establishment of an appropriate legal and regulatory framework, the creation of a basic set of property rights, and an institutional legal and regulatory regime in which these rights can be enforced. There are many areas of law and regulation that need to be established to deliver all this, including those governing accounting, bankruptcy and insolvency, collateral mechanisms, company formation, corporate governance, and disclosure.

Little research has been done on the optimal sequencing path a country should follow to establish an appropriate legal and regulatory framework. Black (2001) has identified a series of legal and institutional preconditions he believes critical for strong securities markets. Most importantly, he argues that a strong securities market must ensure that minority shareholders receive good information about the value of each company's businesses and also have confidence that company managers and controlling shareholders will not steal significant portions of the minority shareholders' investments.

Black stresses that the institutions that support strong securities markets cannot be built quickly. He identifies one area of particular importance as being the development of honest courts, regulators, and prosecutors. He also examines how best to develop good capital market laws and rules. While it is possible to import these from outside the country, it is vital that a country recognize that all the laws in all the relevant areas need to be consistent with each other.

Good corporate governance is critical for the development of capital markets. An increasing body of both theoretical and empirical literature confirms the existence of an economic relationship between investor protection and capital market development. La Porta and others (2002) summarize a key conclusion of this literature as being that, without appropriate investor protection,[5]

> Expropriation of minority shareholders and creditors by the controlling shareholders is pervasive. When outside investors finance

---

[5] See also Johnson (undated), who suggests that countries with more investor protection have better-developed financial markets and more growth and may also be less prone to economic collapse.

firms, they face a risk, and sometimes near certainty, that the returns on their investments will never materialize because the controlling shareholders or managers simply keep them.

Minority investors' rights are generally protected through disclosure and transparency accounting rules. If a company infringes these rights, then they are upheld by enforcement from the legal system, which in an ideal world would provide suitable mechanisms for redress for minority shareholders. Although a company would normally be able to raise finance more cheaply via a capital market in which outsiders and minority interests are protected, the benefits to controlling shareholders or managers of expropriating the assets of outside investors are typically so large that corporations are not ready to embrace reform that would require increased disclosure for the benefit of minority interests and other stakeholders. Lubrano (chapter 14, this volume) reviews the experience of implementing corporate governance reform in Latin America and the Caribbean and highlights the experience of Brazil and Colombia.

La Porta and others (2002) summarize a central conclusion of the recent literature as follows:

> Investor protection encourages the development of financial markets. When investors are protected from expropriation, they pay more for securities, making it more attractive for entrepreneurs to issue these securities. This applies to both creditors and shareholders. Creditor rights encourage the development of lending, and the exact structure of these rights may alternatively favor bank lending or market lending. Shareholder rights encourage the development of equity markets, as measured by the valuation of firms, the number of listed firms (market breadth), and the rate at which firms go public. For both shareholders and creditors, protection includes not only the rights written into the laws and regulations, but also the effectiveness of their enforcement.

The need to enforce the relevant laws and regulations is as important as establishing a sound legal basis for capital markets. Even in environments in which recourse to a country's legal system may not be a practical solution to redressing problems in the securities markets, a regulator may be able to establish sanctions that work. Properly designed securities market rules can work even in countries with quite different legal systems.

Competition

A critical lesson confirmed in many jurisdictions is that competition in securities markets is almost always beneficial and, therefore, barriers to competition may obstruct the development of capital markets. However, the possibility of achieving the full benefits of competition rests on the assumption that there is a market with sufficient economies of scale to permit competition. Thus, for smaller, less developed capital markets, where trade is inconsequential and markets are highly illiquid, the expectation of competition by trading entities, particularly at the national level, is highly optimistic at best. For these smaller markets, competition should be viewed in relation to other national markets; it is the capacity for a national exchange to compete with other benchmark markets in the same region.

One practical example, albeit for a small emerging economy, highlights the merits of competition in the context of trading systems. This particular situation arose in a country with a stock exchange that had for a long time been dominated by a small number of well-established brokers that essentially ran the exchange as a monopolistic club. They ran the exchange inefficiently, restricted access to its trading system, and were not interested in innovation. In response to this situation, one of the international financial institutions supported the establishment of a new, competing exchange.

After much political wrangling and an extended start-up process, the new exchange was finally created. In response to its creation, however, the old incumbent exchange dramatically changed its practices, embracing new technology and seeking to focus on its customers rather than its owners. So successful was the old exchange in doing this that it eventually forced the new exchange out of business. The international financial institution, which had supported the new exchange, was therefore in a paradoxical situation. On the one hand, its investment in the new exchange was a financial failure; on the other hand, its support for the new exchange proved to be an agent of positive development for the country's capital markets.

Competition between trading systems can also occur internationally. In the Latin American context, the Bolsa de Madrid established Latibex to provide international investors a vehicle for investing in Latin American blue chip stocks via a single trading and settlement system, with a single currency (the euro) and with internationally recognized standards of transparency and security. The aim was to help investors invest in Latin America, without their having to deal with a multiplicity of different legal environments, exchange rate and fiscal regimes, and trading and settlement systems.

There is frequently regulatory concern about the perceived problem of fragmentation. There are three main reasons, however, why concerns about fragmentation arising from the existence of multiple dealing systems are likely to be misplaced.[6] First, the experience of competition between trading systems in the equity markets of both Europe and the United States has been unequivocally positive. It has led to lower transaction costs, increased the efficiency and quality of trading systems, and augmented liquidity. It has encouraged the use of better technology in trading and has provided an incentive for trading systems to enhance their product lines. Finally, it has allowed different types of trading systems to come into existence to satisfy the needs of disparate types of traders.

The second reason why fragmentation is unlikely to lead to adverse outcomes is that, notwithstanding the current proliferation of trading systems, there is a powerful reason why trading in any particular class of assets is likely to be concentrated on a single dealing mechanism or at most a small number of competing systems. Successful trading systems benefit from a positive network externality, in that the likelihood of a market participant receiving an execution of an order on a trading system is higher if other participants also send their orders to the trading system. Order flow thus attracts further order flow, and only a few of the best competing trading systems are therefore likely to survive.

The third reason is that the private sector is likely to provide solutions to most of the problems of fragmentation. In a market with multiple trading systems, a key regulatory question is whether some form of infrastructure linking the trading systems should be required. The two most important types of linkage are an order-routing facility and a vehicle to consolidate price and quote information. Both types of mechanisms are likely to be provided by the private sector. In Europe, for example, where competition between the London Stock Exchange and Virt-X for trading the same securities has occurred, various data vendors have combined the data feeds from the London Stock Exchange and Virt-X to provide a single screen on which all competing orders may be ranked against each other.

Many different types of barriers to competition in securities markets may be established, which could harm market development. The taxation of transactions in securities markets, for example, can impose significant disincentives on trading for both local and foreign investors. Such taxation can take many forms, including repa-

---

[6] This and the next few paragraphs draw on Lee and Qin (2002).

triation (or withholding) tax, capital gains tax, and income tax, all of which may be charged differentially to different groups of people, such as local investors, foreign investors, natural persons, legal entities, and nonresidents.

Investors can easily migrate to foreign markets in response to the imposition of a tax. As summarized in Lee and Qin (2002), an example of this arose in Sweden, where a 1 percent round-trip equity transaction tax was imposed on Swedish brokerage services in 1984; the tax was doubled to 2 percent in 1986, reduced back to 1 percent on January 1, 1991, and finally removed on December 1, 1991. The total trading volume in Swedish equities was adversely affected during this episode. It is estimated that 60 percent of the trading volume of the 11 most actively traded Swedish shares migrated to London on the announcement of the mid-1986 tax increase, and the proportion of total Swedish share volume traded in London rose from 48 percent in 1988 to 51 percent in 1989 and 52 percent in 1990.[7] Campbell and Froot (1994) show that trading in Swedish shares by foreigners in Sweden was particularly depressed during the late 1980s, since it was easier for foreign investors than for domestic investors to substitute their trading abroad.

Competition for domestic stock exchanges in emerging markets can also arise if local companies seek listings in or migrate to more established exchanges or trade in American Depository Receipts (ADRs). The way in which cross-listing of companies internationally affects the performance of their domestic markets is complicated. Foerster and Karolyi (2000) and Smith and Sofianos (1997) discuss how a company may choose to list its shares on a foreign exchange, as well as a domestic one, because competitive pressure among the exchanges can narrow the dealing spreads on the domestic market and thereby raise trading activity. However, Domowitz, Glen, and Madhavan (1998) show that cross-listing may not always lead to greater liquidity for a company's shares, especially when the transmission of relevant information between the markets is constrained in some way.

Sanvicente (2000) argues that the listing by Brazilian companies of ADRs on the New York Stock Exchange (NYSE) did not encourage orders to migrate to the NYSE. On the contrary, it appears to have increased domestic trading. In addition, Sanvicente notes that it was hard to predict whether ADR registration and listing led to higher or lower volatility in the domestic market. He concludes that the establishment of ADR programs appears to have had a positive effect on the domestic share prices of Brazilian companies.

---

[7] Figures obtained from the Stockholm Stock Exchange. See Umlauf (1993).

Standards

Following the Asian crisis, a wide consensus has grown that the creation and adoption of international standards covering a range of aspects related to capital market development are critically important (box 16-1). It is, however, both extremely difficult and still relatively early to make a full assessment of the extent to which the adoption of international standards does in fact facilitate the development of capital markets. Further research on this issue is required. Nevertheless, some preliminary lessons have been suggested.

The following benefits of adopting and implementing international standards have been identified (Köhler 2001):

- National authorities have an increased ability to identify relatively rapidly the sources of vulnerability in their financial systems and to select their priorities for institutional and capital market development.
- There is a reduced likelihood of financial crises and their contagious effects across countries.
- International investors are better able to compare the regulatory environments of different regimes, and thus international standards may be useful for attracting foreign capital. It is likely that international investors are more willing to invest in countries that have policies and practices that are closer to

Box 16-1	**Standards for Securities Market Development**

The key international standards relevant for the development of securities markets include the principles and objectives of securities regulation established by the International Organization of Securities Commissions (IOSCO), the international accounting standards established by the International Accounting Standards Board (IASB), the international auditing standards established by the International Federation of Accountants (IFAC), the corporate governance principles established by the Organisation for Economic Co-operation and Development (OECD), and the principles for clearance and settlement systems established by the Committee on Payment and Settlement Systems (CPSS) and the Technical Committee of the IOSCO task force.

The assessment of these standards for countries around the world has been systematized via the World Bank's Financial Sector Assessment Programs and the International Monetary Fund's Financial System Stability Assessments (FSSAs), and the Reports on the Observance of Standards and Codes (ROSCs). Each ROSC module provides a description of country practice in an area that is then benchmarked against the relevant standard.

an international standard. Investors may also be able to price risks more appropriately and make better investment decisions.
- International standards facilitate complementarities and integration among countries and markets.

Moreover, the status of adoption and implementation of standards, as the International Monetary Fund's (IMF's) Reports on the Observance of Standards and Codes indicate, constitutes useful input for the IMF in its surveillance consultations and in the technical assistance programs of the IMF, World Bank, Inter-American Development Bank, and Asian Development Bank.

Several broad concerns of adopting international standards to promote capital market development have also been noted. These include the following (Griffith-Jones 2000):

- The employment of uniform standards assumes that "one size fits all" and may not allow either for the fact that different countries are at different stages of development or for the different cultural, institutional, and legal traditions across countries. Some standards are general enough to allow for variation at the country level, while others are more detailed, making compliance more difficult. It is difficult to balance the need to apply standards uniformly versus the need to apply them pragmatically and according to individual countries' circumstances (IMF 2001).
- The monitoring and adoption of international standards sometimes impose severe administrative burdens on countries.
- The assessment of different countries' adoption of international standards may not take into sufficient account individual countries' capacity for compliance and, hence, may mean that a country that is not fully compliant is at a disadvantage.
- A central issue concerning the adoption of international standards is the pace and sequencing at which they should be instituted. There is controversy about whether a voluntary, gradual approach should be adopted, whether countries should be held to account for nonperforming standards, and whether more rigid approaches should be employed.
- People have different views as to the extent to which international financial standards should be viewed as aspirations or diagnostic tools rather than inflexible requirements.

Creating and Implementing a Capital Market Strategy: Some Recommendations

Chapters 2 to 5 of this book discuss a wide range of areas that could be included in a capital market strategy, including different policies for different types of markets. This section suggests guidelines for these aspects of capital market development and proposes some pragmatic approaches to implementing a strategy.

The creation and implementation of a strategy for capital market development in a particular jurisdiction are complex undertakings and involve a process of reform and adjustments. Nevertheless, there are some useful generalizations, and we make recommendations on three broad aspects of such strategies: the core policy targets of capital market development strategies, the factors affecting an optimal sequencing strategy, and the roles that different types of institutions play in capital market development strategies.

Core Policy Targets—"The Five I's"

In developing a capital market strategy, it is important to identify the key targets for policy. A useful typology for categorizing policy reform may require a focus on the five I's: information, institutions, instruments, infrastructure, and regional integration. Policy initiatives could be developed to address all of these areas and be suitable targets for implementing reform.

Information Disclosure

There is almost universal acceptance of the need to promote corporate disclosure in order to enhance investor protection and to provide the raw data for investor education. Notwithstanding this consensus, recent experiences confirm that corporate disclosure is effectively delivered in only a few countries and requires continuous monitoring and fine-tuning. While there are many policies that may be used to further this goal, one of the most effective in an environment with little corporate disclosure is also extremely simple.

Listed companies are typically required to release basic quarterly and annual financial statements. However, in many developing countries, the underlying framework to promote information disclosure is not in place. Lessons from experience indicate that information disclosure requires a combination of explicit enforcement by improving government agencies (such as the securities regulator) and incentives that reward companies with good disclosure. In practical terms, this requires the use of International Accounting Standards, good monitoring of company reporting, access to specific programs and financing based on good corporate disclosure, updated corporate governance systems, and the prevention of private pension funds from investing in entities that do not subscribe to corporate disclosure. Several Latin American countries, including Colombia, Brazil, Mexico, and Peru, have launched programs in line with these proposals.[8]

The Role of Market Institutions

Goldstein (chapter 5, this volume) demonstrates that institutional investors can be key contributors to the development of capital markets. Institutional investors are relevant because they add liquidity to securities traded in the marketplace, foster innovation and financial development as issuers try to match the investment needs of institutional investors, help uninformed investors to become part of the overall capital markets, and impose market discipline on market participants. The development of institutional investors in the United States has had a range of additional impacts on the securities markets: the advent of competitive bidding for corporate securities, the development of mortgage securitization and derivatives products, the introduction of indexed funds, the modernization of trading and related facilities, and the use of collective bodies and specialized monitors for strengthening corporate governance. It takes time for institutional investors to reach the critical level that would allow them to play a catalytic role in capital market development. Some of the beneficial effects of institutional investors are taking place faster in developing countries because of the experience gained in advanced countries and because of the transfer of financial expertise that electronic technology and globalization make possible.

One of the most clear-cut examples of the impact of institutional investors on the development of capital markets is Chile. As Dowers, Gomez-Acebo, and Masci (chapter 1, this volume) illustrate, Chile has the highest market penetration rates for capital markets in Latin America and the Caribbean and one of the highest among all emerging markets. While there is no one single explanation for this outcome, one of the most important lies in the development of private pension systems. In 1980, Chile introduced a national private pension system that replaced the pay-as-you-go system of the past. This new pension system has several key characteristics, including defined

---

[8] See Lubrano (chapter 6, this volume) for discussion of specific regulatory reforms in Colombia, Brazil, and Mexico pertaining to increased disclosure.

contributions by pension contributors, mandatory participation by all workers, pension associations that compete on the basis of net returns for the funds of each investor, and individual accounts to control the contributions made by each employee. This structure has resulted in a flood of funds directed to the financial system and has stimulated high interest in active market participation.

In spite of the benefits for Chile's capital markets as a result of pension fund reform, Vittas (1998) argues that the promotion of private pension funds and insurance companies should be pursued for their own sake and their potential economic, fiscal, and financial benefits and should not be dependent on the prior development of securities markets. The situation of mutual funds is different because they are unlikely to thrive unless the markets for the instruments in which they specialize are themselves well developed.

Vittas (1998) notes that a limited supply of suitable financial instruments should not be a major obstacle for the creation of pension funds and insurance companies. These institutions will accumulate their long-term financial resources on a gradual but steady basis, providing ample time to allow reforming governments to develop their securities markets. A more important factor than the state of development of securities markets is normally the existence of strong political commitment to a holistic reform program that would need to cover not only pension and insurance reform but also broader macroeconomic, fiscal, banking, and capital market reforms.

Institutional investors can help the development of securities markets. They can act as a countervailing force to the dominant position of commercial banks, stimulate financial innovation, modernize capital markets, enhance transparency and information disclosure, and strengthen corporate governance.

Instruments

This section examines the key types of instruments that exist in the capital markets and attempts to provide pragmatic suggestions to help increase the overall liquidity of these instruments. As equities and fixed-income instruments dominate capital markets, the focus is on these two types of securities. However, this does not negate the potential benefits of instruments such as commercial paper, which in fact is the dominant instrument in many underdeveloped markets, and derivatives instruments, which are more appropriate for advanced capital markets.

Equities. Improving liquidity in equity markets in emerging economies is a difficult endeavor because it requires work on the supply and demand sides and also on the market infrastructure and trading mechanism. As discussed above, perhaps one of the key issues in developing a local securities market as a good and consistent source of funds is to ensure that there is a good local and international investor base. The reality for many countries is that local investors are more dedicated to domestic securities and, if mobilized, provide major demand-side strength for market development.

On the supply side, to increase the amount of securities offered, effort should be directed at increasing the amount of issues through privatization programs with a view to ensuring increased trading and enhanced local market participation. Increasing local issues can also be realized by programs that target SMEs, different tiers for market trading, and the creation of specific incentives for listing securities, including tax holidays, access to specific government financing, and score cards that rate enterprises on the basis of specific desirable capital market qualities.

Recent evidence suggests the need to consider the establishment of alternative trading architectures that can facilitate the path for more medium-size companies to come to the market.[9] This underscores the nascent efforts of the São Paulo Stock Exchange and the Bolsa de Colombia to support greater participation of indigenous medium-size firms. Hannes and Korcsmaros (chapter 12, this volume) present some of the evidence regarding the ability of these SME stock exchanges to increase SME access to capital markets. Hannes and Korcsmaros conclude that the findings are somewhat mixed. While there is some evidence that these SME stock exchanges do play a role, they are more relevant for medium-size companies and those that are advanced in their life cycle. For SMEs at the early stage, bank financing, angel funds, and personal funds tend to be much more relevant sources of financing than access to capital markets.

Fixed-income markets. Bond markets provide a means to fulfill mid- and long-term funding needs. When developed, they contribute to reducing the financial risks of the overall economy, providing the government with a noninflationary source of finance and establishing a basis for pricing assets in the market, creating a well-balanced financial environment, and promoting economic growth. There is also clear evidence that domestic government bond markets are the foundation on which the domestic bond markets are built. These are only a few of the potential benefits of domestic bond markets. The importance of these markets to the entire economy makes it imperative that governments lead the process of developing bond markets by creating

---

[9] However, recent evidence suggests the need for prudence in the establishment of these markets because the early successes of small and medium-size markets that initially showed promise in Germany, France, and Spain, for example, have all suffered declines and outright failure recently.

a domestic government bond market and providing an adequate framework to develop corporate bond markets.

Conroy and Zhang (undated) discuss how best to develop domestic bond markets. They argue that, at the initial stage, a sovereign debt management project and a bond market development program need to be launched in parallel. This requires building a consensus between the government and the central bank regarding the importance of bond market development for effective debt management, consistency between bond market development and macroeconomic policies, and an overall strategy to develop the domestic bond market.

In chapter 10 (this volume), del Valle identifies some specific stages for developing bond markets. In the first stage, the development of an effective primary market for government securities is pursued. Treasury bill markets are typically first developed, and the government is encouraged to gradually extend the maturity spectrum of its treasury bonds. Once again, it is vital for the primary market development to be consistent with the government's sovereign debt management program, including its funding strategy and risk management program, and also with the central bank's open market operations. Various auction methods may be tested with a view to adopting a model that best enhances bond-selling efficiency. A primary dealer system may also be established to ensure competitive bidding in the auctions.

In the second stage, a secondary market for government securities may be developed. Ways to improve market liquidity should be pursued. Market infrastructure can be enhanced, including clearing and payment systems and the market for repurchase agreements. Any legal, regulatory, accounting, and tax impediments to investing and trading in bonds should be identified and removed. The role of intermediaries, such as market makers and dealer-brokers, may be enhanced.

In the third stage, the development of the corporate bond market may be emphasized. Typically, this requires appropriate corporate transparency and disclosure requirements, the presence of credit rating agencies, and also the need for relevant tax and other regulatory issues to be addressed. It is important to be flexible when focusing on corporate bond market development, which can range from developing a viable commercial paper market to structured products.

Market Infrastructure

Market infrastructure is important because all participants in capital markets rely on its smooth and efficient functioning. It represents the intersection of the diverse participants in the market. It is composed of the institutions, mechanisms, and rules that govern the trading, clearing, settlement, and custody of capital market trades. Without a well-functioning infrastructure, capital markets cannot flourish.

For issuers, the infrastructure provides the support for issuing equity, debt, and derivatives instruments. Functions covered include registry of ownership, custody, communication of information, and instructions concerning changes in the status of securities. For investors, including banks, market makers, brokers, institutional investors, nonbank investors, and individuals, infrastructure supports their trading activity and provides custody and related information services. For brokers and securities dealers, infrastructure supports the clearing and settlement of their own and their customers' trades in equity, debt, and derivatives.

The emphasis on market infrastructure is moving from first-generation issues, like appropriate legislation, appropriate institutions, a settlement period of T+3, and delivery versus payment, to new challenges or second-generation issues. According to Hook (chapter 8, this volume), these include achieving a T+1 settlement period, straight-through processing, linkages and/or mergers between clearing and settlement institutions, and closer linkages of securities and derivatives clearing and settlements with payment systems.

While working toward implementing these issues will bring about a more efficient, safe, and well-functioning market infrastructure, further enhancement can be attained by increasing attention to the technology aspects of the infrastructure and the implementation of international standards and best practices in clearing and settlement. Policymakers should provide a vision for the configuration of institutions, regulations, competition, and technologies for the market infrastructure and exercise good management to translate the vision into strategies and action.

Integration of Capital Markets

Many emerging capital markets face a particularly difficult dilemma. On the one hand, their development appears to have stalled, as they are simply too small to be interesting to most international investors. On the other hand, the possibility of making the markets more attractive and viable by participating in some form of regional capital market integration strategy implies that national identity must be subsumed into a broader regional context. Furthermore, the likelihood of success of a regional capital market development strategy, as discussed in Lee (chapter 6, this volume), is low.

Regional capital market integration can take three primary forms. The first form involves cooperative initiatives in the provision of market infrastructure. Such initiatives may originate from the organizations that deliver the following market infrastructure functions: listing, information dissemination, order routing, trading, clearing via a central counterparty, settlement, and marketing.

The second form pertains to policies that are implemented to promote domestic market development but also have an impact on market integration. These may include improvements in supervision and regulation to bring them up to internationally accepted standards. The implementation of these standards helps toward the harmonization of financial regulations internationally and thus may be considered a step toward international integration.

The third form of regional integration refers to policies that arise from the ongoing efforts to develop regional and subregional economic integration and that affect the functioning of securities markets and stimulate their integration. In Latin America and the Caribbean, these subregional initiatives include the Andean Pact, the North American Free Trade Agreement (NAFTA), the Central American Common Market (CARICOM), and Mercosur. It is interesting that many of the regional initiatives have little in terms of explicit policy objectives to formulate regional capital markets. Thus, it comes as no surprise that the impact of these initiatives for regional capital market development has been minimal at best.

The benefits of securities market integration are relevant for investors, issuers, and the economy in general. Some of the specific benefits as summarized by Lee (chapter 6, this volume) include more efficient, liquid, and broader markets; lower net returns (after transaction costs); greater innovation that allows for portfolio diversification; and enhanced risk-return frontiers, particularly for investors who face restricted opportunities.

The literature on ADR and the analysis of overseas listing demonstrate that, based on information economies and target marketing by the issuer, cross-border investment is driven mainly by familiarity and geographic proximity. Sarkissian and Schill (2001) report that there is evidence that firms tend to follow a graduated approach, where they start cross-listing in G-5 economies, then add neighboring countries and other more familiar markets. This approach could be explained in terms of the cost of global information for firms from emerging economies. Lee (2002) discusses the benefits of securities markets, including their contribution toward improving market depth and increasing market liquidity.

The costs of securities market integration can be seen on two levels: the short-term transaction and transition costs for implementation of the process of integration and the costs incurred by independent interests that are directly affected through the loss of market power. Pertaining to the former, the integration process requires appropriate legal/regulatory reform, which can be costly in monetary terms due to the need to establish new rules and regulations and training and to enhance the monitoring processes. In addition, in the short term, some market players may have to bear the additional cost of participating in an unfamiliar cross-border market. In the case of opportunity cost to market participants, securities market integration in essence assumes an element of financial market liberalization, which effects greater competition for limited investment resources. Thus, financial institutions that previously had market advantages, particularly in a domestic setting, will have to compete against cross-border financial firms. Lee (2002) reports that securities market integration may lead to unanticipated protectionism, either from the process being captured by specific vested interests or due to the specific action of institutions or individuals opposed to the process.

Optimal Sequencing of Capital Market Reform

There is no consensus about how capital markets grow or about the most important factors in effecting such growth. Furthermore, different sequencing programs may be optimal for different countries with different cultural, economic, legal, and political histories and different political economies. However, three key factors should go into the determination of an optimal sequencing program for the development of capital markets in a particular country.

The first factor is the link between the macroeconomic status of the country and the types of capital market instruments that could be traded. Many policymakers argue that domestic long-term savings should be increased with the development of capital markets to avoid excessive reliance on external borrowing. They also claim that financing needs differ depending on the stage of development of the economy, and different segments of the capital markets need to be developed to accommodate these evolving financing requirements. An optimal sequencing plan would ideally specify the required actions along all the key policy targets: the legal/regulatory structure, market infrastructure institutions, private sector market participants, and capital market instruments. In addition, the manner in which the proposed capital market development strategy fits into the wider financial sector reform plan needs to be considered.

The second factor is the level of sophistication and complexity in the country and the prerequisites needed for certain instruments and institutions to function appropriately. Glen and Madhavan (1998) suggest that primary market development is related to both macroeconomic factors and market-specific aspects, including the legal and regulatory framework, the nature of the institutional investor community, the tax regime, and the competitiveness of the investment-banking network. While financial market development may aid in achieving macroeconomic goals, such as boosting the growth rate, it is apparent that policymakers must first achieve a minimum of stability in the macroeconomy if financial markets are to grow.

The third factor is government policy. In their study of Peru, Glen and Madhavan (1998) suggest that government policy can play an important role in developing domestic primary markets through a pro-market stance, the creation of a legal framework that establishes rules and favors transparent markets, and the provision of incentives for financial institutions to demand private securities, such as through a private pension fund system. However, subtle institutional details may have a major effect on market development. For example, the constraints on pension fund portfolios create a bias toward debt over equity, which may influence the relative prices of debt and equity and also overall issuance activity.

The Relevance of Institutional Support to Implement Reform Policy

To implement a successful capital market development strategy, different entities must play specific roles in accordance with the principles of creating checks and balances among the various players, which would ultimately constitute the real force to implement the strategy and monitor the fundraising of the systems. Here we discuss the various roles that government, the private sector, and multilateral agencies can play.

Government

Government can take either a passive or an active role in promoting capital market development. In the experience of many countries, the passive government stance is generally associated with two areas: creating the relevant legal/regulatory structure, disclosure requirements, and trading systems and creating incentives for increasing the trading activity of market participants. A case for passive government intervention and relevance in capital market development has been receiving increasing attention in the literature on public goods. Researchers have demonstrated the importance of financial and capital markets for social development and thus have established an important mandate for the public sector and the leadership of policymakers as advocates of establishing a functioning capital market.

Government can also take a more active role in capital market development, both as a market participant involved in issuing tradable instruments and directly as an investor in capital market instruments. The government can provide specific value added if its role as an active market participant does not crowd out private sector initiative and thus reduce the capacity for innovation. As an active participant in stimulating capital market development, the government's role must also have a specific demonstration effect based on the nature of the deal or transaction undertaken.

In addition, the government should ensure that there is equity in the way transactions are completed so that other transactions could be initiated in the future and there is no unfair advantage provided to a select group that can capture the process and retain the gains independent of the functioning of the system. At a minimum, government's action should create a suitable environment to stimulate private sector participation and risk taking.

Private Sector

The private sector, especially market infrastructure institutions, institutional investors, listing companies, and financial intermediaries, clearly has a central role to play in furthering capital market development. Ideally, the objective should be to encourage the private sector to engage in capital market transactions with manageable levels of risk and to limit inequities in the process. This represents a major challenge for many emerging economies, where a basic and, in some instances, relatively well-developed market infrastructure and legal regulatory framework may exist, but where there is little market activity. Companies thus have little incentive to issue securities, investors have few assets in which to invest, and firms find it scarcely profitable to provide financial intermediation.

For many emerging economies, the challenge of private sector involvement occurs alongside the increasing interest in taking capital market activities offshore via ADRs and foreign currency–denominated issues. During the past decade, issues from emerging markets raised an average of $7 billion a year though ADRs, with the average close to $22 billion in more recent years, peaking at $32 billion in 2000. In the early 1990s, Latin American ADRs dominated the market, but these have recently shifted to Asia.[10] However, these markets are relevant only for the largest issuers.

There are many issues that reduce the willingness of the private sector to participate in domestic capital market activities. First, the reinforcing cycle of illiquidity is a common feature of many capital markets in developing economies. The lack of liquidity in local capital markets encourages major private sector issuers to shift to offshore or more developed capital markets, which further reduces the liquidity in the local marketplace. On the investor side, corporate governance particularly concerns the treatment of minority shareholders and discourages some investors from demon-

---

[10] See IMF (2000a, box 3.6) for more details and discussion of depository receipt programs.

strating a keen interest in local issues. The same could be said for lax disclosure requirements that fail to convey appropriate market information to current and prospective investors. On the other hand, as factors such as liquidity and corporate governance move toward acceptable standards, the private sector would likely increase its involvement in capital market development.

Multilateral Institutions

Multilateral institutions can foster capital market development in emerging economies, working at different parts of the process. First, they can provide ex ante guidance to entities to identify specific approaches to capital market development. Second, they can partner with policymakers and country officials to shape a holistic and long-term capital market strategy. Third, multilateral institutions can work together with client countries to provide resources, including finance and advisory services, to implement a capital market strategy. In this capacity, they can bring together officials from different countries to help broker deals for regional integration and ensure that the strategy is consistent with development in other areas.

A key ingredient for a successful capital market strategy is to ensure that there are viable instruments traded in the marketplace. Multilateral institutions can play a direct role in creating structures (such as guarantees, advisory services, and capital contributions) that facilitate increased trading of financial market instruments. However, there must be clear benefits for the overall market and limited moral hazard problems based on free riding or heavy risk taking.

Multilateral institutions may be able to provide various forms of support to facilitate capital market development, including assessment programs, technical assistance programs (reimbursement and nonreimbursement), and different types of loans from multilateral and bilateral agencies, contributing capital and different types of guarantees to support the issue of capital market securities. There are many ongoing assessment programs relating to financial sector activity, including the World Bank/IMF Financial Stability Assessment Programs and Reports on the Observance of Standards and Codes and International Organization of Securities Commission (IOSCO) surveys on country compliance with IOSCO guidelines.

Guarantees to Private Sector Entities

Financial guarantees can support the development of capital markets. The usual scenario is where an AAA-rated entity (generally an international entity or a government entity that has established a robust track record in the domestic market) utilizes the strength of its balance sheet or capital structure to provide support for entities that are interested in tapping the capital market. This type of guarantee helps to mobilize long-term financing for investments and can contribute directly to the development of bond markets as a source of capital. It is also a useful tool for promoting local currency issue. Although the objective of a guarantee is to increase market receptivity for capital market transactions, it may be structured to perform different functions. For example, it may include supporting weak credits, lengthening the maturity of traded instruments, and providing a co-insurance mechanism that encourages the participation of other private sector guarantors.

There are many policy issues to be considered in providing financial guarantees. First, a decision must be made in terms of the level of support that should be provided. The provision of partial financial guarantees, while providing the credit support needed, may ensure that the issuer has a stake in the transaction and may reduce the moral hazard problem of excessive risk taking. Second, it is important to ensure that the guarantee facilitates the entrance of other financial sector players in the guarantee business and thus serves as a catalyst in the capital market. Third, from the guarantor's perspective, it is also important that there is good asset-liability management to ensure that all risks are priced appropriately and incorporated into the management of its risk capital.

Conclusion

This chapter seeks to provide some practical guidelines for implementing capital market strategies, taking the perspective of the government, private sector, or policymaker. It brings together substantive ideas that are presented in several chapters in the book. Starting with a summary of some of the key lessons learnt from past global experiences, the aim is to avoid repeating them in this new focus on capital market development.

The chapter also presents a useful taxonomy to guide policymakers in their attempt to facilitate capital market development, focusing on five key ingredients of market reform. The chapter makes the case that there is some possible role for public sector involvement in fostering the development of capital markets. Public sector involvement could be useful to catalyze the overall market, foster equity and safety, and stimulate a demonstration effect in the types of instruments that are brought to the market.

An important contribution of the chapter, which further helps to integrate the key areas that are developed, is that it emphasizes the importance of sequencing reform in line with developments in the real economy. The chapter ends with a discussion of practical considerations for policymakers (government, private sector, and multilateral institutions) that are involved in the process of capital market development.

Bibliography

Akamatsu, Noritaka. 2001. *World Bank Operations for Capital Market Reform in Asia.* Tokyo Roundtable (ADBI/OECD). Financial Sector Development Department, World Bank, Washington, D.C.

Bekaert, Geert, Campbell R. Harvey, and Christian T. Lundbald. 2001. Does Financial Liberalization Spur Growth? Social Science Research Network. http://www.ssrn.com/.

Black, Bernard S. 2001. *The Legal and Institutional Preconditions for Strong Securities Markets.* John M. Olin Program in Law and Economics, Working Paper No. 179. Stanford Law School. *University of California Los Angeles Law Review,* Vol. 48, pp. 781–858.

Cadogan Financial. 1999. *Rebirth and Development Perspectives for the Russian Capital Markets.* Report prepared for the Centre for Capital Market Development, the World Bank and U.K. Department for International Development.

Campbell, John Y., and Kenneth A. Froot. 1994. International Experiences with Securities Transactions Taxes. Ch. 6 in Jeffrey A. Frankel (ed.), *The Internationalization of Equity Markets.* NBER Project Report. Chicago: University of Chicago Press.

Carmichael, Jeffrey, and Michael Pomerleano. 2002. *The Development and Regulation of Non-Bank Financial Institutions.* World Bank, Washington, D.C.

Chown, John. 2000. *Successful Tax Policies for Emerging Capital Markets.* Oxford Economic Policy Ltd. www.oxford-policy.com/news.

Claessens, Stijn, Thomas Glaessner, and Daniela Klingebiel. 2000. *Electronic Finance: Reshaping the Financial Landscape around the World.* Financial Sector Discussion Paper 4. World Bank, Washington, D.C.

Clayton, Matthew J., Bjorn Jorgensen, and Kenneth A. Kavajecz. 1999. *On the Formation and Structure of International Exchanges.* Working Paper Series. http://www.ssrn.com/.

Coffee Jr., Jack C. 1999. Privatization and Corporate Governance: The Lessons from Securities Market Failure. *Journal of Corporation Law*, Vol. 25, pp. 1–39.

Conroy, Patrick, and Xin Zhang. Undated. *The Role of Government in the Development of Domestic Bond Markets*. APEC Initiative on the Development of Domestic Bond Markets. World Bank, Washington, D.C.

Demirgüç-Kunt, Asli, and Ross Levine. 1996. Stock Market Development and Financial Intermediaries: Stylized Facts. *The World Bank Economic Review* 10(2, May): 291–322.

Department for International Development (DFID). Undated. *Budapest Stock Exchange—Project Evaluation*.

Domowitz, Ian, Jack Glen, and Ananth Madhavan. 1998. International Cross-listing and Order Flow Migration: Evidence from an Emerging Market. *Journal of Finance*, pp. 2001–27.

The Economist. 2001. When Capital Markets Rule. March 5.

Financial Stability Forum (FSF). 2000a. *Follow-Up Group on Incentives to Foster Implementation of Standards*. http://www.fsforum.org/publications/publication_22_27.html.

_____. 2000b. *Task Force on Implementation of Standards*. http://www.fsforum.org/publications/publication_22_27.html.

Fischer, Stanley. 2001. *Asia and the IMF*. IPS Lecture Series.

Foerster, Stephen R., and G. Andrew Karolyi. 2000. The Long-Run Performance of Global Equity Offerings. *Journal of Financial and Quantitative Analysis* 35(4): 499–528.

Glen, Jack, and Ananth Madhavan. 1998. Primary Securities Markets in Emerging Nations: A Case Study of Peru. Working Paper. International Finance Corporation, Washington and Marshall School of Business, USC, Los Angeles.

Goldfinger, Charles, Karel Lannoo, and Ruben Lee. 2002. *Issues Paper: Developing a European Perspective on Disclosure*. Draft. GEF, CEPS and OFG, Brussels.

Griffith-Jones, Stephany. 2000. *Developing Countries and the Global Financial System: Report of Conference*. Commonwealth Secretariat, World Bank, and IMF. Lancaster House, London.

Harwood, Alison (ed.). 2000. *Building Local Bond Markets: An Asian Perspective*. International Finance Corporation, Washington, D.C.

International Monetary Fund (IMF). 2000a. International Capital Markets: Developments, Prospects, and Key Policy Issues. *World Economic and Financial Surveys*, International Monetary Fund, Washington, D.C.

———. 2000b. *Progress in Strengthening the Architecture of the International Financial System: A Fact Sheet*. International Monetary Fund, Washington, D.C.

———. 2001. International Standards and Codes. *IMF Survey*. Vol. 30, No. 7.

International Monetary Fund and World Bank. 2001. *Assessing the Implementation of Standards: A Review of Experience and Next Steps*. International Monetary Fund, Washington, D.C.

International Organization of Securities Commissions. 1998. *Objectives and Principles of Securities Regulation*. Conference Series Proceedings. Federal Reserve Bank of Boston.

Johnson, Simon. Undated. *Coase and the Reform of Securities Markets*. pp. 187–204.

Kenen, Peter. 2000. Financial-Sector Reform in Emerging-Market Countries: Getting the Incentives Right. *Strengthening the Resilience of Global Financial Markets*. Per Jacobsson Foundation. Lucerne.

Köhler, Horst. 2001. Standards and Codes—A Tool for Growth and Financial Stability. IMF/World Bank Conference on International Standards and Codes, Washington, D.C. (July 3).

La Porta, Rafael, Florencio López-de-Silanes, Andrei Shleifer, and Robert W. Vishny. 2002. *Investor Protection: Origins, Consequences, Reform*. http://www.worldbank.org/finance/html/investorprotection.html.

Lee, Ruben. 1998. *What Is an Exchange? The Automation, Management, and Regulation of Financial Markets*. Oxford: Oxford University Press.

———. 2002. The Future of Securities Exchanges. Ch. 1 in Robert Litan and Richard Herring (eds.), *Brookings-Wharton Papers on Financial Services*.

Lee, Ruben, and Duo Qin. 2002. *Securities Trading Systems in the Netherlands*. Report prepared by Oxford Finance Group for the Financial Markets Policy Directorate, Ministry of Finance, The Netherlands.

Levich, Richard M. 2000. *Financial Innovations in International Financial Markets*. New York University Working Paper Series, New York. http://www.ssrn.com/.

Levine, Ross. 1997. Financial Development and Economic Growth: Views and Agenda. *Journal of Economic Literature*, Vol. 35, (June) pp. 688–726.

_____. 1998. *Napoleon, Bourses, and Growth in Latin America.* Working Paper No. 365, Office of the Chief Economist, Inter-American Development Bank, Washington, D.C.

Levine, Ross, and Sara Zervos. 1996. Stock Market Development and Long-Run Growth. *The World Bank Economic Review* 10: 323–39.

_____. 1998. Stock Markets, Banks, and Economic Growth. *American Economic Review* 88: 537–58.

Mathieson, Donald J., and Garry J. Schinasi. 2001. International Capital Markets: Developments, Prospects, and Key Policy Issues. *IMF World Economic and Financial Surveys.* http://www.imf.org/external/pubs/ft/icm/2001/02/eng/pdf/chap1.pdf.

Megginson, W. L., and J. R. Netter. 2001. From State to Market: A Survey of Empirical Studies on Privatization. *Journal of Economic Literature,* Vol. 39, (June) pp. 321–89.

Mortlock, Geof. Undated. Reforms to Global Financial Architecture. *Reserve Bank of New Zealand Bulletin,* Vol. 63, No. 3, pp. 45–58.

Rajan, Raghuram G., and Luigi Zingales. 1998. Financial Dependence and Growth. *American Economic Review,* Vol. 88, (June) pp. 559–586.

Sanvicente. 2000. The Market for ADRs and the Quality of the Brazilian Stock Market.

Sarkissian, Sergei, and Michael J. Schill. 2001. *The Overseas Listing Decision: New Evidence of Proximity Preference.* Working Paper Series. http://www.ssrn.com/.

Schuler, Kurt A., Dennis R. Sheets, and David W. Weig. 1997. *Money Markets in Selected Southern African Countries.* IMCC—Consulting Assistance for Economic Reform II (CAER II), Directed by Harvard Institute for International Development (HIID), Sponsored by USAID Contract PCE-Q-00-95-00016-00. http://www.cid.harvard.edu/caer2/htm/content/papers/bns/dp20bn.htm.

Securities Commission of Malaysia. 2000. *Capital Market Masterplan* (February). Kuala Lumpur.

Smith, Katherine, and George Sofianos. 1997. *The Impact of a NYSE Listing on the Global Trading of Non U.S. Stocks.* NYSE Working Paper 97-02. New York Stock Exchange, New York.

Task Force on the Future of the Canadian Financial Services Sector. 1998a. *Competition Competitiveness and the Public Interest: Change, Challenge, Opportunity.* Background Paper No. 1.

_____. 1998b. *Report of the Task Force: Change, Challenge, Opportunity.*

Umlauf, Steven R. 1993. Transaction Taxes and the Behavior of the Swedish Stock Market. *Journal of Financial Economics* 33(2): 227–40.

United States Agency for International Development (USAID, ANE). Undated. *Creating a Framework for Capital Markets in Sri Lanka.* Washington, D.C.

_____. 1998. Center for Development Information and Evaluation (CDIE). *Impact Evaluation: Developing Romania's Capital Market.* PN–ACA–921 No. 4.

_____. 1999a. *Impact Evaluation: Developing the Capital Market in India.* PN–ACA–922. Center for Development Information and Evaluation (CDIE), USAID, Washington, D.C.

_____. 1999b. *Impact Evaluation: Developing the Capital Market in Kenya and Morocco.* PN–ACA–928. Center for Development Information and Evaluation (CDIE), USAID, Washington, D.C.

_____. 1999c. *Impact Evaluation: Developing the Philippines' Market.* PN–ACA–933. Center for Development Information and Evaluation (CDIE), USAID, Washington, D.C.

_____. 2000. *Efficient Capital Markets: A Key to Development.* USAID Program and Operations Assessment Report No. 26 PN–ACG–620. Center for Development Information and Evaluation (CDIE) – James Fox. USAID, Washington, D.C

Vittas, Dimitri. 1998. *Institutional Investors and Securities Markets: Which Comes First?* ABCD LAC Conference, San Salvador, El Salvador. Development Research Group, World Bank, Washington, D.C.

———. 2000. *Pension Reform and Capital Markets Development: 'Feasibility' and 'Impact' Preconditions.* Development Research Group, World Bank, Washington, D.C.

World Bank Economic Development Institute. 1997. *Securities Market Development: A Guide for Policymakers.* World Bank, Washington, D.C.

World Bank and International Monetary Fund. 2001. *Developing Government Bond Markets: A Handbook.* World Bank, Washington, D.C.

Index

In this index, page numbers in boldface type indicate tables or figures, and page numbers with an italicized *n* indicate footnotes located on that page.

ACCC (Australian Competition and Consumer Commission), 288
access provider regulation, 55
accountability, corporate/government, 131, 377, 452. *See also* corporate governance
accounting and auditing standards
    bond markets, 326
    capital market functioning, 214–18
    corporate governance, 441
    ethical issues, 425
    financial stability, 217–19, 235, 303
    information disclosure, 213–14
    institution of international, 19–20
    for Latin America and Caribbean, 225, **226–27**, 228, **229**, 230
    market liquidity, 102
    policy considerations, 230, 234–36
    SMEs, 395
    U.S. and IAS rules, 136, 220–25, **231–33**
acquisitions and mergers. *See* mergers and acquisitions
ad hoc contracting in Brazil, 448–51
ADRs (American Depository Receipts), 14–15, 43–44, 55–56, 252, 497
African Stock Exchanges Association (ASEA), 47
agency role, 216, 243
aggregate quote size, 180–81
agricultural commodities, 335, 343, 348
AIM, 409
alliances and partnerships
    CME-Singapore agreement, 192–94
    emerging markets, **47**
    equity institutions, 109, 247
    exchanges, 46–47, 248, 251–52, 288
    globalization, 109
    human capital development, 466, **467**, 482–83
    infrastructure improvements, 264
    regulatory issues, 54
    SMEs, 392
    See also demutualization of exchanges; mergers and acquisitions

alternate service providers and infrastructure, 250
alternative trading systems (ATSs)
    competition issues, 249
    demutualization of exchanges, 272, 281
    international linkage discussions, **48**
    regulation of, 62
    self-regulation of exchanges, 277
    types and role of, 49–53, 55
    See also electronic trading systems
Al-Yousif, Yousif Khalifa, 6
American Depository Receipts (ADRs), 14–15, 43–44, 55–56, 252, 497
American Exchange (AMEX), 183–84
Amman Stock Exchange, 111–12
Amsterdam, demutualization of exchanges, 276, 289–90
Amsterdam Stock Exchange, 191, 276, 290–91
analysts, professional securities, and Internet, 65
Andean countries, infrastructure developments, 258–59
ANDIMA (National Association of Open Market Institutions), 255
angel investing, 398–99
annual reports, requirement history, 280
application system provider (ASP), 192
arbitration services, 277, 448
Archipelago, **51**
Argenclear, 257
Argentina
    bond markets, 314
    cattle futures market, 347
    corporate scandals, 443
    credit and money supply, 93
    debt market situation, 305
    depository receipts, 14–15
    derivatives markets, **353**
    financial crisis, 13, 100, 332
    infrastructure development, 256–57
    institutional investing, **124**
    market institutions role, 24, 25
    mergers and acquisitions, 15

Argentina (continued)
    mortgage market, 325
    pension funds, 23, 107, 316
    poor macroeconomic policy, 95–97
    regional market integration, 27
    trading activity, 12
Arrow, K. J., 415
ASEA (African Stock Exchanges Association), 47
Asian markets
    corporate governance development, 140
    vs. Latin American markets, 8
    market capitalization levels, 41–42, 45
    market reforms in, 252
    public sector response to scandal, 458
ASIC (Australian Securities and Investment
    Commission), 279, 287
ASP (application system provider), 192
asset price volatility and crossover investing, 13
assets vs. liabilities, 100. See also capital markets
ASX, Ltd., 288
auction sales method, 163–64, 248, 311, 313,
    344, 349
auditing and accounting standards. See
    accounting and auditing standards
Australia, market changes in, 107, 275–76, 287–88
Australian Competition and Consumer
    Commission (ACCC), 288
Australian Securities and Investment
    Commission (ASIC), 279, 287
Australian Stock Exchange, 277, 279–80, 290,
    404–5
automated clearinghouses, 257
automatic trading halts, 366–67

Bahamas, insurance investing in, 123
Ball, R., 215
Banco Centroamericano de Integración
    Economia (BCIE), 261
Bank for International Settlements (BIS), 303
bankruptcy law, 326
banks
    Argentine crisis, 95–96
    bond markets, 307, 314–15, 319
    vs. capital markets, 16, 92, 97–102
    clearing and settlement role, 320
    vs. commercial credit, 94
    consolidation among, 15, 41
    corporate governance reforms, 448
    cost of crises in, 100, 218n4

    CSDs, 265
    disintermediation of, 303–4, 315, 317, 325
    financial stability goals, 302
    vs. institutional investing, 129
    Latin American developments, 91,
      112–13, 114, 257–58, 272, 315
    Mexican crisis, 304–5, 452
    vs. money market funds, 137
    and mutual funds, 123
    online banking, **71**
    outsourcing of securities processing, 264
    reduction of government dependence on,
      4, 308–9
    regulation of, 303
    risk management, 100, 309–10
    SMEs, 390, 395–96, **397**, 399
    Swedish crisis, 285
    See also central banks
Barbados, 262
basis risk, 341, 342, 344, 359–60
BCIE (Banco Centroamericano de Integración
    Economia), 261
BDS (business development services), 396
Beck, Thorsten, 5, 164–65
Bekaert, Geert, 6
Belgian exchange, 191, 290
benchmarks for government bonds, 311
best bid and offer, 181
bid and ask quotes, 181
bid and offer quotes, 181
BIS (Bank for International Settlements), 303
Black, Bernard S., 493
blue-sky merit regulation, 280–81
BM&F (Bolsa de Mercadoria & Futuros). See
    Bolsa de Mercadoria & Futuros (BM&F)
BNDES (Brazilian national development bank),
    448
boards of directors and corporate governance,
    441, 452, **460**
Bolivia, infrastructure developments, 259, 264
Bolsa de Colombia, 503
Bolsa de Madrid, 495
Bolsa de Mercadoria & Futuros (BM&F)
    derivatives markets, 383–84, 386
    infrastructure development, 255
    origins of, 340
    regional integration, 109
    regulation of, 352
    strength of equity market in Brazil, 94

Bolsa de Valores de Rio de Janeiro (BVRJ), 24, 109, 255, 383
Bolsa Mexicana de Valores, 43–44
Bombay Stock Exchange, 103
bond markets
    corporate, 147, 298, 306, 323–27, 329–30
    financial reform and stability, 302–4
    government, 107, 295–98, 306–22
    Latin America and Caribbean, 304–5, 331–32
    linkages between markets, 327–30
    macroeconomic environment, 300–302
    motives for creating, 16
    pension funds, 135
    reform of, 20, 21, 24
    role of, 295–99
    sequence of development, 306–8
    taxation policy, 315, 327, 330–31
    U.S. performance, 11
Bossone, G., 104
Botazzi, L., 114
Bourse Régionale des Valeurs Mobilières (BRVM), 186–87
BOVESPA (São Paulo Stock Exchange). See São Paulo Stock Exchange (BOVESPA)
Boyd, John, 6
Brazil
    bond markets, 24, 311, 315, 319, 332
    capital market reforms, 20–21, 40
    corporate governance, 40, 444, 445–51
    corporate scandals, 443
    debt market situation, 305
    dematerialization of securities, 253
    depository receipts, 14–15
    derivatives markets, 340, 352, **353**, 355, 365n43, 383–86
    equity market strength, 94
    financial crisis, 13
    infrastructure developments, 254–55
    institutional investing, **124**
    interest rates, 305
    investment in foreign exchanges, 497
    lack of shareholder protection, 145
    market institutions, 24, 25, 459
    mutual funds, 126
    pension funds, 107
    regional market integration, 27, 109
    tiered listing system, 111
    trading activity, 12

broker-customer relations rules, 367–68, 384
broker-dealers
    ATSs as, 52, 55
    automated trading fees, 66, 367–68
    and Internet, 72–73, 78–79, 80–81
    regulation issues, 278, 279
Brown, P., 215
Brussels Exchange, 191, 290
BRUT, **51**
BRVM (Bourse Régionale des Valeurs Mobilières), 186–87
Budapest Stock Exchange, 490
bulletin board markets, 73
Business Coordinating Council (Mexico), 452
business development services (BDS), 396
Business Environment Simplification Task Force (EU), 394
business ethics development, 419–20
business-to-business models, 349n15

Cadogan Financial, 492
Campbell, John Y., 497
Canada
    bond markets, 295, **296**
    harmonization of market rules, 168
    human capital development, 470–71
    retirement savings plans, 134
    timing of settlement, 250
Canadian Securities Administrators (CSA), 168
capital
    allocation and integration benefits, 4, 161–62
    banking resources for, 3–4
    requirements for derivatives, 369–70
    and stock market growth, 165
capital markets
    accounting and auditing role, 214–18
    benefits of, 3–5, 127
    bond markets, 297–98
    changing conditions in, 159–60
    corporate governance role, 437–38
    definitional issues, 465
    vs. derivatives markets, 338, 339
    developmental strategies, 17–28, 487–92, 511–12
    ethical role, 417–18, 429
    financial intermediary role, 92–93
    globalization, 37–40
    human capital imperative, 463

capital markets (continued)
    information and capital flow, 65
    infrastructure for, 239–40
    institutional investor role, 119–23,
        124–25, 126–27
    regulation, 53–59, 61–62
    research review, 5–7
    SMEs, 390, 410–11
    technology, 48–53, 61, 160
    trends in Latin America/Caribbean, 7–17
    world comparison, **9–11**
    See also debt markets; derivatives
        markets; equity markets
capital-based position limits, 367
Caprio, Gerard, Jr., 6
captive finance sources
    bond markets, 307, 310, 312, 314, 317, 327
    Latin American use of, 114
    pension funds as, 106–7
Caribbean basin
    infrastructure developments, 261–62
    insurance investing, 123
    regional market integration, 39
    See also Latin America and Caribbean
Caribbean Community (CARICOM), 146
Caribbean Stock Exchange, 262
Carmichael, Jeffrey, 488
cash markets and derivatives, 341–47, 348, 355.
    See also equity markets
cattle futures market, Argentina, 347
CAVALI, 258
CBLC (Clearing and Depository Corporation)
    (Brazil), 254–55
CCP (central counterparty clearing), 190–94,
    197–98, 243, 256, 364
Cedel, 195–96
cellular phones and online trading, 72
Center for Custody and Financial Settlement of
    Securities (CETIP), 254–55
Central America, infrastructure developments,
    260–61. See also individual countries
central banks
    Argentine crisis, 95–96
    bond markets, 298–99, 322
    Brazil, 385
    cash management by government, 309
    Central America, 260
    clearing and settlement role, 243, 247–48,
        255, 258

    fractional reserve requirements, 99
    Guatemala, 103
    infrastructure developments, 257, 266
    as lender of last resort, 100
    monetary management, 310
    Paraguayan crisis, 101
    See also banks
Central Counterpart Group (CCP-12), 243–44
central counterparty clearing (CCP), 190–94,
    197–98, 243, 256, 364
Central de Registración y Liquidacion de
    Instrumentos de Endeudamiento Público
    (CRYL), 257
central processing unit model for settlement, 195
central securities depositories (CSDs)
    Caribbean, 261–62
    Central America, 260–61
    Chile, 258
    Colombia, 259
    cross-border linkages, 243–44
    infrastructure role, 242–43
    Peru, 258
    regional market integration, 194–98,
        264–65
    strategies for improvement, 23
CETIP (Center for Custody and Financial
    Settlement of Securities), 254–55
Chicago Mercantile Exchange (CME), 192–94,
    273–74, 365n41
Chile
    benchmark instruments, 311
    bond markets, 304, 332
    corporate governance reforms, 444, 445
    corporate scandal in, 443
    depository receipts, 14–15
    derivatives markets, 352, **353**
    fiscal crisis, 100, 113
    infrastructure development, 256–58
    institutional investing, 40, 121–22, **124**,
        501–2
    market capitalization, 45, 126–27
    market reforms in, 21
    mortgage market, 325
    pension funds, 127, 135, 316, 491, 501–2
    social security reform, 106
China and capital market development, 356n23,
    356n25
CISPA (Payment System Inter-bank
    Commission), 258

Clearing and Depository Corporation (CBLC) (Brazil), 254–55
clearing and settlement
    bond markets, 308, 319–20
    derivatives markets, 360, 361, 364–68, 370
    efficiency of, 40
    European developments, 139, 176
    global developments, 247–52
    infrastructure improvement, 23, 245–46
    institutional specialization, 242–43
    as key to market development, 239–40
    Latin American developments, 253–62, 264–65, 384
    regional market integration, 26, 190–98
    technology, 60, 131
clearinghouses, 195–96, 243, 257
Clearnet S.A., 191
Clearstream, 197–98
closed Internet markets, 73–74
closed-end investment companies. See institutional investors
CLS (continuous linked settlement), 246, 248
club structures, avoiding, 23
Cluster Action Plan (MIF), 235–36
CME (Chicago Mercantile Exchange), 192–94, 273–74, 365n41
CNBV (Comisión Nacional Bancaria y de Valores) (Mexico), 126, 452
(CNVs) comisiones de valores, 15. See also securities and exchange commissions
Code of Best Practice of Corporate Governance (Brazil), 452
codes of conduct in market activity, 419–20, 451. See also ethical issues
Coffee, John, 7
collateral issues for SMEs, 395–96
collateralized securities, 325. See also bond markets
Colombia
    bond markets, 314, 319, 332
    captive finance sources, 317
    debt market situation, 305, 312, 325
    information disclosure reforms, 453–56
    infrastructure developments, 258–60
    pension funds, 316
    stock exchange, 503
Comisión Nacional Bancaria y de Valores (CNBV) (Mexico), 126, 452

comisiones de valores (CNVs), 15. See also securities and exchange commissions
commercial financing, 94, **397**
commercial investors and derivatives markets, 339, 349, 367, 374. See also institutional investors
commercial terms in derivatives markets, 348
Commissão de Valores Mobiliarios (CVM), 20, 385
Committee of Wise Men, 161, 174, 206–7, 266
commodities
    Brazilian exchange, 383
    in derivatives market, 335, 338, 340, 343, 348
    self-regulation of exchanges, 277
Commodities and Futures Trading Commission (CFTC) (U.S.), 277, 351, 360n35, 382
communications
    Internet impact, 69, 72
    and regional integration, 26
Companhia de Concessões Rodoviarias (CCR) (Brazil), 448, 450–51
companies, conflict resolution with investors, 21. See also issuers
competition
    ATSs, 249
    banking role in markets, 92, 314–15
    bond markets, 303–4, 307
    capital market environment, 160
    corporate governance reforms, 456
    credit agency, 326
    demutualization of exchanges, 269, 272, 274, 275, 276
    derivatives markets, 347
    European market integration, 162–64, 170, 174–75, 177
    globalization, 39
    importance of market, 239, 245, 263
    and infrastructure improvements, 264
    institutional investors, 142–43
    Latin America, 105, 205–6, 251
    liquidity enhancement to, 128
    market benefits of, 159, 495–97
    North American regional integration, 184–85
    regulation of markets, 21
    self-regulation motivation, 58, 376
    strategies for improving, 22–25
    transaction costs of, 247

computers. See technology
Computershare Ltd., 288
Concept Release, 55, 221n7
confidence, market
    accounting standards, 213, 217
    bond markets, 308
    corporate governance, 509–10
    instability of Latin America, 426, 427
    oversight, 363
    regulation, 479
    shareholder rights, 438
    vs. trust, 422
conflicts of interest
    bond markets, 315
    corporate governance, 440
    demutualization of exchanges, 271, 272,
      276–79
    derivatives markets, 362–63
    electronic trading systems, 53
    issuer-investor negotiations over, 450–51
    self-regulation, 62, 378
    stock exchange role, 46, 58
Conroy, Patrick, 504
Consolidated Quotation System (CQS), 181–82,
    183
Consolidated Tape Association (CTA), 181–82
consolidation
    banking industry, 15, 41
    capital markets environment, 159–60
    exchanges, 255, 262
    See also mergers and acquisitions
consortiums and SME financing, **397**
consulting companies, infrastructure role of, 247
consumer protection in European market
    integration, 175, 176
Continental vs. London exchanges, 163, 179
continuous auction method (open outcry), 248,
    349
continuous linked settlement (CLS), 246, 248
contracts
    ad hoc, 448–51
    derivatives markets, 343–44, 352–53, 356,
      360–62, 372
    ethical issues, 424
    and globalization, 67–68
    self-regulation, 377
    See also enforcement of market rules
cooperation
    Brazilian markets, 254, 255

    business ethics, 417
    clearing procedures, 190–94
    exchange trading, 178–79, 185–90,
      194–98, 247, 269
    information dissemination, 179–82
    integration issues, 159, 177, 199–203
    marketing of markets, 198–99
    order routing, 182–85
    and trustworthiness, 423
corporate bond market, 298, 306, 323–27,
    329–30
corporate governance
    accounting standards, 216–17
    appraisal framework, 439–41, **460–61**
    confidence in market, 509–10
    and debt markets, 4
    demutualization of exchanges, 269, 271,
      273, 274–76, 278, 280–81, 291–92
    disclosure practices, 149, 440–41, 448, 452
    ethical issues, 427
    individual lack of trust in, 474
    infrastructure developments, 266
    institutional investors, 131, 139–41, 453,
      456, 491–92
    Latin America, 19–21, 40, 145, 441–59
    liquidity, 102
    market development process, 7, 493
    protection of shareholders, 18–19,
      140–41, 149, 438, 439–40, 443, 444,
      458
    regional market integration, 201–3
    role in capital markets, 437–38
    strengthening of, 108, 148–49
Corporate Governance Roundtable (Latin
    America), 459
corporate ventures. See venture capital
corporate vs. government-issued debt, 343–44
COSRA (Council of Securities Regulators of the
    Americas). See Council of Securities
    Regulators of the Americas (COSRA)
Costa Rica, 260–61, 305, 315
costs, financial services
    and CCP, 190–91
    cross-border, 160, 251
    futures markets cooperation, 193
    harmonization of market rules, 168
    infrastructure developments, 250, 263,
      266–67
    liquidity, 239

costs, financial services *(continued)*
 regional market integration, 160, 161, 162,
  166, 199–201, 506–7
 SMEs, 8, 399
 See also transaction costs
costs of capital and liquidity benefits, 128
Council of Ministers, Europe, 171, 177
Council of Securities Regulators of the Americas
 (COSRA)
 human capital development, 476, 481
 institutional investors, 147
 market integration role, 47–48
 oversight principles, 378–79
 support for IOSCO principles, 19
counterparty transactions
 CCP, 190–94, 197–98, 243, 256, 364
 common vs. individual, 357
 and credit risk, 365–66
 derivatives markets, 340, 348
CQS (Consolidated Quotation System), 181–82,
 183
credible contract commitments, 203
credit
 enhancement of, 325
 indigenous savings, 474
 and money supply, 93–94, 99–100
 SMEs, **397**
credit bureaus, 19
credit ratings in bond markets, 308, 326–27
credit risk, 311, 342, 343, 365–66, 367–68
creditworthiness and custodians of derivatives,
 363
Crest, 197–98
cross-border trading
 clearing and settlement, 240, 253
 costs of, 160, 251
 demutualization of exchanges, 282–83
 drivers for, 506
 European market integration, 163, 172
 information sharing, 373
 and Internet, 75, 76
 jurisdiction problems, 48
 Latin American development, 40, 146, 495
 linkage establishment, 243–44
 listing arrangements, 179, 497
 self-regulation, 377
 shareholder protection, 56
 standards development, 61, 213, 249
 technology, 53, 54–56, 131
 See also regional market integration

crossover institutional investors, 13
cross-subsidization, demutualization of
 exchanges, 271
CSA (Canadian Securities Administrators), 168
CTA (Consolidated Tape Association), 181–82
cultural issues
 disciplined accounting standards, 234
 futures market cooperation, 194
 human capital development, 464, 466–67,
  467, 472–74, 480, 482
 instability of Latin American, 426
 Latin American market integration, 205
 NOREX success, 186
 SME role, 393
 See also ethical issues
currency issues
 Argentine fiscal crisis, 96
 bond markets, 302, 308
 CLS, 248
 foreign exchange risk, 301, 302
 institutional investors, 24
 Mexican financial crisis, 304–5
custodians, clearing, 243, 250, 264, 320, 363
custody of securities, 23, 243, 255
CVM (Commissäo de Valores Mobiliarios), 20,
 385

Da Rin, M., 114
Danish derivatives exchange, 286–87
day trading and Internet, 81–83, 87
DCV (Deposito Central de Valores) (Chile), 258
dealers. *See* broker-dealers
debt, public
 Argentine fiscal crisis, 95–97
 balanced use of, 91–92
 decline in, 7, 12
 excessive, 95
 external debt levels, **301**
 See also deficits, government budget
debt markets
 corporate governance, 4
 and derivatives markets, 338, 340, 343–44
 vs. equity markets, 93, 97–102, 103, 106,
  114, 127
 Latin American environment, 305, 312, 325
 SME financing, 396–98, 399–400
 See also bond markets
DECEVAL (Deposito Centralizado de Valores de
 Colombia), 259

defaulting of firms and derivatives markets, 368
deferred net settlement systems, 248
deficits, government budget
  bond markets, 308, 327
  Latin American difficulties with, 7, 92, 114, 305
  and poor macroeconomic policy, 95
defined-contribution (401(k)) plans, 134, 144
delivery for derivatives contracts, 348, 360n34, 382
delivery vs. payment (DVP)
  bond markets, 308, 319–20
  Latin America, 253, 255, 257, 258, 260
  market importance of, 243
demand and supply issues, 93, 144, 345–46, 347, 502–3
dematerialization of securities
  bond markets, 308, **320**
  Latin America, 253, 256, 258, 260
  and technology, 110
Demirgüç-Kunt, A., 5–6, 102
democracy and markets, 425, 430–31
demutualization of exchanges
  Amsterdam, 289–90
  Australia, 287–88
  capital market environment, 160
  conflicts of interest, 271, 272, 276–79
  derivatives markets, 362
  flexibility, 46
  globalization, 41, 247, 272–73
  for Latin America and Caribbean, 290–92
  oversight, 374
  process overview, 269–72
  reasons for, 272–76
  regulatory solutions, 279–84
  Sweden, 284–87
deposit insurance facilities in Latin America, 100–102
Deposito Central de Valores (DCV) (Chile), 258
Deposito Centralizado de Valores de Colombia (DECEVAL), 259
depository systems
  ADRs, 14–15, 43–44, 55–56, 252, 497
  bond markets, 308, 320
  and capitalization share, 41–42, **43**
  See also central securities depositories (CSDs); clearing and settlement

Depository Trust and Clearing Corporation (DTCC), 192, 249
deregulation of markets
  capital markets environment, 160
  corporate bond market, 324–25
  derivatives markets, 335
  developing economies' trends, 108–9
  exchange rate issues, 302
  institutional investors, 141–42
  vs. self-regulation, 380
derivatives markets
  bond markets, 298, 318
  in Brazil, 383–86
  capital market trends, 110
  and CCP, 191
  clearinghouses, 243
  CME and SIMEX offset arrangement, 192–94
  day trading risks, 82
  design of, 341–52
  history and current trends, 335–38
  identification of need for, 338–41
  OM, 285–86
  oversight and self-regulation, 355, 362–63, 373–80
  policy recommendations, 381–83
  regulation, 340, 352, 355–73, 385
  Scandinavian futures exchanges, 286–87
  technology impact, 246, 248, 347
Deutsche Börse, 189–90, 198, 251, 404
developed economies, human capital in, 469–72, **473**. See also Canada; Europe; United States
developing economies
  accounting standards, 214
  alliances and partnerships, 46–47
  current status of, 39–41
  depository receipts, 14–15
  financial stability, 219
  globalization strategies, 59
  infrastructure improvements, 240
  institutional issues, 107–12
  and Internet, 66, 69, 86
  long-term credit availability, 6
  market intermediaries, 91–92
  regulation issue, 40, 53, 68, 148
  self-regulation, 57
  share of capitalization, 41–42
  shareholder protection, 438

developing economies *(continued)*
SMEs, 389–90, 393, 403, 411
See also Asian markets; international
investment in local markets; Latin
America and Caribbean; policy issues
development agencies and SMEs, **397**
direct public offering (DPO), 401, 403
direct vs. portfolio investment, 7, 73
discipline, market, and accounting standards, 213,
234
disclosure, information
bond markets, 302–3, 308, 313, 321–22,
325–27, 329–30
Colombian reforms, 453–56
corporate governance, 19, 149, 440–41,
448, 452
demutualization of exchanges, 277, 286
derivatives markets, 348
guiding principles for, **460**
infrastructure development, 302–3
Internet trading, 66, 75, 76
loosening of requirements, 148
policy issues, 500–501
regional market integration, 179–82
regulation in U.S., 136–37, 280, 281
shareholder protection, 326–27, 494
See also accounting and auditing
standards; prices and quotes
discounting of assets in derivatives contracts,
369–70
disintermediation of banking industry, 303–4,
315, 317, 325
dispersed regulations, 20
dispute resolution, 57, 277, 448
distortion risk, 355
diversification, 4, 130, 134–35
domestic capital markets. See local capital markets
Dominican Republic, infrastructure
developments, 261
Domowitz, Ian, 497
DPO (direct public offering), 401, 403
dual listing of stocks, 43, 60
DVP (delivery vs. payment). See delivery vs.
payment (DVP)

Easterly, W., 104
Eastern Europe, market capitalization levels, 45
ECNs (electronic communication networks), **48**,
49–52, 249, 272

Ecuador, infrastructure developments, 258–59
education
ethical issues, 427–28
human capital development, 464, 466,
467
information disclosure, 500
institutional investors, 137
investor program proposal, 149
languages and regional market training,
483
Latin American lack of market, 474, **475**,
476
professional associations, 482
training institutions and programs,
469–72, **473**, 480–81
and trust levels, 430–31
efficiency, market, 6, 215, 217, 241–42, 243, 350
El Salvador, infrastructure developments, 261
El Sitio, 16
electronic bulletin markets, 73
electronic communication networks (ECNs), **48**,
49–52, 249, 272
electronic finance systems, **71**
Electronic Payment Means (MEP), 257
electronic trading systems
Argentina, 257
bond markets, 319
Brazil, 94
demutualization of exchanges, 269, 272,
281, 285, 289
derivatives markets, 349, 350, 359, 366
development competition, 249
vs. floor trading, 202, 248, 269, 277, 285
and IPO, 73
rise of, 41, 48–53, 55
risk and uncertainty with, 60
See also Internet
emerging economies. *See* developing economies
e-money systems, **71**
Employee Retirement Income Security Act of
1974 (ERISA) (U.S.), 134
employment, SMEs as job creators, 392
Enersis, 443
enforcement of market rules
accounting standards, 224
cross-border issue, 373
derivatives markets, 356, 372
European Court weaknesses, 176–77

enforcement of market rules (continued)
 globalization, 67–68
 harmonization problems, 169
 importance of, 19–20
 Internet trading, 74–75
 in Latin America, 116, 426
 oversight of markets, 379
 regulation, 53, 167, 303
 shareholder protection, 494
 See also regulation
Enron Corp., 213–14, 221
entrepreneurs and financial access for SMEs, 389
equity markets
 alliances and partnerships, 109, 247
 Brazil, 94
 capitalization levels, **9–10**
 corporate governance, 4
 current status of emerging, 39–41
 vs. debt markets, 93, 97–102, 106, 114,
  127
 derivatives markets, 341–47, 348, 355
 economic growth, 3, 6, 165
 globalization, 38, 41–48, 59–61, 109, 256
 India, 102–3, 115
 Internet impact, 65–66, 68–75
 market development role, 502–3
 productivity issue, 165
 rating agencies, 19–20
 regulation issues, 53–59, 61–62, 66–68,
  74–87, 98
 safekeeping of securities, 23
 SMEs, 8, 396–98, 399, 405
 technology developments, 48–53, 61
 trade activity, 12
 U.S., 138
 See also capital markets; exchanges,
  securities
ERISA (Employee Retirement Income Security
 Act of 1974) (U.S.), 134
ethical issues
 capital market applicability, 415–16
 framework for market profession, 419–21
 fraud, 74, 83–86, 101–2, 103, 167
 Latin American/Caribbean markets,
  425–31
 and law, 419, 423–25
 manipulation of market, 83–86, 346, 347,
  355, 385
 moral development process, 418n3

 moral hazard problem, 101–2, 314, 424
 role in markets, 416–19
 and self-regulation, 377
 trust, 421–23
 See also conflicts of interest; transparency,
  market
Eurex Clearing, 191–92, 247, 248
EUROCAC, 163
Euroclear, 196
Eurolinks model for settlement, 197
EuroList, 179
Euronext
 alliance partners, 109
 and CCP, 191
 demutualization of exchanges, 289–90
 infrastructure improvements, 264
 institutional investing, 139
 regional market integration, 187–88,
  198–99
 trading cost reductions, 251
Euro.NM, 111, 114, 198
Europe
 benefits/costs/barriers to integration,
  161–66
 capitalization levels, **9–10**, **42**
 clearing and settlement, 139, 176, 190–98,
  248, 251
 demutualization of exchanges, 272–73,
  282
 electronic trading, 48–49
 exchange trading, 185–90, 410
 information dissemination, 179–82
 institutional investing, 139, 140
 integration issues, 46, 146, 177, 199–203,
  251, 264
 and Latin American integration, 27
 listing, 178–79
 marketing of markets, 198–99
 mutual recognition/home country control,
  170–77
 order routing, 182–85
 public sector financing role, 91–92
 regulation issues, 54, 279
 SMEs, 147, 389, 391, 392, 394, 401,
  407–10, 411–12
 standards issues, 169, 221
 technology, 131, 163, 251
 trading activity, 12
 See also individual countries

European Central Securities Depositories
Association, 197
European clearinghouse model for settlement,
195–96
European Commission, 171–72
European Court, 170, 174–75, 176–77
European Options Exchange, 289
European Parliament, 171
European passport, 172–73, 176
European Securities Forum, 191
exchange rate regime and bond markets, 301,
302
exchanges, securities
alliances and partnerships, 46–47, 248,
251–52, 288
Caribbean infrastructure development, 261
as central depositories, 261
clearing and settlement, 242
Colombian developments, 259
consolidation of, 255, 262
corporate governance reforms, 445–48
cross-listing, 497
globalization, 38, 41–48, 59–61
government bond trading in, **318**
human capital development, 476
information dissemination, 179–82
infrastructure developments, 256
Internet use, 73–74, 76–77
investment in foreign, 106, 128, 178–79,
497, 509
and ITS, 183
politicization of Latin American, 425
public interest responsibility, 271, 419
regional market integration, 162–64,
183–94
regulation, 53–59, 61–62, 85, 87
requirements, 19
segmentation of, 114–15
SMEs, 147, 395, 403–10
tailored approach to, 110–12
technology developments, 48–53, 61, 202,
248
viability measurement challenges, 490
See also demutualization of exchanges;
derivatives markets; trading systems;
individual exchanges
exposure supervision in derivatives, 370
extensible business reporting languages, 249–50,
425

Extensible Markup Language (XML), 250
external financing, 165, 301. See also international
investment in local markets
extraordinary items in accounting, 224

fair and equitable treatment in derivatives
markets, 361–62
families, concentration of investor wealth in, 145
FASB (Financial Accounting Standards Board),
214, 220, 222, 223–24
Federation Internationale des Bourses des
Valeurs (FIBV), 246, 269, 403–4
Federation of Euro-Asian Stock Exchange
(FEAS), 47
Federation of European Stock Exchanges (FESE),
47, 179
fees, exchange user, 283–84. See also transaction
costs
FESCO (Forum of European Securities
Commissions), 169
FIABV (Ibero-American Association of Stock
Exchanges), 47, 476
FIBV (Federation Internationale des Bourses des
Valeurs), 246, 269, 403–4
finance ministry, market role, 289, 298–99, 307,
310, 329
Financial Accounting Standards Board (FASB),
214, 220, 222, 223–24
financial engineering, 40, 110
financial guarantees and market development,
510–11
Financial Information Exchange (FIX), 249–50
financial instruments
benefits of capital markets for, 4
choices for market development, 502–4
derivatives markets, 335, 338, 348, 352
and Internet, 69
money markets, 137, 298, 307, 309–10,
327
reform process, 491–92
financial markets and economic growth, 164–65
financial policies, constraints on equity markets,
99
Financial Services Authority (Australia), 280
Financial Services Authority (UK), 355
financial stability
accounting and auditing standards,
217–19, 235, 303
bond markets, 302–4

financial stability (continued)
  capital market contribution, 239
  ethical issues, 415–16
  institutional investors, 129–30
  in local capital markets, 16–17, 60
  mutual and pension funds, 129–30
financial statements
  FASB vs. IASB, 223–24
  functions of, 214
  influence on prices, 215
  quality of, 216–17, 228, **229**, 230
Financial Supervisory Authority (Swedish), 285, 286
Financial Supervisory Authority (UK), 471
financial system, components of, 3
financing of enterprises. See debt markets; small and medium enterprises (SMEs)
Finnish derivatives exchange, 286
fiscal policy
  bond markets, 300
  Latin American crises, 95–97, 100, 113
  need for conservative, 146
  privatization of industries, 7
fiscal stabilization funds and small economies, 105
fitness and propriety of market operators, 363
FIX (Financial Information Exchange), 249–50
fixed commission structures, 141
fixed-income markets
  bond markets, 315–16
  crowding out of private sector offerings, 97
  Latin American, 109, 123, 126, 257, 260
  market development role, 503–4
  mortgage-backed securities, 131, 324–25
  in OECD, 121
  private sector, 323, 324–26
  See also bond markets
fixed-rate investments, 307, 312
floatation option for SMEs, 407–8, **409**
floating rate securities, 311
floor trading
  demutualization of exchanges, 248, 269, 281, 289
  vs. electronic systems, 202
  obsolescence of, 41, 48
Foerster, Stephen R., 497
foreign market investment
  effect on local markets, 43, 107, 128, 135, 497, 509

listings in foreign exchanges, 106, 178–79
mutual recognition approach to, 55, 170–77
SEC regulatory proposals, 55–56
See also international investment in local markets
for-profit organizations, exchanges as, 46, 52. See also demutualization of exchanges
Forum of European Securities Commissions (FESCO), 169
forwards vs. futures, **343**, 347
fractional reserve requirements, 99–100
fragmented markets, 23, 496
France, investment environment, 121, 401
fraud issues, 74, 83–86, 101–2, 103, 167
free riding in derivatives markets, 359
freedom of establishment in European markets, 170–71, 173
freedom of movement in European markets, 170–71, 173
Fretes-Cibils, Vicente, 100
Froot, Kenneth A., 497
fundamental analysis and accounting standards, 214–16
funding, government. See bond markets
funding for demutualization of exchanges, 266–67, 271–72, 284
fungibility of derivatives, 340, 341, 350
futures and options markets. See derivatives markets
Futures Commission Merchants, 193
Futures Exchange of Rio de Janeiro (Brazil), 383
Futures Industry Association, 335

GAAP (Generally Accepted Accounting Principles), 136, 217, 220–25, **231–33**
Garcia, Valeriano F., 93, 100
GDP (gross domestic product), 7, **9**, 165
GDRs (Global Depository Receipts), 14–15, 44
GEM (Global Equity Market), 109, 256
general good issue for European Union, 173, 174–75
Generally Accepted Accounting Principles (GAAP), 136, 217, 220–25, **231–33**
Germany, investment environment, 121, 401
Glass-Steagall Act, 142
Glen, Jack, 497, 507, 508
Global Corporate Governance Forum, 459
Global Depository Receipts (GDRs), 14–15, 44

Global Equity Market (GEM), 109, 256
Global Straight through Processing Association
  (GSTPA), 249, 250
Global Trading System, 94
globalization
      accounting standards, 217, 218–19, 234
      clearing and settlement, 196, 240, 244
      demutualization of exchanges, 41, 247,
        272–73
      enforcement of contracts, 67–68
      ethical issues, 428, 430
      government role in inter-market linkages,
        327
      infrastructure upgrades, 247–52
      institutional investors, 501
      market areas affected, 37–40
      and openness to trade, 6
      regional market integration, 160
      regulation issues, 19–20, 46, 53–59,
        61–62, 85, 87
      self-regulation, 380
      SMEs, 392
      stock market effects, 41–48, 59–61, 109,
        256
      technology, 48–53, 61
      See also integration, global market
Globex Alliance, 383
Gompers, Paul A., 6–7
governance, sector, 466, **467**
government bond market, 107, 295–98, 306–22
government-issued debt vs. corporate debt,
  343–44
governments
      banking dependence of, 4, 308–9
      demutualization of exchanges, 277–78,
        279, 282
      derivatives markets, 374
      ethical issues, 423, 426–27, 428–29, 431
      human capital development, 464
      limitations of market role, 24
      liquidity interference by, 97
      money market role, 327
      motives for creating market economy, 16
      as owners of exchanges, 286
      self-regulation as brake on interference by,
        380
      SME funding, 393, **397**
      support for reforms, 27–28, 105, 145–46,
        207, 508–9

      See also debt, public; deficits, government
        budget; legal issues; policy issues;
        politics
gross domestic product (GDP), 7, **9**, 165
Group of 30, 244, 245
growth, economic
      bond markets, 295
      capital market contribution, 37–38
      democracy, 430
      financial market effects, 3–4, 5–6, 93,
        164–65
      and income levels, 97
      institutional investors, 129, 149–50
      integration benefits, 162
      Latin American equity markets, 7
      small economy challenges, 104
      SMEs, 390–91, 410
Grupo Televisa, 43
GSTPA (Global Straight through Processing
  Association), 249, 250
Guatemala, debt vs. equity markets in, 103

Hallberg, K., 392, 393
harmonization of market rules
      accounting standards, 213, 220–25,
        226–27, 234
      advantages of, 59
      bond markets, 301
      Euronext, 290
      globalization, 54
      regional market integration, 167–69, 172,
        175–76, 205–6
      SMEs, 412
      See also integration, global market
Harvey, Campbell R., 6
hedging. *See* derivatives markets
Helsinki Stock Exchange, 404
heterogeneous vs. homogeneous debt, 344
high-tech industries, new exchanges for, 111. See
  also technology
Hogan, Stokes Report, 275–76
home country control and regional integration,
  170–77
homogeneity and derivatives contracts, 343–44
Honduras, infrastructure developments, 261
Hong Kong financial center, 194
Honohan, P., 104
horizontal vs. vertical market integration, 251
housing market, corporate bond market, 324–25

hub and spokes model for settlement, 196
human capital
    developed markets, 469–72, **473**
    framework for development, 465–69
    Latin America and Caribbean, 472–83
    local market investment in, 40
    need to address, 463–65
    regulation of global markets, 61
Hungarian exchange, 490
Hunter, W., 463–64
hybrid payment systems, 248
hyperlinks and Internet trading issues, 70, 77–78

IASB (International Accounting Standards
    Board), 19–20, 220–25, **231–33**
Ibero-American Association of Stock Exchanges
    (FIABV), 47, 476
Ibero-American Securities Markets Institute, 27
Ibolsa, 16
IDB (Inter-American Development Bank), 207,
    235–36, 261
IFC (International Finance Corporation), 439,
    459
IFIs (international financial institutions), 104
Impavido, G., 7, 106
Improvements Project (IASB), 224
income levels
    equity market growth, 97
    small economy challenges, 104
index funds, U.S. development, 133
indexed securities, 304, 305, 307, 311
India, vibrant equity market of, 102–3, 115
indigenous savings and credit, 474
indirect monetary instruments, 310
individual investors, 41, 65–66, 81–83, 86, 315,
    316
individual retirement accounts (IRAs), 134
industry associations. See professional
    associations
inflation
    bond markets, 295, 300, 302, 310
    Brazil's issues, 254, 385
    inflation-indexed securities, 304
    SME funding, 390
informal financing markets, 101–2
information
    human capital development, 481
    importance in financial services, 65, 66, 86,
        148

Internet, 66–67, 69
liquidity of markets, 102
monetary management, 310
regional market integration, 207
regulation integration, 167
sharing of, 373, 377
timeliness of, 69, 230, 234
vision for infrastructure changes, 265
See also dematerialization of securities;
    disclosure, information; transparency,
    market
infrastructure, market
    bond markets, 318–21
    capital markets, 239–40
    derivatives markets, 381–82
    globalization, 247–52
    information disclosure, 302–3
    Latin American developments, 102–7,
        252–62, 474, 478–79
    multiple trading systems, 496
    policy issues, 488, 489–91, 504–5
    regional market integration, 199–203
    strategies for improvement, 22–25,
        241–47, 262–67
    See also institutions, socioeconomic
initial public offering (IPO)
    Chilean reforms, 21
    demutualization of exchanges, 274
    developed markets, 15
    disclosure requirements, 19
    electronic, 73
    European environment for, 164
    and Internet, 16, 81
    Latin American difficulties with, 8
    need for support, 25
    SMEs, 115, 390, 399, 401–2
    tailored approach to listing, 110
innovation
    globalization challenges, 40
    importance of, 25
    institutional investors, 130–31
    integration benefits, 161
    regulation, 67
    SMEs, 392–93
insider trading protections, 21
instability, political and economic, 415–16, 426,
    427. See also volatility, market
Instinet, 50, 278
Institute of Corporate Governance (Brazil), 459

institutional investors
  bond markets, 308, 316
  capital market role, 5, 6–7, 119–23,
    124–25, 126–27
  corporate governance reforms, 131,
    139–41, 453, 456, 491–92
  crossover, 13
  derivatives markets, 374
  domestic market influences, 127–43
  European market integration, 164
  foreign market access, 56
  vs. individual, 41, 65, 86
  Latin America, 22–25, 40, 110, 143–45
  policy issues, 145–51, 501–2
  SME financing, 395, **397–98**
  See also human capital; institutional
    investors; shareholder protection
institutions, socioeconomic
  alliances and partnerships, 109, 247
  Brazil, 21, 22–24, 459
  developing economies, 6, 107–12
  IFIs, 104
  importance of supporting market
    development, 28
  infrastructure improvements, 241
  in Latin America, 102–7, 206–7
  policy issues, 508–10
  professional associations, 265
  SMEs, **397**
  specialization of, 242–43
  strategies for improving, 22–25
  See also corporate governance; individual
    institutions
insurance investments
  bond markets, 315–16
  competition among investors, 143
  consolidation issue, 41
  and corporate governance, 448
  derivatives markets, 338n2
  economic development role, 492, 502
  investment rules for, 142
  in Latin America and Caribbean, 123
  in OECD, 121
  protection in Europe, 175
  in U.S., 120–21, 133
integration, global market
  accounting standards, 213
  benefits of, 6, 15–16
  challenges of, 59

emerging markets, 28, 41
exchanges, 109, 247
marketing organizations, 198
regulation difficulties, 46
securities commissions' role, 47–48
small economies, 105
See also regional market integration
Inter-American Development Bank (IDB), 207,
  235–36, 261
interest rates
  Argentine fiscal crisis, 95–96
  bond markets, 24, 326
  Brazil's problems, 305
  decline in crossover investment, 13
  Guatemala, 103
  institutional investor independence from,
    129
  liberalization goal, 303
  replacement for private instruments, 114
  vulnerabilities of banking system, 101
Intermarket Trading System (ITS), 183
intermediaries, market
  as alternate trading system sponsors, 51
  banks as, 98
  capital markets as, 92–93
  derivatives markets, 350
  developing vs. developed economies,
    91–92
  economic growth, 164–65
  foreign presence in Mexico, 43, **44**
  globalization, 38
  and Internet, 72–73, 75, 80–81
  lack of trust in Latin America, 479
  large firms as model for, 100
  self-regulation issues, 58
  SME financing, **398**
  See also exchanges, securities; venture
    capital
International Accounting Standards Board
  (IASB), 19–20, 220–25, **231–33**
International Finance Corporation (IFC), 439, 459
international financial institutions (IFIs), 104
international investment in local markets
  benefits for developing economies, 27,
    109
  bond markets, 304, 307, 316, 320
  capital market contribution, 3
  depository receipts, 14–15
  domestic institutions' role, 130

international investment in local markets
  (continued)
    institutional investing restrictions, 144
    in Latin America, 11–13, 43–44, 93–94,
      123, 252, 463
    Latin American reliance on, 6, 307, 472
    regulatory reform, 20
    transparency of market, 60
International Monetary Fund (IMF), 235, 499
International Organization of Securities
  Commissions (IOSCO)
    cross-border trading, 54, 61
    demutualization of exchanges, 269–70
    derivatives markets, 352, 355, 372
    Improvements Project (IASB), 224
    and Internet, 76–83
    market integration role, 47–48
    principles of, 19, 146–47
    regional integration, 166
    regulation integration, 167
    on self-regulation, 374
International Society of Securities Administrators
  (ISSA), 246
Internet
    characteristics of, 68–70
    impact on Latin American markets, 16
    impact on securities trading, 41, 46
    and information transparency, 115
    investment capabilities of, 65–66
    market uses of, 70–75
    regulation issues, 66–68, 74–87
    SEC view of, 55–56
    and SMEs, 392, 404–5
Internet company IPOs, 8, 16
Internet discussion sites (IDSs), 78, 83–84
Internet service providers (ISPs), 85–86, 87
intrinsic value vs. market value, 215
Inversura, 455–56
Investment Company Act of 1940 (U.S.), 136
Investment Services Directive (ISD), 54, 172–73,
  174
investors
    ad hoc contracting, 449–51
    bond markets, 307, 308, 314–17
    capital market benefits, 4
    competition among, 143
    concentration of wealth in families, 145
    conflict resolution with companies, 21
    debt vs. equity markets, 98

    derivatives markets, 349, 350, 357
    education program proposal, 149
    infrastructure role, 242
    institutional vs. individual, 41, 65, 86
    interest in Latin America and Caribbean,
      59–60
    Internet use, 71–72
    investment needs, 15–16
    Latin American deficiency in, 13
    market liquidity needs, 7
    protection of, 75, 81–83, 107–8
    prudent investor rule, 141–42, 148
    regulation as attracting, 18
    retail, 65–66, 81–83, 86, 315, 316
    SME financing, **397**
    STP popularity, 240
    See also institutional investors; shareholder
      protection
IRAs (individual retirement accounts), 134
Ireland and SMEs, 406
ISD (Investment Services Directive), 54, 172–73,
  174
Israeli stock exchange, 43
ISSA (International Society of Securities
  Administrators), 246
issuance methods and derivatives markets,
  346–47
issuers, market instrument
    ad hoc contracting, 449–51
    bond markets, 323
    capital funding options, 3–4
    corporate governance, 278, 443–44,
      455–56
    derivatives markets, 346–47
    governments as, 297, 310–14, 329
    infrastructure support for, 505
    Internet use, 72
    lack of trust in, 479
    website liability issue, 77–78, 80–81
Istanbul Stock Exchange, 47
Italy, institutional investing, 121, **125**
ITG, 50
ITS (Intermarket Trading System), 183
iX (international exchanges plc), 189–90

Jamaica, market developments, 123, 261–62
Jamaica Stock Exchange, 261
Japan, market environment, 121, 351, 360n35,
  391

Jensen, Michael, 216
job creation, SME role in, 392
joint ventures, 192, 202, 392
Jordanian stock exchange, 111–12
judicial system, role of, 18, 102, 448
jurisdiction issues, securities exchanges, 54, 76–77

Karolyi, G. Andrew, 497
Know-how Fund, 490
Kohlberg, L., 418n3
Korea, corporate governance development, 140
Kothari, S., 215
Kray, A., 104
Kuala Lumpur Stock Exchange, 252

La Porta, R., 6, 7, 102, 493–94
Lamfalussy, Alexandre, 140
languages
        coordination of software, 249–50, 425
        and regional market training, 483
large vs. small enterprises, benefits from
        globalization, 109. See also small and medium
        enterprises (SMEs)
Latibex, 495
Latin America and Caribbean
        accounting and auditing standards, 225,
                226–27, 228, **229**, 230, 234, 235–36
        banking industry dependence, 91, 112–13,
                114, 272, 315
        bond markets, 295–97, 301, 304–5, 311,
                313–17, 320, 331–32
        capital market trends, 7–17
        capitalization changes, 41–43, **45**
        constraints on capital markets, 92–107
        corporate governance reforms, 441–59
        cross-border trading, 495
        demutualization of exchanges, 273, 283,
                284, 290–92
        derivatives markets, 338, 340, 344, 346,
                352, **353–54**, 382–86
        developmental strategies, 17–28
        ethical issues, 425–31
        globalization, 39, 44–45
        human capital development, 463–65,
                472–83
        infrastructure development, 252–67
        institutional investing, 120, 121–23,
                124–25, 126–29, 135, 143–51, 150

international investment dependence, 4,
                307, 472
        Internet use, 16, 87
        investment in foreign exchanges, 43, 497
        macroeconomic environment, 112–16
        market reform progress, 3
        mortgate markets, 325
        political instability, 415–16, 426, 427
        regional integration strategy, 203–8
        and SMEs, 412
        stock market developments, 38, 109, 111,
                264, 490
        See also individual countries and regions
Latin America Integration Association (LAIA),
        146
leadership knowledge and human capital
        development, 480
leasing companies and SMEs, **397**
Lee, Ruben, 497
legal issues
        bankruptcy law, 326
        corporate governance reforms, 441–45
        derivatives markets, 355, 356, 357–58,
                364, 368
        ethical standards in markets, 419, 423–25
        first-generation market reforms, 488
        importance for market liquidity, 102
        instability of Latin America, 426
        oversight of markets, 378
        policy role in law and enforcement, 6, 7,
                493–94
        public sector issuance of voluntary codes
                of practice, 452–53
        risk and efficient markets, 241
        and SROs, 375
        See also regulation; self-regulation; tax
                issues
lender of last resort in Latin America, 100–102
Levich, Richard M., 488
Levine, Ross, 5–6, 102, 128, 164–65
Ley de Oferta Públicas de Adquisición de
        Acciones, 21
liabilities vs. assets, 100. See also debt markets
liability issues for issuers in websites, 77–78,
        80–81
LIFFE (London International Financial Futures
        Exchange), 193
liquidity, market
        banking management of, 100, 309–10

liquidity, market *(continued)*
  bond markets, 20, 307–8, 316, 318, 323
  demutualization of exchanges, 274
  derivatives markets, 339, 341, 342, 344,
    349–50, 359, 366, 369
  economic growth, 6, 165
  electronic trading, 50, 53
  government interference in economy, 97
  institutional investor benefits, 128–29
  institutional role in enhancing, 23, 102
  as investor requirement, 15
  lack of physical location, 269
  Latin American issues, 127, 252
  market viability for investment, 509
  measurement of capitalization, 8
  reduced market costs, 239
  regional integration, 26
  risk control, 128, 263
  secondary market reform, 22
  settlement systems, 240, 248
  SME markets, 406
  turnover rate, **11**, 12
listing on stock exchange
  corporate governance, 445–48
  demutualization of exchanges, 277,
    279–81
  dual listing, 43, 60
  future of, 38, 46
  Latin American losses, **45**
  regional market integration, 106, 178–79,
    497
  requirements, 19
  self-listing by exchanges, 271
  SMEs, 147, 395, 405
  tailored approach to, 110–12
loans vs. bonds for corporations, 323–24. *See
  also* debt markets
Loayza, Norman, 164–65
local capital markets
  balancing of, 103–5
  competition with international, 24
  decline in Latin American, 8, **9–10**, 11–13
  foreign market investment effects, 43, 107,
    128, 135, 497, 509
  globalization, 38, 41
  hub and spokes model for settlement,
    196
  institutional investors, 127–43
  liquidity issue, 20

  local exchange challenges, 39
  need for stability in, 16–17, 60
  revitalizing of, 40
  social security reforms, 106
  See also international investment in local
    markets
London Clearing House, 191–92
London International Financial Futures Exchange
  (LIFFE), 193
London Metals Exchange, 360n35
London Stock Exchange (LSE)
  competition from Continent, 247
  deregulation of, 141
  electronic trading rules, 55
  listing authority, 280
  multiple trading systems, 496
  OM attempted takeover of, 287
  regional market integration, 163, 179,
    189–90, 251
Long, M., 104
long-term credit availability, 6
Lopez-de-Silanes, Florencio, 7
Lumsdaine, Robin L., 6
Lundblad, Christian, 6

macroeconomic environment
  bond markets, 300–302, 307
  capital markets in Latin America, 91–102
  derivatives markets, 381, **384**
  institutional investing, 143
  institutional issues in emerging markets,
    107–12
  Latin American history, 7–17
  Mexican financial crisis, 304–5
  need for government commitment to,
    145–46
  policy issues, 112–16
  sequencing of capital market reforms,
    507–8
  structural constraints on capital markets,
    102–7
Madhavan, Ananth, 497, 507, 508
MAE (Mercado Electronico Abierto), 257
Maino, Rodolfo, 100
Maksimovic, Vojislav, 6
Malaysia, market reforms in, 252
mandatory tender offer rule, 444
manipulation, market, 83–86, 346, 347, 355, 385
manufacturing, SMEs in, 391

margin requirements, 322, 364–66
Market Abitration Chamber, Brazil, 21
market capitalization
    Asian markets, 41–42, 45
    Brazilian derivatives markets, **384**
    current world status, **39**
    depth of, **299**
    institutional strategies, 22–25
    levels, **127**
    Mexico, 42–43, 256
    and SMEs, 410
    U.S., **9–10**, 45
    West Africa, 187
market indices, Euronext, 198–99
market makers, 349, 406
market value vs. intrinsic value, 215
marketing of markets, regional market
    integration, 198–99
market-oriented funding strategy for
    governments, 307, 309, 321
maturity transformation and capital market
    benefits, 4
Meckling, William, 216
media systems and regional integration, 26
MEP (Electronic Payment Means), 257
Mercado de Valores de Buenos Aires (Merval),
    257
Mercado Electronico Abierto (MAE), 257
Mercosur shares, pension reform problems, 107
mergers and acquisitions
    vs. cooperative ventures, 203
    costs of, 200–201
    exchanges, 272–73, 289
    Latin American markets, 15, 252–53
    SME financing, **398**
Merval (Mercado de Valores de Buenos Aires),
    257
Metrick, Andrew, 6–7
Mexican Stock Exchange, 256
Mexico
    bond markets, 23, 304–5, 314, 322, 332
    corporate governance reforms, 443–44,
        451–53
    credit and money supply, 93–94
    currency devaluation, 13
    dematerialization of securities, 253
    depository receipts, 14–15
    derivatives markets, 339, **354**
    financial stability relevance, 219

fiscal crisis, 100, 113–14
foreign intermediaries, 43, **44**
infrastructure developments, 255–56
institutional investing, **124–25**
market capitalization, 42–43, 256
market reforms, 21, 126, 250
mortgage-backed securities, 131
pension funds, 24, 144–45, 316
regional market integration, 26
microenterprises, 393
microstates, prosperity of, 104
ministry of finance, market role, 289, 298–99,
    307, 310, 329
minority shareholders. See shareholder
    protection
mobile telephony, 72
modernization of market and institutional
    investors, 130–31
Modigliani-Miller theorem, 98
monetary policy, bond markets, 300, 302, 307,
    308–10
money market instruments, 137, 298, 307,
    309–10, 327
money supply, 93–94, 99–100, 113
moral development process, 418n3
moral hazard problem, 101–2, 314, 424. See also
    ethical issues
Morgan Stanley, 264
mortgage-backed securities, 131, 324–25
multilateral institutions, development role of, 510
Multilateral Investment Program (MIF), 235–36
Musalem, A., 7, 106
mutual funds
    bond markets, 315, 322
    competition among investors, 143
    current importance of, 119
    diversification, 134–35
    European market integration, 146
    in Latin America and Caribbean, 123,
        126
    market stability, 129–30
    in OECD, 121
    retirement savings plans, 134
    in U.S., 120, 133, 137
    See also institutional investors
mutual offset arrangement, CME and SIMEX,
    192–94
mutual recognition approach to foreign market
    access, 55, 170–77

mutual reliance and regional market integration, 168–69
mutualization structure for exchanges, 52, 247

NAFTA (North American Free Trade Agreement), 93–94
Nahas, Naji Robert, 355
NASD (National Association of Securities Dealers), 181–82, 272, 277, 283
NASDAQ
    ATSs, 52
    demutualization of exchanges, 272, 274, 281
    globalization, 109
    listing requirements, 280–81
    regulation debate, 41
    SME encouragement, 147
NASDAQ Europe, 410
national and international accounting standards, 213, 220–25, **226–27**, 234
National Association of Open Market Institutions (ANDIMA), 255
National Association of Securities Dealers (NASD), 181–82, 272, 277, 283
National Market System (NMS), 180, 181
national securities associations, 251. See also NASD
net settlements, 190, 192, 248, 257, 260
Netherlands. See Amsterdam
Neuer Markt (Frankfurt), 110–11, 409, 410, 447n10
new economy companies and Latin American IPOs, 8
new firms and benefits of financial development, 165
New York Stock Exchange (NYSE)
    arbitration role, 277
    demutualization of exchanges, 272, 281
    depository receipts, 15
    disclosure requirements history, 280
    global equity market initiative, 48, 109
    Latin American investment in, 43, 497
    regulation debate, 41
    self-regulation, 283, 445
NMS (National Market System), 180, 181
nonfinancial corporations, 316
noninstitutional savings vehicles, 474
nonprofit organizations, exchanges as, 52, 247.
    See also demutualization of exchanges

nonvoting shares, 21, 111
Nordic Growth Market, 410
NOREX (Nordic Exchange), 109, 185–86, 251, 286–87
North American Free Trade Agreement (NAFTA), 93–94
Norwegian derivatives exchange, 286
Nouveau Marché (Paris, Bruxelles, Amsterdam), 111, 410
novation process, 190, 192
Novo Mercado (Brazil), 20–21, 111, 446–48
Nuovo Mercato (Italy), 410

Oceania, 477–78
OECD (Organisation for Economic Co-operation and Development). See Organisation for Economic Co-operation and Development (OECD)
off-market trading, derivatives markets, 359
offset arrangement, CME and SIMEX, 192–94
OM Gruppen AB (OM), 264, 274–75, 285, 286, 287
OM Technology, 185, 190
Omgeo, 249, 250
100 percent reserve plan for banks, 99–100
online services. See Internet
open outcry auction method, 248, 349
open-end investment companies. See mutual funds
operational risk, 241, 246
opportunity costs, government bond market, 314
Optimark, 51
optimization arrangements for clearing and settlement, 192
options and futures. See derivatives markets
ordering systems
    and integration pressures, 163
    Internet impact, 66, 71–72, 73
    order book execution, **49**
    order routing, 182–85, 200
Organisation for Economic Co-operation and Development (OECD)
    corporate governance principles, 19–20, 439, 459, **460–61**
    institutional investors, 119–21, **122**
    SMEs, 390–93
Osaka Futures Exchange, 360n35
Outreville, J. F., 463

outsourcing and infrastructure changes, 247, 250, 264

oversight of markets
accounting standards, 235
demutualization of exchanges, 271, 282–84
derivatives markets, 351, 362–63, 370, 373–80, 381
and Enron, 214
importance of, 18
institutional investors, 135–37
and Internet, 66
regulation of customer relationship, 279
and self-regulation, 56, 59
surveillance, 74, 84, 167, 370–72, 378

over-the-counter (OTC) markets
bonds in, 318–20, 322
derivatives markets, 335, 340–41, 343–44, 386
vs. exchange futures, **343**, 350, 365, 380

ownership changes and SMEs, 407
ownership of development process, 492

Pagano, Marco, 164
Paine, Thomas, 430
Panama, market environment, 260, 305
Paraguay, banking crisis, 101
Paris Bourse, 290
pay-as-you-go retirement vs. private pension funds, 134, 135, 143–44
Payment System Inter-bank Commission (CISPA), 258
payment systems. See clearing and settlement
pension funds
accounting standards, 222
bond markets, 135, 315–16
capital markets environment, 160
as captive finance sources, 106–7
corporate governance, 448
deregulation of, 148
growth of private, 24, 25
institutional investors, 132–34
in Latin America and Caribbean, 21, 107, 122–23, 127, 143–45, 316, 501–2
market reforms, 491–92
market stability, 129
in OECD, 121
See also social security systems

Peru
bond markets, 322
debt market situation, 305
derivatives markets, **354**
infrastructure development, 257, 258, 259, 264
institutional investing, **125**
mutual funds, 123
pension funds, 316
petroleum market, 345
physical delivery futures requirements, 382
policy issues
accounting and auditing standards, 230, 234–36
and capital market development strategies, 6–7, 487–89, 511–12
competition benefits, 495–97
derivatives markets, 341, 352, 374, 381–83
economic institutions' roles, 508–10
ethical standards in markets, 416, 431
financial guarantees, 510–11
financial instrument choices, 502–4
financial sector reform process, 491–92
general good issue for European Union, 174–75
information disclosure, 500–501
infrastructure enhancement, 241–67, 489–91, 504–5
institutional investors, 145–51, 501–2
international standards, 498–99
law and enforcement, 493–94
macroeconomic environment, 94–97, 112–16
monetary policy, 300, 302, 307, 308–10
ownership of development process, 492
regional integration, 505–7
sequencing of reforms, 507–8
SMEs, 410–13
See also bond markets; fiscal policy; regulation
politics
accounting standards, 219, 234
banking role reforms, 315
bond market restrictions, 328
commitment to reform, 502
democracy and markets, 425, 430–31
demutualization of exchanges, 285
ethical issues, 424–25
European market integration, 171–72

politics *(continued)*
> foreign market access, 55
> harmonization of market rules, 168
> human capital development, 464, 466,
> > **467**
>
> independence of standard-setting bodies,
> > 222
>
> information dissemination, 182
> instability in Latin America and Caribbean,
> > 415–16, 426, 427
>
> interest groups and trade openness, 6
> leadership to institute reforms, 27–28
> and market declines, 13
> regional market integration, 206–7
> sabotaging of structural reforms, 105
> SME role, 393

Pomerleano, Michael, 488
pooling-of-interest method, 224
portfolio investment
> competition among institutional investors,
> > 142–43
>
> vs. direct investment, 7, 73
> in Latin America, 12
> liberalization of requirements, 141–42
> margin measurement systems, 365

POSIT, 50–51
poverty, SME effect on, 393
preferred shares, 21, 111
price discovery, 339–40, 359
price support programs and derivatives, 345
prices and quotes
> accounting method effects, 215
> asset price volatility and crossover
> > investing, 13
>
> capital prices, 93
> components of, 216
> derivatives markets, 335, 339, 340, 344,
> > 355, 364–65, 381
>
> regional market integration, 180–82
> transparency of, 348, 350–51, 358–60

primary dealers, bond markets, 311, 313–14
primary markets, 22, 308, 310–14, 329, 507–8
Primex, 51
principal/agent conflict and corporate
> governance, 438

principle- vs. rule-based accounting systems,
> 221–25

Principles of Corporate Governance (OECD),
> 439, **460–61**

private placements financing, 399
private sector
> capital markets role, 97, 105
> corporate governance reform role, 445,
> > 446–59
>
> financial guarantees for, 510–11
> human capital development, 466, 469
> infrastructure improvement role, 245–46
> market development role, 509–10
> ownership of reforms, 492
> *See also* capital markets

privatization
> benefits for developing economies, 109
> capital markets environment, 160
> corporate bond market, 324–25
> demutualization of exchanges, 269, 285,
> > 288
>
> as essential to market viability, 490
> and Latin American markets, 14, 20,
> > 105–6
>
> motives for, 16
> and public debt decline, 7
> social security, 122–23

productivity, 97, 105, 165, 392–93
professional associations
> Brazil, 254–55
> human capital development, 469, 471–72
> and public sector institutions, 265
> regional development, 481, 482

professionals, market
> developed markets, 469–72, **473**
> ethical issues, 418–19, 422, 426, 427
> framework for development, 465–69
> Latin America and Caribbean, 472–83
> need to address, 463–65
> *See also* institutional investors;
> > intermediaries, market

proprietary futures, 369
prospectus requirements and Internet trading,
> 76

protected industries, integration costs, 162
protection of market users
> derivatives markets, 362, 367
> and Internet, 75, 81–83
> and market freedom, 429
> regulation, 107–8
> *See also* shareholder protection

protectionism in market integration, 162, 169,
> 174–75

prudent investor rule, 141–42, 148
public directors for for-profit exchanges, 271
public disclosure. *See* disclosure, information; transparency, market
public funding institutions, and SMEs, **397**
public good consideration, 4, 27, 214, 217–19, 235
public interest responsibility of exchanges, 271, 419
public offerings
    demutualization of exchanges, 271, 278–79, 281
    direct public offering, 401, 403
    process of making, 81n15, 115
    Swedish exchange, 285
    See also initial public offering (IPO)
public policy. *See* policy issues
public sector
    borrowing decline in, 7
    corporate governance role, 443, 451–59
    human capital development, 466, 469
    See also central banks; governments; policy issues

Qin, Duo, 497
quality control, accounting standards, **226–27**, 228, **229**, 230
quotes, market, 163–64, 180–82, 183. *See also* prices and quotes

Rajan, Raghuram, 6, 7, 165
rating agencies, stock, 19
rational morality and market activity, 420
real estate financing. *See* mortgage-backed securities
Real Plan, Brazil, 385
real-time gross settlement (RTGS)
    global infrastructure developments, 247–48, 250
    Latin America, 255, 257, 258, 260
reciprocal obligation, 417, 423
Redibook, **51**
reforms, market. *See* policy issues
Regional Council for Public Savings and Financial Markets, 186
regional market integration
    benefits and costs, 27, 161–65, 199–201
    bond markets, 301
    clearing and settlement, 190–98
    conditions for, 159–61

cross-border trading, 21–22, 60
    CSDs, 194–98, 264–65
    Europe, 251
    exchanges and trading, 106, 178–79, 185–90, 497
    funding of, 266
    governance issues, 201–3
    information dissemination, 179–82
    institutional role in, 24
    language training, 483
    for Latin America and Caribbean, 26, 39, 109, 146–47, 203–8, 261–62
    marketing of, 198–99
    order routing, 182–85
    policy issues, 505–7
    regulatory issues, 166–77, 182, 188, 264
    strategies for improvement, 25–27
    technology considerations, 26, 147, 201
    See also Europe
RegionClear, 194–95
registration of securities, 253, 256
regulation
    bond markets, 298–99, 303, 308, 311, 313, 315, 321–22, 326–28
    capital market benefits, 4, 5, 6
    clearing and settlement, 241, 248–49
    confidence in market, 479
    CSD standardization, 242–43
    current debate on, 40–41
    demutualization of exchanges, 279–84
    deregulation trends, 108–9, 141–42
    derivatives markets, 340, 351–52, 355–73, 385
    ethical issues, 424
    European market integration, 140, 172, 173–74, 175, 177, 251, 279
    financial statement quality control, 228, 230
    globalization, 19–20, 46, 53–59, 61–62, 85, 87
    human capital development, 469, 470–71, 476, 480–81
    independence of regulatory bodies, 234
    infrastructure developments, 126, 245–46, 256–58, 260–61, 265–66
    institutional investors, 135–37
    and Internet, 66–68, 74–86
    Latin American problems with, 144–45, 146–47

regulation *(continued)*
    market liquidity, 102
    pension funds, 24, 25, 107, 144
    regional market integration, 166–77, 182,
        185–87, 188, 264
    shareholder protection, 54, 107–8
    small economy challenges, 104
    SMEs, 394–95, 412
    strategies for capital market development,
        17–22
    tax distortions and equity markets, 98
    trading systems, 51–53, 496
    transparency of markets, 54, 109, 115–16
    See also demutualization of exchanges;
        oversight of markets; self-regulation
relative efficiency view of markets, 215
repo markets, 307
Reports on the Observance of Standards and
    Codes (ROSCs), 235
reputation capital, 57–58, 376, 421–23
research and development, 115, 393
Resolution 275 (Colombia), 454–56
retail investors, 65–66, 81–83, 86, 315, 316
retirement benefits. *See* pension funds; social
    security systems
revenue recognition principle, 216
Rio de Janeiro Stock Exchange, 24, 109, 255, 383
risk and uncertainty
    banking management of, 100, 309–10
    bond markets, 309, 311, 322
    capital market environment, 4, 160
    clearing and settlement, 190, 248–49
    decline in crossover investment, 13
    differing preferences for investors,
        110–12, 114
    electronic trading, 60
    exchange rate issues, 301, 302
    futures markets cooperation, 193
    integration initiatives, 160
    Internet trading, 75, 81–83
    Latin American IPOs, 8
    liquidity benefits, 128, 263
    need for management of, 23, 25
    operational risk, 241, 246
    poor macroeconomic policy, 95
    regional market integration, 200
    regulation, 54
    See also derivatives markets
risk capital. *See* venture capital

Rodrick, S., 6
ROSCs (Reports on the Observance of
    Standards and Codes), 235
routing orders and regional integration, 26
rule of law, 356, 424
rule- vs. principle-based accounting systems,
    221–25
rules, trading. *See* regulation
Russia, challenges of market reform in, 492

sales of companies and shareholder rights,
    449–50
Sanvicente, 497
São Paulo Commodities Exchange (BMSP), 383
São Paulo Stock Exchange (BOVESPA)
    capital access improvements, 20–21, 40
    consolidation, 255
    derivatives market, 383
    listing reform initiative, 446–48
    market institution role, 24
    regional market integration, 109
    SMEs, 503
    strength of equity market in Brazil, 94
Sarkissian, Sergei, 506
savings, domestic
    capital market contribution, 3
    institutional investors, 23, 129
    Latin American weakness in, 95, 472,
        473–74
    mandatory contribution effects, 106–7
    structural reforms, 105
SAXESS trading platform, 185
scandals, corporate, 437, 442–43
Schill, Michael J., 506
Schulman, Michael Ashley, 405, 407–8
S.D. Indeval, 255–56
SEAQ International (SEAQ-I), 163
secondary markets
    bond, 307–8, 313, 318–21, 322, 323,
        329–30
    derivatives as, 371
    institutional improvements, 22
    SMEs, 395
sector allocation of investments, 160
sector-based approach to human capital
    development, 465–69
securities. *See* equity markets
Securities and Exchange Act of 1934 (U.S.), 136,
    280

Securities and Exchange Commission, U.S. (SEC)
  CSD standardization, 242
  and Enron, 214
  foreign market access issue, 55–56
  listing standards, 280
  and NMS, 180
  regulation, 41, 52–53, 136–37, 221, 222
  self-regulation of exchanges, 283, 284
  settlement improvements, 248–49
securities and exchange commissions (outside
  U.S.), 15, 18, 19, 47–48
Securities Authority of Israel, 43
Securities Board of the Netherlands, 289
securities depositories. See central securities
  depositories (CSDs)
Securities Exchange and Clearing Operations
  Act of 1992 (Sweden), 285
Securities Industry Association (SIA), 250, 282–83
security, job, and SME volatility, 392
security of Internet trading systems, 78–79
seed capital for SMEs, 398–99, 405
segmentation of securities exchanges, 114–15
segregation, derivatives markets, 367–68
self-financing of SMEs, 394, 398–99
self-interest and trustworthiness, 423. See also
  conflicts of interest
self-listing by exchanges, 271
self-policing challenges for markets, 58
self-regulation
  bond markets, 322, 329
  Brazilian markets, 384
  corporate governance, 446–48
  demutualization of exchanges, 269, 271,
    283, 284
  derivatives markets, 355, 362–63, 373–80
  ethical standards, 418, 426, 427
  Guatemala, 103
  information transparency, 116
  in U.S., 136, 273, 375n54, 417–18, 445
self-regulatory organizations (SROs)
  ATSs, 52–53
  demutualization of exchanges, 276–79,
    282–83, 289
  derivatives markets, 374–78
  globalization/technology issues, 53–59
  listing standards in U.S., 280
  role of, 41, 46, 62
SELIC (Special System for Settlement and
  Custody), 255

service sector as focus for SMEs, 391, 393
settlement. See clearing and settlement
shareholder protection
  accounting standards, 216
  corporate governance, 7, 18, 140–41, 149,
    438, 439–40, 443, 444, 458
  cross-border trading, 56
  demutualization of exchanges, 277, 288
  guiding principles, **460**
  information disclosure, 326–27, 494
  as investor requirement, 15
  in Latin America and Caribbean, 19, 21,
    145, 448–51
  market development process, 493–94
  market liquidity, 102
  mergers, 200–201
  prudent investor principles, 142
  regulation, 54, 107–8
Singapore International Monetary Exchange
  (SIMEX), 192–94
Single European Act, 171
Single Market, European, 171, 174
size of cash market, derivatives markets, 345–46
small and medium enterprises (SMEs)
  access to finance, 394–96
  capital access improvements, 20
  deregulation advantages for venture
    capital, 142
  economic role of, 389–93
  exchange markets for, 403–10
  financing instruments, 396–403
  globalization benefits, 109
  Internet advantages, 66
  need for market support, 25, 38, 114–15
  policy issues, 96, 410–13
  stock market operating costs, 8, 399
  strategies to encourage, 147–48
  trading support for, 503
Small Business Investment Company (SBIC), 142
small economies
  balancing of, 103–5
  bond markets, 301
  institutional investing restrictions, 144
Smith, Bruce, 6
Smith, Katherine, 497
social issues. See cultural issues
social security systems, 21, 23, 105–7, 122–23
Sofianos, George, 497
sovereign credit risk, 311

sovereign debt markets, 338, 340
Spain, trading environment, 12, 27
SPAN (Standard Portfolio Analysis of Risk
    Margining), 365n41
special interests and corruption of law, 424
Special System for Settlement and Custody
    (SELIC), 255
special-purpose entities (SPEs), 221
speculation, limitation of excessive, 364
speculators and derivative investor recruiting, 350
spot trade, bond markets, 318
stability, market. See financial stability
stakeholders, needs of, 18, 265, 440
standard margin, 366
Standard Portfolio Analysis of Risk Margining
    (SPAN), 365n41
standards, financial
        corporate governance, 439, **460–61**
        cross-border trading, 61, 213, 249
        CSDs, 242–43
        derivatives markets, 340, 342, 348,
            351–52, 371–72
        Europe, 169, 221
        infrastructure improvements, 240, 244,
            253, 264, 325–26
        Latin America need for, 15
        listing, 280
        policy issues, 498–99
        RTGS, 248
        SMEs, 394
        See also accounting and auditing standards
Starmedia, 16
start-up financing of SMEs, 398–99
statutory restrictions, bond markets, 327–28
Steil, Benn, 56
stock markets. See equity markets
stock options and accounting standards, 222
Stockholm Stock Exchange, 269, 274–75, 277,
    290
straight-through processing (STP), 240, 249–50,
    256, 264
strategic business services, SMEs in, 391
Strike, **51**
structural reforms. See infrastructure, market
structured products, bonds as, 325
Stulz, Renee, 7
substitutions, derivatives markets, 362
Sumitomo, 39n35, 351
Superintendency of Securities (Colombia), 454

supply and demand issues, 93, 144, 345–46, 347,
    502–3
surveillance, market, 74, 84, 167, 370–72, 378
swaps, Colombian debt, 312. See also derivatives
    markets
Swedish exchanges
        demutualization of, 284–87
        loss of investment to foreign exchanges,
            497
        Stockholm Stock Exchange, 269, 274–75,
            277, 290
SWIFT software language, 250
Sydney Futures Exchange, 288
systemic risk, 241, 322

T+1 settlement timing, 240, 245, 248–49,
    250–51, 255
tag-along rights for shareholders, 443, 449–50
Taiwan, SME initiatives in, 396
takeover, corporate, 4. See also mergers and
    acquisitions
Target payments system, 248
tax issues
        as barriers to market development,
            496–97
        bond markets, 315, 327, 330–31
        and equity markets, 98
        institutional investors, 130
        pension funds, 134
        SMEs, 395
techMARK (UK), 410
technology
        bond markets, 316
        Brazil exchanges' use of, 94
        capital market environment, 160
        and cheap information, 46
        clearing and settlement, 192
        computer role in market development,
            23, 39
        cross-border trading, 53, 54–56, 131
        demutualization of exchanges, 272, 275
        derivatives markets, 246, 248, 347
        European market integration, 163, 251
        globalization, 48–53, 60, 61, 109, 110
        infrastructure improvements, 246–47, 263
        institutional investors, 130–31, 137–38, 501
        multiple trading systems, 496
        regional market integration, 26, 147, 201,
            202

technology (continued)
    self-regulation, 53–59
    SME focus on, 407
    See also Internet
Tel Aviv Stock Exchange, 43
telecommunications sector, mergers and
   acquisitions, 15
Telefonos de Mexico (Telmex), 43
tender offer rules, 444
Thailand, currency devaluation, 13
Thornton, Grant, 408, **409**, 409–10
timeliness of information, 69, 230, 234
timing of settlement, 240, 245, 248–49, 250–51,
   255
timing risk, 200
Tokyo Communiqué, 351, 371–72
Tokyo Stock Exchange, 48
Toronto Stock Exchange (TSE), 183–84
total factor productivity, 165
trade associations. See professional associations
trade credit and SMEs, **397**
Tradebook, **51**
Tradepoint, 50, 55, 56, 163
trading activity
    access vs. market ownership, 46
    after-hours, 72
    Argentine fiscal crisis, 96
    automatic trading halts, 366–67
    broker-dealer role, 66, 367–68
    government bonds on exchanges, **318**
    openness and economic growth, 6
    regional market integration, 106, 178–79,
       185–90, 497
    trade shocks and small economies, 105
    worldwide levels, **10**, 12
    See also cross-border trading; derivatives
       markets; exchanges, securities
trading systems
    bond markets, 318–19
    competition benefits, 495–97
    computerization of, 23
    derivatives markets, 349–51
    multiple, 496
    regional market integration, 26, 163–64,
       185–90
    regulation, 51–53, 496
    See also alternative trading systems
       (ATSs); clearing and settlement; floor
       trading; ordering systems

trading volume, 38, 39–40, 79, **335–36**
training institutions and programs. See education
transaction costs
    and day trading risks, 82–83
    dematerialization of documentation, 110
    exchange competition, 247
    government bond market, 314
    and Internet, 65–66, 69, 73, 78
    regulation, 108
    technology, 137–38
transparency, market
    accounting standards, 234
    corporate governance, 440–41, 448
    derivatives markets, 339, 350–51, 358–61
    European market integration, 174, 177
    guiding principles, **460**
    international investment, 60
    and Internet trading, 67, 74
    need for, 19, 115–16
    prices and quotes, 182, 348, 350–51,
       358–60
    regulation, 54, 109, 115–16
    self-regulation, 377
    shareholder protection, 494
    SME funding, 395, 406
    and trust, 421
    See also disclosure, information
treasury bills, 310, 311
treasury bonds, 321–22
Treaty of Rome, 170, 171
Tressel, Thierry, 7
Trinidad and Tobago, 262
trust and ethical issues in markets, 417, 419,
   421–23, 426, 427, 430–31
trustworthiness and ethical behavior, 421–23
TSE (Toronto Stock Exchange), 183–84
Turkish stock exchange, 47
turnover, market, **10, 330**, 345–46
TV Azteca, 443

UEMOA (West African Economic and Monetary
   Union), 186
unemployment and Argentine fiscal crisis, 95
Unger, Laura, 53
unified market and regional integration, 26–27,
   171, 174
United Kingdom
    corporate governance rules, 438
    derivatives markets, 351

United Kingdom (continued)
    human capital development, 471–72
    institutional investing, 121, **125**
    Know-how Fund, 490
    market liquidity, **128**
    pension funds, 107
    SMEs, 401
United States
    bond markets, 295, **296**
    capitalization and trading volume, **39**
    corporate governance rules, 438
    debt vs. equity markets, 97
    demutualization of exchanges, 282–83
    deregulation of markets, 141
    derivatives markets, 350, 351, 352,
      364–65, 367, 369
    foreign market access initiatives, 55
    GAAP and IAS accounting rules, 220–25,
      231–33
    human capital development, 472, **473**
    institutional investing, 119, 120–21, **125**,
      133, 138, 139, 501
    and ITS, 183
    market capitalization, **9–10**, 41, **42**, 45
    market liquidity, **128**
    and Mexico, 93–94
    mortgate market, 325
    pension funds, 107, 133–34
    prices and quotes, 180
    regulation, 41, 136, 279
    self-regulation, 277, 280–81, 283–84, 373,
      375n54, 417–18
    settlement developments, 248–51
    share ownership, 288
    SMEs, 147, 392, 401, 411
    stock market performance, 11
    trading activity, 12
Uruguay, market environment, 27, 100, 257, 305,
   316

valuation models, 216, 274
value traded levels, **10**
variation margin, 366, 368n45
Venezuela, market environment, 259, 305, **354**
venture capital
    deregulation of markets, 142
    new exchanges for, 111
    SMEs, 395, **398**, 400–401, 411, 412

vertical vs. horizontal market integration, 251
viability of market, assessment difficulties, 490–91
vicious circle in bond markets, 328–29
virtual securities commission, 168
virtue, trade as teacher of, 417. See also ethical
   issues
virtuous circle in bond markets, 328
Virt-X, 496
Vittas, D., 106, 492, 502
volatility, market
    asset price and crossover investing, 13
    derivatives, 344, 365, 381
    exchange rate issues, 302
    globalization, 60
    mutual funds, 130
    online system resilience, 79
    SMEs, 392
volume, trading, 38, 39–40, 79, **335–36**

wage flexibility of SMEs, 392
WAP (wireless application protocol), 72
Watts, R., 216
wealth accumulation culture in Latin America, 472
wealth levels and institutional investing, 132
websites, issuer liability issues, 77–78, 80–81. See
   also Internet
West African Economic and Monetary Union
   (UEMOA), 186
Williamson, Roham, 7
wireless application protocol (WAP), 72
workforce development, 466, **467**, 469
workforce mobilization, 466, **467**
World Bank, 235, 439
Wurgler, Jeffrey, 6
Wyplosz, C., 218n5

XML (Extensible Markup Language), 250

yield, bond, 316, 327
Yupi Internet, Inc., 16

Zarb, Frank G., 41
zero-coupon instruments, 311
Zervos, Sara, 5, 6, 165
Zhang, Xin, 504
Zimmerman, J., 216
Zingales, Luigi, 6, 7, 165